Law's History

This book is a study of the central role of history in late nineteenth-century American legal thought. In the decades following the Civil War, the founding generation of professional legal scholars in the United States drew from the evolutionary social thought that pervaded Western intellectual life on both sides of the Atlantic. Their historical analysis of law as an inductive science rejected deductive theories and supported moderate legal reform, conclusions that challenge conventional accounts of legal formalism. Unprecedented in its coverage and its innovative conclusions about major American legal thinkers from the Civil War to the present, the book combines transatlantic intellectual history, legal history, the history of legal thought, historiography, jurisprudence, constitutional theory, and the history of higher education.

David M. Rabban is Dahr Jamail, Randall Hage Jamail, and Robert Lee Jamail Regents Chair in Law and University Distinguished Teaching Professor at the University of Texas School of Law. Rabban is the author of *Free Speech in Its Forgotten Years* (Cambridge 1997), which won the 1998 Morris D. Forkosch Prize presented by the *Journal of the History of Ideas* and the 1998 Eli M. Oboler Award of the American Library Association Intellectual Freedom Roundtable.

Cambridge Historical Studies in American Law and Society

Series Editor
Christopher Tomlins, *University of California, Irvine*

Previously Published in the Series:

Law's History

*American Legal Thought and the Transatlantic
Turn to History*

DAVID M. RABBAN

University of Texas, Austin

CAMBRIDGE
UNIVERSITY PRESS

CAMBRIDGE UNIVERSITY PRESS
Cambridge, New York, Melbourne, Madrid, Cape Town,
Singapore, São Paulo, Delhi, Mexico City

Cambridge University Press
32 Avenue of the Americas, New York, NY 10013-2473, USA

www.cambridge.org
Information on this title: www.cambridge.org/9780521761918

First published 2013

Printed in the United States of America

A catalog record for this publication is available from the British Library.

Library of Congress Cataloging in Publication data
Rabban, David M., 1949–
   Law's history : American legal thought and the transatlantic turn to
history / David M. Rabban, University of Texas, Austin.
      pages   cm. – (Cambridge historical studies in American law and society)
   Includes bibliographical references and index.
   ISBN 978-0-521-76191-8
   1. Law – United States – Philosophy – History – 19th century.   2. Law – United
States – Interpretation and construction – History – 19th century.   3. Law – Study
and teaching – United States – History – 19th century.   I. Title.
   KF380.R33   2012
   349.7309′034–dc23   2012012605

ISBN 978-0-521-76191-8 Hardback

Contents

Acknowledgments

I am pleased to acknowledge the assistance I have received from many people and institutions during the long period I worked on this book. My primary debt is to the University of Texas School of Law. Its generous donors have provided financial support for my research, and my faculty colleagues have contributed to a stimulating intellectual environment. I particularly thank my colleagues who have read and responded to multiple drafts. Hans Baade drew on his deep knowledge of American, English, and German legal history in guiding my research as my project expanded into areas beyond my original expertise. His many clarifications and suggestions saved me from numerous errors. Mark Gergen's broad teaching and research interests in the common law extend to its history. He was eager to learn how the nineteenth-century scholars I discuss in this book dealt with the history of the common law, and his close readings of my drafts helped me sharpen my treatment of the legal issues these scholars addressed. Mark's fascination with this material gives me hope that scholars of the common law, as well as legal historians and philosophers, will find value in this book. Oren Bracha and Willy Forbath were especially helpful and patient in probing my analysis of the historiographical and jurisprudential assumptions of late nineteenth-century American legal thought and its relationship to more general historical developments. In recent years, Bob Bone and Emily Kadens have made incisive comments about late drafts of various chapters. I also thank the students in the reading group that used my final draft as a text. Their reactions prompted me to make additional revisions, and their enthusiastic engagement with what I feared might seem to them an overly specialized treatment of a relatively esoteric subject indicates that this book may appeal to some general readers. Another student, Amina Dammann, wrote an excellent seminar paper drawing on her native fluency in German to analyze the work on the Frankish origins of the jury by Heinrich Brunner, the great nineteenth-century German scholar who was a major influence on his contemporary American and English legal historians.

Colleagues at other institutions have also responded generously to my drafts. Robert Gordon, Thomas Grey, Morton Horwitz, Duncan Kennedy, and

Stephen Siegel, leading recent scholars of late nineteenth-century American legal thought whose work I discuss in the last chapter, have graciously commented on my treatment of them as well as on my own historical interpretations. Their comments have greatly assisted my revisions of this chapter. David Seipp helped me understand key issues in English legal history, and I have built on his research and writing about Melville Madison Bigelow, a major though largely forgotten late nineteenth-century American legal scholar. Tom Green read several chapters, making particularly valuable comments about my chapters on the historical school of American jurisprudence and on Pound, whose important views on criminal justice he had addressed at length in his own scholarship. After I completed my manuscript, I became aware of revisionist scholarship in German on the history of nineteenth-century German legal thought. Hans-Peter Haferkamp, to whom I was introduced via e-mail by my colleague Inga Markovits, provided information about this scholarship, including his own work. He even wrote detailed comments about my draft chapter on nineteenth-century German legal scholarship, pointing out in particular where recent revisionist scholarship in German challenged the traditional interpretations on which I had relied. I made significant changes to this chapter based on his comments.

Throughout my work on this book, I have given talks about it at law schools and conferences in the United States and abroad, including, in roughly chronological order, Yale, the University of Arizona, Rutgers-Camden, the University of Tel Aviv, the University of Chicago, the University of Texas, Ohio State, the University of Southern California, Oxford University, Boston University, UCLA, the University of Michigan, and the German Studies Association. I am especially grateful to the American Society for Legal History, where I have presented twice, and the British Legal History Conference, where I have presented three times and learned an enormous amount about English legal history and historiography. Preparing these talks and conversations following them contributed enormously to the completed book, sometimes through articles based on the talks and now incorporated into the book.[1]

I wrote most of this book while teaching at the University of Texas School of Law, but I was also fortunate to have two year-long research leaves during its preparation, the first as a visiting Fellow at the Whitney Humanities Center at Yale University and a visitor at Yale Law School in 2000–1; the second as a visitor at Harvard Law School in 2004–5. I thank Peter Brooks, the Director of the Whitney Humanities Center; Dean Anthony Kronman at Yale; Dean Elena Kagan at Harvard; and the faculty at all three institutions for making me feel welcome and for their interest in my research.

[1] David M. Rabban, The Historiography of Late Nineteenth-Century American Legal History, 4 Theoretical Inquiries in Law 541 (2003); David M. Rabban, The Historiography of the Common Law, 28 Law & Social Inquiry 1161 (2003); David M. Rabban, From Maine to Maitland via America, 68 Cambridge L.J. 210 (2010); David M. Rabban, Melville M. Bigelow: Boston University's Neglected Pioneer of Historical Legal Scholarship in America, 91 B.U. L. Rev. 1 (2011).

Soon after I completed the manuscript for this book, I was fortunate to receive an invitation from the Hebrew University of Jerusalem to participate in a symposium about it in connection with a new journal, the *Jerusalem Review of Legal Studies*, designed to publish symposia on recent or forthcoming books. The symposium about my book was published in the first issue, 1 *Jerusalem Review of Legal Studies* 71–136 (2010). I am grateful to Adam Hofri-Winogradow, for organizing as well as contributing to this symposium, and to the other Israeli legal historians who published comments on my book: Ron Harris, Assaf Likhovsky, and Roy Kreitner. My response to these four comments concluded the symposium. Fortunately, I was able to take their thoughtful comments into account in the final revision of the manuscript.

The three readers of my manuscript for Cambridge University Press wrote exceptionally comprehensive and perceptive reports that enthusiastically recommended publication while also containing valuable criticisms and suggestions. Each subsequently identified himself to me, and I am pleased to be able to thank Mark Gergen, Joshua Getzler, and John Schlegel by name.

This is the second book I have published in the Cambridge Historical Studies in American Law and Society series. Chris Tomlins was such an outstanding editor of the first book that I was eager for him to edit this one as well. As I expected, my confidence in Chris was rewarded again by his critical yet sympathetic edit. Once again, he tried to understand my own goals for this book and directed his editorial suggestions to helping me achieve them. A very long conversation with Chris about the readers' reports was an intellectual highlight of my professional life. Assisted by the high quality of the reports themselves, we ultimately arrived at a plan for revision that addressed various comments by the readers that initially did not seem interrelated. The revision delayed the completion of the manuscript for more than a year, but I am confident that the published book, whatever its strengths and weaknesses, is much better as a result.

Timeline

Introduction

This book examines the central role of history in late nineteenth-century American legal thought. It argues that historical legal thought dominated American legal scholarship from the 1870s until superseded by the sociological jurisprudence promoted by Roscoe Pound in the decade before World War I. This argument reinterprets the intellectual history of American law while relating it to developments in other countries and in other disciplines. The American scholars who are the primary focus of this book include Henry Adams, James Barr Ames, Melville M. Bigelow, James Coolidge Carter, Thomas McIntyre Cooley, William Gardiner Hammond, Oliver Wendell Holmes, Jr., John Norton Pomeroy, Roscoe Pound, James Bradley Thayer, Christopher G. Tiedeman, and Francis Wharton.

In analyzing these American legal scholars, I will try to convey how they understood their own work. Because they were interested in the evolution of legal doctrine, I will devote substantial attention to it. But this book is neither an attempt to write my own history of legal doctrine, nor an explanation of legal doctrine as ideology. Rather, it is primarily an intellectual history of the historical school of late nineteenth-century American legal scholarship in the context of transatlantic social thought. By trying to understand these scholars on their own terms, I hope to strip away a century of distortions and oversimplifications by twentieth-century commentators often more interested in their own political and intellectual agendas than in recovering what their predecessors actually thought and achieved. I hope to restore a deservedly prominent place in the history of American legal thought to its founding generation of professional legal scholars. More cosmopolitan, more learned, and more internationally respected than many of the people who have misrepresented or neglected them, they should be recognized and engaged as part of a rich intellectual tradition.

Combining transatlantic intellectual history, legal history, the history of legal thought, historiography, jurisprudence, constitutional theory, and the history of higher education, this book should appeal to readers interested in any of these subjects, and particularly to those interested in the connections among them.

Because I provide biographical information about important nineteenth-century legal scholars in Europe and the United States as well as summaries of their major works, the book should also appeal to readers who want to learn more about them. Addressing the backgrounds and political beliefs of these scholars, it portrays them as more diverse and complex than most subsequent commentators have assumed. For people who have never read classics such as *Ancient Law* by Henry Maine, *The Common Law* by Oliver Wendell Holmes, Jr., *The History of English Law* by Frederick Pollock and Frederic Maitland, or the pathbreaking articles by Roscoe Pound on "sociological jurisprudence," my extended discussion and analysis of these texts should provide a useful introduction. To a lesser but still substantial extent, I explore the work of the major German legal scholars who most influenced the Americans, such as Friedrich Carl von Savigny, Heinrich Brunner, and Rudolph von Jhering. My treatment of these scholars within a broad historical and international context, moreover, should enable fresh perspectives even for readers already familiar with much of their work. For example, by illustrating how many historical assumptions and interests all of these scholars shared, I challenge prevailing views about the distinctiveness of Holmes, Maitland, and Pound. Holmes and Pound continued to treat law historically even as they urged lawyers to apply the insights of the emerging social sciences, and Maitland, though justifiably perceived as broadening the focus of legal history to include social and economic history, remained primarily interested in the evolution of legal doctrine. Beyond examining major works of nineteenth-century legal scholarship, the book stresses the important, but lesser known contributions of other scholars, including Henry Adams, whose pioneering work introducing "scientific" legal history in the United States has understandably been overshadowed by his later, much better known histories and autobiography.

Beginning with Holmes and Pound in the decades around 1900 and continuing through most of the twentieth century, American legal scholars have defined their own understandings of law in opposition to the views of their late nineteenth-century predecessors, which they typically characterize, and often ridicule, as "legal formalism" or "classical legal thought." According to many of their successors, the late nineteenth-century scholars attempted to create a timeless structure of legal thought, often built on principles uncovered through the study of legal history, which would yield correct results deduced by formal logic. Many twentieth-century critics added that this timeless structure advanced conservative political goals by denying the possibility of conscious change and by treating the law as an autonomous system divorced from the forces and conflicts of the broader society. Jhering had made similar criticisms of German historical jurisprudence, which Pound often cited and quoted. Some twentieth-century scholars, more often in history and political science than in law itself, ascribed malevolent intent to the nineteenth-century scholars. They charged that intellectually bankrupt formalism was simply a pretext for justifying laissez-faire constitutionalism, a way to enforce individual economic rights to protect the wealthy while invalidating social legislation in the public interest.

Twentieth-century scholars often depicted Holmes as the great exception in the late nineteenth century, a brilliant, highly original thinker who laid the intellection foundations for the sociological jurisprudence developed by Pound in the early twentieth century. Sociological jurisprudence, they declared, finally made law modern by replacing formalism with a pragmatic approach that drew its inspiration from the emerging social sciences. They associated Holmes and Pound with what Morton White famously called the liberal "revolt against formalism" that pervaded American social thought from roughly 1890 to 1930.

The relatively few American legal historians who have addressed the history of their own field have reinforced the negative image of nineteenth-century American legal thought. Ever since J. Willard Hurst founded the "Law and Society" school of legal history at the University of Wisconsin in the 1940s, they have joined Hurst in criticizing the poor quality of prior American scholarship in legal history from its beginnings in the 1870s. They have portrayed Hurst himself as the first sophisticated legal historian in the United States, characterizing the work of his predecessors as dismal, rarely even meeting the minimal standards of professional scholarship in history, and best remembered as an embarrassing reminder of the pitfalls current legal historians should avoid. Ascribing to previous scholarship in legal history many of the faults associated with classical legal thought in general, they have deprecatingly referred to it as doctrinal, internal, formalistic, apologetic, and conservative. They have also criticized its "presentist" orientation, trying to explain current law by connecting it to past law and thereby failing to understand past law in its own, often very different context. Given the low esteem in which they held the earlier scholars, it is not surprising that they have not discussed their work in any detail.

This book reveals that the widely held consensus about late nineteenth-century American legal scholarship is largely inaccurate. It prompts suspicion that this consensus derives more from the progressive intellectual and political agenda of twentieth-century scholars than from a close reading of their nineteenth-century predecessors. Historical understandings of law, not unchanging deductive formalism, pervaded the legal thought of late nineteenth-century American legal scholars. Contemporary scholars both at home and abroad recognized Holmes as part of this distinctively historical school of legal thought even as they indicated that his historical conclusions were both bolder and less accurate than those of his historically minded colleagues. Legal scholars often invoked history to reform rather than to justify existing law and, as some recent revisionist work has observed, were more likely to be Mugwump reformers or Jacksonian democrats than conservative apologists for laissez-faire capitalism. They frequently spoke out against the increasing materialism of American society and denounced the excesses and inequalities produced by the growth of corporate capitalism. Many American legal scholars were extremely well educated, well traveled, and multi-lingual. Some contributed to major literary and political journals of the period and participated actively in public affairs, from opposition to slavery before the Civil War to postwar efforts combating municipal and corporate corruption, promoting civil service reform, and urging better treatment of American Indians. In their scholarly work, they acknowledged their intellectual debts to European scholars, particularly in Germany and England, even as they occasionally criticized the conservatism of the Europeans. Correspondingly, eminent European legal scholars, most impressively the great English legal historian Frederic Maitland, relied on the legal history written by Americans while praising its originality and quality. Even when the late nineteenth-century scholars displayed key characteristics ascribed to them by their later detractors, they typically were much more intellectually sophisticated than the detractors acknowledged. For example, although they frequently focused on the internal development of legal doctrine in an effort to understand current law, they were sensitive to how the past differed from the present, warned against mistaking resemblance for continuity, stressed reversals and dysfunctional survivals as well as progress over time, and recognized the contingency of history while highlighting the influence of external factors on internal legal development.

The emphasis on history as the key to understanding law was part of a general movement toward historical explanation in many disciplines by Western intellectuals on both sides of the Atlantic during the nineteenth century, often in reaction against the metaphysical speculation of the eighteenth century that they associated with the excesses of the French Revolution. This movement began most prominently in Germany. German historical scholarship and the German research university became models for ambitious scholars elsewhere, who frequently studied in Germany to receive professional training as yet unavailable at home. Throughout the nineteenth century, historically oriented scholars in many fields, including law, influenced each other. Savigny, who largely initiated the historical school of law in the early nineteenth century, had been inspired by prior German scholarship on the history of Rome and in turn inspired his student, Jacob Grimm, to investigate medieval German poetry and folk tales. Grimm's philological work on the history of Teutonic languages stimulated English scholars to study Anglo-Saxon language and culture. Their investigations eventually extended to Anglo-Saxon law. Henry Maine's widely read book, *Ancient Law*, published in England in 1861, popularized Savigny's historical jurisprudence in England and the United States. Ultimately more influential in the emerging fields of anthropology and sociology than in law itself, *Ancient Law* made an important contribution to the evolutionary social thought that prevailed on both sides of the Atlantic, preceding and remaining largely independent of Darwin's evolutionary theories based on natural selection. American legal historians who studied the history of English law in the decades after 1870 provided an important though overlooked intellectual link between the two leading English legal scholars, Maine and Maitland, while relying on the research methods and findings of German legal historians who had investigated the history of Teutonic law. The emphasis by the American legal historians on the Teutonic origins of English law encouraged and reinforced the late nineteenth-century American historians and political scientists who maintained that fundamental American institutions, such as the New England town meeting, derived from Teutonic roots. As the text of this book reveals, these illustrations of transatlantic and interdisciplinary connections can easily be multiplied.

The American scholars felt personally connected to the legal history they studied. They identified themselves as members of a unified Anglo-American race derived from Teutonic origins. Bigelow even combined genealogical research into his own family, which he traced to medieval England, with his broader research on the history of the English common law, just as Maitland subsequently picked the county of Gloucester, where he had family connections, as the site of his early original research about medieval English law. Focused primarily on the origins of the Anglo-American legal system, these late nineteenth-century American legal scholars devoted less attention to the history of distinctively American law. Occasionally, they did comment on the history of American common law and constitutional law, often in elaborating their evolutionary legal thought. They also referred to and occasionally wrote about the legal consequences of major current events, such as Reconstruction following the Civil War and industrialization. Yet in contrast to Savigny and other early nineteenth-century German scholars, whose very turn to historical analysis was largely a reaction against the background and aftermath of the French Revolution, American legal scholars did not shape their historical analysis in response to Reconstruction and industrialization. The Americans adapted the evolutionary social thought that originated in Germany and had become pervasive throughout Western intellectual life by the time they began their scholarly careers. This intellectual influence, rather than political or economic factors, best explains the dominance of historical analysis in late nineteenth-century American legal thought.

Overwhelmingly committed to evolutionary conceptions of legal change, the late nineteenth-century American legal scholars did not display the timeless deductive formalism ascribed to them by twentieth-century commentators. They repeatedly stressed that law evolves in response to changing social customs, an approach that recognized external influences on law. Many believed that evolution, at least in Western countries, had produced progress, and a few equated Western progress with the racial superiority of peoples evolved from Teutonic "roots." Yet they did not think that the evolutionary process had stopped, and most did not limit evolutionary progress to Teutonic societies. Often explicitly rejecting deductive theories of law, they emphasized that law is an empirical science based on induction from historical evidence. As part of their inductive approach, they wanted to organize and classify the legal data they observed. When their historical research revealed the survival of laws that made sense in the past but that no longer functioned effectively in the changed society of the present, they urged legal reforms that would eliminate these dysfunctional survivals. They recognized that their classifications were temporary, subject to further revision as part of the continuous process by which law responds to evolving custom. Just as functional laws in the past had become dysfunctional in the present, functional laws in the present could become dysfunctional in the future.

Emphasizing the significance of their evolutionary analysis of law, the late nineteenth-century American legal scholars made clear that they considered it a distinctive jurisprudential school. They explicitly differentiated it from prior jurisprudential schools, particularly natural law and analytic jurisprudence. They especially contrasted the unscientific speculative approach of these prior schools, based on a priori "speculation" and "mere theory," with their own "scientific" reliance on induction from the empirical evidence of history. Their use of induction, they often maintained, was analogous to its use in the natural and physical sciences. Beyond identifying historical legal science as a different and better jurisprudential school than natural law or analytic jurisprudence, the late nineteenth-century legal scholars applied it to some of the most fundamental legal issues of their time. Because they believed that judges were typically in a better position than legislators to respond to evolving custom, they favored adjudication over legislation. Yet they approved legislation in exceptional circumstances, such as periods of rapid social transformation when immediate and substantial changes in the law are required. In response to the dramatic industrialization of the United States, for example, many of them urged legislation governing child labor, the operation of dangerous machines, and tenement housing, thereby challenging the claim by many subsequent scholars that their general opposition to legislation was based on conservative resistance to legislative reform. Their fundamental emphasis on law as a response to evolving custom also explains many of their views about constitutional interpretation. Rather than focusing on the text of the Constitution or the original intent of the framers and ratifiers, they believed that constitutional law, like law generally, evolves as circumstances change. While they generally acknowledged that the written text of the Constitution imposes some interpretive limits on judicial discretion, they urged judges to recognize transformations of popular understandings of the Constitution, such as the definition of citizenship during and after the Civil War, even as some of them cautioned that judges should often defer to legislative interpretations of constitutional meaning.

Among the many late nineteenth-century American legal scholars who made evolutionary legal thought the dominant jurisprudential school in the United States, a few published important original contributions to legal history. Drawing on the methods and findings of German scholars, they investigated the primary sources of English law while emphasizing its Teutonic origins. They mostly dismissed prior English scholarship on the history of English law as amateurish, insular, and unscientific, but they also criticized as pedantic and abstruse the Germans they generally admired. Henry Adams, who introduced the professional study of legal history into the United States when he joined the Harvard history department in 1870, studied the history of Anglo-Saxon law. Together with his students, he used the details of Anglo-Saxon law to test, and often to refute, the provocative generalizations about legal evolution that Henry Maine in *Ancient Law* derived mostly from the history of Roman law. Bigelow, Holmes, Thayer, and Ames, who all lived in the Boston area and were in contact with each other, continued the American study of the history of English law in the last three decades of the nineteenth century. Bigelow and Thayer focused on the history of particular subjects, procedure for Bigelow and evidence for Thayer, whereas Holmes and Ames wrote about numerous issues in the history of the common law. While covering the history of various discrete topics, these scholars addressed broader themes in the history of English law. Within a consensus about the primarily Teutonic origins of English law, they disagreed among themselves as well as with leading German historians, particularly Heinrich Brunner, about the relative influence of Anglo-Saxon and Norman sources and about the extent to which the English mostly continued or independently developed Norman law after the Norman Conquest. Frederic Maitland, the great English legal historian, praised and built on the work of these Americans in his own scholarship on the history of English law. Maitland also developed close professional and personal relationships with Thayer, and particularly with Bigelow. Some American legal scholars, including some who focused on the early history of English law, wrote much less extensively about the history of both common law and constitutional law in the United States.

The historical orientation of the late nineteenth-century American legal scholars was closely tied to the emergence of the American research university in the decades after the Civil War. Many of these scholars emphasized that the historical research they urged could only be accomplished by full-time professional scholars whose teaching loads left them ample time for research. They criticized the prevalence of part-time instructors at American law schools, typically practicing lawyers and judges who had full-time jobs elsewhere. The position of a law professor, they asserted, should be a vocation, as in Germany, not an avocation of busy lawyers, as in England. While characterizing the historical study of law as an inductive science, they explicitly argued that law, like other inductive sciences such as biology and physics, deserved inclusion in the emerging American research university. Many of these American legal scholars devoted themselves to the reform of American legal education. They were among the founding faculties of new, university based law schools devoted to higher academic standards for both teachers and students. Several became deans of these law schools. Others were instrumental in the transformation of Harvard under President Charles W. Eliot from a teaching college to a research university. In 1870, the year after he became president, Eliot appointed Adams as a history professor and Christopher Columbus Langdell as the dean of the law school. Grateful for Eliot's strong support of his teaching and scholarship based on German methods of original research, Adams recognized that his hiring was part of Eliot's fundamental effort to reform education at Harvard. Like scholars throughout the emerging American research universities, many law professors had studied as postgraduates in Germany and wanted to introduce German standards of scholarship in the United States.

The dominance of historical explanation throughout the Western intellectual world declined in the early twentieth century, in law, as in other disciplines. Just as the turn to history in legal scholarship was part of a general transatlantic movement during the nineteenth century, legal scholars on both sides of the Atlantic joined scholars in other disciplines during the decades around the turn of the twentieth century in a broad reorientation of social thought, which protested the excesses of liberal individualism at the expense of the collective public welfare. By promoting "sociological jurisprudence" as an attractive alternative to "historical jurisprudence" in his enormously influential early work during the decade before World War I, Roscoe Pound contributed substantially to the demise of historical explanation in American legal scholarship as well as to what became the prevailing, though importantly inaccurate, view of its role in nineteenth-century legal thought. Like many intellectuals in Europe and the United States, including the leading German and English legal scholars, Rudolf von Jhering and Frederic Maitland, Pound believed that traditional conceptions of individualism and individual rights impeded the attention to collective interests required in the modern world. He linked his intellectual interest in the history of legal thought with his strong conviction that American law, through the "mechanical" reasoning of deductive formalism, promoted extreme individualism at a time when the American public needed and demanded the legal recognition of collective interests to solve the pressing social problems that excessive individualism had largely produced. Various prior jurisprudential schools, he claimed, including the historical school that he recognized as dominant in the United States since 1870, contributed to the formalism and individualism that made American law a barrier to desirable social reform. He particularly criticized Supreme Court decisions that formalistically invoked individual constitutional rights such as "liberty of contract" to strike down progressive legislation enacted in the public interest.

Pound treated historical legal thought in America as largely derivative of the pioneering scholarship of Savigny in Germany and Maine in England, which he explored in substantially more detail than any work produced by Americans. He criticized both Savigny and Maine for their individualism, a criticism that applied much more fairly to them than to the Americans Pound largely ignored and thereby diminished. While developing sociological jurisprudence as an alternative to the outmoded jurisprudential schools of the past, he described it as an amalgam of anti-formalist German legal thought, especially as formulated by Jhering, American philosophical pragmatism, and the emerging social sciences. All of these influences, he stressed, recognized the importance of collective interests. He claimed that Holmes, in articles published in the 1890s and in his opinions as a judge, had anticipated its major themes. Ironically, Pound contributed to the decline of legal history largely through his own work as a legal historian. Using what seemed to be an evolutionary model of historical analysis to deny the continuing importance of history itself, he claimed that legal history at the turn of the twentieth century had value mainly as "preparatory work" for sociological jurisprudence.

The following chapter begins with an analysis of a revealing address to the American Bar Association by James Bradley Thayer, a professor at Harvard Law School. Thayer's address highlights the importance of history in late nineteenth-century American legal thought. The chapter then provides brief biographical sketches of the eleven leading American legal scholars whose writings about legal history provide the focus of this book. The remainder of the book consists of three parts. Part I, "The European Background," summarizes the general turn to historical explanation in nineteenth-century Western thought and examines the major European legal scholars who most influenced the Americans, from Savigny to Jhering in Germany, and Sir Henry Maine in England. Part II, "The Historical Turn in American Legal Scholarship," is the core of the book. Devoting successive chapters to the scholarship of the major American legal historians of the late nineteenth century, it concludes with an analysis of the central themes of the distinctive "historical school of American jurisprudence" that dominated American legal thought during this period and included many scholars who did not themselves write original works of legal history. Part III consists of three long chapters. The first discusses the great English legal historian Frederic Maitland, who built on prior American scholarship on the history of English law while bringing the nineteenth-century study of English legal history to a culmination and, in many respects, to a close. The second portrays Pound's key role in transforming American legal scholarship from historical to sociological understandings of law while creating the portrait of his predecessors that dominated the leading twentieth-century interpretations of late nineteenth-century American legal thought. I review and assess these twentieth-century interpretations in the final chapter.

I

The Historical Study of Law in the United States

In August 1895, James Bradley Thayer, as chairman of the Section on Legal Education of the American Bar Association, read an address entitled "The Teaching of English Law at Universities." The address was published several months later in the *Harvard Law Review*. Nearing the end of a long and varied career, Thayer observed that he based his comments on eighteen years of busy legal practice followed by twenty-one years as a professor at Harvard Law School.[1] His address emphasized that legal scholarship, legal education, and practical law reform all depend on the study of legal history.

According to Thayer, "every man who proposes really to understand any topic, to put himself in a position to explain it to others, or to restate it with exactness, must search out that one topic through all its development."[2] In "thorough historical and chronological exploration," Thayer maintained, "lie hidden the explanation of what is most troublesome in our law." With effective historical research, the "dullest topics kindle" and "the most recondite and technical fall into the order of common experience and rational thought." Thayer stressed that studying the history of any part of the law inevitably reveals "the necessity of restating the subject in hand." Through historical investigation, "many a hitherto unobserved relationship of ideas comes to light, many an old one vanishes, [and] many a new explanation of current doctrines is suggested." Confused topics are disentangled, ambiguities are cleared up, false theories are exposed, and "outworn and unintelligible phraseology" becomes understandable. History, in short, is the best "dissolver and rationalizer of technicality" and enables a "new order" to arise.[3]

The essential work of historical reconstruction as the basis for restating the law, Thayer stressed, must be performed by full-time law professors in universities. To be effective, these professors must specialize in only a few related

[1] James Bradley Thayer, The Teaching of English Law at Universities, 9 Harv. L. Rev. 169, 182 (1895).
[2] Id. at 177.
[3] Id. at 178–9.

subjects and have teaching loads that leave them ample time for research.[4] He wrote that "our law must be studied and taught as other great sciences are studied and taught at the Universities, as deeply, by like methods, and with as thorough a concentration and life-long devotion of all the powers of a learned and studious faculty."[5] But pedagogy was outside the scope of Thayer's concerns. In an introductory footnote to the published version of his address, he emphasized that it would "not deal with mere method of teaching."[6] Perhaps he was indicating, especially through the word "mere," that he considered contemporary debate about the case method of instruction relatively unimportant, at least compared to the scientific study of law through its history. In discussing students, Thayer's main point was that during their three years of law school they, like their professors, should devote their full efforts to legal study rather than spend substantial time working in law offices or observing the courts.[7]

Thayer emphasized the difficult historical task facing legal scholars. Meeting scholarly standards for understanding most current law, he maintained, requires study of the entire written history of Anglo-American law, from the period even before the beginning of English legal reporting six centuries earlier. Much of this vast material, moreover, was unprinted and in the foreign languages of Latin for the old legal records and of Anglo-French for the first two hundred years of legal reporting in the Year Books, the generic name for the anonymous summaries of legal arguments, especially pleadings, that first appeared in the late thirteenth century.[8] Further complicating historical research, the Year Books were poorly edited and often inaccurate.[9] Yet Thayer took pains to underline that the Year Books contained essential information for the legal scholar. "Amidst their quaint and antiquated learning," he remarked, "is found the key to many a modern anomaly; and the reader observes with delight the vigorous growth of the law from age to age by just the same processes which work in it to-day in our latest reports," including "the breaking out of what we call the modern spirit."[10] After the Year Books came more than three hundred and fifty years of reported cases in England and a century of American decisions.[11] Nor was all of this enough, for Thayer, convinced that "if a man would know any one thing, he must know more than one," urged the comparative study of the history of other legal systems, particularly Roman law, in order to understand Anglo-American law.[12]

---

[4] Id. at 173–5, 183.

[5] Id. at 173.

[6] Id. at 169 n. 1.

[7] Id. at 183.

[8] J. H. Baker, An Introduction to English Legal History (London: Butterworths, 1979) (2d ed.), pp. 152–3; S. F. C. Milsom, Historical Foundations of the Common Law (Toronto: Butterworths 1981) (2d ed.), pp. 44–8.

[9] Thayer, supra note 1, at 175–6.

[10] Id. at 177.

[11] Id. at 175–6.

[12] Id. at 178.

After setting forth his historical agenda, Thayer anticipated possible objections to it. To those potentially daunted by such a huge enterprise, Thayer denied that he was recommending an absurd impossibility. Based on his own experience, he claimed that the historical investigation he advocated "is not only practicable, but a necessary preliminary for first-rate work." He did emphasize in this context, however, that legal scholars should limit themselves to a single specialty, or at most several interconnected ones, rather than attempt to explore the entire range of legal subjects.[13] At the opposite extreme, he rejected the possible view that the two great nineteenth-century English works of legal history – Maine's 1861 classic, *Ancient Law*, and Pollock and Maitland's just published *History of English Law* – provided sufficient coverage of the field. Rather, Thayer declared, legal history "is still largely unexplored." For the scholar, he added, "such books are helps and guides for his own research, and not substitutes for it."[14] He predicted that it would take two generations for legal scholars to master the history of law sufficiently to enable its systematic restatement.[15]

Thayer also anticipated objections from those who would urge codification to replace the common law, which would thereby eliminate the need to study the "enormous load" of its history. Refusing to discuss contemporary debates over codification, Thayer simply responded that codification could never be effective without thorough understanding of the law. "To codify what is only half understood," he wrote, "is to perpetuate a mass of errors and shallow ambiguities; it is to begin at the wrong end." In the areas of his own expertise, he confidently reported, "I have never seen any attempt at codification, here or abroad, which was not plainly marked by grave and disqualifying defects." The codifiers, he added, were often people of goodwill who had great ability and practical sense, but who lacked competent knowledge of their subject. Such knowledge, Thayer stressed, must be based on historical study that remained to be done. Codification of law or its systematic restatement for purposes of legislation "should come later, if it come at all."[16]

While urging the academic study of law in universities, Thayer happily reported that the condition of legal education was much better in the United States than in England. He recognized that the study of English law in universities began in England, with the appointment of Blackstone at Oxford in 1758. Lawyers on both sides of the Atlantic welcomed the publication of Blackstone's *Commentaries*, beginning in 1765, as a great achievement, what Thayer called a "really Herculean task of redeeming to orderly statement and to an approximately scientific form, the disordered bulk of our common law."[17] After quoting William Hammond, an American editor of Blackstone's *Commentaries*,

---

[13] Id. at 176.
[14] Id. at 178.
[15] Id. at 183.
[16] Id. at 181.
[17] Id. at 170.

on their enormous immediate and continuing influence in America since their initial publication, Thayer emphasized that Blackstone was "a scholar and a University man, who had the genius to see that English law was worthy to be taught on a footing with other sciences, and as other systems of law had been taught in the Universities of other countries."[18]

In America, Blackstone's example as a university scholar was soon emulated, beginning with the chair of law established in 1779 at the College of William and Mary through the efforts of Thomas Jefferson and followed at other universities even before 1800. But in England itself, legal education in universities languished. Blackstone himself resigned from Oxford in 1766, disappointed by its failure to implement his plan for a college of law. "The conservatism of a powerful profession," Thayer wrote about England, "absorbed in the mere business of its calling, itself untrained in the learned or scientific study of law, and unconscious of the need of such training, did not yield to or much consider the suggestions of what had already been done at Oxford." The traditional method of legal education through office apprenticeship continued, with Blackstone's *Commentaries* simply added to the reading of the apprentice, as if they were the "full and final restatement of the law."[19]

Although apprenticeship continued in the United States as well, Thayer pointed out that the systematic study of law at universities had a continuous, if uneven existence, always flourishing somewhere and more generally accepted than in England. Thayer acknowledged that the situation in England had recently improved, but he also observed that leading English legal scholars looked with understandable envy at the condition of legal education in the United States.[20] American legal scholars, he added, had an obligation to take advantage of their favorable position. They "must not be content with a mere lip service, with merely tagging our law schools with the name of a University, while they lack entirely the University spirit and character," namely, the scientific study of law through history.[21]

Thayer was not impressed by the current quality of scholarship in English law. Despite recent improvements, the number of truly excellent works remained very small. As examples of published work that should serve as models for the kind of legal scholarship he was advocating, he referred first, significantly, to the work of a German scholar on what Thayer called "one of our English topics," Brunner's *History of the Jury*, published in 1872 and still, "to the disgrace of the English-speaking race," not translated into English. Turning next to writing by English scholars, he began with the *History of English Law*, written primarily by Maitland, and complimented Maitland's editing of *Bracton's Note Book*, a selection of previously unpublished judicial records from the thirteenth century. He also cited the great earlier work by Blackstone and by Henry Maine,

---

[18] Id. at 171.
[19] Id. at 171–2.
[20] Id. at 172–3.
[21] Id. at 173.

whose *Ancient Law* he had described as illustrating the advantages of comparative legal history by using Roman law as a mirror that reflected light on English law.[22] He even concluded that *Ancient Law*, published in 1861, "created an epoch" on the same order of importance as Darwin's *Origin of Species*, published almost contemporaneously in 1859.[23] Among other recent English legal scholars familiar to Americans, he praised Dicey, Holland, Markby, and Pollock. Thayer, more delicately, did not mention the names of American legal scholars he admired. Yet he emphasized that scholars in at least seven American university law schools from all parts of the country had recently published outstanding contributions in many areas of law[24] and specifically praised Bigelow for his work in gathering for the first time many of the oldest recorded judicial proceedings in England.[25] Undoubtedly, many of these unnamed scholars, as well as Bigelow and Hammond, American legal scholars Thayer did name, are among those on whom I focus in this book.

Both directly and implicitly, Thayer made many points in this address with which other leading late nineteenth-century American legal scholars overwhelmingly agreed, though they shared numerous additional views as well. The most fundamental consensus among these scholars was that historical research into the entire development of current law is a prerequisite to understanding and, ultimately, to restating it. They believed that history reveals ambiguities, anomalies, gratuitous technicalities, and false theories in current law that should be eliminated through legal reform. Primarily interested in the history of Anglo-American law, they were eager to explore any insights the histories of other legal systems could provide into their own. They believed that an enormous amount of preliminary historical research was needed before a systematic restatement of current law could be properly accomplished, and for this reason they often opposed codification as historically premature. They viewed the historical study of law as a science, which, like other sciences, needed to be housed within research universities staffed by full-time professors and attended by full-time students. Commitment to studying law as a historical science accounted for the time and energy many of them spent in reforming legal education.

As Thayer indicated by referring to Americans at universities throughout the country, many of these professors saw themselves as part of a collaborative effort, extending to Germany and England, to build on the few good prior works of English legal history. Thayer's initial citation to Brunner as a model for future scholarship in the field reflected a broader recognition that German legal scholars had pioneered the historical study of English law as well as, beginning with Savigny in the early nineteenth century, the general field of legal history. The Americans were also familiar with legal historians in England,

[22] Id. at 178.
[23] Id. at 179.
[24] Id. at 180–1.
[25] Id. at 176.

particularly, as Thayer highlighted, the imposing figures of Maine in the middle of the nineteenth century and Maitland at its end. Most, however, were not as generous as Thayer to Blackstone's *Commentaries* of the late eighteenth century, which they often criticized as unhistorical and, therefore, unscientific.

An Overview of the American Legal Scholars

In examining the centrality of history in late nineteenth-century American legal scholarship, I focus on eleven scholars, chosen for the quality and influence of their work. Born between 1820 and 1857, they published their major works from the 1860s through the first decade of the twentieth century. In order of their birth, they are Francis Wharton (1820), Thomas McIntyre Cooley (1824), James Coolidge Carter (1827), John Norton Pomeroy (1828), William Gardiner Hammond (1829), James Bradley Thayer (1831), Henry Adams (1838), Oliver Wendell Holmes, Jr. (1841), James Barr Ames (1846), Melville Madison Bigelow (1846), and Christopher G. Tiedeman (1857).[26] Many of these scholars corresponded with each other and some had close, interlocking relationships. Many also corresponded with major legal scholars in Germany, and especially in England. Some studied law in Germany and did research in England on the history of English law.

Except for Wharton, Carter, Adams, and Holmes, all of these scholars had substantial careers as law professors, often starting as founding members of new law faculties. Cooley was one of the three professors appointed to the original law faculty of the University of Michigan in 1859; Hammond joined the law faculty at the University of Iowa in 1867, one year after its establishment; Bigelow prepared the report that led to the founding of the Boston University School of Law and was part of its initial faculty in 1872; and Pomeroy, after teaching law at New York University, moved to the Hastings College of Law when it opened in San Francisco in 1878. Although Harvard Law School had been founded much earlier, Ames in 1873 and Thayer in 1874 were the initial appointments by Christopher Columbus Langdell, the new dean hired by President Eliot as part of his effort to transform Harvard into a research university, an equivalent undertaking to starting a new school. Drawing on their historical interests, Pomeroy and Hammond initiated curricular and pedagogical innovations that became important variants of the case method of instruction introduced by Langdell and most fully developed by Ames at Harvard. In

---

[26] After selecting these eleven scholars, I realized that many of them had been included in the multi-volume series entitled Great American Lawyers (Philadelphia: The John C. Winston Company, 1909) (William Draper Lewis, ed.) As its subtitle indicated, these volumes profiled "the lives and influence of judges and lawyers who have acquired permanent national reputation, and have developed the jurisprudence of the United States." Volume VII included an essay on Cooley, and volume VIII included essays on Carter, Pomeroy, Hammond, and Thayer. The inclusion of these scholars reinforces my judgment about their importance. These volumes did not profile living lawyers. Adams, Holmes, Ames, and Bigelow were alive in 1909.

addition to their careers as law professors, Cooley, Hammond, Bigelow, Ames, and Tiedeman became law school deans.

Among the scholars who did not become law professors, Adams was the only one who was not a lawyer, though he had studied law in Germany after graduating from Harvard College. Yet during his brief career on the history faculty at Harvard in the 1870s, Adams introduced the professional study of legal history to the United States. Following German models, Adams taught seminars in legal history in which students worked from original sources. In 1876, he financed the publication of the first significant American scholarship in legal history, *Essays in Anglo-Saxon Law*, contributed by him and three of his advanced students. The following year he resigned from Harvard and abandoned his career as a legal historian. Wharton had a varied career, including periods as an Episcopalian priest and solicitor of the Department of State. Carter was a distinguished practicing lawyer in New York City and a leader of the bar. Holmes wrote most of his legal scholarship while in private practice in Boston. He briefly joined the Harvard law faculty in 1882, but he resigned at the end of the year to accept an appointment to the Supreme Judicial Court of Massachusetts. He remained a judge for the rest of his long career, moving to the United States Supreme Court in 1903.

Although all of these scholars emphasized the centrality of history in legal analysis, and often explored the historiographical and jurisprudential implications of evolutionary legal thought, only a few of them produced original scholarship in legal history. In addition to the *Essays in Anglo-Saxon Law* by Henry Adams and his students, the major American works in legal history were written by Bigelow, Holmes, Thayer, and Ames, the four American scholars generously cited by Pollock and Maitland as important predecessors in studying the history of English law.[27] When they began their work in legal history in the 1870s, they all lived in the Boston area and were in regular contact with each other. Both Bigelow and Thayer reported that they recognized the need for original research in legal history while preparing works on substantive law, torts for Bigelow and evidence for Thayer.[28] Hammond, who was in contact with these four scholars from Boston, took extensive notes on the English Year Books and drafted thousands of pages for a projected book on the history of the common law that, sadly, he never completed.

Though unified by a shared commitment to the historical study of law, these scholars had quite diverse family and educational backgrounds. Some, especially Adams and Holmes, were born into prominent and wealthy families; others grew up poor. Some attended elite colleges and law schools; others, including some from wealthy families, received legal training in law offices

---

[27] Frederick Pollock and Frederic William Maitland, The History of English Law before the Time of Edward I (Cambridge University Press, 1899) (2d ed.), vol. 1, p. xxxvii.

[28] Melville M. Bigelow, Placita Anglo-Normannica (Boston: Soule and Bugbee, 1881), p. iii; James Bradley Thayer, A Preliminary Treatise on Evidence at the Common Law (Boston: Little, Brown and Company 1898), p. 1.

rather than law schools, a typical form of legal education in their time. Cooley, one of the most eminent of the entire group, was raised in a pioneering farming family in western New York and did not even attend college.

Many of these legal scholars had intellectual interests beyond the law. Cooley worked as a journalist before becoming a law professor and judge. Thayer wrote literary criticism for serious popular magazines during his years as a practicing lawyer and was offered a chair of rhetoric at Harvard before joining its law faculty. Ames taught literature and history at Harvard College while a student at Harvard Law School. Wharton spent several years teaching history and literature as well as constitutional law at Kenyon College and taught at theological seminaries. Some belonged to discussion clubs in their communities, in which prominent men in business and the professions discussed literary, philosophical, and political issues. Many became active and often held positions of leadership in various professional societies, such as the American Academy of Arts and Sciences, the American Social Science Association, and the American Society for the Advancement of Social Science. They also participated in and often led distinctively legal organizations, such as the Association of American Law Schools, the American Bar Association, the Association of the Bar of the City of New York, and the Selden Society, an organization of legal historians founded in England.

Though some of these scholars did not leave strong traces of their political views, if any, others did. Their political commitments varied. Before the Civil War, Wharton and Cooley were active Democrats in the Jefferson-Jackson tradition, Wharton in Pennsylvania and Cooley in Michigan, though Cooley became an anti-slavery Free Soiler in 1848 and after the Civil War often identified with the Republican Party as he turned increasingly conservative. Hammond, by contrast, was active in the local Republican Party in New York when he worked for a Wall Street firm in the 1850s. After the Civil War, Adams, Ames, Carter, and Thayer were involved in the reformist wing of the Republican Party, often called "independent" or "liberal," and in the later "Mugwump" movement.[29] The independent Republicans became increasingly disappointed that their hopes for the reform of American society, assisted by the discipline that helped win the Civil War, were being undermined by the corruption they associated with the Republican administration of President Grant.[30] They felt that political corruption, particularly the "spoils system" of awarding government positions on the basis of political connections divorced from merit, had replaced slavery as the major threat to republican institutions.[31] Centered in

[29] Geoffrey Blodgett, The Gentle Reformers: Massachusetts Democrats in the Cleveland Era (Cambridge, Mass.: Harvard University Press, 1966), p. 20; Gerald W. MacFarland, Mugwumps, Morals & Politics (Amherst, Mass.: University of Massachusetts Press, 1975), pp. 41, 42, 94, 130, 207, 244 n. 7; John G. Sproat, "The Best Men": Liberal Reformers in the Gilded Age (New York: Oxford University Press, 1968), pp. 90–2, 102.

[30] George M. Fredrickson, The Inner Civil War: Northern Intellectuals and the Crisis of the Union (New York: Harper Torchbook, 1968).

[31] MacFarland, supra note 29, at 12.

the Northeast, they focused particularly on civil service reform. Trying initially to reform the Republican Party from within, some independent Republicans, after repeated failures, become the Mugwumps who left the Republican Party in 1884 to support the Democratic presidential nominee, Grover Cleveland.[32] Cleveland, who won the 1884 election by a slim margin, believed that the Mugwumps had contributed significantly to his victory.[33] Revealingly, the term "Mugwump," the Algonquian word for "great men," was applied ironically to these bolters by Republican Party regulars, to connote that they took themselves and their idealism too seriously.[34]

Northeastern colleges, particularly Harvard, provided substantial leadership for the Mugwumps. People committed to civil service reform and to the creation of the modern research university believed that authority should be based on professional expertise. They often viewed the research university as the training ground for educated public servants committed to the meritocratic values of science and professionalism rather than to the personal politics of the spoils system.[35] In *The Emergence of the American University*, Laurence Veysey calls President Eliot of Harvard "the archetypical Mugwump"[36] and claims that the Mugwumps, while not realizing their hopes for civil service reform, achieved their greatest success by transforming Harvard into a modern research university. "Harvard University, rather than Boston or the United States, became the body politic of the Mugwump's dream."[37]

Though Carter, Cooley, and Tiedeman have been portrayed by subsequent progressive scholars as apologists for the interests of big business, their views were more complex. Carter typically represented large corporations, but in major Supreme Court cases he defended the redistributive policies of the federal income tax and argued for the constitutional rights of Chinese immigrants and criminal defendants. Consistent with his Mugwump ideology, he frequently supported municipal reform, most prominently in representing New York City in a successful prosecution of the Tweed ring for stealing city funds. Beyond opposing corruption, Carter criticized the increasing materialism of American life. Cooley and Tiedeman developed the theory of constitutional limitations on government power, which protected corporations against legislative regulation, but they also opposed government intervention in the economy on behalf of corporate interests. Even when he became increasingly conservative after the Civil War, Cooley criticized the Republican Party for allowing itself to be

---

[32] Blodgett, supra note 29, at 1–18; MacFarland, supra note 29, at 2, 16; Sproat, supra note 29, at 90–3, 112–41.

[33] MacFarland, supra note 29, at 53.

[34] Id. at 11.

[35] Blodgett, supra note 29, at 21; Fredrickson, supra note 30, at 21; Thomas L. Haskell, The Emergence of Professional Social Science (The Johns Hopkins University Press, 2000), pp. 91, 119–21; Laurence R. Veysey, The Emergence of the American University (University of Chicago Press, 1970), p. 72.

[36] Veysey, supra note 35, at 88.

[37] Id. at 98.

corrupted by the interests of the wealthy. More generally, Carter, Cooley, and Tiedeman bemoaned the growing concentration of economic power in the United States, often seeming to look back nostalgically to an era of greater economic competition and equality before the Civil War. In 1887, Cooley became the first chairman of the Interstate Commerce Commission after his appointment to the commission by President Cleveland, the Democratic president elected with the help of the Mugwumps. As chairman of the ICC, as previously as a judge on the Michigan Supreme Court, Cooley frequently upheld government regulation of business. Although Tiedeman was explicitly conservative in his scholarship, warning against attempts by radicals to invoke the power of the state on their own behalf, by 1900 he, too, was more open to the exercise of government authority against concentrated private wealth.

The current reputations of these scholars do not line up neatly with their scholarly accomplishments. Though Adams and Holmes are by far the most famous today, they are not well known for their work in legal history. Adams's important career as the founder of professional legal history in the United States has been largely overshadowed by his great literary accomplishments after leaving Harvard. Even people who are interested in legal history are often unfamiliar with his major contributions to the field. Holmes's reputation as perhaps the greatest American legal thinker has mostly survived the assaults of recent revisionism, but his work as a legal historian, which was influential though often inaccurate, has received relatively little attention. Among the other scholars, Ames, Cooley, Thayer, and Tiedeman are probably best known today, but largely for reasons unrelated to the quality of their scholarship. Progressive historians drew attention to Cooley and Tiedeman by claiming that they provided the intellectual justifications for the Supreme Court's support of laissez-faire capitalism in the late nineteenth and early twentieth centuries.[38] More recent revisionist challenges to this interpretation have extended attention to their work.[39] The reputations of Ames and Thayer have benefited from their association with Harvard Law School during its rise to preeminence at the end of the nineteenth century. Though their writing was excellent, even their colleagues commented that Thayer and especially Ames had not been particularly productive scholars. By contrast, Tiedeman and Cooley were prolific

[38] See, e.g., Clyde E. Jacobs, Law Writers and the Courts: The Influence of Thomas M. Cooley, Christopher G. Tiedeman, and John F. Dillon Upon American Constitutional Law (University of California Press, 1954); Arnold M. Paul, Conservative Crisis and the Rule of Law: Attitudes of Bar and Bench, 1887–1895 (Ithaca, N.Y.: Cornell University Press, 1960); Benjamin R. Twiss, Lawyers and the Constitution: How Laissez Faire Came to the Supreme Court (Princeton, N.J: Princeton University Press, 1942).

[39] Howard Gillman, The Constitution Besieged: The Rise and Demise of Lochner Era Police Powers Jurisprudence (Durham, N.C.: Duke University Press, 1993); Michael Les Benedict, Laissez-Faire and Liberty: A Re-Evaluation of the Meaning and Origins of Laissez-Faire Constitutionalism, 3 L & Hist. Rev. 293 (1985); Alan Jones, Thomas M. Cooley and "Laissez-Faire Constitutionalism": A Reconsideration, 33 J. Am. Hist. 751 (1967); Charles W. McCurdy, Justice Field and the Jurisprudence of Government-Business Relations: Some Parameters of Laissez-Faire Constitutionalism, 1863–1897 61 J. Am. Hist. 970 (1975).

scholars, as were Pomeroy and Wharton, who are much less known today. And Bigelow, who is virtually forgotten today, arguably was the late nineteenth-century American legal scholar who made the greatest contribution to original scholarship in legal history. The following brief biographical sketches introduce in chronological birth order the leading American scholars who studied law historically.

Francis Wharton

Francis Wharton produced major works of legal scholarship while pursuing several careers. Born in Philadelphia in 1820, he graduated from Yale College in 1839. He then returned to Philadelphia to work in his father's law office and was admitted to the bar in 1843. A Jeffersonian Democrat, Wharton was active in the Pennsylvania Democratic Party, through which he obtained a position as an assistant state attorney general. He left legal practice in the 1850s for Kenyon College in Ohio, where he taught English history and literature as well as constitutional law. At the affiliated theological seminary, he gave a series of lectures on "modern infidelity," which he published in a book entitled *Modern Theism*. He also wrote extensively for literary periodicals.[40]

Wharton became an Episcopalian priest in 1862 and the following year moved to Brooklyn, New York, where he worked as a parish priest. After a trip to Europe in 1869, he resigned from his parish to teach at the Seminary of the Episcopal Church in Cambridge, Massachusetts. He also lectured at Boston University School of Law, joining Bigelow on the faculty. Wharton took another extensive trip to Europe in 1881–3 and in 1885 was appointed solicitor of the Department of State in Washington, D.C., a position he held until his death in 1889.[41]

After his resignation as a parish priest in 1869, Wharton wrote continuously on a wide range of topics. He produced major treatises on conflicts of law and criminal law and wrote books about international law and diplomatic history. He also compiled an annotated volume containing historically important state trials in early American history.[42] His receipt of an honorary doctor of laws from the University of Edinburgh[43] reflected his contemporary reputation. Despite his honor from Edinburgh, his long periods of residence in England, and his substantial knowledge of English history,[44] Wharton asserted that his careful study of German scholarship most influenced his own.[45]

Wharton's views on legal history are best reflected in his 1884 *Commentaries on Law*, whose subtitle announced that it embraced "chapters on the nature,

[40] John Bassett Moore, A Brief Sketch of the Life of Francis Wharton (Washington, D.C.?: s.n. 1889), pp. 1–3.
[41] Id. at 2–3, 7.
[42] Francis Wharton, State Trials of the United States During the Administrations of Washington and Adams (Philadelphia: Carey and Hart, 1849).
[43] Moore, supra note 40, at 8–9.
[44] Id. at 3–4.
[45] Id. at 9.

FIGURE 1.1. *Francis Wharton*. From Francis Wharton, *A Memoir* (Philadelphia, 1891).

the source, and the history of law; on international law, public and private; and on constitutional and statutory law."[46] Throughout this work, Wharton stressed that effective law must emanate from the conscience and needs of a people. Consistent with his Jeffersonian ideology, he believed that the conscience and needs of the American people required a limited government that promoted individual freedom and protected the minority against the excesses of majority rule.[47]

Thomas McIntyre Cooley

Born in 1824, Cooley was the tenth of fifteen children in a family of pioneering farmers in western New York. Interested from an early age in becoming a lawyer, Cooley had hoped to attend college as part of his preparatory training. When his father's opposition thwarted his college plans, Cooley began to study law in 1842 in the office of Theron K. Strong, an influential lawyer in Palmyra,

---

[46] Francis Wharton, Commentaries on Law (Philadelphia: Kay & Brother, 1884).
[47] Moore, supra note 40, at 11.

FIGURE 1.2. *Thomas McIntyre Cooley*. Published with permission of the Tarlton Law Library, Jamail Center for Legal Research, University of Texas School of Law.

New York, who had been a Democratic congressman and who later became a judge on the state supreme court. Cooley himself was an avid follower of William Leggett, a Jacksonian Democrat who used laissez-faire ideology to denounce the corruption of government by concentrated corporate power.[48]

Cooley moved west in 1843. Apparently, he intended to travel to Chicago, but he settled in Adrian, Michigan, when his money ran out. He resumed his legal studies in an Adrian law office and was admitted to the Michigan bar in 1846. Cooley's early career as a lawyer was undistinguished. During the decade following his admission to the bar, he devoted substantial time to other

[48] Harry Burns Hutchins, Thomas McIntyre Cooley, in Great American Lawyers, supra note 26, vol. VII, pp. 431, 431–6; Jones, supra note 39, at 753. On Leggett, see Sean Wilentz, The Rise of American Democracy (New York: W. W. Norton & Company, 2005), p. 235; Richard Hofstadter, William Leggett, Spokesman of Jacksonian Democracy, 58 Pol. Sci. Q. 581 (1943).

interests, including farming, real estate, journalism, and politics.[49] He was active in the Democratic Party but alienated himself from its mainstream and probably harmed his incipient political career when he, like other Democrats opposed to slavery and corporate power, helped organize the local Free Soil Party in 1848. In his politics and in his writing in the late 1840s and early 1850s, Cooley attacked slavery and monopolies while defending free trade, free public schools, and free discussion. Concerned that corporate interests had taken over the legislative process, producing "class legislation" that favored the rich and harmed everyone else, he supported efforts to impose constitutional limitations on legislative power.[50]

In the mid-1850s, Cooley was a country lawyer unknown beyond southern Michigan, but his career took off at the end of the decade. In 1857, the Michigan legislature appointed Cooley to compile the laws of the state. His success in efficiently completing this task prompted the newly created state supreme court to select him in 1858 as the reporter of its decisions. Another year later, the University of Michigan established a Department of Law, and the Board of Regents appointed Cooley one of the initial three professors.[51] He remained on the faculty for twenty-five years and during most of that period also was the dean.[52]

Cooley's correspondence with other leading scholars throughout his career indicates his importance. He received letters praising his work and often asking his advice from Hammond,[53] Holmes,[54] Bigelow,[55] Thayer,[56] Wharton,[57] and Tiedeman.[58] Writing that the *North American Review* wanted to publish six articles on the "movement of American thought" in various fields during the last century, including religion, literature, and politics, Henry Adams invited Cooley to write the one about law.[59] Through an introduction by Andrew D. White, the first president of Cornell University and the American Historical Association, James Bryce, professor of law at Oxford, asked Cooley to comment

---

[49] Hutchins, supra note 48, at 436–41.

[50] Jones, supra note 39, at 753–5; On Democrats in the Free Soil Party, see Eric Foner, Free Soil, Free Labor, Free Men (New York: Oxford University Press, 1970), pp. 60, 169.

[51] Hutchins, supra note 48, at 441–6.

[52] Id. at 448–9.

[53] See, e.g., Letter from William G. Hammond to T. M. Cooley (September 18, 1871) (Thomas M. Cooley Papers, Box 6, Bentley Historical Library, University of Michigan) [hereinafter cited as Cooley Papers].

[54] Letter from O. W. Holmes to T. M. Cooley (April 16, 1873) (Cooley Papers, supra note 53, Box 6).

[55] Letter from Melville M. Bigelow to T. M. Cooley (October 31, 1876) (Cooley Papers, supra note 53, Box 1).

[56] Letter from J. B. Thayer to T. M. Cooley (March 24, 1885) (Cooley Papers, supra note 53, Box 2).

[57] Letter from Francis Wharton to T. M. Cooley (May 16, 1885) (Cooley Papers, supra note 53, Box 2).

[58] Letter from C. G. Tiedeman to T. M. Cooley (February 10, 1886) (Cooley Papers, supra note 53, Box 2).

[59] Letter from Henry Adams to T. M. Cooley (August 28, 1875) (Cooley Papers, supra note 53, Box 2). Cooley did not write this article. See G. T. Bispham, Law in America, 1776–1876, 38 North American Rev. 154 (1876).

on his forthcoming book on the American Constitution.[60] Cooley responded, critically and at length, and corresponded with Thayer about Bryce's book, the influential and widely read *American Commonwealth*.[61] Over the years, Cooley received invitations to teach at the University of Chicago[62] and Johns Hopkins University,[63] to give the Storrs lectures at Yale Law School,[64] and to be conferred an honorary doctor of laws during the 250th anniversary of Harvard College.[65]

Five years after his appointment as a law professor, Cooley was elected to fill a vacancy on the Michigan Supreme Court. He served simultaneously on the faculty and the court until he retired from both in 1885.[66] In the 1880s, he developed expertise in the important practical field of railroad regulation. One of three commissioners selected by major railroads in 1882 to determine freight rates on key routes, he wrote the commission's report. In 1886, a federal judge named him receiver of the Wabash railway system, a position that ended just a few months later, when President Cleveland appointed him to one of the five positions on the Interstate Commerce Commission, which had just been established by the Interstate Commerce Act of 1887. Chosen chairman by his colleagues, Cooley remained on the commission until 1891, when poor health forced him to resign.[67] He lived until 1898, becoming president of the American Bar Association in 1894.[68]

Cooley was a prolific author who wrote treatises in many legal fields.[69] Although Cooley himself thought his treatise on torts the best of his books,[69] his first major work, *A Treatise on Constitutional Limitations*, established and maintained his reputation. Published in 1868, and republished in six editions

---

[60] Letter from Andrew D. White to T. M. Cooley (November 15, 1885) (Cooley Papers, supra note 53, Box 2); letter from J. Bryce to T. M. Cooley (December 23, 1885) (Cooley Papers, supra note 53, Box 2).

[61] See Cooley notebook on Bryce's draft (Cooley Papers, supra note 53, Box 7); letter from J. B. Thayer to T. M. Cooley (August 11, 1887) (Cooley Papers, supra note 53, Box 3). Bryce thanked Cooley "most heartily for just criticisms." Letter from J. Bryce to T. M. Cooley (October 15, 1887) (Cooley Papers, supra note 53, Box 3). After completing his revisions, Bryce wrote Cooley that he had removed statements to which Cooley objected and occasionally had "placed in a note an extract from your remarks on some passage in the text of my book correcting or adding to it." Letter from J. Bryce to T. M. Cooley (Mar. 2, 1888) (Cooley Papers, supra note 53, Box 3). See generally Everett S. Brown, The Contribution of Thomas M. Cooley to Bryce's "American Commonwealth," 31 Mich. L. Rev. 346 (1933).

[62] Letter from James R. Boise to T. M. Cooley (March 11, 1876) (Cooley Papers, supra note 53, Box 1).

[63] Letter from D. C. Gilman to T. M. Cooley (November 16, 1880) (Cooley Papers, supra note 53, Box 1).

[64] Letter from Letter from Simeon E. Baldwin to T. M. Cooley (January 27, 1890) (Cooley Papers, supra note 53, Box 3).

[65] Letter from Charles W. Eliot to T. M. Cooley (October 20, 1886) (Cooley Papers, supra note 53, Box 8).

[66] Hutchins, supra note 48, at 450, 455.

[67] Id. at 484–7.

[68] Twiss, supra note 38, at 35.

[69] A. C. McLaughlin, Cooley, Thomas McIntyre, 3 Dictionary of American Biography 392, 393 (1930).

through 1903, *Constitutional Limitations* was at a minimum the most important treatise on constitutional law written in the second half of the nineteenth century and was arguably the most influential legal treatise ever produced by an American.[70]

In writing *Constitutional Limitations*, Cooley became the first scholar to focus on state rather than federal constitutional law.[71] He accumulated and organized the multiple limitations on state constitutional power found in state court decisions throughout the country, including limitations that were only implicit or accepted in a minority of states.[72] From these decisions, Cooley built what Benjamin Twiss, writing in the 1940s, called "a constitutional ideology for individualism"[73] that by the end of the nineteenth century dominated decisions by the United States Supreme Court as well as by state courts.[74]

Doctrinally, *Constitutional Limitations* played a significant role in transforming the concept of due process from a procedural guarantee into a substantive principle that protected individual rights against abridgment by the state. From congressional debates over the Fourteenth Amendment and scattered judicial opinions, Cooley constructed a broad interpretation of its due process clause that the Supreme Court subsequently and repeatedly cited while declaring progressive legislation unconstitutional.[75] Building on his earlier writings, Cooley also opposed "class legislation" throughout *Constitutional Limitations*, a position that, in the view of some subsequent scholars, paved the way for the Supreme Court a generation later to develop "liberty of contract," a term never used by Cooley himself.[76] According to these scholars, "liberty of contract" complemented substantive due process as another doctrinal weapon to invalidate legislation on constitutional grounds. By providing intellectual support for constitutional limitations on legislative powers, scholars maintained, Cooley helped reverse presumptions in favor of the validity of legislation that had prevailed from roughly 1830 to 1850.[77]

Even scholars who portrayed Cooley as a key figure in creating constitutional support for laissez-faire capitalism have observed that corporate lawyers and judges sympathetic to the interests of big business extended his views in more conservative directions than he originally intended in *Constitutional Limitations*.[78] For example, Cooley included a chapter on "the police power of the state," which justified substantial state authority to legislate in the public

[70] Hutchins, supra note 48, at 472–3; Jacobs, supra note 38, at 29; Jones, supra note 39, at 759.

[71] Twiss, supra note 38, at 33; Jacobs, supra note 38, at 29; Jones, supra note 39, at 759.

[72] Twiss, supra note 38, at 26; Jacobs, supra note 38, at 30.

[73] Twiss, supra note 38, at 18 (title of chapter II).

[74] Jacobs, supra note 38, at 22, 29.

[75] Twiss, supra note 38, at 26; Jacobs, supra note 38, at 32; Jones, supra note 39, at 760.

[76] Twiss, supra note 38, at 28; Jacobs, supra note 38, at 12–13, 26–7, 30. See Jones, supra note 39, at 760 (subsequent scholars miscited Cooley to support "liberty of contract").

[77] Twiss, supra note 38, at 29; Jacobs, supra note 38, at 107; Morton J. Horwitz, The Transformation of American Law 1870–1960 (New York: Oxford University Press), p. 22.

[78] Twiss, supra note 38, at 22, 34, 41; Jacobs, supra note 38, at 30.

interest.[79] In an early edition, moreover, he criticized Chief Justice Marshall's
decision in the *Dartmouth College* case for allowing corporations to have
more influence on legislation "than the states to which they owed their corporate existence."[80]

Cooley's careers as a judge on the Michigan Supreme Court and as chairman of the Interstate Commerce Commission reinforced the textual language
in *Constitutional Limitations* that demonstrated independence from the ideology and interests of big business. Believing in judicial restraint, he often upheld
regulatory legislation against constitutional challenges by affected corporations. Indeed, Thayer frequently cited Cooley in support of his own subsequent
defense of judicial restraint and wrote directly to Cooley to acknowledge his
influence.[81] At times, Cooley did strike down legislation as unconstitutional,
but these decisions could harm as well as benefit corporate interests. One of his
best known opinions, consistent with his long-standing hostility to corporate
influence on government, invalidated legislation that authorized municipalities
to issue bonds for railroad construction. In a decision subsequently reversed by
the United States Supreme Court, Cooley emphasized that the state power of
taxation is limited to public purposes and called railroad construction a private
interest of the railroad corporations.[82] As chairman of the Interstate Commerce
Commission, Cooley again acted against the interests of the railroad corporations. He rejected the claim that the determination of rates by the commission
constituted an unconstitutional deprivation of the railroads' property rights in
violation of substantive due process. Rather, Cooley defended the fairness of
the commission's administrative due process in reaching its decisions on appropriate rates.[83]

On the other hand, scholars have observed that in subsequent editions of
Constitutional Limitations Cooley often incorporated into his characterization of the positive law the conservative extensions of his original language
in numerous intervening judicial decisions.[84] And while Cooley retained his
aversion to the abuse of corporate power that he first expressed as a young
Jacksonian Democrat, by the end of his life he had become a moderate conservative, who often identified with but never became an active supporter of the
Republican Party.[85] Even Alan Jones, the scholar who has done most to challenge Cooley's reputation as a defender of business interests, acknowledged the
increasingly "conservative mood" of his thought.[86] Yet Jones also stressed that
Cooley opposed what he perceived to be the corruption of the Republican Party

[79] Twiss, supra note 38, at 29–30.
[80] Jones, supra note 39, at 755.
[81] Jones, supra note 39, at 762.
[82] Hutchins, supra note 48, at 467–72. The Supreme Court, by contrast, upheld the same legislation. Id. at 472. See also Twiss, supra note 38, at 24–5; Jones, supra note 39, at 766.
[83] Jones, supra note 39, at 762.
[84] Twiss, supra 38, at 31; Jacobs, supra note 38, at 30.
[85] Hutchins, supra note 48, at 491.
[86] Jones, supra note 39, at 457–8.

after the Civil War. Cooley himself believed that his criticism of Republicans for becoming the party of wealthy individuals and corporations cost him an appointment to the United States Supreme Court.[87] Deploring the focus on wealth during the "Gilded Age" of the late nineteenth century, Cooley's increasing conservatism was nostalgic for the values of individualism, independence, and equality that he recalled as more prevalent before the Civil War.[88]

Like many of the other scholars I discuss, Cooley had a deep interest in history throughout his life that informed his legal scholarship even though he never became a professional legal historian. While growing up on an isolated farm, Cooley spent many of his evenings reading history by firelight.[89] He continued to read widely in history as an adult, especially about the development of political institutions in England and the United States.[90] When he became a professor and a judge, he immersed himself in English legal history.[91] Cooley relied heavily on his historical knowledge and sensibility in his legal scholarship. "Constitutional law is so inseparably connected with constitutional history, and is so vital a part of general history," he wrote in 1889, "that I hardly know where to draw the line."[92] Many of the views Cooley expressed in *Constitutional Limitations* derived from his reading in both American and English history. His knowledge of the period surrounding the framing of the Constitution convinced him that the founding generation had good reasons to be skeptical of governmental action.[93] Though a legal scholar and not a professional historian, Cooley even wrote a history of Michigan published in 1885.[94] Recognizing his historical learning, the University of Michigan appointed him professor of American history as well as dean of the School of Political Science after his retirement from the law school and the state supreme court.[95]

James Coolidge Carter

Born in Massachusetts in 1827, Carter graduated in 1850 from Harvard College, where he excelled academically and athletically. After a year as a tutor, he entered Harvard Law School in the fall of 1851. During the middle of the spring 1853 term, he left to join a prominent Wall Street firm in New York City, where he worked until his death in 1905.[96] Carter and Christopher Columbus Langdell were close friends in law school, and in 1869 Carter played a crucial

[87] Id. at 770.
[88] Id. at 769–71.
[89] Hutchins, supra note 48, at 432.
[90] Id. at 451.
[91] Jones, supra note 39, at 757.
[92] Id. at 757 n. 26.
[93] Hutchins, supra note 48, at 474.
[94] Id. at 452.
[95] Id. at 448.
[96] George Alfred Miller, James Coolidge Carter, in Great American Lawyers, supra note 26, vol. VIII, pp. 3, 3–6.

FIGURE 1.3. *James Coolidge Carter*. Published with permission of the Tarlton Law Library, Jamail Center for Legal Research, University of Texas School of Law.

role in convincing President Eliot to appoint Langdell dean of Harvard Law School.[97] Carter remained actively involved in law school affairs and became the first president of the Harvard Law School Association, an alumni group founded in 1886. In that role and from the perspective of an accomplished Wall Street lawyer, he praised the case method of instruction introduced by Langdell as "a vast improvement" in legal training over the pedagogy used when he was a student.[98]

In his Wall Street practice, Carter handled cases involving high financial stakes and covering various subjects, including real property, commercial law,

[97] William P. LaPiana, Logic and Experience: The Origin of Modern American Legal Education (New York: Oxford University Press, 1994), pp. 12–13.
[98] Id. at 101.

admiralty and maritime law, and wills.[99] Beginning in 1888, he argued many important cases before the United States Supreme Court on a wide range of issues. Carter often represented businesses, sometimes against competitors, and sometimes against the government, whose asserted power to regulate business he repeatedly denied. Representing a freight association, for example, he invoked freedom of contract as an argument against application of the Sherman Antitrust Act and the Interstate Commerce Act. In a very different context, he raised First Amendment objections to a federal statute that prohibited the circulation of lottery advertisements through the mails. Yet Carter did not limit his Supreme Court advocacy to corporate clients. He represented individuals against the government while attacking the constitutionality of the Chinese Exclusion Act and asserting the constitutional right of a witness to refuse to give incriminating testimony.[100]

Nor did Carter always challenge government action. In one of the most visible cases of his career, he defended the constitutionality of the federal income tax law and the redistributive economic policies it embodied. According to his law partner, George Alfred Miller, Carter's argument in this case reflected his own deeply held convictions.[101] For this reason, and because his position presents a more complex ideology than the conservatism portrayed by some commentators,[102] Carter's argument merits attention. He began by proudly observing that he had been retained by the Continental Trust Company, "one of the companies which, it might be supposed, represent interests which would be the especial subjects of income taxation," but "which avows its readiness to submit itself without controversy or contention to the law of the country."[103] Observing "the growing concentration of large masses of wealth in an ever diminishing number of persons," Carter viewed the income tax law as an attempt by Congress to remedy this unfortunate development. The purpose of the law "was to redress in some degree the flagrant inequality by which the great mass of the people were made to furnish nearly all the revenue, and leave the very wealthy classes to furnish very little of it in comparison with their means."[104] To the charge that the income tax was "class legislation" because it made "a distinction between the rich and the poor," Carter readily assented. Such a distinction was "its very object and purpose," one "which should always be looked to in the business of taxation." Unfortunately, he added, the

---

[99] Miller, supra note 96, at 14–15, 23.

[100] Id. at 23–5; Twiss, supra note 38, at 179–80, 191–2.

[101] Miller, supra note 96, at 33–4.

[102] See Horwitz, supra note 77, at 139; Mathias Reimann, The Historical School Against Codification: Savigny, Carter, and the Defeat of the New York Civil Code, 37 Am. J. Comp. L. 95, 118–19. Lewis A. Grossman, James Coolidge Carter and Mugwump Jurisprudence, 20 L. & Hist. Rev. 577 (1989), challenges this conventional conservative interpretation.

[103] Pollock v. Farmers' Loan and Trust Company, 157 U.S. 429, 513–14 (1895) (Mr. Carter's Argument for Appellee).

[104] Id. at 517.

distinction had previously "been observed in the wrong direction," with "the poorer class prodigiously overburdened."[105]

In addition to defending the income tax as a proper means of redressing class inequality, Carter stressed the importance of judicial deference to democratic legislation on matters of economic policy. Carter granted, as he had argued in many cases for corporate clients, that the Constitution provides for "a government of delegated and limited powers." He urged the Supreme Court to "declare that the limit has been passed, when it is clearly convinced of the fact." But he also urged the Court to "decline the office of judgment in cases where the question does not assume a purely judicial form," especially "when there is mingled with the question any element of legislative discretion which cannot be separated from it." The constitutional structure of government, Carter stressed, limits the Supreme Court as well as the Congress, and the limits of the judicial function "are already transgressed" when the Court "finds itself even considering whether this or that view of a question of political economy or of the wisdom of taxation, is a sound one."[106] Carter closed by observing without elaboration that Americans "have had some experiences in our history of the futility of attempting to convert political into judicial questions, and the result has not added to the authority of this tribunal." Courts, he concluded, should "avoid attempts at the solution of problems which must and will be finally settled in another forum."[107]

Carter's legal work extended to municipal affairs. After the overthrow of the corrupt Tweed ring in New York City, Carter was retained by the city's corporation counsel to prosecute those accused of stealing city funds, including Tweed himself, and to defend the city against suits brought by people who claimed they had been defrauded while Tweed was in control. According to Carter's partner, the prosecution against Tweed resulted in a verdict for the city of more than six and a half million dollars, and Carter's successful defenses of the city against numerous claimants saved millions more.[108] During this period, Governor Tilden appointed Carter to a commission designed to suggest reforms that would prevent a recurrence of corruption. Carter wrote the commission's report, which was condemned by the general public for recommending that only voters who met certain property qualifications should be eligible to vote for a Board of Finance with authority over city funds. Carter remained interested in municipal reform for the remainder of his life. From his experience with the Tweed ring, he became convinced that partisan state and national politics should be eliminated from municipal affairs, a position he reiterated and elaborated when he became president of the National Municipal League twenty years later.[109] By this time Carter had become concerned about the

---

[105] Id. at 518.
[106] Id. at 531.
[107] Miller, supra note 96, at 35–6 (quoting Carter).
[108] Id. at 9–12.
[109] Id. at 12–13.

corruption of municipal government "by the great monied interests" as well as by "party interests."[110]

In an address to his fiftieth Harvard College reunion in 1900, Carter reiterated, at a more general level, the concern about the negative influence of great wealth on American life that informed his position in the income tax cases and as a municipal reformer. He complained that "our society both in thought and action is under the control of an enormous pressure of material interests which hold in disdain any appeals to the universal principles of truth and right." He advocated defiance against "the pressure of material interests, the denunciations of politicians, and the clamors of yellow journalism." At least among the "priesthood of the great and good" at Harvard, Carter urged his listeners, "let truth, liberty and justice be held in ever-increasing honor, and assert the everlasting supremacy of the moral over the material world."[111] How appropriate that this florid declaration of the dying Mugwump creed be delivered at the center of its greatest strength.

Particularly important among his various civic and professional activities, Carter was a founder and leader of the Association of the Bar of the City of New York. As part of its many activities, the association sponsored lectures, including by Cooley and Tiedeman.[112] Carter served five terms as president and led its successful opposition to the Field Code, which was designed to supersede the common law of New York.[113] Carter had previously encountered Field, who had defended Tweed when Carter prosecuted him on behalf of New York City.[114] Carter cited his experience as a practicing lawyer under the New York code of procedure as a warning against further codification. While conceding that the original code of procedure was adequate, Carter asserted that it had become incomprehensible by incessant legislative amendments and that even its author had disowned it. By 1883, Carter pointed out, uncertainty over its meaning had generated more than six thousand reported cases and many more unreported ones.[115] At a more theoretical level, Carter claimed that judges are better able than legislators to conform law to its foundations in evolving custom. In preparing numerous pamphlets and speeches against the Field Code, Carter relied particularly on Savigny's arguments against codification in Germany, which he first encountered in lectures while a law student.[116] He reiterated these arguments as part of his historical analysis of law in his posthumously published book, *Law: Its Origin, Growth and Function*, the work Roscoe Pound described as the best example of "the historical school in America."[117]

---

[110] Id. at 14.
[111] Id. at 39–40.
[112] Twiss, supra note 38, at 172.
[113] Miller, supra note 96, at 17–18.
[114] Id. at 10.
[115] Id. at 7.
[116] Reimann, supra note 102, at 103–6.
[117] Roscoe Pound, Book Review, 24 Harv. L. Rev. 317 (1909).

John Norton Pomeroy

The son of a probate judge in Rochester, New York, Pomeroy was born in 1828 and graduated from Hamilton College in 1847. He then taught school for three years, first in Rochester, and later near Cincinnati, where he also began studying law in the office of Senator Thomas Corwin, who soon became secretary of the Treasury. Pomeroy returned to Rochester, was admitted to the bar in 1851, and practiced law there for a decade while becoming active in its local literary club composed of lawyers, physicians, businessmen, and professors. Rather unsuccessful as a lawyer, Pomeroy moved to New York City in 1861 in a failed effort to improve his legal practice, which he abandoned within a year to become the principal of an academy in Kingston, New York.

While in Kingston, Pomeroy wrote his first book, *An Introduction to Municipal Law*, published in 1864. Its frontispiece announced that it was "designed for general readers and for students in colleges and higher schools." For Pomeroy, the subject of municipal law was not the law of municipal corporations, as some have mistakenly maintained, but the entire positive law of the state. Widely and favorably reviewed, the book gained Pomeroy substantial acclaim, an honorary degree from his alma mater, and a professorship at New York University (NYU) Law School. He taught at NYU from 1865 until 1871, when poor health prompted him to resign and move back to Rochester, where he became a full-time writer. He earned a modest living by producing heavily annotated editions of existing law books and by contributing hundreds of articles on legal topics for an encyclopedia that he also edited. In addition, he wrote frequently for the *Nation* and the *American Law Review*, mostly on international and constitutional law. During his years as a writer in Rochester, Pomeroy also wrote an original work on remedies.[118]

In 1878, Pomeroy moved to San Francisco to accept the chair of municipal law at the new Hastings Law College of the University of California. At Hastings, Pomeroy developed an elaborate three-year curriculum, with different functions assigned to each of the three years of instruction. The first year introduced the student to the basic classifications of the law as they had developed historically. The second year was more practical, exposing the student to the work of the typical lawyer. The third year focused on remedies. Pomeroy also varied the pedagogy in each of the three years. The first year consisted of a combination of lectures and general discussion of the assigned readings, largely from treatises. Although Pomeroy was skeptical about the wisdom of codification, he also assigned many statutes to first-year students for the pedagogical purpose of demonstrating the boundaries of legal classifications. The second year, like the first, included a combination of lectures and discussion, but cases, not treatises, were the primary reading assignments, and the discussion was

[118] John Norton Pomeroy, Jr., John Norton Pomeroy, in Great American Lawyers, supra note 2, vol. VIII, pp. 91, 91–8, 106–8; Thomas Gardner Barnes, Hastings College of Law: The First Century (San Francisco: University of California, Hastings College of Law Press, 1978), pp. 94–5, 99–100.

FIGURE 1.4. *John Norton Pomeroy*. Published with permission of the Tarlton Law Library, Jamail Center for Legal Research, University of Texas School of Law.

much more narrowly focused on technical analysis of the cases than on the broader themes of the first year. Lectures predominated in the third year, when much of the student work involved exercises in drafting and oral argument. To some extent, therefore, Pomeroy developed a variant of the case method of instruction. But he used the case method more sparingly than Langdell and created a much more systematic curriculum in which every course related to a coherent structure. He particularly ridiculed as "most preposterous" the failure of Harvard Law School to provide elementary instruction in legal principles in the first year. The curriculum developed by Pomeroy culminated in a comprehensive final examination, with separate oral and written portions, covering all three years.[119]

---

[119] Barnes, supra note 118, at 101–5; Pomeroy, supra note 118, at 99 n. 7 ("most preposterous").

In addition to his curricular innovations, Pomeroy continued to produce substantial scholarship at Hastings, most impressively a three-volume treatise on equity jurisprudence published between 1881 and 1883. Reviewing the third edition in 1906, H. R. Hutchins, the dean of the University of Michigan Law School, wrote that during the previous twenty years this "epoch-making" treatise had more influence on American jurisprudence than any other.[120] Much more recently, Thomas Barnes asserted in 1978 that as a scholar Pomeroy exceeded his equally distinguished peers in both his range of subjects and his conceptual boldness. Conceding that Pomeroy was not a scholar whose research uncovered new information, Barnes emphasized his brilliance in synthesizing existing information in ways that yielded novel insights.[121]

Although Pomeroy did not write legal history based on intensive study of primary sources, both as a scholar and as a teacher he emphasized the centrality of history in legal analysis. *An Introduction to Municipal Law*, the book that established his reputation in 1864, covered the historical origins of Anglo-American law and included discussion of the history of Roman and continental European law.[122] In *An Introduction to the Constitutional Law of the United States*, published in 1868 and, like his book on municipal law, "especially designed for students, general and professional,"[123] Pomeroy also included substantial historical analysis. "The method and habit of the lawyer are essentially identical with those of the historical critic or the biblical student,"[124] he wrote at a time when German historical scholarship largely influenced biblical criticism. In this book, he tried to rethink the subject of constitutional law in the immediate aftermath of the Civil War and relied heavily on European scholars who wrote about the origins of concepts such as sovereignty and the state. Although Pomeroy's discussion of case law quickly became obsolete as the Supreme Court revolutionized constitutional law during Reconstruction, the book remained influential for scholars of constitutional history and theory, including Thayer, and judges, including Chief Justice Chase.[125] In his inaugural address at Hastings in 1878, Pomeroy again expressed his profound belief that "the law must be studied historically." Implicitly contrasting his own approach to Langdell's, he added that "while the historical method of study is thus absolutely essential, it is one thing to study the present existing law of the United States historically, and a very different thing, under the name of the historical method, to study only the law which existed and was in full operation in England a century ago."[126]

[120] H. R. Hutchins, Book Review, 4 Mich. L. Rev. 248 (1906).

[121] Barnes, supra note 118, at 91–3.

[122] Id. at 95.

[123] John Norton Pomeroy, An Introduction to the Constitutional Law of the United States (Littleton, Colo.: Fred B. Rothman & Company 1997) (reprint of 4th ed., 1879) (frontispiece).

[124] Id. at 13.

[125] Barnes, supra note 118, at 93–4; Pomeroy, supra note 118, at 102–6.

[126] Pomeroy, supra note 118, at 100.

Like many of his contemporaries, moreover, Pomeroy became very interested in the codification movement. After initially thinking that the movement might usefully be extended beyond procedure, Pomeroy changed his mind and opposed it as a result of his intensive study of California's experiment in broad codification. Carter and his allies in the Association of the Bar of the City of New York relied heavily on Pomeroy's writing against general codification, which they circulated broadly during their campaign in 1885 against codification in New York.[127]

William Gardiner Hammond

Born to a wealthy and prominent Rhode Island family in 1829, Hammond received an excellent education before college and read broadly, particularly in history. After graduating from Amherst College, where he was salutatorian and editor in chief of its literary magazine,[128] Hammond, like many of his contemporaries, prepared for the bar in a law office rather than in law school. He subsequently joined a Wall Street law firm and became active in the local Republican Party. In 1856, he left his firm for health reasons and sailed to Europe. He spent two years abroad, traveling extensively, but also studying law at Heidelberg. He became fluent in German and, by reading German legal scholarship, developed a lifelong interest in the historical study of the civil law. Not long after returning to the United States, he visited his brother in Iowa and decided to settle there.[129]

While practicing law in Iowa, Hammond prepared a digest of decisions of the Iowa Supreme Court, which he hoped would enable him to specialize in representing clients before it. Probably as a result of his work on the digest, in 1867 Hammond became the founding editor of *The Western Jurist*, advertised as the only legal journal published west of the Allegheny Mountains, and started teaching at the Iowa Law School, which had been established the previous year. Hammond soon gave up his legal practice to devote full time to the law school, as a professor and its head, with the title of chancellor.[130] He remained until he became dean of St. Louis Law School in 1881, serving there until his death in 1894.[131] Hammond became involved in national organizations concerned about legal education. As chairman of the Committee on Legal Education of the American Bar Association and of the Department of Jurisprudence of the American Social Science Association, he delivered several papers on legal education.[132]

---

[127] Id. at 115–17.

[128] Emlin McClain, William Gardiner Hammond, in Great American Lawyers, supra note 26, vol. VIII, pp. 191, 194–202.

[129] Id. at 208–12.

[130] Id. at 213–14.

[131] Id. at 231–2.

[132] Id. at 221–2. McClain misidentifies the American Social Science Association as the American Association for the Advancement of Social Science. Id. at 222. William G. Hammond Papers,

FIGURE 1.5. *William Gardiner Hammond*. Courtesy of University of Iowa.

Hammond corresponded with leading American and English scholars about their mutual interests in legal history, including Holmes,[133] Thayer,[134] and the English scholar Edward Freeman.[135] While giving lectures on the history of the common law in Boston, he met socially with Ames, Bigelow, Holmes, Thayer,

University of Iowa College of Law, vol. 2 [hereinafter cited as Hammond Papers]; Haskell, supra note 35, at 221.

[133] Letter from Oliver Wendell Holmes, Jr. to William Gardiner Hammond (March 25, 1875) (Hammond Papers, supra note 132, vol. 2).

[134] Letter from James Bradley Thayer to William Gardiner Hammond (March 22, 1890) (Hammond Papers, supra note 132, vol. 4); letter from William Gardiner Hammond to James Bradley Thayer (March 25, 1890) (Hammond Papers, supra note 132, vol. 4).

[135] Letter from William Gardiner Hammond to Edward A. Freeman (August 27, 1884) (Hammond Papers, supra note 132, vol. 3); letter from Edward A. Freeman to William Gardiner Hammond (December 25, 1884) (Hammond Papers, supra note 132, vol. 3); letter from Edward A. Freeman to William Gardiner Hammond (October 4, 1885) (Hammond Papers, supra note 132, vol. 3); letter from Edward A. Freeman to William Gardiner Hammond (November 1, 1886) (Hammond Papers, supra note 132, vol. 3).

and Wharton.[136] He particularly enjoyed a small dinner party at Thayer's home, where he, Thayer, Ames, and Bigelow, who "were all interested in the same studies," had a "delightful chat" about "old law books and other things that most men would find dry!"[137] Hammond also had a long-standing relationship with Cooley,[138] who attended one of Hammond's lectures on the history of the common law while visiting St. Louis.[139] Reflecting Hammond's international prominence, Frederick Pollock asked him to contribute an article to the *Law Quarterly Review*.[140]

As a teacher, Hammond rejected the traditional pedagogy of lectures and recitations from textbooks. He tried to recreate for his students the way that a lawyer or judge would actually analyze a case. To some extent, he developed a form of the case method analogous to the one that Langdell would soon introduce at Harvard. Like Langdell, he assigned cases and discussed them interactively with students to elicit general legal principles. But Hammond prevented the frustration experienced by many of Langdell's students, for in every course he prepared synopses that organized the cases under analytical classifications.[141] More like Pomeroy than Langdell, Hammond did not view the case method as the exclusive method of legal instruction. Believing that the case method, on its own, proceeds too slowly, he argued that it should be combined with lectures and treatises.[142]

From the beginning of his career as a professor, Hammond demonstrated his interest in legal history. He reviewed Maine's *Ancient Law* in *The Western Jurist*[143] and began teaching a course on the history of law.[144] In numerous public lectures, he stressed that law developed historically from the basic principles of Anglo-Saxon civilization.[145] Hammond intended to write a book on the history of the common law and prepared an outline of this work in 1871, a decade before Holmes published *The Common Law*. He bemoaned how little others appreciated the historical study of law and realized that his proposed work

---

[136] Letter from William Gardiner Hammond to "My dearest wife" (March 1, 1876) (Hammond Papers, supra note 132, vol. 2); letter from William Gardiner Hammond to "My dearest wife" (March 5, 1876) (Hammond Papers, supra note 132, vol. 2); letter from William Gardiner Hammond to "My dearest mother" (January 10, 1882) (Hammond Papers, supra note 132, vol. 3).

[137] Letter from William Gardiner Hammond to "My dearest mother" (January 22, 1888) (Hammond Papers, supra note 132, vol. 3).

[138] Letter from William Gardiner Hammond to "My dearest mother" (January 28, 1888) (Hammond Papers, supra note 132, vol. 3).

[139] Notes, Law Journal, May 19, 1882, Hammond Papers, supra note 132, vol. 3.

[140] Letter from Frederick Pollock to William Gardiner Hammond (November 18, 1886) (Hammond Papers, supra note 132, vol. 3).

[141] McClain, supra note 128, at 219–21.

[142] William Gardiner Hammond, Legal Education and the Study of Jurisprudence in the West and North-west (Boston: American Social Science Association, 1876), p. 14.

[143] McClain, supra note 128, at 214–15.

[144] Id. at 217, 230.

[145] Id. at 222.

would take years to complete. Yet he began collecting original sources, learned Anglo-Saxon in order to read them, and took extensive notes on the English Year Books, sometimes even translating entire cases into modern English. He also studied German scholarship on Anglo-Saxon laws and institutions, which far surpassed anything previously written in England or the United States. Although Hammond lectured on the history of the common law at various law schools, including Boston University and the University of Michigan, he never produced a book and did not even publish shorter articles or essays derived from his extensive historical research.[146]

Hammond wrote thousands of pages of unpublished notes and drafts for his unpublished "History of the Common Law." He projected a book of thirty chapters, which would have exceeded Pollock and Maitland's monumental two-volume work, *The History of English Law*, in coverage and length. Like Pollock and Maitland, Hammond divided his book into two main parts, a general historical overview followed by chapters about specific doctrines. He began with "primitive Germanic law," devoted separate chapters to church law and Roman law, and discussed the law of persons, property law, inheritance, contracts, torts, and jurisdiction.[147] His drafts, though clearly unfinished, reveal extensive learning based on thorough study of primary sources as well as existing American, English, and German scholarship. The final chapter, "Theory of Law," which Hammond completed to page proofs, emphasized that the historical study of law had become a distinctive jurisprudential school, which used induction from national experience to replace the deductive, syllogistic reasoning of prior legal thought.[148] His friend and colleague Emlin McClain maintained that completing this book became Hammond's "chief ambition,"[149] that he moved from Iowa to St. Louis expecting to have more time there to work on it,[150] and that he viewed his lectures on the history of the common law as preliminary treatments of subjects he would elaborate in his book.[151] Hammond did draw on his historical research, however, in his many substantive notes to his edition of Blackstone's *Commentaries*, published in 1890. Like previous editors, Hammond commented on Blackstone and on related subsequent developments in American law. But he emphasized in his preface that attention to "the historical theory of law" would be the distinguishing feature of his edition. This historical approach, Hammond maintained, had developed a fundamentally "different theory of the law from any known in the eighteenth century," when Blackstone wrote. It took issue with Blackstone on many

---

[146] Id. at 230–2. Hammond's daughter gave his manuscript notes on the Year Books to the Harvard Law School library. Id. at 231 n. 3.

[147] William Gardiner Hammond, Historical Outlines of the Common Law, Hammond Papers, supra note 132, vol. 4.

[148] William Gardiner Hammond, Theory of Law, Hammond Papers, supra note 132, Box V.

[149] Emlin McClain, Biographical Sketch of William Gardiner Hammond, Chapter VI, The History of the Common Law and Blackstone, 1, Hammond Papers, supra note 132, vol. 1.

[150] Id. at 5.

[151] Id. at 6.

important points and "must be understood by any one who would know the common law as it is now administered in America, to say nothing of its past development."[152]

Hammond's study of the history of the common law complemented his continuing interest in the history of civil law, which he first developed as a student in Germany. He became convinced by his historical research that civil and common law had many more similarities than most of his contemporaries acknowledged. In 1876, fourteen years before his edition of Blackstone, he published an American edition of Sandars's *Institutes of Justinian*, a key document of the Roman civil law. The introduction, subsequently published separately under the title *System of Legal Classification of Hale and Blackstone in its Relation to the Civil Law*, addressed the parallels between common and civil law systems. Many nineteenth-century English writers favorably contrasted the scientific system of classification of the Roman civil law with the messiness of the English common law, which they saw as scientific only to the limited extent that it adapted concepts from the civil law. Hammond, by contrast, maintained that both civil and common law had developed historically. The main purpose of his introduction, he declared, was to demonstrate that "many principles in matters of Roman law are strictly analogous to those of the common law of England and America."[153] Hammond sent a copy to Maine, who replied that he "read it with very great interest" and agreed with much of it. Maine graciously attributed his surprise that Hammond produced this work in Iowa to the "arrogant ignorance of an Englishman."[154] Hammond also drew on his knowledge of the history of civil law in his edition of Francis Lieber's *Legal and Political Hermeneutics*.[155]

For Hammond, as for Carter, appreciation of the historical foundations of law led to skepticism about codification. Hammond actually served as a commissioner appointed to revise the statutes of Iowa. He was selected by his fellow commissioners to prepare their final report to the legislature, which accepted most of their recommendations in the Iowa Code of 1873. The code contained four parts: public law, civil practice, criminal procedure, and the relatively few prior legislative changes of private law. Though the code was largely a restatement of existing law, Hammond made an original contribution by including provisions that expanded the personal and property rights of married women. Based on his extensive historical knowledge of both civil and common law, Hammond resisted attempts to reduce the entire common law of private law into a code. He stressed that a formal code of private law would undermine the benefits the common law derived from allowing gradual development over time.[156]

---

[152] McClain, supra note 128 at 233–5.
[153] Id. at 227–8.
[154] Iowa Abroad, Hammond Papers, supra note 132, vol. 2 (newspaper article quoting letter from Maine to Hammond).
[155] McClain, supra note 128, at 229.
[156] Id. at 224–6.

James Bradley Thayer

Born in 1831, Thayer spent eighteen years as a practicing lawyer in Boston before joining the Harvard Law School faculty in 1874, one year after Ames. Thayer's father, Abijah, was a newspaper editor in Haverhill, Massachusetts, devoted to the program of moral reform associated with the Whig Party. He became best known for his support of temperance, but he was also committed to the more controversial cause of abolition. Abijah Thayer was a friend of the famous abolitionist William Lloyd Garrison, whose poetry he published and with whom he founded the Haverhill abolitionist society. Reaction against abolitionism had a dramatic impact on the Thayer family after Abijah became editor of the *Commercial Herald* in Philadelphia. The poet John Greenleaf Whittier lived with the Thayers in Philadelphia while editing an abolitionist newspaper, the *Pennsylvania Freeman*. After a proslavery mob burned Whittier's offices, the Thayers and Whittier returned to Massachusetts, where the family finances declined as Abijah unsuccessfully attempted to establish a business cultivating silkworms in Northampton. Young James Thayer fortunately received financial assistance from a wealthy local widow, Anne Lyman, who helped many promising poor boys receive a good education. Lyman enabled Thayer to attend preparatory school and Harvard College.[157] After graduating Phi Beta Kappa in 1852, Thayer taught private school for two years, entered Harvard Law School in 1854, and, two decades before Harvard extended attendance requirements from two to three years,[158] graduated with an outstanding record in 1856.[159]

Thayer became a partner in two eminent Boston law firms during his eighteen years of legal practice, predominantly as a corporate lawyer. In the late 1860s, Holmes became an associate in Thayer's firm and worked with him to win an important case before the Supreme Judicial Court of Massachusetts in 1867.[160] Chosen two years later to edit the twelfth edition of Kent's famous *Commentaries*, Thayer asked Holmes to assist him. Holmes ultimately did the major work on this project, which eventually appeared under his name alone, as Thayer limited his participation to editorial revision.[161] Perhaps Thayer was distracted from this project by his service in the early 1870s as counsel to a committee that investigated the Marginal Freight Railway Company, a public service company accused of wrongdoing. The committee's report, written by Thayer, prompted the Massachusetts legislature to revoke the company's charter.[162]

---

[157] Jay Hook, A Brief Life of James Bradley Thayer, 88 Nw. U.L. Rev. 1, 1–2 (1993).

[158] The Centennial History of the Harvard Law School, 1817–1917 (Boston: The Harvard Law School Association, 1918) [hereinafter Centennial History], p. 32.

[159] James Parker Hall, James Bradley Thayer, in Great American Lawyers, supra note 26, vol. VIII, pp. 345, 347–50.

[160] Hook, supra note 157, at 3.

[161] Hall, supra note 159, at 351. See Mark DeWolfe Howe, Justice Oliver Wendell Holmes: The Proving Years, 1870–1882 (Cambridge, Mass.: Harvard University Press, 1963), pp. 11–16.

[162] Hall, supra note 159, at 351.

FIGURE 1.6. *James Bradley Thayer*. Courtesy of Historical & Special Collections, Harvard Law School Library.

While practicing law, Thayer found time for many other activities. He was a member and kept the journal of the Septum Club, a group of young Harvard graduates who met to give papers and discuss contemporary philosophical and policy issues. Club members, who included Charles William Eliot, the future president of Harvard, had a particular interest in the reform of higher education. Perhaps influenced by his father, during the Civil War Thayer joined Charles Eliot Norton, the future editor of the influential *North American Review*, in directing the Loyal Publication Society, which provided subscribing newspapers with information loyal to the Union cause. After the war, Thayer helped found the American Social Science Association and served as secretary of its Jurisprudence Committee.[163]

---

[163] Hook, supra note 157, at 3–4; Haskell, supra note 35, at 221.

Thayer became a close friend of Ralph Waldo Emerson after his marriage in 1859 to Sophia Ripley, Emerson's niece. Thayer helped Emerson with many practical matters. He prepared his will, handled his investments, booked his lectures, and even bought his cigars. Thayer also became an intellectual intimate of Emerson, with whom he discussed religion and literature. Thayer published an account of his 1871 trip to California with Emerson. Emerson and Norton helped Thayer become a frequent contributor of literary criticism to leading periodicals, such as the *North American Review*, the *Nation*, and the *Atlantic Monthly*. Thayer most frequently reviewed English translations of the classics and of contemporary poetry and literature.[164]

Thayer's extensive participation in intellectual and literary activity may indicate that he never became "wholly absorbed in the practice of law," as James Parker Hall, the dean of the University of Chicago School of Law, asserted in a 1909 biographical essay. Hall also maintained that Thayer, though respected and successful during his years of practice, never reached the "highest rank as a lawyer," perhaps because he was "too judicially-minded," "saw the merits of opposing views," and was "not enough of a partisan."[165] In any event, Thayer's growing reputation as a literary critic and his long relationship with Eliot prompted Harvard to offer him the Boylston Chair in Rhetoric in 1872 and to enlist Emerson's help in recruiting him. Thayer refused this chair but two years later accepted the more lucrative Royall Professorship at Harvard Law School after much hesitation based on the substantial financial cost of leaving his legal practice.[166]

Upon joining the Harvard law faculty, Thayer immersed himself in teaching, scholarship, and the educational reforms that transformed Harvard Law School from mediocrity to preeminence. He focused especially on learning the historical roots of his two main subjects, evidence and constitutional law. His most important work, *A Preliminary Treatise on Evidence at the Common Law*, was dedicated to Carter.[167] Thayer never followed up his "preliminary" treatise with the more complete treatment of the law of evidence that he hoped to produce. That task was finished by Thayer's student and admirer, John Wigmore, who dedicated his great treatise on evidence to Thayer.[168] Thayer also wrote a classic historical essay about constitutional law,[169] and his casebook on constitutional law contained a substantial amount of historical material.[170] During his years at Harvard, Thayer corresponded extensively with leading American and foreign legal scholars, including Bigelow, Brunner, Carter, Cooley, Dicey,

---

[164] Hook, supra note 157, at 4–5; see Hall, supra note 132, at 373.

[165] Hall, supra note 159, at 351.

[166] Id. at 352; Hook, supra note 157, at 5.

[167] Hall, supra note 159, at 355; Hook, supra note 157, at 5; John Chipman Gray, 15 Harv. L. Rev. 601–2 (1902); Jeremiah Smith, 15 Harv. L. Rev. 602 (1902).

[168] Hook, supra note 157, at 5; Hall, supra note 159, at 362–3.

[169] James Bradley Thayer, The Origin and Scope of the American Doctrine of Constitutional Law, 7 Harv. L. Rev. 129 (1893).

[170] Hall, supra note 159, at 369.

Hammond, Holmes, Maitland, Pollock, and Wigmore. Much of this correspondence is filled with praise for Thayer's scholarship.

The publication of the *Preliminary Treatise on Evidence at the Common Law* generated positive reviews on both sides of the Atlantic. Yet after he died, colleagues observed that he had not been a particularly productive scholar. Jeremiah Smith commented on "the failure of Professor Thayer to accomplish more in the line of legal authorship," attributing it to his helpfulness to others as critic and reviser and to his primary commitment to teaching, which included extensive class preparation.[171] Remarking that Thayer most loved his historical work, John Chipman Gray acknowledged that its "bulk is not large."[172] As an explanation, Gray emphasized Thayer's fastidious scholarship,[173] a point Samuel Williston reinforced by praising "the depth of his historical research"[174] and his "patience in wearisome investigation."[175] The extensive notes on the German law of evidence in Thayer's papers support the testimony of his colleagues.[176] Like other colleagues at Harvard, Thayer prepared casebooks,[177] which diverted his energies from more substantial scholarship.

It is, therefore, somewhat ironic that Thayer only belatedly conformed to the case method of instruction pioneered by Langdell. At the beginning of his teaching career, Thayer used the more traditional teaching method of assigning a chapter from a treatise and lecturing on that topic.[178] Even after adopting the case method, Thayer did not follow the pedagogy most closely associated with Langdell. Unlike many professors at Harvard, Williston observed, Thayer did not use a decision by a court "merely as a starting point for analytic discussion." Thayer "had little inclination to develop from his own mind a perfectly logical or entirely consistent body of legal doctrine." Rather, he attempted to illuminate as precisely as possible "what the law was." If the law was illogical or inconsistent, Thayer tried to explain "how it had grown up in this way rather than to work out a more systematic and logical theory than the courts had made."[179] Even in his pedagogy, Thayer remained a historian.

Fully engaged in his work at Harvard, Thayer did not maintain his literary criticism after becoming a professor.[180] Yet he did find time for civic and political activity, some of which seemed to extend the Whig moral reformism of his father. In the 1880s, Thayer was member of the Mohonk Conference, a group of elite easterners concerned about the oppression of American Indians in the West, and wrote an article in the *Atlantic Monthly* supporting congressional

---

[171] Smith, supra note 167, at 605.
[172] Gray, supra note 167, at 601–2.
[173] Id. at 602.
[174] Samuel Williston, 15 Harv. L. Rev. 607 (1902).
[175] Id. at 609.
[176] James Bradley Thayer Papers, Box 12, Folders 1–4, Harvard Law School Library.
[177] Centennial History, supra note 158, at 38.
[178] Id.
[179] Williston, supra note 174, at 608.
[180] Hall, supra note 159, at 375.

legislation intended to improve their situation.[181] He supported tariff reform and protested political corruption, particularly the granting of valuable franchises by municipalities.[182] These positions prompted Thayer to become an active Mugwump in 1884. Jay Hook has plausibly speculated that Thayer's support of judicial deference to legislation in his famous article "The Origin and Scope of the American Doctrine of Constitutional Law" derived at least in part from his abolitionist and radical Republican roots. Thayer might have been thinking about the Reconstruction legislation designed to protect freed blacks, which the Supreme Court invalidated as unconstitutional in the *Civil Rights Cases*, while advocating the alternative of judicial deference.[183]

Putting his scholarly expertise to use, Thayer participated in drafting the state constitutions of North and South Dakota.[184] He acted on his long-standing interest in educational reform, which dated at least from his membership in the Septum Club as a young man, when he helped found the Association of American Law Schools in 1900 and became its first president. He also participated in the Selden Society, an organization of legal historians founded in England, in which Maitland took a leading role, and tried to involve other Americans in its work.[185]

Henry Adams

Born in 1838 into one of the most famous families in the United States, Henry Adams was the great-grandson and grandson of presidents, John Adams and John Quincy Adams, and the son of the future American minister to Great Britain during the Civil War, Charles Francis Adams. Today Adams is well known to a broad educated public for his two books that have become classics, *Mont Saint Michel and Chartres* and *The Education of Henry Adams*. His multi-volume histories of the United States during the administrations of Thomas Jefferson and James Madison, though overshadowed today by his two classics, were a great accomplishment of nineteenth-century American historical writing and, thanks to a recent book by Gary Wills, have been reintroduced to general readers.[186] Adams's brief career as a historian at Harvard from 1870

---

[181] Id. at 379; Hook, supra note 157, at 6–7. See James Bradley Thayer, The Dawes Bill and the Indians, 61 Atlantic Monthly 315 (1888). Thayer, however, did not believe that the increased rights of citizenship for Indians should include the right to vote. James Bradley Thayer, A People without Law, II, 68 Atlantic Monthly 676, 682–3 (1891). See also James Bradley Thayer, A People without Law, I, 68 Atlantic Monthly 540 (1891); Carol Nackenoff, Constitutionalizing Terms of Inclusion: Friends of the Indian and Citizenship for Native Americans, 1880s–1930s, in The Supreme Court & American Political Development (Lawrence: University Press of Kansas, 2006) (Ronald Kahn and Ken I. Kersch, eds.), pp. 366, 379–80.

[182] Hall, supra note 159, at 379.

[183] Hook, supra note 157, at 6.

[184] Hall, supra note 159, at 370.

[185] Id. at 372.

[186] Gary Wills, Henry Adams and the Making of America (Boston: Houghton Mifflin Company, 2005).

FIGURE 1.7. *Henry Adams.* Courtesy of University of Harvard University Archives as requested in letter from Harvard granting permission to publish: HUP Adams, Henry, A. B. 1858 (2a).

to 1876, by contrast, is little known, even among professional historians. Yet during those years, Adams introduced to the United States the professional study of legal history based on original sources.

After graduating from Harvard College in 1858, Adams spent two years in Europe, initially attending lectures in law at the University of Berlin, and then continuing his legal studies on his own while mastering the German language. Upon returning to the United States in 1860, he began to study law in the office of Horace Gray, a distinguished Massachusetts judge, who later became a justice on the United States Supreme Court. Only three weeks later, however, he moved to Washington to become private secretary to his father, who was a member of the House of Representatives from Massachusetts. When President

Lincoln appointed his father the American minister to Great Britain in 1861, Henry continued as his father's private secretary in London.[187] Before Adams left for England, the editor of the New York Times hired him as its London correspondent. In order to avoid compromising his father, and possibly violating State Department regulations, Adams kept his relationship with the Times secret, informing only his brother Charles, and publishing his articles anonymously.[188] Remaining in England until 1868, Adams socialized extensively with important figures in England and with eminent Americans who visited London. Though the highest levels of the English aristocracy were mostly sympathetic to the Confederacy and remained distant from the American minister and his circle, Adams met many English liberals and radical reformers who supported the Union.[189] He was most impressed with John Stuart Mill, whom he met in 1863 and called "the ablest man in England."[190]

On his return to Washington in 1868, Adams began contributing articles on history and current affairs to leading journals, including the North American Review and the Nation. Adams mostly wrote on history and current affairs, but he also contributed a long article to the North American Review reviewing the tenth edition of Sir Charles Lyell's Principles of Geology and its relation to Charles Darwin's theories of evolution. Many of his articles protested political and financial corruption in the United States. An article called "Civil Service Reform," which he reprinted as a pamphlet and distributed to members of Congress, invoked the constitutional separation of powers to protest the spoils system by which members of Congress influenced appointments to the civil service. Subsequent articles revealed and criticized the attempt by officers of the Erie Railroad to corner the market on gold. Focusing on Jay Gould, its president and treasurer, and James Fisk, its vice president, Adams called them "a band of unshrinking scoundrels."[191] He also excoriated their prestigious lawyer, David Dudley Field, the proponent of codification who later unsuccessfully represented the Tweed Ring when Carter prosecuted them for stealing funds from New York City. Adams portrayed Field as an example of the decline of the legal profession in America.[192] When the Senate rejected the nomination of his friend, Attorney General Hoar, to the Supreme Court, Adams wrote an article asserting that a "cabal" composed of the "dregs of the Senate" voted against Hoar because he had appointed "competent men to office regardless of political combinations."[193]

In 1870, Adams left Washington to become an assistant professor of history at Harvard. Although he had initially refused President Eliot's offer to join the Harvard faculty, his father and brothers as well as Eliot and his colleagues urged

[187] Ernest Samuels, The Young Henry Adams (Cambridge, Mass.: Harvard University Press, 1948), p. 96.
[188] Id. at 97–8, 105.
[189] Id. at 122–6.
[190] Id. at 136.
[191] Id. at 196.
[192] Id. at 198–9.
[193] Id. at 190; see generally id. at 150–208, 317–18 (listing articles by Adams during this period).

him to accept. The political situation in Washington that he had been criticizing in his journalism also influenced his decision. Even though "I hate Boston and am very fond of Washington," Adams wrote to his close English friend, Charles Milnes Gaskell, most of his political friends were out of power during the Grant administration, which "reconciles me to going away."[194] Adams only stayed at Harvard for six years, largely because he continued to hate Boston and missed Washington. But during those years he became America's first professional legal historian.

Drawing on his two years in Germany after his graduation from Harvard College, Adams introduced the German seminar and German methods of historical scholarship to the United States. In both his teaching and his scholarship, Adams worked from original documents, which often required knowledge of Latin, Anglo-Saxon, and German. The *Essays in Anglo-Saxon Law,* published by Adams and three of his students in 1876 and personally financed by Adams, was the first work of original legal history to appear in the United States. This volume was widely reviewed in the United States and England, including by Maine and Holmes. It served as a model for the later work in legal history by Bigelow, Holmes, Ames, and Thayer as well as for historians of the United States, particularly in stressing the Teutonic origins of English and American laws and institutions. During his years at Harvard, Adams also published numerous reviews of books on legal history by leading English and German scholars, bringing this scholarship to the attention of American readers. Even while an academic at Harvard, Adams remained interested and involved in American political life. He was active in efforts by liberal Republicans to reform the Republican Party from within and worked hard but unsuccessfully in 1876 to secure the Republican presidential nomination for a candidate he associated with reform.[195]

Though his own work in legal history stimulated other law professors and historians, Adams abandoned the field after he left Harvard. Despite his resolution to "keep clear of politics" when he returned to Washington in 1877, Adams remained involved for a while with the continued reform efforts of liberal Republicans.[196] He joined the Mugwumps who bolted the Republican Party in 1884 and voted for the successful Democratic presidential candidate, Grover Cleveland. Yet Adams did not attend the major Mugwump meeting in New York that supported Cleveland. Though he did attend a similar meeting in Boston, he was too absorbed in his writing to participate in the presidential campaign.[197] Increasingly, Adams devoted himself to his literary work, writing the histories, novels, and memoirs that made him famous. He became less active in politics even as he wrote about it in his many books.

---

[194] Id. at 207.
[195] Id. at 282–4; Ernest Samuels, Henry Adams: The Middle Years (Cambridge, Mass.: Harvard University Press, 1958), p. 14; Sproat, supra note 29, at 90–3.
[196] Samuels, supra note 195, at 15.
[197] Id. at 156.

Oliver Wendell Holmes, Jr.

Three years younger than his lifelong friend, Henry Adams, Oliver Wendell Holmes, Jr., born in 1841, was a member of another prominent Boston family. Son of Dr. Oliver Wendell Holmes, Sr., the well-known physician and essayist who first used the word "Brahmin" to describe the upper-class intellectuals of New England,[198] Holmes grew up in this environment. His maternal grandfather, Charles Jackson, had been a financially successful merchant before becoming an associate justice of the Supreme Judicial Court of Massachusetts.[199] His paternal grandfather, Abiel Holmes, was minister of the First Congregational Church in Cambridge and wrote biography, history, and poetry.[200] Today Holmes is probably even better known than Adams, largely the result of his long tenure as a justice on the United States Supreme Court and widespread continuing debate about his judicial and intellectual legacy. *The Common Law*, the ambitious book he published in 1881, just before his appointment to the Supreme Judicial Court of Massachusetts, brought him acclaim among lawyers in England as well as the United States. Though more known than read, it remains a classic of American legal scholarship, probably the most famous book about law ever written by an American. Best known for its many aphorisms and for its innovative analysis of legal concepts, much of *The Common Law* is based on Holmes's extensive study of legal history.

Entering Harvard College in 1857, Holmes graduated in 1861[201] and served as a Union officer in the Civil War from July 1861 until July 1864.[202] Acquiescing to his father's strong pressure, he enrolled in Harvard Law School in the fall of 1864.[203] He left law school in December 1865 to work in the office of a Boston lawyer.[204] Holmes sailed to England in April 1866 and remained in England and Europe until he returned to Boston the following September. Although mostly a tourist on the Continent, in England Holmes met leading figures in English intellectual and political life, often through introductions from eminent Bostonians, including members of the Adams family. Holmes's visit to England reinforced through personal experience the close cultural and intellectual connections between Boston Brahmins and the English intellectual elite in which he already was saturated.[205]

Upon his return from Europe, Holmes joined a major Boston law firm in which Thayer was one of the three named partners.[206] In his early years of legal

---

[198] G. Edward White, Justice Oliver Wendell Holmes: Law and the Inner Self (New York: Oxford University Press, 1993), p. 11.

[199] Id. at 17; Mark DeWolfe Howe, Justice Oliver Wendell Holmes: The Shaping Years, 1841–1870 (Cambridge, Mass.: Harvard University Press, 1957), p. 29.

[200] White, supra note 198, at 18.

[201] Howe, supra note 199, at 35.

[202] Id. at 80–175.

[203] Id. at 176.

[204] Id. at 204.

[205] Id. at 223–44.

[206] Id. at 245.

FIGURE 1.8. *Oliver Wendell Holmes.* Courtesy of Historical & Special Collections, Harvard Law School Library.

practice, Holmes worried that the law would not satisfy his intellectual ambitions. He was particularly interested in broad philosophical issues, which he frequently discussed with William James, who had not yet committed himself to the philosophical career in which he became prominent.[207] Like other legal scholars of the period, Holmes joined various informal clubs for serious conversation. He participated in the Metaphysical Club, founded in Cambridge in 1872 and composed of an exceptionally able group of members.[208] Chauncey Wright, Thayer's high school friend, college roommate,[209] and a member with Thayer of the Septum Club in the 1850s,[210] was a spectacular conversationalist who provided the social glue for the Metaphysical Club.[211] Several of its members, especially William James and Charles S. Peirce, later became identified as founders of the important philosophical movement known as pragmatism. Holmes himself, however, did not become one of the more active members in the Metaphysical Club[212] or endorse the basic program of philosophical

---

[207] Id. at 255.
[208] Louis Menand, The Metaphysical Club (New York: Farrar, Straus & Giroux, 2001), pp. 200–1.
[209] Hall, supra note 159, at 347, 350.
[210] Menand, supra note 208, at 214.
[211] Id. at 205–6.
[212] Id. at 216; J. W. Burrow, Holmes in His Intellectual Milieu, in Robert W. Gordon, The Legacy of Oliver Wendell Holmes, Jr. (Stanford, Calif.: Stanford University Press, 1992), p. 23; Thomas C. Grey, Holmes and Legal Pragmatism, 41 Stan. L. Rev. 787, 865 (1989).

pragmatism.[213] Yet with others in the Metaphysical Club he expressed skepticism about the possibility of discovering absolute truths and confidence that scientific investigation of empirical evidence, rather than metaphysical speculation, was the method by which any meaningful knowledge, however provisional, could be discovered.[214]

Despite substantial doubts about law as a career, Holmes quickly became reconciled to his choice. "Law," he wrote to William James in 1868, "as well as any other series of facts in this world may be approached in the interests of science."[215] And in 1876, while sending a copy of one of his early legal essays to Ralph Waldo Emerson, another Boston Brahmin with whom Holmes, like Thayer, was acquainted through family connections, Holmes expressed confidence that legal study could be a route to philosophical analysis. "I have learned," Holmes wrote to Emerson, "after a laborious and somewhat painful period of probation, that the law opens a way to philosophy as well as anything else, if pursued far enough, and I hope to prove it before I die." He asked Emerson to accept his essay "in that faith and as a slight mark of the gratitude and respect I feel for you who more than anyone else first started the philosophical ferment in my mind."[216]

By the early 1870s, Holmes had immersed himself in his legal career. Following Thayer's invitation in 1869, he worked hard as editor of a new edition of Kent's *Commentaries on American Law*, which he completed in 1873. In 1871, he opened his own law firm and became coeditor of the *American Law Review*, which had been founded in 1867 by his Boston friends John Gray and John Ropes and to which Holmes had already contributed. He became sole editor of the *American Law Review* in 1872, the same year that President Eliot appointed him to the faculty of Harvard College as university lecturer on constitutional law.[217] Holmes married in 1872.[218] Yet as Mark DeWolfe Howe wrote in his biography of Holmes, during "at least the first ten years of their marriage the story of their life was, in its essentials, the story of his striving for and achievement of intellectual eminence."[219]

Holmes joined a new law firm in 1873, giving up his teaching at Harvard College and his editorship of the *American Law Review*. While working in private practice throughout the 1870s, however, Holmes invested his great ambition in legal scholarship, perhaps spending more time on it than on his practice.[220] He wrote important articles during that decade, and his scholarship

213 Menand, supra note 208, at 217; Grey, supra note 212, at 864–70.

214 Howe, supra note 199, at 256.

215 Letter from Oliver Wendell Holmes, Jr. to William James (April 18, 1868), in Oliver Wendell Holmes Papers, Harvard Law School Library, Cambridge, Massachusetts (Frederick, Md.: University Publications of America), Microfilm, Reel 34, 0387.

216 Howe, supra note 199, at 203.

217 Howe, supra note 161, at 61; White, supra note 198, at 127–8.

218 Howe, supra note 161, at 9.

219 Id. at 10.

220 Id. at 135; White, supra note 198, at 112, 128.

culminated in his book, *The Common Law*, published in 1881, just days before his fortieth birthday. Reflecting his enormous desire for success, Holmes later wrote to a friend that he rushed to get the book out because "it was said that if a man was to do anything he must do it before 40."[221]

In pursuing his legal scholarship, Holmes self-consciously rejected his father's intellectual style of wide-ranging and eclectic essays for the rigorous professionalism of specialized study. Though psychological tension between father and son might account to some extent for this difference,[222] Holmes's attachment to professional values reflected a broader generational change. Holmes joined the many young American intellectuals who committed themselves to professionalism after the Civil War,[223] perhaps in part because wartime service impressed on them the general importance of discipline and rigor.[224]

Holmes's growing scholarly reputation prompted President Eliot to invite him to join the Harvard law faculty, whose four full-time professors were Ames, Gray, Langdell, and Thayer. Appointed in February 1882, Holmes began attending faculty meetings in March and started teaching in the fall. In December 1882, however, Holmes shocked his colleagues by resigning to accept a position as associate justice on the Supreme Judicial Court of Massachusetts, the highest court of the state.[225] Elevated to chief justice in 1899, he served on that court until 1903, when he became an associate justice on the United States Supreme Court. Holmes remained a Supreme Court justice until his retirement in 1932.

James Barr Ames

Like Carter, Thayer, Adams, and Holmes, Ames was a native of Massachusetts, a graduate of Harvard College, and, like all but Adams, a graduate of Harvard Law School. Born in Boston in 1846, Ames remained there his entire life. After graduating from the Boston Latin School, he received three degrees from Harvard, his B.A. in 1868 and his M.A. and J.D. in 1872. He taught at a private school in Boston in 1868–9, studied at German universities in 1869–70, and returned home to enter Harvard Law School in the fall of 1870. Throughout his two years of law school, Ames taught modern languages at Harvard College, and, while remaining at the law school for an additional year of graduate study in 1872–3, taught two undergraduate courses in history: the history of England in the seventeenth century and the history of medieval institutions. On the basis of his extremely successful undergraduate teaching and his outstanding record as a law student, he received an appointment to the Harvard law faculty in 1873, the year before Thayer, while finishing his graduate study.[226]

---

[221] Howe, supra note 161, at 135.
[222] Howe, supra note 199, at 11–12.
[223] Menand, supra note 208, at 58–9; see generally Haskell, supra note 35.
[224] Frederickson, supra note 30, at 174–5, 180.
[225] Howe, supra note 161, at 260–72; White, supra note 198, at 198–205.
[226] Charles W. Eliot, James Barr Ames, 23 Harv. L. Rev. 321, 321–2 (1910); Centennial History, supra note 144, at 175–6.

FIGURE 1.9. *James Barr Ames.* Courtesy of Historical & Special Collections, Harvard Law School Library.

Ames's first year as a law student coincided with Langdell's introduction of the case method of legal instruction. According to President Eliot, Langdell strongly urged the appointment of Ames to the faculty because he had been his best student. Eliot stressed that hiring Ames was a "remarkable step" because the law school had never previously appointed a person without experience in practice.[227] To Ames, Eliot added, "is largely due the success of the Langdellian method, and no one was clearer in the recognition of that fact than Professor Langdell himself, whose own teaching power was diminished by his very defective eyesight and a certain constitutional slowness in making a careful statement."[228] Samuel Williston, who became Ames's colleague at Harvard, agreed. He wrote that "Mr. Ames's success in adapting for practical use the fundamental idea of his predecessor, Dean Langdell, unquestionably had much to do with the ultimate triumph of the case system."[229]

---

[227] Eliot, supra note 226, at 321–2.
[228] Id. at 322.
[229] Samuel Williston, James Barr Ames – Services to Legal Education, 23 Harv. L. Rev. 330 (1910); see also id. at 332.

Assisted by his fluency in Latin, French, and German,[230] Ames read widely in legal history.[231] From the beginning of his career, he spent his summers taking notes on the English Year Books. These notes formed the basis for his essays on legal history, first published in the *Harvard Law Review*[232] and posthumously collected in a book.[233] Ames corresponded about substantive issues in legal history with Holmes, Maitland,[234] Pollock, and, in German, with Brunner.

In an address "The Vocation of the Law Professor," delivered in 1901, Ames reiterated many of the points that Thayer had made in "The Teaching of English Law at Universities." After almost thirty years as a law professor, Ames urged American legal scholars over the next generation to follow "the modern spirit of historical research."[235] They should produce treatises on every important branch of the law "exhibiting the historical development of the subject and containing sound conclusions based upon scientific analysis."[236] Discovering the origins of legal doctrines, he added, could help clarify current law.[237] As models, Ames cited Pollock and Maitland's *History of English Law*[238] and the work of several German legal scholars, Savigny, Windscheid, Jhering, and Brunner.[239] Ames characterized American legal scholars as "distinctly poor" compared to the Germans, though he recognized some admirable exceptions. He attributed this scholarly poverty to "the absence of a large professional class."[240] Praising the development of university law schools in the United States in contrast to England,[241] Ames nevertheless lamented that while some law schools were composed almost entirely of full-time faculty, most were not. Among all law professors in the United States, three-fourths were active practitioners or judges. Yet to produce the historically based legal scholarship he advocated, the job of a law professor must be a vocation, as in Germany, not an avocation of busy lawyers.[242] The resulting scholarship, in addition to improving the legal education of students, would provide guidance to the judge and the legislator.[243] The best modern codes, Ames observed, are found in Germany, the country where full-time professors produced outstanding scholarship. He urged Americans

---

[230] Id. at 331.

[231] Id. at 323.

[232] Id. at 330.

[233] James Barr Ames, Lectures on Legal History and Miscellaneous Legal Essays (Cambridge, Mass.: Harvard University Press, 1913).

[234] H. D. Hazeltine, Gossip about Legal History: Unpublished Letters of Maitland and Ames, 2 Cambridge L.J. 1 (1924).

[235] Ames, supra note 233, at 365.

[236] Id. at 366.

[237] Id. at 368.

[238] Id. at 366.

[239] Id. at 364.

[240] Id. at 365.

[241] Id. at 354–60.

[242] Id. at 361–2.

[243] Id. at 364–8.

to resist the current "spirit of codification" until they developed comparable scholarship along the lines he recommended.[244]

Ames never wrote the major work in legal history that many hoped and expected from him. Much of the commentary about Ames when he died recognized and accounted for his lack of scholarly productivity. He was an enormously successful and accessible teacher for whom the needs of his students came first.[245] He taught widely throughout the curriculum. By his death in 1910, he had taught half the courses then offered at Harvard Law School.[246] There were no casebooks for many of these courses when Ames first taught them, and Ames, in the words of Samuel Williston, "took enthusiastic pleasure in preparing them."[247] As dean from 1895 until his death, Ames immersed himself in the details of administration.[248] And to the dismay of his colleagues, even when undertaking scholarly research he spent too much time "merely collecting authorities and printing them in notes."[249] Joseph Beale, his colleague at Harvard, wrote that Ames "always looked forward to the time when he had finished, just the little case-book he was at work upon, so that he might devote his time" to scholarly work in various fields, "above all, to legal history." Ames "promised his colleagues again and again to give up the making of case-books and get down to serious work – after just one more." But he never did. He "chose to be the friend of his pupils rather than the great author he might have been."[250] Professor Kirchway of Columbia Law School made the same point somewhat more sympathetically and defensively: "Ames never fell victim to the academic superstition that the true and only end of scholarship is the production of printed matter. His writings were only the by-product of his real work, chips from his workshop. His workshop was the classroom."[251] Many of Ames's students themselves became law professors and deans, and, after spending most of his professional career focused on Harvard Law School, Ames became more active in advising other institutions about legal education and served as a leader of the Association of American Law Schools.[252]

Melville Madison Bigelow

Relatively unknown today, Bigelow arguably made the greatest contributions to legal history of any American scholar of his generation.[253] Born in Michigan

[244] Id. at 368.

[245] Williston, supra note 229, at 333–4; Joseph H. Beale, James Barr Ames – His Life and Character, 23 Harv. L. Rev. 325, 327 (1910); Julian W. Mack, James Barr Ames – His Personal Influence, 23 Harv. L. Rev. 336, 337 (1910).

[246] Beale, supra note 245, at 326.

[247] Williston, supra note 229, at 331.

[248] Centennial History, supra note 158, at 183.

[249] Beale, supra note 245, at 327.

[250] Id. at 328.

[251] Centennial History, supra note 158, at 178–9.

[252] Id. at 185–6; Mack, supra note 245, at 337.

[253] See generally David M. Rabban, Melville M. Bigelow: Boston University's Neglected Pioneer of Historical Legal Scholarship in America, 91 B.U. L. Rev. 1 (2011).

FIGURE I.IO. *Melvin Madison Bigelow*. From *Boston University Law Review,* January 2011 issue. Permission granted by *Boston University Law Review.*

in 1846, Bigelow graduated from the University of Michigan, A.B. 1866, LL.B. 1868, A.M. 1871. His father was a Methodist minister. Bigelow attended public schools throughout Michigan, often in frontier country, as his father received various assignments from the Detroit Conference of the Methodist Church. After practicing law in Michigan in 1868 and Tennessee in 1869, Bigelow, who already had strong interests in the historical evolution of the law, moved to Boston in 1870 with the intention of becoming a legal scholar. He soon became involved with others in Boston who in 1872 founded the law school at Boston University, a Methodist institution, as a response to their shared dissatisfaction with existing standards at American law schools. He helped prepare the report that led to the establishment of the law school and read it to the trustees. The new law school was the first in the United States to require three years of attendance, graded courses, and systematic examinations as conditions of graduation, requirements other American law schools soon adopted. Bigelow taught at Boston University School of Law from its inception until his death nearly fifty years later and served as its dean from 1902 to 1911. Throughout his career, Bigelow explored English legal history, an interest that extended both to English history in general and to genealogical research into his own family, which he traced to Edward I. For Bigelow, links to the English past were personal as well as intellectual.[254]

Bigelow published his first work, a treatise on estoppel, in 1872, but he made his reputation with two works of legal history: *Placita Anglo-Normannica*, published in 1879, and *History of Procedure in England from the Norman Conquest, 1066–1204*, published in 1880. *Placita Anglo-Normannica* was the printed version of Bigelow's Ph.D. thesis at Harvard, which Bigelow received in 1879 while teaching law at Boston University. Ames was one of the Harvard professors who approved Bigelow's thesis. A committee at Harvard chose Bigelow to read an essay based on it during the commencement at which he received his Ph.D. In writing to Bigelow about his selection, Thayer reported that as the legal scholar on the committee, he "was able to recognize the great value and interest of your researches." That summer President Eliot wrote to Bigelow that his "essay lent weight and dignity to the exercises of Commencement."[255]

In a tribute to Bigelow shortly after his death in 1921, Edward Avery Harriman, a professor at Northwestern Law School and a former student of Bigelow's at Boston University, identified him as among the small group of Americans who, beginning around 1870, developed historical jurisprudence based on the history of the English common law. After calling Holmes "the most brilliant and original" of this group, Harriman astutely concluded that Bigelow was the "most active in giving to the world the results of his studies in published works." Indicating that Harriman's praise of Bigelow was not simply eulogistic exaggeration, H. A. L. Fisher, Maitland's brother-in-law and literary executor, wrote that Maitland's *Pleas of the Crown for the County of Gloucester*, published in 1884, was the first major work on English legal history written by an Englishman. "All the really important books," Fisher wrote, "were foreign – Brunner's *Schwurgerichte*, Bigelow's *Placita Anglo-Normannica* and *History of Procedure in England*, the Harvard *Essays on Anglo-Saxon Law*, Holmes' brilliant volume on the *Common Law*." Fisher thus put Bigelow, the only author of two books among his list, in very eminent company.[256]

Bigelow never matched the quality of his two great early works on English legal history. Yet in some of his essays in the early twentieth century, he stressed the dangers of individualism in American society and law. He urged legal scholars and educators to connect their work more closely to the actual conditions

[254] Id. at 7–8.
[255] Id. at 8–9.
[256] Id. at 7.

of life. These were the themes that Roscoe Pound, a generation younger than Bigelow, was influentially emphasizing in his own early scholarship written at the same time. In his own intellectual development, Bigelow embodied the major transformation in American legal thought from historical interpretations to a focus on the social conditions law should address.[257]

Christopher G. Tiedeman

Christopher Tiedeman, the final scholar I discuss and by eleven years the youngest of the group, has frequently been treated as Cooley's junior and more conservative collaborator in providing the legal justification for laissez-faire capitalism on which judges relied in the late nineteenth and early twentieth centuries. Born in 1857 in Charleston, South Carolina, Tiedeman grew up in a prosperous family and received his A.B. and A.M. from the College of Charleston before he turned nineteen. He then studied law in Germany, spending almost two years there in 1877 and 1878, first at Gottingen and then at Leipzig. He returned to the United States to enter Columbia Law School in the fall of 1878 and received his LL.B. after only one additional year of study. He practiced law for the next two years, first back home in Charleston and then in St. Louis. In 1881, Tiedeman joined the faculty of the University of Missouri Law School, where he remained until he became a law professor at the University of the City of New York in 1891. Eager to devote more time to scholarship, he resigned this position in 1897. He became dean of the University of Buffalo Law School in 1902 and died the following year at the age of forty-six.[258]

During his short career, Tiedeman was a prolific author. He was best known for *A Treatise on the Limitations of the Police Power in the United States,* published in 1886, which reinforced the growing influence of Cooley's *Constitutional Limitations* in providing judges with scholarly arguments they could use to declare legislation unconstitutional. Much more explicitly conservative than Cooley, Tiedeman stated in the preface that he wrote his book "in the cause of social order and personal liberty." It was an "attempt to awaken the public mind to a full appreciation of the power of constitutional limitations to protect private rights against the radical experimentations of social reformers."[259] Acknowledging that the doctrine of laissez-faire had previously limited government power, Tiedeman warned about recent political pressure for increased government activity. "Socialism, Communism, and Anarchism," he lamented, "are rampant throughout the civilized world" and are calling upon the state to protect the weak.[260] The growth of universal suffrage, he

---

[257] Id. at 3, 33–41.

[258] Jacobs, supra note 38, at 59.

[259] Christopher G. Tiedeman, A Treatise on the Limitations of Police Power in the United States (St. Louis: F. H. Thomas Law Book Company, 1886), pp. vii–viii.

[260] Id. at vi.

FIGURE I.11. *Christopher G. Tiedeman.* Image courtesy of SUNY Buffalo Law School.

added, gave unprecedented power to this "great army of discontents." As a result, the "conservative classes stand in constant fear of the advent of an absolutism more tyrannical and more unreasoning than any before experienced by man, the absolutism of a democratic majority." The primary purpose of his book, Tiedeman proclaimed, was to prevent this "democratic absolutism" by demonstrating the limitations on government action contained in both federal and state constitutions.[261]

Tiedeman's conservatism, however, did not translate into unrestrained support for corporate interests. Like Cooley, he applied his laissez-faire principles consistently and resisted government intervention in the economy whether sought by business or by labor. He opposed tariffs designed to protect American businesses from foreign competition as well as the maximum hour and minimum wage legislation favored by workers and unions. Extending

[261] Id. at vii.

his laissez-faire principles beyond economic matters, Tiedeman also opposed anti-miscegenation laws that many conservatives endorsed.[262]

By the end of the nineteenth century, Tiedeman concluded that the growth of concentrated capital in large corporations rivaled big government as a threat to the traditional American economy. He even advocated the nationalization of businesses such as railroads, insurance companies, and public utilities as a preferable alternative to private monopolies. Tiedeman wanted to preserve economic competition where possible. But for enterprises that seemed inevitably to become monopolies, he preferred nationalization for the benefit of the entire population to the extraction of huge profits by large private corporations. He also justified the organization of labor unions as a needed counterweight to corporate power. In his preference for a laissez-faire economy in which roughly equal small competitors would be free from the pressures of either big government or big business, Tiedeman shared Cooley's nostalgia for an earlier America. Hopeful in the 1880s that this America could be preserved by resisting the pressures of democratic majorities for an activist state that would benefit the unproductive weak, by 1900 he seemed to view the state as a necessary check on the lamentable economic concentration of the intervening decades.[263]

Although he is best known for his support of constitutional limitations on government power, Tiedeman was also a vigorous proponent of the historical analysis of law. During his years as a law student in Germany, he became familiar with German legal scholarship and responded especially to the work of Jhering. Tiedeman's major work of constitutional interpretation, *The Unwritten Constitution of the United States*, is in large part an application of Jhering's theories to American constitutional law. Just as Jhering viewed law as evolving in response to society's changing needs, Tiedeman maintained that even the written Constitution of the United States must constantly be reinterpreted through unwritten constitutional law derived from changes in the "prevalent sense of right" among the American people. American constitutional law, Tiedeman emphasized, constantly evolves without any formal amendments to the written Constitution. Citing Jhering repeatedly, Tiedeman made clear his preference for Jhering's view that these changes emerge from contests among opposing forces within society rather than as a smooth development over time, as assumed by Savigny and Puchta, Jhering's eminent German predecessors.[264] Tiedeman attempted to reconcile his historical understanding of legal development with his belief in constitutional limitations. He maintained that the unwritten law

---

[262] Thomas C. Grey, Introduction to Christopher G. Tiedeman, The Unwritten Constitution of the United States (Buffalo, N.Y.: William S. Hein & Company, Inc., reprint ed. 1974) (original ed. 1890), p. iv.

[263] Louise A. Halper, Christopher G. Tiedeman, 'Laissez-Faire Constitutionalism,' and the Dilemmas of Small-Scale Property in the Gilded Age, 51 Ohio State L.J. 1349, 1350, 1353, 1383–4 (1990).

[264] See generally, id. at 1263; Grey, supra note 262, at iv–v.

in America generally prohibits the state's exercise of its police power.[265] The dangerous absolutism of democratic majorities, he claimed, often demonstrates popular whims that do not reflect the people's actual sense of right.[266]

These introductory portraits of major late nineteenth-century legal scholars provide the background for examining their joint contributions to the historical turn in American legal thought. Whatever their individual biographical or political differences, this founding generation of professional legal scholars in the United States constituted a distinctive historical school of American jurisprudence. Often in contact with each other as well as with their counterparts in England and Germany, the historical approach of these scholars dominated American legal thought from the end of the Civil War to the first decade of the twentieth century.

The following three chapters place the turn to history in late nineteenth-century American legal scholarship in a broader intellectual context. The first examines the European background of the emphasis on historical explanation in transatlantic intellectual life. The second and third explore the historical turn among the European legal scholars who most influenced the Americans. The chapter on the Germans begins with Savigny, discusses the Pandectists who followed him, compares the Romanist and Germanist schools of German legal scholarship, and concludes with Jhering. The third chapter treats the leading English legal scholar, Sir Henry Maine, through whom many Americans learned about German scholarship in legal history and whose generalizations about legal evolution provoked much of the initial American research into English legal history by Henry Adams and his students. The book then returns to these leading American scholars themselves, moving from the overview and biographical sketches of this chapter to a detailed discussion of their treatment of history.

---

[265] See Jacobs, supra note 38, at 61.
[266] Tiedeman, supra note 262, at 80, 164–5.

PART I

THE EUROPEAN BACKGROUND

II

The Historical Nineteenth Century

Historical explanation dominated nineteenth-century intellectual life throughout the Western world. Although twentieth-century critics generally neglected the central role of history in late nineteenth-century American legal thought, it is not surprising that such a major transatlantic intellectual trend influenced legal studies as well. The turn to history in the nineteenth century, scholars have convincingly observed, rivaled the scientific revolution of the seventeenth century as a fundamental transformation of Western thought.[1] Historians have called the nineteenth century "the Golden Age of History"[2] and "the Historical Era in humanistic scholarship."[3] They have identified "historical sophistication" as "the characteristic virtue of nineteenth-century thought"[4] and one of its most distinctive features.[5] Just as historical thinking pervaded philology, biblical studies, classics, philosophy, literature, and art; the emerging social sciences of anthropology, politics, and economics; and natural sciences such as geology, paleontology, and biology,[6] it also dominated legal scholarship. As Roscoe Pound recognized in the early twentieth century, "in law as in everything else," the nineteenth century was the "century of history."[7]

---

[1] John Higham, Preface, pp. 8–9, in John Higham with Leonard Krieger and Felix Gilbert, History (Englewood Cliffs, N.J.: Prentice-Hall, Inc., 1965), citing Herbert Butterfield, Man on His Past (Cambridge University Press, 1960), p. vii.

[2] Felix Gilbert, European and American Historiography, pp. 317, 340, in History, supra note 1.

[3] John Higham, Theory, pp. 87, 102, in History, supra note 1.

[4] J. W. Burrow, Evolution and Society: A Study in Victorian Social Theory (Cambridge University Press, 1966), p. 173.

[5] Maurice Mandelbaum, History, Man and Reason: A Study in Nineteenth-Century Thought (Baltimore: Johns Hopkins Press, 1971), p. 41.

[6] See, e.g., Peter Brooks, Reading for the Plot (Cambridge, Mass.: Harvard University Press, 1984), pp. xi, 6; Burrow, supra note 4, at 108–9; Higham, supra note 1, at xi; Higham, supra note 3, at 102; Dorothy Ross, The Origins of American Social Science (Cambridge University Press, 1991), p. 4.

[7] Roscoe Pound, Book Review, 35 Harv. L. Rev. 774 (1922); accord G. P. Gooch, History and Historians in the Nineteenth Century (London: Longmans, Green, and Company, 1913), p. 42.

European scholars, often led by lawyers, had been attentive to historical issues before the nineteenth century. French legal scholars in the sixteenth century studied Roman law on its own terms, recognizing the differentness of the past while examining the relationship between past and present law.[8] English scholars during the seventeenth century discovered that the laws and liberties of Anglo-Norman feudalism differed from those of previous Anglo-Saxon and subsequent post-feudal England.[9] Scottish legal thinkers in the eighteenth century developed a "conjectural" school of historical jurisprudence that posited stages of historical progress from barbarism to civilization and urged law reform to eliminate vestiges of feudal law that had become obsolete and harmful in their new, commercial age.[10] Yet the historians of historical thought who have done most to illuminate it in earlier centuries themselves highlight the distinctiveness of the nineteenth-century historical turn. Prior work was often eclectic and unsystematic,[11] not based on original sources,[12] and did not join historical insight with historical narrative.[13] J. G. A. Pocock wrote *The Ancient Constitution and the Feudal Law*, his pathbreaking 1957 "study of English historical thought in the seventeenth century," in opposition to the prevalent view that serious historical thought began in nineteenth-century Germany. But he also emphasized that it was only in the nineteenth century that "history became a distinct and self-conscious way of looking at things,"[14] an accomplishment of "historians whom we may feel to be still our own contemporaries."[15] Historical scholarship displayed its "modern character," extending to all aspects of the human condition, he more recently observed, when the reorganization of academic and intellectual life in the nineteenth century made history a profession. Even in the late eighteenth century, history remained in a "pre-modern condition."[16] Dorothy Ross similarly traced the "modern understanding of history" to the early nineteenth century, when "history as a continuous procession of qualitative changes came fully into view" and when "many European thinkers began to interpret the whole of reality, including

---

[8] J. G. A. Pocock, The Ancient Constitution and the Feudal Law: A Study of English Historical Thought in the Seventeenth Century (Cambridge University Press, 1957) (1990 reprint), pp. 1–29; Donald R. Kelley, Foundations of Modern Historical Scholarship: Language, Law, and History in the French Renaissance (Columbia University Press, 1970).

[9] Pocock, supra note 8, at 208.

[10] Peter Stein, Legal Evolution: The Story of an Idea (Cambridge University Press, 1980), pp. 8–9, 23–50; David Lieberman, The Province of Legislation Determined: Legal Theory in Eighteenth-Century Britain (Cambridge University Press, 1989), pp. 148–58, 172–5; J. G. A. Pocock, Barbarism and Religion: Narratives of Civil Government, vol. 2, (Cambridge University Press, 1999), pp. 310–29.

[11] Kelley, supra note 8, at 307.

[12] Lieberman, supra note 10, at 149.

[13] Pocock, supra note 10, at 224–6, 248.

[14] Pocock, supra note 8, at 251.

[15] Id. at 228.

[16] Pocock, supra note 10, at 7.

what had earlier been conceived as absolute and unchanging, in contextual historical terms."[17]

The general turn to history in nineteenth-century Western thought is a huge subject. Relying on a broad range of secondary sources, I focus here on aspects of the historical turn that relate most to the work of the American legal scholars. This focus encompasses the fascinating interactions among historically oriented scholars in different emerging disciplines, especially in Germany, England, and the United States.

Many nineteenth-century scholars viewed history as a continuous process of connected events that reveals meaning over time. Well before Darwin, they often compared history to an evolving organism, though they had varied, and sometimes incompatible, views of evolutionary change. The turn to history began at different times in different countries, starting most significantly in Germany at the end of the eighteenth century, followed by England, primarily after the Napoleonic wars, and then the United States, primarily after the Civil War. Yet throughout the period in which historical thought dominated Western intellectual life, scholars in these countries influenced each other. For example, three English writers, the historians Edward Gibbon and Edmund Burke and the lawyer and philologist William Jones, contributed substantially to early German interest in history. In the first half of the nineteenth century, German scholars, particularly philologists, stimulated English research into Anglo-Saxon language, history, and law. And toward the end of the nineteenth century, American legal scholars, themselves influenced by previous German scholarly methods and research on the history of Teutonic law, produced work that Frederic Maitland, the great English legal historian, relied on in his masterpiece, *The History of English Law*.

German interest in historical explanation arose in the late eighteenth century largely in opposition to the universal rationalism of the French Enlightenment, an opposition intensified, and often associated with patriotic nationalism, by the reaction against the French Revolution and Napoleon's subsequent occupation of Germany. Johann Herder aroused historical consciousness by challenging Enlightenment conceptions of language as a universal and rational structure. Herder maintained instead that language is the key to distinctive group cultures with which it grows organically. Subsequent German scholars, building on Herder's views, related classic texts, such as the *Odyssey* and the Hebrew Bible, to the cultures that produced them, often concluding that these works were written by multiple authors at different times. Convinced that all aspects of a group's culture are organically related, scholars were simultaneously interested in many of them and contributed to each other's work. For example, Savigny, who reported that previous work in Roman history stimulated his own ambitious scholarship on the history of Roman law, awakened the historical interests of his student and research assistant Jacob Grimm. From helping Savigny with his research on Roman law, Grimm began to study

---

[17] Ross, supra note 6, at 4.

medieval German poetry and folk tales. These studies led to his research on
the history of Teutonic languages as well as to his collections of early German
legal decisions that paralleled his much better known collections of folk tales.
His work on the history of Teutonic languages attracted the English scholar
John Mitchell Kemble, who spent time with Grimm in Gottingen and applied
Grimm's techniques to the study of Anglo-Saxon culture, from poetry to legal
history.

Kemble is just one example of the influence of German historical scholarship
in England. In some fields, such as biblical studies and classics, religious resistance delayed the eventual acceptance of German scholarship that challenged
the historical authenticity of major texts, particularly the Bible. In other fields,
especially English history, the impact of German scholarship was early, continuous, and substantial. William Stubbs, who followed Kemble as the leading
historian of English history, similarly relied on German scholarship in emphasizing the Teutonic origins of English institutions and laws. Henry Adams, as
he was beginning his own career teaching medieval history and law at Harvard,
complimented Stubbs for immersing himself in previous German scholarship
while writing his major work on the constitutional history of England. Stubbs's
familiarity with German scholarship, Adams concluded, allowed him to avoid
the amateurism that had dominated prior work by Englishmen on their own
history. When Maitland began his investigations into the legal records of
medieval England, he, too, built on the work of leading German historians
of Teutonic law. In a very different project formulating theories of social and
legal development, Henry Maine's *Ancient Law* extended the mostly German
research into the historical relationships among Aryan languages and cultures.
One of the most influential books published in the nineteenth century, *Ancient
Law* ultimately had more impact on the emerging disciplines of anthropology
and sociology than in the field of legal history itself.

In the United States, as previously in Germany and England, scholars in
many fields turned to historical explanation in the late nineteenth century. As
in Germany and England, moreover, intellectual influences moved freely among
disciplines and countries. For example, the historically oriented German political economists, who often praised Savigny's historical jurisprudence as an
important intellectual model, were themselves models for political economists
in the United States. The historical study of Teutonic laws and institutions,
which originated in Germany and spread to England, was one of the major
intellectual transplants to the United States. Many American historians became
interested in how Teutonic "seeds" or "germs" had developed in America as
well as England. In their detailed studies of Anglo-Saxon law, Henry Adams
and his students challenged Maine's broad theories of historical change.

The research university was a major institutional force in the transatlantic
turn to historical explanation. Many of the pioneers of historical scholarship in
Germany taught at the University of Gottingen, which had become well known
by the end of the eighteenth century for its quality and academic freedom, and
many subsequent scholars developed their historical interests as students at

Gottingen. The University of Berlin, founded in 1810 with Savigny among the initial faculty, became another center of historical studies in many fields and a model for other German research universities. Lacking similar research universities in their own countries, English and American students frequently studied in German universities. The American research universities that emerged in the decades after 1870, whose faculties included many people who had studied in Germany, in many respects emulated their German predecessors. The research university, both in Germany and later in the United States, provided an institutional home to people who wanted to devote their lives to scholarship and enabled the development of history as a professional career rather than an avocation of wealthy amateurs. By contrast, English universities in general, and law schools in particular, resisted transformation into research institutions. As leading English scholars and government reports periodically complained, this resistance impeded scholarship in England.

Evolutionary Historical Thought

The widespread historical orientation of nineteenth-century thought encompassed different and sometimes conflicting views about the study and meaning of the past. Within this variety, many nineteenth-century scholars, including legal scholars, were attracted to the particular form of historical analysis often described by the term "historicism," the belief that the meaning of a phenomenon depends on its place within a process or stream of historical development.[18] Historicists were not simply interested in the past. Often differentiating historical from mathematical or mechanical models of explanation, they emphasized that the human world is not eternal. They viewed history as a continuous series of events that were both connected to and qualitatively different from each other. This process continued to the present and would extend into the future.[19] Just as the great nineteenth-century novelists revealed meaning through the sequences of narrative plots,[20] legal scholars examined the connections between past and present law.[21]

Historicists frequently expressed their conceptions of history through the analogy of a living organism. They were interested in the entire life of the organism and attempted to describe the course of its changes over time. They frequently referred to these changes as development or evolution, using "evolution" as a synonym for development rather than in its later, more specific Darwinian sense as a theory of natural selection extending over multiple generations. Many were especially eager to identify and explore the organism's

---

[18] Mandelbaum, supra note 5, at 42–3; Morton White, Social Thought in America: The Revolt against Formalism (Oxford University Press, 1976 ed.) (original ed. 1947), p. 12.

[19] Ross, supra note 6, at 474–5; Frederick C. Beiser, Historicism, in Oxford Handbook of Continental Philosophy (Oxford University Press, 2007) (B. Leiter and M. Rosen, eds.), pp. 155, 158–61.

[20] Brooks, supra note 6, at xi–xii, 113.

[21] Gooch, supra note 7, at 51.

infancy, from which its subsequent development or evolution could be traced and explained.[22] The state was the organism whose continuous evolution they particularly wanted to explore.[23] The search for the origins of the modern state accounts for the enormous attention nineteenth-century historians in Europe and the United States devoted to the Middle Ages, the time, they believed, when the roots of the modern state first formed. Typically, the initial major project of a professional historian, including those who intended to concentrate on modern history, focused on the Middle Ages.[24] The image of the state as an organism included the view that the different parts of an organism must be understood in functional relationship to each other and to the organism as a whole. What is true of the body is also true of the state. Just as the heart and brain, arms and legs, are related parts of the body, language and law, art and religion, are related parts of the state. These historians treated the population of the state as a unitary entity sharing fundamental characteristics that expressed themselves throughout social life and evolved over time.[25]

As numerous recent scholars have concluded, evolutionary conceptions of time dominated social thought well before Darwin published his theories of biological evolution.[26] "When the cradle of evolutionary social theory was being prepared," J. W. Burrow vividly observes, "Darwin was in his hammock and three thousand miles away."[27] The American legal scholar Francis Wharton cited Burke and Savigny to make this point in the nineteenth century.[28] Indeed, Darwin himself relied on philological investigations into the evolution of related Aryan languages to illustrate his own observations about biological evolution.[29] Rather than stimulating evolutionary conceptions of time, Darwin's theories of biological evolution reinforced and helped diffuse them.[30] Even after Darwin published, much scholarship on social evolution proceeded without significant reliance on him. For example, the founders of evolutionary anthropology in England during the 1860s drew more on prior legal and philosophical thought than on Darwin's theories of biological evolution.[31] And the young American economists who founded the American Economic Association in 1885, though sympathetic to Darwinian evolutionary theory, treated it mostly as support for the general idea of development over time. Like many of their American peers

---

[22] Higham, supra note 3, at 102; John Higham, American History, in History, supra note 1, at 160; Mandelbaum, supra note 5, at 47.

[23] Jurgen Herbst, The German School in American Scholarship: A Study in the Transfer of Culture (Cornell University Press, 1965), p. 119; Peter Novick, That Noble Dream: The "Objectivity Question" and the American Historical Profession (Cambridge University Press, 1988), p. 87.

[24] Gilbert, supra note 2, at 333–4; Mandelbaum, supra note 5, at 55.

[25] Mandelbaum, supra note 5, at 55–7.

[26] Higham, supra note 3, at 94; Burrow, supra note 4, at 21, 135, 152–3; Mandelbaum, supra note 5, at 77–8; see generally Stein, supra note 10.

[27] Burrow, supra note 4, at 100.

[28] Francis Wharton, Commentaries on Law (Philadelphia: Kay & Brother, 1884), p. 69.

[29] Mandelbaum, supra note 5, at 97; Burrow, supra note 4, at 109.

[30] Burrow, supra note 4, at 114.

[31] Id. at 135.

in other disciplines, they looked more to the German historical school than to Darwin as the model for their own evolutionary approach to economics.[32]

Evolutionary theories of history took many different forms. Some viewed evolutionary change as having a deterministic tendency to move in a particular pattern or direction. Others maintained instead that evolution is the contingent sum of unpredictable changes over time, which can only be understood retrospectively.[33] The German scholar Johann Herder prominently popularized the concept of a distinctive Volksgeist, or folk spirit, which developed autonomously and often unconsciously within a particular culture.[34] More specifically, many historians and legal scholars in England and the United States endorsed the "Teutonic germ-theory," which treated the traditions and institutions of England and the United States as the culmination of internally developing positive traits that originated in the German forests of the remote past, reached England with the migration of Teutonic tribes in the fifth and sixth centuries, and arrived in America during the English colonization of the seventeenth century. As examples of the maturity of Teutonic germs in contemporary society, Americans emphasized local self-government, particularly as manifested in the New England town meeting, and individual freedom.[35] Evolutionary theories of history often differentiated meaningful history, which exhibited the process of development, from history that was merely "accidental" or "superficial" and, therefore, unimportant.[36]

Whether or not they viewed historical development as contingent or determined, evolutionary theories of history often assumed that history proceeded in distinctive stages toward higher or better levels. Depending on the preferred evolutionary theory, this progression could reflect the gradual unfolding of what was already immanent from the beginning, the impact of governing laws over time, or simply the fortuitous result of temporal change.[37] When confronted with evidence that change had not occurred or had occurred in directions that were not higher or better, they considered the situation abnormal.[38]

Many nineteenth-century scholars were ambiguous, ambivalent, or even contradictory about the extent to which the course of evolution was contingent,

---

[32] Richard Hofstadter, Social Darwinism in American Thought (Boston: Beacon Press, 1970) (rev. ed.), p. 147.

[33] Mandelbaum, supra note 5, at 109; see James T. Kloppenberg, Uncertain Victory: Social Democracy and Progressivism in European and American Thought, 1870–1920 (Oxford University Press, 1986), p. 157.

[34] Ross, supra note 6, at 5; Gooch, supra note 7, at 54; Franz Wieacker, A History of Private Law in Europe (Oxford: Clarendon Press, 2003) (translated by Tony Weir), p. 285; Isaiah Berlin, Herder and the Enlightenment, in The Proper Study of Mankind: An Anthology of Essays (New York: Farrar, Straus & Giroux, 1998) (Henry Hardy and Roger Hausheer, eds.), pp. 359, 400, 408, 413–14.

[35] Novick, supra note 23, at 87–8; Herbst, supra note 23, at 117–19; Higham, supra note 22, at 158–61; Hofstadter, supra note 32, at 172–5.

[36] Mandelbaum, supra note 3, at 49, 59.

[37] Id. at 43–7, 103–8.

[38] Id. at 109.

determined, or progressive. For example, Henry Maine, one of the most influential evolutionary theorists, focused on the progression from primitive to civilized legal systems. In his most famous passage, he declared "that the movement of the progressive societies has hitherto been a movement *from Status to Contract*."[39] But he did not clarify whether this history disclosed actual laws of social and legal evolution, as many of his followers subsequently claimed.[40] Maine asserted the "necessity of taking the Roman law as a typical system,"[41] perhaps because the history of other legal systems, such as the English, was much less accessible.[42] Maine may have only been generalizing from the evidence most readily available to him, primarily from the history of Roman law, rather than proposing deterministic laws governing evolution. Based on his extensive analysis of Maine's work, J. W. Burrow concluded that he was an unsystematic thinker who gave conflicting and irreconcilable signals about whether he was an evolutionary determinist or simply an inveterate generalizer.[43] Numerous English and American scholars accepted versions of the "Teutonic-germ theory," yet at the same time stressed the contingency of historical events, such as the Norman Conquest of England and much of the subsequent course of English history. Henry Adams, who introduced professional legal history in the United States, struggled to find laws of historical evolution until the complexity of the data he scrupulously gathered and studied prompted him to give up. Theories of biological evolution generated similar uncertainties. Darwin seemed to view biological evolution as a progressive, developmental process, even though his explanation based on natural selection did not entail change in a particular pattern or direction.[44]

Evolutionary historical thought spanned the ideological and political spectrum. Much of the emphasis on historical evolution in the late eighteenth and early nineteenth centuries was a conservative reaction against the perceived excesses of the French Revolution. The conception of gradual evolutionary change over time provided a comfortable continuity with the past, a reassuring alternative to the drastic changes in social and political life advocated by a priori theorists and translated terrifyingly into practice during the most violent phases of the French Revolution.[45] Evolutionary theories similarly seemed an attractive antidote to the rapid change threatened by the Industrial Revolution.[46] Beyond emphasizing the necessary continuity between past and present that should not be disrupted by revolutionary change, conservative

---

[39] Henry Maine, Ancient Law (Washington, D.C.: Beard Books, 2000) (original ed. 1861), p. 100.
[40] Stein, supra note 10, at 114; George Feaver, From Status to Contract: A Biography of Sir Henry Maine 1822–1888 (London: Longmans, Green and Company Ltd., 1969), p. 55.
[41] Maine, supra note 39, at xv.
[42] Frederick Pollock, Introduction, Maine's Ancient Law (New York: Henry Holt and Company, 1889), pp. xi, xx–xxi.
[43] Burrow, supra note 4, at 164.
[44] Mandelbaum, supra note 5, at 109.
[45] Burrow, supra note 4, at 265.
[46] Novick, supra note 23, at 87; Ross, supra note 6, at 63–4.

evolutionists often idealized and venerated the present precisely because it was the product of an evolutionary process.[47] They, therefore, resisted conscious efforts to change the status quo, including modifications that did not threaten revolution. Critics who otherwise valued their respect for historical continuity faulted them for undermining "the creative energies of the present."[48]

Though evolutionary theories of historical change arose largely as a conservative response to the French Revolution, liberals also invoked them to support social reform.[49] Whereas conservative evolutionists stressed the gradual and often inevitable evolution of national and racial unity, liberals often portrayed evolution as a continuous struggle of interests and goals that could be affected by human intervention and societal change.[50] Unlike conservative evolutionists, who celebrated the past as the source of values that should be venerated in the present, liberal evolutionists often studied history to emancipate the present from the dysfunctional survivals of a more primitive past.[51] E. B. Tylor, the eminent English anthropologist, was largely responsible for directing his discipline into a search-and-destroy mission against dysfunctional survivals, particularly in religious practice.[52] Borrowing explicitly from Tylor, Oliver Wendell Holmes, Jr., similarly studied legal history to emancipate current law from dysfunctional legal survivals.

In specific political views, as well as in general ideological orientations, the evolutionary historical thought of leading nineteenth-century scholars correlated with both conservative and liberal positions. Throughout the nineteenth century, German evolutionary historians reflected the spectrum of political views from conservatism to socialism.[53] Among legal scholars, a significant political divide arose between "Romanists," who studied Roman law, and "Germanists," who increasingly viewed Roman law as a foreign infection that undermined the organic native law of Germany. In the late 1830s, Germanists largely associated themselves with the revolutionary liberalism of the political Left, playing a leading role in the Revolution of 1848. They accused Romanists, who often supported the Prussian Crown, of invoking scholarly neutrality to hide their reactionary political views.[54] The historically oriented German economists at the end of the century praised Savigny as an intellectual model, though their political views were considerably to his left.[55]

[47] Novick, supra note 23, at 27.

[48] Gooch, supra note 7, at 47.

[49] Burrow, supra note 4, at 265.

[50] Higham, supra note 22, at 172–3; Hofstadter, supra note 32, at 68, 71, 75–6, 107–8, 115, 118, 125.

[51] Burrow, supra note 4, at 257, 267–8.

[52] Id. at 256.

[53] Georg G. Iggers, The German Conception of History: The National Tradition of Historical Thought from Herder to the Present (Middletown, Conn.: Wesleyan University Press, 1968), p. 4.

[54] James Q. Whitman, The Legacy of Roman Law in the German Romantic Era (Princeton University Press, 1990), pp. 200–5; Mathias Reimann, Nineteenth-Century German Legal Science, 31 Boston College L. Rev. 837, 869–70 (1990).

[55] Herbst, supra note 23, at 132, 145–7.

In England, as in Germany, evolutionary understandings of history corre-lated with a broad range of political views. Historians of the medieval village community, a major subject of investigation in nineteenth-century England, well illustrate this political diversity. While agreeing that evolutionary links connected the medieval village community with contemporary English society, they varied widely, as Maitland later observed, both in their political aspira-tions and in the extent to which they saw those aspirations foreshadowed in the Middle Ages. Scholars who disagreed about current politics could agree about the characteristics of the medieval village community, just as scholars who agreed about current politics could disagree about those characteristics. Conservatives as well as liberals depicted the medieval village community as either socialist or individualist, democratic or unfree.[56]

Just as English historians of the medieval village community exhibited diverse political views, so did the many Americans who emphasized the Teutonic roots of English and American institutions. While many adherents of the "Teutonic-germ theory" were politically conservative, favoring restrictions on immigra-tion at home and supporting imperialism abroad,[57] others were progressive, emphasizing the liberality and representativeness of the American institutions that had evolved from Teutonic origins.[58] Conservatives often stressed the evo-lution of the strong national state as the protector of individual rights, espe-cially property rights. Yet many historically oriented American scholars tried to influence the continued organic evolution of Anglo-Saxon liberties into a more communal and egalitarian society that would reform the excesses and inequalities of capitalist individualism. Some participated extensively in the late nineteenth-century movement of genteel reform against perceived polit-ical corruption, particularly in the civil service, and often opposed American imperialism. Further to the left, American students of German historical econo-mists frequently endorsed cooperative versions of socialism, many based on Christian doctrine, while rejecting Marxist socialism.[59]

The Historical Turn in Germany

The turn to history as a mode of explanation in Western intellectual life began most intensely in Germany, largely in reaction against French influ-ence. Initially a response to the universal rationalism of the eighteenth-century French Enlightenment, historical thought in Germany became more pro-nounced, and more associated with German nationalism, in the wake of the

---

[56] J. W. Burrow, "The Village Community" and the Uses of History in Late Nineteenth-Century England, in Historical Perspectives: Studies in English Thought and Society, in Honour of J. H. Plumb (London: Europa, 1974) (Neil McKendrick, ed.), pp. 255, 258–61.

[57] Herbst, supra note 23, at 120–2; Hofstadter, supra note 32, at 172, 179–82.

[58] Novick, supra note 23, at 87, 99; Hofstadter, supra note 32, at 173–4.

[59] Ross, supra note 6, at 104–6, 111–14, 139; Herbst, supra note 23, at 189; Daniel T. Rodgers, Atlantic Crossings: Social Politics in a Progressive Age (Cambridge, Mass.: Harvard University Press, 1998), pp. 98–101.

French Revolution and the subsequent French occupation of Germany during the Napoleonic wars. The major thinkers of the French Enlightenment were confident in the capacity of human reason progressively to discover a universal and timeless reality subject to general, often mechanistic laws. They speculated about the rational principles assumed to underlie both the natural world and human affairs. When they did think about the past, they typically characterized it as a more primitive period that the development of human reason was gradually overcoming in its search for universal truths.[60] Contemporary Germans directly challenged these fundamental ideas of the French Enlightenment. Denying the possibility of universal laws governing human experience, they emphasized the individuality and diversity of different cultures. In contrast to philosophical speculation about the rational and the universal, they sought explanations in the organic growth of each distinctive culture, rooted in language and extending to all aspects of national life.[61] Attitudes toward medieval Europe well illustrated these differences. Whereas the French Enlightenment dismissed this period as a primitive, even barbaric, era that devalued rational thought, German thinkers embraced it as part of the continuous unity of their culture.[62]

Germans perceived the French Revolution and the extension of French rule over Europe as the tragic political and military consequences of Enlightenment thought, attempts to impose universalism, as understood by the French, on the rest of the Continent. In the years after the French Revolution, German historical thinking, as a particularistic alternative to Enlightenment universalism and revolutionary absolutism, increasingly became associated with German nationalism. Politically fragmented and occupied by the French, many Germans looked to their historical traditions, and especially to the medieval German empire, as an inspirational source for a future German state. The substantial subsidization of historical scholarship by the Prussian government in the early nineteenth century reflected this nationalistic goal.[63]

"German Schools of History," Lord Acton's lead article in the first issue of the *English Historical Review* in 1886, dramatically conveyed, through the florid and self-assured style of his time, the German turn to history in response to the French Revolution. "Historical writing was old, but historical thinking was new in Germany when it sprang from the shock of the French Revolution. Condemnation of history had been the strongest plank in the platform of 1789." The French revolutionaries "who struck at the misery inflicted by traditional authority believed no dogma so firmly as that of the folly of their ancestors." This dogma was the flag under which the French armies conquered Germany.

---

[60] Herbst, supra note 23, at 9, 55–6, 102; Mandelbaum, supra note 5, at 49, 55; Ross, supra note 6, at 9; Berlin, supra note 34, at 415, 431.

[61] Mandelbaum, supra note 5, at 47, 49, 56; Ross, supra note 6, at 9–10; Berlin, supra note 34, at 415.

[62] Mandelbaum, supra note 5, at 55–6.

[63] Ross, supra note 6, at 21; Novick, supra note 23, at 99; Gooch, supra note 7, at 64–6.

The German reaction "was the revolt of outraged history." The Germans maintained that recovering the lost knowledge of the past made "it possible to understand, to appreciate, and even to admire things which the judgment of rationalism condemned in the mass of worthless and indiscriminate error." German writers "admitted India to an equality with Greece" and "medieval Rome with classical." They viewed history "as a remedy for the eighteenth century and the malady of vain speculation."[64] Eventually, the German historical school, "having abolished the law of nature which was the motive of 1789, instituted the law of nationality, which became the motive of 1848," the year of liberal revolution in Germany.[65]

Johann Herder was the most influential eighteenth-century German opponent of Enlightenment thought and a significant spur to historical scholarship in Germany. Herder synthesized, popularized, and built upon the work of others while contributing original ideas of his own.[66] From his study of language, Herder derived broad implications that subsequently stimulated historical studies across disciplines. He challenged the Enlightenment search for a single universal and rational structure underlying all languages as well as its assumption that the contents of language express truths about the world.[67] Instead, Herder viewed language as an organism having a natural growth, to be studied genetically and comparatively as an independent entity, without the distraction of a futile search for a unifying rationality.[68] Language could be modified and reformed, but not created through logic alone.[69] Convinced that song and poetry were among the earliest forms of language, Herder himself compiled an international collection of folk songs, an extremely popular precursor of Grimm's fairy tales.[70]

For Herder, the study of language was simultaneously the study of culture.[71] He considered language the key to forming, and thus to understanding, a distinctive group culture, which he called a volk. Language linked the group together and expressed its collective experience not just in literature itself, but throughout all aspects of its culture as well, from art and religion to social and political life.[72] German poetry thus resembled German art or German law more than it resembled the poetry of other cultures.[73] Languages and cultures not only differed from each other; like other living organisms, but they changed over time and thus must be studied historically.[74] Rather than a sign of philosophic truth,

---

[64] Lord Acton, German Schools of History, 1 English Hist. Rev. 7, 8–9 (1886).

[65] Id. at 10.

[66] Berlin, supra note 34, at 361–6; Hans Aarsleff, The Study of Language in England, 1780–1860 (University of Minnesota Press, 1983), pp. 147–8.

[67] Aarsleff, supra note 66, at 143–7; Berlin, supra note 34, at 385, 415.

[68] Aarsleff, supra note 66, at 151–3; Berlin, supra note 34, at 383.

[69] Berlin, supra note 34, at 384.

[70] Aarsleff, supra note 66, at 151.

[71] Id. at 324.

[72] Stein, supra note 10, at 58; Berlin, supra note 34, at 368, 380–1, 384.

[73] Berlin, supra note 34, at 413–14.

[74] Ross, supra note 6, at 5; Berlin, supra note 34, at 416.

language provided the historical record that revealed the distinctive national characteristics of a people.[75] Among the multiplicity of languages and cultures, Herder did not perceive hierarchies of value. He loved German language and culture but did not consider them superior to others and criticized those who did.[76] In addition to urging the recovery of early German poetry, he encouraged study of the Hebrew Bible as the national poem of the Jews that revealed their distinctive volk[77] and wrote an important work, *The Spirit of Hebrew Poetry*.[78] Nor did he celebrate, as did many of his contemporaries, a presumably classic past as the source of universal values for the present. He emphasized that culture is necessarily attached to the organic development of a people, that any attempt to impose the past on the present is artificial and, therefore, impossible.[79] Avoiding the false promise of resurrecting an idealized past, each people must develop its accumulated culture in the context of its own era.[80]

By emphasizing history rather than reason as the way to understand the complexities of human activity, Herder provided a major impetus for the German turn to historical scholarship in the nineteenth century. He most directly influenced philology, whose attention to the history of language pervaded German scholarship throughout the nineteenth century and affected virtually all fields, including law.[81] Indeed, the extent to which Herder's successors followed his historical approach made it so familiar that his own pioneering contributions were often overlooked.[82]

German scholars in different fields, often in contact with and inspired by each other, wrote the earliest works that examined their subjects historically.[83] In biblical criticism, classics, law, and German literature, important original scholarship carried out the historical analysis previously advocated by Herder. J. G. Eichhorn is widely considered the first scholar to study the Old Testament historically, beginning with his book *Introduction to the Old Testament*, published in 1783.[84] Sharing both a close friendship and intellectual affinities with Herder, Eichhorn, like Herder, treated the Israelites portrayed in the Old Testament as a volk. The Old Testament itself, they believed, expressed the mental world of the Israelites, a world they often called "orientalism."[85] In

---

[75] Aarsleff, supra note 66, at 146–7.

[76] Berlin, supra note 34, at 368, 415.

[77] Id. at 374 n. 1, 403; Gooch, supra note 7, at 521.

[78] T. K. Cheyne, Founders of Old Testament Criticism: Biblical, Descriptive, and Critical Studies, (London: Methuen & Company, 1893), p. 17.

[79] Berlin, supra note 34, at 398, 431.

[80] Id. at 431; Ross, supra note 34, at 431.

[81] Aarsleff, supra note 66, at 152–3; Berlin, supra note 34, at 361 n. 2, 385, 416; Gooch, supra note 7, at 38, 54.

[82] Berlin, supra note 34, at 367, 417.

[83] Gooch, supra note 7, at 42, 54; Acton, supra note 64, at 11.

[84] Gooch, supra note 7, at 521; Cheyne, supra note 78, at 13; Bible, The Encyclopaedia Britannica (Cambridge University Press, 11th ed. 1911), vol. III, pp. 849, 862.

[85] Gooch, supra note 7, at 521; Cheyne, supra note 78, at 14–15; John Rogerson, Old Testament Criticism in the Nineteenth Century: England and Germany (London: SPCK, 1984), p. 17.

the first edition of his *Letters on Theology*, published before Eichhorn's book, Herder acknowledged that "we have not as yet a proper critical introduction to the Old Testament." In his second edition, Herder added in a footnote "We now have it in Eichhorn's valuable Introduction."[86]

Applying literary analysis for the first time to the Old Testament, Eichhorn concluded that it, like the ancient texts of other cultures, was written and edited at different times by different people. Yet he believed that the Old Testament, if understood through the worldview of its multiple authors, is essentially an accurate historical record.[87] For example, he maintained that the account in Genesis of the expulsion of Adam and Eve from the Garden of Eden reflected the historical experience of a couple becoming aware of their sexual differences after eating a poisonous fruit. The references to God and a talking serpent, while not historically accurate, reflected the way the early Semitic authors of Genesis, with their oriental mentality so different from the orientation of Eichhorn's contemporaries, could comprehend and narrate these actual events.[88] The interdisciplinary connections in the German turn to history are well illustrated by the Eichhorn family. Eichhorn's son, Karl Friedrich, worked closely with Savigny during the first decades of the nineteenth century in developing historical approaches to law.[89]

In the field of biblical criticism itself, scholarship moved from the largely literary analysis of Eichhorn to a consideration of the value of the Old Testament as a historical record. In a major work published in 1806–7, W. M. L. De Wette challenged Eichhorn's apologetic explanation of the essential accuracy of the Old Testament. Most originally, he denied the historical authenticity of the books of Chronicles in the Old Testament, which portrayed Moses as giving the Israelites a legal and religious system that had been followed from the time of King David. The Chronicles, De Wette maintained, were written long after the events they described and anachronistically projected the religious practices of this later period onto the earlier one. Turning then to the historical books of the Old Testament that dealt with the earlier period – Judges, Samuel, and Kings – De Wette observed that they portrayed very different religious practices than in the Chronicles. Thus, the "Mosaic" law of the Chronicles and, De Wette also maintained, of most Old Testament books from Genesis through Numbers was not the law given by Moses or followed in the generations immediately following his death.[90] Subsequent German scholars, though differing on many particulars with De Wette and each other, tried to reconstruct the actual history and religion of Israel during the period described in the Old Testament, emphasizing a story of change and development over time.[91]

---

[86] Cheyne, supra note 78, at 18.
[87] Id. at 23; Rogerson, supra note 85, at 25–7; Encyclopaedia Britannica, supra note 84, at 862.
[88] Rogerson, supra note 85, at 17–18.
[89] Cheyne, supra note 78, at 21; Gooch, supra note 7, at 43–4.
[90] Rogerson, supra note 85, at 29, 33–4; Encyclopaedia Britannica, supra note 84, at 862.
[91] Rogerson, supra note 85, at 34, 71–2, 78; Encyclopaedia Britannica, supra note 84, at 862–63.

Influenced by the turn to historical scholarship, Jewish scholars in Germany also began to study their religious texts historically. Though excluded as Jews from professorial positions in German universities,[92] some of them had been students of leading German professors, such as Wolf, Eichhorn, and De Wette.[93] The Jewish scholars typically focused on rabbinic literature rather than the Old Testament, which had attracted the substantial attention of Christians.[94] Like the Christians, Jewish scholars challenged the historical accuracy of many of their religious texts and viewed Judaism as an organically evolving culture.[95] Just as Germans in the nineteenth century tied German history to nationalistic goals, German Jews viewed Jewish history as a source of collective pride, continuity, and preservation.[96]

A similar turn to historical analysis occurred in classical studies. In his book on Homer, published in 1795, F. A. Wolf maintained that the texts ascribed to Homer were composites of different traditions and authors, a conclusion Herder endorsed while claiming that he had reached it first.[97] By referring to Homer as "the Bible of Greece," Wolf associated his work with biblical criticism declaring multiple authorship of the Bible, which helps explain religious resistance to historical scholarship in classics as well as biblical studies.[98] Drawing on Wolf's earlier work on ancient Greece, B. G. Niebuhr used poetry to investigate the early history of Roman institutions.[99] Outraged by the French Revolution and the Napoleonic occupation of Germany, he viewed Rome as a great state, whose history could strengthen the resolve of Germans to create a great state of their own.[100] Observing that Niebuhr emancipated history from its prior subservience to other fields, giving it intellectual independence and eventual dominance, Lord Acton called him the originator of true historical studies in Germany and the model for subsequent German historians.[101]

Niebuhr inspired research on the history of Greek civilization[102] as well as Savigny's investigation of the history of Roman law. According to Savigny, Niebuhr's accomplishment gave him the courage to undertake his own ambitious project. Savigny also helped Niebuhr. Based on a hunch by Savigny, Niebuhr discovered in 1816 a manuscript by the Roman scholar Gaius, which provided the first reliable information about classical Roman law, a boon

---

[92] Ismar Schorsch, From Text to Context: The Turn to History in Modern Judaism (Hanover, N.H.: University Press of New England for Brandeis University Press, 1994), p. 352.

[93] Id. at 222, 235, 237, 340.

[94] Id. at 350.

[95] Id. at 185, 247, 316, 348.

[96] Id. at 288–9.

[97] Gooch, supra note 7, at 28–9.

[98] Norman Vance, Niebuhr in England: History, Faith, and Order, in British and German Historiography, 1750–1950: Traditions, Perceptions, and Transfers (New York: Oxford University Press, 2000) (Benedikt Stuchtey and Peter Wende, eds.), pp. 83, 90–1.

[99] Gooch, supra note 7, at 19.

[100] Id. at 18, 22.

[101] Acton, supra note 64, at 7; accord, Gooch, supra note 7, at 14.

[102] Gooch, supra note 7, at 31.

to nineteenth-century legal scholars.[103] Echoing Herder, Savigny rejected the Enlightenment glorification of codification as the embodiment of the universal law of reason and argued instead that law, like language, reflects the distinctive organic development of a people. Both language and law are found, not made.[104] The French *Code civil*, he ruefully observed, was a by-product of the French Revolution that disastrously illustrated the evils of codification.[105] Similarly following Herder, Savigny saw law as part of the general history of a culture and treated it more as a literary tradition than as a social reality.[106] Just as Jewish scholars in Germany adapted theories of organic cultural evolution and techniques of historical criticism of religions texts, they emulated the historical jurisprudence of Savigny in studying Jewish law.[107]

Influenced generally by Herder and directly by Savigny, Jacob Grimm examined German literature and language historically. Best known for the collection of fairy tales he compiled with his brother Wilhelm, Grimm was the son of a lawyer, who encouraged him to study law. He became interested in historical research as a student of Savigny. In his autobiography, Grimm wrote that Savigny's lectures "exercised a decisive influence on my whole life," and he dedicated his book on German grammar to Savigny. When Savigny traveled to Paris in 1805 to collect sources for his work on the history of Roman law, he invited Grimm to accompany him as his assistant. While helping Savigny, and encouraged by Wilhelm, Grimm discovered at the Bibliotheque Nationale manuscripts of medieval German literature, a field he had first encountered in Savigny's personal library.[108] Grimm's interest in medieval German poetry and folk tales extended to analysis of language, particularly etymology. Convinced by criticism of his early work for failing to apply the insights of scholarship on grammar to the study of literature, Grimm devoted himself to the systematic investigation of German grammar.[109] He produced a pioneering multi-volume study that received high praise, including from the leading critic of his earlier work.[110] Drawing on the recent scholarship of others, Grimm participated in the transformation of philology from a philosophical to a historical discipline. In contrast to the eighteenth-century speculative tradition, which attempted to create a universal grammar based on logic and to study words for insights into the ideas they named, he joined the movement to study language empirically and comparatively as an organic growth, tied to the development of national culture. Rather than prescribe rules of language based on logic, Grimm believed that philologists should investigate how language had been

---

[103] Wieacker, supra note 34, at 330.
[104] Id. at 295; Gooch, supra note 7, at 50; Action, supra note 64, at 9.
[105] Wieacker, supra note 34, at 296.
[106] Wieacker, supra note 34, at 305–6.
[107] Schorsch, supra note 92, at 191, 261–2.
[108] Gooch, supra note 7, at 55; Otto Jespersen, Language: Its Nature, Development and Origin (London: George Allen & Unwin Ltd., 1922), pp. 40–1.
[109] Gooch, supra note 7, at 56–7; Jespersen, supra note 108, at 41.
[110] Gooch, supra note 7, at 58.

used and transformed over time, particularly through the changes in the end-ings of words.[111] For him, the attempt to impose uniformity in language con-stituted the linguistic parallel to the absolutism of the Terror during the French Revolution.[112]

Grimm concluded that all Teutonic languages were part of a related fam-ily whose current forms could only be understood by tracing them to their origins. More broadly, he and his philological colleagues claimed that the study of related languages provided knowledge about the people who used them. The history of language opened the path to the entire history of human experience.[113] In a separate book, *Legal Antiquities*, which Savigny welcomed as an extension of his own work, Grimm relied on medieval German legal deci-sions, literature, and legend to emphasize that law, like language and literature, revealed the different stages of German experience and that the judge as well as the poet conveys the thought of the people. Just as he produced collections of early German sagas and fairy tales, he edited multiple volumes of Weistumer, or dooms, early legal decisions that, he wrote, would "make important contri-butions to a knowledge of law, mythology and customs, and give warmth and color to our early history."[114] Grimm's *Legal Antiquities* was a major impe-tus to the subsequent study of early Germanic law throughout the nineteenth century.[115]

German universities played an important role in the turn to history in German scholarship. In the late eighteenth century, the University of Gottingen led a resurgence of German universities to a higher standard than had existed in any European country for centuries. Gottingen allowed great freedom of thought, perhaps attributable both to its location in Hanover, the part of Germany least subject to the influence of absolutist princes, and its relatively recent founding in 1736, which enabled it to develop without the constraints of less liberal aca-demic traditions from an earlier era. Known for the quality of its scholarship and teaching, by the last decades of the eighteenth century it had become the center of emerging historical studies. Borrowing the seminar format of teaching from schools of theology, professors at Gottingen used it to encourage active learning by students engaged in independent, original scholarship.[116] Herder had substantial contact with the Gottingen faculty, and many leading schol-ars first developed their historical interests as students there, including both Eichhorns and the Grimms.[117] The establishment of the University of Berlin in 1810 was another major impetus to historical scholarship in Germany. At the

---

[111] Id. at 57.
[112] Id.
[113] Id. at 58; Jespersen, supra note 106, at 33.
[114] Gooch, supra note 7, at 59.
[115] Patrick Wormald, The Making of English Law: King Alfred to the Twelfth Century (Oxford: Blackwell Publishers Ltd., 1999), vol. 1, p. 11.
[116] Aarsleff, supra note 66, at 179–80; Whitman, supra note 54, at 85–6.
[117] Rogerson, supra note 85, at 17; Gooch, supra note 7, at 42–3, 61–2, 521; Cheyne, supra note 78, at 13–14.

University of Berlin, which became a model for other German universities, history for the first time became an autonomous discipline.[118] Greek and Roman history flourished there,[119] and Savigny joined its initial faculty, making it a center for historical jurisprudence.[120]

The Historical Turn in England

Early nineteenth-century German historical scholarship had an enormous, though often delayed, impact in England. The study of history as a professional discipline occurred later in England than in Germany and other continental European countries. Not until the 1860s did Oxford and Cambridge appoint serious scholars to chairs in history. History first became a subject of concentration for undergraduates in 1875. The *English Historical Review*, founded in 1886, began publication later than the national historical journal of any other major European country.[121]

Yet even before the nineteenth century, work by leading late eighteenth-century English writers had provided an important stimulus to the German historical turn. Edward Gibbon's *Decline and Fall of the Roman Empire* became an intellectual sensation in Germany.[122] During the years Gibbon published it in England, it was partially translated into German, beginning in 1779.[123] The translation of Gibbon's chapter on the history of Roman law in 1789, with comments by Gustav Hugo, an eminent law professor at Gottingen, had a particularly great impact, stimulating the German revival of scholarship on Roman law most impressively associated with Savigny.[124] While acknowledging their debt to Gibbon, German scholars often treated him as an erudite dilettante, criticizing him for paying insufficient attention to original sources and for generalizing too broadly from inadequate evidence.[125] Like Gibbon's *Decline and Fall*, the German translation of Edmund Burke's *Reflections on the Revolution in France* in 1793 was widely read and enormously influential,[126] including for major scholars such as Niebuhr[127] and Savigny.[128] Germans endorsed Burke's praise of the organic continuity of a tradition over time in contrast to the uniform and mechanical rationality of the French Enlightenment and the reforms imposed by the French

---

[118] Gilbert, supra note 2, at 324–5.

[119] Gooch, supra note 7, at 42.

[120] Id. at 47–8.

[121] Gilbert, supra note 2, at 335–6.

[122] Whitman, supra note 54, at 83; Charles E. McClelland, The German Historians and England: A Study in Nineteenth-Century Views (Cambridge University Press, 1971), p. 13; Wilfried Nippel, Gibbon and German Historiography, in British and German Historiography, supra note 98, at pp. 67, 67–8.

[123] Nippel, supra note 122, at 67–8.

[124] Id. at 68; Whitman, supra note 54, at 84–5; Gooch, supra note 7, at 43.

[125] Nippel, supra note 122, at 69, 75, 79; Iggers, supra note 53, at 29.

[126] McClelland, supra note 122, at 37–8.

[127] Id. at 49; Gooch, supra note 7, at 16.

[128] Stein, supra note 10, at 57.

Revolution.[129] For the Germans, as for Burke, history provided an intellectual defense against the French as well as a source of national identity.[130]

The philological work by William Jones was a third major English stimulus to historical scholarship in Germany. During the English rule of India, Jones was appointed a judge in Bengal in 1783. He had previously distinguished himself as an orientalist, studying Arabic and Persian languages and literature, and as a practicing lawyer. Deciding that he needed to know Hindu law to be an effective judge in India, Jones learned the Hindu language. After two years in India, Jones began to study Sanskrit as well. The Sanskrit drama by Calidas that he translated into Latin and then English, *Sakuntala, or the Fatal Ring*, was in turn translated into German in 1791 and stimulated intensive study of Indian religion and literature in Germany.[131] Beginning in 1789, Jones wrote essays, often based on his previous lectures, which were frequently republished and translated throughout Europe over the next decades.[132] Perhaps his most famous essay highlighted the resemblances, in the roots of verbs and the forms of grammar, among Sanskrit, Greek, and Latin. The affinities among these languages, he observed, were stronger "than could possibly have been produced by accident; so strong indeed, that no philologer could examine them all three, without believing them to have spring from some common source, which, perhaps, no longer exists."[133] In related and equally influential essays, Jones connected etymology with ethnography, maintaining that systematic resemblances of words among different languages often indicate affinities of kinship among the peoples who spoke them.[134]

Jones recognized that that his work was just a starting point for future collection and comparison of linguistic and ethnographic data,[135] which he did not pursue himself before his death in 1794.[136] This additional work did not at first occur in England. Most English interest in India, including its languages, was limited to the practical concerns of business and government. Many people in England took a dim view of Indian culture and character. English philologists, moreover, remained focused on language as the key to thought rather than as a guide to history.[137] In Germany, by contrast, where sensitivity to historical accounts of origins and development already had a powerful hold, Jones provided a major spur to the comparative historical study of language and culture, including the work of Grimm.[138]

---

[129] Iggers, supra note 53, at 33; McClelland, supra note 122, at 37.

[130] Benedikt Stuchtey and Peter Wende, Introduction, in British and German Historiography, supra note 98, at 1, 10.

[131] Aarsleff, supra note 66, at 115–20.

[132] Id. at 123.

[133] Id. at 133.

[134] Id. at 125–9.

[135] Id. at 234–5.

[136] Jespersen, supra note 106, at 34.

[137] Aarsleff, supra note 66, at 139–40.

[138] Id. at 143; Burrow, supra note 4, at 149.

As history became a serious subject of professional inquiry in England, many English scholars relied heavily on prior work by Germans. In some fields, especially biblical studies but also classics, there was substantial resistance to German influence, largely on religious grounds. Although German critical scholarship on the Old Testament was known in England as early as the 1790s, only toward the end of the nineteenth century did English scholars generally accept it.[139] The lingering impact of seventeenth-century Christian revivals in England contributed to a widespread religious conservatism that equated German biblical criticism with unbelief, an equation that occurred much less frequently in Germany itself.[140] Even after the broad English acceptance of German biblical criticism in the late nineteenth century, many in England rejected works that used it to deny the historical accuracy of the Old Testament.[141]

Wariness about German analysis of the Old Testament extended to German scholarship on classical Greece and Rome. The English understood that the same critical techniques used to question the unity and accuracy of ancient classical texts, such as Homer and Livy, had been applied to the ancient text that mattered most to many of them, the Old Testament.[142] English social and religious progressives translated Niebuhr in the 1820s and 1830s, thereby introducing German critical analysis of Roman history but also provoking hostility from conservatives. Niebuhr himself had challenged literal readings of the Old Testament by suggesting in his studies of Rome that different peoples might have been created at different times.[143]

Philological scholarship in Germany on Teutonic languages, itself stimulated by Jones, had the earliest impact on historical studies in England and can be traced directly to subsequent English work on the history of Anglo-Saxon law. After 1812, the end of the continental blockade during the Napoleonic wars that cut off travel between England and Germany, generations of English students studied in Germany.[144] These students included John Mitchell Kemble, who first went to Germany in 1829 and returned there throughout his life. In 1834, Kemble visited Gottingen, where he spent much of his time with Grimm and met his future wife, the daughter of a philosophy professor. Like the German philologists, Kemble had historical interests that encompassed language and literature, archaeology, ancient law, and history itself. Just as Grimm and other German philologists had initiated the historical study of all Teutonic languages, Kemble focused on applying the new historical philology to Anglo-Saxon, the language brought to England by migrating Teutonic tribes. In 1833, Kemble published the first full edition in England of the Anglo-Saxon poem *Beowulf*, based on a manuscript to which he added footnoted corrections

---

[139] Rogerson, supra note 85, at 5, 147, 158, 178–80, 234, 247; Encyclopaedia, supra note 84, at 863.

[140] Rogerson, supra note 85, at 250, 252.

[141] Id. at 218–19.

[142] Id. at 172; Vance, supra note 98, at 88–90.

[143] Vance, supra note 98, at 83, 86–8; Gooch, supra note 7, at 319.

[144] Aarsleff, supra note 66, at 221.

derived from his careful study of the Anglo-Saxon language. Four years later, he published the first complete English translation of *Beowulf*, which included a lengthy glossary.[145] Kemble dedicated both volumes to Grimm,[146] who in turn praised Kemble and Benjamin Thorpe, the other great English scholar who first applied the new techniques of continental philology to Anglo-Saxon. According to Grimm, Kemble and Thorpe deserved great honor for "rescuing the study of the Anglo-Saxon tongue (which for every Englishman should be a patriotic subject) from the long debasement into which it has hitherto been sunk." Grimm was confident that the work of Kemble and Thorpe would help Germans investigate their own language and literature.[147]

Kemble's interests moved increasingly from literature to history in the 1840s. He collected, transcribed, and published a huge number of Anglo-Saxon documents and used them to reconstruct the history of early England, including its legal history. In 1849, Kemble published his most important book, *The Saxons in England*, which relied on his own previous collection of documents and a compilation of old laws by Thorpe.[148] Kemble emphasized that the social structure as well as the language of Anglo-Saxon England were essentially Teutonic.[149] He claimed that the Saxons brought to England the *mark* community, or village community, whose centrality to Teutonic societies Grimm had emphasized.[150] English interest in Anglo-Saxon England had been revived before Kemble wrote by Sharon Turner's three-volume *History of the Anglo-Saxons from the Earliest Period to the Norman Conquest*, published between 1799 and 1805. The first serious study of England in the Anglo-Saxon period, Turner's volumes remained extremely popular until superseded by Kemble's more sophisticated scholarship, which was informed by the advances of German philology.[151] Resembling an encyclopedia more than a historical narrative, Kemble's book dominated subsequent English scholarship on the Anglo-Saxons for a generation. Translated into German by Konrad Maurer, it also became a key reference for German scholars of medieval institutions.[152]

William Stubbs, who viewed Kemble as his greatest predecessor,[153] became the leading English scholar of English medieval history in the 1860s and 1870s. Like Kemble, Stubbs relied heavily on German scholars, especially successors of Grimm who studied the history of Germanic law, including Waitz, Gneist, Maurer, Brunner, and Sohm. Stubbs knew many of these Germans personally[154]

---

[145] Id. at 181–2, 190, 193–4.
[146] Id. at 190.
[147] Id.
[148] Gooch, supra note 7, at 289.
[149] Id. at 290; Wormald, supra note 115, at 12.
[150] J. W. Burrow, A Liberal Descent: Victorian Historians and the English Past (Cambridge University Press, 1981), p. 124.
[151] Id. at 120; Aarsleff, supra note 66, at 167–9; Gooch, supra note 7, at 282.
[152] Gooch, supra note 7, at 289–90.
[153] Id. at 343.
[154] Id. at 343, 345; Wormald, supra note 115, at 13.

and was the most important English consumer of German historical scholarship before Maitland.[155] Maitland himself filled his correspondence with praise for Stubbs.[156] He commented when Stubbs died that in historical methodology "we must look to the very greatest of the Germans to find the peers of Dr Stubbs,"[157] adding that German scholars recognized Stubbs as the outstanding English historian.[158] Stubbs believed that his work was more broadly and intelligently received in Germany than in England, possibly reflecting the greater historical sophistication of German scholars.[159]

Beginning in 1863 and for the next twenty-five years, Stubbs wrote substantial prefaces to editions of medieval English chronicles.[160] According to Maitland, "under the pretext of introducing chroniclers Dr Stubbs was writing excellent history on a large scale."[161] His most important work, *Constitutional History*, was praised upon its publication in 1874 as one of the major historical works in the English language. Stubbs was concerned that English students were taught more about ancient Greece and Rome than about the history of their own country. Covering the long period from the Roman occupation of England to the first Tudors and broader in scope than its title indicated, *Constitutional History* was the first comprehensive survey of English history. It emphasized the history of institutions and reflected his view that all history should be understood against the background of constitutional history. Like Kemble, Stubbs not only emulated German historical scholarship, but also concluded that English law and institutions had Teutonic origins.[162] Subsequent scholars have observed that Stubbs's chapters on the Anglo-Saxon period were the shortest and weakest in *Constitutional History*, though better than any previous work on this period. Hampered by a dearth of primary sources, he relied heavily on the prior interpretations of German scholars.[163] Praising Stubbs's work on ecclesiastical documents, Maitland wished that Stubbs "had given one of many lives to the Anglo-Saxon charters,"[164] which would have provided some of the missing primary evidence. Stubbs was the first trained historian to hold the chair of modern history at Oxford when he was appointed in 1866, and he remained there until he became a bishop

---

[155] Wormald, supra note 115, at 13.

[156] The Letters of Frederic William Maitland (Cambridge, Mass.: Harvard University Press, 1965) (C. H. S. Fifoot, ed.), pp. 87, 225–6, 283.

[157] Frederic William Maitland, William Stubbs, Bishop of Oxford, in The Collected Papers of Frederic William Maitland (Cambridge University Press, 1911) (H. A. L. Fisher, ed.), vol. III, pp. 495, 498–9.

[158] Id. at 500.

[159] Gooch, supra note 7, at 343.

[160] Id. at 340–1.

[161] Maitland, supra note 157, at 501.

[162] Id. at 504–5; Gooch, supra note 7, at 242–3; Wormald, supra note 115, at 14.

[163] Maitland, supra note 157, at 506, 508; Gooch, supra note 7, at 343; Wormald, supra note 113, at 14.

[164] Maitland, supra note 157, at 510.

in 1884.[165] He was instrumental in creating an "Oxford School" of English historians, whose other leading members included Edward Freeman and John Green.[166]

Kemble and the Oxford historians believed that the Teutonic influence on Anglo-Saxon England extended into the nineteenth century. Kemble called the Anglo-Saxon period "the childhood of our own age, – the explanation of its manhood."[167] Its "rational and orderly liberty" was "full of the seeds of future development."[168] The Oxford historians, Stubbs, Freeman, and Green, described the village communities taken to England by the Saxons as self-governing primitive democracies, the embryonic sources of English freedom and stability.[169] Freeman particularly romanticized the village community, identifying his goals as a nineteenth-century Gladstonian liberal as the natural extension of Teutonic freedoms.[170] Playing off Freeman's famous dictum – "History is past politics, and politics is present history" – Lord Bryce wittily commented that "he sometimes made history present politics as well as past."[171]

For these scholars, the Norman Conquest interrupted but did not break the continuity between Anglo-Saxon and modern England.[172] Stubbs portrayed the Anglo-Saxon seeds of continuous English values as resources, preserved in local institutions and available throughout English history in struggles against potential tyrants.[173] The Norman Conquest began as a despotic alien force in Anglo-Saxon England but eventually fused with Saxon traditions in ways that ultimately benefited the English people. The Normans halted the feudalism into which Anglo-Saxon England had been degenerating and imposed a unity subsequently transformed by the English from a tool of oppression into a healthy national consciousness that fostered the development of the best Anglo-Saxon traditions.[174] Green identified the itinerant royal courts as a key impetus to national unity.[175] The fusion of the Anglo-Saxon with the Norman and "the subsequent growth of the English constitution," Stubbs maintained, was not predetermined or teleological. Rather, it was the result of the "subtle and intricate" reciprocal influences of "the national character, the external history, and the institutions of the people."[176]

---

[165] Gooch, supra note 7, at 341, 345.
[166] Id. at 346 and generally at 340–58.
[167] Wormald, supra note 115, at 14.
[168] Id. at 13.
[169] Burrow, supra note 56, at 263, 269–70, 280); Burrow, supra note 150, at 124–6, 290.
[170] Burrow, supra note 56, at 264–9; Gooch, supra note 7, at 344; John Burrow and Stefan Collini, The Clue to the Maze: The Appeal of the Comparative Method, in Stefan Collini, Donald Winch, John Burrow, That Noble Science of Politics: A Study in Nineteenth-Century Intellectual History (Cambridge University Press, 1983), pp. 208, 222.
[171] Burrow, supra note 150, at 163–4.
[172] Id. at 193–4; Wormald, supra note 115, at 13–14.
[173] Wormald, supra note 115, at 14.
[174] Burrow, supra note 150, at 139–48.
[175] Id. at 204.
[176] Id. at 144, 147.

The Historical Turn in the United States

The historical turn in nineteenth-century Western thought eventually arrived in the United States, largely corresponding with the emergence of the American research university in the decades following the Civil War. As previously in Germany and England, historical scholarship in the United States typically focused on evolutionary development and pervaded many disciplines simultaneously, including philology, biblical scholarship, philosophy, law, political science, economics, anthropology, and, of course, history itself. American scholars in these fields saw themselves as collaborators in a shared commitment to historical explanation and recognized their debt to European scholars.[177] For example, J. Franklin Jameson, a founder of the American Historical Association who became its president and the editor of the *American Historical Review*, wrote in 1890 that historical and comparative work in religion and jurisprudence in Europe had stimulated the expansion of historical scholarship.[178] European influences were institutional as well as intellectual. The American research university, in many ways emulating its German predecessor, made professional historical scholarship possible by providing employment for trained scholars. These university professors, committed to the "scientific" study of history, were a "new social type," supplanting the patrician amateurs who had been responsible for most of the history written in the United States before the Civil War.[179] In order to understand the historical turn in the United States, it is helpful to recognize its institutional setting.

American universities underwent a revolutionary transformation between the Civil War and 1900 as teaching colleges became research universities.[180] Innovations in American universities based on German models included the creation of graduate schools staffed by professors with Ph.D.s, the availability of fellowships for graduate students and sabbaticals for faculty, and the introduction of the scientific laboratory and the research seminar as pedagogical methods for immersing students in scholarship.[181] In the United States during the late nineteenth century, as previously in Germany, the growth of scholarly research in universities prompted the organization of disciplinary journals and associations.[182]

Many of the professors in the new research universities had studied in Germany and returned home imbued with the German conception of the

---

[177] Higham, supra note 3, at 102.

[178] Id.

[179] Higham, The Historical Profession, in History, supra note 1, at 3–4.

[180] Id. at 4; Walter P. Metzger, Academic Freedom in the Age of the University (Columbia University Press, 1961), pp. 3, 85; Laurence R. Veysey, The Emergence of the American University (University of Chicago Press, 1965), pp. 1–2, 74, 128.

[181] Veysey, supra note 180, at 153–5, 175–6; Herbst, supra note 23, at 32–8; Rodgers, supra note 59, at 97.

[182] Herbst, supra note 23, at 38–46; Higham, supra note 179, at 5, 16; Thomas L. Haskell, The Emergence of Professional Social Science: The American Social Science Association and the Nineteenth-Century Crisis of Authority (The Johns Hopkins University Press, 2000), p. 145.

professor as a research scholar. German universities held many attractions for American students. They were the best in Europe and provided specialized advanced training that was unavailable in the United States before the 1870s. They were open to foreigners, were inexpensive to attend, and allowed students great personal and academic freedom.[183] American students had studied in German universities from the early nineteenth century, especially in medicine and law. Their numbers increased substantially in the 1850s and continued to grow through the 1880s and 1890s.[184] Students in the humanities and social sciences produced the late-century burst,[185] encouraged by the developing ambitions of American universities that promised careers for research scholars in those fields.[186] By 1895, roughly half the historians teaching in American universities had been trained in Germany.[187] A decade later, a survey of more than one hundred leading economists and sociologists in the United States and Canada revealed that a little more than half had studied at least a year in Germany. Five of the initial six officers of the American Economic Association, founded in 1885, had studied in Germany, as had at least twenty of its first twenty-six presidents.[188] Advanced study in Germany made many Americans more intellectually cosmopolitan and helped the United States become part of a transatlantic intellectual community.[189]

The transformation of American higher education in the late nineteenth century extended to legal education. American law schools became serious academic institutions in conjunction with the creation of the research university. Full-time professors devoted to scholarship increasingly became the norm in American law schools attached to universities, supplanting practicing lawyers and judges who taught part time. As in other fields, a significant number of these law professors had studied in Germany and were instrumental in creating professional associations and specialized journals, though uniquely in law schools the journals were edited by students.

The first generation of professional historians in the United States in the decades after 1870 assimilated the commitment to historical understanding based on original sources that first flourished in Germany. They self-consciously differentiated themselves from the antebellum patrician amateurs who wrote history before the Civil War. They criticized their predecessors for treating historical writing as a form of literature, cultivating a florid style that emphasized personalities and "mere narrative," intruding their own subjective moralizing and political preferences to intruding in their work, and "copying" secondary sources. By contrast, they saw themselves as scientific empiricists, who

[183] Herbst, supra note 23, at 13, 18–22; Ross, supra note 6, at 55; Rodgers, supra note 59, at 85.
[184] Herbst, supra note 23, at 6–7; Metzger, supra note 180, at 94; Veysey, supra note 180, at 10, 130; Rodgers, supra note 59, at 76.
[185] Herbst, supra note 23, at 8, 17–18; Rodgers, supra note 59, at 76, 86.
[186] Metzger, supra note 180, at 93–4, 101–2; Veysey, supra note 180, at 174–6.
[187] Higham, supra note 3, at 92 n. 1.
[188] Rodgers, supra note 59, at 86.
[189] Id. at 111.

carefully induced their conclusions from the facts disclosed by painstaking research into primary sources and who dispassionately focused on the evolution of institutions,[190] an interest largely stimulated by Maine's efforts to demonstrate continuities over large periods.[191] Historical criticism of the Bible in the most distinguished American seminaries and divinity schools, itself heavily influenced by prior work in Germany, provided a particularly important model for historical scholarship generally.[192]

These features that differentiated professional from amateur history, American scholars generally believed, all originated in Germany. Prior German scholars had pioneered the use of original sources as the methodological basis for history and the evolution of institutions as its fundamental subject matter. Yet by also attributing to Germans the emphasis on induction from the empirical evidence of original sources, the Americans underestimated the lingering idealism of the German historical scholarship they thought they were emulating. The widespread misunderstanding of the great German historian Leopold von Ranke by American historians illustrated their apparent conflation of German historical scholarship with the English empirical tradition. American historians frequently praised Ranke as the embodiment of empiricism, who focused on establishing historical facts through rigorous analysis of original sources.[193] Yet as his colleagues in Germany recognized, whether supporters or critics, Ranke was an idealist as well as a careful investigator of historical facts "as they were." He emphasized that historians must intuit from the unique and the individual in order to uncover the "essences" and "spiritual content" beyond "external appearance."[194] American historians, Peter Novick astutely observes, venerated Ranke "for being precisely what he was not"[195] and "naturalized" the German idealist tradition into Anglo-American empirical science.[196]

The American historians generally viewed themselves as applying the empirical scientific method, as originally set forth by Francis Bacon in the early seventeenth century, to the study of history. They understood this method to require careful empirical observation of phenomena, followed by their classification, while resisting all speculative hypotheses.[197] For historians, observation entailed gathering facts from the critical evaluation of original documents.[198] Harnessed to their interest in the history of institutions, the scientific method

[190] Herbst, supra note 23, at 101; Novick, supra note 23, at 45–6; Higham, supra note 3, at 97.
[191] Higham, supra note 22, at 159.
[192] Herbst, supra note 23, at 101 and generally at 73–97.
[193] Novick, supra note 23, at 28–31; Georg G. Iggers, The Image of Ranke in American and German Historical Thought, 2 History and Theory 17, 18, 21 (1962).
[194] Novick, supra note 23, at 28; Herbst, supra note 23, at 108; Iggers, supra note 53, at 76–80; Iggers, supra note 191, at 18, 30.
[195] Novick, supra note 23, at 28.
[196] Id. at 31. See also Higham, supra note 3, at 99; Iggers, supra note 53, at 63–5; Iggers, supra note 193, at 18, 21.
[197] Novick, supra note 23, at 33–4; Higham, supra note 3, at 99.
[198] Higham, supra note 3, at 99.

involved studying the changes in their structures over time, much as a biologist examines the evolving structures of organisms.[199] Most of these historians were wary of attempts to induce general laws of historical change, considering them at best premature before more historical facts were gathered and classified.[200]

The search for the Teutonic origins of contemporary society, begun in Germany and continued in England, was a particularly visible and influential manifestation of the historical turn in the United States, dominating research in the closely related fields of history, law, and political science.[201] Many American scholars in these fields were exposed to the "Teutonic-germ theory" while studying in German universities, including its most prominent American advocates, Herbert B. Adams, who taught history at Johns Hopkins, and John W. Burgess, who taught political science at Columbia.[202] These scholars also relied on the English scholars who had already applied German theories of Teutonic influence to the study of English history, especially Kemble, Stubbs, and Freeman.[203] Just as the English historians found the origins of modern English liberties in the traditions the Teutonic Saxons imported from Germany, American historians, most notably Adams, maintained that the English colonists took these Teutonic traditions to North America.[204] Herbert Adams himself reported that Henry Adams, who was already studying and teaching at Harvard about the continuity between Teutonic and Anglo-Saxon law, encouraged him at the beginning of his career in the early 1870s to extend the study of Teutonic influences to the New England town meeting,[205] as Henry Maine had hypothesized.[206] In the first volume of the Johns Hopkins Studies in Historical and Political Science, published in 1882–3, Herbert Adams contributed the essays "The Germanic Origin of New England Towns," "Saxon Tithing-Men in America," and "Norman Constables in America."[207] Adams maintained, for example, that the democratic features of the ancient German village communities were carried by Teutonic settlers first to England and then to America, where they were perfected in the New England town meeting.[208] Freeman and Adams were friends, and Freeman lectured extensively about the Teutonic origins of English and American institutions during a series of lectures in the

[199] Higham, supra note 22, at 159.
[200] Novick, supra note 23, at 33; Higham, supra note 3, at 99.
[201] Novick, supra note 23, at 81, 83, 87; Higham, supra note 22, at 160; Ross, supra note 6, at 24–5; Hofstadter, supra note 32, at 172–84.
[202] Herbst, supra note 23, at 112–16; Ross, supra note 6, at 95; Hofstadter, supra note 32, at 174.
[203] Higham, supra note 22, at 160; Hofstadter, supra note 32, at 172.
[204] John Higham, Herbert Baxter Adams and the Study of Local History, 89 Journal of American History 1225, 1228 (1984).
[205] Herbert B. Adams, New Methods of Study in History, in Johns Hopkins University Studies in Historical and Political Science (Baltimore: John Murray & Company, 1884) (Herbert B. Adams, ed.), vol. II (Institutions and Economics), pp. 25, 101.
[206] Higham, supra note 22, at 160.
[207] Higham, supra note 204, at 1229.
[208] Herbst, supra note 23, at 115–16; Ross, supra note 6, at 74; Novick, supra note 23, at 87–8.

United States in 1881–2.[209] Freeman was thrilled "to see the Germans of Tacitus live once more in the popular gatherings of New England."[210]

Many of the scholars in this tradition, like Herbert Adams, applauded the progress, and often the superiority, of Teutonic peoples. The "seeds" or "germs" of freedom and democracy, originating in early continental Teutonic communities, had progressively "matured" or "flowered" over centuries, finally "ripening" in England and especially in the United States of their own era. Though they criticized antebellum American historians for their unscientific moralizing, the empirically based evolutionary histories of the professional historians after the Civil War typically conveyed pride in the progressive achievements of the Anglo-Saxon race.[211] Racial pride in Anglo-Saxon virtues sometimes took the form of smugness or overt racism. For example, while proclaiming the superiority of Teutonic peoples, Burgess justified imperialism abroad and restrictions on immigration at home. Racial superiority, he believed, created the "Teuton's burden" of world leadership and justified the use of force by "civilized" Teutonic nations against "barbaric" peoples. He worried about preserving American "Aryan nationality" and urged extending citizenship to "only such non-Aryan race-elements as shall have become Aryanized in spirit and in genius by contact with it." Burgess made clear that even many European populations, including Slavs, Czechs, Hungarians, and South Italians, were "rabble" who had not become "Aryanized in spirit."[212]

American legal scholars in the late nineteenth century generally endorsed the "Teutonic-germ theory." Much of their original historical research in primary sources explored the Teutonic origins of English and American law. They focused especially on the technical legal history of Anglo-Saxon and Norman England, but they also traced subsequent developments in England and the United States. Like the English historians who preceded them, they often viewed the Norman Conquest as an interruption but not a break in the continuous history of English law. And like their many American colleagues in departments of history and political science, they often described American freedom and democracy as the "descendants" of ancient Teutonic practices. For legal scholars, as for historians and political scientists, histories of Teutonic progress sometimes contained claims of racial superiority, including justifications for imperialism and for restrictions on immigration.

The American legal historians expressed their scholarly debts to their German and English predecessors. They most frequently acknowledged Savigny for emphasizing that law, like literature, reflects the evolving organic development of a culture; the German legal historian Heinrich Brunner for his research into the Teutonic influences on English law; and Maine for his provocative theories

---

[209] Herbst, supra note 23, at 117; Novick, supra note 23, at 81.
[210] Herbst, supra note 23, at 117.
[211] Novick, supra note 23, at 81, 85, 89; Higham, supra note 22, at 158.
[212] Herbst, supra note 23, at 121–2; John W. Burgess, Reminiscences of an American Scholar (Columbia University Press, 1934), pp. 254–5, 397–8.

of legal development, which American scholars variously refuted or endorsed. In discussing the extent to which history was deterministic or contingent, the American legal scholars reflected the same wide range of often ambiguous and contradictory views as other nineteenth-century evolutionary thinkers on both sides of the Atlantic. Also reflecting general themes in transatlantic thought, they used history both to justify current law and to advocate its reform. And just as they endorsed the Teutonic-germ theory, they also agreed with their colleagues in history departments that the empirical method of scientific induction should govern their research. They focused on gathering and classifying the data of legal history and often believed that generations of additional historical work were required before current law could be systematically restated.

This chapter has attempted to place the historical turn in late nineteenth-century American legal scholarship in the broader context of the widespread movement toward historical explanation in many disciplines on both sides of the Atlantic. In the following two chapters, I discuss in more detail the European legal scholars whose work most influenced the Americans, first the Germans and then the Englishman Henry Maine. The European background helps explain and evaluate the historical thought and research of the American legal scholars themselves.

III

German Legal Scholarship

In legal scholarship, as in other fields, Germans initiated the emphasis on historical explanation. German legal scholars during the late eighteenth and early nineteenth centuries increasingly rejected the Enlightenment view that natural law based on reason can produce universally and eternally valid legal principles. They protested the imposition of such presumed principles by the state. They looked instead to the historical evolution of law, which they often associated with the Volksgeist, the national spirit of the people, as the legitimate source of legal authority.[1] In this chapter, as in the previous chapter on the general turn to history in nineteenth-century thought, I provide a general overview, emphasizing the German legal scholarship that helps explain the turn to history by late nineteenth-century American legal scholars.

Particularly important for the development of the historical study of law, a number of German scholars, beginning in the late 1780s, invoked the constitutionalism they ascribed to the Holy Roman Empire of the sixteenth century in favorable contrast to the absolutism they linked to the Enlightenment. They thereby stimulated the study of the Roman law that was introduced in Germany during the Holy Roman Empire. Gustav Hugo, a professor at Gottingen, was the leading figure in the revival of Roman law in the 1790s. His hostility to the Enlightenment law of reason was intensified by its use in justifying the excesses of the French Revolution, as portrayed by Edmund Burke in England and by various scholars in northern Germany. Inspired by Gibbon's admiring chapter on Roman law in *The Decline and Fall of the Roman Empire*, which he reviewed and translated into German, and influenced by the historical studies of his colleagues at Gottingen, Hugo was the first to apply their historical methods to legal history. He integrated original sources discovered by others into a historical narrative of Roman law, which he hoped would serve as a

---

[1] James Q. Whitman, The Legacy of Roman Law in the German Romantic Era (Princeton University Press, 1990), p. 42; Franz Wieacker, A History of Private Law in Europe (Oxford: Clarendon Press, 2003) (translated by Tony Weir), pp. 279–80, 283–5.

model for German law in his own day. Despite his importance, Hugo was soon overshadowed by his disciple, Friedrich Carl von Savigny.[2]

For many German legal scholars in the nineteenth century, legal history was not an independent field of study, but the source of empirical data for a science of law, which would supersede the speculative natural law theories of the Enlightenment. Savigny stressed the "two-fold spirit" required of the jurist, the "historical" and the "systematic." Savigny himself exemplified this spirit in his own scholarship, but many of his successors favored the systematic over the historical. They produced impressive treatises based on the Roman law found in the Pandects, the opinions by the classical jurists of the third century in Rome compiled at the direction of the emperor Justinian in Constantinople during the sixth century. They, therefore, became widely known as "Pandectists." Other German legal scholars studied the history of distinctively Germanic law, in contrast to the Roman law that was the focus of Savigny and the Pandectists. Although Savigny himself favored research in both fields and worked collaboratively with leading scholars of Germanic law, by the late 1820s significant intellectual and political tensions emerged between many "Romanists," who wanted to revive Roman methods of legal analysis in Germany, and many "Germanists," who viewed Roman law as a foreign intrusion on indigenous Germanic law. Rudolph von Jhering, who dominated German legal thought in the late nineteenth century as Savigny had earlier, began his career as a Pandectist. In the years around 1860, however, Jhering dramatically changed intellectual course, asserting that the Pandectists, by erroneously treating law as a mathematical system of a priori reasoning, divorced it from social reality. For the remaining three decades of his life, Jhering emphasized the social context of law. Claiming that Savigny and his successors had incorrectly treated legal history as the gradual, largely unconscious evolution of an organic national tradition, Jhering insisted instead that it should be studied as a struggle of competing interests.

Late nineteenth-century American legal scholars relied heavily, though not uncritically, on Savigny's historical understanding of law. Many of them were familiar with the Pandectists and sought to emulate them by producing systematic treatises on subjects of American law. Yet in the early twentieth century, Roscoe Pound ascribed Jhering's critique of the Pandectists to his American predecessors, a mischaracterization that persisted throughout the twentieth century. In addition to Jhering's substantial influence on Pound, several late nineteenth-century American legal scholars, particularly Holmes and Tiedeman, agreed with his criticisms of Savigny. The "Germanist" legal scholars became particularly influential for the American legal historians who did original research in English legal history, especially those Germanists who convinced the Americans that English law derived primarily from Teutonic origins.

[2] Whitman, supra note 1, at 84, 87–8; Wieacker, supra note 1, at 300–3.

Savigny

Through his prodigious scholarship, literary excellence, and personal background and characteristics, Savigny became the dominant German legal scholar of the first half of the nineteenth century. He was familiar to a broad public and to foreign scholars as well as to his professional colleagues in Germany. Born into the high ranks of the German nobility, the sole heir of an extremely wealthy family, and described by his contemporaries as handsome, dignified, and charismatic, Savigny made good use of these enormous advantages. After studying law in the late 1790s, he became one of the few people of his social background and wealth to choose an academic career. His decision probably contributed to the prestige of German professors in the nineteenth century, encouraged other talented people to follow his professional example, and may even help account for the flourishing of academic scholarship in Germany earlier than in other countries, including England and the United States.[3] In addition to his important work as a scholar and as the cofounder of the *Journal for Historical Legal Science*, Savigny helped organize and became the rector of the University of Berlin, took an active role in the reorganization of other universities, became involved at several points in his career in the revision of Prussian legislation, and tutored the future King Frederick Wilhelm IV.[4]

Recent scholars describe Savigny's politics as initially moderate,[5] reform,[6] or bourgeois[7] conservatism, but becoming increasingly reactionary after 1830.[8] Savigny initially understood his work as a professor and university administrator in the second decade of the nineteenth century as part of the program of Prussian reform in the wake of its liberation from Napoleonic domination.[9] In 1837 Savigny prominently revealed his increasing tendency to submit to the authority of the state by refusing to give public support to seven professors at Gottingen, including his good friends the Grimms, whose refusal to accept the abrogation of the existing Hanoverian Constitution by a new monarch led to their resignation and exile. Although Savigny disagreed with the abrogation of the Constitution and admired the moral integrity of the professors, he did not want to become associated with their political commitment to constitutional

---

[3] Whitman, supra note 1, at 106, 110; Wieacker, supra note 1, at 303–4; Hermann Kantorowicz, Savigny and the Historical School of Law, 53 Law Quarterly Rev. 326, 331–2 (1937).

[4] Wieacker, supra note 1, at 304; Kantorowicz, supra note 3, at 329.

[5] Wieacker, supra note 1, at 304; John E. Toews, The Immanent Genesis and Transcendent Goal of Law: Savigny, Stahl, and the Ideology of the Christian German State, 37 Am. J. Comp. L. 139, 160 (1989).

[6] Whitman, supra note 1, at 112, 184; Karl A. Mollnau, The Contributions of Savigny to the Theory of Legislation, 37 Am. J. Comp. L. 81, 86 (1989).

[7] Hermann Klenner, Savigny's Research Program of the Historical School of Law and its Intellectual Impact in 19th Century Berlin, 37 Am. J. Comp. L. 67, 76 (1989).

[8] Whitman, supra note 1, at 203; Wieacker, supra note 1, at 304–5; Michael John, Politics and the Law in Late Nineteenth-Century Germany: The Origins of the Civil Code (Oxford: Clarendon Press, 1989), pp. 20, 24.

[9] Toews, supra note 5, at 150–2.

FIGURE 3.1. *Friedrich Karl von Savigny.* From Alfred Gudeman, *Imagines Philologarvm,*
Druck und Verglag von B.G. Teubner, 1911.

liberalism.[10] Three years later Frederick Wilhelm IV became king of Prussia and
in 1842 appointed Savigny minister of justice in charge of legislation. In revising the Prussian divorce law, Savigny, after some hesitation and discomfort,
sided with conservatives who, rejecting popularly supported tendencies toward
liberalization, wanted to limit divorce to adultery and malicious desertion, the
only grounds allowed by the Lutheran theology of the sixteenth century.[11]

In an early lecture in 1802, when he was just twenty-three years old,
Savigny advocated the link between historical research and systematic analysis to which he adhered throughout his lifetime of scholarship. He regarded
legal history primarily as the history of scholarly analysis of legal texts. This
history, he believed, uncovers the material upon which to build a legal system that is logically ordered, and, therefore, philosophical and scientific.[12] It

---

[10] Id. at 157.
[11] Id. at 160–1.
[12] Wieacker, supra note 1, at 293–4, 305.

is a necessary but preliminary step in the creation of legal science. The title of the journal he cofounded revealingly referred to "historical legal science," not "legal history."[13]

Published a year after his lecture, Savigny's first major book, *The Law of Possession*, exemplified the combination of historical research and systematic analysis he advocated. From his comprehensive research into the classical Roman law of possession, Savigny extracted basic principles from which he constructed a theory of possession based on intent.[14] He believed his theory addressed the needs of contemporary Germany, particularly by facilitating the gradual disappearance of lingering feudal relations. While not abolishing feudalism through legislation, the goal of more progressive reformers, basing possession on intent would allow the modification of feudal property rights, which previous theories of possession had treated as eternally valid.[15] This book established Savigny's international reputation and became the model for future legal scholarship.[16] In his two major multi-volume projects, Savigny continued to pursue both historical and systematic studies according to the plan he announced at the beginning of his career. His *History of Roman Law in the Middle Ages*, published in six volumes between 1815 and 1831, focused on the historical development of Roman law, and his *System of Roman Law Today*, published in eight volumes between 1840 and 1849 but never completed, stressed the continuing influence of Roman law in Germany.[17] Echoing his lecture of 1802 more than a generation later, he wrote in the introduction to the first volume of the *System* that "the essence of the systematic method" lay "in the recognition and demonstration of the internal coherence or relationship, through which the individual concepts and rules are united into one great whole."[18]

In a short work published in 1814, *Of the Vocation of Our Age for Legislation and Jurisprudence*, Savigny forcefully and influentially set forth his views on legal history and legal science in opposition to the Enlightenment law of reason and its attempted codification. Though some American scholars, particularly those who did original work in legal history, read or at least consulted his subsequent multi-volume works, this slim volume was the major route through which Americans became exposed to his fundamental ideas. Savigny originally planned it as an attack on the French influence in German law and as the introduction to his *History of Roman Law in the Middle Ages*. But when Anton Friedrich Justus Thibaut, a professor of Roman law at Heidelberg who believed in natural law based on reason, wrote a pamphlet, *On the Need for a*

---

[13] Id. at 308; Mathias Reimann, Nineteenth Century German Legal Science, 31 Boston College L. Rev. 837, 892 (1990).

[14] Wieacker, supra note 1, at 306–7, 307 n. 15.

[15] Whitman, supra note 1, at 183–4.

[16] Id. at 183–4; Wieacker, supra note 1, at 306–7; Reimann, supra note 13, at 856.

[17] Wieacker, supra note 1, at 294–5, 314–15; Reimann, supra note 13, at 856–7.

[18] Reimann, supra note 13, at 855.

Civil Code for All Germany, Savigny reconceived his argument as a response to Thibaut and published it as a separate volume. In the aftermath of the defeat of Napoleon and the end of French rule in Germany, Thibaut saw a code for all of Germany as a way to unite the German states while removing the inefficient complexities of existing Roman law in Germany. For Savigny, Thibaut's call for codification, and particularly his reliance on the French *Code civil*, exemplified the problems with French law, so responding to Thibaut achieved his original purpose.[19]

Near the beginning of *Vocation*, Savigny connected the abstract and unhistorical rationalism of the Enlightenment with arguments for codification. Since the middle of the eighteenth century, he observed, "a blind rage for improvement" leading toward "a picture of absolute perfection" prevailed throughout Europe. As a result, all historical sensibility was lost. Most familiar in religion and government, this attitude also affected law, particularly in the widespread longing for codes based "on the conviction that there is a practical law of nature or reason, an ideal legislation for all times and all circumstances, which we have only to discover to bring positive law to permanent perfection." Such codes, expressed in the language of "pure abstraction," would "be divested of all historical associations." Fortunately, he added, recent times had awakened a "historical spirit," which left no room for this "shallow self-sufficiency."[20] Among German jurists, he singled out Hugo for praise, complimenting his systematic use of history to challenge the prevailing theories of the Enlightenment.[21]

Reiterating the central theme of his earliest work while opposing codification based on abstract reason, Savigny stressed the need for jurists to develop systematic analysis of law grounded in historical research. "A two-fold spirit is indispensable to the jurist; the historical, to seize with readiness the peculiarities of every age and every form of law; and the systematic, to view every notion and every rule in lively connection and co-operation with the whole, that is, in the only true and natural relation."[22] He analogized law to geometry. Just as it is possible to "deduce" the whole triangle from "two sides and the included angle," the law has "points," which Savigny called "leading axioms," from which the entire legal system can be deduced. Legal science consists in identifying these "leading axioms" and deducing "from them the internal connection, and the precise degree of affinity which subsist between all juridical notions and rules."[23]

---

[19] Wieacker, supra note 1, at 294–5, 308–10; Kantorowicz, supra note 3, at 336; John, supra note 8, at 18; Reimann, supra note 13, at 851; Mathias Reimann, The Historical School Against Codification: Savigny, Carter, and the Defeat of the New York Civil Code, 37 Am. J. Comp. L. 95, 97 (1989).

[20] Frederick Charles von Savigny, Of the Vocation of Our Age for Legislation and Jurisprudence (North Stratford, N.H.: Ayer Company Publishers, Inc., 2000) (reprint of 1831 English edition), pp. 20–3.

[21] Id. at 31.

[22] Id. at 64–5.

[23] Id. at 38–9.

Most of *Vocation* elaborated the historical rather than the systematic aspects of this "two-fold" enterprise. Addressing himself to the history of law "amongst nations of the nobler races," Savigny claimed that law, like language and manners, is tied to the history of a particular people, bound in "the kindred consciousness of an inward necessity, excluding all notion of an accidental and arbitrary origin."[24] History reveals and maintains "the indissoluble organic connection of generations and ages," which, if lost, deprives "every people the best part of its spiritual life."[25] Like many nineteenth-century historians, Savigny added that not every part of a people's history relates to this organic connection. A main purpose of legal history, therefore, "is to trace every established system to its root, and thus discover an organic principle, whereby that which still has life, may be separated from that which is lifeless and only belongs to history."[26] By revealing the distinctiveness of a national tradition, Savigny emphasized, historical research protects against the recurrent "self-delusion" of "holding that which is peculiar to ourselves to be common to human nature in general."[27] The failure to investigate the history of Roman law, he observed in a telling example, led many prior jurists to mistake it as natural law emanating from pure reason rather than as a distinctive product of the experience of a particular people.[28] Historical knowledge, moreover, is necessary to understand, evaluate, and apply existing law effectively.[29] And while historical knowledge cannot bring back the past, it can recall its best features "and thus guard our minds against the narrowing influence of the present."[30]

In an important elaboration of his view that law, like language and manners, is tied to the organic history of a particular people, Savigny maintained that as civilization progresses, "national tendencies become more and more distinct, and what otherwise would have remained common, becomes appropriated to particular classes." For law, the particular class is jurists. In progressive societies, "law perfects its language, takes a scientific direction, and, as formerly it existed in the consciousness of the community, it now devolves upon the jurists, who thus, in this department, represent the community."[31] Savigny immediately added that the development of law "by internal silently-operating powers, not by the arbitrary will of a law-giver,"[32] continued even as law became "more artificial and complex"[33] and jurists supplanted the general community as its primary interpreters.

[24] Id. at 24.
[25] Id. at 132, 136.
[26] Id. at 137.
[27] Id. at 134.
[28] Id. at 134–5.
[29] Id. at 103, 132–4.
[30] Id. at 136.
[31] Id. at 28.
[32] Id. at 30.
[33] Id. at 28.

The organic legal history of Germany, Savigny asserted, is based on both Roman and Germanic law. Until very recently, he observed, a uniform system of common law, modified in part by provincial law, prevailed throughout Germany. This common law, known as the *ius commune*, derived from the Roman law contained in the legal works of Justinian. Pointing out that German jurists had devoted most of their attention to the *ius commune*, Savigny also reported that many in Germany had objected to the foreign influence of Roman law, claiming that it prevented the development not only of indigenous Germanic law, but, more broadly, of German nationality. Savigny dismissed these complaints as hollow and groundless. He emphasized that the reception of Roman law in Germany "would never have come to pass, or, at any rate, would never have endured, without some internal necessity." Just as national development in religion and literature often incorporates foreign elements, he pointed out, so it does in law.[34]

Even if Roman law had never been introduced, Savigny added, Germany could not have relied on indigenous Germanic law. A sound legal system, he maintained, can only arise in an "unmoved locality," such as ancient Rome. The constant emigrations and conquests of German history, by contrast, precluded a similar "unmoved locality" in Germany, a problem exacerbated by the many revolutions within Germanic nations. As soon as the feudal system was established in Germany, "nothing peculiar to the old race of people was left; every thing, even to forms and names, had undergone a radical change, and this entire revolution was already decided, when the Roman law was introduced."[35] Yet Savigny acknowledged that Germanic law might be revived through further study.[36]

Savigny, therefore, concluded that both Roman law and Germanic law could contribute to contemporary legal reform in Germany. Based on its "high state of cultivation," Roman law could "serve as a pattern and model for our scientific labours."[37] He especially praised Roman law for its ability to move easily back and forth from the particular to the general.[38] Though lacking the cultivation of Roman law, Germanic law had the advantage of being "directly and popularly connected" to the German people.[39]

The Roman law that contemporary German jurists should study, Savigny emphasized, should be the law of its classical age in the third century. Justinian's Pandects made classical Roman law available to contemporary jurists, though Savigny observed that they were compiled in "a season of decline" and did not fully reflect the excellence of the previous classical period.[40] Expressing one of his "liveliest convictions," Savigny maintained that classical Roman law should not be studied merely as "a dead letter," but should be "regenerated" for use in

[34] Id. at 53–4.
[35] Id. at 54–5.
[36] Id. at 137.
[37] Id.
[38] Id. at 47.
[39] Id. at 137.
[40] Id. at 44–5.

the present. Citing Hugo as a model, he urged his colleagues to immerse them-selves in the classical Roman scholars so thoroughly that they could "compose in their style, and on their principles, and thus continue, in its true spirit, the work they were prevented from consummating."[41] While stressing the impor-tance of grappling with "Roman law at its root" in the classical period, Savigny also felt that its entire history should be mastered. Compared to the classical period, he acknowledged, studying the inferior literature on Roman law since the Middle Ages is "often a repulsive labor," but he felt it was necessary to develop a mature understanding of the subject.[42]

Savigny maintained that while recovering legal history, whether Roman or Germanic, scholars should seek "the gradual purification of the present system from that which has been produced through the mere ignorance and dullness of uncultivated times, without any real practical demand for it."[43] He was confident that his scientific approach to law, based on "an organically progressive jurispru-dence"[44] developed by university professors in communication with the courts,[45] was a more effective means to the same goal of Thibaut and other advocates of codification, the creation of effective national law for a unified Germany.[46]

Throughout *Vocation*, Savigny reiterated his opposition to codification as a poor alternative to historical legal science. He took special pleasure in criticiz-ing the French *Code civil*, the code that he particularly disliked and that Thibaut took as a model. Despite their "ordinary self-commendations," even the French, Savigny remarked, recognized its many imperfections. The code posed a "more pernicious and ruinous" threat to Germany than to France itself, for Napoleon attempted to impose it "as a bond the more to fetter nations." Fortunately, the defeat of Napoleon saved Germany from this threat.[47] Though Savigny con-sidered the French *Code civil* an especially "melancholy spectacle,"[48] he also criticized the codes of Prussia and Austria.[49] More generally, he maintained that codification, which attempts to anticipate correct results in all future cases, inevitably fails "because there are positively no limits to the varieties of actual combinations of circumstances" that may arise.[50] Citing the history of Roman law to strengthen his argument against codification, Savigny pointed out that the Romans did not need or devise a code as long as their law "was in active progression" during its classical period. Only in the sixth century, when "all intellectual life was dead" and the law was in a state of "extreme decay," were codes of Roman law compiled from "the wrecks of better times."[51]

[41] Id. at 139–40.
[42] Id. at 140–1.
[43] Id. at 138–9.
[44] Id. at 182.
[45] Id. at 149.
[46] Id. at 173, 182.
[47] Id. at 73–4.
[48] Id. at 83.
[49] Id. at 99–130.
[50] Id. at 38.
[51] Id. at 50–2.

In certain rare and limited circumstances, Savigny conceded, codification is appropriate, even beneficial.[52] Codes can preserve and confirm commendable views of the public, even if they cannot produce them.[53] Codes can also resolve controversies in the law and reflect political decisions.[54] But Savigny stressed that "the requisites of a really good code" are rarely found in any age.[55] One of these requisites, of particular relevance to the Germany of his own day, is a mature legal system on which to base a code. In contrast to the Romans, who had the benefit of their classical jurisprudence when they subsequently enacted codes, the Germans had not produced any jurisprudence of remotely comparable quality. Emphasizing the "great danger inevitably impending when a very defective and shallow state of knowledge is fixed by positive authority,"[56] Savigny asserted that until German legal science is improved, "I deny our capacity for the production of a good code."[57] For Savigny, his "two-fold" program of historical research combined with systematic analysis was the way to improve German legal science.

Although Savigny encouraged research into both Roman and Germanic legal history in *Vocation*, for the rest of his long scholarly career he himself wrote about the history of Roman law. Within the field of Roman legal history, moreover, Savigny concentrated on private law rather than public law, and even within the field of private law, he concentrated on the ideas of learned jurists rather than on the actual operation of legal rules. By narrowing his historical focus in these ways, Savigny advanced his own intellectual and ideological goals, though it is possible that the historical material he studied itself helped shape his goals. The classical Roman jurists on whom he most relied emphasized logical consistency and the contours of individual spheres of freedom within society, precisely the features Savigny wanted to encourage in the German law of the nineteenth century.[58] Ironically, Savigny's emphasis on logical consistency, though based on the sources of an organic historical tradition rather than the speculation of the Enlightenment law of reason, in many ways fostered the formal rationalism he criticized in Enlightenment thought and expected historical research to combat.[59]

Romanists and Germanists

Because they focused on Roman legal sources, Savigny and the Pandectists were known as "Romanists." Other German legal scholars focused on indigenous Germanic sources and, therefore, were known as "Germanists." Americans were familiar with both the Romanists and the Germanists. Understandably,

[52] Id. at 31.
[53] Id. at 63.
[54] Id. at 152.
[55] Id. at 42.
[56] Id. at 67.
[57] Id. at 65 and generally at 64–7.
[58] Wieacker, supra note 1, at 297–8. Reimann, supra note 13, at 857–8, 888.
[59] Wieacker, supra note 1, at 295.

FIGURE 3.2. *Heinrich Brunner*. Courtesy of Historical & Special Collections, Harvard Law School Library.

they were more attracted to the Germanists, whose research illuminated the origins of English law.

Karl Friedrich Eichhorn, who cofounded the *Journal for Historical Legal Science* with Savigny in 1814, is generally considered the leading early Germanist. In his *History of Law and State in Germany*, published in 1808, Eichhorn collected and presented in a coherent historical narrative the findings of previously disperate studies of Germanic sources, just as Hugo had done for the history of Roman law. As the joint editorship of the *Journal for Historical Legal Science* suggests, early Romanists and Germanists worked closely together. Although Savigny was a Romanist, he maintained in *Vocation* that indigenous Germanic law as well as classical Roman law could provide mutually reinforcing sources for legal reform in nineteenth-century Germany.[60] Eichhorn and other Germanists shared Savigny's "two-fold" program of historical and systematic scholarship. And just as Georg Friedrich Puchta, the Romanist who became Savigny's most influential successor, subsequently emphasized the systematic over the historical, so did the Germanist, Karl Friedrich Wilhelm Gerber.[61]

---

[60] Savigny, supra note 20, at 137–8.
[61] Wieacker, supra note 1, at 320–1, 325–6; Munroe Smith, A General View of European Legal History and Other Papers (Columbia University Press, 1927), pp. 119–20; Reimann, supra note 13, at 868–70.

By the late 1820s, however, a bitter split had arisen between the Romanists and the Germanists. Drawing on Savigny's view that law is the product of the organic history of a people, Germanists claimed that indigenous Germanic law constituted the organic law of Germany and, unlike Savigny, portrayed Roman law as a foreign infection. Tension between Germanists and Romanists increased in the 1830s and peaked in the 1840s. In contrast to the collaboration of the Romanist Savigny and the Germanist Eichhorn in founding the *Journal of Historical Legal Science* in 1814, in 1839 two Germanists started a new journal devoted exclusively to Germanic studies, the *Journal of German Law and German Legal Science*. Georg Beseler, who was active in liberal national politics and served in the Prussian parliament, became the leading Germanist critic of the Romanists. He challenged Romanists in his inaugural lecture when he became a professor in 1835 and attacked Puchta directly in the book he published in 1843, *People's Law and Jurists' Law*. He condemned Puchta for elevating "jurists' law" over "people's law." Beseler himself favored "people's law" while calling for increased use of lay judges and juries in the tradition of indigenous Germanic law. The reception of Roman law in Germany, Beseler charged, had been a "national disaster," for which he held the jurists responsible. Puchta reacted angrily, further exacerbating the rift between Germanists and Romanists.[62]

By the late nineteenth century, many German legal scholars, both Germanists and Romanists, no longer subscribed to Savigny's "two-fold" program of a legal science based on the systematic analysis of the "organic" material historical research had uncovered. They studied legal history as an independent subject, not as the means for developing legal science. The separation of legal history from legal science came more easily to Germanists, who, as a group, had been less attracted than Romanists to systematic analysis and more familiar with humanist scholarship in related fields. Particularly significant for English and American scholars interested in the history of their own law, several Germanists illuminated Germanic sources of English law and became interested in the history of English law itself.[63]

Rudolph Sohm and Heinrich Brunner were the Germanist scholars who most influenced the Americans. Sohm and Brunner were prolific authors who wrote on many topics of legal history. For the Americans, one book by each of them had particular significance: Sohm's *Der Procesz der Lex Salica* (1867), on the procedure of the Salic law, and Brunner's *Die Entstehung der Schwurgerichte* (1872), which investigated the early history of the jury.[64] Although their work was not translated into English, as the Americans occasionally observed with

---

[62] Wieacker, supra note 1, at 322–5; Reimann, supra note 13, at 869.

[63] Reimann, supra note 13, at 872–4; Wieacker, supra note 1, at 335–40.

[64] Felix Liebermann's important publications on English legal history flourished from 1892 to 1902, too late for the pioneering American scholars but in time for Maitland to recognize its importance. H. W. C. Davis, Felix Liebermann, 41 English Hist. Rev. 91, 93–5 (1926); Patrick Wormald, The Making of English Law: King Alfred to the Twelfth Century (Oxford: Blackwell Publishers Ltd., 1999), vol. 1, p. 21.

regret and even shame, most of the major American legal historians were sufficiently fluent in German to read it. Thayer, who apparently could not read
German, thanked his cousin in print for reading German books to him and
specifically mentioned Brunner's.[65]

Sohm's book was particularly useful to historians of English law because, as
Henry Adams emphasized in his review of the French edition, the Lex Salica,
the law of the Salian Franks in the fifth century, was the best preserved example
of the archaic Teutonic law. Adams maintained, and other American legal historians soon agreed, that archaic Teutonic law influenced all territories settled
by Germans, including England. Sohm's book, Adams observed, established his
reputation in Germany, enabling him to become a professor at Freiburg, where
his additional work placed him "at the head of his profession."[66] Adams's
lengthy abstract of the book in his review in 1874 remains the fullest description in English of its contents. Sohm identified executive procedure, procedure
for the recovery of lost property, and judicial procedure as the central varieties
of Salic procedure. Executive procedure was an ex parte proceeding, involving
a series of legal formalities but not requiring a judicial judgment, by which
private rights could be satisfied. Sohm reconstructed the details of executive
procedure by examining allusions to it in the three areas of the Lex Salica in
which it was used: the enforcement of contracts, the collection of loans, and
the prevention of a newcomer from acquiring a legal residence within a village
community. The procedure for the vindication of movables was more complicated because it combined civil and criminal procedure. It was a summary
process but under certain circumstances could become a case conducted in a
court. It, therefore, linked the earlier executive procedure, which reflected a
society that lacked courts, with the emerging judicial procedure. "It is a curious phenomenon in legal history," Adams remarked in his review, "and offers
a striking example of the effort of archaic law to adapt its procedure to the
nature of the complaint, instead of including the greatest possible variety of
complaints within one procedure." Judicial procedure was directed at obtaining a judgment from a court and arose in criminal cases. Originally, only personal property rather than land could satisfy a judgment, and a person could
be seized only in a limited number of cases. After covering these three varieties of Salic procedure, Sohm briefly sketched the decline of the earlier private
procedure and the expansion of judicial procedure to include civil as well as
criminal actions.[67]

Although Sohm's work on Salic law was extremely valuable to American
scholars in presenting an early version of Teutonic law from which they could
trace subsequent developments in England, Brunner's book on the early history

---

[65] James Bradley Thayer, A Preliminary Treatise on Evidence at the Common Law (Boston: Little
Brown, and Company 1898), p. 9 n. 2.
[66] Henry Adams, Sohm's Procedure de la Lex Salica (April 1874) North American Review 416
(book review).
[67] Id. at 417–25.

of the jury had an even greater influence on the leading Americans legal historians who were vitally interested in this subject. Brunner corresponded with Ames and Thayer, reviewed Bigelow's book, and apparently met Henry Adams when Adams visited Germany shortly after he began teaching medieval law and history at Harvard. Many German legal scholars before Brunner had addressed the history of the jury, often in connection with general nineteenth-century German interest in the contemporary function of the jury.[68] Brunner, however, was the first to study the history of the jury both historically and comparatively. He extended his study to French, Norman, and English sources, comparing these "sister laws" as part of his effort to understand the origins and development of the Teutonic jury, particularly in Frankish law. Brunner did not simply compare these different laws; he detected a historical relationship among them.[69] This approach, he wrote to Ames in 1872, isolated him from his German colleagues.[70]

Reviewing a subsequent book by Brunner, Maitland wrote that his "thorough knowledge of the English law of the Norman and Angevin periods has from the first distinguished Dr. Brunner from most of his fellow Germanists, who, however learned they may be in the Anglo-Saxon dooms, are apt to leave England to itself so soon as the Normans have conquered it." Maitland observed that Brunner's knowledge of English law repeatedly helped him make more informed judgments about developments on the Continent. Just as "the key to many a problem of French and German history is to be found in England," Maitland added, "it is equally true that the key to many an English problem must be found in France or Germany." Brunner's work thus "has thrown a noble and a stable bridge over the high seas."[71] Brunner returned Maitland's compliment in his review of *The History of English Law* by Pollock and Maitland. Switching metaphors, Brunner wrote that when he began to study the history of English law in the 1860s he "often felt as if German and English legal history were separated by an impassable mountain range." During the intervening three decades, he asserted, "the ceaseless labor of science has driven a tunnel through the heart of the mountains," with Pollock and Maitland now playing "a prominent part."[72] Beginning with Henry Adams and his students in the early 1870s, American scholars had contributed to this "ceaseless labor."

Brunner maintained that the original Frankish *inquisitio* heavily influenced subsequent Norman law, which the Norman Conquest of 1066 introduced to

---

[68] Amina Dammann, Heinrich Brunner and the Frankish Origins of the Jury (September 2006) (unpublished draft of seminar paper, University of Texas School of Law), pp. 22–4, 31.

[69] Id. at 4. Amina Dammann, Heinrich Brunner and the Frankish Origins of the Jury (December 2006) (unpublished seminar paper, University of Texas School of Law), p. 6.

[70] Letter from Heinrich Brunner to James Barr Ames (September 28, 1872) (James Barr Ames Papers, Harvard Law School Library, Box 1, Folder 7).

[71] F. W. Maitland, Book Review of Heinrich Brunner, Forschungen zur Geschichte des Deutschen und Franzosischen Rechtes, 9 English Hist. Rev. 593, 594 (1896).

[72] Heinrich Brunner, Pollock and Maitland's History of English Law, 11 Political Science Quarterly 534, 544 (1896).

England and which gradually superseded prior Anglo-Saxon law.[73] He challenged previous scholars in Germany and England who had asserted that the English jury derived from Roman, Nordic, pre-Conquest English, or canon sources.[74] English scholars who had studied the history of the English jury, Brunner observed, reached erroneous conclusions because they had limited their research exclusively to English sources.[75] Insisting on the Frankish influence on Norman law, Brunner also rejected the view of his German predecessor, Konrad Maurer, who believed that the jury developed independently within each Germanic tribe, including the Normans.[76] In discussing the development of the English jury following the Norman Conquest, Brunner asserted that the *inquisitio* initially retained its "testimonial" function from the original Frankish law. Jurors were chosen for their knowledge of disputed facts rather than, as in the later English jury, to make a "judicial" decision based on facts presented to them for the first time by witnesses.[77] Used in the Domesday inquiry of 1086 soon after the Norman Conquest, essentially for fiscal purposes in determining ownership of land as a basis for taxation, the *inquisitio* expanded, first as a privilege granted by the king. During the reign of Henry II from 1154 to 1189, the *inquisitio* became regularly available to all litigants in the king's courts in connection with litigation over title to land, which continued to have fiscal implications.[78] Brunner provided an overview of the subsequent mutation of the *inquisitio* into the modern English jury while maintaining that the details were beyond the primary scope of his book. He observed that the jury's function increasingly became more "judicial" than "testimonial." Yet he also maintained that the jury in England performed both testimonial and judicial functions for more than three hundred years and did not become fully limited to the judicial role of evaluating the testimony of independent witnesses until 1650.[79]

Jhering

Rudolph von Jhering became the most prominent German legal scholar of the late nineteenth century, eclipsing even Savigny in reaching a broad popular and international audience. A leading Pandectist at the beginning of his career, Jhering became a polemical opponent of Pandectism in the late 1850s. Ridiculing the German Pandectists for their extreme abstractness and logical formalism, which divorced law from social reality, Jhering viewed law as a struggle of concrete individual and social interests. Jhering revised his

---

[73] Dammann, supra note 68, at 5.

[74] Id. at 12–13.

[75] Id. at 11.

[76] Id. at 12.

[77] Id. at 13–15.

[78] Mike Macnair, Vicinage and the Antecedents of the Jury, 17 Law & Hist. Rev. 537, 541 (1999).

[79] Dammann, supra note 68, at 17.

FIGURE 3.3. *Rudolph von Jhering.* Courtesy of Historical & Special Collections, Harvard Law School Library.

understanding of legal history as part of his transformation from Pandectism to the analysis of competing interests. He no longer treated legal history as the intellectual history of legal concepts, reflecting gradual and mostly unconscious evolution. Instead, he examined the history of law in social context, identifying the various individual and social interests that consciously competed for dominance and often produced dramatic and rapid change. Among American scholars of the late nineteenth century, Tiedeman and Holmes particularly identified with Jhering's changed views. A major predecessor of the "free law" movement in Germany, which extended his critique of legal formalism and fostered sociological interpretations of law, Jhering was also an important influence on Roscoe Pound, who frequently acknowledged the extent to which his own program of sociological jurisprudence and interest balancing, developed in the first decade of the twentieth century, derived from Jhering's earlier work. Pound, moreover, explicitly applied to his American predecessors Jhering's critique of German scholars for creating a mathematical, a priori jurisprudence divorced from social realities.

In his early career as a Pandectist, Jhering admired Puchta "as master and model of the correct jurisdic method,"[80] which Jhering called "the jurisprudence of constructs."[81] He tried to derive new legal principles from the logical structure of classical Roman law.[82] Frequently analogizing legal science to natural science, Jhering maintained that the logical derivation of new legal principles paralleled similar processes in chemistry and biology. Just as new chemical compounds are formed from existing elements, and just as new beings are formed through biological procreation, legal "concepts are productive, they mate and conceive new ones."[83] Jhering tried to "construct" from the materials of Roman law a practical commercial law for nineteenth-century Germany.[84] Recent scholars identify Jhering's development of *culpa in contrahendo* in contract law, the principle that contracting parties have a mutual duty of care even before a contract has been formally concluded, as the most impressive example of his construction of a new legal principle out of Roman materials.[85]

While still in his Pandectist phase, Jhering challenged the nationalistic interpretation of Roman legal history by Savigny and his followers, emphasizing instead the universal characteristics of Roman law. In the first volume of his *Spirit of Roman Law in the Different Stages of Its Development*, published in 1852, Jhering criticized "the one-sided insistence upon the principle of nationality," the "doctrine of the historical school that law develops purely from within each nation."[86] Unlike Savigny, who maintained that the distinctive "internal necessity" of German national development accounted for the German reception of Roman law, Jhering asserted that "the reception of foreign legal institutions is not a question of nationality, but simply one of expediency, of need. No one will fetch a thing from abroad when he has as good or better at home." He added, "But only a fool will reject the bark of the cinchona because it did not grow in his vegetable garden."[87]

To "combat" the erroneous nationalistic interpretation of legal history, Jhering stressed the "international communication and influence" that had become the "universal rule of civilization." He maintained that law, like language, morals, religion, industry, art, and science, was subject to this "universal rule." The idea of "universality," he proclaimed, "furnishes the key to the present era." Jhering agreed with the "historical school" that the previous

---

[80] Smith, supra note 61, at 133.

[81] Wieacker, supra note 1, at 317.

[82] Id. at 356 n. 25.

[83] Reimann, supra note 13, at 883.

[84] Whitman, supra note 1, at 215, 217, 221–2, 225.

[85] Wieacker, supra note 1, at 355 n. 24; Reimann, supra note 13, at 866 n. 110.

[86] Smith, supra note 61, at 116, 122.

[87] Id. at 122.

theorists of natural law had been methodologically unscientific. Yet Jhering also believed, contrary to the historical school, that in asserting "the doctrine of the universality of law, elevated above time and place," theorists of natural law had correctly perceived "the peculiar course of modern history."[88]

Consistent with his general emphasis on the evolution of law toward universalism, Jhering focused on the universal aspects of Roman law in his treatment of its history.[89] Departing from the periodization of Roman legal history by previous German scholars, Jhering identified three successive stages: the Indo-European, followed by the national Roman, and culminating in the universal Roman.[90] The universal Roman law, Jhering stressed, was the Roman law received in Germany and throughout medieval Europe.[91] This later reception by a different culture, he added, reinforced its universality.[92] Complementing his emphasis on universal law, Jhering innovated by incorporating comparative legal history into his discussion of Roman law. He wanted to compare what was common, and presumably universal, in different legal cultures. Throughout the *Spirit of Roman Law*, he minimized what was distinctively national in Roman law, often ignoring entirely aspects of Roman legal history covered by other scholars but not, in his view, related to universal themes.[93]

In the years around 1860, Jhering dramatically rejected many of his previous views, frequently mocking himself as well as his famous predecessors, especially Puchta and Savigny. Describing his own intellectual transformation, Jhering reported that his "revulsion" against the "*a priori* logical construction" of his prior work resulted from his practical experience in "active intercourse with practitioners," who often asked him to provide opinions in cases they were handling. These collaborations, he revealed, "not infrequently led me to recoil in terror from the application of theories that I had previously defended."[94] With the passion of a convert, Jhering disparaged prior German legal thought, including his own, and proceeded to develop theories of law and legal history rooted in social reality.[95]

What Jhering once lauded as "the jurisprudence of constructs," he now criticized as "the over-valuation of the logical element in law."[96] Legal scholars "must abandon the delusion" that law "is a system of legal mathematics, without any higher aim than a correct reckoning with conceptions."[97] "Principles," he maintained, "are not written in the stars, nor have they fallen from the skies;

[88] Id. at 115–16.
[89] Id. at 172; Albert Kocourek, Introduction, Rudolph von Jhering, The Struggle for Law (Chicago: Callaghan and Company, 1915), p. xxvi.
[90] Smith, supra note 61, at 172.
[91] Id. at 122–3.
[92] Id. at 124.
[93] Id. at 173–4.
[94] Id. at 133–4.
[95] Id. at 129–33; Whitman, supra note 1, at 317–18; Wieacker, supra note 1, at 356; Reimann, supra note 16, at 861 n. 93.
[96] Smith, supra note 61, at 138.
[97] Id. at 135.

man makes them for himself."[98] In *The Struggle for Law* (1877), Jhering's most accessible and frequently translated work, he wrote that "the one-sidedness of the purely scientific standpoint" of looking at law logically, as "a system of abstract legal principles," had given German legal theory "a character not in harmony with the bitter reality."[99] Jhering, moreover, did not really think the approach he criticized was meaningfully logical or scientific. He accused conceptual jurisprudence of "making a scientific method out of slogans."[100] Although Jhering's critique remained influential throughout the twentieth century, recent German scholarship, largely not translated into English, disputes his attribution of deductive formalism to prior German scholars.[101] Hans-Peter Haferkamp maintains that the typical Pandectist treatise tried to be "highly rational, but also elastic."[102]

Jhering's rejection of his previous views extended to legal history. In *The Struggle for Law*, Jhering acknowledged that he had once shared what he called "the Savigny-Puchta theory of the origin of law." "According to this theory," he wrote, "the formation of the body of principles of jurisprudence is effected by a process as unnoticed and as painless as the formation or growth of language." The process involves "no strife, no struggle," and occurs "slowly but surely" as "minds gradually open" to "the quiet working power of truth."[103] Legal principles display "a peaceable, gentle evolution" that derives from "the inner consciousness of popular conviction."[104] Equating the "Savigny-Puchta theory" with "the Historical School in law," Jhering claimed that it "might just as well have been called the romantic" because it was "based on a false idealization of past conditions."[105] Not fully altering his previous views, he admitted that "the law, like language, has an unintended, unconscious development, or, to call it by the traditional expression, an organic development from within outward." Yet he maintained that this "autonomous" development of law, which could be analyzed through traditional scientific abstraction and deduction, was relatively minor compared to "the struggle for law" he now identified among consciously competing interests.[106]

---

[98] Id. at 195.

[99] Jhering, supra note 89, at 5.

[100] Wieacker, supra note 1, at 344.

[101] See, e.g., Ulrich Falk, Ein Gelehrter wie Windscheid. Erkundungen auf den Feldern der sogenannten Begriffsjurisprudenz (Frankfurt: Klosterman) (2d ed. 1999); Hans-Peter Haferkamp, Karl Adolph von Vangerow (1808–1870) – Pandeckterecht und 'Mumiencultus,' 16 ZEuP 813 (2008); Regina Ogorek, Richterkonig oder Subsumtionsautomat? (Frankfurt: Klosterman, 1986). See Hans-Peter Haferkamp, Positivism as a Concept of Legal Historians, 17 Juridica International 101, 105–6 (2010).

[102] Hans-Peter Haferkamp, The Science of Private Law and the State in Nineteenth Century Germany, in Beyond the State: Rethinking Private Law (Tubingen, Germany: Mohr Siebeck, 2008) (Nils Jansen and Ralf Michaels, eds.), pp. 245, 253.

[103] Jhering, supra note 89, at 7–8.

[104] Id. at 17.

[105] Id. at 16.

[106] Id. at 9.

While peace is the end of the law, Jhering wrote in the opening sentences of *The Struggle for Law*, war is the means to that end. "The life of the law," he asserted, "is a struggle, – a struggle of nations, of the state power, of classes, of individuals."[107] Force, not logic, lies at the root of law.[108] The history of law is thus the history of struggle.[109] Although Jhering did not "presume any judgment on the correctness of the Darwinian theory," he recognized that the "results at which I personally have arrived in reference to the historical development of law confirm it to the fullest extent in my sphere."[110]

Jhering wrote *The Struggle for Law* while preparing his multi-volume work, *Law as a Means to an End*,[111] in which he elaborated the relationship between individual and social interests and recognized that they could sometimes conflict. "The individual acts voluntarily in the service of society," Jhering maintained, "where his interest coincides with that of society." He identified four fundamental areas where individual and social interests typically overlap: "*preservation of life, reproduction of same, labor, and trade.*" Yet Jhering acknowledged that individual interests and social interests could conflict even in these four fundamental areas.[112] And when conflict occurs, he reiterated throughout the book, social interests must prevail. He stressed that "society is stronger than the individual; and that therefore where it is obliged to summon its power in order to assert its right against the individual, the preponderance is always found on its side."[113] Referring to the "historical step-ladder of social purposes," Jhering claimed that interests are first asserted by the individual, then by associations of individuals who share interests, and ultimately by the State. "If inference from the past to the future be justified," Jhering wrote while clearly indicating his belief that it is, "the State will in the final future take up within itself all social purposes."[114] In a famous passage reflecting the title of his book, Jhering concluded that law is "not an end in itself; but merely a means to an end, the final end being the existence of society." If existing law cannot sustain society or adapt to do so, he added, "then force must step in and do what is demanded."[115] He defined law "as the form of the *security of the conditions of social life*, procured by the power of the State."[116]

As part of his revised theory of law, Jhering developed a conception of rights that differed radically from the views of previous German legal scholars. Instead of defining rights as necessary to protect the expression of individual will, Jhering treated them instrumentally, as "powers allocated for the purpose

[107] Id. at 1.
[108] Id. at 5, 15.
[109] Id. at 13.
[110] Rudolf von Ihering, Law as a Means to an End (Boston: Boston Book Company, 1913) (Modern Legal Philosophy Series, vol. V), p. lviii.
[111] Smith, supra note 61, at 151–2 (translating book as Teleology of Law).
[112] Jhering, supra note 110, at 338.
[113] Id. at 222.
[114] Id. at 230.
[115] Id. at 188, 317.
[116] Id. at 330.

of satisfying interests worth protecting."[117] Applying this analysis, Jhering rejected Savigny's famous theory that possession is protected as a manifestation of individual will, the intent to hold property against the world. He argued instead that it should be protected to foster practical individual and social needs in proving probable ownership.[118]

Consistent with his analysis of interests, Jhering emphasized "the *social* character of private rights."[119] The state allows many private rights for the protection of private interests because the expression of those private interests ultimately benefits the social ends of the public. On the other hand, if the state determines that private interests will not benefit the public, it will not extend legal rights to protect them.[120] "All rights of private law," Jhering maintained, "even though primarily having the individual as their purpose, are influenced and bound by regard for society." An individual cannot legitimately say, I have a right "exclusively for myself, I am lord and master over it, the consequences of the concept of right demand that society should not limit me." Jhering was confident that the "social conception of private law will continually gain ground over the individualistic." He predicted, for example, that the law would eventually limit individual property rights, that "society will no more recognize the alleged right of the individual to gather together as much as possible of the goods of the world, and combine in his hand a landed possession upon which hundreds and thousands of independent farmers might live, than it recognizes the right of life and death of the ancient Roman father over his children." While dismissing the "vain folly" of socialistic and communistic arguments for the abolition of private property and inheritance, Jhering looked forward to the time when taxes imposed by the state would limit the excess accumulation of private property and use the surplus in the social interest, "to lighten the pressure upon the other parts of the social body."[121]

Jhering's treatment of legal history reflected his transformed views about law as a struggle among competing interests. He continued to examine the evolution of law over time. But instead of exploring the autonomous evolution of legal ideas, he directed attention to the evolution of social forces that produced conflicting interests.[122] The national differences that Savigny and his numerous followers had often attributed to the "inward necessity" of the organic consciousness of the Volksgeist, which excluded "all notion of an accidental and arbitrary origin," Jhering ascribed to the contingencies of different external influences.[123] And in contrast to Savigny and his followers, who maintained that legal evolution was largely unconscious as well as internal, Jhering

---

117 Wieacker, supra note 1, at 356.
118 Smith, supra note 61, at 143–5; Kocourek, supra note 89, at xxvii–xxvii.
119 Jhering, supra note 110, at 396.
120 Wieacker, supra note 1, at 356; Smith, supra note 61, at 152, 154–5, 163; Kocourek, supra note 89, at xviii–xx.
121 Jhering, supra note 110, at 396.
122 Wieacker, supra note 1, at 356–7; Smith, supra note 61, at 183.
123 Smith, supra note 61, at 190.

emphasized that much legal evolution was purposive, the conscious attempt of individuals and groups to assert and gain their perceived interests.[124] In his late work *History of the Evolution of Roman Law* (1894), Jhering reiterated this point. "Against the doctrine of the unconscious growth of law," he wrote, "I for my part assert ... the doctrine of its conscious making. The law is not an efflux of the sense of right, discharging its creative function naively under obscure impulse – that mysterious process which would cut off (and deliver the legal historian from) further investigation." Rather, it is "the work of human purpose and calculation, exerting themselves in every stage of social development to find what is suitable. The history of law is the history of human thought in reference to the practical realization of the conditions of existence of the human community." He, therefore, concluded that all law "has been *made*." In what was probably an indirect criticism of his predecessors, he added that if law "seems to have grown of itself, it is because in many instances insight into the making is denied us."[125] Typically, Jhering believed, the impetus for legal change comes from the most enlightened members of society, who recognize the social conditions that require it.[126]

Savigny's mistaken views about legal history, Jhering wrote in *The Struggle for Law*, are not merely false, but politically dangerous. They offer the false optimism "that things will take care of themselves," that people can confidently wait for gradual improvement through the unconscious development of organic national law. Instead, Jhering urged, people "should act, and act with a full and clear consciousness of the object aimed at," with all their strength.[127] If people understand the teachings of history only after it is too late, he asserted, it is their own fault, not the fault of history.[128] Perhaps Jhering was alluding to and disagreeing with Hegel's famous statement "The owl of Minerva spreads its wings only with the falling of the dusk."[129]

In *Spirit of the Roman Law*, Jhering observed approvingly that the same legal doctrine, without altering its form, could develop a new substantive meaning over time as an effective adaptation to changing social needs.[130] Yet Jhering also believed that this process does not always work and that many legal doctrines simply outlive their usefulness as society evolves. In *Struggle for Law*, he pointed out that much Roman law was inappropriate in contemporary Germany. "Institutions and principles which in Rome were, considering the circumstances and customs of the time there, intelligible, became here, on account of the complete disappearance of their conditions precedent, a real

---

[124] Id. at 167; Kocourek, supra note 89, at xiv.

[125] Smith, supra note 61, at 185.

[126] Id. at 183–4.

[127] Jhering, supra note 89, at 14–15.

[128] Id. at 105.

[129] G. F. W. Hegel, Hegel's Philosophy of Right (London: Oxford University Press, 1967), p. 13.

[130] Mathias W. Reimann, Holmes's *Common Law* and German Legal Science, in Robert W. Gordon, The Legacy of Oliver Wendell Holmes, Jr. (Stanford, Calif.: Stanford University Press, 1992), pp. 72, 103.

curse."[131] When legal doctrines or institutions no longer work, he maintained, new ones should replace them. In *Law as a Means to an End*, for example, he identified the jury as an institution that had outlived its original usefulness and objected to laissez-faire doctrines in contract law as failing to recognize the social interest in subordinating individual freedom to justice.[132]

Jhering emphasized that people with powerful interests often resist needed legal change even when public opinion overwhelmingly favors it. The resistance is greatest, he added, when interests have been protected as vested rights. While recognizing that the struggle for change can last a century, Jhering encouraged it.[133] New legal principles and institutions won by long struggle are stronger, making the struggle "not a curse, but a blessing."[134] And major legal change, Jhering stressed, must be achieved through legislation, which he defined as "the action of state power." He declared, "It is not mere chance, but a necessity, deeply rooted in the nature of the law, that all thorough reforms of the mode of procedure and of positive law may be traced back to legislation."[135] Pointing out "the aversion of Savigny and of all his disciples to the interference of legislation,"[136] Jhering attributed his support of legislation to his "diametrically opposed" views about law and legal change.[137]

The historically oriented American legal scholars in the late nineteenth century were familiar with these developments in German legal scholarship and often cited the works of the German legal scholars discussed in this chapter. Savigny and Jhering, whose major works were translated into English, had the greatest impact on the American scholars. Most interested in the theoretical discussions of the historical process by these two great German scholars, the Americans also referred to their historical studies of Roman law. The Americans were familiar with but less interested in the Pandectists. Like the Pandectists, the Americans tried to organize and classify their own law. But they did not view themselves as constructing a system of legal mathematics, the criticism that Jhering leveled against the Pandectists but that recent German revisionists deny. The relatively few American legal scholars who worked from primary sources to write original histories of English law shared the more widespread interest in Savigny and Jhering. Yet they also had specialized interests in the Germanist scholars, especially Sohm and Brunner, whose works helped them explore the Teutonic origins of English law. The Americans addressed many of the subjects and themes raised by the Germans, often adding distinctive American nuances. Like the Germans themselves, the Americans shared many views about the centrality of history in understanding law but also disagreed with each other about numerous specific issues.

---

[131] Jhering, supra note 89, at 121–2.
[132] Jhering, supra note 110, at 105–6 (contract), 310–11 (jury); see Smith, supra note 68, at 160; Kocourek, supra note 112, at xxx–xxxi.
[133] Jhering, supra note 89, at 11–12.
[134] Id. at 19.
[135] Id. at 9–10.
[136] Id. at 15.
[137] Id. at 17.

IV

English Legal Scholarship

Sir Henry Maine

In contrast to Germany, which already had a distinguished tradition of historical legal scholarship by the middle of the nineteenth century, in England historical legal scholarship essentially began in 1861 with the publication of Henry Maine's enormously influential *Ancient Law*. Readers immediately compared Maine to Blackstone, Bentham, and Austin, the great British jurists of the previous hundred years, and his book became a classic.[1] *Ancient Law* popularized historical understandings of law in the English-speaking world and stimulated original "scientific" scholarship in legal history, most directly in the United States through the work of Henry Adams and his students at Harvard in the early 1870s. Beyond the world of legal scholarship, *Ancient Law* was a major contribution to the evolutionary social thought that attracted scholars in many fields and countries during the middle of the nineteenth century. It also helped initiate the disciplines of anthropology and sociology, where it had more lasting impact than among legal scholars themselves.[2]

Maine's reliance on the German historical school of jurisprudence was apparent both to his contemporaries and to his successors, although Maine himself did not address its influence on his work. Many concluded that *Ancient Law* introduced the German historical school to England and was the first book by an English scholar to exhibit its central characteristics, including its emphases on the organic development of law, the continuity of national traditions, the parallels between law and language, and the defects of statutes.[3]

[1] George Feaver, From Status to Contract: A Biography of Sir Henry Maine 1822–1888 (London: Longmans, Green and Company Ltd., 1969), p. 128; George Feaver, The Victorian Values of Sir Henry Maine, in The Victorian Achievement of Sir Henry Maine: A Centennial Reappraisal (Cambridge University Press, 1991) (Alan Diamond, ed.) [hereinafter Feaver-Victorian Values], p. 28; Frederick Pollock, Introduction, Maine's Ancient Law (New York: Henry Holt and Company, 1889), pp. xi, xl.

[2] Feaver, supra note 1, at 55; Alan Diamond, Introduction, in The Victorian Achievement of Sir Henry Maine, supra note 1, at 1, 1–3; Calvin Woodard, A Wake (or Awakening?) for Historical Jurisprudence, in id. at 217, 228.

[3] Ernest Barker, Political Thought in England 1848 to 1914 (London, Oxford University Press, 1928) (2d ed.), p. 142; J. W. Burrow, Evolution and Society: A Study in Victorian Social Theory

A review of *Ancient Law* hailed Maine as the English Savigny and predicted that it would begin a new era of jurisprudence in England, just as Savigny founded historical jurisprudence in Germany.[4] Like many of the German legal scholars, Maine used the categories of Roman law to analyze all legal systems, and his extensive discussions of Roman law derived largely from the previous work of the Germans.[5] Maine also embraced the distinctively English scientific tradition committed to induction from empirical evidence. History, he believed, provides the empirical data for an inductive science of law.[6] He endorsed historical jurisprudence as a convincing scientific alternative to the prior jurisprudential schools of natural law and analytic jurisprudence, which were based on abstraction and speculation.

Maine became best known for his sweeping and memorably phrased generalizations based on historical data uncovered by others. *Ancient Law* contains what has become his most famous generalization: "The movement of progressive societies has hitherto been a movement *from Status to Contract*."[7] The movement from status to contract, he believed, was one example of the more fundamental transformation in the history of all progressive societies from collectivism to individualism, the central theme in his work. Among his other important generalizations, Maine asserted that primitive societies were uniformly patriarchal, that law in progressive societies becomes less formal and more specialized, that the practices of primitive societies in the present provide evidence of the forgotten past of civilized societies, and that social change requires corresponding changes in law.

Although Maine was vitally interested in contemporary English law and society, *Ancient Law* did not explore English legal history, which had been much less studied than the history of Roman law. Frederick Pollock, the eminent English legal scholar, later remarked apologetically on Maine's behalf that "the English materials were not in a fit state, when Maine was writing 'Ancient Law,' to be used with effect for any purpose of historical generalization or comparison; and he had no choice but to leave them alone for the most part, and build on other and at that time safer ground."[8] In contrast to subsequent legal historians, beginning with Henry Adams and other Americans scholars in the

(Cambridge University Press, 1966), pp. 142–3; Peter Stein, Legal Evolution: The Story of an Idea (Cambridge University Press, 1980), p. 89; Paul Vinogradoff, Introduction to Historical Jurisprudence (London: Oxford University Press, 1920), p. 139; Paul Vinogradoff, The Teaching of Sir Henry Maine, 78 Law Quarterly Rev. 119, 125 (1904) [hereinafter Vinogradoff-Maine]; letter from Frederick Pollock to Oliver Wendell Holmes, Jr. (February 16, 1923), in Holmes-Pollock Letters (Cambridge, Mass.: Harvard University Press, 1941) (Mark DeWolfe Howe, ed.), vol. 2, p. 112.

4 Feaver, supra note 1, at 44.
5 Stein, supra note 3, at 90; Peter G. Stein, Maine and Legal Education, in Diamond, supra note 1, at 195, 204–5, 208.
6 Burrow, supra note 3, at 145–6, 156, 178; Vinogradoff-Maine, supra note 3, at 126.
7 Sir Henry Maine, Ancient Law (Washington, D.C.: Beard Books, 2000) (reprint of 1861 ed.), p. 100.
8 Pollock, supra note 1, at xx–xxi.

1870s and culminating in the heroic achievements of Frederic Maitland from the mid-1880s until his death in 1906, Maine did not want to undertake the thorough investigation of original sources that would put the English materials in "a fit state." Rather, he built on the "safer ground" of Roman law, which had already been extensively investigated by Savigny and his German successors.

Yet Maine emphasized that his generalizations from the history of Roman law had implications for his own country. He observed that Roman law directly influenced the legal thought of modern Europe, including England. More importantly than any direct influence, he stressed, the history of Roman law provided insight into the evolution of England's own legal system by revealing the "typical" progression from primitive to civilized legal societies. Like many evolutionary thinkers in the nineteenth century, Maine did not clarify whether this progression followed historical laws or was merely a pattern. But even if only reflecting the "typical" pattern of legal progress, Maine did not acknowledge any exceptions and assumed that it applied to English as well as to Roman law. Indeed, he may simply have used increased individualism as the characteristic that determines whether or not a society is progressive.[9] Maine's fundamental generalization that progressive societies moved from collectivism to individualism provided intellectual support for his political concerns about the dangers of popular democracy in England, first expressed in early journalistic essays and reiterated in publications toward the end of his life. Maine warned that popular democracy produced pressures for egalitarianism and collectivism that undermined the individualism upon which progressive societies depend.

Biographical Background

Relatively little is known about Maine's childhood between his birth in 1822 and 1840, when he won a scholarship to Pembroke College, Cambridge. An outstanding student at Cambridge, where he won prizes for his work in Greek and Latin as well as for English verse, Maine was elected to the exclusive Apostles' Club, whose members prepared and discussed papers dealing with "higher philosophy" and "contemporary problems of England."[10] Immediately after his graduation in 1844, he accepted a junior tutorship at the Cambridge law college, Trinity Hall, where he focused on Roman law. Just three years later, Maine became the Regius Professor of Civil Law at Cambridge. Yet this position, which others described as "an ill-paid sinecure,"[11] did not provide Maine sufficient income, so he also worked as a barrister.[12]

In the 1840s, when Maine began his career, there was very little academic study or teaching of law in England, a situation that became widely publicized

---

[9] John W. Burrow, Henry Maine and mid-Victorian Ideas of Progress, in Diamond, supra note 1, at 55, 56.

[10] Feaver, supra note 1, at 11.

[11] Id. at 19.

[12] Id. at 1–17, 24.

FIGURE 4.1. *Henry Maine*. Courtesy of Historical & Special Collections, Harvard Law School Library.

through the report of a select committee established by the House of Commons in 1846 to review the condition of legal education. The report concluded that the situation in England and Ireland was vastly worse than "in all the more civilized states of Europe and America."[13] Particularly impressed by legal education in Germany, where the academic study of law as a science preceded practical professional training, the select committee recommended a similar system in England and urged the formal training of English lawyers in both Roman and English law. Maine agreed with and benefited from these recommendations.

[13] Stein, supra note 5, at 196.

The report of the committee both provoked Maine to aspire to a career as a law professor devoted to the scientific jurisprudence it encouraged and led to the establishment of more remunerative teaching positions, which Maine soon filled.[14]

Maine himself urged changes in legal education in testimony to the Oxford and Cambridge Commission of 1850. He observed that the endowments of the law professorships at Cambridge were so low that it was hard to attract able people. After referring to his own supplementary work as a barrister, he pointed out that his "two immediate predecessors were beneficed clergy men, and in none of these cases can it be said that the University was the theatre of the Professor's most engrossing labours."[15] In addition to providing better salaries to professors, Maine recommended a broader and more academic legal curriculum that would incorporate the historical, comparative, and philosophical study of law. He also suggested a more rigorous system for examining students. The commission accepted many of Maine's recommendations, but Maine himself left Cambridge to accept a readership in jurisprudence and civil law at the Inns of Court in London, one of the five readerships created at the Inns of Court in 1852, a response to the 1846 report of the select committee.[16]

Finding his higher salary as a reader still inadequate and the burdens of private legal practice a strain on his always precarious health, Maine turned increasingly to journalism. Beginning in 1847, he contributed unsigned articles about domestic and international politics to a political journal, the *Morning Chronicle*, and wrote steadily for the important journal *Saturday Review* from its inception in 1855. His polemical articles in the *Saturday Review*, written during the period he was composing *Ancient Law*, praised the individualism whose historical development he traced in his book. Maine often directed his articles against the disciples of Jeremy Bentham, who were making utilitarian arguments on behalf of universal suffrage and other democratic reforms. Maine warned that popular democracy had produced the tyranny of the majority, particularly in France, and a decline in cultural standards, particularly in the United States. He approved the British political reforms of the 1830s and 1840s, which promoted freedom of contract by favoring free trade. But a truly democratic system of government in Britain, he feared, would replace this healthy individualism with a leveling state collectivism and social egalitarianism.[17]

Although *Ancient Law* was not published until 1861, Maine had prepared much of it earlier for lectures he gave at the Inns of Court in the 1850s and might have previously delivered similar lectures in Cambridge.[18] Maine revised

---

[14] Id. at 195–8; Feaver, supra note 1, at 18–22.

[15] Feaver, supra note 1, at 21.

[16] Id. at 21–4; Stein, supra note 5, at 197.

[17] Feaver, supra note 1, at 29–36; J. W. Burrow, 'The Village Community' and the Uses of History in Late Nineteenth-Century England, in Historical Perspectives: Studies in English Thought and Society, in Honour of J. H. Plumb (London: Europa, 1974) (Neil McKendrick, ed.), pp. 255, 273.

[18] Feaver, supra note 1, at 41–3; Burrow, supra note 3, at 139–40.

these lectures throughout the late 1850s and was delighted when John Murray, who published Darwin's *Origin of Species* in 1859, agreed in 1860 to publish *Ancient Law* as well. *Ancient Law* had as great an impact for many lawyers, historians, and other students of society as *Origin of Species* had for natural scientists.[19] It sold well and was used widely in law schools in Europe and the United States as well as in Great Britain.[20] Yet it is important to emphasize that the evolutionary social thought to which *Ancient Law* made a major contribution preceded Darwin's theories of biological evolution, as the lengthy gestation of Maine's book itself reveals. Even after Darwin published *Origin of Species*, many of the founders of evolutionary social theory, including Maine, remained much more interested in combating utilitarian views, which assumed a universal and unchanging human nature unaffected by history, than in harmonizing their thought with Darwin's theories about biological evolution.[21] Maine and many other pre-Darwinian social evolutionists were not attracted to mechanistic and deterministic understandings of evolutionary theory. They did not generally become Social Darwinists, who derived political implications from inflexible biology laws such as natural selection.[22]

The success of *Ancient Law* enabled Maine to become legal member to the Viceroy's Indian Council. Perhaps most importantly, Lord Acton, after reading *Ancient Law* "with extreme delight," used his political influence to lobby for Maine's appointment. Maine served in India from 1862 until he returned to England in 1869. While in India, Maine tried to modernize Indian law on English models by promoting individual rights, including freedom of contract.[23] Appointed vice-chancellor of Calcutta University by Lord Elgin, he saw education of the Indian "enlightened classes" as the best vehicle for achieving the transformation of Indian law and society from collectivism to individualism without excessive disruption.[24] During his years in India, Maine took extensive notes on his observations of village communities in northern India, intending this research to amplify his conclusions in *Ancient Law*.[25]

Maine returned to England in 1869, becoming Corpus Professor of Jurisprudence at Oxford.[26] He only had to lecture at Oxford two days a week, a schedule that enabled him to resume his journalism.[27] While continuing his journalism, he moved from Oxford to Cambridge in 1877 to become master of Trinity Hall, primarily an administrative position,[28] which he retained until his death in 1888. Maine's lectures at Oxford in 1870 formed the basis

---

[19] Feaver, supra note 1, at 41–4.
[20] Id. at 128–9.
[21] Burrow, supra note 3, at 26–7, 97–8, 135–6, 216–17.
[22] Id. at 115, 157, 163–4, 174–5.
[23] Feaver, supra note 1, at 62, 73, 89.
[24] Id. at 87, 89–90.
[25] Id. at 109.
[26] Id. at 61–5; Burrow, supra note 3, at 140–1.
[27] Feaver, supra note 1, at 114, 122.
[28] Id. at 174.

for *Village-Communities in the East and West*, published in 1871. Relying on his own observations in India and on recent German scholarship on the history of Teutonic law, Maine claimed that these materials reinforced the conclusions he derived in *Ancient Law* from the history of Roman law. Maine's subsequent volumes, *Lectures on the Early History of Institutions* (1875) and *Dissertations on Early Law and Custom* (1883), were also drawn from his lectures and continued to explore the themes he first addressed in *Ancient Law*. *Lectures on the Early History of Institutions* focused on ancient Irish law, and *Dissertations on Early Law and Custom* collected essays on a variety of subjects loosely related by the book's title. His final book, *Popular Government* (1885), revisited the dangers of democracy that he had initially addressed in his *Saturday Review* articles in the 1850s. Increasingly conservative and polemical over his lifetime,[29] he worried that the liberal program of electoral reform in late nineteenth-century England would reestablish the collectivism from which England had the rare good fortune to escape. He admired the House of Lords in England and the Senate and Constitution of the United States as checks against democratic excesses.[30] For Maine, the collectivism he portrayed so negatively as the key feature of the medieval village community served as a warning against his contemporaries who advocated democracy and socialism.[31] None of the books Maine wrote after his return from India approached the impact of *Ancient Law*, one of the most influential books of the nineteenth century and the key to understanding his thought.

The Central Themes of *Ancient Law*

"The chief object of the following pages," Maine announced in the first sentence of his preface to *Ancient Law*, "is to indicate some of the earliest ideas of mankind, as they are reflected in Ancient Law, and to point out the relation of those ideas to modern thought."[32] He maintained that the "rudimentary ideas" found in early legal conceptions "are to the jurist what the primary crusts of the earth are to the geologist. They contain, potentially, all the forms in which law has subsequently exhibited itself."[33] Through this analogy, Maine indicated his intent to study law scientifically and, more specifically, his view that in law, as in geology, examining the history of continuous change over time provides the key to scientific understanding of the current world. He asserted that prior legal scholars had not proceeded scientifically, a failure to which

---

[29] Stefan Collini, Democracy and Excitement: Maine's Political Pessimism, in Diamond, supra note 1, at 88, 90.

[30] Feaver, supra note 1, at 222, 230; Barker, supra note 3, at 147; R. C. J. Cocks, Sir Henry Maine: A Study in Victorian Jurisprudence (Cambridge University Press, 1988), p. 131; Stefan Collini, Public Moralists: Political Thought and Intellectual Life in Britain, 1850–1930 (Oxford University Press, 1991), p. 279.

[31] Burrow, supra note 17, at 272–3.

[32] Maine, supra note 7, at xv.

[33] Id. at 2.

Maine attributed the inadequacies of existing jurisprudence. "The inquiries of the jurist," he complained, "are in truth prosecuted much as inquiry in physics and physiology was prosecuted before observation had taken the place of assumption." Jurists developed unverified legal theories instead of engaging in the scientific work of "sober research into the primitive history of society and law."[34]

As part of his justification for the historical study of law, Maine elaborated his general criticism of previous jurisprudence. He expressed reservations about the prevalent analytical school in England, primarily associated with Bentham and Austin. With more hostility and at much greater length, he castigated the state of nature school associated with Hobbes, Locke, Blackstone, and, most perniciously from Maine's perspective, Rousseau.

The focus of the analytical school on law as a command of the lawgiver, Maine conceded, accurately, though not precisely, described the "mature jurisprudence" of nineteenth-century England. Yet it typically incapacitated its practitioners from recognizing the differences of other societies at other times and frequently prompted them to judge people living in the past by the morality of the present. Lacking historical perspective, analytical jurisprudence tended erroneously to treat all societies alike and to describe in universal terms characteristics that may be unique to the modern world.[35]

Though Maine had his differences with the analytical school, he identified the earlier state of nature school as the primary continuing impediment to the historical method of legal scholarship that he advocated and tried to exemplify in his book[36] and that he occasionally described as "historical jurisprudence."[37] The state of nature school assumed "a nonhistorical, unverifiable, condition of the race" in a presocial state. State of nature theorists, most famously Hobbes and Locke, differed about the characteristics of the presocial natural state and about how social organization emerged from it, but they agreed that "a great chasm separated man in his primitive condition from man in society."[38] Maine blamed Rousseau for extending the influence of the state of nature school[39] and for aligning it with the political and social views that led to the "grosser disappointments" of the French Revolution.[40] He called Rousseau a "remarkable man who, without learning, with few virtues, and with no strength of character, has nevertheless stamped himself ineffaceably on history by the force of a vivid imagination, and by the help of a genuine and burning love for his fellow-men, for which much will always have to be forgiven him."[41] Under his influence, the state of nature school stimulated "disdain of positive law,

---

[34] Id.
[35] Id. at 4–5, 182–3.
[36] Id. at 52, 53.
[37] Id. at 133.
[38] Id. at 68.
[39] Id. at 51.
[40] Id. at 53.
[41] Id. at 51.

impatience of experience, and the preference of *a priori* to all other reasoning."
During the French Revolution, it encouraged anarchy and was invoked more
frequently as the times grew worse.[42]

Legal theorists in both the analytical and the state of nature schools, Maine
concluded, failed to investigate the law of archaic societies that differed from
their own. At most, they simply speculated about the past. This failure, he
stressed, is analogous to the error of investigating the physical universe without paying attention to "the particles that are its simplest ingredients" and
is no more defensible in jurisprudence than in other fields of science. Just as
physical science should begin with its simplest ingredients, Maine declared,
jurisprudence should begin "with the simplest social forms in a state as near as
possible to their rudimentary condition."[43] It is, therefore, necessary to explore
the "history of primitive societies,"[44] precisely the task he assigned himself in
Ancient Law.

Although Maine opened *Ancient Law* by comparing the historical study
of law with geology, he subsequently invoked another, seemingly closer analogy: comparative philology. Maine did not elaborate the parallel between
comparative philology and the historical study of law. But by using the term
"comparative jurisprudence" to describe his method, he indicated that just as
comparative philologists had been examining "with surprising results" the history of language in different societies at different stages of development, he
would undertake similar comparisons of legal systems. More specifically, Maine
was interested in the legal systems of the same societies, the "Indo-European
stock," whose languages the comparative philologists had already studied.[45]

In his preface, Maine informed his readers that his book would focus on
Roman law because two of its characteristics were crucial to his project. First,
the available records of the earliest period of Roman law contained evidence
of the practices of even more remote antiquity. Second, the later periods of
Roman law produced rules and civil institutions that continue to influence
modern society. Aware that a high proportion of the illustrations in his book
were from Roman law, Maine stressed that he had not intended to write a
treatise on Roman jurisprudence and that his book should not be read as one.
Rather, Maine referred to the "necessity of taking the Roman law as a typical
system," thereby indicating that the records of no other legal system were similarly available for comparative analysis.[46] Yet when he could find other evidence of the practices of archaic societies, Maine relied on it, most notably in
discussing the village communities of India and Russia in his chapter on "the
early history of property."[47]

---

[42] Id. at 54.
[43] Id. at 70.
[44] Id. at 71.
[45] Id. at 72.
[46] Id. at xv.
[47] Id. at 153–7.

Early passages in *Ancient Law* set forth Maine's general conception of legal change. The initial customs of a society, he maintained, typically reflect its needs. If these customs are preserved until the society develops new needs, requiring new practices, "the upward march of society is almost certain." But in many societies, old customs reflecting actual social needs are extended by inappropriate analogies to new contexts, thereby generating unreasonable usages.[48] For example, though Romans and Hindus derived from the same ethnic stock and originally had strikingly similar customs, the Roman code protected Romans from the corruption of these customs that occurred in Hindu culture, in which irrational analogies produced "an immense apparatus of cruel absurdities."[49] Prohibitions against the consumption of certain kinds of food, originally based on sanitary concerns, were extended to all similar foods, "though the resemblance occasionally depends on analogies the most fanciful." Similarly, customs that helped insure cleanliness became "long routines of ceremonial ablution." Perhaps most perniciously, class divisions that were necessary for national preservation "degenerate[d] into the most disastrous and blighting of all human institutions – Caste."[50]

In "progressive societies," Maine generalized, "social necessities and social opinion are always more or less in advance of Law." Because law is stable, whereas a progressive society changes by definition, a gap arises between society and law. "We may come indefinitely near to the closing of the gap between them," he observed, "but it has a perpetual tendency to reopen." Happiness in a progressive society, Maine concluded, depends on how quickly developing gaps are narrowed. He identified three techniques for bringing law "into harmony with society": legal fictions, equity, and legislation. Though claiming that these techniques had always appeared historically in the chronological order in which he listed them, Maine acknowledged that sometimes two of them have operated simultaneously and that some legal systems have not exhibited all of them.[51]

Maine defined a legal fiction as "any assumption which conceals, or affects to conceal, the fact that a rule of law has undergone alteration, its letter remaining unchanged, its operation being modified."[52] The use of legal fictions, Maine believed, provides an invaluable way to overcome the rigidities of law during times of social progress. By ridiculing legal fictions, Bentham merely revealed his own broader ignorance of the role of history in legal analysis. Yet Maine also disagreed with unnamed theorists who argued that legal fictions should remain a permanent part of a legal system. Over time, he maintained, legal fictions turn into mere shells, hiding new rules inside. These shells become barriers to the symmetrical classification of the law that Maine favored. While

---

[48] Id. at 11.
[49] Id. at 12.
[50] Id. at 11.
[51] Id. at 15.
[52] Id. at 16.

recognizing the value of legal fictions as an instrument to close the gap between law and a developing society, he felt that after serving this purpose they should be pruned away to maintain structural order in a legal system.[53]

After discussing legal fictions, Maine addressed the other two techniques for adapting law to society. He defined equity as "any body of rules existing by the side of the original civil law, founded on distinct principles and claiming incidentally to supersede the civil law in virtue of a superior sanctity inherent in those principles." Legislation, by contrast, originates in a source acting on behalf of the entire society, such as an autocratic ruler or a parliamentary body. Whereas equity derives its authority from the presumed higher nature of its principles, the force of legislation depends on its external source.[54]

Maine alerted readers at the beginning of his book that he was only interested in progressive societies, which, he emphasized, were extremely rare.[55] According to Maine, "the stationary condition of the human race is the rule, the progressive the exception."[56] In most societies, he asserted, the influence of religion reinforced the rigidity of primitive law and prevented it from developing. He added that many societies in his own time had remained in a primitive condition.[57] Eastern societies in general, and India in particular, were Maine's primary examples of stagnant societies.[58]

Only a few fortunate races, Maine repeatedly observed, had the "marvellous fate" to escape this "calamity."[59] Roman law was for Maine the primary example of the experience of a fortunate race, for it improved continuously while "the rest of human thought and action materially slackened its pace, and repeatedly threatened to settle down into stagnation."[60] Roman law also had the advantage of a long and well-known history, whose changes could be easily ascertained.[61] Maine summarized the progression of Roman law from its beginnings in the isolated judgments and commands of the patriarchal head of household. After these judgments and commands began to accumulate, results in similar situations became the "germ or rudiment of a Custom." Tweaking his contemporaries, who assumed "*a priori* that the notion of a Custom must precede that of a judicial sentence, and that a judgment must affirm a Custom or punish its breach," Maine confidently reiterated that "the historical order of the ideas" was precisely the opposite.[62]

When early customs first became codified, Maine added, they applied to the patriarchal heads of families rather than to individuals, who remained subject

[53] Id. at 16–17.
[54] Id. at 17.
[55] Id. at 13–15.
[56] Id. at 14.
[57] Id. at 79.
[58] Id. at 10–12, 15.
[59] Id. at 45.
[60] Id. at 15.
[61] Id. at 14.
[62] Id. at 3.

to the family patriarch. Over time, through the application of legal fictions, equity, and legislation, the role of civil law increased, ultimately transferring power over both personal rights and property from the family patriarch to public tribunals.[63] Legislation, which at first was limited to "the removal of some great abuse, or the decision of some incurable quarrel between classes and dynasties,"[64] eventually extended to "private concerns," which no longer were ruled "by the behests of a despot enthroned by each hearthstone."[65] The "final reconstruction" of Roman law in the Justinian Code of the sixth century, Maine concluded, expressed the most mature stage of Roman law, in which "few traces of archaism" remained. Some aspects of this mature Roman law "descended unimpaired to the modern world, while others, destroyed or corrupted by contact with barbarism in the dark ages, had again to be recovered by mankind."[66] The barbarians reintroduced much primitive law that had previously disappeared as Roman law progressed, but the new primitive law combined, often uneasily, with the mature Roman law that survived. Maine believed that the English law of his own time was still shedding the vestiges of primitive law reintroduced by the barbarians, thereby implying that it had not reached the same stage of maturity that the Justinian Code provided Roman law in the sixth century.[67]

Announcing the major thesis of his book, Maine concluded that the transformation from primitive to progressive societies has uniformly "been distinguished by the gradual dissolution of family dependency and the growth of individual obligation in its place. The Individual is steadily substituted for the Family, as the unit of which civil laws take account." Contracts among free individuals slowly replace dependent family relationships in defining reciprocal rights and duties.[68] In his most famous expression of this transformation, Maine wrote that "the movement of the progressive societies has hitherto been a movement *from Status to Contract*."[69] Maine acknowledged that the movement from family to individual, from status to contract, had occurred at different rates in different progressive societies. He insisted, however, that this movement is not subject to reversal unless a society absorbs archaic customs from a foreign source,[70] as happened in Europe after the fall of Rome to barbarian tribes.[71]

Reporting that most of his contemporaries viewed primitive societies as collections of individuals,[72] Maine ascribed this misperception to lack of historical

---

[63] Id. at 98.
[64] Id. at 25.
[65] Id. at 98.
[66] Id. at 99.
[67] Id. at 79–80.
[68] Id. at 99.
[69] Id. at 100.
[70] Id. at 99.
[71] Id. at 99, 135, 174–5.
[72] Id. at 74.

sensibility, in particular to the anachronistic inability of nineteenth-century scholars to realize that primitive people had different ideas from their own.[73] Almost exclusively on the basis of evidence from Indo-European societies,[74] Maine asserted that primitive societies correctly perceived themselves to be aggregations of patriarchal families. Ancient law naturally reflected this social structure. The power of the patriarchal head of the family, for example, left relatively little room for legal regulation, accounting for the scantiness of ancient law.[75] The most distinctive feature of ancient law, Maine emphasized, was the conception of the family as a perpetual entity. Because the family is immortal, it is subject to indefinite liability. Under this view, individuals without personal responsibility may nevertheless be held liable for acts committed by the family.[76] Maine suggested that in many respects the patriarchal family can be compared to a small independent corporation.[77]

Primitive societies, Maine observed, uniformly viewed themselves as derived from a single original stock, even though their own traditions and records indicated otherwise. He explained that this assumption was necessary to justify joining a political community and that it was maintained through the legal fiction of adoption, which permitted the artificial creation of family relations and enabled the absorption of outsiders. Just as people with no blood relationship could be absorbed into the family, Maine added, blood relations could be excluded from it if they withdrew from the empire of the patriarch.[78] Pointing out that the patriarchal family was vastly different from the modern family, Maine stressed that it "stamped itself on all the great departments of jurisprudence" and accounted for "many of the most important and most durable characteristics" of ancient law.[79]

Elaborations in Specific Contexts

Much of the text of *Ancient Law* elaborated Maine's general assertions about the transformation from primitive to progressive societies by examining in successive chapters the early history of wills, property, contract, and criminal law. As he alerted his readers at the beginning of the book, he focused especially on the Roman law related to these subjects. Although he is best remembered for his famous generalization "the movement of the progressive societies has hitherto been a movement *from Status to Contract*,"[80] Maine did not reiterate this phrase throughout his chapters on particular areas of the law. Rather, in each

[73] Id. at 78.
[74] Id. at 72.
[75] Id. at 74.
[76] Id. at 75.
[77] Id. at 74.
[78] Id. at 76–9.
[79] Id. at 79.
[80] Id. at 100.

of these chapters, he emphasized the contrast between the family as the basic unit of primitive law and the individual as the basic unit of modern law.

Wills, Maine asserted, is the area of law that best reveals the superiority of historical investigation over prevailing jurisprudential approaches.[81] Perhaps that is why he chose wills as the first specific topic to illustrate the general themes he discussed in the introductory chapters. Examining the continuous history of wills, he pointed out, demonstrates that assumptions about their necessary or natural qualities are merely unjustified extrapolations from their current characteristics. In fact, Maine stressed, ancient wills did not contain any of these current characteristics, which all arose more recently.[82]

The shift from the family to the individual as the fundamental unit of law, Maine asserted, accounts for the fundamental differences between the ancient and the modern will. He warned against anachronistically attributing the modern functions of the will to the ancient will. The will in ancient law, he stressed, was one of several ways to transfer the representation of the family to a new head after the death of the previous one. Family goods were included in this transfer, but only because the responsibility of governing the family included control over its common property. The Romans invented the will to provide better protection than the rules of intestate succession for the members of a family upon the death of its head. Only much later did the will become a powerful instrument for distributing the property of the dead man to individuals, including to individuals outside the family. Eventually, the will exerted enormous influence in modifying society, second only to the contract, for it stimulated the circulation of property and plasticity in proprietary rights.[83]

Even after the revolution from familial to individual relations that transformed the functions of wills, Maine observed, the origins of the will as a method to protect the family affected modern law. Although the magistrate and the civil tribunal took the place of the patriarch and the domestic forum, "the whole scheme of rights and duties administered by the judicial authorities remained shaped by the influence of the obsolete privileges and coloured in every part by their reflection." For example, "the prolongation of a man's legal existence in his heir, or in a group of co-heirs, is neither more nor less than a characteristic of *the family* transferred by a fiction to *the individual*."[84]

In his discussion of wills, Maine devoted substantial attention to primogeniture, which he defined as the mode of succession "whenever a single son or descendant succeeds to the authority over a household or society."[85] He referred to primogeniture as "one of the most difficult problems of historical jurisprudence."[86] The emergence of primogeniture in feudal Europe is a

---

[81] Id. at 101.
[82] Id. at 102–3.
[83] Id. at 114–15.
[84] Id. at 109.
[85] Id. at 140.
[86] Id. at 133.

historical puzzle, Maine observed, because neither Roman law nor barbarian custom, the two available sources for feudal institutions, gave any preference to the eldest son in inheriting property.[87] How, then, did this practice arise? In his answer, Maine recognized the contingency of legal history.

Primogeniture, Maine asserted, originated in benefices, the grants of Roman provincial land from invading barbarian chieftains conditioned on the performance of military service by the beneficiary. The benefices, though not initially hereditary, gradually evolved into hereditary fiefs. Individual negotiation between grantor and beneficiary determined the rules for the succession of fiefs, which occasionally, but neither necessarily nor even typically, were inherited by the eldest son. Yet the minority practice of primogeniture soon superseded all other forms of succession.[88] Maine speculated that as civil authority disintegrated under the pressure of barbarism, people fell back on the earlier, patriarchal form of social organization. The new patriarchal form did not develop by adoption, as in primitive times, but through infeudation, the relationship between lord and vassals. And succession by primogeniture prevented the division of feudal land, which would have invited attack during this violent era. Primogeniture did not disinherit others in favor of the eldest son but provided a safe method for protecting the entire community.[89]

Eventually, rule by a hereditary chief ended in Europe, as it had ended in the ancient world. But primogeniture remained in Europe, whereas in the ancient world, including Rome and the Germanic tribes, the demise of the hereditary chief led to the equal division of property among all male members of the family.[90] Maine explained this difference by stressing the use of advanced Roman jurisprudence to interpret the new feudal system. "The ideas and social forms which contributed to the formation of the system were unquestionably barbarian and archaic, but, as soon as Courts and lawyers were called in to interpret and define it, the principles of interpretation were those of the latest Roman jurisprudence, and were therefore excessively refined and matured." Under the ancient law of patriarchal societies, the patriarch had absolute control over the family's property but also correlative duties to the members of the family that prevented him from being a proprietor of property in the modern sense. Yet later Roman jurisprudence, which remained influential in feudal Europe, viewed absolute control over property as ownership, which was not limited by the correlative duties that had prevailed in the ancient law of primitive patriarchal societies. The contact of the refined Roman law with the barbarous practice of absolute control by the patriarch of the family property, Maine concluded, "had inevitably for its effect the conversion of the eldest son into legal proprietor of the inheritance."[91]

---

[87] Id. at 135.
[88] Id. at 134–6.
[89] Id. at 138–9.
[90] Id. at 135, 139.
[91] Id. at 140.

Maine's discussion of property closely tracked his treatment of wills. He criticized scholars for anachronistically ascribing universal qualities to current law, maintained that the historical shift from the family to the individual explained changing conceptions of property, and explored the combination of primitive law with Roman law in feudal Europe. Singling out Blackstone for special scorn, Maine ridiculed the prevailing impression of property in primitive society. Blackstone's "sketches of the plight of human beings in the first ages of the world," Maine sarcastically observed, "are effected by first supposing mankind to be divested of a great part of the circumstances by which they are now surrounded, and by then assuming that, in the condition thus imagined, they would preserve the same sentiments and prejudices by which they are now actuated, – although, in fact, these sentiments may have been created and engendered by those very circumstances of which, by hypothesis, they are to be stripped."[92] Maine specifically disagreed with the dominant view, expressed by Blackstone, that in primitive society property began by physical possession of land through occupancy. This view, Maine asserted, "directly reverses the truth"[93] by transposing the modern conception of property, derived from the mature stage of Roman law, to the primitive past.

Reiterating his fundamental theme that the individual replaced the family in legal analysis as primitive societies became modern, Maine explained that occupancy is an individualistic conception, as Blackstone indicated by always portraying property as occupied by an individual.[94] The occupant becomes the owner, Maine observed, only when "all things are presumed to be somebody's property."[95] He concluded that Blackstone and others had been misled by relying on the mature Roman law of property, which already reflected the transformation from the family to the individual, for their theory that "individual ownership is the normal state of property right, and that ownership in common by groups of men is only the exception to a general rule."[96] Maine believed that Roman law "has rendered precisely its greatest service to civilisation in enfranchising the individual from the authority of archaic society."[97] Yet this very accomplishment meant that mature Roman law could not have accurately described the primitive law of property, before the individual was liberated from the family. Given the central role of the family in primitive society, Maine reasoned, it is most likely that property in ancient law was based on joint ownership.[98]

To support his conclusion about joint ownership, Maine referred to contemporary research on the village community in India. Nineteenth-century India provided a much better guide to primitive law than the much earlier mature

---

[92] Id. at 149–50.
[93] Id. at 151.
[94] Id. at 152.
[95] Id. at 151.
[96] Id. at 153.
[97] Id. at 152.
[98] Id. at 153.

law of Rome, Maine stressed, because India, unlike Rome, had never progressed from a primitive to a modern society. Having remained the least developed of all societies in the Indo-European family, India was the best place to look for the primitive institutions that can no longer be found or even traced in modern societies, including, of course, Maine's England and its common law. However much a primitive institution may have changed in India, Maine asserted, "it will seldom be found to have entirely cast aside the shell in which it was originally reared." And Maine reported that intelligent observers of India, who had no theoretical stake in the origin or nature of property law, had portrayed the Indian village community as a society of "immense antiquity" that is both patriarchal and "an assemblage of co-proprietors."[99] Russian villages, Maine added, resemble those in India, as do other European societies that, with more variations, have retained the patriarchal form.[100] All of this evidence from different village communities, Maine concluded, "renders less presumptuous the conjecture that private property, in the shape in which we know it, was chiefly formed by the gradual disentanglement of the separate rights of individuals from the blended rights of a community."[101]

In his chapter on property, more specifically than in his treatment of wills, Maine addressed the process by which ancient law became modern. Primitive societies, he maintained, initially designated as property the objects they most enjoyed. They subsequently extended the concept of property to other objects but placed them in a different and lower category. This subsequent category, precisely because it was lower, did not require as many or as stringent rules governing transfer and descent as the original, more valuable property. As primitive communities progressed, they applied to all property the more flexible and convenient rules that governed the lesser category, and the distinction between classes of property often disappeared.[102] Maine concluded that "by a gradual course of innovation the plasticity of the less dignified class of valuable objects is communicated to the classes which stand conveniently higher."[103] As a happy result, the "embarrassing formalities" governing the earliest property, which often had become "stumbling blocks to good faith and stepping stones to fraud," were abandoned.[104] Maine gave several examples of this process. In Roman law, the original forms of property, which required a formal ceremony of conveyance, were assimilated into lesser categories of property, which did not. In continental Europe, the Roman law of movables subverted the feudal law of land. And in England, the law of personalty was absorbing and annihilating the law of realty.[105]

[99] Id.
[100] Id. at 156–8.
[101] Id. at 158–9.
[102] Id. at 160–4.
[103] Id. at 160.
[104] Id. at 162.
[105] Id. at 160–1.

Maine concluded his chapter on "the early history of property" by discussing developments in feudal Europe. Though he did not refer to his analysis of primogeniture in his treatment of wills, he made many similar points. He especially emphasized that feudal property law combined barbarian customs and Roman law,[106] a combination he had stressed in dealing with primogeniture and reiterated at the end of the following chapter on contract law. The Roman law of contract, Maine asserted, was both the tie that bound together the earliest feudal communities and the feature that "principally distinguishes the feudal institutions from the unadulterated usages of primitive races."[107]

Strikingly, in his chapter on contract, Maine neither repeated nor paraphrased the "from status to contract" language that has subsequently received more attention than anything else in *Ancient Law* and that for many has become a cliché to which they have reduced the entire book. More broadly, even though Maine had previously stated that contract "is the tie between man and man which replaces by degrees those forms of reciprocity in rights and duties which have their origin in the Family,"[108] the actual chapter on contract did not focus on his fundamental theme about the transformation from the family to the individual as society progressed. The most important point about primitive societies, he nevertheless reiterated in passing, is that the individual has few or no rights and duties but is governed by rules derived from his station of birth or commanded by the head of his household.[109]

In his specific discussion of contract, Maine elaborated his earlier criticism of the state of nature school of jurisprudence. Many theorists of the state of nature, he observed, assumed that "all Law had its origin in Contract." This assumption had become so prevalent that "it seemed easy to give a fallacious reality and definiteness to the contractual origin of Law by insisting on the Social Compact as a historical fact."[110] While rejecting this historical assumption as entirely unfounded, Maine conceded that primitive societies had rudimentary conceptions of contract. He observed that in primitive societies, in contrast to modern ones, the formalities associated with a promise were more important than the promise itself. The "delicate analysis which mature jurisprudence applies to the conditions of mind under which a particular verbal assent is given," he wrote, "appears, in ancient law, to be transferred to the words and gestures of the accompanying performance."[111] In ancient law, the omission of any required word or gesture rendered a promise unenforceable, just as their performance precluded any claim of duress or deception. Echoing his discussion of the removal of "embarrassing formalities" during the gradual and progressive development of property law, Maine described a similar

[106] Id. at 174–5.
[107] Id. at 214–15.
[108] Id. at 99.
[109] Id. at 183.
[110] Id. at 182.
[111] Id. at 184.

process in contract law. Gradually, some of the ceremonies accompanying the contract were eliminated and others were either simplified or easily avoided. Later, contracts that are necessary for "social intercourse" were differentiated, and no formalities were required to enter them. Ultimately, "mental engagement, signified through external acts," replaced "the external shell of form and ceremony," which were retained only as "guarantees of authenticity, and securities of caution and deliberation."[112]

Writing about contracts, but apparently generalizing to the overall transformation from primitive to modern law, Maine added that "ancient conceptions and ancient terms are subjected to a process of gradual specialisation." Originally, a technical term covered all the things that modern law subsequently distinguishes through separate names. Modern law does not abandon the original term but limits it to only a subset of the things it initially covered. So, for example, the original Latin term for patriarchal power covered everything controlled by the patriarch. But as Roman society advanced, new terms emerged to describe patriarchal power over specific subjects, such as material commodities and children. But the original term continued to describe the patriarchal power over a wife.[113]

The historical relationship between conveyances and contracts, Maine stressed, illustrates this process of gradual specialization. Initially, the same ceremonial act, called a nexum, covered all solemn transactions. But soon the concepts of contract and conveyance became differentiated. Although the same ceremony continued to apply to both, a new term, mancipation, designated the conveyance of property, while the original term nexum still covered the making of a contract.[114] Early in this differentiation, the formalities of the ceremony remained more important than the agreement itself. But over time, as Maine had already indicated in general terms, the ceremony of the nexum became simplified. Later, even the simplified ceremony could easily be waived. Later still, partial performance of a contract by the parties precluded its repudiation based on formal deficiencies. Ultimately, the mental state of the contracting parties became determinative, and external circumstances were only evidence of that mental state. Maine acknowledged that information about other ancient societies was insufficient to support the generalization that this progression in the Roman law of contracts "exemplifies the necessary progress of human thought on the subject of Contract." But he immediately expressed confidence that it did so "up to a certain point," which he never specified.[115] Whatever the universality or particularity of the Roman history of contracts, Maine added, its enormous influence on modern thought provides an independent reason to study it.[116]

[112] Id. at 185–6.
[113] Id. at 186–7.
[114] Id. at 187.
[115] Id. at 199.
[116] Id. at 199–200.

Following this rather technical analysis of the emerging Roman law of contracts, Maine made the much broader claim that Roman law in general, and
especially its contract law, helped shape virtually every intellectual activity of
modern Europeans except physics.[117] The description of reciprocal rights and
duties developed in Roman contract law, he particularly stressed, provided
the ideas and the terminology that enabled the articulation of emerging ideas
about political obligation in Europe after the decay of feudalism.[118] Although
there were plenty of models for obedience to rulers, "the consciousness of correlative rights possessed by the governed would have been entirely without
the means of expression if the Roman law of Obligation had not supplied a
language capable of shadowing forth an idea which was as yet imperfectly
developed."[119]

In the final chapter of *Ancient Law*, Maine turned to the history of criminal law, which he largely interpreted through his familiar emphasis on the
relationship between the patriarchal family and ancient law. Virtually all commentators agree, Maine observed, that the proportion of criminal law is much
higher in ancient than in modern legal systems. Yet the standard explanation
for this difference, the presumed greater degree of violence in primitive societies, seemed incomplete to Maine. A full explanation, he maintained, required
attention to the power of the patriarchal family in primitive societies.

Maine identified the law of persons, property, inheritance, and contract as
the overwhelming majority of the legal subjects that compose the law of civilized societies but are largely irrelevant in a primitive society governed by
the patriarchal family. If the wife, son, and ward are subject to the patriarchal power of the man who is husband, father, and guardian, Maine asserted,
there is virtually no role for a law of persons. Nor is there much need for laws
governing property and succession if land and goods remain within the family
and are never distributed to outsiders. Observing the absence of contract in
ancient law, which he considered its most substantial difference from modern
law, Maine asserted that contract depends on moral notions that had not developed in primitive societies.[120] "There are no corresponding reasons," he concluded, "for the poverty of penal law, and accordingly, even if it be hazardous
to pronounce that the childhood of nations is always a period of ungoverned
violence, we shall be able to understand why the modern relation of criminal
law to civil should be inverted in ancient codes."[121]

At the beginning of his account of the early history of criminal law, Maine
stressed that, though he used the term "criminal law" for convenience, primitive societies did not really have the modern, civilized conception of criminal
law as an offense against the community or the state. Rather, they treated all

[117] Id. at 200.
[118] Id. at 202–4.
[119] Id. at 203.
[120] Id. at 216–17.
[121] Id. at 217.

offenses as wrongs, roughly equivalent to torts in later English law. Offenses such as theft, assault, and violent robbery, which modern law treats as crimes, primitive law treated as wrongs to be remedied by financial compensation[122] measured by the injured person's assumed impulse for revenge.[123]

In tracing the subsequent development of criminal law, Maine again relied on Roman law, as he had in previous chapters, because it best exemplified the history of legal progress.[124] He identified four stages of the primitive history of criminal law in Rome. First, the conception of crime as any injury to the community or state became differentiated from a wrong, and the collectivity interposed itself to punish the evildoer. Second, a legislature delegated its power over crimes to an independent body, which investigated a particular accusation and, if proved, punished the offender. Third, the legislature, instead of responding to actual crimes, periodically created the independent body in anticipation of their commission. Finally, the independent body became a permanent court, governed by rules for the future selection of judges and by specified penalties for designated crimes.[125] As the Roman commonwealth decayed, Maine reported, the emperors gained power over these tribunals from the Senate, and the emperor increasingly was perceived as the guardian of justice for all the people. Because modern European societies retained this late Roman view of the sovereign's responsibility for justice, Maine concluded, they did not have to recapitulate every stage of the development of the Roman criminal law.[126]

After *Ancient Law*

Maine continued to publish regularly after his return to England from India in 1869. As Maine himself acknowledged, much of this work elaborated *Ancient Law*. He reiterated many of its major themes, qualified some of its broad generalizations, extended its comparative historical method to the history of early Germanic and Irish law, and, in contrast to *Ancient Law*, addressed how the legal history of various Indo-European societies illuminated the history of English law. Maine's last book, *Popular Government*, expressed his concerns about the growth of democracy in the nineteenth century, particularly in Britain, but he viewed his analysis as an application of the historical method he had used ever since *Ancient Law*. Although dwarfed in importance by *Ancient Law*, Maine's later work helps clarify his ideas and their impact on subsequent scholars, who themselves read and responded to it both as illuminating Maine's classic book and as raising provocative issues about the history of English law.

Reiterating his commitment to evolutionary thought, Maine emphasized that institutions and law, "like forms of organic life, are subject to the great law

---

122 Id. at 217–18.
123 Id. at 224.
124 Id. at 231.
125 Id. at 226–7.
126 Id. at 232–3.

of evolution."[127] He criticized the tendency, particularly of "German juridical opinion" but also of Bentham and Austin, to exaggerate the admitted stability of legal conceptions into the assumption that "they are absolutely permanent and indestructible," part of a framework subject to discovery through reason.[128] Pointing out that legal conceptions decay and perish, Maine declared that "even jurisprudence itself cannot escape from" evolutionary law.[129] He continued to point out analytical errors caused by the insensitivity of legal scholars to historical change. Modern scholars who contemptuously blame the Roman system of legal classification for not clearly identifying rights, he observed, fail to understand that "the legal idea of a Right was very slowly evolved." He condemned those scholars for "in effect taxing persons who had not yet attained to the conception of a legal Right, with not having anticipated methods of classification of which Rights are the basis."[130]

Maine viewed his new work as contributing to the "comparative jurisprudence" he had begun in *Ancient Law*.[131] While often praising recent German scholarship on the history of European landownership, he complained that "the Historical Method in their hands has not yet been quickened and corrected by the Comparative Method." In particular, the Germans had failed to recognize that the current law of India reveals the ancient law of Europe.[132] "The great difference between the East and West," Maine wrote in a typically catchy phrase, "is that the Past of the West lives in the Present of the East."[133] Echoing his connection between law and philology in *Ancient Law*, Maine claimed that these German legal scholars remained "condemned for awhile to struggle with the difficulties which embarrassed" philologists before they recognized the importance of Sanskrit in understanding the history of Indo-European languages.[134] In addition, as in *Ancient Law*, Maine repeatedly emphasized the movement from collective to individual ownership of land in various societies.[135]

While reiterating many of his key themes from *Ancient Law*, Maine added some qualifications. He indicated limits to his analogy between comparative philology and comparative jurisprudence. Stressing that comparative jurisprudence was far from matching the accomplishments of comparative philology, Maine explained this distance in part by pointing out that society and law are

---

[127] Sir Henry Sumner Maine, Dissertations on Early Law and Custom (London: John Murray, 1907), p. 302.

[128] Id. at 360.

[129] Id. at 361.

[130] Id. at 366.

[131] Sir Henry Sumner Maine, Lectures on the Early History of Institutions (Port Washington, N.Y.: Kennikat Press, Inc., 1966) (reprint of 7th ed., 1914), p. 21.

[132] Sir Henry Sumner Maine, Village-Communities in the East and West (London: John Murray, 7th ed., 1913).

[133] Maine, supra note 127, at 131.

[134] Maine, supra note 132, at 224.

[135] Id. at 81, 141, 227; Maine, supra note 127, at 352.

much more influenced by external circumstances irreducible to rules than is language. He urged extreme caution in speculating from parallel usages in different societies[136] even as he continued and encouraged others to do so. Despite the difficulties in applying the comparative method to law, he remained committed to the effort because the results, if successful, would be so significant.[137] Maine similarly warned against the dangers of parallels between language and race. In *Ancient Law*, he had referred to the "Indo-European stock"[138] in explaining that he was following the comparative methods philologists had applied to their languages. In his later work, he emphasized that philologists had modified their earlier assumption that people speaking similar languages shared a common racial descent, now believing it no more than "approximately true"[139] and subject to "considerable qualification."[140] He pointed out that the Irish are a very mixed race and that the Italians can only be called a race "by a perversion of language."[141] His experience in India taught him to be on "guard against certain extravagances in the modern theory of Race" and to "be slow to believe that identity of language and religion necessarily imply identity of ethnic origin."[142]

Maine, moreover, tempered his frequent assertions in *Ancient Law* about the ubiquity of the patriarchal family in primitive societies. He discussed respectfully and at length the subsequent challenges to his patriarchal theory by J. F. McLennan and L. H. Morgan.[143] Recognizing recent scholarly disagreements about the historical role of the patriarchal family, he acknowledged in 1875 that all societies may not have emerged from it.[144] Eight years later, he even asserted that many societies did not. "There are unquestionably many assemblages of savage men so devoid of some of the characteristic features of Patriarchalism," he confidently proclaimed, "that it seems a gratuitous hypothesis to assume that they had passed through it." He also admitted, in tension with his treatment of the patriarchal family in *Ancient Law*, that some societies approached the condition of the patriarchal family rather than emerged from it.[145] Yet he continued to insist, as in *Ancient Law*, that whenever a joint family or village community appeared in an Aryan society, a patriarchal family preceded it.[146] He also maintained that all patriarchal families, whenever or however they appeared, had "the same character and composition."[147]

---

[136] Maine, supra note 132, at 8–9.
[137] Id. at 230.
[138] Maine, supra note 7, at 72.
[139] Sir Henry Sumner Maine, Popular Government (London: John Murray, 1886) (2d ed.), p. 27.
[140] Maine, supra note 132, at 209.
[141] Maine, supra note 139, at 27.
[142] Maine, supra note 132, at 128.
[143] Maine, supra note 127, at 195; see generally id. at 192–228.
[144] Maine, supra note 131, at 118, 310.
[145] Maine, supra note 127, at 204.
[146] Maine, supra note 131, at 118.
[147] Id. at 310.

In much of his later work, Maine broadened his use of the comparative historical method by citing examples from more societies than in *Ancient Law*, particularly the Teutonic and the Irish. While continuing to claim that the current law of India reflects the ancient law of other Indo-European societies in the West that had progressed from this earlier stage,[148] Maine added many examples from early Teutonic and Irish law. Maine referred frequently to German scholars, particularly Maurer, Nasse, and Sohm, for his evidence about early Teutonic law. Crediting Sohm for the first full interpretation of Salic law,[149] he asserted that its appearance in the fifth century was "the oldest of the Teutonic codes, the oldest portrait of Germanic institutions drawn by a German."[150] The structure of Salic law, he observed, demonstrates that it did not derive from the latest periods of Roman law, which preceded it in time, but was analogous to the early Roman law, which was almost certainly unknown in the fifth century and from which it could not have borrowed directly.[151] As he drew connections among different Indo-European societies, Maine concluded that Maurer's description of the Teutonic township could "pass for an account, so far as it goes, of an Indian village."[152] The resemblances of the Indian village community and the Teutonic township, he insisted, "are much too strong and numerous to be accidental."[153]

Lectures on the Early History of Institutions focused on ancient Irish law, otherwise known as Brehon law,[154] as another "authentic monument of a very ancient group of Aryan institutions."[155] Stressing that ancient Irish law, unlike the law of the European continent, developed independently of Roman law, and perhaps earlier,[156] Maine proclaimed it "wonderful" that it contained "some very strong analogies to another set of derivative Aryan usages, the Hindoo law, which was similarly developed."[157] Consistent with his comparative approach, he maintained that the student of either Irish or Indian law had to take account of both systems.[158] He also compared ancient Irish with ancient German laws and institutions, concluding that the Irish were "nothing more" than the German "at an earlier stage of barbarism."[159] This similarity, he emphasized, "is almost enough by itself to destroy those reckless theories of race which assert an original, inherent difference of idea and usage between Teuton and Celt."[160] Maine found ancient Irish law particularly useful in

[148] Maine, supra note 132, at 53, 62, 148, 154.
[149] Maine, supra note 131, at 269, 271.
[150] Maine, supra note 127, at 167.
[151] Id. at 373.
[152] Maine, supra note 132, at 113.
[153] Id. at 12.
[154] Maine, supra note 131, at vii.
[155] Id. at 11.
[156] Id. at 20.
[157] Id. at 11–12.
[158] Id. at 12.
[159] Maine, supra note 127, at 179.
[160] Maine, supra note 131, at 282.

revealing an Aryan race that, while settled on the land, retained many concepts and rules from an earlier period when kinship, rather than land, was the foundation of "social union." The role of kinship, he added, explains the "natural communism" of their primitive forms of property.[161]

Throughout his later work, Maine connected his comparative analysis of ancient Indo-European law with the history of English law, which he had essentially ignored in *Ancient Law*. He stressed that there is no country whose legal history is more obscure than England.[162] As partial explanations, he cited the scarcity of records and the extraordinary technicality of English law.[163] Yet employing the comparative historical method he endorsed, he indicated that the evidence of other ancient Aryan societies, particularly the Indian and the Teutonic, provided insight into ancient English law.[164] Maine also claimed that Teutonic law, in addition to being a source of information about ancient law in all Aryan societies, including England, had a direct impact on the development of English law. While acknowledging that Roman law "influenced the stubborn body of Germanic custom prevailing in Great Britain,"[165] he stressed it had much less impact in England than in continental Europe. Roman law became ascendant over ancient customs on the Continent,[166] but not in England, which escaped the "overwhelming disturbance" produced by Roman law in other Germanic societies.[167] Even though the origins of the English common law remained obscure in many ways, Maine asserted confidently that "it was undoubtedly in the main a version of Germanic usage, generalised by the King's courts and justices."[168]

Relying especially on a monograph by Nasse, Maine asserted that "vestiges" or "traces" of the ancient Teutonic law regulating collective property in village communities "survived" in England even after the Norman Conquest.[169] Such evidence, Maine stressed, undermined the popular English theory that through feudalism in general, or the Norman Conquest in particular, all land in England was confiscated and became the property of lords.[170] Maine also emphasized that the crucial role of the king in the administration of justice in England derived from ancient Teutonic law.[171] Salic law revealed "the first feeble and uncertain steps of royal authority towards the ascendency which in all Teutonic countries it has gained over the primitive popular justice." Although the king appeared to have no function in the Salic popular court, called the Hundred Court, he had the "ultimate residual authority" to enforce the court's

[161] Id. at 188.
[162] Maine, supra note 127, at 167.
[163] Maine, supra note 132, at 168–9.
[164] Id. at 11–12, 61–2, 147–8, 215; Maine, supra note 131, at 270.
[165] Maine, supra note 131, at 21.
[166] Maine, supra note 127, at 189–90.
[167] Id. at 167.
[168] Id. at 190.
[169] Maine, supra note 132, at 77, 85; Maine, supra note 131, at 1–4.
[170] Maine, supra note 132, at 84.
[171] Maine, supra note 127, at 167.

judgments.[172] Royal authority in the popular courts grew over time, profoundly changing the old system of popular justice into one in which deputies of the king became powerful, first "insisting that justice be administered in the King's name, and finally administering a simpler justice of their own amid the ruins of the ancient judicial structures fallen everywhere into disrepute and decay."[173] While identifying the English jury as "a survival of the old popular justice" of ancient Teutonic tribunals,[174] a "representative system that has done so much to continue the English form of Teutonic liberty,"[175] Maine emphasized the power of the king to compel attendance of people summoned.

In struggles between the king and the ancient popular courts, Maine added, the king gained power by moving around the country carrying royal justice with him. Instead of the litigant going to the king, as in the past, the king went to the litigant.[176] Maine observed that the justice dispensed by the itinerant king had numerous advantages over the popular courts. Because the king moved with his officials and military, the justice he dispensed was executed promptly, based on expertise, and irresistible. Less subject to the corruption that often infected the popular courts, the king's justice also reformed the law by simplifying its procedures and relaxing its severity.[177] As English society became wealthier and more complex, the king could no longer provide individual justice,[178] leading to the provision in the Magna Carta that "the Common Pleas shall no longer follow the King." This provision, Maine concluded, "marked a revolution in judicature" and established the modern English judicial system.[179] Maine acknowledged that much later, during the Tudor and Stuart period, royal justice was viewed as a barrier to popular liberty and reached its nadir with the Star Chamber.[180] "The royal judicial authority was once the most valuable and indeed the most indispensable of all reforming agencies," Maine concluded, "but at length its course was run." Throughout the civilized world, elected legislatures, which Maine called "the children of the British Parliament," assumed what was once the role of the king.[181] He took great pleasure that in his own day the English were passing on to India, the long stagnant society from which he derived evidence of ancient law in the West, the principle of progress they had been fortunate to experience over centuries. He was confident that similar progress could occur in India[182] and referred to the "marvellous destiny which has brought one of

[172] Id. at 171.
[173] Id. at 172.
[174] Id. at 175.
[175] Id. at 176.
[176] Id. at 178.
[177] Id. at 185–6.
[178] Id. at 189.
[179] Id. at 188.
[180] Id. at 190–1.
[181] Id. at 191.
[182] Maine, supra note 132, at 230.

the youngest branches of the greatest family of mankind from the uttermost ends of the earth to renovate and educate the eldest."[183]

While discussing the history of English law, Maine included other observations, often in passing, that subsequent important scholars elaborated. For example, he asserted the probability that "our English law of Evidence would never have come into existence if we had not continued much longer than other Western societies the separation of the province of the judge from the province of the jury."[184] The significance of the law of actions in the early English courts, he also concluded, demonstrates that "substantive law has at first the look of being gradually secreted in the interstices of procedure; and the early lawyer can only see the law through the envelope of its technical forms."[185]

Maine described his last book, *Popular Government*, as an effort to apply to "political institutions" the "Historical Method" that he first used in *Ancient Law* to study the "the private laws and institutions of Mankind." Just as a priori theories about the state of nature had obstructed his effort in *Ancient Law*, Maine observed, so they obstructed his attempt to extend the historical method to political institutions. He ascribed these theories in the political sphere to Rousseau's belief that democracy prevailed in the state of nature, making every other form of government illegitimate.[186] But just as evidence from ancient societies had enabled Maine to challenge a priori theories in *Ancient Law*, he asserted that during the previous fifty years many facts from the experience of countries throughout the civilized world enabled him to assess current a priori theories about "Popular Government as it verges on Democracy."[187] Based especially on "the terrible events and bitter disappointments" in the wake of the French Revolution,[188] Maine was convinced that democracy threatened civilization and progress.

Maine wrote at length about the United States as a country that avoided the excesses of democracy better than his own country, thanks largely to its written Constitution. The language of the Constitution establishing the presidency, he asserted, made clear that the office had powers similar to those exercised by kings in Europe, particularly the British king.[189] Indeed, Maine believed that by the late nineteenth century, the American president had become much more powerful than the increasingly diminished British king.[190] Moreover, the written United States Constitution, with its stringent process for amendment, created a welcome barrier to the kind of new legislation that had transformed the very foundations of the political system in Great Britain.[191] Maine also emphasized

---

[183] Id. at 294.
[184] Id. at 302.
[185] Maine, supra note 127, at 389.
[186] Maine, supra note 139, at v–vii.
[187] Id. at ix.
[188] Id. at 127.
[189] Id. at 211.
[190] Id. at 214.
[191] Id. at 240.

the importance of the clause in the Constitution that prohibited states from impairing the obligation of contracts. This clause, as helpfully extended by the Supreme Court's decision in the famous *Dartmouth College* case, "is the bulwark of American individualism against democratic impatience and socialistic fantasy." Under its interpretation by the federal courts, "certain communistic schemes of American origin, which are said to have become attractive to the English labouring classes because they are supposed to proceed from the bosom of a democratic community, have about as much prospect of obtaining practical realization in the United States as the vision of a Cloud-Cuckoo-borough to be built by the birds between earth and sky."[192] Maine did not cite the federal court decisions upon which he based this conclusion.

Ironically, just five years after Maine published *Popular Government*, the American scholar Christopher Tiedeman used the *Dartmouth College* case and its aftermath to illustrate his conception of "the unwritten constitution of the United States," by which courts transform the written meaning of the Constitution in response to changes in public opinion. This conception mirrored Maine's own discussion in *Ancient Law* of legal fictions to close the gap between existing law and transformed social views in a progressive society. Citing many decisions, Tiedeman maintained that subsequent case law had "substantially modified, if not abrogated altogether"[193] the *Dartmouth College* case by allowing states to exercise their "police power" to invalidate contracts. This was precisely the outcome Maine had assumed was precluded by the written United States Constitution and the *Dartmouth College* case.

Maine's Legacy

Maine's work, particularly *Ancient Law*, the book that catapulted him into international prominence, received widespread critical attention from his contemporaries and from later generations. Admirers endorsed historical jurisprudence as a welcome new alternative to the a priori theorizing of earlier jurisprudential schools. They applauded Maine's emphasis on the relationship between past and present law and his inductive use of history to identify broad patterns and processes in the evolution of legal ideas. By making the historical method comparative, they added, Maine avoided the parochialism of the German historical school. Many commented on Maine's brilliant style and his powers of synthesis and generalization, which made his work accessible to a broad audience. Even while acknowledging the many criticisms of the book that accumulated over the years, his defenders observed that Maine deserved substantial credit for inspiring this corrective scholarship and for helping to found the new disciplines of anthropology and sociology.[194]

---

[192] Id. at 248.

[193] Christopher G. Tiedeman, The Unwritten Constitution of the United States (Buffalo, N.Y.: William S. Hein & Company, 1974) (reprint of 1890 ed.), p. 66.

[194] Burrow, supra note 3, at 153–4, 235–7; Vinogradoff, supra note 3, at 139–40; Feaver, supra note 1, pp. xv–xvi, 133; Vinogradoff-Maine, supra note 3, at 121, 129–30; Pollock, supra note 1,

The criticisms of Maine's work frequently reflected the same qualities that others praised. Critics condemned it for being antiquarian rather than theoretical and systematic, for examining the origins of current rules rather than analyzing whether these rules made sense. They objected to its sweeping and unjustified generalizations, its inaccuracy and inattention to detail, and its allusive and vague style. They reproached Maine as a vulgarizer who lacked erudition and who limited his crude comparisons to Aryan societies. They disagreed with virtually all of his conclusions, including his patriarchal theory of primitive society, his description of Roman law, his assumption that the mechanisms of Roman law applied to the history of the English common law, and his treatment of Indian society as static.[195] Many who accepted Maine's general method of historical jurisprudence objected that he artificially froze legal evolution at the stage of individualism. They maintained instead that law would continue to evolve toward a more progressive collectivism.[196]

Most of Maine's contemporaries and immediate successors regarded his strengths as much more significant than his weaknesses. The advantages of Maine's historical approach to legal analysis, they particularly stressed, far outweighed the many errors produced by his inattention to detail and his tendency to overgeneralize.[197] Such errors could be corrected by additional, if often more prosaic, scholarship. Essays written by Frederick Pollock and Paul Vinogradoff, two of the most important English legal historians in the generation following Maine, vividly expressed these views while defending his work and praising his legacy.

In an introduction to an edition of *Ancient Law* published in 1906, Pollock called it "a classical text" whose fundamental ideas had been largely confirmed and supplemented by more than a generation of additional research and speculation. Pollock acknowledged that some of this additional scholarship had also revealed flaws in Maine's work, but he emphasized that the subsequent discovery of error is inevitable in "progressive" disciplines such as history and law. According to Pollock, the "wonder is not that Maine's results ... should

---

at xiv, xvi–xvii; Alan D. J. Macfarlane, Some Contributions of Maine to History and Anthropology, in Diamond, supra note 1, pp. 111, 111–19; letter from Oliver Wendell Holmes, Jr. to Frederick Pollock (March 4, 1888), in Holmes-Pollock Letters, vol. 1, supra note 3, at 31.

[195] Burrow, supra note 3, at 153; Feaver, supra note 1, at 56–7, 136–43; Pollock, supra note 1, at xii; Vinogradoff-Maine, supra note 3, at 120, 130; Woodard, supra note 2, at 219; Macfarland, supra note 194, at 119; C. A. Bayly, Maine and Change in Nineteenth-Century India, in Diamond, supra note 1, at 389, 395; Adam Kuper, The Rise and Fall of Maine's Patriarchal Society, in Diamond, supra note 1, at 99, 105–8; letter from Holmes to Pollock, supra note 194; letter from Oliver Wendell Holmes, Jr. to Lady Pollock (July 2, 1895), in Holmes-Pollock Letters, vol. 1, supra note 3, at 58; letter from Frederick Pollock to Oliver Wendell Holmes, Jr. (February 13, 1922), in Holmes-Pollock Letters, vol. 2, supra note 3, at 89.

[196] Feaver, supra note 1, at 120–1; Macfarlane, supra note 194, at 139; John Burrow and Stefan Collini, The Clue to the Maze: The Appeal of the Comparative Method, in Stefan Collini, Donald Winch, John Burrows, That Noble Science of Politics: A Study in Nineteenth-Century Intellectual History (Cambridge University Press, 1983), pp. 208, 218–19.

[197] Burrow, supra note 3, at 153.

stand in need of some correction, but that, in fact, they need so little as they do."[198] To those who challenged Maine's originality, Pollock responded that Maine's views had become so widely accepted that many forgot how novel they were when he published *Ancient Law*. According to Pollock, Maine "did nothing less than create the natural history of law."[199] Maine "showed, on the one hand, that legal ideas and institutions have a real course of development as much as the genera and species of living creatures, and in every stage of that development have their normal characters; on the other hand, he made it clear that these processes deserve and require distinct study, and cannot be treated as mere incidents in the general history of the societies where they occur."[200] To those, particularly in continental Europe, who claimed that Maine never developed a symmetrical system of legal analysis, Pollock replied that Maine never promised such a system and that his development of historical jurisprudence was ambition enough.[201] And to those who faulted *Ancient Law* for its lack of technical detail and accuracy, Pollock emphasized that Maine never pretended to be a "technical antiquary" and recalled Maine's introductory statement that he did not intend his book to be a treatise about the Roman law on which he so heavily drew. Rather, Maine relied on previous work in legal history, which primarily focused on Roman rather than English law, "to disclose the right lines of antiquarian research, and rescue it from the state of mere dilettante curiosity."[202]

Pollock expressed similar views about Maine in correspondence with Holmes. He wrote to Holmes that very few people in England knew about "the historical school before *Ancient Law* was published."[203] About the same time that he was writing his introduction to *Ancient Law*, Pollock gave Holmes his balanced but essentially favorable view of Maine. Pollock acknowledged that Maine, relying on "imperfect materials," had made "quite odd mistakes in detail" and often viewed historical "processes as shorter and simpler than they are." But Maine's "larger views and instincts," Pollock immediately added, "are almost always sound – more than once right against what seemed then the best information."[204]

Vinogradoff used the occasion of his inaugural lecture in 1904 as the Corpus Chair of Jurisprudence at Oxford, the chair first held by Maine and then by Pollock,[205] to assess Maine's work. Vinogradoff reported that Maine had been one of his greatest intellectual influences, even though he had only

---

[198] Pollock, supra note 1, at xi–xii.
[199] Id. at xv.
[200] Id. at xiv.
[201] Id. xii–xiii.
[202] Id. at xix.
[203] Letter from Frederick Pollock to Oliver Wendell Holmes, Jr. (February 16, 1923), in Holmes-Pollock Letters, vol. 2, supra note 3, at 112.
[204] Letter from Frederick Pollock to Oliver Wendell Holmes, Jr. (July 15, 1905), in Holmes-Pollock Letters, vol. 1, supra note 3, at 121.
[205] Vinogradoff-Maine, supra note 3, at 119.

recently emigrated from Russia to England. Acknowledging that many of his contemporaries superciliously condemned Maine's "lack of erudition and accuracy" and the "allusiveness and vagueness" of his writings, Vinogradoff dismissed "such cheap criticisms" as failing to account for Maine's impact as a "potentate" in European thought.[206] For Vinogradoff, Maine's attempt to connect past with present law,[207] to undertake "historical investigation of the growth of legal rules and ideas,"[208] revealed his central importance.

Like Pollock, Vinogradoff acknowledged that Maine was not a builder of systematic theories in the continental manner. Vinogradoff praised Maine's lack of system as a virtue, which avoided the unfortunate tendency among Germans and French to build systems that lost contact with reality. The Germans too often exaggerated "their unrivalled learning" into "a phantastic region of their own, where they accumulate and dispose their materials according to requirements of speculation without much regard for the facts of life." The French weakness for formalism exaggerated lucidity and order in ways that obscured the complexity of reality.[209] Vinogradoff conceded that Maine did not closely study historical evidence or secondary scholarship.[210] Nor was his work sufficiently comparative, for by limiting his research to Aryan societies Maine failed to recognize that not all primitive societies had been patriarchal.[211] Vinogradoff admonished his contemporaries "to be more careful in the analysis of single cases, more critical in our historical investigations, less prompt to generalize and less sanguine of getting quickly to ultimate results in the shape of laws of development." But Vinogradoff declared himself to be Maine's follower in the field of historical jurisprudence[212] and praised Maine's work, "which will ever stand as a monument of creative thought, and an incentive to further study."[213]

Maine's contemporaries used his theories for vastly different political and intellectual purposes. Advocates of laissez-faire individualism invoked his generalization about the movement of progressive societies from status to contract as a novel justification for opposing government restrictions on freedom of contract. Already convinced that government intervention in the economy was bad policy, they read Maine as arguing that it was more fundamentally a misguided attempt to alter the natural course of history and to reverse the fortunate progress that only a few societies had managed to achieve. They ignored Maine's qualification that progress had "hitherto" been from status to contract, a qualification that left open the possibility that the progression

---

[206] Id. at 120.
[207] Id. at 121.
[208] Id. at 127.
[209] Id. at 120.
[210] Id. at 129.
[211] Id. at 130.
[212] Id. at 132.
[213] Id. at 129.

of the past might not necessarily continue in the future. Rather, they turned a historical generalization into an iron law of legal evolution.[214]

Others accepted Maine's historical theories of progressive legal evolution but refused to freeze the evolutionary process at the current individualistic stage of development. In an essay published in 1871, John Stuart Mill remarked that Maine's historical approach in *Ancient Law* "is a most powerful solvent of a large class of conservative prejudices," although Mill added that Maine did not have any such intent in writing the book. Mill asserted, as had Maine, that ideas evolved from the past may not be suited to the changed circumstances of the present and future. Seeing no necessity to prefer individualism to collectivism, Mill suggested that efforts to reconvert property into collective forms would be appropriate.[215] Karl Marx, unsurprisingly, criticized Maine for not recognizing that in progressive societies individualism would be superseded by collectivism, for not being enough of an evolutionist to recognize that evolution would reach later and better stages.[216] Vinogradoff saw the "collectivist tendencies in modern society" as a new stage of evolution.[217] And Dicey, whose dislike of collectivism rivaled Maine's, reluctantly reached the conclusion that, beginning in 1865, collectivism had superseded individualism in England.[218] In legislation such as the Workman's Compensation Act of 1897, Dicey and others saw a reversion from contract to status.[219]

Over time, Maine had much less influence on jurisprudence and legal history, his main areas of interest, than on the emerging fields of sociology and anthropology, which his own work helped initiate.[220] The great German sociologist Ferdinand Tonnies observed that his famous distinction between Gemeinschaft and Gesellschaft bore a close similarity to Maine's earlier distinction between status and contract.[221] Tonnies's survey of the history of German sociology, moreover, dealt at length with Maine's work.[222] At a conference in 1988 to mark the centenary of Maine's death, eminent sociologists and anthropologists emphasized his lasting importance. According to Edward Shils, "No writer has entered, so penetratingly and so pervasively, into the fundamental outlook of sociologists of the twentieth century as has Maine."[223] Alan Macfarlane observed that anthropologists, even while rejecting many of Maine's specific views, especially his description of primitive society as patriarchal, have recognized many of his ideas about kinship as the foundation of modern social

[214] Feaver, supra note 1, at 55; Stein, supra note 3, at 112–14; Woodard, supra note 2, at 226–7.

[215] Feaver, supra note 1, at 120–1.

[216] Macfarlane, supra note 194, at 139.

[217] Burrow and Collini, supra note 196, at 219.

[218] Feaver-Victorian Values, supra note 1, at 47–8.

[219] Feaver, supra note 1, at 54.

[220] Feaver, supra note 1, at 55; Diamond, supra note 2, at 1–3; Woodard, supra note 2, at 228.

[221] Peter Stein, Roman Law in European History (Cambridge University Press, 1999), p. 127; Edward Shils, Henry Sumner Maine in the Tradition of the Analysis of Society, in Diamond, supra note 1, pp. 143, 153.

[222] Burrow and Collini, supra note 196, at 210 n. 1.

[223] Shils, supra note 221, at 144.

anthropology.[224] More generally, by comparing his own society with very different societies in both the remote past and the present, Maine displayed a "wide and relativistic mind that can suspend moralizing," a virtue that "foreshadowed much that was best in the anthropology of the next century."[225] Maine was "able to stand back and question his own society's assumptions, and to see the apparently natural as cultural," the main task of contemporary anthropology.[226]

Within jurisprudence and legal history, by contrast, Maine's dominant position waned, eventually reduced to insignificance after World War I. The same generalizations that provided fertile ground for anthropologists and sociologists, even as they challenged many of his conclusions, seemed dated and even unprofessional as legal historians, like historians generally, increasingly stressed the importance of historical detail and particularity based on careful attention to primary sources. Even *Ancient Law*, Maine's most influential book, lost its place as a standard text and was no longer read by law students.[227] Yet Maine continued to influence legal scholarship for decades. He had important successors, who often acknowledged their intellectual debts to him. Recent scholars have claimed that Pollock and Vinogradoff "virtually lived off his intellectual capital,"[228] and Vinogradoff himself wrote that "the whole of my generation of students of law and history have had to deal directly or indirectly with the ideas propagated by him or similar to his."[229]

As subsequent chapters of this book will elaborate, Maine had a major impact on American legal scholars in the last three decades of the nineteenth century. The historical method that he contrasted to prior schools of analytical jurisprudence and natural law dominated American legal scholarship. Henry Adams, who initiated the "scientific" study of legal history in the United States, wrote to Maine that he took *Ancient Law* as his starting point. Adams encouraged his students to challenge Maine's theories through their own studies in the history of English law.[230] The essays published by Adams and his students prominently disputed Maine's conclusion in *Ancient Law* that the modern state developed from the patriarchal family. Bigelow described himself as a follower of the historical school founded by Maine.[231] While treating the English law of evidence as "the child of the jury,"[232] Thayer acknowledged that Maine had

---

[224] Macfarlane, supra note 194, at 111–18.

[225] Id. at 137.

[226] Id. at 136.

[227] Cocks, supra note 30, at 95–9; William Twining, Maine and Legal Education: A Comment, in Diamond, supra note 1, pp. 209, 209–10, 215–16.

[228] Burrow and Collini, supra note 196, at 210.

[229] Vinogradoff-Maine, supra note 3, at 119.

[230] Letter from Henry Adams to Henry Maine (February 10, 1875), in H. D. Cater, Henry Adams and His Friends; A Collection of His Unpublished Letters (Boston: Houghton Mifflin Company, 1947), p. 63.

[231] Melville M. Bigelow, A Scientific School of Legal Thought, 17 Green Bag 1 (1905).

[232] James Bradley Thayer, A Preliminary Treatise on Evidence at the Common Law (Boston: Little, Brown, and Company, 1898), p. 47.

made this point thirty years before in the context of discussing how the English might adapt their system of evidence in governing India.[233] Thayer's own emphasis on the importance of royal power in the development of the jury, he recognized, illustrated Maine's generalization that in early periods the king was the great reformer of the law.[234] Holmes, who was famous for exaggerating his own originality, minimized Maine's influence on him, but both contemporaries and subsequent scholars have convincingly observed substantial similarities in their historical analysis of law, and even the extent to which *The Common Law* reproduced the organizational structure of *Ancient Law*.[235]

Although Hammond never wrote the book he contemplated on the history of the common law, he reviewed *Ancient Law* at length in 1868, before Adams and his American successors began publishing their original contributions to English legal history. "It has often been said of late," his first sentence declared, "that the characteristic feature of the nineteenth century, is the substitution of the historic method of study for the dogmatic, in all the sciences which relate to human life or action."[236] After bemoaning the delayed "acceptance of the historical method in our jurisprudence,"[237] Hammond praised Maine for "his very great service" in remedying that defect. Despite this initial praise, Hammond proceeded to criticize *Ancient Law* at length, both for its treatment of specific topics, such as primogeniture and occupancy, and, more importantly, for its broader conclusions. He asserted that the title "was too extensive." Rather than "a general treatise on Ancient Law, we have a series of essays on the light thrown upon that subject by the history of Roman jurisprudence." Roman law, Hammond emphasized, "does not alone constitute Ancient Law." Even in discussing Roman law, moreover, Maine relied too uncritically on recent secondary sources. Although Maine himself realized that "the seventeenth and eighteenth century reads Anglo-Saxon jurisprudence by its own theory and preconceived notions," he did not apply the same scrutiny when he relied on "the meagre second-hand accounts" available on the history of Roman law.[238] *Ancient Law*, Hammond observed, was "acute rather than comprehensive." Granting "we have no right to expect that the first essay in a new field shall have all the thoroughness and completeness of an elaborate treatise upon a familiar science," Hammond nevertheless concluded that "the necessary imperfection and sketchiness of the present work are brought into contrast by the promise of the title."[239]

Writing at the very end of the nineteenth century, Frederic Maitland, the great and famously generous English legal historian, was atypically

---

[233] Id. at 508.

[234] Id. at 509.

[235] David M. Rabban, From Maine to Maitland via America, 68 Cambridge Law Journal 410, 426–8 (2009).

[236] William Gardiner Hammond, Ancient Law, 2 Western Jurist 1 (1868).

[237] Id. at 3.

[238] Id. at 8.

[239] Id. at 10.

critical of Maine. He privately criticized Maine's sloppiness and unsupported overgeneralizations[240] while devoting much of his own work to the patient excavation of the original sources for English legal history that Maine ignored. In print, Maitland challenged, both directly and indirectly, many of Maine's conclusions. Most dramatically, he reversed Maine's most famous theory, detecting a movement from individualism to collectivism in English legal history.[241]

Much more significant than Maitland's disapproval, legal scholars in both England and the United States generally lost interest in historical approaches to law. In England, Vinogradoff, Maine's last successor, did not leave an intellectual legacy in a later generation of scholars,[242] and Bryce, in a book published in 1921, essentially wrote a mournful epitaph for the comparative and historical approach that Maine pioneered and epitomized.[243] In the United States during the decade before World War I, Roscoe Pound effectively disparaged "historical jurisprudence" while promoting "sociological jurisprudence" as a promising new approach to legal scholarship. This movement away from history in legal scholarship reflected a broader trend in many academic fields on both sides of the Atlantic. For many scholars at the turn of the twentieth century, historical analysis, especially evolutionary theories of historical change, no longer seemed to explain the world they studied.

---

[240] Letter from Frederic Maitland to Frederick Pollock (January 21, 1901), in The Letters of Frederic William Maitland (Cambridge, Mass.: Harvard University Press, 1965) (C. H. S. Fifoot, ed.), p. 222.

[241] Frederick Pollock and Frederic William Maitland, The History of English Law before the Time of Edward I (Cambridge University Press, 1899) (2d ed.), vol. I, pp. 616–17, 620, 627–8, 630, 687–8; vol. 2, pp. 240, 245, 402, 433.

[242] Cocks, supra note 30, at 188.

[243] Burrow and Collini, supra note 196, at 245–6.

PART II

THE HISTORICAL TURN IN AMERICAN LEGAL SCHOLARSHIP

V

Henry Adams and His Students

The Origins of Professional Legal History in America

Original scholarship in legal history by Americans began with the publication in 1876 of *Essays in Anglo-Saxon Law*, written by Henry Adams and three of his advanced students at Harvard, Henry Cabot Lodge, Ernest Young, and J. Laurence Laughlin. During an understandably overlooked period of his varied and productive career, Adams taught history at Harvard from 1870 until he resigned in 1877 to pursue a more active and cosmopolitan life in Washington, D.C. Neither Adams himself nor subsequent biographers and scholars attached much significance to his few years as a Harvard professor.[1] Compared to his subsequent multi-volume works of American history and especially to his great books, *The Education of Henry Adams* and *Mont Saint Michel and Chartres*, his brief career at Harvard seems minor. For an understanding of the history of legal history in the United States, however, the years Adams spent at Harvard were crucial. During this period, Adams and his students virtually created the field and provided a model for subsequent legal historians in England as well as in their own country. Most importantly, Adams applied the methods and the findings of German legal historians to the study of Anglo-American law while emphasizing its Teutonic origins.

Between his graduation from Harvard College in 1858 and his appointment to the Harvard faculty by President Eliot in 1870, Adams studied law in Germany and spent many years in England. During a year's interlude of travel after joining the Harvard faculty, he met leading historians and legal scholars in Germany and England. Throughout this period, he read extensively in both German and English historical and legal scholarship, and as a young professor at Harvard he immersed himself and his students in the primary sources of

[1] For discussions of Adams at Harvard, see Henry Adams, The Education of Henry Adams (New York: Random House, 1931) (original ed. 1918), pp. 291–307; Mark DeWolfe Howe, Justice Oliver Wendell Holmes: The Proving Years 1870–1882 (Cambridge, Mass.: Harvard University Press, 1963), pp. 27, 142–8; Ernest Samuels, The Young Henry Adams (Cambridge, Mass.: Harvard University Press, 1948), pp. 208–18, 245–58, 266–75, 289–93; Gary Wills, Henry Adams and the Making of America (New York: Houghton Mifflin Company, 2005), pp. 87–95.

Anglo-Saxon law. He declared German "scientific" scholarship vastly superior to the mostly insular and amateurish work produced in England, which was constrained by the historical fictions of the English common law and the weaknesses of the English educational system. He praised Maine's *Ancient Law* as a brilliant exception to the poverty of English scholarship. Yet Adams and his students spent much of their energy questioning and refuting many of the central themes in *Ancient Law*. They challenged Maine's reliance on the history of Roman law as the basis for his broad generalizations about stages of legal evolution, particularly his assumption that all societies pass through a stage resembling the patriarchal Roman family before developing the modern state. Much of their work in Anglo-Saxon law emphasized that the Teutonic family structure, taken to England by the Anglo-Saxons, was fundamentally different from the Roman patriarchy. Their *Essays in Anglo-Saxon Law*, published in 1876, asserted the Anglo-Saxon roots of the English common law and of positive English values, including equal rights and democratic government. Though Adams and his students did not pursue legal history after the publication of this volume, their essays laid the foundation for subsequent American scholarship in this field. Research by some of the American legal scholars who followed Adams, particularly Bigelow, Holmes, Thayer, and Ames, contributed to Maitland's great work on the history of English law, as Maitland himself graciously acknowledged.

The Legal Education of Henry Adams

Like many American legal scholars of his generation, Adams studied law in Germany after his graduation from college in the United States. While discussing his negative reaction to his undergraduate years at Harvard College in his autobiographical *The Education of Henry Adams*, Adams reported that from the beginning "he wanted to be done with it." He sought a path into the larger outside world but was dismayed that so many paths "lay mostly through Boston, where he did not want to go." Studying with James Russell Lowell, professor of belles-lettres at Harvard, showed Adams his "first door of escape" from Boston, and that door "led into Germany," where Lowell himself had studied, convinced that Germans had set the highest standards of scholarship.[2] When Adams graduated from Harvard College in 1858, he wrote in his autobiography, his "exceedingly indulgent" parents "dutifully consented" to his request to study civil law at a German university, "although neither he nor they knew what the Civil Law was, or any reason for his studying it."[3] Despite this typically dismissive tone toward his education that Adams took throughout his autobiography, both he and his parents probably had good reasons for his study of civil law in Germany. They were familiar with the importance Henry's great-grandfather, President John Adams, placed on reading civil law in

[2] Adams, supra note 1, at 61.
[3] Id. at 71

its original languages and aware that knowledge of continental civil law would be useful to ambitious American lawyers in their own time, when many were urging the codification of American law on the continental model. Perhaps most importantly, Senator Charles Sumner, a close friend of the Adams family and a man Henry particularly admired, had studied in Europe to prepare for what became an eminent legal career in the United States.[4]

Soon after Adams arrived in Berlin in the fall of 1858, he responded to an inquiry about his plans from his older brother, Charles Francis Adams, Jr. "When I left America," Adams wrote to his brother, "my intention was first to accustom myself to the language, then to join the University and systematically attend lectures on the Civil Law, at the same time taking a Latin tutor and translating Latin into German; and to continue this course in Heidelberg or in Paris or in both."[5] He expected to spend two years in Europe, return to Boston for two years to study law, and then "emigrate" to Saint Louis, where he would practice law and try to resist the traditional tendency of the Adams family "to quit law for politics."[6]

Exposure to the University of Berlin prompted Adams to change his immediate plans. "He had thought Harvard College a torpid school," he wrote in his autobiography, "but it was instinct with life compared with all that he could see of the University of Berlin." The instruction in civil law, he reported, reflected "the lecture system in its deadliest form as it flourished in the thirteenth century." Adams concluded that students could have learned in a day more from books or discussion than they could learn from the mumbling professor in a month. He decided that the study of civil law would be worthless without previous knowledge of the common law, and that a student with a sufficient background in common law "had only to read the Pandects or the commentators at his ease in America, and be his own professor." According to Adams, his "first lecture was his last" at the University of Berlin,[7] although his biographer speculated that Adams exaggerated his absenteeism.[8]

Though quickly abandoning formal legal studies, Adams continued to learn German and to read law. Following the advice of one of his American acquaintances in Berlin, he decided to enroll for three months in a gymnasium attended by much younger students.[9] Both in contemporary letters to his brother and in his subsequent autobiography, Adams reported that the gymnasium and informal conversation with the students had improved his German.[10] He also wrote

[4] Samuels, supra note 1, at 54–5.

[5] Letter from Henry Adams to Charles Francis Adams (November 3, 1858), in Letters of Henry Adams (1858–1891) (Boston: Houghton Mifflin Company, 1930) (W. C. Ford, ed.) [hereinafter Letters], pp. 1, 3.

[6] Id. at 4–5.

[7] Adams, supra note 1, at 75–6.

[8] Samuels, supra note 1, at 56.

[9] Adams, supra note 1, at 77.

[10] Id.; letter from Henry Adams to Charles Francis Adams (February 9, 1859), in Letters, supra note 5, at 14, 15–17.

to his brother that he was reading "a few pages of Roman law every day"[11] and was "going on in a general course of German reading mostly in the constitutional history of various countries." "So far as learning a trade goes," he added, "idle I'm likely to remain. So far as education goes, I consider these two years as the most valuable of my life."[12] When he subsequently claimed that his education in Germany had been "a total failure," that his "only clear gain – his single step to a higher life – came from time wasted; studies neglected; vices indulged; education reversed,"[13] Adams was engaging in the self-deprecatory exaggeration that pervaded his autobiography.

Teaching Medieval History at Harvard

In the summer of 1870, Charles W. Eliot, recently appointed president of Harvard after Adams's father, Charles Francis Adams, declined the position in 1869, offered Henry Adams a position as assistant professor of history. Adams at first declined the offer, but he soon changed his mind and agreed to teach medieval history at Harvard.[14] Explaining his decision to his close English friend, Charles Milnes Gaskell, Adams reported that his father and brothers, as well as Eliot and the dean of Harvard College, Ephraim Gurney, had put great personal pressure on him to accept. In accepting the professorship, Adams also agreed to succeed Gurney as the editor of the *North American Review*. Acknowledging that he was "utterly and grossly ignorant" of medieval history, Adams explained that "I gave the college fair warning of my ignorance, and the answer was that I knew just as much as anyone else in America knew on the subject, and I could teach better than anyone that could be had." Adams recognized that "I am brought in to strengthen the reforming party in the University," led by Eliot, which assured him "of strong backing from above."[15] Soon after his appointment, Adams indicated his commitment to Eliot's reforms by publishing an article in the *North American Review* stating that successful education must "make the scholar its chief object of interest."[16]

As he started teaching, Adams described to friends how hard he was working and how much he was learning by reading heavy history books in German,[17]

---

[11] Letter from Henry Adams to Charles Francis Adams (May 15–17, 1859). in Letters, supra note 5, at 35, 36.

[12] Letter from Henry Adams to Charles Francis Adams (November 23, 1859), in Letters, supra note 5, at 50, 51.

[13] Adams, supra note 1, at 80.

[14] Samuels, supra note 1, at 203–5.

[15] Letter from Henry Adams to Charles Milnes Gaskell (September 29, 1870), in Letters, supra note 5, at 193–5; see Adams, supra note 1, at 293–4.

[16] Samuels, supra note 1, at 213.

[17] Letter from Henry Adams to Henry Lee Higginson (October 24, 1870), in Letters, supra note 5, at 195; letter from Henry Adams to Charles Milnes Gaskell, supra note 15, at 195; letter from Henry Adams to Charles Milnes Gaskell (December 19, 1870), in Letters, supra note 5, at 199–202; letter from Henry Adams to Charles Milnes Gaskell (November 13, 1871), in Letters, supra note 5, at 217; letter from Henry Adams to Charles Milnes Gaskell (December 14, 1871), in Letters, supra note 5, at 218; Adams, supra note 1, at 299–300.

made possible, as he recognized in his autobiography, by "his two lost years of German schooling" after college.[18] Adams derived great satisfaction from his teaching even as he asserted that he returned to Harvard "not so much to teach as to learn."[19] "You would be proud," he wrote to his English friend Gaskell, to know as much as his students had learned about medieval English history, a subject, Adams believed, that was not even taught in England itself.[20] Adams taught lecture courses and seminars, and his teaching was well received, particularly his seminars.[21]

After his wedding in June 1872, Adams and his wife spent a year traveling in Europe. During this time, he met leading historians and legal scholars in Germany and England. In Germany, Adams was particularly interested in Heinrich Rudolph von Gneist, the preeminent European scholar of English constitutional and administrative law, whose work overlapped most with the early English constitutional history Adams was so diligently studying and teaching. A letter from Brunner to Ames that year mentioned that he was looking forward to a prospective visit from Adams.[22] While in England, Adams traveled to Oxford, where he met Stubbs and socialized extensively with Maine.[23] In addition to meeting leading scholars abroad and continuing his reading of their work, Adams did his own original research while in Europe. Soon before returning to the United States, he wrote to his student Henry Cabot Lodge, "I have this year been engaged in investigating and accumulating notes upon some points of early German law, out of which I expect in time to make a pamphlet or small book."[24]

When Maine sent Adams his latest book in February 1875, Adams included in his response a description of one of his courses at Harvard. "I have again this year taken a class through your Ancient Law, encouraging them to dispute, and overthrow if they could, every individual proposition in it." Reassuring Maine "that I only wish I could ever do anything myself that was half as good," Adams added that attacking Maine's opinions "amuses me, and won't hurt you." Next, Adams continued, "we read the Germania," by Tacitus, "and are now half way through the Lex Salica, translating and commenting on every sentence." Reading "everything else they could lay their hands on, including

---

[18] Adams, supra note 1, at 304.

[19] Letter from Adams to Higginson, supra note 15, at 195.

[20] Letter from Henry Adams to Charles Milnes Gaskell (February 13, 1871), in Letters, supra note 5, at 201, 202.

[21] Samuels, supra note 1, at 211–13, 339–41 (listing courses).

[22] Letter from Heinrich Brunner James Barr Ames (April 17, 1872) (James Barr Ames Papers, Harvard Law School Library, Box 1, Folder 7).

[23] Samuels, supra note 1, at 237–41; letter from Henry Adams to Charles Milnes Gaskell (June, 1873), in Letters, supra note 5, at 251; letters from Clover (Mrs. Henry Adams) to Pater (Robert W. Hooper) (June 1, 1873, June 29, 1873, July 11, 1873), in The Letters of Mrs. Henry Adams 1865–1883 (Boston: Little, Brown, and Company, 1936) (Ward Thoron, ed.), pp. 115, 128, 132.

[24] Letter from Henry Adams to Henry Cabot Lodge (June 11, 1873), in Letters, supra note 5, at 252, 254.

much Roman law and other stuff," the students, Adams reported, "are deep in theses on numerous abstruse points, and argue in the lecture room by the hour."[25] Apparently describing the same course in his autobiography, he wrote that he "could only think of law as subject; the Law School as end." The course "began with the beginning, as far as the books showed a beginning in primitive man, and came down through the Salic Franks to the Norman English." "Since no textbooks existed," Adams added, he "refused to profess, knowing no more than his students, and the students read what they pleased and compared their results." Adams considered his pedagogy a triumph. "The boys worked like rabbits, and dug holes all over the field of archaic society; no difficulty stopped them; unknown languages yielded before their attack, and customary law became familiar as the police court." The students learned to "chase an idea, like a hare, through as dense a thicket of obscure facts as they were likely to meet at the bar."[26] Former students recalled that "they read and searched many times the whole collection of Anglo-Saxon laws, and ploughed through 25,000 pages of charters and capitularies in Medieval Latin," in addition to reading primary and secondary sources in German.[27]

Adams best revealed his emerging views on legal history in letters to Henry Cabot Lodge and in reviews of books by German and English scholars in the *North American Review*. Based on his "vague curiosity" about the subject, Lodge had "stumbled" into the undergraduate course Adams taught on medieval history. "For the first time," Lodge recalled in his autobiography, "I got a glimpse of what education might be and I really learned something." Adams "roused the spirit of inquiry and controversy in me, and I was fascinated."[28] Responding to a letter from Lodge in 1872, Adams encouraged his interest in pursuing a career in history. Lodge later wrote that this letter had "a profound effect" at a crucial "turning point of my life."[29] While traveling in Europe in 1872–3, Adams continued to write to Lodge with advice about his career. When Adams returned to Harvard in the fall of 1873, Lodge, who was then attending Harvard Law School, enrolled in his advanced class in medieval institutions and eagerly accepted Adams's offer to become assistant editor of the *North American Review*.[30]

In one of his letters to Lodge, Adams described how his interests had developed from the time Harvard "pitchforked me into medieval history, of which I knew nothing." Knowing nothing did not bother Adams because "it makes little difference what one teaches; the great thing is to train scholars for work, and for that purpose there is no better field than medieval history to future

---

[25] Letter from Henry Adams to Henry Maine (February 10, 1875), in Harold Dean Cater, Henry Adams and His Friends (Boston: Houghton Mifflin Company, 1947), p. 63.

[26] Adams, supra note 1, at 303.

[27] Samuels, supra note 1, at 215.

[28] Henry Cabot Lodge, Early Memories (New York: C. Scribner's Sons, 1913), pp. 186–7.

[29] Id. at 238.

[30] Id. at 238–41; Samuels, supra note 1, at 242–3; John A. Garraty, Henry Cabot Lodge: A Biography (New York: Knopf, 1953), pp. 37–8.

historians." Wanting to "give a practical turn to my men," Adams gave his course "a strong legal bent." From this starting point, he "found at the outset the Family was the centre of early law." From the family, Adams saw various possible

lines of development. The organization of the Family, the law of inheritance, of testaments, of land tenure, of evidence and legal procedure, the relations of the Family to the community, in its different forms of village, county and state, as well as many other parallel lines of study lay open before me and I have only to indicate them to true students whether of law or of history, and let them go to work and develop them.

Adams immediately added that neither he nor anyone else had mastered these subjects. But he suggested that Lodge and Ames, who was then a graduate student at Harvard Law School while teaching undergraduate courses in history, "can win a reputation by following up any one line of investigation." Writing to Lodge from Egypt, Adams indicated that he was eager to hear about the progress of Ames's ongoing research and that he wanted to write to Ames once Adams himself had "got some sort of order into my ideas."[31]

Historical scholarship, Adams advised Lodge, "requires patient study, long labor, and perseverance that knows no limit." Observing that the "Germans have these qualities beyond all other races," Adams encouraged Lodge to learn and use "the German historical method." Although Adams did not consider style a German virtue, he was confident that Lodge could develop it at his leisure.[32] When Lodge wrote to Adams that he was reading Sohm, Adams responded that he should also read other German historians, including von Maurer and Brunner. Disclaiming any intention to "set up the Germans as exclusive models," Adams nevertheless stressed their high scholarly standards. "An ignorant, or a superficial work," he observed, "could hardly come from any distinguished German student," a statement he could not make "for other countries." Turning to the English, he claimed that Freeman, despite his "parade of knowledge," had "never written anything solid." Adams had a higher opinion of Maine, whose work he assigned to students "to admire and to criticize." "I know of no writer," he wrote to Lodge, "who generalizes more brilliantly." "But everyone of his generalizations," he immediately added, "requires a lifetime of work to prove it."[33] Through this comment, Adams clearly indicated his view that Maine himself had not provided such proof.

In addition to German and Latin, Adams encouraged Lodge to learn Anglo-Saxon, which Adams was studying himself and finding "quite amusing."[34] He also suggested that Lodge consult the English Year Books for their possible

---

[31] Letter from Henry Adams to Henry Cabot Lodge (January 2, 1873), in Letters, supra note 5, at 235, 236–7.

[32] Letter from Henry Adams to Henry Cabot Lodge (June 2, 1872), in Letters, supra note 5, at 227, 228.

[33] Letter from Adams to Lodge, supra note 31, at 235–6.

[34] Letter from Henry Adams to Henry Cabot Lodge (June 11, 1873), in Letters, supra note 5, at 252, 253.

insight into Saxon law. Acknowledging that most cases in the Year Books dealt with "modern law," Adams had "glanced over the volumes enough to see that here and there are some very pretty hints" about the earlier Saxon period.[35] Adams wrote to Lodge that any field of legal history is worthy of study, observing in a letter from Luxor that he was tempted to write an essay on Egyptian law and encouraging Lodge to "choose whatever you think best suits your tastes." Yet Adams emphasized in the same letter that "our own law and institutions are what we aim at, and we only take German institutions so far as they throw light on English affairs."[36] Lodge's tastes, in any event, matched Adams's own interest in the early history of English law. When Adams asked Lodge to investigate "the exact procedure both manorial and royal in cases of theft charged as committed in time past" as part of a broader study of "the development of capital jurisdiction,"[37] Lodge responded with notes that delighted Adams, who proposed that Lodge develop his research into a monograph. Adams also encouraged Lodge to undertake further study of the history of procedure, which would "connect the machinery of the state" as well as "illustrate law."[38]

Assessing German and English Scholarship

A series of book reviews by Adams in the *North American Review* more formally elaborated the themes of his letters to Lodge and set forth additional views about legal history. Writing self-confidently about leading European scholars, Adams made clear his preference for German over English scholarship while identifying weaknesses in both. He maintained that Germanic law differed substantially from Roman law and concluded that English law derived primarily from Germanic rather than Roman sources. Like Maine, Adams was interested in the stages of development from primitive to modern law, but he was much less confident than Maine that existing data enabled meaningful conclusions about legal evolution.

Stressing that history is a science, Adams repeatedly criticized the English for not emulating the scientific history practiced in Germany. "A scientific training," he wrote, "is as necessary to the historian as to the mathematician, and it is the misfortune of England that she has never yet had a scientific historical school."[39] Particularly embarrassing for the English, Adams emphasized, German historical science had produced "a mass, one might even say a library,

---

[35] Letter from Henry Adams to Henry Cabot Lodge (June, 1874), in Letters, supra note 5, at 259, 260.

[36] Letter from Adams to Lodge, supra note 31, at 237.

[37] Letter from Henry Adams to Henry Cabot Lodge (Sept, 1874), in Letters, supra note 5, at 262, 263.

[38] Letter from Henry Adams to Henry Cabot Lodge (September 26, 1874), in Letters, supra note 5, at 264.

[39] Henry Adams, Book Review, Stubbs's Constitutional History of England (July 1874) North American Review 233.

of German books, all of which bear more or less directly on the history of England, and none or few of which have ever been utilized for the explanation of that history" by the English themselves.[40] Indeed, little of this outstanding German scholarship had even been translated into English.[41] Adams recognized that German historical scholarship was "undeniably hard reading, even for specialists." Yet he warned that without mastering this scholarship any historian of early English law and society "will throw his labor away."[42]

The great gap between German and English scholarship, Adams believed, had an "obvious explanation" in the different professional backgrounds of the authors. German scholarship was the work "of jurists rather than of historians, and there never has been a time when the training of an English lawyer admitted of the possibility of such speculations." Adams attributed this deficiency to the common-law tradition in England, which he characterized as insular and practical, skeptical of theory, and based on historical fictions. "The whole fabric of the common law," he wrote, "rests on a quantity of assumptions which as history are destitute of any sound basis of fact, and these assumptions have decisively influenced the ideas even of those English historians who, technically speaking, knew no law." Adams maintained that the historical fictions of the common law, which he did not specify, impaired the development of scientific legal history in England as much as the religious assumptions of monks distorted the history they wrote during the Middle Ages. In Germany, by contrast, "the lawyer was also a jurist, and his study of codes, rendered necessary as it was by his situation, has forced him to develop a faculty for comparison and criticism, for minute analysis and sweeping generalization, such as no Englishman, except perhaps Austin and Maine, has ever dared to conceive." Adams conceded that as a legal system, the English common law might be superior to German law, which, in contrast to the "spontaneous and healthy" development of the common law, "may have been warped and biased by its connection with Rome." But for the study of legal history, the English common-law tradition was, Adams felt, an enormous disaster.[43]

Adams was hopeful that this deplorable situation was changing in England. With the old historical school "practically worn out,"[44] Adams saw a "chance that English critical literature will spring into new life, and that English history will perhaps at last be written."[45] In reviewing *The Constitutional History of England in Its Origin and Development* by William Stubbs, Regius Professor of History at Oxford, Adams applauded Stubbs for relying on and acknowledging previous German scholarship even as he complained about Stubbs's

---

[40] Henry Adams, Book Review, Maine's Village Communities (January 1872) North American Review 196, 198.

[41] Henry Adams, Book Review, Sohm's Procedure de la Lex Salica (April 1874) North American Review 416, 417.

[42] Id. at 425.

[43] Adams, supra note 40, at 198–9.

[44] Id. at 196.

[45] Id. at 199.

dull style and insufficient theorizing.[46] He hoped its publication was a sign that Oxford, where the study of English history remained "in comparatively slight esteem, overshadowed as it is by the prescriptive authority of the classics," intended "at last ... to tolerate no longer that indifference which has thus far left the national annals in the hands of Scotchmen or amateurs."[47] Yet even Stubbs limited himself to public law. He did not examine existing German works on early English private law, a subject "destined to remain untouched" in its own country "until Germany has forced England into scholarship."[48]

The work of Henry Maine, Adams repeatedly observed, was a key indication that a new and better historical school was arising in England. In *Ancient Law*, Maine "sketched out with great breadth and boldness one principal path which the new student would be obliged to follow."[49] Maine's great contribution, Adams wrote, was developing the idea of "a science of comparative archaic jurisprudence." Maine conceived this science, sketched its outlines, and "described or divined some portions of its vast domain," combining extensive knowledge and a fascinating imagination with a delightful style.[50] Placing Maine at the same level of intellectual importance as Darwin and Spencer, Adams emphasized his enormous influence on young lawyers and historians.[51] Adams acknowledged the criticisms of Maine's work and freely added his own. "Science has not been idle," Adams wrote in 1875, since Maine published *Ancient Law* in 1861. Many of the opinions Maine provocatively asserted there had been substantially corrected and even refuted by subsequent scholarship. "But all the essentials of the purely historical investigation" that Maine pioneered remained "unchanged and unchangeable." Adams also defended Maine from critics of his frequent speculations, declaring that Maine himself "would certainly be the first to recognize their provisional character." Maine, he wrote, "is too brilliant to be dogmatic."[52]

In his own criticisms of Maine, Adams nevertheless complained that he often advanced theories he did not attempt to prove.[53] Echoing his comment to Lodge that each of Maine's generalizations would take a lifetime to prove, Adams wrote that "without denying the beauty or ingenuity or even the probable truth of Sir Henry's theories, it may be safely said that there is hardly a theory advanced by him which does not require that two or three volumes should be written by way of a preliminary clearing of the ground before it will be possible to arrive at an approximate decision of the point in question."[54]

---

[46] Adams, supra note 39, at 235.

[47] Id. at 233.

[48] Id. at 235.

[49] Adams, supra note 40, at 196–7.

[50] Henry Adams, Book Review, Maine's Early History of Institutions (April 1875) North American Review 432, 438.

[51] Id. at 432.

[52] Id. at 433.

[53] Id. at 436–8.

[54] Id. at 437.

Regarding Maine's provocative theory of successive stages of legal development, Adams emphasized that legal science was "still seeking painfully for the most essential facts," in great contrast to the philologists, who had actually reconstructed the stages of archaic Indo-European language. Until legal scholars actually uncovered and compared ancient legal codes, Adams maintained, Maine's "brilliant hypotheses" remained "hazardous guesses."[55] Adams specifically questioned Maine's conclusions about primogeniture[56] and, most significantly, his assumptions in *Ancient Law* that Roman law was typical of all law[57] and that all societies organized by the family and the tribe before they developed the state.[58]

Adams relied on the findings of German historical scholarship to challenge prevailing English understandings of English history. English lawyers and historians, Adams observed, had not investigated the history of England before the Norman Conquest. They assumed that by introducing the feudal system to England, William the Conqueror had produced a break in English legal and historical continuity. Uninterested in the period before this break, they began their studies with the Norman Conquest and assumed that the manor was the source of land law. They recognized the existence of feudal law in England and "very unwillingly but at last frankly, accepted Roman law as modifying feudal law." They fought desperately, however, "against the idea that the Germans as such, before they were feudalized or Romanized, had an actual system of personal and proprietary law of their own, a system as elaborate, as fixed, and as firmly administered by competent and regular courts, as ever was needed to guarantee security of person and property in a simply constructed, agricultural community."[59]

German scholars, Adams emphasized, had demonstrated what English scholars resisted. The Germans had convincingly proved that the laws of this archaic German society, rather than Roman law or "William the Conqueror's brain," were the source of the English common law and of its constitutional system.[60] Commenting on an English translation of Nasse's *Agricultural Communities of the Middle Ages*, Adams praised Nasse for using English materials to demonstrate the Germanic sources of English law. That Nasse, "a plodding, obscure, and far from lively German," had put "a new face on English history and law," Adams asserted, should be an embarrassment to English scholars, who had overlooked what had been lying under their eyes for six centuries. "If they were not too thoroughly convinced both of the merits of English law, and of the merits of English historians, to feel any slight sense of mortification," he

---

[55] Id. at 433.

[56] Id. at 436–8.

[57] Henry Adams, Book Review, Coulange's Ancient City (April 1874) North American Review 390, 392–3.

[58] Adams, supra note 50, at 434.

[59] Adams, supra note 40, at 197–8.

[60] Id. at 198.

acidly commented, "one would suppose that this translation ... would be likely to stimulate it."[61]

In several reviews, Adams singled out Rudolf Sohm as the most impressive of the many German scholars whose research informed the history of English law.[62] Adams drew special attention to Sohm's book on the procedure of the Lex Salica while reviewing a French translation. Criticizing the English again for ignoring German scholarship while observing that Sohm's important books had not even been translated into English, Adams used the French translation as an opportunity to write an abstract of Sohm's central themes. He began his review by underlining the importance of the Lex Salica, the law of the Salian Franks in the fifth century, to English legal history. The Lex Salica, Adams proclaimed, was "the most perfect type that has been preserved of the German system of archaic law." This archaic German law, which remained the law in parts of Germany until the fourteenth century, became the dominant legal system "wherever the German race, throughout the Dark Ages, set its conquering foot," including Scandinavia, Iceland, France, Italy, and, most importantly for Adams, England. Adams maintained that from the latter half of the fifth century, when the Germanic Angles and Saxons conquered England,[63] until the Plantagenets seven centuries later, the archaic German law preserved in the Lex Salica was the common law of England. These seven centuries, he observed, were a longer period than the time between the Plantagenets and the present. Even after the Plantagenets transformed English law through royal courts of equity, Adams added, the prior common law based on German archaic law continued to influence the developing law of England.[64]

Though English scholars generally ignored Sohm and other German scholars who could have helped them "clear the darkness which rests on this portion of their history,"[65] Adams applauded Stubbs as a promising exception.[66] Most importantly, Stubbs, relying on German scholars, recognized German archaic law and society as the foundation of English law and rejected Roman law as an early influence in England. Stubbs realized that the German "hundred" was the basic organizational division of early Anglo-Saxon society in England.[67] Yet Adams repeatedly criticized Stubbs for lack of clarity and for substantive errors, particularly for not appreciating the extent to which the hundred remained at the core both of English constitutional machinery[68] and of subsequent manorial jurisdiction, which Adams called a "private hundred."[69]

---

[61] Id. at 197–8.
[62] Adams, supra note 40, at 198; Adams, supra note 41, at 416.
[63] Adams, supra note 39, at 236.
[64] Adams, supra note 41, at 416–17.
[65] Id. at 417.
[66] Id. at 416; Adams, supra note 39, at 235–6.
[67] Adams, supra note 39, at 236.
[68] Id. at 239.
[69] Id. at 243.

Germanic law, Adams stressed, was both different from and older than Roman law. He conceded the prevailing views that Roman law was the best legal system ever developed and that familiarity with its history was necessary for any scientific study of legal history or of modern legal systems. Yet he vigorously rejected the common assumption that Roman law was the typical legal system. He observed that even Maine, who brilliantly advocated the study of comparative jurisprudence and at least illustrated some of his conclusions by reference to Hindu law, shared this erroneous assumption. Maine treated Roman law as "the pure, typical, legal history, to be illustrated rather than to be used for illustration, to be studied as an end rather than to be used as a subject for classification."[70] Adams argued, by contrast, that Roman law and family structure were not typical of archaic law and the archaic family.[71] He emphasized the extent to which archaic German law and family structure differed substantially from their Roman counterparts and concluded that "hardly a trace is to be found in the German family of that elaborate religious and legal formalism which is so prominent in Rome."[72] The absolute power of the Roman paterfamilias did not exist in Germany, where a son had unlimited rights to acquire and own property, a daughter was not excluded from her family when she married, a wife could easily obtain a divorce to protect herself against her husband's authority, and kinship was determined through the mother's as well as the father's side of the family.[73]

Others had explained these differences by the "easy assumption" that the Germans had originally resembled the Romans and had developed differently after they began their wanderings. Yet it is equally likely, Adams asserted, that the Romans developed differently as a result of their distinctive contacts with other races. There was no good reason, he concluded, for the common assumption that the original Aryan family system was Roman.[74] Adams repeatedly emphasized that a definitive answer about its origins could only be determined by comparing the laws of vastly different archaic societies, an effort that had barely begun.[75] "The early history of law," he declared, "has never been written; indeed, it is safe to say that hardly an attempt has been made to collect, far less to study on any scientific system, the materials for such a history."[76]

The need for further study, however, did not prevent Adams from expressing his own conviction that original Aryan law was German. He took obvious delight in citing recent work by Maine, who in *Ancient Law* had famously treated Roman law as original Aryan law, to support his own contrary argument for Germany. Maine's description of the property rights of married women in ancient Hindu law, Adams pointed out, much more closely resembled the

[70] Adams, supra note 57, at 391.
[71] Id. at 392.
[72] Id. at 396.
[73] Id. at 395.
[74] Id. at 396.
[75] Id. at 391, 396.
[76] Id. at 391.

liberality of ancient German law than the "religious autocracy" Roman law conferred in the paterfamilias. Adams, therefore, maintained that Roman law modified and even "perverted" the original Aryan law exhibited in both India and Germany. Maine's own evidence, Adams radically asserted, "points to the inevitable conclusion that the Roman family and the law derived from it were not universal to the archaic society; that they were peculiar to Rome; that they were in their peculiarities essentially perversions of the Indo-European customs, and that these perversions mark the whole history of Roman jurisprudence." For the scholar of English law, this important conclusion should lead to the realization that the study of its history must go "back through the German hundred, as well as through the Roman city, to its Aryan source."[77]

Throughout his reviews, Adams expressed fascination with the concept of stages of social and legal evolution. The history of England during the seven centuries between the settlement of the German tribes and the Magna Carta, he excitedly observed, included "the entire conversion of an archaic, pagan community into a nation." Those centuries were the period when England "passed through all the stages of change both in public and private law, from pure archaism down to the latest germs of future institutions now struggling into life, either in her own soil or that of her offshoots." England, moreover, was unique in its development because "in all this mass of public and private law it can hardly be said that there is a single interruption of legal continuity."[78] Yet Adams was skeptical about the "mania" for theories that assumed all societies passed through fixed stages of development. Evidence that one society passed through a particular stage, he maintained, did not provide grounds for concluding that all societies did. Adams was confident that stages of Aryan law would eventually be discovered through the scientific investigation of comparative law that Maine advocated but had barely begun himself. He doubted, however, that this discovery would lead to a broader science of social and legal development.[79]

Based on the findings of the German scholars, Adams specifically challenged Maine's claim that all societies passed through stages in which the family and the tribe predominated. The earliest forms of German law revealed that German society was not tribal, that the state "was already supreme," and that the family, "however powerful it might be, was in law wholly subordinate to the state." Individuals, associated with each other in "artificial groups, constituted the state." No evidence indicated that archaic German society was ever organized in any other way. "There is just as much ground," Adams concluded, "for assuming that many small families associated together from the first as equals, as there is for supposing," as Maine had, "that one large family developed into a tribe with a patriarchal head."[80]

---

[77] Id. at 396–7.
[78] Adams, supra note 39, at 234–5.
[79] Adams, supra note 50, at 437.
[80] Id. at 434.

Correspondence with Morgan on Stages of Development

Adams elaborated his views on stages of development in letters to Lewis H. Morgan, an American lawyer who contributed to the *North American Review* while Adams was editor and whose influential scholarship on the Indian tribes of his native New York reflected his own interest in this issue. Morgan is best known for using his research on American Indians to challenge Maine's theory of patriarchal authority in the primitive family.[81] Adams, however, was most interested in the implications of Morgan's research for understanding how archaic German society fit into general theories of social and legal development. In letters to Morgan in 1876, Adams asked his opinions about whether the stage of society represented by the American Indians preceded the stage of archaic German society and whether earlier stages preceded the American Indians.[82] He was particularly "curious to know whether our American Indians had any trace of the political and judicial organization which characterizes the earliest Germans known to us. Had they any legal modes of obtaining compensation for personal injuries? Had they any notion of a suit at law? Had they any means of recovering lost or stolen property? Had they a court of law or a legal procedure?"[83]

No letters from Morgan are included in the Adams or Morgan papers, but Adams addressed the relationship between the American Indians and the archaic Germans after reading Morgan's book *Ancient Society*, published in 1877. Praising the book as "the foundation of all future work in American historical science," Adams wrote to Morgan declaring his conviction that the two societies differed substantially. He reasoned that the archaic Germans had either "leaped" the stage of American Indian development or "had not come to it." Adams chose the first alternative, adding that "if so, the Germans must have possessed a very remarkable instinct for the organization of political society." He observed that in studying the archaic Germans he could not find "a trace of religious or priestly influence, not a sign of arbitrary power vested in either the family or the state, not even a vestige of that social denigration of women and children which is so common elsewhere." He highlighted the German "genius for reconciling liberty with law; broad political organization with the utmost individual license." Their laws proved to Adams that "they clung to their old communal assembly as their favorite machinery of society" and, as a result, rendered "the family a mere private and politically nonexistent organization."[84]

---

[81] George Feaver, *From Status to Contract: A Biography of Sir Henry Maine 1822–1888* (London: Longmans, Green and Company Ltd., 1969), pp. 133–5, 160–8.

[82] Letter from Henry Adams to Lewis Henry Morgan (April 29, 1876), in Cater, supra note 25, at 77; letter from Henry Adams to Lewis Henry Morgan (May 4, 1876), in Cater, supra note 25, at 78; letter from Henry Adams to Lewis Henry Morgan (May 21, 1876), in Cater, supra note 25, at 79; letter from Henry Adams to Lewis Henry Morgan (October 16, 1876), in Cater, supra note 25, at 80.

[83] Letter from Adams to Morgan (April 29, 1876), supra note 82.

[84] Letter from Henry Adams to Lewis Henry Morgan (July 14, 1877), in Cater, supra note 25, at 83, 84.

Pleased by a statement in Morgan's book about the influence of domestic animals in Aryan racial development, Adams wanted to illustrate this point "in a legal sense." He claimed that substantial ownership of cattle as private property required the elaboration of legal conceptions and observed that the procedure for recovery of stolen cattle was one of the oldest Anglo-Saxon laws. Summarizing his argument, Adams wrote: "Circumstances prescribe a pastoral life. The pastoral life favors the development of high physical and mental powers, as compared with a less favored state of existence. The most successful of the pastoral races find new necessities for the protection of property; they turn their practical minds to law; and all the rest follows by logic of the environment; the most capable branches of the stock, the strongest shoots, grow and flower; in time we have a Lex Salica, a Corpus Juris Civilis, and an English Common Law."[85]

In praising Aryan and particularly German and English social and legal development, Adams did not preclude the possibility that other races could make similar progress. He wrote to Morgan that reports by Schweinfurth, a German traveler to Africa, had indicated such possibilities and expressed regret that Schweinfurth had not examined the law of the large cattle-growing tribes of central Africa. Doing so would have enabled the comparative study of archaic law that Adams frequently encouraged and would have provided evidence of whether or not valid generalizations about pastoral societies could be made across races. "The history of property," Adams concluded, "is the history of law, and the history of law is the best that man has to show."[86]

Essays in Anglo-Saxon Law

The publication in 1876 of *Essays in Anglo-Saxon Law* was the culmination of Adams's career as a teacher and scholar. In 1874, Adams proposed a graduate seminar in Anglo-Saxon law for Ph.D. candidates. Approved by President Eliot, this seminar inaugurated graduate study in history at Harvard.[87] *Essays in Anglo-Saxon Law*, whose publication Adams financed,[88] included an introductory essay by Adams and the doctoral dissertations of the three students in the seminar, which earned the first Ph.D.s in the History Department.[89] Adams wrote "The Anglo-Saxon Courts of Law," Henry Cabot Lodge "The Anglo-Saxon Land Law," Ernest Young "The Anglo-Saxon Family Law," and J. Laurence Laughlin "The Anglo-Saxon Civil Procedure." As a group, they treated many of the "lines of development" of legal history that Adams had identified as potential subjects in his earlier letter to Lodge. Adams dedicated the book to Eliot, calling it the "fruit of his administration."[90]

---

[85] Id. at 84–5.

[86] Id. at 85.

[87] Samuels, supra note 1, at 245, 341 n. 4.

[88] Letter from Henry Adams to Charles Milnes Gaskell (June 14, 1876), in Letters, supra note 5, at 288.

[89] Cater, supra note 25, at xxxix.

[90] Essays in Anglo-Saxon Law (Boston: Little, Brown, and Company, 1876) (1905 ed.), frontispiece.

Working collaboratively with his students throughout the editorial process, Adams met them at his house to review drafts, suggested changes, and revised their work.[91] He took great pride in the result. The week before publication, he wrote to his English friend, Charles Milnes Gaskell, that it had been "a really satisfactory piece of work."[92] Warning Gaskell that the book was "fearfully learned," something Gaskell himself "cannot read," Adams doubted he would recoup the money he had spent in producing it. Rather, his reward would be the success of his students. "Their success is mine," he wrote to Gaskell, "and I make the investment for them, expecting to draw my profit from their success." Adams was confident that the essays exceeded the standards of previous English scholarship. He told Gaskell he had "contradicted every English author, high and low,"[93] and was "curious to learn whether your universities think they can do better. If so," he teased, "they have hitherto hidden their powers very carefully."[94]

Though each essay dealt with technical topics specific to its subject, some important general themes pervaded the collection. Not surprisingly, these general themes often reflected points Adams had made in his previous correspondence and book reviews. The essays particularly stressed the Germanic origins of Anglo-Saxon law in England, and thus the relevance of archaic German law on the Continent to understanding the history of English law. Many of them differentiated this Germanic law from Roman law and stressed that the archaic German family did not resemble the Roman patriarchal family, whose structure Maine assumed had been a universal stage of social development. Like the Oxford historians, they portrayed the Norman Conquest as a major intrusion into the history of English law, changing it in many ways but not ultimately eradicating continuous threads of Germanic influence. Though relying much more heavily on the methods and conclusions of prior German than of English scholarship, the essays self-confidently criticized German as well as English scholars on many points. They announced a new school of American legal history.

Adams on "The Anglo-Saxon Courts of Law"
In his introductory essay, "The Anglo-Saxon Courts of Law," Adams elaborated points he had made in his earlier review of Stubbs, particularly with respect to the continuing importance of the Germanic "hundred" in English law. Relying on German scholarship, Adams opened his essay by declaring "the

---

[91] Letter from Henry Adams to Henry Cabot Lodge (February 23, 1876), in Letters, supra note 5, at 280, 281; letter from Henry Adams to Henry Cabot Lodge (June 25, 1876), in Letters, supra note 5, at 290–1; letter from Henry Adams to Henry Cabot Lodge (June 30, 1876), in Letters, supra note 5, at 292–93.

[92] Letter from Henry Adams to Charles Milnes Gaskell (September 8, 1876), in Letters, supra note 5, at 299, 300.

[93] Letter from Henry Adams to Charles Milnes Gaskell (June 14, 1876), in Letters, supra note 5, at 287, 288.

[94] Letter from Adams to Gaskell, supra note 92, at 300.

fundamental historical principle, that the entire Germanic family, in its earli-est known stage of development, placed the administration of law, as it placed the political administration, in the hands of popular assemblies composed of the free, able-bodied members of the commonwealth." He emphasized in his essay, as he had not in his review of Stubbs, the broader political importance of this historical principle. It enabled the historian to trace "the slender thread of political and legal thought," which, "through two thousand years of vicissi-tudes and dangers," including the "confusion of feudalism," extended from "the wide plains of northern Germany," where the "State and the law may well have originated," to the present. The "slender thread of political and legal thought" highlighted by Adams "embraced every free man, rich or poor, and in theory at least allowed equal rights to all." Following this thread, Adams declared, "gives to the history of Germanic, and especially of English, institutions a roundness and philosophic continuity" that has "practical value" as well as intrinsic inter-est. He did not specify this "practical value," but he seemed to be suggesting to his readers that they themselves should recognize and safeguard this demo-cratic thread that their ancestors had preserved "through two thousand years of vicissitudes and dangers."[95]

Immediately after announcing his central theme, Adams dismissed the rel-evance of Maine's theories of development from the patriarchal family to the state, though he did not cite Maine himself. "There is no occasion," Adams maintained, "for introducing theories in regard to the development of fami-lies into tribes, of family heads into patriarchal and tribal chiefs, of the tribe into the state, of the tribal chief into the king, of the family council into the state assembly, or of family custom into public law." He observed that schol-ars remained ignorant of societies antedating the Indo-European family but did have sufficient information to reach meaningful conclusions about early Germanic society. The evidence of early German laws indicated a society of small families without a patriarchal chief, whose able-bodied male members united in a council as "individuals equally entitled to a voice" rather than as families. The council elected civil and military officers, protected property, and arbitrated disputes, proving that in these matters "the state was already supreme." The council did not, however, control the private affairs of families, which decided according to family custom.[96]

As the central goal of his essay, Adams wanted to prove the continuity of Germanic institutions in England from the conquest of the Anglo-Saxons in the late fifth century. He began by describing early German society as a con-federation of states, which themselves were divided into districts. The essen-tial characteristic of the district was the assembly of all free men who lived within it, which met frequently and which served as a court of law.[97] To prove

---

[95] Henry Adams, The Anglo-Saxon Courts of Law, in Essays in Anglo-Saxon Law, supra note 90, at 1.

[96] Id. at 1–2.

[97] Id. at 3–5.

continuity, Adams felt he had to demonstrate that "the Anglo-Saxons brought with them from Germany and established in England, not merely German law, but German courts of law, and the German territorial district which was the theatre of activity of the German district court."[98] Citing evidence beginning with the first written compilations of customary law in England around 600, Adams claimed that it was easy to prove the identity of the English and the earlier Germanic law court.[99] "The procedure, the nature of the business performed, the very names of the courts" in England, he concluded, "are mere repetitions of what is found in the barbarian codes of the continent." He doubted any one would dispute this conclusion.

Much more difficult, Adams conceded, was proving the identity of the territorial district in which the courts operated.[100] The district had different names in different German states, but eventually the word "hundred" came into general use to describe it.[101] Yet in England, there was no evidence before the ninth century of a territorial district called a "hundred."[102] Lacking evidence, some scholars denied that the hundred previously existed in England. Other scholars claimed that the English hundred was an aggregation of smaller territories. Either view, Adams recognized, undermined the theory of identity and, therefore, continuity between the Germanic and the Anglo-Saxon territorial districts.[103]

Adams ingeniously attempted to overcome this difficulty by citing legal sources from the eighth and ninth centuries that, he claimed, proved the existence throughout Anglo-Saxon England of the territory that was known in Germany as the hundred. The same territory, he reasoned, must have existed in the seventh century as well, thus filling the gap from the Anglo-Saxon settlement of England until the ninth century.[104] Adams agreed that there was no evidence of the use of the word "hundred" in England before the ninth century, but he claimed that during the intervening centuries different words were used to describe the same territorial division as the German hundred. The actual word "hundred," when eventually introduced in England, probably in imitation of Frankish usage, thus restored the original German terminology to describe a territorial division that, whatever its name, had continuous existence from early German society through the centuries the Anglo-Saxons dominated England.[105] Thus preserving the identity of the territorial district as well as of the courts, Adams concluded that the Anglo-Saxons in England never lost sight of "their original democratic starting-point" in the popular assemblies of the earliest Germanic societies.[106]

---

[98] Id. at 7–8.
[99] Id. at 8–11.
[100] Id. at 11.
[101] Id. at 5.
[102] Id. at 7, 11.
[103] Id. at 11–12.
[104] Id. at 13–18.
[105] Id. at 20–1.
[106] Id. at 22.

After proclaiming the continuity of German democracy in the judicial system of Anglo-Saxon England, Adams examined the extent to which it was transformed by "the increasing tendency toward aristocracy and feudalism." This tendency, though much less pronounced and harmful than in continental Europe, nevertheless "produced the only considerable changes that can be detected in the long history of the Anglo-Saxon judicial constitution." The introduction of manorial jurisdiction, which transferred judicial power from the state to a private landowner, was for Adams the key indicator of feudalism in the judicial system. Recognizing that previous scholars in England and Germany, most prominently the German scholar Konrad Maurer, had concluded that manorial jurisdiction existed in Anglo-Saxon England from a relatively early period, Adams, "with the utmost diffidence," disagreed. The laws, charters, and historical literature of Anglo-Saxon England, he stressed, did not support this early dating. He found "something forced in the assumption that an institution so revolutionary as a private common-law court could have existed unknown to the written law."[107]

Adams agreed with Maurer that landed proprietors at a relatively early time had substantial authority over their household and the occupants of their lands. He even conceded that in exercising this authority, the lord "developed for his own use, a certain system of law," which was based on "the ordinary hundred law, – the only code known to England." Yet Adams denied that this authority created legal jurisdiction in the manorial lord. It was rather an alternative form of dispute resolution. It did not remove the dependents of the lord from the jurisdiction of the hundred court but encouraged them to resolve their disputes within the manor, without exercising their right to sue in the hundred court. Given the "clumsy organization and procedure" of the hundred court, Adams thought it likely that the manorial alternative to legal jurisdiction was more likely to provide justice and preserve order.[108] Based on detailed analysis of original charters, Adams rejected other arguments for early manorial jurisdiction. Royal grants of authority that allowed landed proprietors to collect fines and to exclude royal officials, he maintained, did not confer jurisdiction. He also claimed that the term "socn," which previous eminent scholars had translated as jurisdiction, related to fiscal rather than judicial matters.[109]

Manorial jurisdiction, Adams concluded, dated from the reign of Edward the Confessor, just before the Norman Conquest, and reflected a revolutionary new theory of constitutional law largely attributable to Norman influences. Adams stressed that Edward the Confessor, "half Norman by birth, and wholly Norman by education and sympathies," filled as many offices as possible with Normans and wanted the duke of Normandy to succeed him as king of England. It was, therefore, not surprising that his constitutional practice was

[107] Id. at 27–8.
[108] Id. at 28–9.
[109] Id. at 29–45.

also Norman.[110] Using extensive quotations from Edward's charters as evidence that he introduced manorial as well as ecclesiastical jurisdiction to England,[111] Adams reiterated that they produced a revolution in English constitutional law by transforming state jurisdiction into private property.[112] This revolutionary change, Adams observed, probably made little difference in practice, especially given the extensive prior use of manorial authority as an alternative to the public tribunals of the hundred court.[113] After this change, as before, "the freemen met in their courts of law, heard pleas and decided them, as they had done from time immemorial. It mattered not so much to them whether the king's, the abbot's, or the lord's reeve presided over their court, as it did that whoever presided should not abuse his power." Nevertheless, and importantly for Adams, the theory of the Anglo-Saxon constitution "was irretrievably lost. Justice no longer was a public trust, but a private property." As the judicial system of England was "torn in pieces" and privatized, "a new theory of society, known as feudalism, took its place."[114]

Adams clearly regretted the introduction of feudalism, which he attributed to the Normans. But he was not clear about its implications. Both in his review of Stubbs and in his essay, he referred to the new manorial jurisdiction as "a private hundred." In his review, he emphasized that in this private hundred, the freemen, not the lord, "declared the law," thus maintaining the freemen's central role in a chain that extends to "our modern judicial constitution."[115] But he did not include a similar comment about such a chain to the present at the end of his essay, even though he reiterated that "the law administered in the manorial court was hundred law" and that the freemen continued to decide cases. Instead, he concluded much more pessimistically by declaring that the manorial court, as a private hundred, served to "perpetuate the memory of the most archaic and least fertile elements of both the Saxon and the feudal systems." Yet Adams included in the concluding paragraph of his essay the statement that "whatever historical interest the manorial system possesses, as part of the English judicial constitution, is due to the fact that its origin was not feudal, but Anglo-Saxon." This statement, especially when coupled with his introductory comment about the continuity through two thousand years of "Germanic, and especially of English, institutions" based on equal individual rights, indicates that he retained his earlier views about the importance of "the freemen's central role" in the manorial courts. For Adams, feudalism, as manifested in manorial jurisdiction, was one of the "vicissitudes and dangers" posed to this continuous tradition but apparently did not break it.[116]

---

[110] Id. at 46.
[111] Id. at 46–52.
[112] Id. at 52.
[113] Id. at 52–3.
[114] Id. at 54.
[115] Adams, supra note 39, at 243.
[116] Adams, supra note 95, at 1.

Lodge on "The Anglo-Saxon Land Law"

Lodge's essay, "The Anglo-Saxon Land Law," reiterated in the context of a different subject many of the themes Adams stressed in his treatment of the courts of law. Lodge, like Adams, emphasized the distinctiveness of Germanic law and its continuity in Anglo-Saxon England until disrupted but not destroyed by the Norman Conquest. An early passage captured Lodge's most general conclusions. Referring to Anglo-Saxon England, Lodge maintained that its racial purity and physical isolation "gave a scientific development to the pure Germanic law hardly to be found elsewhere. Free from the injurious influences of the Roman and Celtic peoples, the laws and institutions of the ancient German tribes flourished and waxed strong on the soil of England." He boldly connected the pure Germanic law of the Anglo-Saxons to the modern common law of England. "Strong enough to resist the power of the church in its infancy, stronger still to resist the shock of Norman invasion, crushed then, but not destroyed, by foreign influences, the great principles of Anglo-Saxon law, ever changing and assimilating, have survived in the noblest work of the race, – the English common law."[117]

The purpose of his essay, Lodge wrote, was to identify the key principles of Anglo-Saxon land law, classify them, and trace their growth or decay. He believed that for this purpose, many intricate details were irrelevant, and, therefore, promised to exclude them as "objects of only antiquarian interest."[118] He criticized previous unspecified "eminent writers" for "trying to extract, from the authorities, evidences of a system, rounded, defined, and of arithmetical proportions." According to Lodge, the Anglo-Saxon histories and charters demonstrated, above all, that "such a system did not exist, – that it was something inconceivable to the Anglo-Saxon mind." Based on the origins of Anglo-Saxon land law, Lodge classified it into two categories: estates originating in custom and estates originating in a written instrument, known as boc-land, land created by book. He further subdivided estates originating in custom into family land, common land, and folc-land, the land of the nation or state.[119] A single individual, Lodge stressed, in theory, and often in practice, could hold all four of these types of land.[120]

Without referring to Maine, Lodge conceded as "a fair inference" that the family in prehistoric times functioned more as a legal entity than as an aggregation of individuals.[121] Yet by historic times, even well before the introduction of written laws and charters, the family, as an entity, no longer held land. Rather, individuals held family land, either as the head of a household or in a

---

[117] H. Cabot Lodge, The Anglo-Saxon Land Law, in Essays in Anglo Saxon Law, supra note 90, at 55, 56.a.

[118] Id. at 56–7.

[119] Id. at 56.

[120] Id. at 58.

[121] Id. at 74 n. 3.

FIGURE 5.1. *Henry Cabot Lodge.* Courtesy of Harvard University Archives, HUP Lodge, Henry Cabot, A.B. 1871 (2a).

purely individual capacity.[122] Family land was inalienable[123] and untaxed.[124] Distinguishing the common land from the folc-land, Lodge identified common land as land of the local community available for use by all its members and not taxable, whereas the folc-land was treated as revenue bearing for the benefit of the entire nation.[125] Over time, individual estates grew at the expense of the common land,[126] a process, Lodge maintained, analogous to the later "substitution of the lord for the community in judicial affairs."[127] Similarly, as government became more centralized and royal power increased, the folc-land

[122] Id. at 74; see also id. at 69.
[123] Id. at 75.
[124] Id. at 80.
[125] Id. at 82–3.
[126] Id. at 84.
[127] Id. at 85.

became the land of the kings rather than of the entire people, particularly with the advent of Norman influence in England.[128] "What had happened to the Continental tribes six hundred years before, now happened in England." Regarding land law, as in other areas, the "monarchical and centralizing forces of the age proved too strong for the old Germanic principles." None of these three customary sources of land law provided for transferring property to the church, and boc-land originated as a means to do so through written instruments.[129] Boc-land eventually provided for marriage settlements, mortgages, and wills.[130] In the written instruments, Lodge emphasized, "women appear as in every respect equal to men," illustrating the "fundamental principle of the equality of women before the law, in every thing relating to land, except the family land."[131]

At the end of his essay, Lodge addressed the development of feudal land law in England. He acknowledged that the "germs of feudalism" arose and slowly expanded in England before the Norman Conquest. As an example, he cited the growth of large estates, which he identified as one of the prevailing causes of feudalism.[132] Yet these germs, he emphasized, existed only "in embryo."[133] For Lodge, the key indicator of feudalism was military tenures in land, the holding of land on condition of military services. Citing evidence of the Germanic system of universal military service throughout the history of Anglo-Saxon England, he maintained that military tenures in land did not replace this system until after the Norman Conquest.[134] In his last paragraph, Lodge observed that some form of feudalism would have arisen in England as a natural native development even if there had been no Norman Conquest. It was impossible to know, he added, whether a native English feudalism would have resembled the continental version. He was certain, however, "that the slow, strong progress of England was rudely broken, and on the nascent feudalism of the Anglo-Saxons was superimposed the full-grown system of William and Normandy."[135]

Frustratingly, Lodge never returned to his early assertion that the Anglo-Saxon land law, though "crushed" by the Norman invasion, was not "destroyed" by it, but "survived" in the English common law. Like Adams, Lodge never elaborated his broad claim that basic principles of pure Germanic law continued in England after the devastating impact he ascribed to the imposition of feudalism through the Norman Conquest. Both ended their chronological accounts with the immediate aftermath of the Norman Conquest. Adams provided hints of an argument for continuity by citing the retention of the freemen and the hundred law, both based on Germanic democratic principles,

---

[128] Id. at 99–100.
[129] Id. at 100–1.
[130] Id. at 106.
[131] Id. at 113.
[132] Id. at 117.
[133] Id. at 118.
[134] Id. at 117–19.
[135] Id. at 119.

in the feudal manorial court. By identifying mortgages and wills, which survived into the common law, as products of Anglo-Saxon boc-land, Lodge provided some evidence of continuity, but he did not even attempt an argument that these technical instruments reflected "the great principles of Anglo-Saxon law."[136]

Young on "The Anglo-Saxon Family Law"

Young's essay, "The Anglo-Saxon Family Law," like the prior essays of Adams and Lodge, stressed the Germanic origins of Anglo-Saxon law. While differentiating the German from the Roman family, Young devoted much more space than Adams or Lodge to criticizing Maine's theory of the patriarchal Roman family as the archetype of a primitive Aryan family. For Young, as for Adams and Lodge, feudalism "corrupted" the "purity" of much Germanic Anglo-Saxon law[137] but did not obliterate it. Young maintained that the Germanic law of the household revealed "the origin of modern laws and customs."[138] Yet this continuity between Germanic Anglo-Saxon and modern law was less central to Young than it was to Adams or even to Lodge. Young made little effort to establish this continuity beyond asserting it, though he did give some examples. Rather, he emphasized the interest and importance of the Germanic law of the household "for the student of comparative history, as furnishing a type – perhaps the most archaic type of which we have any knowledge – of a primitive Aryan institution."[139] It was in this context of comparative history that Young directly and extensively criticized Maine.

At the beginning of his essay, Young observed the difficulty of reconstructing the earliest history of Germanic family law. The first written German laws, he pointed out, were not compilations of existing unwritten laws, but expressed changes in them. Family law, the area of law most rooted in custom and most resistant to change, was, therefore, least reduced to writing. Nevertheless, early written laws among various German tribes did reflect two significant gradual modifications of customary family law. Public law limited the family in dealing with private feuds that threatened the peace, and the church limited some of the harshest features of family custom. These two modifications proved to Young that the Anglo-Saxons had essentially the same system of family law as all the other German tribes. Young associated himself with a scholarly consensus that the family was the central institution of all early "Indo-Germanic" societies, the point Adams made in an earlier letter to Lodge.[140]

The word "family," Young stressed, referred both to the entire group of kindred and to the smaller group, which Young called the household, consisting of husband, wife, and children. He cited the law that the wife upon marriage did

---

[136] Id. at 56.
[137] Ernest Young, The Anglo-Saxon Family Law, in Essays in Anglo-Saxon Law, supra note 90, at 121, 142.
[138] Id. at 148.
[139] Id. at 148.
[140] Id. at 121–2.

FIGURE 5.2. *Ernest Young.* Courtesy of Harvard University Archives, HUP Young, Ernest, A.B. 1873 (1).

not become kin to her husband's kin as proof that the household was not simply a subdivision of the larger kindred, but a distinct group.[141] Young maintained that distinct laws governed these distinct groups[142] and proceeded to discuss each set of laws in turn. The laws of the kindred, he concluded, did not survive beyond the introduction of feudalism, when the Roman law of determining degrees of kinship superseded it.[143] By contrast, the laws of the household, dealing with marriage and the relations among its members, extended into the modern common law. Young called the household "the basis, the corner-stone" of Aryan society. Modifications occurred over time, but "the essential characteristics of the modern household already existed in the earliest Teutonic law."[144]

Although he observed the significant continuities between the Anglo-Saxon and modern households, Young was most interested in establishing that the early Germanic family, reflected in Anglo-Saxon law, was the best example of an early Aryan institution. A central part of Young's argument involved refuting Maine's claim that the patriarchal Roman family was typically Aryan.

[141] Id. at 123.
[142] Id. at 125.
[143] Id. at 147.
[144] Id. at 148.

Young did not challenge Maine's treatment of the Roman family. He agreed that in Roman law kinship was agnatic, based on descent through males from a common ancestor, and that the power of the father in the Roman family was virtually absolute. Young parted from Maine in vigorously insisting that the German family differed from the Roman in "radical" ways.[145] Maine's characterization of the German family as subject to the authority of a patriarchal chief, Young maintained, "is as much in error as when he ascribes the Roman agnation to the primitive German system." For Young, nothing was more certain in Germanic law than that the maternal kin played a crucial role in the family.[146] Even after marriage, the wife remained in her kinship group, which protected her against the abuse of her husband's power. The children belonged to the kinship groups of both parents, enabling the maternal kin to intervene against the father on their behalf as well.[147] In the German family, moreover, sons became independent of their fathers at an early age, illustrating that "the German system is utterly opposed to the patriarchal theory."[148]

Reiterating the absence of patriarchal power in Anglo-Saxon England, Young also disagreed with Maine's assertion that private property in English as well as Roman land law derived from the ownership of a patriarchal chief. As had Lodge in his essay on land law, Young maintained that in Anglo-Saxon England "the individual predominated over the family." Even in prehistoric times, when the children and grandchildren of a deceased man often lived together without a division of property, there was no patriarchal system. Rather, all adult members of the group had equal rights. "It is not the subjugation of all descendents to the will of an ascendant, but the voluntary association of the near kindred; and the control exercised by the family council in such a group as little resembles the despotic power of a patriarchal chief ... as the free democratic constitution of primitive Germany resembled the highly aristocratic constitution of early Rome."[149] To support his argument that the patriarchal Roman family was not typical, Young noted the research on the American Indian family by Lewis Morgan, who demonstrated that the Indians, like the early Germans, had a democratic rather than a patriarchal family structure.[150]

Laughlin on "The Anglo-Saxon Legal Procedure"
The final essay in the collection, by J. Laurence Laughlin, addressed "The Anglo-Saxon Legal Procedure." Like the other essays, Laughlin's emphasized the Germanic origins of Anglo-Saxon law while differentiating it from Roman law. He particularly stressed that "to justly estimate the Anglo-Saxon laws,

[145] Id. at 149.
[146] Id. at 150.
[147] Id. at 149.
[148] Id. at 152.
[149] Id. at 151–2.
[150] Id. at 152 n. 2.

FIGURE 5.3. J. *Laurence Laughlin.* Courtesy of Harvard University Archives, HUP Laughlin, James Lawrence, A.B. 1873 (1a) B. 1873.

appeal must be made to the Saxon law of the continent, and to other German codes; and the primitive German procedure must be kept clearly in view."[151] While commenting on continental German law, he relied heavily on the prior scholarship of Germans. Most broadly, Laughlin followed Adams and Young in highlighting the German commitment to democracy. "The democratic character of German political institutions," he wrote in his opening paragraph, "finds a parallel in the large judicial powers vested in the individual" in matters of legal procedure.[152] More than his colleagues, Laughlin directly compared Germanic with Roman law throughout his essay, not only observing their many differences, but also warning that their occasional similarities typically did not reflect influence. In contrast to the others, however, he rarely addressed the impact of feudalism. Rather, he drew attention to the persistence of the old law of Germanic procedure throughout the Anglo-Saxon period of English

[151] J. Laurence Laughlin, The Anglo-Saxon Legal Procedure, in Essays in Anglo-Saxon Law, supra note 90, at 183, 185.
[152] Id. at 183.

history. He emphasized that in this old law, in great contrast to current law, "proof came *after*, not *before*, the judgment."[153]

Laughlin divided Anglo-Saxon legal procedure into four categories: action for debt, action for movables, action for real property, and criminal procedure. These categories largely, but not entirely, overlapped with the categories Sohm identified in his book on the procedure of the Lex Salica, as described by Adams in his review. The action for debt, Laughlin observed, was the first of these procedures to emerge.[154] He emphasized the role of individual self-help throughout the various steps of the action for debt, from the original summons to private execution.[155] Pointing out that this action was founded on a unilateral contractual obligation, Laughlin stressed differences between German and Roman ideas of contract while acknowledging some similarities.[156]

At the beginning of his discussion of the action for movables, Laughlin similarly contrasted German with Roman law. Relying on German scholars who had corrected their predecessors, Laughlin asserted that the German action for movables did not distinguish between actions *in rem*, against a borrower, and *in personam*, against a third possessor. To make such a distinction, he claimed, reflected "the great mistake of trying to engraft on German law the judicial conceptions of the Romans, with whom this distinction was original, – a development which was never reached by the German law of the middle ages, and which, moreover, is opposed to the fundamental principles of German procedure."[157] Rather, the proper division of the action for movables was between the action for return of an object "when the object had passed out of the owner's hand with his consent," and the action "when the object was lost against the owner's will."[158] Laughlin treated these two categories at length, elaborating in great detail the different procedures that pertained to each.[159] Again stressing the inapplicability of Roman law, Laughlin observed that the later Saxon sources varied in the time of unconcealed possession allowed as a defense to a charge of theft. "Perhaps nothing shows better the freedom from Roman influences enjoyed by Anglo-Saxon law," he commented, than the absence of a fixed period of time.[160]

Turning to the action for real property, Laughlin began by observing that in early Germanic societies the community rather than private individuals held property. When private property in land was first recognized and disputes over the rights of individuals to this property arose, the procedures that already governed movables were extended to land as well.[161] Eventually, however,

---

[153] Id. at 188.
[154] Id. at 189.
[155] Id. at 196.
[156] Id. at 189–91.
[157] Id. at 197.
[158] Id. at 199.
[159] For a summary, see id. at 226–7.
[160] Id. at 225–6.
[161] Id. at 227.

disputes over land produced what Laughlin called a "remarkable revolution" in Germanic procedural law. He identified the end of the sixth century as the "turning point" in this revolution. Procedure came under the supervision of the court, and, under the influence of the Roman church, written documents for the first time became the means of proof.[162] "It is through the procedure for land," Laughlin concluded, "that a break was made with the narrower conditions of the old law, and that questions of right were decided on wider principles of justice, and opened to the larger influences of jurisprudence." He stressed the progression from the original action for debt, through the better action for movables, to the action for real property, which brought the law of procedure "nearer to the more perfect system of to-day."[163] As in his discussions of the other procedural categories, Laughlin repeatedly contrasted German and Roman law,[164] emphasizing differences and pointing out that even apparent similarities were "correlative" rather than "synonyme."[165]

Criminal procedure, the fourth and final category of Anglo-Saxon legal procedure identified by Laughlin, prompted his broadest generalizations about historical change. In primitive German societies, he observed, there were no courts. Individuals used self-help to punish crimes. "The German was himself judge and warrior; he levied execution and exacted blood for blood by the sovereign powers vested in himself by that most democratic of all constitutions." In modern England, the situation had changed dramatically, for only the king could initiate prosecutions against criminals. Laughlin, therefore, concluded that the development of criminal procedure "is one of the most instructive lessons in the history of English law." Through this history, it is possible "to trace the growth of the power of government over the individual; the establishment of courts of justice; the gradual suppression of private warfare; [and] the substitution of permanent kings for temporary leaders."[166]

In the earliest period of German legal history, Laughlin maintained, two different procedures existed, though they sometimes mingled. One procedure was vengeance and feud, operating outside the state but allowed by it. The other procedure was outlawry, in which a person charged with breaching the peace appeared before a court, and the community, through the court, determined whether or not to declare him an outlaw. Such a declaration enlarged the right of vengeance to the entire community.[167] Over time, the law limited the offenses subject to outlawry, allowing a growing number that could be expiated through "composition," the payment of a fixed sum as a compensatory fine.[168] A third system "arose by slow development from the slightest germ"

---

[162] Id. at 230.
[163] Id. at 229.
[164] See, e.g., id. at 233–4, 255–6, 258, 261.
[165] Id. at 261.
[166] Id. at 262.
[167] Id. at 270, 303.
[168] Id. at 272–3, 304.

alongside the other two and eventually prevailed over them.[169] This third system, called "true punishment" by Laughlin,[170] was based on "civilized conceptions" of "wrongs against society, and the energies of the state were directed more and more to the repression of crime and the punishment of offenders."[171] Anglo-Saxon criminal procedure, he concluded, was in the midst of the transition from the second system to the third.[172]

Responses by Holmes and Maine to the Essays

The *Essays in Anglo-Saxon Law* were favorably reviewed in the United States and in England, where they were published in an English edition.[173] Reviews in both countries emphasized with pleasure that the *Essays* initiated the American study of Anglo-Saxon law.[174] An American review attributed the prior neglect of this subject to its "lack of immediate practical utility," observing that Anglo-Saxon lawsuits had as little relevance to modern American judges and lawyers as precedents from the Old Testament. Citing Adams's dedication of the *Essays* to Eliot, the reviewer praised Harvard's "new spirit of learning," which rejected the traditional American view of law as a "purely commercial" subject, "nothing but a pathway for sharp wits to wealth and place," and instead treated it as "an elevated branch of learning" that deserved to be called a "science."[175]

Adams's friend Oliver Wendell Holmes, Jr., wrote a particularly thorough and thoughtful review. Pointing out that the research for the essays had been conducted collaboratively under the "general supervision" of Adams, Holmes opened his review by accurately and approvingly stressing "their entire and almost polemical renunciation of English models," praising instead "their adoption not only of German methods, but of the authority and opinions of the now dominant German school."[176] He observed that the *Essays* admirably revealed "a more minute and painful scrutiny of the obscure sources of Anglo-Saxon law" than "any parallel English work we know." Yet Holmes also had his criticisms, even of Adams. For example, Holmes disagreed with Adams that manorial jurisdiction was a late development imposed under Norman influence, arguing instead that

---

[169] Id. at 304; see id. at 273–5.

[170] Id. at 273, 304.

[171] Id. at 277.

[172] Id. at 275, 304.

[173] Samuels, supra note 1, at 255; Herbert B. Adams, New Methods of Study in History, in Johns Hopkins University Studies in Historical and Political Science (Baltimore: John Murray & Company, 1884) Herbert B. Adams, ed.), vol. II (Institutions and Economics), pp. 25, 88.

[174] 43 Atlantic Monthly (February 1879) 263; Law Magazine and Review (London: Stevens and Haynes, 1878) Fourth Series, vol. III, 120.

[175] 43 Atlantic Monthly (February 1879), supra note 174, at 264.

[176] Holmes, Book Review, in The Collected Works of Justice Holmes (University of Chicago Press, 1995) (Sheldon M. Novick, ed.), vol. 3, p. 16.

it was a "gradual growth."[177] Holmes mingled criticism with overall praise of the other essays as well, challenging details of analysis and suggesting that Laughlin was not sufficiently expert to tackle his important and neglected subject. More broadly, Holmes maintained that "there is a limit to historical explanation," that some subjects, such as the origins of the concept of property, are better understood by analyzing "human nature" rather than history.[178] Yet Holmes concluded his review by emphasizing "that such monographs as these prepare the ground for a truly philosophical history of the law, and that, without such a history, the foundations of jurisprudence will never be perfectly secure."[179]

Maine himself responded to the *Essays* in a letter to Adams thanking him for sending the book. Admitting that he had not yet read the book "with half the care which it deserves," Maine felt he could no longer defer a reply and wrote to Adams that it "has interested me greatly." Adams was fortunate, Maine initially observed, in having "a considerable advantage over us at Oxford," students who could read German. Maine then turned to the contents of the essays. "I am gratified by the attention which your pupils seem to have given to my books," he wrote, "and even when they differ from me, I have no reason to complain." Yet Maine immediately seemed to complain by criticizing Young's essay on family law, the essay that challenged him most directly and at greatest length. Maine refused to be "corrected" about the prevalence of the patriarchal family. "In regard to family law," Maine acknowledged, "I should not view that of the German system with the same brevity as in my 'Ancient Law,' written now more than twenty years ago. But I think Mr. Young greatly underrates the evidence in favor of the Patria Potestus and agnatic among the Germans." Maine also accused Young of inadvertently attributing to him an unspecified position about the origin of private property that he did not hold. After disposing of Young, Maine proceeded to praise Adams, telling him that his "own essay appears to me to have very great value," though Maine did not elaborate.[180]

The Mixed Legacy of Adams and His Students

Despite the success of *Essays in Anglo-Saxon Law*, neither Adams nor his students pursued a career in legal history. In his lecture "The Primitive Rights of Women" at the end of 1876, the year the *Essays* were published, Adams criticized Maine's views of the patriarchal family.[181] This lecture, however, was his valedictory to early legal history. He was in the process of transferring his intellectual interests at Harvard to seventeenth-century English legal and constitutional history and to American history.[182] In 1877, he resigned from Harvard

---

[177] Id. at 17.
[178] Id. at 19.
[179] Id. at 20.
[180] Letter from Henry Maine to Henry Adams (December 26, 1876) (Henry Adams Papers, Lamont Library, Harvard University).
[181] Samuels, supra note 1, at 260–2.
[182] Id. at 266–7.

and moved back to Washington, D.C., where he wrote the books that made him famous but abandoned the subject of legal history. Yet he left a major legacy at Harvard, where his students dominated the Harvard history department for decades.[183] Adams made another significant, though indirect, contribution to academic history soon after his arrival in Washington by stimulating Herbert B. Adams, an important historian at Johns Hopkins, to investigate possible continuities between Teutonic and American institutions.[184] Perhaps most importantly, Adams was a major influence on subsequent work on the history of English law. He stimulated Holmes's turn from analytic to historical approaches to law in the 1870s and, more specifically, helped convince Holmes that the common law derived from Germanic rather than from Roman sources.[185] Other major historians of English law built on the *Essays* and cited them throughout their work.

In his autobiography, Adams suggested some reasons for his change of career. Frustrated that he "had no theory of evolution to teach, and could not make the facts fit one," he concluded that history is essentially "incoherent and immoral" and "had either to be taught as such – or falsified." Adams was unwilling to do either.[186] He enjoyed his students but found he had nothing useful to teach them. He had written to Lodge that he taught legal history to give his course "a practical turn."[187] Yet he ultimately concluded that though his students had become excellent researchers, "his wonderful method led nowhere, and they would have to exert themselves to get rid of it in the Law School even more than they exerted themselves to acquire it in the college." Apart from its lack of practicality for law school, Adams came to believe that history "had no system, and could have none, since its subject was merely antiquarian." Though he tried, he "could not make it actual."[188] Much worse than these frustrations, Adams recalled, was the poverty of faculty life. He found Cambridge "a social desert that would have starved a polar bear." Even those brilliant and agreeable faculty who "were greedy for companionship, all were famished for want of it. Society was a faculty meeting without business."[189] He happily returned to Washington, writing to Gaskell that it "is the only place in America where society amuses me, or where life offers variety."[190]

All three of Adams's students who contributed to *Essays in Anglo-Saxon Law* joined the Harvard faculty, but none continued to publish in legal history.

---

[183] Ephraim Emerton, History, in Samuel Eliot Morison, The Development of Harvard University Since the Inauguration of President Eliot, 1869–1929 (Cambridge, Mass.: Harvard University Press, 1930), p. 156.

[184] Herbert B. Adams, supra note 173, at 101.

[185] Howe, supra note 1, at 146–7.

[186] Adams, supra note 1, at 301.

[187] Letter from Adams to Lodge, supra note 31, at 236.

[188] Adams, supra note 1, at 303.

[189] Id. at 307.

[190] Letter from Henry Adams to Charles Milnes Gaskell (November 25, 1877), in Letters, supra note 5, at 302.

Adams successfully urged President Eliot to appoint Lodge to teach American history, to be paid from Adams's own professorship and, therefore, at no additional cost to Harvard. Reflecting his belief in the educational value of student exposure to conflicting faculty positions,[191] Adams wrote to Eliot that Lodge's "views being federalist and conservative, have as good a right to expression as mine which tend to democracy and radicalism. The clash of opinions can hardly fail to stimulate inquiry among the students."[192] Lodge taught at Harvard until 1879, but he was a very unpopular teacher and soon turned his attention to politics, in which he had a long and distinguished career as senator from Massachusetts.[193] Young also taught a variety of courses in the Harvard history department, including Roman law, and continued his study of early legal institutions. He did not, however, complete any major additional work. He committed suicide in 1888, apparently after a long period of depression and mental illness.[194] "Had he lived," one obituary declared, "he would doubtless have written works that would have given him a wide reputation."[195] Laughlin became an eminent political economist, at Harvard until 1888, and later at Cornell and the University of Chicago, where he was head of the department of political economy and remained on the faculty until his retirement in 1916.[196]

Although Adams and his students abandoned legal history, other American scholars built on their work, particularly in applying the "Teutonic-germ theory" to English and American law and institutions. In addition to the direct impact of Henry Adams on Herbert B. Adams and on Oliver Wendell Holmes, Jr., a generation of American legal and historical scholarship in the new American research universities traced the Teutonic roots of later developments in England and the United States. During the remainder of the nineteenth century, Bigelow, Ames, and Thayer made major contributions to the history of English law. Following the example of Adams and his students, they mastered German scholarship on the history of Teutonic law and immersed themselves in the primary sources of English legal history. Maitland, who is still enormously respected as the most significant scholar of English legal history, relied heavily on these American legal scholars, corresponded extensively with them, and developed a close friendship with Bigelow. In his important book published in 1999, *The Making of English Law: King Alfred to the Twelfth Century*, Patrick Wormald called the *Essays in Anglo-Saxon Law* "serious, though now rarely cited," and praised the one by Adams as "lastingly important."[197]

---

[191] Adams, supra note 1, at 303–4.

[192] Letter from Henry Adams to Charles W. Eliot (March 27, 1877), in Cater, supra note 25, at 81.

[193] Garraty, supra note 30, at 51–3; Emerton, supra note 183, at 156–7.

[194] Death of Professor Young, Harvard Crimson, March 5, 1888.

[195] Boston Post Times, Ernest Young Biographical Folder, Harvard University Archives.

[196] Alfred Bournemann, Laughlin, James Laurence, Dictionary of American Biography (New York: Charles Scribner's Sons, 1944), vol. XI, Supplement One (Harris E. Starr, ed.), pp. 487–8.

[197] Patrick Wormald, The Making of English Law: King Alfred to the Twelfth Century (Oxford: Blackwell Publishers Ltd., 1999), vol. 1, p. 13.

VI

Melville M. Bigelow

From the History of Norman Procedure to Proto-Realism

As commentators recognized on both sides of the Atlantic, the publication of two books by Melville W. Bigelow, *Placita Anglo-Normannica* (1879) and *History of Procedure in England* (1880), continued the American study of English legal history begun by Adams and his students in *Essays in Anglo-Saxon Law*. Whereas Adams and his students stressed the Anglo-Saxon origins of modern English common law, Bigelow maintained instead that it derived from Norman law, imported from Normandy but developed distinctively in England during the "Norman Period" of English history, which Bigelow dated from 1066 to 1204. He stressed that the Norman Conquest had dealt a "fatal blow" to Anglo-Saxon law, replacing most of it with distinctively Norman law, whose own Germanic characteristics had been largely modified by exposure to Roman law. Challenging the eminent German scholar Heinrich Brunner, Bigelow also claimed that the key developments in the transformation of the Norman inquisition into the modern English jury occurred in England after the Norman Conquest, not, as Brunner claimed, previously in Normandy. Bigelow's books gained him international acclaim. He became better known in England than in the United States, developed extensive professional relationships with legal scholars in both countries, and became especially close, personally as well as professionally, to Frederic Maitland.

Two decades after publishing the books on the history of English law that established his international reputation, Bigelow questioned the approach of the "historical school" of legal scholarship while acknowledging his own prior participation in it. By focusing on the history of law as a process of continuous evolution from the remote past, Bigelow came to believe, the historical school diverted attention from the pressing issues that law should address in the present. Like other scholars at the beginning of the twentieth century, most famously Roscoe Pound in his early articles promoting "sociological jurisprudence," Bigelow asserted that the destructive individualism and related inequality in the United States threatened democracy and urged legal scholars to undertake a "scientific" study of the social and economic forces to which law must respond.

When he was dean of the Boston University School of Law, Bigelow proposed, but never implemented, a broader curriculum designed to introduce students to external influences on law. As part of this "plan of legal extension," Bigelow sponsored a series of lectures, including two by him, intended to illustrate the conception that "law is the expression, more or less deflected by opposition, of the dominant force in society."[1] Morris Cohen, the eminent legal philosopher, declared in the 1930s that these lectures, published in 1906 as *Centralization and the Law*, constituted the "first pronouncement" of legal realism.[2] Though Bigelow questioned the value of the purely historical study of law to which he himself had made major contributions, he endorsed the use of history to evaluate whether or not survivals of past law served useful functions in the present. His final essays,[3] published in 1920, invoked historical examples to warn against "undisciplined individualism" and to illustrate the more desirable social unity provided by religion and family. Bigelow's proto-realism, though much less influential than Pound's sociological jurisprudence or Bigelow's own earlier work in legal history, illustrates in the career of one scholar the major transformation in American legal thought from the historical school that dominated in the late nineteenth century to the more socially conscious "law and society" orientation that prevailed during most of the twentieth century.

Placita Anglo-Normannica was the published version of Bigelow's Harvard Ph.D. dissertation. It compiled all "known legal monuments" related to litigation in the period between the Norman Conquest in 1066 and the beginning of the reign of Richard I in 1189,[4] a period before law reports and legal treatises. Bigelow relied on a variety of printed records for his compilation. Bigelow maintained that the Domesday Book, the survey of England undertaken by William the Conqueror in 1085–6, was "the most valuable monument of the Norman time."[5] He also relied on charters, formulaic documents that often recorded legal actions in an epistolary form,[6] and chronicles, the histories of the period, which typically read more like diaries assembling the facts of current events than works of modern history,[7] making clear that he did not include charters or chronicles that lacked information relating to litigation. Remarking on the difficulty in finding "authoritative information" about the history of English law during this period, Thayer observed in his own subsequent work

[1] Melville M. Bigelow, Preface to Centralization and the Law: Scientific Legal Education (Boston: Little, Brown, and Company, 1906) (Melville M. Bigelow, ed.), p. v.

[2] Morris Cohen, A Critical Sketch of Legal Philosophy in America, in Law: A Century of Progress 1835–1935 (New York University Press, 1937) (Alison Reppy, ed.), vol. 2, pp. 266, 304.

[3] Melville M. Bigelow, Medieval English Sovereignty, in Papers on the Legal History of Government (Boston: Little, Brown, and Company, 1920), pp. 71, 150–1.

[4] Melville M. Bigelow, Placita Anglo-Normannica: Law Cases From William I to Richard I Preserved in Historical Records (Boston: Soule and Bugbee, 1881), pp. iii, vi.

[5] Id. at xlix–l. For a complete list of Bigelow's sources, see id. at xlvi–lv.

[6] Emily Kadens, Diplomatics, in Dictionary of the Middle Ages (New York: Scribner, 2004) (William Chester Jordan, ed.), Supplement 1, p. 160.

[7] N. F. Blake, Chronicles, in Dictionary of the Middle Ages (New York: Scribner, 1989) (Joseph R. Strayer, ed.), vol. 3, p. 325, 326–7.

that most existing knowledge derived from Bigelow's "competent and careful hand" in collecting the materials in *Placita Anglo-Normannica*.[8]

History of Procedure in England also covered the Norman period, extending the ending date to 1204. Reversing the proportion of text to original material in *Placita*, *History of Procedure in England* constituted Bigelow's book-length analysis of the subject. The first part of the book focused on the courts, particularly the jurisdiction and procedure of the Ecclesiastical Court, the rise of the King's Court, and the corresponding decline of the ancient popular courts, including the County, Hundred, and Manorial courts.[9] He also devoted a long section to the Exchequer, pointing out that it became a purely fiscal court.[10] The second part of the book dealt with the rise of trial by recognition, the judicial duel, the decline or transformation of previous modes of trial, and the conduct of causes from the initial process to the final judgment.[11]

Both books revealed Bigelow's familiarity with the *Essays in Anglo-Saxon Law*, and reviewers on both sides of the Atlantic admiringly described Bigelow as continuing the scholarship on English legal history the *Essays* initiated. Bigelow's personal relationship to Henry Adams and his students, however, is difficult to ascertain. Brooks Adams, Henry's brother, wrote after Bigelow died in 1921 that he had met Bigelow, he believed in 1872, when Bigelow was working on his first scholarly project in the library of the old courthouse in Boston and Adams was still a law student. Over the years, he added, "so far as the law was concerned, Bigelow became my most intimate friend."[12] It seems likely, though I have found no direct evidence, that Bigelow knew Henry Adams through Brooks Adams and their shared interest in the early legal history of England. Bigelow probably knew Lodge, Young, and Laughlin as well, either through Henry Adams or perhaps, after Adams left Harvard in 1877, while Bigelow was a Ph.D. student there in the years immediately before the publication of *Placita* in 1879. During his years as a student at Harvard, Bigelow was acquainted with President Eliot, a relationship indicating that he also knew people closer to his field. In the preface to *Placita*, Bigelow acknowledged "the aid and encouragement of friends, both in his own country and in England."[13] I suspect these American friends included Henry Adams and his students.

The History of Procedure in Norman England

Bigelow's interest in the history of procedure in Norman England originated during his preparation of a casebook on tort law. Research for the casebook

---

[8] James Bradley Thayer, A Preliminary Treatise on Evidence at the Common Law (Boston: Little, Brown, and Company, 1898), p. 50.

[9] Melville M. Bigelow, History of Procedure in England from the Norman Conquest: The Norman Period (1066–1204) (Boston: Little, Brown, and Company, 1880).

[10] Id. at 103–31.

[11] Id. at 147–349.

[12] Brooks Adams, Melville M. Bigelow, 1 B.U. L. Rev. 168 (1921).

[13] Bigelow, supra note 4, at viii.

convinced him of "the importance of a careful study of the litigation, and especially of the writs, of the Norman and sub-Norman time."[14] Bigelow intended his *Leading Cases on the Law of Torts* (1875) to present the "essential doctrines" of tort law.[15] For many of the doctrines he identified, Bigelow included often extensive notes on "historical aspects of the subject." Bigelow confessed his own "partiality" to these historical portions of his book, though he acknowledged that "in this swift age" they would probably "pass unnoticed" by many readers. "The practicing lawyer of to-day," he acknowledged, "has little time, and possibly less inclination, for historical study; and the old law, having lost much of its force as authority, is rapidly passing into oblivion." Bigelow hoped, however, that his notes had rescued the historical sources from "the crabbed books" in which they previously existed and made them accessible even to busy lawyers. More importantly for Bigelow, and reflecting the emergence of the modern American law school staffed by full-time scholars and teachers, he identified "a growing class of persons devoted more or less to the *study* of the law, rather than to its practice; and for such the historical notes are especially intended." The notes, he explained, "will show how those subjects first took form in the English Courts, after the Norman Conquest, and their subsequent growth and development."[16] In only one of these notes, on assault and battery, did Bigelow refer to earlier Anglo-Saxon law.[17]

By the time he wrote *Placita Anglo-Normannica* and *The History of Procedure in England*, Bigelow believed that the history of procedure was the key to understanding the relationship between Norman law and modern English common law. He made this crucial point most clearly in his unpublished 1879 commencement address at Harvard. "The legal results produced by the Norman Conquest," he declared at the beginning of his address, "touch mainly on the subject of procedure." Through the reign of Richard I, who died in 1199, there had been no "material change" in laws relating to property, contracts, or domestic relations. Even criminal law remained largely unchanged. In legal procedure, by contrast, the "far-reaching effects" of the Norman Conquest "have extended down the course of time to the present-day, and have not yet spent their force."[18]

Bigelow claimed scholarly originality for his *History of Procedure in England*. Anticipating similar comments by Frederic Maitland in his great work on the history of English law,[19] Bigelow asserted in his preface that constitutional

---

[14] Id. at iii.

[15] Melville M. Bigelow, Leading Cases on the Law of Torts Determined by the Courts of America and England: With Notes (Boston: Little, Brown, and Company, 1875), p. v.

[16] Id. at 6.

[17] Id. at 222.

[18] Melville M. Bigelow, Legal Results of the Norman Conquest (June 25, 1879) (manuscript available in the Howard Gotlieb Archival Research Center, Boston University, Bigelow Collection, Box 1, Bigelow Commencement Folder) [hereinafter Bigelow Collection], p. 1.

[19] Frederick Pollock and Frederic Maitland, The History of English Law before the Time of Edward I (Cambridge University Press, 1899) (2d ed.), vol. I, p. xxxvii.

historians, while dealing with aspects of the subject, had ignored the "technical processes of law" on which he would focus. German scholarship, he acknowledged, had made enormous contributions to understanding Germanic procedure but had not explored "the conduct of causes in England."[20] Bigelow was more pointed in the unpublished manuscript version of his preface. He recognized that his treatment of the courts went over ground covered by previous writers but emphasized that he was the first to do so from the perspective of a lawyer, which, he observed, required "a fresh examination of the whole subject." He hoped this part of his book would appeal to the general student of history as well as to those interested in the technical system of law. The second part of his book, Bigelow maintained, consisted of entirely new ground. German scholars had touched incidentally on English procedure while addressing the law of the Continent. But they had not reconstructed the English procedural system during the Norman period "as a consistent whole," as Bigelow attempted in his book. He called this "undertaking far more arduous ... than the reconstruction of a general system of Teutonic procedure without regard to its actual existence as a whole in any one country."[21]

Bigelow's historical scholarship addressed two major themes that engaged transatlantic scholars then and since: (1) the extent to which the modern English common law derived from Anglo-Saxon or Norman sources and (2) the extent to which English law in the century after the Norman Conquest followed the previous law of Normandy or emerged independently in England. In his introduction to *Placita Anglo-Normannica*, Bigelow challenged the frequent assertion that the English common law originated in "ancient" or "primitive" Germanic law.[22] Although Henry Adams and his students had endorsed this assertion in their *Essays in Anglo-Saxon Law*, Bigelow did not direct his criticism at them but instead cited Heinrich Brunner, the eminent German legal historian, as his example.[23] More specifically, Bigelow rejected the claim that ancient Germanic influences remained as evident in the English common law as they did in the English language. "Every page of our literature," Bigelow observed, "bears the stamp of early German origin." The common law, by contrast, "is essentially different" from Anglo-Saxon law, though he conceded the existence of a "few scattered remains" that could be traced "in unchanged lines to find their origin in the primitive times of the Germanic or Anglo-Saxon

---

[20] Bigelow, supra note 9, at v. Bigelow did not further identify the previous scholars. Among the constitutional historians, he surely was thinking of the English bishop, William Stubbs, whose Constitutional History of England was published in three volumes between 1873 and 1878. Maitland specifically identified Stubbs in explaining why his great work on the history of English law did not include constitutional history. Pollock and Maitland, supra note 19, at xxxvi. Among the German scholars, Bigelow surely was thinking of Heinrich Brunner, with whom he debated how much the law of Normandy influenced subsequent English law.

[21] Melville M. Bigelow, Preface to History of Procedure in England 1–2 (May 1, 1880) (unpublished manuscript) (on file with Harvard University Archives).

[22] Bigelow, supra note 4, at ix.

[23] Id., at ix n. 1.

procedure."[24] Even these remains, he added, have been obscured by numerous subsequent influences that have formed modern English law, including Norman feudalism, Roman law, and the development of commerce. "The existing law, whether of contracts, torts, real property, equity, or even of crimes, disconnected from intermediate stages in history, would fail, in its characteristic parts, to reveal 'the very form and features' of ancient German law, – Salic, Saxon, or Anglo-Saxon. Nor do the old codes of the German nations contain the 'promise and potency' of the present common law of England."[25] Maintaining that it is impossible to speculate how the Germanic law of Anglo-Saxon England would have developed on its own without these subsequent influences, Bigelow was confident that "it could not have resulted in the common law and procedure of the nineteenth century."[26]

Bigelow conceded that most, though far from all, external influences on English law had been Germanic. Yet he immediately qualified this concession by stressing that "the most potent by far of all external Germanic influences, the Norman, had itself been modified, to a considerable extent," by what he called "non-German" or "broken German" law, particularly the "semi-Roman law and civilization" of southern France. The "pure" German law of Anglo-Saxon England, Bigelow concluded, received "a fatal blow at the hands of the Normans."[27] As described by Bigelow, this "fatal blow" occurred gradually between the Norman Conquest of 1066 and the end of the reign of Edward I in 1307. During this transitional period, Anglo-Saxon and Norman law existed side by side, as most Anglo-Saxon law gradually disappeared. Evidence of decline of Anglo-Saxon procedures, Bigelow observed, was often "entirely negative." It could not be found in direct statements of the chronicles and laws. But Bigelow considered the absence of Anglo-Saxon procedure in civil litigation during later Norman and subsequent times, in contrast to its frequent use just after the Norman Conquest, "very marked and suggestive."[28] The legal documents of the century and a half following the Norman Conquest, Bigelow concluded, made it possible to look both backward and forward. These documents revealed many elements of old Germanic law of the past as well as "features, dimly outlined,"[29] of nineteenth-century English common law.

Throughout *History of Procedure in England*, Bigelow provided examples of the continuation and eventual disappearance of Anglo-Saxon law in Norman England. The Anglo-Saxon procedure of ordeal – which used physical tests such as hot and cold water, a hot iron, or swallowing a large morsel of bread or cheese as "a solemn appeal to heaven to decide the dispute" – was gradually replaced by Norman procedures, including the duel as a trial by

[24] Id. at ix.
[25] Id. at x.
[26] Id. at xi.
[27] Id.
[28] Id. at xiii.
[29] Id. at xii.

battle and fact finding through the inquisition.[30] The ordeal received a "fatal" but not yet terminal "blow" when the Lateran Council of 1215 ordered its discontinuance throughout Christendom, though it lasted in practice in England a while longer.[31] In his chapter on the summons to trial, Bigelow maintained that the Anglo-Saxon summons, which was "always a private, extra-judicial act," persisted after the Norman Conquest, but "as time progressed, the custom of sending summons by an officer furnished with the king's writ became established, and finally entirely superseded the ancient mode."[32] Stressing the differences between popular and royal courts, Bigelow observed that in the popular courts of the county, hundred, and manor, Anglo-Saxon procedure "ran its course with little interruption – certainly with no sudden change – during the Norman period"[33] before eventually disappearing, different specific procedures at different times.[34]

Although he stressed the extent to which Norman law superseded Anglo-Saxon law, Bigelow occasionally identified important features of Anglo-Saxon law that persisted beyond the Norman period and contributed to the development of the modern common law. He traced the fundamental distinction between contracts and torts in modern English common law to the early Germanic Salic law, which allowed the right of distraint, the seizure of personal property, as a remedy for a breach of contract, but not as a remedy for a tort. Bigelow concluded that this distinction in Salic law, "under modifications, has continued throughout the history of English law."[35] Most broadly, Bigelow emphasized that the earliest forms of action, through which the common law identified compartments of law, arose from the convergence of the count, the formal statement of the claim originating in Anglo-Saxon law, and the writ, the official authorization to begin legal proceedings introduced from the Continent by the Norman Conquest.[36] The count and the writ, Bigelow explained, existed side by side in Norman England, moving closer together over time and finally converging in the thirteenth century. The "count is unbroken," he declared, "from Alfred to Victoria," from Anglo-Saxon to nineteenth-century England.[37] He repeatedly identified the forms of action of the common law as the "direct lineal descendents" of Anglo-Saxon Germanic law.[38] A "gradual progress" without "any sudden change" marked the transition from the Germanic procedure to the forms of action, which assumed their modern characteristics during

---

[30] Bigelow, supra note 9, at 322, 325–6.
[31] Id. at 323.
[32] Id. at 217.
[33] Id. at 1–2.
[34] Id. at 2.
[35] Id. at 201.
[36] Id. at 147–8; see also J. H. Baker, An Introduction to English Legal History (London: Butterworths, 2002) (4th ed.), pp. 53–4, 56; S. F. C. Milson, Historical Foundations of the Common Law (Toronto: Butterworths, 1981) (2d ed.), p. 39.
[37] Bigelow, supra note 9, at 148.
[38] Id.; see id. at 247.

the reign of Edward I at the end of the thirteenth century.[39] By identifying these continuities, Bigelow tempered his more general rejection of the view that the common law derived from ancient Germanic origins. Despite some inconsistent language, he seemed most interested in denying the strong claim that the essential features of English common law were already contained, in embryonic and preordained form, in ancient Germanic law.

In discussing the extent to which English law after the Norman Conquest followed or developed independently of prior Norman law, Bigelow focused on the role of the King's Court in the development of new writs, including the writ of novel disseisin, which led to the modern jury. His Harvard commencement address highlighted the growth of the King's Court as the major legal development following the Norman Conquest.[40] Whereas in Anglo-Saxon times the king had not been involved in the administration of justice, after the establishment of Norman power in England, he became the "fountain of justice" as the King's Court rose to "permanent power."[41] Of greatest importance, the King's Court created "a remarkable innovation," the use of writs to initiate lawsuits. These writs, in turn, led to modern forms of action and to the jury trial.[42] Commenting on this significant "period of transition," Bigelow observed that "the most permanent impressions made upon civilization have generally been unpremeditated." Neither William the Conqueror nor his sons or grandson had consciously intended the major changes in procedure that occurred during their reigns from 1066 to 1154, yet "the changes actually produced by the advent of the Normans far exceeded in effect any of the purposely-wrought inventions" of their successors.[43]

Bigelow maintained in *History of Procedure in England* that the emergence of the King's Court was an important development in the gradual change from local to central authority that had begun long before. He described the King's Court and indicated how it prevailed over other courts, which tenaciously tried to maintain their ancient privileges.[44] Through new writs, the King's Court acquired jurisdiction "by direct usurpation, in derogation of the rights of the popular courts and manorial franchises."[45] The dominance of the King's Court, he concluded, was completed between 1154 and 1189 during the reign of Henry II, who succeeded in establishing his courts throughout his kingdom and in providing them with jurisdiction over all causes – civil and criminal, legal and equitable. The basic machinery of these courts, Bigelow asserted without any attempt at proof, continued in essentially unaltered form into the nineteenth century, with only a few additions until the 1870s, just before Bigelow published his book.[46]

---

39 Id. at 247.
40 Bigelow, supra note 18, at 7.
41 Id. at 7, 10.
42 Id. at 8.
43 Id. at 1–2.
44 Bigelow, supra note 9, at 75.
45 Id. at 78.
46 Id. at 101–2.

Bigelow emphasized that the writs developed by the King's Court had Norman origins but developed in distinctive English ways. In his introduction to *Placita*, he asserted that the writs manifested a "gradual growth" after the Norman Conquest, at times receding but generally advancing to their permanent form by the late twelfth or early thirteenth century. Invoking the standard biological metaphor of nineteenth-century historical thought, he asserted that the "Norman germs have had their natural development on English soil" and denied any "transplanting of developed forms" from Normandy to England. Just as a characteristically English church architecture arose during this period, "there appears in the history of English law a distinctively English writ procedure."[47] Most importantly for Bigelow, these writs "became the fixed precedents for the peculiar forms of action which have characterized the English law from the time of Edward the First to the present day."[48] Noting that the same form of some of these early English writs may have previously existed in Normandy, Bigelow asserted that Brunner's argument for this position was not well supported, rising "little above conjecture," and even if accurate, did not contradict Bigelow's central point about the significant development of writs in England before they reached their "final, settled form."[49]

Bigelow elaborated his analysis in *History of Procedure in England* while discussing the history of writs that had reached a fixed form by the time of Glanvill in the 1180s,[50] whose treatise on "the laws and customs of England" became a major landmark in the history of English law. Bigelow emphasized that these writs "were not created by a stroke of the pen, or imported into perfect form from Normandy" by Glanvill or anyone else. Rather, "though of continental origin, they were gradually developed on English soil, out of rough and even shapeless material."[51] They lacked any formal language until they reached a definite framework prior to Glanvill, who subsequently wrote about the writs that had already been put into final form.[52] Before the reign of Henry I between 1100 and 1135, writs typically did not indicate the type of action involved in the case or even the subject matter.[53] The connection of the writs to the forms of action, he observed, mostly occurred after the Norman period.[54]

The inquisition introduced from Normandy, Bigelow maintained, was the "great feature of procedure in the Norman period"[55] and had a "direct lineage" to the modern jury. It developed through the writ of novel disseisin, dealing with disputes over property.[56] Though differing little in formal language from previous writs, the writ of novel disseisin importantly added a procedure, the

---

[47] Bigelow, supra note 4, at xxvi.
[48] Id. at xxvii.
[49] Id. at xxvii & n. 1.
[50] Bigelow, supra note 9, at 149.
[51] Id. at 147.
[52] Id. at 191.
[53] Id. at 156.
[54] Id. at 147.
[55] Id. at 331.
[56] Id. at 334.

summons that led to a jury trial.[57] The recognition was a "species of the inquisition."[58] In an inquisition, the court itself served as the inquisitors, whereas the recognition was a chosen group of men who were not part of the court. Both the inquisition and the recognition inquired into the facts in dispute, but the recognition had to report (*recognoscere*) its findings.[59] The recognition was "a body of impartial men, summoned by an officer of the law, to speak the truth concerning the matter in dispute, of which body the officer was never a member. That body in the end was the modern jury."[60] Bigelow conceded that the recognition developed from common Norman and English materials and may have been used for a short period in Normandy before being introduced in England.[61] Yet he challenged Brunner's claim that the transformation of the recognition into a matter of right from a matter of grace had already occurred in Normandy, when the future King Henry II of England was still duke of Normandy.[62] Claiming that Brunner's position "cannot be sustained," Bigelow insisted instead that the change occurred more than sixty years after Henry II had become king of England. Bigelow attributed this major reform to Stephen Langton, the archbishop of Canterbury, who "as the head of the clergy, baronage, and people ... struck the effective blow at the vicious practice (prerogative) of selling justice" through varying the fees charged for obtaining the recognition.[63] The key step from the recognition to the modern jury, Bigelow observed, was the developing view that it was inconsistent for the same person to be both a juror and a witness. Jurors became people unfamiliar with the facts, who were informed about them by the testimony of witnesses, who did know the facts. This differentiation of juror and witness, which occurred after the Norman period, ended the long tradition of judicial examination of jurors, except as to competency.[64]

More generally, while introducing *History of Procedure in England* with the "principles of criticism" that would inform the book, Bigelow warned against the assumption that records from Normandy provide "infallible suggestions" about the details of English law after the Norman Conquest.[65] Although Bigelow believed that "procedure in Normandy offered general types of procedure in England," he maintained that the details often varied.[66] Only in those relatively rare circumstances when the details of procedure were uniform among all Teutonic nations in continental Europe did Bigelow feel comfortable inferring that those details also prevailed in England. Bigelow added that no

---

57 Id. at 172–3.
58 Id. at 335.
59 Id. at 175 n. 4.
60 Id. at 334.
61 Id. at 186 n. 1.
62 Id. at 186.
63 Id. at 186–90.
64 Id. at 336–7.
65 Id. at 1, 4.
66 Id. at 4.

English borrowings from Normandy occurred after 1204 and that there was little or no borrowing during the prior third of a century.[67]

In the course of analyzing the history of procedure, Bigelow displayed historiographical sophistication that refutes the condescension of twentieth-century legal historians toward their nineteenth-century predecessors. Contrary to twentieth-century claims that the nineteenth-century scholars were so focused on the origins of modern legal categories that they misunderstood how legal concepts actually operated in the past,[68] Bigelow repeatedly warned against the anachronistic danger of mistaking apparent similarities between the law of the Norman period and modern common law for actual influences. He maintained that his classification of writs should remove the prior confusion caused by treating writs only in chronological order and by mistaking resemblances between earlier and later writs as proof of a direct lineage. To trace lineage, he declared, "each class must be kept by itself, or its connection with another carefully pointed out."[69] He warned that even when an earlier writ contained language similar to the technical terminology of a later writ requiring a particular mode of trial, it would be dangerous to infer that the earlier writ anticipated the mode of trial of the later writ.[70] The earliest writs for the redress of trespasses did not exhibit "in any settled form" the characteristics of the "familiar writ of trespass of later times," though an "approach to the modern form" could be detected in the last quarter of the twelfth century.[71] He also pointed out that, despite their verbal similarity, the writ of the right of debt was not the source of the modern writ of debt, whose "parent" was instead the writ for money loaned. Yet the old writ of the right of debt was the source of the very differently named modern writ of entry.[72]

Nor did Bigelow view history as progressive, a fault twentieth-century legal scholars frequently ascribed to their predecessors. In his introduction to *Placita Anglo-Normannica*, Bigelow made clear that he did not consider the subsequent history of English law to be a story of progress. During the Anglo-Norman period, he maintained, the administration of justice was simple but efficient. Legal knowledge was minimal, but sufficient for "an age before rights had become complicated by the results of commerce and invention."[73] He especially lamented the loss of the king's prerogative to issue new writs even as he acknowledged that kings had used them to sell justice. "Within proper limits, to guard against abuse, the right to issue writs whenever a case proper for redress or relief was presented was salutary, and its continuance," he added

---

[67] Id. at 6–7.

[68] See, e.g., D. J. Boorstin, Tradition and Method in Legal History, 54 Harv. L. Rev. 424, 424–32 (1941); Gordon, J. Willard Hurst and the Common Law Tradition in American Legal Historiography, 10 Law & Soc'y Rev. 9, 27 (1975).

[69] Bigelow, supra note 9, at 148.

[70] Id. at 156.

[71] Id. at 160.

[72] Id. at 165.

[73] Placita, supra note 4, at xxxix.

using the same phrase as in his commencement address, "would have saved the English law from centuries of constant and deserved reproach." As a result of depriving the king's chancellor of this right, actions on the case emerged, producing "the endless train of subtleties reaching down to the present day, which have so often resulted in the perversion of justice."[74] Like many of his contemporaries, Bigelow clearly favored law reform that would provide more justice by eliminating these subtleties. His regrets about the history of English law and his desire for legal reform challenge twentieth-century assumptions that late nineteenth-century American legal scholars shared naïve beliefs in historical progress and displayed smug satisfaction with existing law.[75]

International Critical Responses

The publication of *Placita Anglo-Normannica* and *History of Procedure in England* brought Bigelow international acclaim. They were reviewed in Germany and England as well as in the United States. Both American and English reviews described *Placita Anglo-Normannica* as a continuation of the work of Adams and his students in *Essays in Anglo-Saxon Law*.[76] One English review observed that *History of Procedure in England* "fulfilled the promise" of Bigelow's previous casebook on torts, which was widely respected in England.[77] The reviews often highlighted the enormous amount of work necessary to produce these volumes, praising Bigelow for his "indefatigable industry"[78] and his "heroic love of learning for its own sake."[79] Brunner wrote the longest and most critical review,[80] though his detailed attention to Bigelow's books itself reveals that Brunner took him seriously.

Most broadly, commentators observed that Bigelow's books contributed to the recent flourishing of interest in the historical study of law in both the United States and England.[81] An English review of *Placita Anglo-Normannica* asserted that the prior work of the leading English scholars Henry Maine and William Stubbs had enlarged the potential audience for Bigelow's book.[82] English reviewers commented, sometimes with embarrassment, that an American had published more detailed scholarship on early English law than any Englishman had

---

[74] Id. at xxx. See Bigelow, supra note 18, at 10.

[75] See, e.g., Morton J. Horwitz, The Conservative Tradition in the Writing of American Legal History, 17 Am J. Legal Hist. 275, 281–3 (1973).

[76] E. J. G. Mackay, The History of Legal Procedure in England, 19 The Academy 219 (March 26, 1881); Placita Anglo-Normannica, 29 The Nation 298, 299 (1879)[hereinafter The Nation].

[77] Mackay, supra note 76, at 219.

[78] Id.

[79] Placita Anglo-Normannica, 13 Am. L. Rev. 737, 738 (1879) [hereinafter American Law Review].

[80] Heinrich Brunner, Litteratur, 2 Zeitschrift der Savigny-Stiftung fur Rechtsgeschichte 202 (1881).

[81] Placita Anglo-Normannica, The Athenaeum, July 19, 1879, at 74–5 [hereinafter The Athenaeum]; The Nation, supra note 76, at 298.

[82] The Athenaeum, supra note 81, at 74.

yet produced. "It deserves the fullest recognition, however mortifying to our national vanity," wrote an English reviewer of *History of Procedure in England*, "that America has challenged the title of German legal scholars to be the only thorough expositors in the present day of our more ancient law before anything of importance has been done in this direction in England itself." The reviewer also observed that together with the *Essays on Anglo-Saxon Law*, Bigelow's book afforded "a gratifying testimony to the zeal and learning of the school of legal history at Harvard."[83] In thanking Bigelow for sending him a copy of *Placita Anglo-Normannica*, Stubbs began a decade of extensive correspondence with him by observing the American contribution to the legal history of England. "It is very pleasant," Stubbs wrote, "to find that on your side of the Atlantic there is so much interest felt and so much good work done in a department of history which at present in England is a little neglected for more exciting political questions."[84] Stubbs also admired *History of Procedure in England*.[85]

By comparing Bigelow's conclusions to those of previous scholars, reviewers helpfully placed his work in historiographical context. One review pointed out that Bigelow had stepped outside the ongoing debate between Germanists and Romanists in England. Bigelow corrected the view that modern English common law derived primarily from ancient Germanic sources, which itself was a reaction against the earlier position that the basic principles of English common law originated in Roman jurisprudence established before the Norman Conquest. For Bigelow, the Norman period in English law constituted a transition between Anglo-Saxon and modern English law in which numerous influences mingled in varying degrees.[86] Reviews observed that Bigelow effectively challenged specific positions of English scholars. Contrary to Edward Freeman's claim that there was no clear evidence of military tenures during the reign of William the Conqueror, Bigelow demonstrated their existence.[87] And contrary to Kenelm Digby's claim about the freedom to alienate property in Norman England, Bigelow cited many cases in which freemen were unable to do so.[88] Bigelow thus saw less freedom in the English past than did the English scholars, a point that the reviewers did not make explicitly but that was implicit in both of their examples. Another review cited Bigelow's challenge to Brunner's view that the English writs were introduced from Normandy. Yet the review minimized the significance of this challenge by observing that Bigelow accepted Brunner's most important conclusions, which linked the origin of inquisitions to the growth of royal power and viewed them as a more civilized form of procedure than the strict popular forms they superseded.[89]

---

[83] Mackay, supra note 76, at 219.

[84] Letter from William Stubbs to Melville Madison Bigelow (June 12, 1879) (Bigelow Collection, supra note 18, Box 2, Stubbs folder).

[85] Letter from William Stubbs to Melville Madison Bigelow (July 2, 1880) (Bigelow Collection, id.).

[86] The Athenaeum, supra note 81, at 74.

[87] The Nation, supra note 76, at 299.

[88] The Athenaeum, supra note 81, at 75.

[89] American Law Review, supra note 135, at 738.

Though generally favorable, the reviews contained some significant criticisms. One suggested that Bigelow exaggerated the importance of the Norman Conquest in the history of English law. Commenting on Bigelow's central claim that the Norman Conquest had delivered a "fatal blow" to Anglo-Saxon law, the review pointed out Bigelow's own acknowledgment that many of the changes in English law during the Norman period would have developed naturally even if the Conquest had not occurred.[90] Another review maintained that Bigelow had slighted the importance of criminal law and especially of canon law in the development of English legal procedure.[91] A particularly negative review accused him of insufficient knowledge of the general history of the Norman period, which produced errors in dating and failure to recognize forgeries,[92] complaints echoed in a letter to Bigelow from Freeman.[93] In private correspondence, Stubbs informed Bigelow that lots of additional records "would have to be searched before anything like a complete repertory of 'Placita Anglo Normannica' could be made up." While eager to talk with Bigelow in England, Stubbs also warned him that "when your book comes to a second edition I shall have a few small points to criticize."[94]

Several reviews, moreover, suggested that Bigelow's admittedly heroic labors in *Placita Anglo-Normannica* had produced a technical and even antiquarian work of limited appeal. One English reviewer observed that practicing lawyers in England "have neither time nor taste for antiquarian researches, and a law-book relating to the ancient procedure of the courts under the Anglo-Norman kings would be regarded as an eccentricity which was likely to do more injury than service to the writer in his profession."[95] While conceding that "a philosophical understanding of law as it is, is impossible, without some well-directed researches into the history of law as it has been," an American review warned that "nothing is easier than to be beguiled from serious questions into curiosities; and it may be asked whether these reports do not fall under the latter head." Though *Placita Anglo-Normannica* fell "upon the border-land between antiquarianism and those studies which are of profit to the profession," the reviewer concluded that it would be useful both to practicing lawyers and to scholars, though not to students.[96] More generously, another American review of *Placita Anglo-Normannica* described it as "designed to assist in the study of the history of law rather than general history," adding that "it has at the same time great value for the student of constitutional and general history."[97]

---

90 The Athenaeum, supra note 81, at 74.

91 Mackay, supra note 76, at 220.

92 Placita Anglo-Normannica: Law Cases from William I to Richard I, [ser. 5] vol. 11 Notes and Queries 519, 519–20 (1879) [hereinafter Notes and Queries]

93 Letter from Edward Freeman to Melville Madison Bigelow (May 30, 1879) (Bigelow Collection, supra note 18, Box 2, Freeman Folder).

94 Letter from William Stubbs to Melville Madison Bigelow (October 20, 1879) (Bigelow Collection, id. Box 2, Stubbs Folder).

95 Notes and Queries, supra note 92, at 519.

96 American Law Review, supra note 79, at 738.

97 The Nation, supra note 76, at 298–9.

Heinrich Brunner wrote the most detailed critical evaluation of Bigelow's two books in a long review essay in *Zeitschrift der Savigny-Stiftung fur Rechtsgeschichte*, a leading German journal. While praising Bigelow's work as very useful, Brunner joined the criticism that Bigelow often misdated and mistakenly accepted the authenticity of the sources he cited. Brunner attributed these failings to Bigelow's unfamiliarity with the history of continental Germanic law and to his reliance on printed materials rather than manuscripts for his original sources. In favorable contrast to Bigelow, Brunner cited his German colleague, Felix Liebermann, who in 1879 had published for the first time previously unpublished original sources on Anglo-Norman law.[98] Substantively, Brunner engaged Bigelow most extensively on the relationship between the prior law in Normandy and the Anglo-Norman law following the Norman Conquest. Brunner observed that German and Anglo-American scholars understandably approached this relationship from different perspectives. The Germans, Brunner believed, were interested in the connections between Anglo-Norman law and the prior Germanic law of the Continent, whereas English and American scholars were interested in the Anglo-Norman roots of the subsequent English common law. Brunner also agreed with Bigelow that it was dangerous to treat apparent similarities between the law of Normandy and Anglo-Norman law as reflecting continuities of legal ideas and institutions. Despite these concessions, Brunner stressed that much Anglo-Norman law can be traced in a continuous link back to the law of Normandy to a much greater extent than Bigelow realized. While acknowledging the emergence of some deep differences between the law of Normandy and English law in the Anglo-Norman period, Brunner maintained that these differences were easily understandable. Only in the thirteenth century, he maintained, did English law become so distinctive that it seemed strange to continental jurists.[99]

Brunner specifically held his ground against Bigelow's claim that Brunner had incorrectly placed the development of the recognition in Normandy rather than in England.[100] If Bigelow knew more about the law of Normandy, Brunner suggested, Bigelow would have noticed these continuities himself. Indeed, Brunner concluded his review by maintaining that it is dangerous to write about Anglo-Norman law without accurate knowledge of continental legal history.[101] Intriguingly, Brunner described Bigelow's chapter in *History of Procedure in England* on the development of writs in Anglo-Norman England as the most valuable in the book, even though Bigelow stressed that the writs were not "imported into perfect form from Normandy" but mostly developed on English soil.[102] Brunner claimed that Bigelow's own evidence reinforced Brunner's conclusion that they originated on the Continent.[103]

---

[98] Brunner, supra note 80, at 204.
[99] Id. at 202.
[100] Id. at 212.
[101] Id. at 214.
[102] Bigelow, supra note 9, at 147.
[103] Brunner, supra note 80, at 211.

Placita Anglo-Normannica and *History of Procedure in England* generated far more praise than criticism and established Bigelow as a major legal scholar with an international reputation. He maintained personal and professional relationships with leading scholars of English legal history both in the United States and in England, where he was better known and appreciated than in his own country.[104] Bigelow and Holmes knew each other well during the 1870s. Holmes later recalled that he "saw a good deal of" Bigelow "in those early years." "How much I was impressed," Holmes wrote, "by his disinterested love of scholarship that led to his counter emigration eastward to get access to the material that he wanted. Without riches he accumulated a part of those materials and gave to the world his very valuable Placita Anglo–Normannica."[105] At a dinner honoring Bigelow in 1913, Brooks Adams, Henry's brother, remarked that in the early 1870s Bigelow and Holmes often worked in the library of the old Boston courthouse. Adams was confident that they "retired to some secret place there to read German law."[106] In late 1875 and early 1876, Holmes read Bigelow's casebook on torts.[107] In the preface of this casebook, Bigelow graciously acknowledged that Holmes's 1873 article "The Theory of Torts" had "a controlling influence" on his own "division of topics."[108] Mark DeWolfe Howe speculated in his biography of Holmes that the discussion of history and policy in Bigelow's casebook in turn probably "stimulated Holmes's interest" in these topics "to a new curiosity."[109]

Throughout the last decades of the nineteenth century, Bigelow remained in contact with Ames and Thayer, his neighbors in Cambridge. They shared and commented on each other's drafts and publications and those of their mutual friends in England.[110] Thayer's son, Ezra, wrote to Bigelow in 1910, gratefully remembering that his father and Bigelow had a "valued friendship of many years."[111] Bigelow and Holmes also maintained their relationship. After

[104] Edward Avery Harriman, 1 B.U. L. Rev. 157, 161–3 (1921).

[105] Id. at 159.

[106] Adams, supra note 12, at 158.

[107] Eleanor N. Little, the Early Reading of Justice Oliver Wendell Holmes, 8 Harvard Library Bulletin 163, 191 (1954).

[108] Bigelow, supra note 15, at vii.

[109] Mark DeWolfe Howe, Justice Oliver Wendell Holmes: The Proving Years, 1870–1882 (Cambridge, Mass.: Harvard University Press, 1963), p. 187 n. 8.

[110] See, e.g., Letter from James Barr Ames to Melville Madison Bigelow (February 16, 1901) (Bigelow Collection, supra note 18, Box 2, Ames Folder); Letter from Melville Madison Bigelow to James Bradley Thayer (November 21, 1898) (James Bradley Thayer Papers, Box 17, Folder 4, Harvard Law School Library) [hereinafter Thayer Papers]; Letter from Melville Madison Bigelow to James Bradley Thayer (October 4, 1892) (Thayer Papers, Box 19, Folder 7); Letter from Melville Madison Bigelow to James Bradley Thayer (February 5, 1892) (Thayer Papers, Box 18, Folder 1), Letter from Melville Madison Bigelow to James Bradley Thayer (November 22, 1889) (Thayer Papers, Box 24, Folder 2); Letter from Melville Madison Bigelow to James Barr Ames (April 20, 1889) (James Barr Ames Papers, Box 1, Folder 5, Harvard Law School Library) [hereinafter Ames Papers]; Letter from Melville Madison Bigelow to James Bar Ames (March 27, 1888) (Ames Papers, Box 1, Folder 5).

[111] Letter from E. R. Thayer to Melville Madison Bigelow (April 14, 1910) (Bigelow Collection, supra note 18, Box 2, E. R. Thayer Folder).

becoming a judge, Holmes asked Bigelow to cite him a case dealing with waiver of contractual conditions. "Of all beneath the Star Spangled banner," Holmes wrote Bigelow, "you I assume know most touching the doctrine of Waiver." Mentioning one of his own decisions, Holmes complained that "I grieve not to see it" in Bigelow's "noble work" on estoppel.[112] When Bigelow's son died, Holmes sent a condolence, prompting a long letter of thanks from Bigelow, who reminisced appreciatively about a lunch for his son that Holmes once gave.[113] In response to a letter from Bigelow congratulating him on his appointment to the Supreme Court, Holmes expressed delight at this "natural expression of mutual friendship": "Among many pleasant letters yours is one of the altogether pleasantest and nicest. We have been alongside for many years, always with great pleasure to me. And time has only increased my respect and warm regard."[114]

Addressing the appropriately named Bigelow Club at Boston University School of Law in 1920, the year before Bigelow died, former President Eliot of Harvard spoke about Bigelow the person as well as the scholar. Eliot gave the impression of knowing Bigelow quite well, referring to various conversations with him when Bigelow was a graduate student at Harvard in the 1870s. Eliot called Bigelow's personal history and experience – presumably his years growing up in Michigan – "remarkable." Already a scholar when he entered Harvard, Bigelow was "a persistent, industrious, and devoted student." Among Bigelow's prodigious scholarly output, Eliot highlighted his book on torts as having had "lasting value" and *Placita Anglo-Normannica* as "his most scholarly work," which "has given him his widest distinction as a scholar in Europe, as well as America." Observing that Bigelow's books were also used in Asia, Africa, and Australia, Eliot maintained that they had "a constant sale in more continents than any American law publication with which I am acquainted." Bigelow's name, Eliot confidently but inaccurately predicted, would "live for generations in the history of legal authorship."[115]

Eliot's address also gave rare insight into Bigelow's private life and personality. Sickly and "of nervous temperament," Bigelow led an isolated and reclusive life, had few intimate friends, and was difficult to contact even by his admirers. Eliot called him "one of the most modest and retiring persons I have ever known" and claimed that Bigelow was uncomfortable when people praised him.[116] To illustrate, Eliot described a dinner in London at which many learned lawyers were eager to meet Bigelow and convey their respect for his excellent scholarship. For Bigelow, this dinner was "a positively painful operation" from

---

[112] Letter from Oliver Wendell Holmes, Jr. to Melville Madison Bigelow (August 15, 1902), microformed on reel 28, 0417 (University Publications of America, Oliver Wendell Holmes Papers) [hereinafter Holmes Papers].

[113] Letter from Melville Madison Bigelow to Oliver Wendell Holmes, Jr. (Apr. 30, undated), microformed on reel 28, 0414–16, Holmes Papers, id.

[114] Letter from Oliver Wendell Holmes, Jr. to Melville Madison Bigelow (August 15, 1902), microformed on reel 28, 0424, Holmes Papers, id.

[115] Charles W. Eliot, Melville M. Bigelow and the Legal Profession, 2 B.U. L. Rev. 17 (1920)

[116] Id. at 17–18.

which he "shrank," "so much so that he did not adequately convey his thanks to those who congratulated him."[117] Reflecting another aspect of Bigelow, as well as Eliot's lifelong contact with him, Eliot told his listeners that Bigelow had recently visited him at home with a book of Bigelow's own poetry. Previously unaware of Bigelow's "poetical side," Eliot praised many of the poems for their high quality.[118]

Just as Bigelow kept in touch with American colleagues, he regularly corresponded, sometimes extensively, with numerous English scholars. They included William Anson, James Bryce, H. A. L. Fisher, Edward Freeman, T. E. Holland, Frederick Pollock, and especially Frederic Maitland. He visited many of them on his trips to England, and they reciprocated when they traveled to Boston.[119] A friend who accompanied Bigelow to England in 1894 recalled visiting Maitland in Cambridge, having dinner with Pollock in London, and seeing many other eminent jurists.[120] According to Brooks Adams, Bigelow's reputation as a scholar, especially for *Placita Anglo-Normannica*, made him "known as our most learned man, the person beyond all others, to whom learned strangers" from England "turned to at once when they visited America."[121]

Bigelow's Close Relationship with Maitland

Bigelow's relationship with Maitland is particularly revealing. That Maitland, the greatest English legal historian, throughout his career maintained a close professional and personal friendship with Bigelow itself provides impressive testimony of Bigelow's importance. Bigelow initiated their correspondence in 1885, at the beginning of Maitland's career. Responding that he taught torts at Cambridge, Maitland wrote to Bigelow: "You therefore are no stranger to me for your books are constantly in my hands and your name in my mouth."[122] Over the remaining twenty years of Maitland's life, he and Bigelow corresponded regularly and at length. "I have lately had occasion to use your Placita Anglo-Normannica and your History of Procedure," Maitland wrote to Bigelow in 1887, "and see that when writing the Appendix for Pollock's Torts I ought to have referred to what you have said about the check put to the invention of writs by the Provisions of Oxford." Maitland added that he had read but not remembered Bigelow's important discussion of this check, which corrected English scholars, who "are too much given to thinking of the original writs as having existed from all eternity." In the same letter, Maitland wrote that Bigelow's "little book on Torts is now definitely established at the head of

---

[117] Id. at 19.
[118] Id. at 18.
[119] See Bigelow Collection, supra note 18, Box 2.
[120] Harriman, supra note 104, at 161–3.
[121] Adams, supra note 12, at 169.
[122] Letter from F. W. Maitland to Melville Madison Bigelow (October 31, 1885), in Warren O. Ault, The Maitland-Bigelow Letters, 37 B.U.L. Rev. 285, 287 (1957). I have not found a copy of the earlier letter from Bigelow to Maitland that prompted this response.

the books on that subject which we recommend to law students." Many copies, Maitland reported with pleasure, were at the local bookstore. Yet Maitland also reported that his friend R. T. Wright, a barrister and lecturer at Cambridge, had urged him to ask Bigelow to prepare an English edition in which English rather than American cases would be given more prominence.[123] Bigelow pursued this suggestion,[124] eventually producing three editions of his English version to complement the eight editions of the original American volume.[125] He dedicated the English edition to Maitland and Wright.[126] A similar dedication in a subsequent edition prompted Maitland to respond that nothing could have given him "a pleasanter proof of our friendship" and to exclaim "what a good book it is!"[127]

Throughout their twenty years of correspondence, Bigelow commented substantively on Maitland's work, and Maitland typically responded with gracious appreciation. On one occasion, Bigelow found a mistranslation in one of Maitland's books. Maitland thanked him "for exposing the blunder" and promised to correct it.[128] Maitland even praised Bigelow behind his back. Apparently referring to the same mistranslation, he wrote to Thayer that a remark by Bigelow "will force me to an 'erratum.' How wonderfully keen he is."[129] Maitland wrote to Bigelow that he had "adopted your opinion about distress for rent arrear"[130] and would make use of his "valuable contribution" in a "note about the liability of townships."[131] Maitland found a letter from Bigelow about corporate liability so interesting that he read it during one of his lectures.[132] While working with the English Year Books, Maitland wrote that he would soon send the finished volume, which he hoped would satisfy Bigelow.[133]

Maitland and Bigelow expressed mutual admiration in print as well as in correspondence. In Maitland's preface to *Bracton's Note Book*, his first major

---

[123] Letter from F. W. Maitland to Melville Madison Bigelow (May 13, 1887), in Ault, supra note 122, at 290.

[124] Letters from F. W. Maitland to Melville Madison Bigelow (June 23, 1887, August 11, 1887, and January 1, 1888), in Ault, supra note 122, at 290–3.

[125] Ault, supra note 122, at 285.

[126] Id. at 294 n. 19.

[127] Letter from F. W. Maitland to Melville Madison Bigelow (August 9, 1903), in Ault, supra note 122, at 318.

[128] Letter from F. W. Maitland to Melville Madison Bigelow (February 24, 1889), in Ault, supra note 122, at 294–5.

[129] Letter from F. W. Maitland to James Bradley Thayer (February 18, 1889) (Thayer Papers, supra note 110, Box 18, Folder 14).

[130] Letter from F. W. Maitland to Melville Madison Bigelow (February 24, 1889), in Ault, supra note 122, at 295.

[131] Letter from F. W. Maitland to Melville Madison Bigelow (February 1, 1891), in Ault, supra note 122, at 299.

[132] Letter from F. W. Maitland to Melville Madison Bigelow (April 19, 1891), in Ault, supra note 122, at 300.

[133] Letter from F. W. Maitland to Melville Madison Bigelow (August 9, 1903), in Ault, supra note 122, at 318.

work, he expressed his "best thanks" to Bigelow and Thayer "for the encouragement given me by friendly letters from a land where Bracton is at least as well known and at best as highly honoured as he is in England."[134] Thanking Maitland for sending him a copy, Bigelow responded: "You are far too modest in your Preface. You have done a lasting service to students of the history of our law, and with such sound *sense* [and] scholarship as leave no chance for caviling."[135] Eight years later, Maitland sent Bigelow his masterpiece, *The History of English Law before the Time of Edward I*. Bigelow wrote a lengthy favorable review in the inaugural issue of the *American Historical Review*,[136] prompting Maitland to express his "heartily grateful" thanks.[137] In commenting on the book's "fresh, ready, almost conversational" style, Bigelow drew on his personal friendship with Maitland. "To one who knows Mr. Maitland," he observed, "it is his living voice, or at least his epistolary pen."[138] In a letter accompanying the copy of his book he sent Bigelow, Maitland expressed his own warm personal feelings. "With my share of the gift," Maitland wrote, "go pleasant memories of hours spent over the Placita Anglo Normannica and of pleasant talks with its author. I hope that when looking at the book you will remember Downing and Horsepools," Maitland's homes in England that Bigelow and his wife had visited.[139] After one of Bigelow's visits, Maitland wrote to Bigelow "that to have had you and Mrs. Bigelow as my guests has been one of the greatest pleasures of my life."[140] Their subsequent letters, and the correspondence between their wives, are filled with intimate details of family life.[141]

In addition to their mutual engagement with the history of medieval English law, Maitland and Bigelow shared their disappointment with the condition of legal education and legal history in their countries. "I am sorry to say," Maitland wrote to Bigelow in a letter enclosing a list of law lectures delivered at Cambridge, "that at present we have a great deal of Roman Law and of what is called General Jurisprudence in our scheme – but I hope that a projected alteration may give English law a fairer chance."[142] A few months later, Bigelow wrote to Maitland that the publication of *Bracton's Note Book* should help the cause of legal history in the United States. No American law school,

---

[134] Bracton's Note Book (London: C. J. Clay & Sons, 1887) (F. W. Maitland, ed.), vol. 1, pp. vii–viii.

[135] Letter from Melville Madison Bigelow to F. W. Maitland (December 19, 1887) (Frederic William Maitland Papers, Cambridge University Library, Add 7006).

[136] Melville M. Bigelow, The History of English Law Before the Time of Edward I, 1 Am. Hist. Rev. 112 (1895).

[137] Letter from F. W. Maitland to Melville Madison Bigelow (November 3, 1895), in Ault, supra note 122, at 304.

[138] Bigelow, supra note 136, at 113.

[139] Letter from F. W. Maitland to Melville Madison Bigelow (March 30, 1895), in Ault, supra note 122, at 302.

[140] Letter from F. W. Maitland to Melville Madison Bigelow (June 5, 1889), in Ault, supra note 122, at 295.

[141] See Ault, supra note 122 passim.

[142] Letter from F. W. Maitland to Melville Madison Bigelow, supra note 123, at 289.

Bigelow informed Maitland, had a chair in legal history, and "what we do in teaching we must smuggle in or get in as best we may in connection with other work." Bigelow did not think that American law schools were hostile or even indifferent to legal history. The problem was that no funds existed to endow positions in the subject. Bigelow believed that Maitland's book would encourage the "growing feeling" that such positions were needed. He specifically hoped that Harvard would establish a professorship in the history of English law. "A noble field of work," he added, "will the first incumbent have!"[143]

From Legal History to Proto-Realism

In the decades following *Placita Anglo-Normannica* and *History of Procedure in England*, Bigelow received professional acclaim and continued to publish steadily. He received the LL.D. from Northwestern and Michigan and became a fellow of the American Academy of Arts and Sciences.[144] In addition to the English editions of his torts book and his lengthy review of *The History of English Law*, he published eight editions of *Bigelow on Torts*; six editions of *Bigelow on Estoppel*; and three editions each of *Bigelow's Bills, Notes and Cheques*; *Bigelow on Equity*; *Bigelow on Wills*; and *Bigelow on Fraudulent Conveyances*. He followed Cooley as the editor of Story's *Commentaries on the Constitution of the United States* and also became the editor of Story's *Commentaries on the Conflict of Laws*.[145] His articles appeared in the early volumes of the *Law Quarterly Review*[146] and the *Harvard Law Review*,[147] leading legal publications in England and the United States. Scholars from abroad solicited work from Bigelow. As organizer of the Cambridge Modern History series, Lord Acton asked Bigelow to contribute a chapter on early American constitutional history.[148] Bigelow wrote the chapter Acton requested,[149] but he apparently did not pursue a flattering invitation to contribute an article to the *Allahabad Law Journal* in India, whose editor wrote to him that "there is probably at the present moment no American text-writer who is held in greater respect in India than yourself."[150]

---

[143] Letter from Melville Madison Bigelow to F. W. Maitland, supra note 122.

[144] Ault, supra note 122, at 285.

[145] David J. Seipp, Who Was Melville Madison Bigelow?, B.U. School of Law Alumni Magazine, Winter 1996, pp. 6, 7.

[146] Melville M. Bigelow, Definition of Circumvention, 5 L.Q. Rev. 140 (1889); Melville M. Bigelow, Definition of Fraud, 3 L.Q. Rev. 419 (1887); Melville M. Bigelow, Mistake of Law as a Ground of Equitable Relief, 1 L.Q. Rev. 298 (1885).

[147] Melville M. Bigelow, Alterations of Negotiable Instruments, 7 Harv. L. Rev. 1 (1893).

[148] Letter from Lord Acton to Melville Madison Bigelow (June 11, 1897) (Bigelow Collection, supra note 18, Box 2, Acton Folder).

[149] Melville M. Bigelow, The Constitution (1776–1789), in The Cambridge Modern History: The United States (New York, The MacMillan Company, 1903) (A. W. Ward et al. eds.), vol. 7, pp. 235–304.

[150] Letter from S. C. Banerji to Melville Madison Bigelow (December 6, 1907) (Bigelow Collection, supra note 18, Box 2, Banerji Folder).

In 1902, Bigelow became dean of the Boston University Law School, resigning when he turned sixty-five in 1911. Bigelow's old friend, Brooks Adams,
joined the faculty in 1903 and stayed for the remainder of Bigelow's deanship.[151] Bigelow and Brooks Adams collaborated on a series of essays published in 1906 under the title *Centralization and the Law*. In this book of
proto-realism and in other writing, Bigelow emphasized the growing inequality in the United States produced by the rapid social and economic changes of
the late nineteenth century.[152] He maintained that law schools must develop a
"scientific spirit" to understand and respond to these forces,[153] for which traditional legal education was insufficient.[154] In an article entitled "A Scientific
School of Legal Thought," published in 1905 and reprinted in *Centralization
and the Law* as the chapter "Scientific Method in Law," Bigelow elaborated
his views in ways that questioned and modified his earlier interest in legal history while making many of the same points that Roscoe Pound was stressing
more influentially in his contemporaneous early articles promoting "sociological jurisprudence."

At the beginning of his article, Bigelow asserted that both in England and
in the United States two successive schools of legal thought had dominated.
The analytic school, associated with Jeremy Bentham and John Austin, had
been followed by the historical school, founded by Henry Maine. The analytic
school, Bigelow maintained, "threw aside the teachings of history, except such
as were permanent in nature – and these could hardly be called historical – and
planted itself on its own conception of the nature of rights and law." It could,
therefore, "serve up codes and constitutions according to taste." Though the
analytic school enjoyed some "palmy days of *a priori* law," it did not take
root in either country and in both was superseded by the historical school,
which still prevailed. The historical school studied legal history "as the true
and main source of our present law. The whole of the past, as far back as the
Norman era, is to be placed before the student, not because all of this, or the
greater part of it, may be necessary to explain the judicial law of our day, but
because there is one continuous stream of law from the earliest times to our
own." Bigelow acknowledged that he had been an "interested witness, and to a
considerable extent a follower myself" of the historical school.[155] But he wrote
his article because he had become persuaded, probably in large part by Brooks
Adams, "that there is something better than either the analytic or the historical school, better than both combined," namely, the "scientific school of legal
thought."[156]

Bigelow barely elaborated what he meant by the "scientific school of legal
thought." He spent most of his article maintaining that current law was

[151] Seipp, supra note 145, at 6–7.
[152] Bigelow, supra note 1, at 4.
[153] Id. at 12–13, 17–18.
[154] Id. at 12–13.
[155] Melville M. Bigelow, A Scientific School of Legal Thought, 17 The Green Bag 1 (1905).
[156] Id. at 1–2.

"losing connection with life,"[157] thereby creating an unhealthy though understandable public skepticism about the legal system.[158] He used the law of procedure as an example. Just as he had complained in his introduction to *Placita Anglo-Normannica* that the "endless subtleties" of procedural law had produced "the perversion of justice" that continued in the present,[159] Bigelow declared that "procedure had become a prison-house for the law. Many a crippled rule of substantive law traces its appearance back sooner or later to some phase of procedure – to set forms of action, jurisdiction, 'niceties' of pleading."[160]

The goal of the scientific school of legal thought, Bigelow apparently believed, was to regain the lost connection between life and law by studying "the actual conditions of life in our day."[161] It should examine all the sources of law, "not merely the history of doctrine founded upon peculiar conditions of the past, which, notwithstanding all changes, still more or less prevails, but the direct and immediate sublegal sources."[162] For Bigelow, these "sublegal sources" included the activities of business and government and, more generally, "political, economic, psychological, and personal influences."[163] Legal education, he emphasized, should include all of these subjects.[164]

In pursuing his new "scientific" approach to law, Bigelow continued to consider legal history important, but only when it informed the study of current law. Legal history, he maintained, could help explain what otherwise seems obscure or meaningless in current law.[165] It could also provide grounds for changing laws that made sense in the past but that have actually become meaningless or even dysfunctional in the changed conditions of the present. "If we govern ourselves to-day by laws laid down yesterday," he reasoned, "it is or should be because those laws are suited to us; they are our own laws, not *a priori* laws made for us by another set of men." Even if laws were effective in the past, why when they no longer work should they "have a posthumous life, to trouble men living under other conditions?"[166] Any law, whether ancient or relatively modern, "which has been kept alive after the conditions under which it was laid down have essentially disappeared, has become from the time of the change an *a priori* rule, and so out of touch with sound theory."[167] Such laws should be left to die.[168] As he wrote in the introduction to *Centralization and the Law*, "the law is handicapped in all its branches with historical survivals"

[157] Id. at 9.
[158] See, e.g., id. at 3.
[159] Bigelow, supra note 4, at xxx.
[160] Bigelow, supra note 155, at 8.
[161] Id. at 2, 9, 16.
[162] Id. at 14.
[163] Id. at 14–15.
[164] Id. at 12–16.
[165] Id. at 14.
[166] Id. at 13.
[167] Id. at 11.
[168] Id. at 13.

and "should be constantly laying aside the grave-clothes of a dead past." Past law should remain only "so long as it is adapted to maintaining the order for which it was intended."[169] Bigelow's friends and contemporaries Holmes and Thayer had been making similar points about the importance of uncovering and discarding dysfunctional survivals in current law.[170]

Based on this analysis, Bigelow concluded that legal history was valuable in assessing the extent to which the past should govern the present but should not be taught simply as a continuous stream. To do so, he believed, would "be not merely waste – it would be positively misleading – it would be putting the chase on the wrong scent." "A clear distinction," he immediately added, "should be made between what influences the declaration of law and what may be useful for other purposes." When legal history "fails to shed light upon our own path," he maintained, it should "be turned over to the historian," to be studied for its intrinsic interest and for "broadening of the mind," even of law students, but not for "teaching our own law."[171] Bigelow seemed to feel that teaching legal history as a continuous stream would encourage people to think that past law should influence "the declaration of" present law simply because they both formed part of this stream. That, apparently, was the "wrong scent" he wanted to avoid.

In an interesting letter responding to Bigelow's new approach, Paul Vinogradoff, a leading scholar of English legal history who had emigrated from Russia to England, indicated his general agreement. "Law ought not to remain indefinitely behind life," Vinogradoff wrote. Yet his "only misgiving" about "scientific, that is, theoretical thought" was significant. Vinogradoff expressed his "apprehension that the needs of today may make us forget that we are products elaborated by a long organic process, and that neither language nor laws can be altered like a set of clothes." Changing metaphors, Vinogradoff asked: "Should we not call a poor surgeon one who would look with contempt on the study of anatomy because he wants to operate on the living and not on the dead?" He reminded Bigelow that medieval legal institutions had more to offer the present than "only dust."[172] In these comments, Vinogradoff defended the assumptions of the traditional "historical school" to which Bigelow admitted he once belonged and from which from he was trying to differentiate himself in his work with Brooks Adams.

During the years Bigelow served as dean, Boston University School of Law increased its admissions requirements, requiring a long list of courses in the liberal arts, and moved from an elective to a required curriculum. It also reduced the pedagogical choices of its faculty from "all approved systems and methods" to a prescribed combination of cases, problems, and exposure to the

---

[169] Bigelow, supra note 1, at 2.

[170] Oliver Wendell Holmes, Jr., The Common Law (Cambridge, Mass.: Harvard University Press, 1963) (Mark DeWolfe Howe ed.) (original ed. 1881); Thayer, supra note 8.

[171] Bigelow, supra note 155, at 13–14.

[172] Letter from Paul Vinogradoff to Melville Madison Bigelow (July 2, 1904) (Bigelow Collection, supra note 18, Box 2, Vinogradoff Folder).

courtroom.[173] But the School of Law never implemented the broad study of the political, economic, and psychological "sublegal sources" of law that Bigelow advocated in his manifesto encouraging the "scientific method in law." Nor did Bigelow's proto-realistic scholarship take hold. Charles Eliot wrote that it was "more theoretical, more philosophical, and also less hopeful" than Bigelow's other work "and, therefore, not likely to live as long." Observing Bigelow's close relationship with Brooks Adams, "his most intimate friend" at the time, Eliot added that Adams's "eccentricities," particularly his position as "a cynical critic of democracy and American society," had hampered Bigelow's own contributions to their joint project, *Centralization and the Law*.[174]

The emergence of Roscoe Pound as a major legal scholar probably contributed to the minimal impact of Bigelow's proto-realism. A generation younger than Bigelow, Pound wrote a series of enormously influential articles in the decade before World War I that explored similar themes while developing what Pound called "sociological jurisprudence."[175] Pound's articles, which propelled him to academic preeminence, overshadowed Bigelow's less scholarly, more polemical, and more pessimistic work with Brooks Adams. In contrast to Bigelow, who himself recognized his own prior participation in the historical school, Pound was a fresh scholarly voice who presented sociological jurisprudence as superseding the historical jurisprudence he criticized as a historian of legal thought.

Late Work in Legal History: The Perils of "Undisciplined Individualism"

After he left the deanship in 1911, Bigelow returned to the study of legal history. In 1920, the year before he died, he published a collection of his historical essays in a book entitled *Papers on the Legal History of Government*. Much more overtly ideological than his early work in *Placita Anglo-Normannica* and *History of Procedure in England*, many of these essays invoked the "chastening page" of history to warn against the "undisciplined individualism" that he, like many scholars on both sides of the Atlantic in the early twentieth century, viewed as the central threat to democracy in his own time.[176] He maintained that "the most stable and efficient government is found where the individual is blended into a common or collective consciousness and will, in the hands of an executive fully backed by and responsible to the people."[177] His essays emphasized the historical role of religion and the family as sources of unity and

---

[173] Elizabeth Kahn, Dean Bigelow's "Scientific School of Legal Education" (unpublished student seminar paper on file with author), p. 8.

[174] Eliot, supra note 115, at 18.

[175] Roscoe Pound, The Scope and Purpose of Sociological Jurisprudence I, 24 Harv. L. Rev. 591 (1911); Roscoe Pound, The Scope and Purpose of Sociological Jurisprudence II, 25 Harv. L. Rev. 140 (1912); Roscoe Pound, The Scope and Purpose of Sociological Jurisprudence III, 25 Harv. L. Rev. 489 (1912).

[176] Bigelow, supra note 3, at 149–51.

[177] Id. at 148–9.

bulwarks against "undisciplined individualism." He simultaneously stressed that unity in a collective consciousness "cannot be rendered under guise or disguise of accredited privilege."[178]

One of Bigelow's essays in this volume, "Becket and the Law," illustrated his central themes through a crucial episode in the historical period covered by the books that made his reputation forty years earlier. The conflict between King Henry II and Thomas Becket in the middle of the twelfth century, he believed, resulted in the defeat of an emerging and healthy collectivism by "self-interested individualism."[179] Bigelow sadly concluded that this defeat was a significant turning point that had devastating and continuing consequences for English law and society.[180]

According to Bigelow, Becket was a collectivist who believed that morality, as expressed by church canons, must be the basis of law.[181] For Becket, any distinction between law and morals encouraged undisciplined and self-aggrandizing individualism that would divide society.[182] He maintained that canon law, which expressed principles of equity,[183] had priority over all inconsistent secular law.[184] Becket's commitment to this general position took a concrete form in his dispute with King Henry II over the Constitutions of Clarendon in 1164, an attempt to resolve the respective roles of church and state.[185] Bigelow stressed that the primary dispute between Becket and King Henry II concerned the division of jurisdiction between church and secular courts, not the substantive law to be applied in each court. The king knew and supported Becket's commitments to equitable principles in all courts while helping him become chancellor and archbishop.[186] In the actual controversy over the Constitutions of Clarendon, moreover, the king demonstrated his respect for canon law by sending them to the pope for ratification.[187] As to matters of substantive law, the king wanted only to exclude from the equitable principles of canon law matters directly related to his ability to raise funds.[188] The king had no objection, by contrast, to the operation of equity in secular courts regarding private matters between men that did not involve the state.[189]

Becket's dispute with the king over jurisdiction, Bigelow maintained, could have been avoided by compromises on each side. But once the jurisdictional dispute was engaged, he indicated, issues of substantive law could not be avoided.[190] For Bigelow, the "pity" of the controversy over the Constitutions of

---

178 Id. at 151.
179 Melville M. Bigelow, Becket and the Law, in Papers, supra note 3, at 186.
180 Id. at 218–20.
181 Id. at 193–4.
182 Id. at 200–1.
183 Id. at 205, 213, 217.
184 Id. at 212.
185 Id. at 199.
186 Id. at 215.
187 Id. at 217 & n. 1.
188 Id. at 214–17.
189 Id. at 238–39 n. 1.
190 Id. at 218.

Clarendon was that "the great moral idea of establishing the rule of equity in secular affairs was to be caught and broken on the wheel of an issue which did not involve the existence of Church authority and should never have arisen."[191] Bigelow believed that England faced a choice between collectivism and individualism during the period immediately before the Constitutions of Clarendon. This emergency "put an end to England's better hope," collectivism, "upon an issue that was not vital," the king's power to finance his ambitions.[192] After Becket, Bigelow sadly observed, no other Englishman arose to champion his related causes of collectivism, morality, and equity. As an unfortunate result, England muddled along under the influence of selfish individualism "until muddling should come to be defended as the proper way."[193]

Bigelow elaborated the disastrous effects of the decline of equity in secular courts after the controversy over the Constitutions of Clarendon. Though principles of equity had considerable influence in secular courts at the time of Becket and the potential for substantially more,[194] they were eliminated from virtually every area of secular law after the Constitutions of Clarendon. In particular, the developing secular law ignored equity's attention to subjective states of mind and focused instead on the objective effects of acts.[195] Criminal law looked to the body, rather than to the mind, as the criminal agent, and, therefore, allowed brutal bodily mutilation and barbarous forms of capital punishment.[196] Though the church had come close to enforcing promises through principles of equity, the writ process that developed in the thirteenth century "drove equity out of the common law courts"[197] and postponed the development of contract and tort law.[198] The courts became immersed in "technicalities concerning matters of mere form," such as debt and covenant, and justice became "hopelessly ensnared" in "an interminable web of subtle and useless refinements and distinctions."[199] The situation became so intolerable that, at the end of the fourteenth century, the Court of Chancery was established as a "stop-gap" court of equity,[200] which for centuries provoked "the marvel of judges of rival courts flinging jurisdictional fictions at each other with all the effect of reality." In America, issues of justice were severed entirely from the law.[201]

---

[191] Id. at 218–19.

[192] Id. at 217–18.

[193] Id. at 219. Other discussions of the Constitutions of Clarendon are much clearer and more detailed about the jurisdictional disputes and historical background, but do not focus on their implications for the role of equity in secular law, Bigelow's distinctive interest. See, e.g., The History of English Law, supra note 19, vol. I, at 124–5, 137, 447–57; vol. II, at 198–9; G. O. Sayles, The Medieval Foundations of England (New York: A. S. Barnes & Company, 1961), pp. 342–51.

[194] Bigelow, supra note 179, at 202, 206.

[195] See id. at 230.

[196] Id. at 220–1.

[197] Id. at 225.

[198] Id. at 223–4.

[199] Id. at 223.

[200] Id. at 226.

[201] Id. at 227.

If only Becket had prevailed! "All this long-drawn-out waste"[202] would have been avoided. Legal collectivism would have granted equitable powers to all courts, allowing them to take subjective as well as objective factors into account.[203] Bigelow conceded that even if Becket had won or avoided the controversy over the Constitutions of Clarendon, his legal collectivism might not have taken hold. But if it had become permanent, the legal history of England "would have changed for the better."[204]

Bigelow ended his paper by bringing his story and lesson up to the present. He claimed that legal collectivism, and, more specifically, the equitable emphasis on states of mind, were "steadily gaining ground" in legal analysis.[205] Yet he warned that the utilitarian doctrines of Jeremy Bentham and John Stuart Mill were "a modern reaction against tendencies to consider states of the mind, or equity, in all courts, as the true test of conduct." Thus, "the great struggle of legal history," in which Becket, the leader of one camp, fell to a side issue of jurisdiction, continued for Bigelow and his readers.[206]

Though Bigelow remained productive throughout his career, *Placita Anglo-Normannica* and *History of Procedure in England*, his original work in English legal history written in his first decade as a law professor, constitute his major scholarly legacy. As reviewers observed at the time, they built on the work of Henry Adams and his students in *Essays on Anglo-Saxon Law*. These two books were widely respected on both sides of the Atlantic, most impressively by Frederic Maitland, the great English legal historian. Maitland praised them in his own scholarship and maintained a lifelong friendship with Bigelow that combined professional engagement and personal intimacy. Bigelow was the most prolific of the late nineteenth-century scholars who initiated the professional study of legal history in the United States through their research on early English law. Building on his work, Holmes, Thayer, and Ames made major additional contributions. Their scholarship underlines the general importance of the turn to history by American legal scholars in the decades after the Civil War.

---

[202] Id. at 225.
[203] Id. at 228.
[204] Id. at 220.
[205] Id. at 229.
[206] Id. at 230.

VII

Holmes the Historian

The Common Law, published in 1881 by Oliver Wendell Holmes, Jr., was the next major American work of legal history after the *Essays in Anglo-Saxon Law* in 1876 and Bigelow's two books in 1879 and 1880. Perhaps the most influential book about law ever written by an American, *The Common Law* had an enormous impact in the United States and abroad. Unlike any other work of legal history written by an American in the nineteenth century, it has received widespread and continuous scholarly attention since its publication. From the original reviews to the present, scholars have accurately portrayed it as combining legal history with jurisprudential analysis.[1] It soon became a classic of legal scholarship, more for its treatment of the core concepts of the common law than for the legal history on which Holmes purported to ground his analysis. As numerous scholars have observed, Holmes repeatedly exaggerated his own originality while minimizing the contributions of others to his thought.[2] He thereby obscured his relationship to the intellectual history of his age, including the substantial extent to which he shared widespread views about the role of history in legal analysis.

---

[1] See, e.g., Albert V. Dicey, Holmes's *Common Law*, The Spectator (June 3, 1882), reprinted in 10 Hofstra L. Rev. 712; 51 Saturday Review 758 (1881); Mark DeWolfe Howe, Justice Oliver Wendell Holmes: The Proving Years, 1870–1882 (Cambridge, Mass.: Harvard University Press, 1963), pp. 137, 182, 192–3, 204, 211, 228; Morton J. Horwitz, The Transformation of American Law 1870–1960: The Crisis of Legal Orthodoxy (New York: Oxford University Press, 1992), p. 41; G. Edward White, Justice Oliver Wendell Holmes: Law and the Inner Self (New York: Oxford University Press, 1993), p. 112; Robert W. Gordon, Holmes' *Common Law* as Legal and Social Science, 10 Hofstra L. Rev. 719 (1982); Thomas C. Grey, Holmes and Legal Pragmatism, 41 Stan. L. Rev. 787, 805–6 (1989); Mathias Reimann, Holmes's *Common Law* and German Legal Science, in The Legacy of Oliver Wendell Holmes, Jr. (Stanford, Calif.: Stanford University Press, 1992) (Robert W. Gordon, ed.), pp. 72, 79; J. W. Burrow, Holmes in His Intellectual Milieu, in Gordon, id. at 17, 20.

[2] See, e.g., White, supra note 1, at 115, 146, 194; Reimann, supra note 1, at 97–8, 102–4, 252 n. 65, 258 n. 110, 260–1 n. 145; Howe, supra note 1, at 71–2, 84–5; Bruce A. Kimball, The Inception of Modern Professional Education: C. C. Langdell, 1826–1906 (University of North Carolina Press, 2009), pp. 103–6; Grey supra note 1, at 841 n. 263.

Yet both English and American reviews of *The Common Law* recognized that Holmes contributed to an emerging American historical school of legal analysis. An American review began by identifying Holmes as "but one of several New England gentlemen who have lately made valuable contributions to the philosophical and the historical literatures of the common law." The accompanying footnote cited the *Essays in Anglo-Saxon Law* and Bigelow's two books.[3] Just as an English reviewer praised Bigelow's *History of Procedure in England* for surpassing the English themselves in the study of English legal history,[4] Frederick Pollock started his review of *The Common Law* by observing that he had previously "called attention to the danger in which English lawyers stand of being outrun by their American brethren in the scientific and historical criticism of English institutions and ideas." Holmes's book, Pollock maintained, "adds considerably to the advantage gained on the American side in this friendly contest."[5] Pollock closed his review by calling the book a valuable, even indispensable "companion to the scientific student of legal history,"[6] and an American review described it as "legal embryology."[7] As some contemporaries and subsequent scholars have observed, Holmes owed major intellectual debts to Savigny and Maine. Holmes's important relationships with his American contemporaries have received less notice. Of particular significance, Henry Adams helped direct Holmes from his early philosophical analysis of law in the early 1870s toward more historical explanations.

Although Holmes was in the mainstream of the historical turn in late nineteenth-century American legal thought, he was distinctive in several significant respects. Exceptionally ambitious, he took the entire common law as his subject, in contrast, for example, to Henry Adams and his students on aspects of Anglo-Saxon law, Bigelow on procedure, Thayer on evidence, and Ames on discrete topics in the common law. Perhaps fueled by his ambition, Holmes frequently manipulated history to serve his analytical goals, often sacrificing historical accuracy in ways that made him a much less reliable historian than Adams and his students, Bigelow, Thayer, and Ames. Yet Holmes, perhaps also reflecting his ambition, often addressed the role of history in legal analysis more directly, more vividly, and with more attention to theoretical concerns than the other late nineteenth-century American legal historians. Their views on the historiographical and jurisprudential implications of evolutionary legal thought were more embedded and less developed in their work, even as they produced more original and significant research in legal history than Holmes ever undertook or accomplished.

Holmes's commitment to objective and external standards as the underlying principle of the common law helps explain much of the treatment of history

---

[3] The Common Law, 26 Albany L.J. 484 & n (1882).

[4] E. J. G. Mackay, The History of Legal Procedure in England, 19 The Academy 219 (March 26, 1881).

[5] 51 Saturday Review 758 (1881), supra note 1, unsigned but ascribed to Pollock in White, supra note 1, at 188.

[6] Id. at 759.

[7] Holmes's *Common Law*, 15 Am. L. Rev. 331, 332 (1881).

in his book, including his analysis of survivals of previous law in current legal doctrine, his disparagement of Roman law, his emphasis on the Germanic origins of the English common law, his frequent historical inaccuracies, his use of history alternatively to support or undermine existing doctrine, and his neglect of historical detail and of historical issues whose interest and importance he readily conceded. Moral and subjective language in contemporary common law, Holmes frequently maintained, either had been reinterpreted over time to enforce objective and external standards or constituted a dysfunctional survival that should be reformed. Holmes believed that Roman law stood as a barrier to objective and external standards because it had been interpreted by influential German legal scholars under the pernicious spell of the moralism and individualism rampant in German metaphysical thought. He maintained that traditional Germanic law, by healthy contrast, had not been infected by German metaphysics and actually expressed objective and external standards. The inaccuracies detected by Holmes's contemporaries and successors were often attempts to provide historical support for his thesis that objective and external standards pervaded the common law. Holmes cited history as authority when he felt it could support the objective and external standards he favored but used history to undermine current doctrine that did not support such standards.

When Holmes was appointed to the Supreme Judicial Court of Massachusetts in 1882, he mostly left the world of scholarship for a long and distinguished career as a judge. Yet he continued to publish occasional papers. Leading American legal scholars, from Roscoe Pound at the beginning of the twentieth century to Morton Horwitz at its end, have asserted that Holmes abandoned historical explanations of the law by the late 1890s. For both Pound and Horwitz, Holmes's rejection of history provided key evidence that he had left the nineteenth century behind and stimulated the very different legal thought of the twentieth. I disagree, finding in his later essays substantial reiteration of the same historical themes that predominated in his scholarship through the publication of *The Common Law* in 1881. I agree with Pound and Horwitz that by the late 1890s Holmes expressed confidence that the emerging social sciences would provide useful tools for the analysis of policy that should guide law reform. Like Bigelow a few years later, he endorsed many of the positions Pound soon popularized as "sociological jurisprudence." Yet Holmes, also like Bigelow, continued to view legal history as playing a key role in legal analysis, particularly in identifying and eliminating dysfunctional survivals. Holmes, moreover, retained his conception of law as the product of evolving history, from which it could not escape. To invoke one of Holmes's most famous aphorisms, he did not believe that "continuity with the past" was "a duty," but he did believe that it was often "a necessity," however regrettable.[8] Holmes anticipated the sociological jurisprudence of the twentieth century without

---

[8] Oliver Wendell Holmes, Law in Science and Science in Law, 12 Harv. L. Rev. 443 (1899), reprinted in Oliver Wendell Holmes, Collected Legal Papers (New York: Harcourt, Brace and Company, 1921) [hereinafter Collected Legal Papers], pp. 210, 211.

abandoning the evolutionary historical approach that dominated American legal thought in the late nineteenth century.

The Influence of Savigny and Maine

In analyzing Holmes's scholarship through the publication of *The Common Law*, recent commentators have observed his typically unacknowledged intellectual debts, particularly to Savigny and Maine. At the most general level, they have pointed out, Holmes endorsed many of the central themes of the evolutionary historical approach to legal analysis that originated with Savigny, even though he rarely referred to Savigny's historical contributions and minimized them when he did.[9] Throughout the 1870s, Holmes read and reread major works by Savigny,[10] taking extensive notes,[11] and he reviewed what he called a "bad translation" of Savigny into English.[12] Recent scholars have speculated, moreover, that Holmes absorbed Savigny's historical orientation by reading Pomeroy, whose own work was saturated with Savigny's influence.[13] Equally important as their shared historical orientation, Savigny might have served as a model for Holmes's own remarkable ambition. Just as Savigny had reconstructed Roman law through historical analysis, Holmes wanted to reconstruct the common law through the study of its history. Tellingly, the year Holmes turned ninety Frederick Pollock wrote that he could "sum up" Holmes's career as a legal scholar "in one sentence by saying that what Holmes has done for the Common Law, taking it broadly and apart from obvious technical differences, is much like what Savigny did for modern Roman law."[14]

Maine's influence on Holmes was more obvious though similarly unacknowledged. As early as 1872, James Fitzjames Stephen responded from England to an article by Holmes by writing, "I am amused to find you so deep in the historical method, which my friend and neighbor, Sir H. Maine invented to a certain extent in this country."[15] A review of *The Common Law* in the *Nation* highlighted its similarities to Maine's earlier work, particularly in tracing the progress of legal systems from savagery to civilization and in using "analogies afforded by existing savage customs to bear upon the obscurities of the past." Holmes, the review accurately observed, applied Maine's approach to a

---

9   Reimann, supra note 1, at 99, 258 n. 114.
10 Eleanor N. Little, The Early Reading of Justice Oliver Wendell Holmes, 8 Harvard Library Bulletin 163, 181, 193, 194, 198 (1954).
11 Oliver Wendell Holmes, Black Book (Oliver Wendell Holmes, Jr., Papers, Harvard Law School Library), pp. 18–20, 105–7.
12 7 Am. L. Rev. 320 (1873), in The Collected Works of Justice Holmes (University of Chicago Press, 1995) (Sheldon M. Novick, ed.), vol. 1, p. 322.
13 White, supra note 1, at 149; Reimann, supra note 1, at 258 n. 110.
14 Frederick Pollock, Ad Multos Annos, 31 Colum. L. Rev. 349 (1931); see Reimann, supra note 1, at 98–9.
15 Letter from James Fitzjames Stephens to Oliver Wendell Holmes, Jr. (November 17, 1872), microformed on reel 37, 0884, 0886 (University Publications of America, Oliver Wendell Holmes Papers) [hereinafter Holmes Papers].

different subject. Whereas Maine studied ancient Aryan law, Holmes focused on the history of the common law, which had previously been addressed primarily by German scholars.[16] Though Holmes followed Maine's focus on the progress from savagery to civilization, he reached a different conclusion. Where Maine famously found "a movement *from Status to Contract*,"[17] and, more generally, from the family to the individual as the unit of legal analysis,[18] Holmes emphasized the progression from moral and subjective standards of legal liability to external or objective ones.[19] Like Maine before him, Holmes also stressed that old legal forms survive even as their substance changes over time.[20]

At least as striking as these thematic similarities, the organizational structure of *The Common Law* in many ways mirrors Maine's *Ancient Law*. Just as Maine included chapters on "testamentary succession," "property," "contract," and "delect and crime," Holmes, though in a different order, included chapters on "criminal law," "torts," "possession," "contract," and "successions." These "equivalent chapters," Mark DeWolfe Howe noted in his pioneering study of Holmes, were "surely something more than a coincidence."[21] "It would not, I think, be a great exaggeration," Howe remarked in his introduction to a reprinted edition of *The Common Law*, "to say that Holmes borrowed from Maine the spectacles which the Englishman had used for observing the law of ancient Rome and looked through them at the common law of England."[22]

Holmes read *Ancient Law* in 1865–6 and reread it in 1868.[23] He also read Maine's books, *Village Communities* (1871) and *Early History of Institutions* (1875), in the 1870s.[24] During his trip to England in 1874, Holmes met and socialized with Maine.[25] Holmes also sent Maine copies of his early legal writings, and Maine responded with brief but fulsome praise.[26] He cited Maine frequently in his edition of Kent's *Commentaries*.[27] Yet when his English friend Harold Laski asked Holmes in 1922 where he "picked up the notion of the historical examination of the common law, and suggested that Maine might have been the source,"[28] Holmes replied, "I don't think Maine had anything to do

---

[16] The Nation (June 30, 1881), p. 464; see also The Common Law, supra note 3, at 484.

[17] Sir Henry Maine, Ancient Law (Washington, D.C.: Beard Books, 2000) (reprint of 1861 ed.), p. 100.

[18] Id. at 99.

[19] Oliver Wendell Holmes, Jr., The Common Law (Cambridge, Mass.: Harvard University Press, 1963) (Mark DeWolfe Howe, ed.) (original ed. 1881), p. 33; see Grey, supra note 1, at 841–2.

[20] Reimann, supra note 1, at 252 n. 65.

[21] Howe, supra note 1, at 149 n. 31.

[22] Howe, Introduction to Holmes, supra note 19, at xiv.

[23] Little, supra note 10, at 184, 189.

[24] Id. at 184, 189.

[25] Howe, supra note 1, at 100.

[26] Id. at 105.

[27] Oliver Wendell Holmes, Holmes's Notes to Kent's Commentaries, in Novick, supra note 12, vol. 2, at 5, 88–90, 409–15.

[28] Letter from Harold Laski to Oliver Wendell Holmes, Jr. (May 15, 1922), in Holmes-Laski Letters (Cambridge, Mass.: Harvard University Press, 1953) (Mark DeWolfe Howe, ed.), vol. 1, p. 427.

with it except to feed the philosophic passion" and quickly added, "I don't think of any special book that put me on the track."[29] In his biography of Holmes, G. Edward White read this denial as evidence of Holmes's disagreeable tendency to deprecate others while asserting his own originality.[30] Commenting in 1888 on the "great loss" of Maine's death in a letter to Frederick Pollock, Holmes wrote that *Ancient Law* "most brilliantly caught and popularized in the form of established propositions the ideal ends toward which more truly scientific students on the continent had long been striving." Maine, he added, "seems to have been impatient of investigation himself and I do not think will leave much mark on the actual structure of jurisprudence, although he helped many others do so."[31] Perhaps Holmes was thinking of himself as one of many others Maine had helped.

Holmes and His American Contemporaries

Holmes's intellectual debts and relationships with his American contemporaries are easier to assess, particularly through the extensive correspondence he had with many of them. Among the American scholars, Holmes knew his neighbors in the Boston area best. In addition to Bigelow, Holmes was in periodic contact with Adams, Thayer, and Ames. Holmes and Adams were social friends, and both were members of "The Club," a group of young Boston intellectuals founded in 1868 who met for monthly dinners to discuss ideas.[32] During his trip to England in 1866, Holmes spent time with the Adams family, including Henry, while Charles Adams was still serving as the American minister to England.[33] When Holmes returned to England in 1874, Henry Adams gave him letters of introduction to many of his English friends and acquaintances, including Maine.[34] During the 1870s, Holmes read many of the books by German scholars on the history of Teutonic law that Adams reviewed in the *North American Review*, indicating that Adams might have influenced Holmes's own attention to this German scholarship and to the Teutonic origins of English common law.[35] Holmes himself reviewed and praised the *Essays in Anglo-Saxon Law* written by Adams and his students. Holmes's notes on his reading stated that he read "nearly all of it twice" and "very carefully"

---

[29] Letter from Oliver Wendell Holmes, Jr. to Harold Laski (June 1, 1922), in id. at 429–30.

[30] White, supra note 1, at 115, 146, 194.

[31] Letter from Oliver Wendell Holmes, Jr. to Frederick Pollock (March 4, 1888), in Holmes-Pollock Letters (Cambridge, Mass.: Harvard University Press, 1941) (Mark DeWolfe Howe, ed.), vol. 1, pp. 30, 31.

[32] Howe, supra note 1, at 142; Louis Menand, The Metaphysical Club: A Story of Ideas in America (New York: Farrar, Straus & Giroux, 2001), pp. 215–16.

[33] Mark DeWolfe Howe, Justice Oliver Wendell Holmes: The Shaping Years (Cambridge, Mass.: Harvard University Press, 1957), p. 225.

[34] Harold Dean Cater, Henry Adams and His Friends (Boston: Houghton Mifflin Company, 1947), p. 65 n. 4.

[35] Howe, supra note 1, at 142–6; see generally Little, supra note 10.

made "notes and references."[36] In December 1876, apparently in response to an inquiry from Holmes, Adams wrote to Holmes a long letter describing his work in legal history. He addressed Holmes as "Wendell," probably reflecting their close friendship. Indicating his preference for German over English scholarship, Adams wrote to Holmes that he knew he "would have a fight with the Britishers" about his "revolutionary" interpretation of socn in his essay but was confident that the "best Germans will be with me." Adams added that "there is no man in England whose opinion, unbacked by proof, is worth having."[37]

When Holmes published *The Common Law* in 1881, a review in the *Nation*, after stressing its reliance on German scholars to assert the Teutonic origins of the common law, called it an equally excellent sequel to the *Essays on Anglo-Saxon Law*.[38] Later that year, Adams sent Holmes the books he had used in his research on Anglo-Saxon law, hopeful that Holmes would continue the work in English legal history that Adams himself had abandoned. Adams urged Holmes to "put them all to the best use in your power," adding that "I shall then feel as though I were still teaching – by proxy."[39] Years later, when Adams disparaged his own prior work in legal history in *The Education of Henry Adams*, Holmes, in a rare expression of intellectual indebtedness, wrote to his old friend, "I, for one, have owed you more than you in the least suspect, and I have no doubt that there are many others not to be neglected who do the same."[40] In an admitted display of his more frequent "egotism" even in his nineties, Holmes wrote to Wigmore that "a hint from Henry Adams" about an article by Beseler, a German scholar, had allowed him to precede Maitland's work on the origins of the equitable trust.[41]

Thayer helped Holmes begin his scholarly career by reading critically drafts of his earliest essays,[42] written while Holmes worked as an associate in Thayer's law firm, and by inviting him in 1870 to help edit a new edition of Kent's *Commentaries on American Law*. Although it was originally designed as a joint project, Holmes did most of the work and claimed most of the credit.[43] A decade later, Thayer was instrumental in securing the endowment that convinced Holmes to join the faculty of Harvard Law School in 1882.[44] When Hammond wrote to Thayer commenting on *The Common Law*, Thayer passed on Hammond's reactions in a letter to Holmes. "One who has put his heart into

---

[36] Little, supra note 10, at 194; Holmes, supra note 11, at 23–9.
[37] Letter from Henry Adams to Oliver Wendell Holmes, Jr. (December 5, 1876), microformed on reel 27, 0672–5, Holmes Papers, supra note 15.
[38] The Nation, supra note 16.
[39] Letter from Henry Adams to Oliver Wendell Holmes, Jr. (November 3, 1881), microformed on reel 27, 0678, Holmes Papers, supra note 15.
[40] Letter from Oliver Wendell Holmes, Jr. to Henry Adams (December 31, 1907), microformed on reel 27, 0659, Holmes Papers, id.
[41] Letter from Oliver Wendell Holmes, Jr. to John Wigmore (March 14, 1932), microformed on reel 38, 1002, Holmes Papers, id.
[42] Little, supra note 10, at 165–6.
[43] Howe, supra note 1, at 11–16.
[44] Id. at 263–5.

a piece of work," Thayer wrote to Holmes, "likes to hear sympathetic criticism of another who has a right to express opinions."[45] Reflecting their continued relationship, Thayer attended the lecture Holmes delivered at the dedication of a new building in 1897 at the Boston University School of Law, where Bigelow taught. Several days later, Thayer wrote to Holmes praising the lecture but also suggesting that Holmes revise it before publication to emphasize the importance of history as the foundation of legal reform.[46] As subsequently published in the *Harvard Law Review* under the title "The Path of the Law," it became one of Holmes's most famous essays.

Throughout the 1870s, Holmes read casebooks published by Ames on torts, pleading, and bills and notes as well as some of his lectures.[47] They briefly became colleagues on the Harvard law faculty in 1882, and for decades after Holmes left the faculty to become a judge, they maintained a close and respectful, if sometimes testy, intellectual relationship as Ames developed interpretations of the history of the common law that specifically challenged Holmes's earlier writings. I examine one of these conflicts in detail in the subsequent chapter on Ames. Despite his notorious reluctance to give credit to others, in "The Path of the Law" Holmes himself recognized Ames, Bigelow, and Thayer as having "made important contributions" to legal history "which will not be forgotten," though he did not acknowledge any influence they may have had on his own scholarship.[48]

From the beginning of his career, moreover, Holmes corresponded with leading American legal scholars who did not live in the Boston area and who did not themselves produce original work in legal history. Particularly in the early 1870s, Pomeroy and Holmes were in close intellectual contact, reading and commenting on each other's work. Holmes received a long and admiring letter from Pomeroy about one of his earliest essays, "Codes, and the Arrangement of the Law," published in 1870,[49] and a subsequent letter praising his edition of Kent's *Commentaries*.[50] After Holmes sent Pomeroy his essay and asked for his opinion of it, Pomeroy thanked Holmes for his "very flattering letter." He praised Holmes for his ambitious effort to classify the law while suggesting that it would ultimately fail. "An arrangement of our jurisprudence upon some general principle, – in some manner different from that suggested by the convenience of text writer and book seller – would be of immense benefit both

45 Letter from James Bradley Thayer to Oliver Wendell Holmes, Jr. (September 15, 1881), microformed on reel 38, 0531–2, Holmes Papers, id.
46 Letter from James Bradley Thayer to Oliver Wendell Holmes, Jr. (January 11, 1897), microformed on reel 38, 0547, Holmes Papers, id.
47 Little, supra note 10, at 188, 190, 199.
48 Oliver Wendell Holmes, The Path of the Law, 10 Harv. L. Rev. 457 (1897), reprinted in Collected Legal Papers, supra note 8, at 167, 194.
49 Letter from John Norton Pomeroy to Oliver Wendell Holmes, Jr. (February 6, 1871), microformed on reel 36, 0685–93, Holmes Papers, supra note 15.
50 Letter from Oliver Wendell Holmes, Jr. to John Norton Pomeroy (May 22, 1872), microformed on reel 36, 0679, Holmes Papers, id.

in the theory and the practice of law even though it was but partially success-ful."[51] Pomeroy mentioned that he had considered attempting such an arrange-ment himself but ultimately became doubtful about its practicability. Almost all lawyers, he wrote to Holmes, relied on Blackstone "and would simply gaze at you in stupid amazement if you showed" that Blackstone's work "was not perfection."[52]

Yet Pomeroy added that it was a "real kindness" for Holmes "to startle" these lawyers "with ideas above and beyond their common experience."[53] He recognized as well the pedagogical value of attempts to classify law. When he was a law professor, Pomeroy reported, he tried to teach students "gen-eral notions according to which they might arrange and classify the partic-ular rules. They were thus enabled also to see at a glance the inconsistency of certain rules."[54] Reflecting another central theme in late nineteenth-century American legal thought, Pomeroy also expressed delight that Holmes "gave a side blow" to the proposed codification of law in New York.[55] "Nothing is truer," Pomeroy wrote, "than your statement that a code to work must be *complete*. Introducing into the mass of judicial law a partial code," he added, "would immensely increase the difficulty of administering justice, and add an unnecessary element of uncertainty which would throw the whole system into confusion."[56]

In articles and correspondence in 1871, Holmes and Pomeroy engaged in substantial and respectful debates over the constitutionality of two responses to Reconstruction: the "Force Bill" passed by Congress to enforce the newly rati-fied Fourteenth Amendment against the violent efforts of the Ku Klux Klan to undermine Reconstruction and the attempt by conservatives in North Carolina to amend the state constitution of 1868 in ways that would limit the power of the state's Radical Republican government. Whereas Pomeroy claimed that the Fourteenth Amendment only prohibited state action, Holmes believed that it allowed Congress to legislate against private acts that undermined federal law. And while Pomeroy invoked theories of popular sovereignty to justify efforts by Democrats in North Carolina to amend the 1868 constitution by major-ity vote, Holmes maintained that courts should decide whether or not to fol-low the constitution's provision requiring approval by three-fifths of the state legislature before a proposed amendment could be submitted to the people.[57] The next year, Holmes asked Pomeroy to send him "articles on politico-legal subjects which are from time to time before the public." Holmes explained that "all my time is taken up by the law and I know nothing about politics and live questions, as of necessity I am wholly buried in dead ones for some

[51] Letter from Pomeroy to Holmes, supra note 49, at 0685–6.
[52] Id. at 0686; see also id. at 0692.
[53] Id. at 0692.
[54] Id. at 0688.
[55] Id. at 0686.
[56] Id. at 0687.
[57] Howe, supra note 1, at 35–42.

time to come."[58] Holmes wrote to Pomeroy's son that his father "was my most valued contributor" to the *American Law Review* and a "serious and original thinker." "I felt to him," Holmes added, "the gratitude of a younger man for early encouragement not only in personal relations but in print."[59]

In 1881, Holmes wrote a long letter to Pomeroy praising his book on equity, even in comparison to work on the subject by Langdell, "of whose abilities I have also an exceedingly high opinion." Holmes commended Pomeroy for producing the first systematic study of the development of equitable doctrines in the United States,[60] though he later regretted that his own article on early English equity, "which might have induced a remodeling" of Pomeroy's own "preliminaries," appeared four years after Pomeroy's book.[61] Offering reciprocal praise the following year, Pomeroy wrote to Holmes that he had read *The Common Law* "as soon as it came with much interest and much instruction." He complimented its "accurate learning" and originality, observing that Holmes had clearly shown the errors of many "historical notions" about the common law. "While I fully agree with much that you say," Pomeroy nevertheless wrote, "some of your conclusions I don't find myself able to accept." In particular, Pomeroy added, "I should be very sorry to see the *moral* element entirely eliminated from the law,"[62] whereas Holmes emphasized throughout *The Common Law* that the elimination of the moral was a sign of progress.

Despite this major difference between Holmes and Pomeroy, recent scholars have convincingly observed substantial parallels, linguistic as well as thematic, between Pomeroy's *Municipal Law*, published in 1864 and read by Holmes in 1871,[63] and *The Common Law*, published in 1881. Like Pomeroy before him, Holmes emphasized the historical development of law as part of the progressive evolution of a nation and its customs. More specifically, they identified past law as the key to understanding current law and maintained that the evolutionary process prevents a legal system from becoming formally consistent and complete.[64] The linguistic similarities between portions of *The Common Law* and *Municipal Law* are so great that Mathias Reimann "almost suspects plagiarism" by Holmes.[65] Rather than indicating plagiarism, I think these significant similarities, which can also be found in the writing of other late nineteenth-century American legal scholars, reflect their shared views about legal evolution.[66]

---

[58] Letter from Holmes to Pomeroy, supra note 50.

[59] Letter from Oliver Wendell Holmes, Jr. to John Norton Pomeroy, Jr. (January 6, 1909), microformed on reel 36, 0683, Holmes Papers, supra note 15.

[60] Letter from Oliver Wendell Holmes, Jr. to John Norton Pomeroy (November 21, 1881), microformed on reel 36, 0681, Holmes Papers, id.

[61] Holmes to Pomeroy, supra note 59.

[62] Letter from John Norton Pomeroy to Oliver Wendell Holmes, Jr. (December 31, 1882), microformed on reel 36, 0734, 0735, Holmes Papers, id.

[63] Little, supra note 10, at 183.

[64] White, supra note 1, at 149, 524 n. 13; Reimann, supra note 1, at 258 n. 110.

[65] Reimann, supra note 1, at 258 n. 110.

[66] Albert W. Alschuler, Law without Values: The Life, Work, and Legacy of Justice Holmes (University of Chicago Press, 2000), pp. 252–3 n. 88 (agreeing with Reimann regarding the similar "historicism" of Pomeroy and Holmes but not suspecting plagiarism).

Holmes sent Hammond copies of his earliest published articles in 1871, and Hammond responded by telling Holmes that he was already familiar with and admired his work. "I shall always reserve time enough to answer any letter from you," Hammond closed his letter, "and regard myself as a gainer by the exchange."[67] This exchange initiated substantial correspondence between Holmes and Hammond about significant legal issues, including the relationship between civil and common law, codification, and efforts to arrange and classify the law. Hammond praised Holmes for his efforts to analyze "the fundamental principles of the law," adding that Holmes was one of the few people who could do so because he did "not overlook those customs of the Germanic tribes in which the common law of England had its basis far more truly and completely than the Roman law by which it was afterward modified." Like Holmes and his friends at Harvard Law School, Hammond tied the study of fundamental legal principles to the transformation of legal education. "I have long been convinced," he wrote to Holmes, "that the growth of our law schools, and the marked change of the method of professional training from mere office-work to systematic instruction must logically involve a re-formulation of the law itself."[68] Hammond had earlier thanked Holmes for his "flattering opinion" of Hammond's writing about legal education.[69] Yet Hammond, responding to an article by Holmes on the theory of torts, was skeptical about "the possibility of a strictly scientific arrangement of the whole law," which Holmes attempted. Even if feasible, Hammond added, such an arrangement would not be an improvement over what he called "empirical generalizations."[70] Hammond had previously written to Holmes that the classification of legal principles should be derived from what "has grown up in long usage" and "proved" over time rather than by "a single thinker from the force and meaning that a few important terms might have in his own mind."[71] And in his comments about *The Common Law* that Thayer passed on to Holmes, Hammond wrote that Holmes was "clearly right" about torts and bailment, but "clearly wrong" about contracts.[72]

From the early 1870s through the publication of *The Common Law*, Holmes also had substantial interaction with Cooley. In 1871, Holmes reviewed Cooley's treatise on *Constitutional Limitations*, praising it as a very valuable and original work. Although *Constitutional Limitations* did not explicitly discuss the attempt to amend the North Carolina constitution of 1868, the topic Holmes and Pomeroy were contemporaneously debating in correspondence

[67] Letter from William Gardiner Hammond to Oliver Wendell Holmes, Jr. (February 22, 1871), microformed on reel 33,0061–2, Holmes Papers, supra note 15.

[68] Letter from William Gardiner Hammond to Oliver Wendell Holmes, Jr. (August 25, 1879), microformed on reel 33, 0072, 0073, Holmes Papers, id.

[69] Letter from William Gardiner Hammond to Oliver Wendell Holmes, Jr. (January 20, 1874), microformed on reel 33, 0069, Holmes Papers, id.

[70] Id. at 0071.

[71] Letter from William Gardiner Hammond to Oliver Wendell Holmes, Jr. (February 1, 1873). microformed on reel 33, 0067, Holmes Papers, id.

[72] Letter from Thayer to Holmes, supra note 45, at 0531.

and in print, Holmes maintained that it supported his own position.[73] In his only criticism of the treatise, Holmes revealed his early interest in the importance of legal history. He observed the "absence of historical explanation of the famous 'except by the judgment of his peers or the law of the land.'" Holmes stressed that "meanings undreamed of by the framers of Magna Charta have been imported into it." Since Cooley devoted a chapter to this concept, Holmes politely suggested, "it might not have been out of place to trace the growth of the modern interpretations."[74] Cooley asked Holmes in 1873 about the status of his work on Kent's *Commentaries*, and Holmes ended his response with the hope that the book would "win the approval of one who has rendered such distinguished services to the law as the author of Constitutional Limitations."[75] A year later, Holmes had his publisher send Cooley his edition of Kent's *Commentaries*, and Cooley responded that Holmes's notes were "clear, accurate, faithful and thorough," work of quality "so uncommon now that it deserves special acknowledgment."[76]

In 1882, the year after he published *The Common Law*, Holmes wrote to Cooley to complain about improper borrowing in a book by Rufus Waples on *Proceedings in Rem*, for which Cooley wrote an introduction. The borrowing, Holmes asserted, was from his article in the *American Law Review*, "Primitive Notions in Modern Law," which was the foundation of chapter 1 of *The Common Law*. The letter vividly illustrates the ceaseless quest for professional recognition that biographers have frequently ascribed to Holmes. "It is not merely that he takes for his starting point ideas which I have no reason to doubt were original with me and which I spent much time and labor in stating and proving," Holmes protested, "but that the citations which I gathered from various sources occur in such wise as to earmark the indebtedness to my mind." "I am very glad that my work which is directed to the establishment of general principles only," Holmes condescendingly added, "should assist those who are engaged in making text books." But he insisted that his assistance to Waples "should be acknowledged" and urged Cooley, "whose name will secure the book a respectful treatment, to ask if there is any explanation to be made."[77] Cooley sent Holmes's letter to Waples,[78] who responded in a letter Cooley forwarded to Holmes. "I am surprised," Waples wrote, "that he should claim any ideas of my treatise. It was written before I ever knew of the article in the Review. I have never seen his book." Waples acknowledged citing five

---

73 6 Am. L. Rev. 140 (1871), in Collected Works, supra note 12, vol. 1, p. 268.

74 Id. at 269.

75 Letter from Thomas M. Cooley to Oliver Wendell Holmes, Jr. (April 16, 1873), microformed on reel 30, 0203, Holmes Papers, supra note 15.

76 Letter from Thomas M. Cooley to Oliver Wendell Holmes, Jr. (March 30, 1874), microformed on reel 30, 0210–11.

77 Letter from Oliver Wendell Holmes, Jr. to Thomas M. Cooley (September 22, 1882), microformed on reel 30, 0213, Holmes Papers, id.

78 Letter from Thomas M. Cooley to Oliver Wendell Holmes, Jr. (October 2, 1882), microformed on reel 30, 0212, Holmes Papers, id.

or six sources that Holmes had cited in his earlier article but claimed that he found those sources independently to illustrate his own ideas and only later read Holmes's article.[79]

Early Legal Scholarship: From Philosophical to Historical Analysis of Law

From the beginning of his legal career, Holmes exhibited interests in history and philosophy, subjects on which he had focused as an undergraduate.[80] While preparing his edition of Kent's *Commentaries* between 1870 and 1873, his first major project as a legal scholar, Holmes subtly combined these interests in concise annotations that satisfied but ambitiously went beyond the practitioner's desire for relevant decisions and statutes since the previous edition. In response to Pomeroy's praise of his work on Kent, Holmes cautioned "against expecting too much from me." Confined by deadlines, limitations of space, and directions not to change anything Kent wrote in his text and notes, Holmes also had "to keep a civil tongue while I am his valet." Loosening his pen in his letter to Pomeroy, Holmes wrote that Kent's "arrangement is chaotic – he has no general ideas – except wrong ones – and his treatment of special topics is often confused to the last degree." Yet Holmes added that Kent had "merits and there is lots of law in his book if you can only find it." Informing Pomeroy that he had worked very hard on his edition of Kent for two and a half years, Holmes ruefully remarked that he "could have almost easier made a new book."[81] Almost a decade later, Holmes did just that when he published his own book, *The Common Law*.

Although Kent himself had included some information about legal history in his original *Commentaries*, he did not incorporate historical analysis into his jurisprudence and explicitly disapproved of the "new historical school of the civil law" in Germany.[82] Holmes, by contrast, discussed and provided references to recent European scholarship on legal history, though most of his notes discussed case law. In his original *Commentaries*, Kent treated property as the absolute right of an individual, based in natural law and the authority of the Bible. While not commenting directly on this passage in Kent, Holmes implicitly challenged Kent's conception of property by relying on new scholarship from Europe to provide short summaries of the role of villages in primitive societies; the history of property in Greece, Rome, and England; and the law of descent and alienation in different cultures and times. In one of his longest notes, on the history of the law of alienation, Holmes frequently referred to Nasse's *Agricultural Community in the Middle Ages* and Maine's *Village*

---

[79] Letter from Rufus Waples to Thomas M. Cooley (October 6, 1882), microformed on reel 30, 0213, Holmes Papers, id.

[80] Howe, supra note 1, at 26, 31; White, supra note 1, at 42.

[81] Letter from Holmes to Pomeroy, supra note 50.

[82] Howe, supra note 1, at 17.

Communities.[83] In another note, he urged readers "curious as to the origin of individual property" to compare Nasse's book with "the much more lucidly and brilliantly written" book by Maine.[84] Holmes referred as well to Stubbs,[85] Jhering,[86] and Windscheid.[87] Holmes invoked history and philosophy more extensively in his contributions to the *American Law Review* during the three years he worked on his edition of Kent.[88]

Although Holmes displayed early interests in history as well as philosophy, his initial scholarly goals were more philosophical than historical. For several years in the early 1870s, he grappled with and tried to reorient the analytic jurisprudence associated with the great English legal philosopher John Austin. Holmes first read Austin when he was a senior at Harvard College in 1861. By 1871 Holmes had read at least twice Austin's influential *Lectures in Jurisprudence*, which were published in 1863.[89] The young Holmes shared Austin's goal of substituting the rigor of "scientific" philosophical analysis of law for the unverifiable speculation of religious and metaphysical thought.[90] He also shared the widespread view that traditional legal analysis, organized according to the forms of action of the common law, had reached a conceptual dead end.[91]

Holmes followed Austin in seeking a philosophically satisfying alternative classification of law. Like many other American legal scholars of the period, Holmes was impressed by the methods of the natural sciences and tried to apply them to legal analysis, often invoking various fields of science while doing so.[92] He aspired to classify legal subjects as scientifically as biologists classified natural phenomena. In an 1869 book notice of a *Treatise on the Law of Sale of Personal Property*, for example, Holmes asserted that "a book of reference on any subdivision of the law, in order to be satisfactory, must set forth at length, not only the principles constituting the specific difference of the subject-matter, but also those common to it and to many other classes of the same genus."[93] In an 1878 article on the law of possession, Holmes reiterated that the "business of the jurist is to make known the content of the law; that is, to work upon it from within, or logically, arranging and distributing it in order from its *summum genus* to its *infima species.*"[94]

---

[83] Holmes, supra note 27, at 410–15.
[84] Id. at 88–9.
[85] Id. at 88, 412.
[86] Id. at 90.
[87] Id.
[88] Howe, supra note 1, at 17–21.
[89] Frederic Rogers Kellogg, The Formative Essays of Justice Holmes: The Making of an American Legal Philosophy (Westport, Conn.: Greenwood Press, 1984), p. 6.
[90] Id. at 4.
[91] Howe, supra note 1, at 65–6; White, supra note 1, at 117.
[92] White, supra note 1, at 115–16.
[93] Id. at 116.
[94] Oliver Wendell Holmes, Jr., Possession, 12 Am. L. Rev. 688 (1878), reprinted in Kellogg, supra note 89, at 167, 181.

Austin's *Lectures in Jurisprudence* asserted that the analysis of legal rights should be the basis for classifying law across specific subjects. In his scholarship in the early 1870s, Holmes suggested that analysis of duties rather than rights provided better grounds for classification.[95] He experimented over several years with different conceptions of duty.[96] In articles published in late 1872 and 1873, however, Holmes began to doubt the very method of analytic classification. He lost confidence that purely logical analysis of any sort could yield a universal system of legal classification. Like other American legal scholars in the late nineteenth century who rejected Austin's analytical jurisprudence, Holmes increasingly sought explanations for legal doctrine in its historical evolution rather than its logical structure.[97]

Holmes provided additional evidence of his turn toward historical explanation in the early 1870s while challenging Austin's famous definition of law as the command of a politically superior sovereign, a challenge made by other historically oriented American legal scholars. When he first wrote about Austin, Holmes focused on his system of classification without addressing the topic of sovereignty. But as Holmes began to question Austin's analytic approach to law, he also criticized his equation of law with sovereign power.[98] In his lectures on jurisprudence at Harvard College in the spring of 1872, which he summarized in a short essay in the *American Law Review*, Holmes asserted that many factors limit the power of the sovereign. By twice identifying "custom"[99] among those factors, Holmes pointed to the influence of history and joined the many late nineteenth-century American legal scholars who stressed custom as a source of law.

In the early 1870s, Holmes studied the civil law of Rome and the law of England after the Norman Conquest, primarily to understand current Anglo-American law.[100] "A rule of law that has been gradually developed," Holmes wrote in 1871, "can only be understood by knowing the course of its development; and that is more or less known by good lawyers, if the rule took its rise in England."[101] He expressed the consensus that at least part of the English common law is founded on the civil law of Rome[102] and confidently asserted that "every lawyer who aims at being more than a practitioner should know, at least, so much of the Roman law as to intelligently estimate its influence on our own."[103] Holmes also believed that "it would be hard to name any

95 Howe, supra note 1, at 67; Kellogg, supra note 89, at 6.
96 Howe, supra note 1, at 79; Kellogg, supra note 89, at 25.
97 Howe, supra note 1, at 69, 82, 91–2; White, supra note 1, at 123–4; Kellogg, supra note 89, at 7–10; Reimann, supra note 1, at 79.
98 Howe, supra note 1, at 72.
99 Oliver Wendell Holmes, Jr., 6 Am. L. Rev. 723 (1872), reprinted in Kellogg, supra note 89, at 91, 92.
100 Howe, supra note 1, at 92–3, 141.
101 Oliver Wendell Holmes, Jr., Misunderstandings of the Civil Law, 6 Am. L. Rev. 37 (1871), reprinted in Novick, supra note 12, vol. 1, at 257, 260.
102 Id.
103 Oliver Wendell Holmes, Jr., 5 Am. L. Rev. 715 (1871), reprinted in Novick, supra note 12, vol. 1, at 250–1.

one who has thrown new light on such general problems of jurisprudence as the arrangement of the law, who has not known something of the labors of the civilians" in ancient Rome.[104]

But Holmes was interested in more than the influence of the past on the present. Like Thayer's later work on the history of evidence, Holmes sought in history a rational explanation for current legal rules that seemed irrational.[105] He warned that "doctrines get swerved from their true meaning and extent, because we do not remember their history and origin." In many instances, he observed, "an ignorant misunderstanding of the Roman classification," produced by lack of attention to its history and origin, had created confusion in current Anglo-American law.[106] As an example, Holmes cited a passage from Kent's *Commentaries* asserting the presumption in English common law that people born deaf and dumb are legally incompetent. This passage, Holmes claimed, demonstrated "the illicit relationship of the common and civil law, and would never have been written, had not texts of the latter been adopted into the former, and at first misunderstood and later wholly perverted from their meaning and from reason."[107] Holmes pointed out that the original Roman law only prevented persons born deaf and dumb from entering agreements through a legal form that required speech and hearing. Yet when Bracton attempted to incorporate this Roman law in his thirteenth-century English treatise, he failed to perceive that it did not preclude such persons from contracting by other means. Subsequent English lawyers repeated and extended Bracton's mistake.[108] Similarly, and more significantly, Holmes complained that the retention of the Roman concept of bailment in English law derived from a failure of historical understanding. Tracing the history of the law of bailment, he suggested, would indicate that it "consists of fragments of the Roman structure, which have been built into the body of the common law in such a place and manner as to entirely miss the ends which they originally answered, while at the same time they are equally ill adapted to any new purpose."[109]

While writing about legal evolution, Holmes occasionally connected evolving custom more with social conflict than with national and racial consensus. In this important respect, he resembled Jhering and Tiedeman and differed from most of his contemporaries. Holmes's 1873 article in the *American Law Review* on the famous gas-stokers strike in England particularly stressed the role of conflict in social and legal evolution. Referring his readers to other articles for more information about "the immediate social aspects of this case," Holmes focused on its relationship to evolutionary theory, and especially to the Social Darwinian thought of Herbert Spencer. Expressing his emerging skepticism about purely logical analysis of law, Holmes first observed the "singular

[104] Holmes, supra note 101, at 260.
[105] Howe, supra note 1, at 141.
[106] Holmes, supra note 101, at 260.
[107] Id. at 258.
[108] Id. at 257–60.
[109] Id. at 261; see Howe, supra note 1, at 89–90.

anomaly" that Spencer and other "believers in the theory of evolution and in the natural development of institutions by successive adaptations to the environment, should be found laying down a theory of government intended to establish its limits once for all by a logical deduction from axioms." Rather than developing this point, which presumably referred to Spencer's laissez-faire theories, Holmes objected instead that timeless theories assume "an identity of interest between the different parts of a community which does not exist in fact." The "tacit assumption of the solidarity of interests in society is very common," Holmes added, "but seems to us to be false." According to Holmes, the "struggle for life" that creates conflicts between humans and other species "does not stop in the ascending scale with the monkeys, but is equally the law of human existence." In legislation, as in all areas of life, "man rightly prefers his own interest to that of his neighbors." Legislation, "like every other device of man or beast, must tend in the long run to aid the survival of the fittest," a rare allusion to Darwin by a legal evolutionist. Communism and other theories of social improvement designed to reduce inequality could only combat this biological imperative by limiting or ending "the propagation of the species." Holmes tartly added that "it may be doubted whether this solution would not be as disagreeable as any other."[110]

Holmes applied his discussion of "survival of the fittest" to the "class legislation" that punished the striking gas workers for criminal conspiracy while imposing no penalties on the employer whose allegedly unjust dismissal of an employee provoked the strike. "The objection to 'class legislation,'" he observed, "is not that it favors a class, but either that it fails to benefit the legislators, or that it is dangerous to them because a competing class has gained in power, or that it transcends the limits of self-preference which are imposed by sympathy." He suggested that the conviction and jailing of the gas stokers under the law of criminal conspiracy could be criticized under the second objection because "it requires to be backed by a more unquestioned power than is now possessed by the favored class." Yet he reiterated that legislation, whether or not advisable, "is necessarily made a means by which a body, having the power, put burdens which are disagreeable to them on the shoulders of somebody else."[111]

In 1873, the year he finished his work on Kent's *Commentaries*, Holmes resigned from his positions as editor of the *American Law Review* and as lecturer at Harvard College to form a new law partnership. Although these important changes might have signaled that Holmes intended to abandon legal scholarship for the more active life of a practicing lawyer, in fact he immersed himself in an ambitious program of reading that informed his work when he resumed publishing in 1876. Holmes kept a journal of his reading from 1865 until the end of his life. The entries between 1873 and 1876, while covering a broad range of subjects, indicate particular interests in historical studies of

[110] Oliver Wendell Holmes, Jr., The Gas-Stokers' Strike, 7 Am. L. Rev. 582 (1873), reprinted in Novick, supra note 12, vol. 1, at 323, 323–4.

[111] Id. at 325.

English, French, German, and Roman law and in the emerging field of cultural anthropology, which Maine had stimulated. During this period, Holmes mastered a reading knowledge of German, which enabled him to read many works by German legal scholars, though he read plays and other literature in German as well.[112] Holmes may have learned German to read the sources recommended by Henry Adams in his book reviews and in the *Essays in Anglo-Saxon Law*, but he did not limit his reading of German legal history to this "Germanist" school. He also read many works by the "Romanist" school of German legal history.[113] Holmes's reading list includes many references to Savigny,[114] Sohm,[115] Brunner,[116] and Jhering.[117] His Black Book of notes on his reading covers Savigny,[118] Sohm,[119] Brunner,[120] Windscheid,[121] and Jhering.[122]

Holmes's reading in legal history between 1873 and 1876 extended his earlier movement from Austin's purely logical analysis of legal issues to more historical approaches, but he continued to share Austin's goal of organizing and classifying law. For Holmes, history became a more effective means than logic alone to reach this goal.[123] In an 1879 letter to James Bryce, the eminent English scholar, explaining his continued commitment to scholarship while in practice, Holmes wrote that his goal was "to analyze what seem to me the fundamental notions and principles of our substantive law, putting them in an order which is a part of or results from the fundamental conceptions."[124] In contrast to his earliest scholarship under the influence of Austin, but in common with other late nineteenth-century American legal scholars, Holmes recognized these principles as historically evolved rather than logically determined, and he conceived the resulting order as subject to change rather than fixed. Yet he still sought conceptual order in law.[125] By attempting to achieve conceptual order in the present that he assumed would change in the future, Holmes anticipated views later expressed by John Chipman Gray in *The Nature and Sources of the Law*.

Holmes emphasized his use of history to reinforce analysis when he resumed publishing after his three-year hiatus. His article "Primitive Notions in Modern Law," which appeared in two parts in the *American Law Review* in 1876 and

---

[112] Little, supra note 10. See Howe, supra note 1, at 24; White, supra note 1, at 129–30; Kellogg, supra note 89, at 35; Reimann, supra note 1, at 80, 249–50 n. 41.

[113] Howe, supra note 1, at 142–53; White, supra note 1, at 129–30, 523 n. 160.

[114] Little, supra note 10, at 181, 193, 194, 196.

[115] Id. at 189, 190, 192, 196.

[116] Id. at 195, 199, 201, 202.

[117] Id. at 197, 200, 202.

[118] Holmes, supra note 11, at 18–20, 105–7.

[119] Id. at 36–7, 114.

[120] Id. at 42–9.

[121] Id. at 60–3.

[122] Id. at 76–9.

[123] White, supra note 1, at 129; Reimann, supra note 1, at 79.

[124] White, supra note 1, at 130.

[125] Reimann, supra note 1, at 111.

1877, attempted to rely on historical arguments to support analytical conclusions he had previously reached. Holmes was most explicit about his goal in the second part of this article. "The object of the following investigation," it began, "is to prove the historical truth of a general result, arrived at analytically" in an earlier article, "Privity," he had published in 1872. In answering the question "How can a man sue or be sued on a contract to which he was not a party?" Holmes in the 1872 article made the analytic point that cases created "a fictitious identification of distinct persons for the purpose of transferring or completing the right." In the 1877 article, Holmes considered "what light history will throw on the same question."[126] After examining various Roman and German sources, he concluded that "the question propounded at the beginning of this article has now been answered by history in a way which confirms the results of analysis."[127] Yet the historical process that achieved this fictitious identification was based "not in reasoning, but in a failure to reason."[128] Holmes preserved his original analytical conclusion, but through a different method of proof. Uncovering the irrational evolution of legal doctrine replaced logical legal analysis of existing law.[129]

In the first part of his article "Primitive Notions in Modern Law," Holmes similarly used history to support his previous analysis. He focused on the historical origins of current doctrine on liability, a subject at which he had only given a "glance" in his 1873 article "The Theory of Torts." After examining Jewish, Greek, Roman, and Teutonic "primitive" legal cultures, Holmes concurred with his earlier analytic conclusion: "that, more generally than has been supposed, civil liability depends not on culpability as a state of the defendant's consciousness, ... but upon having failed to come up to a more or less accurately determined standard in his overt acts or omissions."[130] His historical analysis of liability disclosed the limits of pure logic, just as his historical analysis of privity disclosed "a failure to reason." The policies typically thought to lie behind primitive theories of liability, Holmes maintained, "have in fact been invented at a later period to account for what was already there, a process familiar to all students of legal history."[131] According to Holmes, reasons given for the contemporary survival of primitive rules are different from the reasons that actually led to their creation in the past by primitive people themselves.[132] For example, procedures justified by theories of vengeance in primitive societies became justified by theories of compensation in modern ones.[133] Various

---

[126] Oliver Wendell Holmes, Jr., Primitive Notions in Modern Law, No. II, 11 Am. L. Rev. 641 (1877), reprinted in Kellogg, supra note 89, at 147.

[127] Id. at 159.

[128] Id. at 160.

[129] Howe, supra note 1, at 88; Kellogg, supra note 89, at 40.

[130] Oliver Wendell Holmes, Jr., Primitive Notions in Modern Law, 10 Am. L. Rev. 422 (1876), reprinted in Kellogg, supra note 89, at 129.

[131] Id. at 130.

[132] Howe, supra note 1, at 161.

[133] Holmes, supra note 130, at 137.

"anomalies"[134] and "confusion"[135] in current law, Holmes stressed, can be traced to the survival of doctrines that are based on discarded policies but cannot be justified by new ones.

The Importance of History in *The Common Law*

In *The Common Law*, his most ambitious work and his only book, Holmes continued to combine history and analysis as tools in his search for conceptual order in law. Based on twelve lectures delivered in late 1880 and published in March 1881, *The Common Law* included revised versions of articles he had published in the *American Law Review* during the prior decade as well as previously unpublished material dealing with criminal law and contracts.[136] While frequently praising the ambition and breadth of *The Common Law* and quoting its many memorable aphorisms, subsequent scholars have as often criticized its style, characterizing it, for example, as obscure, turgid, elusive, elliptical, cryptic, and even unreadable.[137] Despite its stylistic difficulties, *The Common Law* is the best source for understanding Holmes's mature thought.

The Common Law begins with three paragraphs that reveal how much he shared the evolutionary legal thought that pervaded American legal scholarship in the late nineteenth century. These paragraphs highlight the importance of history to Holmes and introduce many of his positions on its role in legal analysis. Written in clear and sometimes aphoristic language, much of which has since become famous, they merit quotation in full.

The object of this book is to present a general view of the Common Law. To accomplish the task, other tools are needed besides logic. It is something to show that the consistency of a system requires a particular result, but it is not all. The life of the law has not been logic: it has been experience. The felt necessities of the time, the prevalent moral and political theories, intuitions of public policy, avowed or unconscious, even the prejudices which judges share with their fellow-men, have had a good deal more to do than the syllogism in determining the rules by which men should be governed. The law embodies the story of a nation's development through many centuries, and it cannot be dealt with as if it contained only the axioms and corollaries of a book of mathematics. In order to know what it is, we must know what it has been, and what it tends to become. We must alternately consult history and existing theories of legislation. But the most difficult labor will be to understand the combination of the two into new products at every stage. The substance of the law at any given time pretty nearly corresponds, so far as it goes, with what is then understood to be convenient; but its form and machinery, and the degree to which it is able to work out desired results, depend very much upon its past.

In Massachusetts to-day, while, on the one hand, there are a great many rules which are quite sufficiently accounted for, by their manifest good sense, on the other, there are some

---

[134] Id. at 140.
[135] Id. at 143.
[136] Howe, supra note 1, at 136.
[137] Holmes's Common Law, supra note 7, at 338; 25 J. Jurisprudence 646, 647 (1881); White, supra note 1, at 154, 181–3, 193; Horwitz, supra note 1, at 110; Alschuler, supra note 66, at 114, 125; Gordon, supra note 1, at 719; Grey, supra note 1, at 787, 832.

which can only be understood by reference to the infancy of procedure among the German tribes, or to the social condition of Rome under the Decemvirs.

I shall use the history of our law so far as it is necessary to explain a conception or to interpret a rule, but no further. In doing so there are two errors equally to be avoided both by writer and reader. One is that of supposing, because an idea seems very familiar and natural to us, that it has always been so. Many things which we take for granted have had to be laboriously fought out or thought out in past times. The other mistake is the opposite one of asking too much of history. We start with man full grown. It may be assumed that the earliest barbarian whose practices are to be considered, had a good many of the same feelings and passions as ourselves.[138]

Holmes signaled his interest in history near the beginning of his first paragraph in a sentence that has become one of his most quoted aphorisms: "The life of the law has not been logic: it has been experience." History recounts the "experience" that has been the "life of the law." By juxtaposing history with "logic" and the "syllogism," Holmes indicated his agreement with other late nineteenth-century American legal scholars who treated historical analysis of law as a distinctive jurisprudential school, in contrast to legal theories generated by deductive logic. In writing that "law embodies the story of a nation's development through many centuries," Holmes reflected the widespread view of late nineteenth-century legal scholars that history is a process of evolutionary growth over time and that the nation is the basic unit of historical study. He also shared the interest of his contemporaries in studying legal history as a means to understand current law and even to project its future. "In order to know what it [law] is," he observed, "we must know what it has been, and what it tends to become." More specifically, he maintained that some legal rules "can only be understood by reference to" the early history of the German tribes or of ancient Rome. Although the substance of law mostly reflects contemporary notions of convenience, "its form and machinery, and the degree to which it is able to work out desired results, depend very much upon its past." In a marginal note inserted by Holmes at this point in his copy of *The Common Law*, he wrote, "Imagination of men limited – can only think in terms of the language they have been taught. Conservative instinct."[139] Holmes also joined many of his contemporaries in stressing the contingency of legal development. A proper understanding of history, he observed, helps prevent the frequent mistake of treating the law of the present as natural and inevitable. By asserting the derivation of current law from issues that "had to be laboriously fought out or thought out in past times," he indicated that the fighting and thinking of the past could have turned out differently.

These three paragraphs illustrate the limits as well as the benefits of history for Holmes. The "general view of the Common Law" sought by Holmes requires "other tools" beyond logic alone, but history is only one of them. Biology as well as history explain law. Even the "earliest barbarian" was a

---

[138] Holmes, supra note 19, at 5–6.
[139] Id. at 5 n.a.

"man full grown," who probably "had a good many of the same feelings and passions as ourselves." And while logic does not fully explain the law, which is more than "the axioms and corollaries of a book of mathematics," logic can "show that the consistency of a system requires a particular result." Such a demonstration "is not all," but it "is something." Holmes emphasized that the "most difficult labor" for the scholar is to understand how "existing theories of legislation" combine with history "into new products at every stage" of legal development. And Holmes's interest in history seemed confined to his basic goal of presenting "a general view of the Common Law." Like so many of his American contemporaries, he examined "the history of our law so far as it is necessary to explain a conception or to interpret a rule, but no further."[140]

Throughout *The Common Law,* Holmes elaborated the observations about legal history with which he introduced his book. He repeatedly justified his excursions into legal history by emphasizing its essential role in understanding current law. For example, Holmes traced "with some care" the derivation of the English common law of bailment from German law because the German doctrine "has had such important influence upon the law of the present day."[141] Knowing the history of the action of debt, Holmes similarly observed, is necessary "in order to understand the enlightened rules which make up the law of contract at the present time."[142] Because the reign of Edward III was "the time when the divisions and rules of procedure were established which have lasted until the present day," Holmes thought it "worth while to repeat and sum up the condition of the law at that time."[143] More generally, Holmes believed that the "true principle" underlying a legal rule "can only be arrived at after a careful analysis of what has been thought hitherto."[144] Yet history can also disclose the sources of error in current law.[145]

On the other hand, Holmes did not pursue history if it could not help explain current law. He did not discuss the duel because "it soon ceased to be used in debt" and, therefore, "has no bearing on" existing contract law.[146] Because warranty "so wholly disappeared" in the Norman period, Holmes concluded that "it can have no influence upon the law of consideration" and assumed that there was no point in discussing it.[147] And because "the heir of modern English law gets his characteristic features from the law as it stood after the Conquest,"[148] there was "no need to go back further than the early Norman period" and consider whether the English law identifying the heir with the ancestor was of German or Roman origin.[149]

---

[140] Id. at 6.
[141] Id. at 138–9.
[142] Id. at 198.
[143] Id. at 208.
[144] Id. at 72.
[145] Id. at 232.
[146] Id. at 201.
[147] Id. at 205.
[148] Id. at 274.
[149] Id. at 270.

While stressing the connections between past and current law, Holmes remained alert to the dangers of anachronism. He warned against transposing the categories of present law back into the past. The modern distinction between torts and breaches of contract, and especially between their different remedies, he pointed out, "is not found ready made." The "region of what we should now call contract" might not have been so identified in the past.[150] Holmes also chastised the condescension of modern commentators toward the reasoning of their predecessors. "It is not justifiable," he wrote, "to assume that a contemporary explanation of a new rule had nothing to do with its appearance." To the suggestion that Bracton's discussion of a legal issue "is only a piece of mediaeval scholasticism," Holmes responded that Bracton was more likely to have a proper understanding of legal developments in his own time than the nineteenth-century scholars who might dismiss him as an obfuscating Scholastic.[151]

In multiple variations of his introductory contrast between logic and experience, Holmes characterized law as a process of development. "However much we may codify the law into a series of seemingly self-sufficient propositions," Holmes concluded at the end of his first chapter, "those propositions will be but a phase in a continuous growth."[152] Like many of his contemporaries, moreover, Holmes maintained that this growth of the law reflected the broader development of society. Introducing his discussion of the history of "liability for harm inflicted by another person or thing," Holmes asserted that in addition to tracing the changes that explain current law, his "story will also afford an instructive example of the mode in which the law has grown, without a break, from barbarism to civilization."[153] Holmes maintained that many societies moved from early theories of liability, based on moral standards associated with the "passion of revenge" against those at fault, to current theories of liability, based on external or objective standards in which fault played no role.[154] The early theories of liability, he stressed, "could not last when civilization had advanced to any considerable height."[155] Emphasizing the limits of logic, Holmes observed that the process of development from early to current theories of liability was "largely unconscious." His historical explanation, Holmes confidently asserted, accounted for "the failure of all theories which consider the law only from its formal side, whether they attempt to deduce the *corpus* from *a priori* postulates, or fall into the humbler error of supposing the science of the law to reside in the *elegantia juris*, or logical cohesion of part with part."[156] Elsewhere in *The Common Law*, Holmes attributed other transformations of legal doctrine to the development of society. In explaining

[150] Id. at 214; see also id. at 289.
[151] Id. at 293.
[152] Id. at 32.
[153] Id. at 8.
[154] Id. at 8, 33.
[155] Id. at 16.
[156] Id. at 32.

changes in the law of property, he observed that absolute protection of titles, while "natural to a primitive community more occupied in production than in exchange, is hardly consistent with the requirements of modern business."[157] Rules of succession similarly changed with "the advance of civilization."[158]

Holmes frequently invoked organic metaphors to describe legal evolution. Just as Savigny and Herbert Spencer had endorsed evolutionary theories of legal development before Darwin published, Holmes read Savigny and Spencer before finally reading Darwin in 1907.[159] Summarizing the development of theories of liability, he referred to the Roman and German "parents" whose "offspring" took root "on English soil." His history of liability revealed that "a single germ," which he characterized as "the desire of retaliation against the offending thing itself," had been "multiplying and branching into products as different from each other as the flower from the root."[160] In his chapter on criminal law, he identified the presentment and the appeal as the "parents" of current criminal procedure, which developed through a process of slow improvement.[161] And in his chapter on the history of contract law, he inferred that "the 'good suit' of the later reports was the descendant of the Saxon transaction witnesses."[162] Occasionally, moreover, Holmes connected legal to racial development. In discussing developments in the law of bailment, for example, he stated that "in this as in other respects, the English followed the traditions of their race."[163] The difference between the English and Roman laws of possession, he emphasized, "are due to the sturdy persistence of the early traditions of our race."[164]

Legal Survivals: "The Paradox of Form and Substance"

Although many late nineteenth-century American legal scholars endorsed evolutionary theories of legal development, Holmes, more than any of the others, elaborated general evolutionary theory in exploring the history of legal ideas. In his frequent and lengthy discussions of legal survivals that reveal what he called "the paradox of form and substance in the development of law,"[165] Holmes presented his most detailed application of evolutionary theory to law. Several nineteenth-century social scientists had employed the concept of survivals before Holmes. E. B. Tylor, the great English scholar often described as the

---

[157] Id. at 80.

[158] Id. at 280–1.

[159] J. W. Burrow, Evolution and Society: A Study in Victorian Social Theory (Cambridge University Press, 1966), pp. 183, 186; Howe, supra note 33, at 156; Howe, supra note 1, at 44–9; White, supra note 1, at 149, 152; Reimann, supra note 1, at 97–8.

[160] Holmes, supra note 19, at 30–1.

[161] Id. at 34–5.

[162] Id. at 203.

[163] Id. at 138.

[164] Holmes, supra note 94, at 167.

[165] Holmes, supra note 19, at 31.

founder of social anthropology as an academic discipline,[166] was the first major figure to focus on identifying survivals of the past in contemporary cultures, although others, including Spencer in an essay Tylor might have read, had previously used the concept.[167] Nor was Holmes the first to apply the concept of survivals to legal analysis. Maine and Jhering had referred to legal survivals in works read by Holmes before he wrote *The Common Law*.[168]

The analysis of legal survivals had a central role in *The Common Law*. An early reviewer recognized this role in calling the book

an historical essay describing the influence of the primitive conceptions of the childhood of the Teutonic races upon the common-law of to-day, an explanation of the savage or mediaeval origin of certain anomalies which we have retained in our modern legal system from convenience, in spite of the logical confusion caused by their survival, while they still bear the traces of conceptions, beliefs, and arguments so strange that we can hardly realize that they ever seemed for a moment true.[169]

The Common Law especially reveals the crucial influence of Tylor on Holmes's treatment of legal survivals.[170]

Tylor most fully elaborated his views on survivals in his classic work, *Primitive Culture*, published in two volumes in 1871. While sharing the widespread nineteenth-century confidence that civilization progresses gradually over time, Tylor believed that some primitive practices and thoughts survive in later stages of civilization. These contemporary survivals of the primitive past, he maintained, often seemed irrational and dysfunctional in the present, but they can be explained historically, by understanding why they made sense when they first arose. Revealing why survivals were rational and functional in primitive times frequently explains as well why they had become irrational and dysfunctional in the very different and more civilized present. It should not be surprising that what worked for the savage barbarian did not work for the nineteenth-century Englishman. Occasionally, the "ruder ancient doctrine" of a survival can be "re-shaped to answer modern needs," but, more typically, a survival is "but time-honoured superstition in the garb of modern knowledge."[171] Uncovering the primitive origins of survivals that have become dysfunctional in the present justifies abandoning them in the future. History, he wrote, not only demonstrates progressive development; it also enables the scholar "to expose the remains of the crude old culture which have passed into harmful superstition, and to mark these out for destruction."[172] Holmes quoted

---

[166] Burrow, *supra* note 159, at xiv.

[167] Id. at 14, 240–1, 257.

[168] Id. at 171; Reimann, *supra* note 1, at 103, 252 n. 65.

[169] The Nation, *supra* note 16.

[170] Morton White, Social Thought in America: The Revolt against Formalism (Oxford University Press, 1976 ed.) (original ed. 1947), pp. 17–18; Burrow, *supra* note 1, at 27; Grey, *supra* note 1, at 811 n. 100.

[171] Edward B. Tylor, Primitive Culture: Researches into the Development of Mythology (London: J. Murray, 1871), vol. 2, p. 403.

[172] Id. at 410; see generally Burrow, *supra* note 159, at 249–50, 255–9.

a lengthy passage from "Mr. Tylor's great work on Primitive Culture" in his 1876 article, "Primitive Notions in Modern Law,"[173] and cited this work twice in the opening chapter of *The Common Law*, "Early Forms of Liability."[174]

In summarizing his first chapter, Holmes wrote that his history of "early forms of liability" had implications beyond this specific topic because it "well illustrates the paradox of form and substance in the development of law." His discussion of these implications provides the most concise statement of his theory of legal survivals. As a purely formal matter, Holmes observed, the growth of the law is logical. "The official theory," he wrote, "is that each new decision follows syllogistically from existing precedents." Holmes immediately challenged this "official theory" with his theory of survivals. "But just as the clavicle in the cat only tells of the existence of some earlier creature to which a collar-bone was useful, precedents survive in the law long after the use they once served is at an end and the reason for them has been forgotten. The result of following them must often be failure and confusion from the merely logical point of view."[175] By using an explicit biological analogy to make his legal point, Holmes indicated the influence of evolutionary theory in the natural sciences as well as in the social sciences on his concept of legal survivals.

Just as Tylor conceded that some survivals could be "re-shaped to answer modern needs," Holmes acknowledged through his elaboration of "the paradox of form and function" that legal survivals similarly could be adapted in the present. Despite the "official theory" that the law develops syllogistically from precedents, Holmes considered it fortunate that "the law is administered by able and experienced men, who know too much to sacrifice good sense to a syllogism." Rather, "when ancient rules maintain themselves" as survivals disconnected from their original rationales, "new reasons more fitted to the time have been found for them." They "gradually receive a new content, and at last a new form, from the ground to which they have been transplanted."[176]

Without explicitly mentioning survivals or "the paradox of form and substance," Holmes wrote another revealing paragraph about his understanding of this evolutionary process earlier in his first chapter:

A very common phenomenon, and one very familiar to the student of history, is this. The customs, beliefs, or needs of a primitive time establish a rule or a formula. In the course of centuries the custom, belief, or necessity disappears, but the rule remains. The reason which gave rise to the rule has been forgotten, and ingenious minds set themselves to inquire how it is to be accounted for. Some ground of policy is thought of which seems to explain it and to reconcile it with the present state of things; and then the rule adapts itself to the new reasons which have been found for it, and enters on a new career. The old form receives a new content, and in time even the form modifies itself to fit the meaning which it has received.[177]

---

[173] Holmes, supra note 130, at 135–6.
[174] Holmes, supra note 19, at 13 n. 25, 19 n. 53.
[175] Id. at 31.
[176] Id. at 32.
[177] Id. at 8.

From this historically informed perspective, Holmes reiterated his objection to the purely formal logical analysis of law. "The truth is," he wrote, "that the law is always approaching, and never reaching consistency. It is forever adopting new principles from life at one end, and it always retains old ones from history at the other, which have not yet been absorbed or sloughed off. It will become entirely consistent only when it ceases to grow." Any attempt to codify existing law in the logical form of "self-sufficient propositions," Holmes observed, "will be but a phase in a continuous growth" and will unravel as changing times demand new laws. The need to rationalize or abandon law that has survived from the past continues as long as human history itself. If "in large and important branches of the law the various grounds of policy on which the various rules have been justified are later inventions to account for what are in fact survivals from earlier times," it makes sense to reconsider these "inventions" to determine whether the reasons given for them are convincing. Many of these subsequently invented reasons, he acknowledged, might be convincing. After all, "if old implements could not be adjusted to new uses, human progress would be slow." But "scrutiny and revision are justified" when these reasons are not convincing.[178]

Holmes's understanding of legal survivals prompted him to recognize and approve "judicial legislation." Though logical in form, he emphasized that "in substance the growth of the law is legislative." Holmes maintained that in general judicial legislation derives from evolving custom, "our practice and traditions, the unconscious result of instinctive preferences and inarticulate convictions." Yet, Holmes connected his interpretation of evolving custom to "considerations of what is expedient for the community concerned," which are "at bottom the result of more or less definitely understood views of public policy." Holmes regretted that judges seldom acknowledged, or perhaps even recognized, what they were doing. "The very considerations which judges most rarely mention, and often with an apology, are the secret root from which the law draws all the juices of policy." While acknowledging that "hitherto this process has been largely unconscious," Holmes joined the many evolutionary legal thinkers in America who urged "a more conscious recognition of the legislative function of the courts."[179] He maintained that "judges as well as others should openly discuss the legislative principles upon which their decisions must always rest in the end, and should base their judgments upon broad considerations of policy to which the traditions of the bench would hardly have tolerated a reference fifty years ago."[180]

Examples of Legal Survivals

While agreeing that Holmes placed great emphasis on legal survivals, important recent scholars have criticized him for not pursuing the historical implications

178 Id. at 33.
179 Id. at 31–2.
180 Id. at 64.

of this concept. Holmes, they protest, never really explained why a current survival made sense when it first arose. Nor did he examine the conditions that prompted people to invent new justifications enabling old concepts to survive. Holmes, in brief, should have investigated social history. Not only did he decline this task, he even left insufficiently explored the internal history of legal doctrine that revealed survivals. As a result, they claim, Holmes rendered history marginal to his book, which is better understood as a work of theory.[181]

Some of these criticisms have substantial merit. But Holmes illustrated the concept of legal survivals in much greater detail than the current critics indicate, and he occasionally provided some of the explanations they find lacking. I will, therefore, discuss specific examples of survivals that Holmes provided throughout *The Common Law*. These examples best reveal how Holmes actually applied his most important theory of history.

In his first chapter, "Early Forms of Liability," Holmes illustrated the extent to which current law retained the terminology of morals from primitive theories of liability based on the desire for revenge. He concluded that different primitive legal systems, independently of each other,[182] justified "vengeance on the immediate offender," which could be a person, an animal, or an inanimate thing. As support for this conclusion, he cited the findings of Tylor and others about "the personification of inanimate nature common to savages and children"[183] and quoted a passage from Tylor describing the "rude Kukis of Southern Asia": "If a tiger killed a Kuki, his family were in disgrace till they had retaliated by killing and eating this tiger, or another; but further, if a man was killed by a fall from a tree, his relatives would take their revenge by cutting the tree down, and scattering it in chips."[184] The connection of liability to vengeance against the offender, Holmes added, extended to matters that have come to be called contractual.[185] A creditor could kill a debtor, and if a debtor owed several creditors, the creditors could divide the debtor's dead body among themselves. Holmes concluded that "the right to put to death looks like vengeance, and the division of the body shows that the debt was conceived very literally to inhere in or bind the body."[186]

With the advance of civilization, Holmes maintained, vengeance was no longer extracted by surrendering the physical body of the offending person, but by the payment of damages. If owners did not properly supervise slaves or animals, instead of surrendering them as in the more barbarous past, they became personally liable for the damages they caused. Eventually, liability expanded to situations in which a person had no personal responsibility for damages. Owners of ships and innkeepers were held liable for wrongs committed by

---

[181] Gordon, supra note 1, at 729–34; White, supra note 1, at 152, 154, 169.
[182] Holmes, supra note 19, at 9.
[183] Id. at 12.
[184] Id. at 19.
[185] Id. at 14.
[186] Id. at 15.

their employees without their knowledge. According to Holmes, the real reason for this extension of liability was the "exceptional confidence which was necessarily reposed in carriers and innkeepers." But many judges retained the previous language of fault in their decisions, blaming the owners for hiring bad employees.[187]

These cases involving shipowners and innkeepers introduced what Holmes called the "startling innovation" of holding one man, the owner, responsible for the wrongs of another man, the employee, who himself, unlike the slave, was subject to a lawsuit. Holmes observed that "the principle introduced on special grounds in a special case, when servants were slaves, is now the general law of this country and England, and under it men daily have to pay large sums for other people's acts, in which they had no part and for which they are in no sense to blame." This principle, which originated in the substitution of "buying off vengeance by agreement, of paying the damage instead of surrendering the body" of the offending slave, ended up as a justification for the "universal and unlimited responsibility" of innocent employers for the acts of their employees.[188]

Maritime law, Holmes added, also illustrated that primitive concepts of vengeance against a personified thing continued to influence the law. As recently as major Supreme Court opinions by Marshall and Story, he maintained, great judges treated the ship, rather than its owner or crew, as the offender to be punished.[189] Reinforcing his earlier examples, Holmes stressed that liability based on vengeance extended to contract as well as tort. The "same metaphysical confusion which naturally arose as to the ship's wrongful acts," Holmes observed, "affected the way of thinking as to her contracts." The value of a ship, for example, became the limit of its owner's liability for contractual damages.[190] Though there may be a "hidden ground of policy" for the results in maritime cases, judicial reasoning "still clothes itself in personifying language" derived from primitive attributions of blame to inanimate things.[191]

At the end of his chapter on "early forms of liability," Holmes reiterated that his purpose had been "to show that the various forms of liability known to modern law spring from the common ground of revenge."[192] For Holmes, these forms of liability, like the clavicle in the cat, are survivals that illustrate "the paradox of form and substance in the development of the law."[193] Modern justifications of policy for rules attributed to these survivals, such as holding carriers and innkeepers to a high standard of care based on their special responsibilities[194] or limiting the risk of a shipowner to an amount that is easily

---

[187] Id. at 16.
[188] Id. at 16–17.
[189] Id. at 27.
[190] Id. at 30.
[191] Id. at 27.
[192] Id. at 33.
[193] Id. at 31.
[194] Id. at 16.

calculable,[195] are divorced from their original justifications as revenge. The survival of the rule provides the form of current law, while the new justification provides its substance. By demonstrating the disjunction between the surviving form and the current substance, Holmes believed he had provided grounds for reevaluating whether the current justification for a rule makes sense and, if it does not, whether the rule itself should be revised.[196]

Subsequent chapters of *The Common Law* provided many other examples of survivals that illustrated "the paradox of form and substance in the development of the law." In the chapter on "bailment," Holmes challenged existing explanations for the strict responsibility of common carriers by attempting to prove that it is "a fragmentary survival from the general law of bailment." Modifications of the old law of bailment, he maintained, derived from "a confusion of ideas" accompanying changes in procedural law and from later conceptions of public policy that were read into earlier precedents.[197] At a time when bailors did not have any remedies against third parties but could only recover from bailees, the common law made bailees absolutely liable to bailors. When procedural developments provided bailors at least some remedies against third parties, exceptions to the absolute liability of bailees arose. These exceptions, however, did not modify the absolute liability of common carriers retained from the old law of bailment.[198] Yet no general principle had emerged to justify treating the common carrier as an insurer.[199] By uncovering this forgotten history, Holmes claimed that he had provided the basis for reconsidering on grounds of policy the extent to which absolute liability should apply.[200]

Holmes proceeded to discuss the anomalous treatment of servants in the law of possession as another illustration of the survival of an old rule that had lost its original justification. The general law of possession, Holmes maintained, is based on "an intent to exclude others."[201] Yet the law regarding possession by servants does not follow that test. A servant with "as much the intent to exclude the world at large as a borrower" is denied the possession the borrower would have. With respect to servants, the law of possession depends on status, not intent. Holmes stressed that history rather than logic accounts for this anomaly. The free servant, he observed, retains many marks of slavery.[202] Slaves could not possess because they had no legal standing apart from their masters. The fictional absorption of legal identity into the master survived emancipation, leaving the free servant in substantially the same position as the slave.[203] According to Holmes, "there is no adequate and complete explanation

---

[195] Id. at 29.
[196] Id. at 33.
[197] Id. at 143.
[198] Id. at 130–61.
[199] Id. at 159–60.
[200] Id. at 161–2; see generally, Howe, supra note 1, at 206–12.
[201] Holmes, supra note 19, at 174.
[202] Id. at 179.
[203] Id. at 180, 183.

of the modern law, except by the survival in practice of rules which lost their true meaning when the objects of them ceased to be slaves."[204] For Holmes, "so long as the fiction which makes the root of a master's liability is left alive, it is as hopeless to reconcile the differences by logic as to square the circle." And Holmes did not just suggest reconsideration of current law, as in many of his previous examples of survivals. He hoped that "common sense" and "the instinct of justice" would limit the application of this anomalous survival.[205]

The history of contract law provided an additional context for Holmes to illustrate the importance of survivals. Just as Maine believed that in early law substance was "gradually secreted in the interstices of procedure,"[206] Holmes observed that "whenever we trace a leading doctrine of substantive law far enough back, we are very likely to find some forgotten circumstance of procedure at its source."[207] He elaborated by demonstrating how the substantive doctrine of consideration derived from procedures associated with the action of debt, the topic on which he and Ames had a subsequent testy disagreement. Under the action of debt, the debt could be proved either by the defendant's seal on a written document or by a group of witnesses, called the *secta*, who swore under oath that they had observed the defendant receive a quid pro quo from the plaintiff. A writing was a more convincing method of proof than an oath, so this method dominated when seals became commonly available. The *secta*, moreover, was losing its general function as a method of proof to procedures that were the origins of trial by jury.[208] It "had shrunk to a form" and had become "a mere survival."[209] But it did not disappear completely. No new actions for the enforcement of contracts developed while the emerging jury trial was replacing the *secta* as a general method of proof, and the *secta* continued as a requirement whenever an action of debt did not rely on the more typical proof of a sealed writing.[210] The requirement of a *secta* "became strictly limited to cases in which the debt arose from the receipt of a *quid pro quo*."[211] What had been "an accident of procedure," the *secta*, "had become a doctrine of substantive law," the quid pro quo.[212]

Subsequently, and independently of the action of debt to recover money, a new procedure, the action of assumpsit, began to develop. Originating as an early form of tort law that allowed recovery for negligent performance of an undertaking that resulted in harm,[213] assumpsit expanded to include cases

---

[204] Id. at 183.

[205] Id. at 182.

[206] Sir Henry Maine, Dissertations on Early Law and Custom (London: John Murray, 1907), p. 389.

[207] Holmes, supra note 19, at 199.

[208] Id. at 203–7.

[209] Id. at 208–9.

[210] Id. at 207–8.

[211] Id. at 208.

[212] Id. at 209.

[213] Id. at 217.

"arising out of a promise as a source of the defendant's obligation" and thus also became "a new and distinct action of contract."[214] Whereas the action of debt applied to contracts in which the defendant had received a quid pro quo from the plaintiff, the new action of assumpsit applied to contracts in which the defendant had harmed the plaintiff by failing to perform a promise.[215]

The "bastard origin" of assumpsit in tort as well as contract, Holmes concluded, thus enabled a broader conception of consideration than was available under the traditional action of debt.[216] The role of the *secta* in actions of debt led to the substantive requirement of a quid pro quo as consideration for a contract. Holmes described this quid pro quo as "a benefit to the promisor."[217] No such requirement applied in assumpsit, in which "detriment to the promisee" was sufficient consideration.[218]

Illustrating again that history rather than logic explains current law, Holmes maintained that the "larger view" of consideration associated with the development of assumpsit "was a change in the substantive law, and logically it should have been applied throughout." But it was not. Instead, "the new doctrine prevailed in the new action, and the old in the old," producing the "anomaly of inconsistent theories carried out side by side."[219] In other words, the new doctrine of consideration "was not separated or distinguished from the remedy which introduced it."[220] For Holmes, this account of confusion in the substantive law of consideration proved once more the value of uncovering survivals from the forgotten past.[221]

In the two chapters on "successions" that concluded *The Common Law*, Holmes provided his final examples of survivals. Paralleling his treatment of the history of contract law, Holmes maintained that historical survivals from two different sources had produced confusion in the current law of property. Just as the action of debt and the action of assumpsit generated different and inconsistent theories of consideration, "the conception of succession or privity" and "that of rights inhering in a thing" generated "two competing and mutually inconsistent principles into our law."[222]

The law of succession, Holmes reported, originated in the early law dealing with succession after death, which was "founded upon a fictitious identification between the deceased and his successor."[223] This fictitious identification arose first for the heir and later was extended to the executor, a process that illustrated a more general phenomenon: "the help of a fiction, which shadows, as

---

[214] Id. at 222.
[215] Id. at 225.
[216] Id. at 224.
[217] Id. at 213.
[218] Id. at 225.
[219] Id. at 213.
[220] Id. at 225.
[221] See generally Howe, supra note 1, at 226–9; White, supra note 1, at 172–4.
[222] Holmes, supra note 19, at 300.
[223] Id. at 266.

fictions often do, the facts of an early stage of society, and which could hardly have been invented had these facts been otherwise."[224] Eventually, the fictional identity of persons "silently modified" the law beyond the original context of inheritance and encompassed "dealings between the living."[225] Observing the "obvious analogy between purchaser and heir,"[226] Holmes asserted that in some contexts involving the transfer of land, the cases assumed a fictional identity of the buyer and the seller similar to the one between the heir and the deceased. The "analogy of the inheritance" is "hidden at the root" of this fictional identification.[227]

On the other hand, Holmes emphasized, cases involving transfers of rights to wrongful possessors were not governed by assumptions of fictional identity. Even as a fiction, it would be difficult to sustain an identity between an owner and a wrongful possessor. Yet wrongful possessors did have rights to easements in land. Reiterating his language from a previous article, he found the explanation "not in reasoning, but in a failure to reason." And the "failure to reason" can be understood historically because it derived from the unthinking retention of the primitive tendency to personify things, the same tendency Holmes discussed at length in his analysis of theories of liability. "The language of the law of easements," he pointed out, "was built up out of similes drawn from persons." Over time, "as often happens, language reacted upon thought, so that conclusions were drawn as to the rights themselves from the terms in which they happened to be expressed. When one estate was said to be enslaved to another, or a right of way was said to be a quality or incident of a neighboring piece of land, men's minds were not alert to see that these phrases were only so many personifying metaphors, which explained nothing unless the figure of speech was true."[228] In other words, "easements have become an incident of land by an unconscious and unreasoned assumption that a piece of land can have rights." Through this process, "absurd or not," rules of law were derived "from the figures of speech without attracting attention, and before any one had seen that they were only figures, which proved nothing and justified no conclusion."[229] A wrongful possessor of land, who could not claim to be a successor to the rightful owner, could obtain the benefits of easements attached to it.

Having thus explained historically "one of the great antinomies of the law,"[230] Holmes proceeded to address more generally the difficulty in distinguishing "between covenants that devolved only to successors, and those that went with the land."[231] Observing that over time the distinction itself had been

[224] Id. at 269.
[225] Id. at 275.
[226] Id. at 276.
[227] Id. at 296.
[228] Id. at 297–8.
[229] Id. at 299.
[230] Id. at 296.
[231] Id. at 306.

forgotten, Holmes concluded the law "has failed to settle the disputed line between conflicting principles."[232] He also concluded that "general reasoning" could not produce a convincing distinction.[233] In this "necessarily vague" state of the law, Holmes simply tried to summarize the rules that had emerged under each category of covenant.[234]

Functional Survivals

Although Holmes devoted much of his scholarship to uncovering anomalous and dysfunctional survivals from the past, often suggesting that they should prompt reconsideration and reform of current law, it is important to remember his fundamental belief that most survivals have become functional through the invention of new policies that replaced their original justifications. As he wrote in the first page of *The Common Law*: "The substance of the law at any given time pretty much corresponds, so far as it goes, with what is then understood to be convenient; but its form and machinery, and the degree to which it is able to work out desired results, depend very much on its past."[235] And at the end of his opening chapter, while advocating the reconsideration of subsequently invented justifications for rules that are survivals from the primitive past, Holmes acknowledged that these justifications might turn out to be convincing. Much human progress, he observed, depends on the adjustment of "old implements" to "new uses."[236]

Consistent with his belief in the adaptability of most survivals to current needs, Holmes referred throughout *The Common Law* to the "good sense" of surviving rules. He sometimes did so even in the midst of discussing anomalous survivals that produced conceptual confusion due to the lingering impact of old justifications. In discussing a rule of liability for the wages of sailors, Holmes remarked that the rule, though a survival, has "as usual" a "plausible explanation of policy."[237] A case exhibiting the "echo of primitive notions" also revealed "that the working rules of the law had long been founded on good sense."[238] According to Holmes, "it does not matter" that "the historical origin of the rule was different" than its current justification.[239] During his analysis of the fictional identifications that survived from the primitive law of inheritance, Holmes observed that "[c]ommon sense kept control over fiction here as elsewhere in the common law."[240] He complimented Bracton for extending a legal fiction with technical skill but also "with good sense, as fictions generally

---

[232] Id. at 311.
[233] Id. at 315.
[234] Id. at 314. See Howe, supra note 1, at 247–8; White, supra note 1, at 178–9.
[235] Holmes, supra note 19, at 5.
[236] Id. at 33.
[237] Id. at 28.
[238] Id. at 94.
[239] Id. at 95.
[240] Id. at 287.

have been used in English law."[241] And Holmes maintained that a rule based on personifying metaphors "which proved nothing and justified no conclusion" nonetheless "was just as good as any other, or at least was unobjectionable."[242] Most importantly, Holmes underlined the adaptability of survivals while reiterating a central theme in *The Common Law*, the transformation of moral and subjective standards into external and objective ones. In virtually every area of the common law, he emphasized, surviving rules originally based on moral grounds, while often retaining the language of morality, currently enforced external standards justified by contemporary considerations of policy.[243]

Just as Holmes compared legal survivals that had lost their original functions to the clavicle in the cat,[244] he seemed to compare the entire common law to the body of the cat. Neither the common law nor the cat could have survived unless it had adapted to its changing environment. Some rules of the common law, like the clavicle in the cat, are survivals that served functions in the past but have no use in the present. But a cat, despite its useless clavicle, must have a functional physiology in order to remain alive. So, too, the common law as a whole must have "convenient"[245] rules "expedient for the community concerned"[246] to survive in the modern world.

If most legal survivals are functional, why did Holmes focus so much of his historical discussion on those he suspected are not? The answer lies in his view that the role of history in legal analysis, like its role in anthropology for Tylor, is to emancipate the present and future from the irrational constraints of the past. If the legal forms derived from outmoded justifications had been adapted effectively to current needs, there was no need to engage in historical analysis. "The doctrine of contract," Holmes revealingly wrote at the beginning of his chapter on its history, "has been so thoroughly remodeled to meet the needs of modern times, that there is less necessity here than elsewhere for historical research."[247] In his discussion of tort law, Holmes similarly explained that he would not explore "the possible historical connection" of certain forms of liability with primitive theories "because, whether that origin is made out or not, the policy of the rule has been accepted as sound."[248] But because Holmes believed that the evolution of law, while mostly unconscious in the past, could be consciously directed in the future, he wanted to uncover the historical origins of surviving rules that are confusing, irrational, or dysfunctional in order to determine whether they could be revised and "adjusted to new uses"[249] through the "legislative function of the courts"[250] or should be abandoned.

---

[241] Id. at 292.
[242] Id. at 299.
[243] Id. at 33, 107–9, 128–9, 253–4.
[244] Id. at 31.
[245] Id. at 5.
[246] Id. at 32.
[247] Id. at 195.
[248] Id. at 124.
[249] Id. at 33.
[250] Id. at 32.

Holmes's Instrumental Use of History in Legal Analysis

As Holmes announced in his opening paragraphs and reiterated throughout *The Common Law*, he subordinated historical explanation to legal analysis. That is why Holmes repeatedly introduced his discussions of legal history by underlining their importance for understanding current law and alternatively justified his lack of attention to history by maintaining that it was irrelevant to the present.

Although he limited the scope of his own historical inquiries, Holmes acknowledged the value of broader historical scholarship. Like many other late nineteenth-century American legal scholars, he recognized the importance of external influences on legal doctrine and occasionally alluded to them while addressing other issues. He observed without elaboration, for example, that the growth of trade made exchange more important than production and led to the erosion of absolute protection for property.[251] Holmes similarly appreciated but did not pursue broad possibilities in studying the intellectual history of legal ideas. At the end of his chapter on the history of contract law, Holmes intriguingly speculated that the growing importance of contract as the basis for legal rights and duties might be related to "the similar prominence which it soon acquired in political speculation." Yet he immediately closed the chapter by calling such speculation "beyond my province to inquire."[252] In a revealing comment at the end of his chapter on "early forms of liability," he recognized "the materials for anthropology contained in the history of the law" while emphasizing that he would be focusing instead on the origins of modern forms of liability.[253]

In applying history to legal analysis, Holmes especially emphasized its value as a means to the goal he identified in the first sentence of his book: "to present a general view of the Common Law."[254] His use of history to support his earlier attempts to organize and classify existing legal doctrine, which marked his return to scholarship in 1876 after an intensive period of reading, remained central in *The Common Law*.[255] In a letter to Pomeroy in August 1881, five months after the publication of *The Common Law*, Holmes wrote that his book was "intended to give the rationale of the cardinal doctrines of the common law – using analysis only where that is sufficient but resorting to history where the particular outline of a conception or a rule could not be explained without it."[256] Holmes combined history and analysis throughout *The Common Law*,

---

[251] Id. at 80.
[252] Id. at 226.
[253] Id. at 33.
[254] Id. at 5.
[255] Grey, supra note 1, at 819–25; Reimann, supra note 1, at 112.
[256] Letter from Oliver Wendell Holmes, Jr. to John Norton Pomeroy (August 8, 1881), microformed on reel 36, 0680, Holmes Papers, supra note 15.

and some chapters are almost entirely analytical.[257] Introducing his two chapters on tort law, Holmes wrote that their object was "to discover whether there is any common ground at the bottom of all liability in tort, and, if so, what that ground is." These chapters, he intimated, would "reveal the general principle of civil liability at common law."[258] Interestingly, the review of *The Common Law* in the *Nation* found the analytic portions much less valuable than its historical analysis. The review referred to the book's "rather unsatisfactory metaphysical discussion of the modern theory of criminal law, of torts," and of other subjects, which would "weary our readers by describing."[259] Although "novel and brilliant" and "reflecting unusually profound legal study," *The Common Law* "is injured by long philosophical discussions" that give it "a tediously discursive and aimless air" and "hide its real historical value."[260]

The pervasiveness of objective and external standards in all areas of the common law is the analytical theme that emerges most clearly from Holmes's book.[261] Emphasizing that "the general principles of criminal and civil liability are the same,"[262] Holmes asserted that civil as well as criminal law punishes people "who have been guilty of no moral wrong." He observed that the predominant "purpose of the criminal law is only to induce external conformity to rule."[263] For most substantive crimes, "acts are rendered criminal because they are done under circumstances in which they will probably cause some harm which the law seeks to prevent."[264] He insisted that the subjective state of mind accompanying the criminal act, however evil, is largely irrelevant.[265] Similarly in tort law, intent is "really an external standard of conduct under the known circumstances, and the analysis of the criminal law holds good here." Analyzing contract law, Holmes also stressed that liability for making a promise depends on objective rather than moral considerations. "In the moral world it may be that the obligation of a promise is confined to what lies within reach of the will of the promisor," but the "consequences of a binding promise at common law are not affected by the degree of power which the promisor possesses over the promised event." Rather, the promisor "takes the risk of the event" and must pay damages if "the promised event does not come to pass."[266] Holmes's analysis of survivals and his treatment of German legal scholarship illustrate how he

---

[257] See, e.g., Holmes, supra note 19, lecture II ("The Criminal Law") and lecture IX ("Contract. – III. Void and Voidable").

[258] Id. at 63.

[259] Nation, supra note 16, at 464.

[260] Id. at 465.

[261] See Howe, supra note 1, at 188–9, 195, 237–8, 252; White, supra note 1, at 154, 161–2, 168, 171, 174–5; Horwitz, supra note 1, at 110–11; Grey, supra note 1, at 816.

[262] Holmes, supra note 19, at 38.

[263] Id. at 42.

[264] Id. at 61.

[265] Id. at 41–2, 61.

[266] Id. at 234–5; see also id. at 236.

harnessed history to support his claim about the pervasiveness of objective and external standards throughout the common law.

Survivals

The many references to the language of morality in current law posed a major obstacle to Holmes's theory of objective and external standards. He dealt with this obstacle by treating moral language as survivals from primitive theories of liability that were grounded in revenge but that no longer governed the law. New grounds of policy eventually transformed rules originally based on morality into rules that enforced objective and external standards.

Holmes set as his goal in *The Common Law* to prove that "while the terminology of morals is still retained, and while the law does still and always, in a certain sense, measure legal liability by moral standards, it nevertheless, by the very necessity of its nature, is continually transmuting those moral standards into external or objective ones, from which the actual guilt of the party concerned is wholly eliminated."[267] For example, in summarizing the law of torts, Holmes maintained that "as the law has grown, even when its standards have continued to model themselves upon those of morality, they have necessarily become external, because they have considered, not the actual condition of the particular defendant, but whether his conduct would have been wrong in the fair average member of the community, whom he is expected to equal at his peril."[268] Holmes concluded that "the actual wickedness of the kind described by" words such as "fraud," "malice," and "intent" was "not an element in the civil wrongs to which these words are applied."[269] Similarly, he reiterated in his discussion of contracts that "although the law starts from the distinctions and uses of the language of morality, it necessarily ends in external standards not dependent on the actual consciousness of the individual."[270] "The morality phraseology," he added, "has ceased to be apposite, and an external standard of responsibility has been reached."[271]

Holmes seemed to be arguing that many surviving rules were functional precisely because they escaped their origins in morality and, through subsequently invented justifications, had been applied to enforce external standards. His treatment of particular survivals illustrated this transformation. For example, modern rules governing the liability of innkeepers and shipowners, though they originated in moral theories of revenge, were justified by the modern needs to hold innkeepers to a high standard of care for their guests and to enable shipowners to calculate with some certainty the risks to which they were exposed.[272]

---

[267] Id. at 33; see also id. at 107–8.
[268] Id. at 128; see also id. at 109.
[269] Id. at 104.
[270] Id. at 253.
[271] Id. at 254.
[272] Id. at 16, 29.

On the other hand, Holmes attributed some of the confusing, irrational, or dysfunctional survivals he uncovered, such as broad liability of employers for the acts of their employees, to the regrettable, if unconscious, retention of moral standards from early law that, in contrast to most survivals, had not been revised and adapted to new conditions as civilization progressed.[273]

Resembling the unsupported conclusions of Henry Maine, Holmes often asserted the historical progression from moral to external standards without reviewing the actual historical process by which this alleged transformation took place. He cited precedents more frequently to demonstrate that external standards had come to prevail than to show how the "old forms" of laws based on morality received a "new content" expressing external standards justified by current policy concerns.[274] Critics are correct, moreover, in observing that Holmes did not explore topics in social history that seemed to arise naturally from his own theory of survivals. He did not address in any detail the social context that might explain why a society first developed a legal concept, the social changes that made the original reasons for a doctrine obsolete, or the extent to which a survival with a new justification actually worked in practice. As Robert Gordon has succinctly observed, Holmes had "an expressly social theory of law without a society anywhere in sight."[275] Holmes's instrumental use of history explains his lack of interest in these broader historical issues. Once Holmes had invoked survivals to explain that a legal doctrine, even if phrased in moral and individualistic language, enforces objective and external standards and is therefore functional, or that a survival is dysfunctional because it has not been so transformed, he achieved his main goal in *The Common Law*. Broader historical issues, even ones raised directly by his theory of survivals, remained peripheral to the object he announced in his first sentence: "to present a general view of the Common Law."[276]

Treatment of German Legal Scholarship

Holmes's constant attacks on German scholars of Roman law, combined with his repeated assertions that the common law derived mostly from Germanic rather than Roman origins, provide related additional examples of his use of history to reinforce his fundamental analytical claim that the modern common law is based on objective and external standards. According to Holmes, German scholars since Savigny read the moral and individualistic principles of German metaphysical thought into their interpretations of Roman law. Expressing skepticism but not attempting to refute the German interpretations of Roman law, Holmes instead emphasized the Germanic sources of the common law, which were not contaminated by German metaphysics and often supported

---

[273] Id. at 16–17.
[274] Id. at 8.
[275] Gordon, supra note 1, at 735.
[276] Holmes, supra note 19, at 5.

objective and external standards. In examining the Germanic sources of the English common law, Holmes followed the prior "Germanist" legal scholars in Germany as well as Henry Adams, who might have introduced Holmes to this "Germanist" scholarship. In contrast to his constant disparagement of the German scholars of Roman law, Holmes did not refer explicitly to the separate Germanist school.[277] Yet he did cite Germanist scholars, including Sohm[278] and Brunner,[279] as well as Adams[280] and Bigelow,[281] while elaborating his historical assertions about the Germanic origins of the common law. Holmes departed from the earlier scholars in his analytic claim that these Germanic sources promoted objective and external legal standards.

From the beginning of his legal career, Holmes rejected the sentimental moralizing about individual freedom, autonomy, and will that he believed characterized German metaphysical thought, especially as expressed by Kant and Hegel.[282] His most direct attack on Kant and Hegel, and on the German scholars of Roman law for incorporating their theories, was in his chapter on possession in *The Common Law*. Holmes complained in the opening paragraph that the theory of possession had "fallen into the hands of the philosophers," in particular the "*a priori* doctrines of Kant and Hegel," which "are worked out in careful correspondence with German views of Roman law." Most leading German speculative jurists from Savigny to Jhering, Holmes observed, had been professors of Roman law and were "profoundly influenced if not controlled by some form of Kantian or post-Kantian philosophy."[283]

Kant and Hegel, Holmes asserted, emphasized free will as the essence of humanity and applied this fundamental principle to the law of possession by focusing on whether a person had brought an object "within the sphere of his will."[284] Holmes portrayed most German jurists as endorsing this view of possession and finding support for it in Roman law.[285] In this manner, German philosophy "adjusted itself to the Roman law, and thus put itself in a position to claim the authority of that law" for its own metaphysical views.[286] The treatment of the Roman law of possession by German scholars, Holmes observed, exhibited "a characteristic yearning of the German mind," demanding "an internal juristic necessity drawn from the nature of possession itself" without any consideration of "empirical reasons."[287] He summarized their position as maintaining

---

[277] Reimann, supra note 1, at 97.

[278] Holmes, supra note 19, at 18 n. 44, 131 n. 1, 191 n. 89, 196, n. 4, 203 n. 25, 269 n. 12, 277 n. 38, 278 n. 42.

[279] Id. at 81 n. 35, 148 n. 62, 203 n. 25.

[280] Id. at 131 n. 1, 196 n. 5, 203 n. 28, 290 n. 2, 310 n. 86.

[281] Id. at 81 n. 36, 214 n. 71, 72.

[282] Howe, supra note 1, at 151, Reimann, supra note 1, at 90–1.

[283] Holmes, supra note 19, at 163; see also id. at 133.

[284] Id. at 164.

[285] Id. at 164–6.

[286] Id. at 166.

[287] Id. at 164.

that a man's physical power over an object is protected because he has the will to make it his, and it has thus become a part of his very self, the external manifestation of his freedom. The will of the possessor being thus conceived as self-regarding, the intent with which he must hold is pretty clear: he must hold for his own benefit. Furthermore, the self-regarding intent must go to the height of an intent to appropriate; for otherwise, it seems to be implied, the object would not truly be brought under the personality of the possessor.[288]

Holmes, by contrast, maintained that "a far more civilized system than the Roman is framed upon a plan which is irreconcilable with the *a priori* doctrines of Kant and Hegel."[289] That "more developed, more rational, and mightier body of law than the Roman" was the English common law,[290] which did not require the "self-regarding" intent to exclude and thus, unlike the German interpretation of Roman law, protected broader rights of possession, including by tenants and bailees.[291] And the English common law of possession, Holmes emphasized in his chapter on bailment, was of "native origin,"[292] by which he meant "of pure German descent."[293] By extending the early Germanic law, Holmes added, "the English followed the traditions of their race."[294] Evidence of the Germanic origins of the common law, "of which philosophy has not yet taken account," enabled Holmes to counter the "hasty assumption" of too many English legal scholars that the analysis of Roman law by German scholars under the influence of Kant and Hegel revealed universal first principles applicable to all legal systems, including the English common law.[295] German metaphysical thought, Holmes asserted instead, distorted German legal scholarship and deprived it "of its claim to universal authority."[296] Although Holmes did not specifically name the English scholars to whom he was referring, he was probably thinking of Maine, who openly generalized from Roman law throughout *Ancient Law*.

Holmes added with some bemusement that contemporary German statutes resembled the English common law of possession, prompting a leading German Romanist to declare, "as the spirit of the Kantian theory required him to say, that this is a sacrifice of principle to convenience." This declaration provided Holmes a wonderful opportunity to reiterate his contempt for German philosophy. He found it difficult to take seriously a principle that was admittedly inconvenient and inconsistent with existing law. Because "it is pretty certain that men will make laws which seem to them convenient without troubling themselves very much what principles are encountered by their legislation," he

[288] Id. at 173.
[289] Id. at 163.
[290] Id. at 166.
[291] Id. at 166–7, 174–5.
[292] Id. at 133.
[293] Id. at 138.
[294] Id.
[295] Id. at 133.
[296] Id. at 163.

snidely observed, "a principle which defies convenience is likely to wait some time before it finds itself permanently realized."[297]

In a letter to a friend about the earlier articles from which he derived his chapters on bailment and possession in *The Common Law*, Holmes expressed his views more concisely. His research, Holmes reported, had revealed that English scholars of the common law "were following the theories of Savigny – which are those of a Romanist inspired by the Kantian philosophy." He wanted "to show by the way our law dealt with bailees that theories based on the Roman law *as the Germans understand it* (it is immaterial whether they have distorted it or not), would not fit our law and that our law was in this respect truly national – Teutonic & not borrowed from Rome." By doing so, Holmes believed, "it is easier to maintain that what has been put out by the German Jurists who are all Kantians or Hegelians, as the theory of possession in all possible systems is in truth only a theory carefully adapted to the facts of the only system known to the writers – although stated as if it were developed apriori."[298] In a letter to Frederick Pollock the following year, Holmes did address whether German scholars had distorted Roman law. Thanking Pollock for a reference to Gaius, the Roman legal scholar who wrote in the second century, Holmes wrote that it "tends to confirm a suspicion which I have often had that even the Roman law as the Roman lawyers understood it would give but partial support to the theories of German philosophers upon possession."[299]

Holmes made many similar points in discussing additional areas of the common law. In advancing his preventive theory of criminal law, he criticized the retributive theories of punishment he associated with Kant and Hegel. Hegel posited "a mystic bond between wrong and punishment" based on his "quasi-mathematical" philosophical position that "wrong being the negation of right, punishment is the negation of that negation, or retribution." For Hegel, "the punishment must be equal to the crime, because its only function is to destroy it." Kant objected to the preventive theory because it "treats man as a thing, not as a person; as a means, not an end in himself," thus violating the "equal rights to life, liberty, and personal security."[300] Responding with scorn to this moralistic "dogma of equality," Holmes emphasized that "justifiable self-preference" is the real basis for human behavior. "If a man is on a plank in the deep sea which will only float one, and a stranger lays hold of it, he will thrust him off if he can. When the state finds itself in a similar position, it does the same thing." To the objection that man should not be treated as a means, Holmes contemptuously responded, "If man lives in society, he is liable to find himself so treated." He immediately proceeded to reiterate his general

---

[297] Id. at 167.
[298] Letter from Oliver Wendell Holmes, Jr. to Arthur Sedgwick (July 12, 1879), microformed on reel 36, 0702, Holmes Papers, supra note 15.
[299] Letter from Oliver Wendell Holmes, Jr. to Frederick Pollock (June 17, 1880), in Holmes-Pollock Letters, vol. 1, supra note 31, at 14, 15.
[300] Holmes, supra note 19, at 37.

proposition that both criminal and civil law typically punish people "who have been guilty of no moral wrong"[301] and emphasized that "the purpose of the criminal law is only to induce external conformity to rule."[302]

In his analysis of contract law, Holmes stressed its Germanic origins and objective standards while rejecting the morally based "will" theories ascribed to the Roman law of contracts. Disagreeing with those "who adopt their phraseology and classification from Rome," Holmes maintained that the action of debt, which became part of the common law of consideration, "is of pure German descent."[303] Because the action in debt focused on the benefit to the promisor,[304] it was a formal and objective standard, in contrast to the importance of consent and will in the Roman theory of contract law that English as well as German scholars presumed was universal. His own risk theory of contract, Holmes added, "has the advantage of freeing the subject from the superfluous theory that contract is a qualified subjection of one will to another, a kind of limited slavery."[305] Holmes conceded that in "the moral world it may be that the obligation of a promise is confined to what lies within reach of the will of the promisor."[306] But in the real world the "consequences of a binding promise at common law are not affected by the degree of power which the promisor possesses over the promised event." Rather, the promisor pays damages "if the promised event," an objective fact, "does not come to pass,"[307] even if the promisor has no power over it.

Holmes did not always explicitly connect his attacks on German metaphysics and on German interpretations of Roman law with his rejection of moral theories of law, his preference for objective and external standards, and his claims for the Germanic sources of the common law. But he often did, and even when he only made explicit connections among some of these points, the rest of his book indicated their implicit connections to the others. Holmes repeatedly asserted his views that throughout the common law, external and objective standards had replaced moral and individualistic ones; that German metaphysical thought superimposed a sentimental moralism on legal analysis; that German scholars applied this misguided metaphysical analysis to their study of Roman law and falsely assumed their conclusions had universal validity; and that the English common law, derived mostly from Germanic rather than Roman sources, was free from the moral and individualistic theories of the German study of Roman law, and actually expressed external and objective standards. Holmes's constant reiteration that the common law had Germanic rather than Roman origins was often shorthand for his fundamental claim that it had not incorporated the moralism and individualism attributed by German

[301] Id. at 38.
[302] Id. at 42.
[303] Id. at 198–9.
[304] Id. at 213.
[305] Id. at 235.
[306] Id. at 234.
[307] Id. at 236.

scholars to Roman law but instead expressed objective and external standards. His interpretation of the origins of the common law thus reinforced his association of the functionality of survivals with the extent to which their moral terminology had been reinterpreted to support objective and external standards. In both contexts, Holmes employed history to support his "general view of the Common Law."

The Historical Inaccuracy of *The Common Law*

Ever since the publication of *The Common Law* in 1881, even scholars who have praised Holmes's ambition, learning, and legal analysis have challenged the accuracy of his historical explanations. They have frequently claimed that Holmes not merely subordinated historical explanation to legal analysis, but actually manipulated historical evidence in order to support his analytical arguments and policy goals. Mark DeWolfe Howe repeatedly observed that Holmes had distorted history in this way. He called *The Common Law* "an endeavor in philosophy – a speculative undertaking in which the author sought to find in the materials of legal history data which would support a new interpretation of the legal order." Contrasting Holmes "the jurist" with Maitland "the historian," Howe reiterated that "Holmes was searching the recorded data for items which would support a thesis."[308] Howe recognized that Holmes's treatment of history in *The Common Law* was neither accurate nor complete.[309] The mistakes Holmes's eminent contemporaries – Ames, Pollock, and Maitland – found in his historical discussion of contract law, Howe maintained, "somewhat marred" his presentation but enabled Holmes to "de-Romanize the law of consideration" by asserting non-Roman sources and thus to oppose Kantian legal theory.[310] Commenting on Holmes's objective theory of tort law, Howe doubted that Holmes would have reached this conclusion had he been writing only as a historian of the common law.[311] Based on the work of historians who wrote after Holmes, Howe agreed that in his interpretation of tort, as of contract, Holmes had "distorted and misinterpreted the legal past" as part of his "dominating eagerness to sustain his philosophical thesis."[312] Howe even believed that Holmes himself would have accepted the historical criticism that "he had pressed decisions into a philosophically favorable shape."[313] Somewhat apologetically on Holmes's behalf, Howe frequently added that Holmes's conclusions, however inaccurate historically, contributed original and provocative ideas that stimulated outstanding future scholarship, particularly the idea that a single standard of liability based on objective and external standards pervaded the common law.[314] He also maintained that

308 Howe, Introduction to Holmes, supra note 19, at xx; see also Gordon, supra note 1, at 719.
309 Howe, Introduction to Holmes, supra note 19, at xi.
310 Howe, supra note 1, at 229–30.
311 Id. at 192.
312 Id. at 193.
313 Id. at 194.
314 Id. at 194, 229–30, 274–5.

Holmes even made significant contributions to legal history itself by calling attention to historical evidence that previously had been neglected.[315]

Grant Gilmore, who could be as sardonic as Holmes himself, extended these criticisms of Holmes's use of history without adding any of Howe's softening praise. Although Gilmore never completed the book on Holmes's judicial career that he intended as a sequel to Howe's biography,[316] which followed Holmes's life until he became a judge, he did write about Holmes elsewhere. In developing his objective theory of contract, Gilmore maintained, Holmes asserted philosophical, economic, and social justifications but also devoted much energy to "pretending" that "it also had the sanction of history." Observing that subsequent scholars who endorsed Holmes's objective theory did not follow him in trying to justify it historically, Gilmore speculated that any attempt to do so "would have overtaxed even their own very considerable ingenuity."[317] More generally, Gilmore asserted that the "historical underpinning" for the fundamental principles that Holmes expressed in *The Common Law* "was patently absurd, even when it had not been deliberately distorted."[318] Gilmore was startled that Holmes, as part of his attempt to support his objective theory of liability, treated cases from the English Year Books of the fourteenth and fifteenth centuries anachronistically, as if they announced principles that made practical sense in late nineteenth-century America.[319] According to Gilmore, *The Common Law*, though dressed up in the "misleading guise of pseudo-history," was "a highly original, essentially philosophical statement about the nature of law." Like Howe, Gilmore suggested that Holmes knew what he was doing. Acknowledging that Holmes was an excellent historian, Gilmore speculated that he intentionally misrepresented history to disguise the originality of his analytical claims and thereby to increase the probability of their general acceptance by making them seem familiar. Gilmore even speculated that Holmes might have been using history to play a joke on his audience – probably more of a reflection on Gilmore's sardonic state of mind than on Holmes's.[320] More plausibly, Gilmore read the closing lines of Holmes's short preface to *The Common Law* as a subtle signal of his sacrifice of history to theory. Anticipating readers who "should reproach me for a want of greater detail," Holmes indicated that he was constructing a theory rather than writing a real legal history.[321]

Some eminent twentieth-century historians of the common law have associated Holmes's historical inaccuracies with broader methodological problems. C. H. S. Fifoot disagreed with Holmes's historical treatment of bailment, tort liability, and consideration and stressed more broadly that Holmes, among others, should be viewed as "a striking and not unentertaining warning against

---

[315] Howe, Introduction to Holmes, supra note 19, at xi.

[316] Grant Gilmore, The Ages of American Law (Yale University Press, 1977), p. 127.

[317] Grant Gilmore, The Death of Contract (Ohio State University Press, 1974), p. 43.

[318] Gilmore, supra note 316, at 52; see also Grey, supra note 1, at 841–2.

[319] Gilmore, supra note 316, at 54.

[320] Id. at 52.

[321] Id. at 127–8 n. 19.

the temptation of historians to assume the presence of some recurrent theme" and then "to 'find the facts' necessary to disclose or to support it."[322] A. W. B. Simpson criticized those who, in "the tradition of Holmes," try to "link their theories about the modern law to their account of the history of the subject, always a methodological error for a legal historian."[323] More recently, Mathias Reimann observed that Holmes's discussion of legal history often left the impression that all the historical evidence supported his conclusions.[324] Rather than engage in critical evaluation of historical sources, Thomas Grey pointed out, Holmes frequently "gave ingenious but tendentious lawyerly readings in support of controversial propositions of law he favored."[325]

The historical weaknesses of *The Common Law*, however, should not overshadow the importance of its historiographical themes. Holmes's evolutionary theories of law, particularly his emphasis on legal survivals, are important keys not only to understanding his thought, but also to recognizing that his influential book, though conceptually original in many ways, was part of a broader American school of historical legal thought in the late nineteenth century.

Holmes's Lingering Historical Interpretation of Law

To what extent did Holmes continue to pursue the historiographical themes that pervaded *The Common Law*? Although *The Common Law* culminated Holmes's work as a scholar, he continued to publish speeches and essays after he became a judge in 1882. In an oration before the Harvard Law School Association in 1886, Holmes reiterated his historical approach to legal analysis while connecting it to the case method of pedagogy pioneered by Langdell. In so doing, he echoed points made by the full-time faculty at Harvard Law School, including Ames, Gray, and Thayer, as well as by Langdell himself. After proclaiming that law professors should be scientific specialists, uniting "democracy with discipline ... in the service of Truth, their only queen,"[326] Holmes asserted the primacy of history in legal analysis. The "simple philosophizing" of the previous generation, Holmes maintained, no longer satisfies because legal scholars have realized that principles and doctrines depend on "historical knowledge." "Under the influence of Germany," Holmes happily added, "science is gradually drawing history into its sphere."[327]

Connecting pedagogy to scholarship, Holmes emphasized that the movement from "simple philosophizing" to scientific historical analysis corresponded to

---

[322] C. H. S. Fifoot, History and Sources of the Common Law: Tort and Contract (London: Stevens, 1949), pp. 159, 187, 396.

[323] A. W. B. Simpson, A History of the Common Law of Contract: The Rise of the Action of Assumpsit (Oxford, England: Clarendon Press, 1975), p. 417 n. 1.

[324] Reimann, supra note 1, at 105.

[325] Grey, supra note 1, at 813.

[326] Oliver Wendell Holmes, The Use of Law Schools, in Novick, supra note 12, vol. 3, at 474, 475.

[327] Id. at 477.

the change in teaching from the textbook to the casebook. He belittled the "rag-bag full of general principles, – a throng of glittering generalities" that satisfied earlier generations. Holmes maintained instead that "to make a general principle worth anything you must give it a body" by showing "how it has gradually emerged." And principles must be understood in "historic relations to other principles, often of very different date and origin."[328] During the brief period he taught at Harvard Law School, Holmes declared, he successfully taught torts using Ames's casebook and discussing cases in "Langdell's method." He agreed with Langdell that there are only a small number of legal principles, and that a legal principle is better taught by studying "its embryology and the lines of its growth" than by seeing it "lying dead before you on the printed page."[329]

As early as Roscoe Pound at the beginning of the twentieth century and as recently as Morton Horwitz in the 1990s, eminent scholars have asserted that Holmes abandoned historical explanations of law in the decades following publication of *The Common Law*. By his essays of the 1890s, they maintained, Holmes focused instead on presciently modern policy analysis based on the frank recognition of competing social interests and respect for the insights of the emerging social sciences. Comparing his later essays to *The Common Law* reveals that this claim is overstated. In his later essays, Holmes often expressed optimism that statistics and economics would be useful tools in guiding the future development of law. But just as Holmes had recognized competing social interests and engaged in policy analysis in *The Common Law* and even earlier, throughout his long career he continued to endorse the evolutionary theories of history that were a central theme of *The Common Law*. It was Pound himself who actually made the break with historical explanation that he incorrectly attributed to Holmes.

Pound observed that Holmes "had done notable work in the historical interpretation of Anglo-American law in the hey-day" of the historical school[330] and had developed "the best possibilities of its method."[331] He emphasized, however, that Holmes soon "parted ways with the then dominant historical school" and anticipated by a generation "the definite break with the historical method" that differentiated twentieth-century from late nineteenth-century legal analysis.[332] In his classic early article "Liberty of Contract," Pound associated Holmes with the "sociological jurisprudence" Pound himself advocated. Pound cited Holmes's dissent in *Lochner v. New York* as "the best exposition of it we have" and Holmes's 1897 essay "The Path of the Law" as a scholarly

---

[328] Id.

[329] Id. at 478.

[330] Roscoe Pound, Interpretations of Legal History (Cambridge University Press, 1923), p. 10.

[331] Roscoe Pound, Justice Holmes's Contributions to the Science of Law, 34 Harv. L. Rev. 449, 450 (1921).

[332] Id. at 449–50, 464 and n. 63. See also Roscoe Pound, The Scope and Purpose of Sociological Jurisprudence III, 25 Harv. L. Rev. 489, 513–14 and n. 54 (1912).

example.[333] When Pound reviewed Holmes's *Collected Papers* of the 1890s, published in 1921, he seemed to identify Holmes as the originator of sociological jurisprudence. These papers by Holmes "might have been written in the second decade of the twentieth century instead of the last decade of the nineteenth." Rereading them convinced Pound that Holmes "has done more than lead American juristic thought of the present generation. Above all others he has shaped the methods and ideas that are characteristic of the present as distinguished from the immediate past."[334] Pound elaborated Holmes's "definite break with the historical method" by citing his interest in issues Pound associated with sociological jurisprudence, including "the relation between the law-finding element in judicial decisions and the policies that must govern law-making," the conscious "harmonizing or compromising conflicting or overlapping interests," a "functional point of view," and "giving up the idea of jurisprudence as a self-sufficient science."[335]

Somewhat inconsistently, Pound at least once recognized that Holmes relied on historical explanation in his later essays. He contrasted Holmes's use of legal history in those essays with the "metaphysical" approach to legal history that dominated American scholarship in the 1870s and 1880s. According to Pound, the metaphysical approach, derived from Savigny and Maine,[336] assumed that "law is something which may only grow and is not to be shaped consciously" and "seeks to deduce everything from and measure everything by a metaphysically given ultimate datum of individual free self-assertion." In "The Path of the Law," Pound asserted, Holmes rejected this approach. Instead, "with the assurance of a master of historical method," Holmes illustrated "the functional use of legal history" by showing "what is behind particular legal traditions, what their course of development has been, and how we may use them intelligently for the ends of today instead of remaining slaves to them."[337] Yet Holmes had taken the same approach to legal history in *The Common Law*, published in 1881, the time when Pound placed him at the center of the "dominant historical school" of that period. Pound seemed to suggest, inconsistently, that Holmes in the 1890s either had abandoned historical explanation entirely or had transformed himself from a "metaphysical" to a "functional" historian. The basic continuity in Holmes's treatment of history from *The Common Law* through his essays of the 1890s demonstrates that both of Pound's alternative suggestions are incorrect.

Using much more dramatic and unambiguous language than Pound, Morton Horwitz has recently asserted that during the sixteen years between *The Common Law* and "The Path of the Law," Holmes rejected the explanatory power of history and custom while recognizing that law is the product of

---

[333] Roscoe Pound, Liberty of Contract, 18 Yale L.J. 454

[334] Pound, supra note 331, at 449.

[335] Id. at 450.

[336] Roscoe Pound, 24 Political Science Quarterly 317 (1912).

[337] Pound, supra note 331, at 450–1.

social struggle among competing interest groups. In the first chapter of *The Common Law*, Holmes bemoaned that "hitherto" the process by which legal rules survived "has been largely unconscious" and made clear that his explanation of legal history would "insist on a more conscious recognition of the legislative function of the courts" based on their views of public policy.[338] Yet Horwitz maintained that in *The Common Law* Holmes himself accepted the approach to legal history that he actually criticized in others. According to Horwitz, Holmes's "effort in *The Common Law* to tie law to custom – to turn from an autonomous 'logic' to social 'experience' – created a picture of law as simply a mirror or reflection of unconsciously evolving social conventions. Law thus continued to be thought of as independent of human will and as not susceptible of being transformed by social engineering."[339] Horwitz stressed that by equating objective legal standards with customary standards, Holmes, like many of his contemporaries, treated historically evolved custom as mediating between the individual and the state.[340] Under this interpretation, the evolving law, albeit with some exceptions, produced a functional rationality.[341]

The substantial social and economic conflicts in the United States during the 1890s, Horwitz maintained, prompted Holmes to abandon such historical explanations and the objective legal standards derived from them.[342] "For Holmes, the customary theory of law had collapsed. Law is the product of social struggle. Nothing stands between the individual and the state."[343] Unlike *The Common Law*, in which Holmes combined analysis and history, in "The Path of the Law" the analysis of policy "virtually obliterates history."[344] By the time Holmes wrote "The Path of the Law," Horwitz concluded, he fully recognized law as an entirely social creation, unrestrained by custom and subject to transformation through social engineering.[345] Echoing Pound, Horwitz asserted that with this essay Holmes "pushed American legal thought into the twentieth century."[346]

Contrary to the assertions of Pound and Horwitz, Holmes reiterated in his essays of the 1890s most of the central historiographical themes of *The Common Law*, which themselves tracked the general historical turn in late nineteenth-century American legal thought. He continued to describe legal history in evolutionary terms. He began his 1899 address, "Law in Science and Science in Law," by stressing that by the late nineteenth century historical science had replaced religion as the fundamental mode of explanation. "A hundred years ago," he wrote, "men explained any part of the universe by showing

---

[338] Holmes, supra note 19, at 32.
[339] Horwitz, supra note 1, at 127.
[340] Id. at 125.
[341] Id. at 130.
[342] Id. at 138–9.
[343] Id. at 130.
[344] Id. at 141.
[345] Id. at 127.
[346] Id. at 142.

its fitness for certain ends, and demonstrating what they conceived to be its final cause according to a providential scheme. In our less theological and more scientific day," he added, "we explain an object by tracing the order and progress of its growth and development from a starting point assumed as given." He called this process of explanation "historical" and reminded his listeners that in their own profession of law the historical method had achieved substantial recent success.[347]

Citing examples from his historical discussion of liability theories in *The Common Law*, Holmes maintained that the development of legal conceptions illustrates the existence of "evolution in this sphere of conscious thought and action no less than in lower organic stages."[348] Using another legal example to make the same point, Holmes expressed confidence that "a flower is not more unlike a leaf, or a segment of a skull more unlike a vertebra, than the executor as we know him is remote from his prototype." Holmes again stressed that developments in law and in biology reflect an underlying evolutionary process when he observed that the law provided many examples of "the paucity of original ideas in man, and the slow coasting way in which he works along from rudimentary beginnings to the complex and artificial conceptions of civilized life." This characteristic of law, he claimed, "is like the niggardly un-inventiveness of nature in its other manifestations, with its few smells or colors or types, its short list of elements, working along in the same slow way from compound to compound until the dramatic impressiveness of the most intricate compositions, which we call organic life, makes them seem different in kind from the elements out of which they are made, when set opposite to them in direct contrast."[349] Yet in addition to describing evolution as a "slow, coasting process," Holmes, as he had in his 1873 discussion of the gas-stokers strike, also recognized "the struggle for life among competing ideas, and of the ultimate victory and survival of the strongest."[350] A decade later, Holmes compared law to a tree, which "has grown as we know it. The practical question is what is to be the next organic step."[351] Holmes even continued to view legal development in racial terms. In "The Path of the Law," he claimed that the "law is the witness and external deposit of our moral life. Its history is the history of the moral development of the race."[352]

More specifically, in his essays of the 1890s, as previously in *The Common Law*, Holmes applied the concept of survivals to legal analysis and maintained that dysfunctional survivals justify revision of the law. Frequently, the language as well as the arguments of the later essays bore remarkable similarities to *The*

---

[347] Holmes, supra note 8, at 210–11.
[348] Id. at 217.
[349] Id. at 215–16.
[350] Id. at 220.
[351] Oliver Wendell Holmes, Holdsworth's English Law, Law Quarterly Review (1909), reprinted in Collected Legal Papers, supra note 8, at 285, 289.
[352] Holmes, supra note 48, at 170.

Common Law. For example, at the end of the first chapter of *The Common Law*, Holmes wrote,

When we find that in large and important branches of the law the various grounds of policy on which the various rules have been justified are later inventions to account for what are in fact survivals from more primitive times, we have a right to reconsider the popular reasons, and, taking a broader view of the field, to decide anew whether those reasons are satisfactory.

If they are not, "scrutiny and revision are justified."[353] In "Law in Science," Holmes wrote that "when a lawyer sees a rule of law in force he is very apt to invent, if he does not find, some ground of policy for its base. But in fact some rules are mere survivals." "History," Holmes observed, "sets us free and enables us to make up our minds dispassionately whether the survival which we are enforcing answers any new purpose when it has ceased to answer the old."[354] Just as Holmes devoted much of his historical analysis in *The Common Law* to uncovering dysfunctional survivals for "scrutiny and revision," in "Law in Science" he stressed that his use of history was "mainly negative and skeptical," a help in "clearing away rubbish," the survivals that "no longer meet their original ends."[355]

Similarly, in "The Path of the Law," Holmes maintained that historical research should play a substantial role in the rational study of law because "it is the first step toward an enlightened skepticism, that is, towards a deliberate reconsideration of the worth" of legal rules. "When you get the dragon out of the cave on to the plain and in full daylight," Holmes added, "you can count his teeth and claws, and see just what is his strength. But to get him out is only the first step. The next step is either to kill him, or to tame him and make him a useful animal."[356] In other words, once you get the "dragon" of a current legal rule out of the "cave" of historical obscurity, you can assess it. If the legal rule is a survival that cannot be "tamed" and made "useful" for contemporary purposes, it must be abandoned and "killed," precisely the point Tylor had made in 1871 while advocating the "destruction" of dysfunctional survivals. "It is revolting," Holmes added, "to have no better reason for a rule of law than that so it was laid down in the time of Henry IV. It is still more revolting if the grounds upon which it was laid down have vanished long since, and the rule simply persists from blind imitation of the past."[357]

As in *The Common Law*, Holmes made clear in his later essays that he limited his own study of history to "the light it throws on the present,"[358] even though he recognized the value of broader historical inquiries. He respected those who studied history as a pleasurable "end in itself" or as a "great anthropological

---

[353] Holmes, supra note 19, at 33.
[354] Holmes, supra note 8, at 225.
[355] Id. at 225–6.
[356] Holmes, supra note 48, at 186–7.
[357] Id. at 187.
[358] Id. at 195.

document," but he emphasized its "practical" utility.[359] After citing the many valuable contributions to legal history by Bigelow, Ames, Thayer, Pollock, and Maitland, Holmes warned against "the pitfall of antiquarianism," especially since Pollock and Maitland's recent book on the history of early English law had "lent that subject an almost deceptive charm."[360] Yet as Pound and Horwitz correctly asserted, in his later essays Holmes expressed reservations even about the continued study of history for practical purposes. "I look forward to the time," Holmes wrote immediately after reiterating the importance of history in understanding the present, "when the part played by history in the explanation of dogma shall be very small." He hoped that "ingenious" historical research would be replaced by "a study of the ends sought to be attained and the reasons for desiring them."[361] He repeatedly stressed that statistics and economics would be the most important tools in such a study,[362] confidently predicting that "the man of the future is the man of statistics and the master of economics"[363] Holmes apparently felt by his essays of the 1890s that his own previous scholarship, particularly his analysis of survivals, had accomplished much of the "negative and skeptical" work he had assigned to history and had thereby enabled the rational analysis of policy choices that should determine the future course of law.

Despite these hopes for the future, Holmes acknowledged that they were probably an unattainable ideal. "Very likely it may be," he concluded, "that with all the help that statistics and every modern appliance can bring us there never will be a commonwealth in which science is everywhere supreme."[364] Though Holmes did not specify the obstacles to his scientific ideal, he seemed to identify them in his repeated assertion throughout his career that law must reflect the views of the dominant members of the community. Presumably, dominant community views about the proper ends and means of a legal system, necessarily shaped by historical experience, would not always coincide with the conclusions of "the man of statistics and the master of economics."

The dominant power in a community, Holmes observed, changes over time, but at any particular time the dominant power might not want change. Judgments of public policy, which are "not capable of exact quantitative measurement," reflect "battle grounds where the means do not exist for determinations that shall be good for all time, and where the decision can do no more than embody the preference of a given body at a given time and place."[365] Eternal law is impossible, for "the intensity of competing desires, varies with the varying ideals of the time."[366] Just a "slight change in the habit of the

---

359 Holmes, supra note 8, at 211–12.
360 Holmes, supra note 48, at 194.
361 Id. at 195.
362 Id. at 187, 189, 195; Holmes, supra note 8, at 242.
363 Holmes, supra note 48, at 187.
364 Holmes, supra note 8, at 242.
365 Holmes, supra note 48, at 181.
366 Holmes, supra note 8, at 231.

mind," Holmes stressed, can open much of the current legal system to reconsideration.[367] On the other hand, the sense of historical continuity between past and present often "limits the possibilities of our imagination, and settles the terms in which we shall be compelled to think." If people living in the present are able to overcome these limits, they should feel free to change the law to make it better "without the slightest regard to continuity with the past." But often they are not able to do so. That is why Holmes, in one of his more famous aphorisms, declared that "continuity with the past is only a necessity and not a duty."[368]

Writing in "Law in Science" after he became a judge, Holmes recognized that in doubtful cases, in which legal analogies help both sides, "what is really before us is a conflict between two social desires," and judges must exercise "the sovereign prerogative of choice." Holmes was nevertheless "slow to consent to overruling a precedent," not because precedent "represents an eternal principle," but because people "have become accustomed" to existing law.[369] Holmes subsequently stated that his recognition of the contingency and artificiality of law had led him to "an unconvinced conservatism." He acknowledged that a society could be as well off if it had adopted a different system of law. "But that if," he emphasized, "is a very great one." Even though "the history of law encourages skepticism when one sees how a rule or a doctrine has grown up" and reveals the extent to which people have assumed that their "social prejudices" constitute "eternal principles," Holmes was reluctant to depart dramatically from current law. Because "men should know the rules by which the game will be played," mere doubt as to the value of current law is not a sufficient reason for judicial innovation.[370] Legal principles are not eternal, but neither should they be changed "until we have a clear vision of what different thing we want."[371] As long as battles among contending forces and ideas in society have not been clearly resolved, "the time for law has not come." A judge should not read "his conscious or unconscious sympathy with one side or the other prematurely into the law." As an example of such premature action, Holmes cited the judicial fear of socialism, which unfortunately "was translated into doctrines that had no proper place in the Constitution or the common law."[372]

The historiographical themes that figured so prominently in *The Common Law* continued to appear in Holmes's later writings. He never abandoned his views that history is often the key to understanding current law, that law reflects the general process of evolution, and that uncovering dysfunctional survivals through historical analysis provides grounds for legal reform. Even as he hoped that the "negative and skeptical" work of history would enable

[367] Holmes, supra note 48, at 181.
[368] Holmes, supra note 8, at 211.
[369] Id. at 239.
[370] Holmes, supra note 351, at 289.
[371] Id. at 290.
[372] Oliver Wendell Holmes, Law and the Court, reprinted in Novick, supra note 12, at 505, 507.

policy analysis, informed by the modern sciences of statistics and economics, to guide future legal development, he recognized the enormous extent to which history influences the dominant power in the community and constrains legal change. To use the kind of evolutionary imagery Holmes himself favored, he, like Bigelow and Pound, was a transitional figure between the historical legal thought of the late nineteenth century and the sociological jurisprudence of the early twentieth.

VIII

Thayer on the History of Evidence

James Bradley Thayer continued the excavation of the history of English law begun by Adams, Bigelow, and Holmes. He wrote about legal history most extensively in his major work, *A Preliminary Treatise on Evidence at the Common Law*, which received great praise on both sides of the Atlantic, including from Brunner in Germany and Maitland in England. Thayer began his original research in the period of the first judicial records, dating from 1194, and Year Books, dating from 1292.[1] He built on and cited the previous scholarship on earlier periods, including Adams on the Anglo-Saxon period, and particularly Bigelow on the century following the Norman Conquest and Brunner on the earlier development of the jury in continental Europe.[2] In his focus on the jury, Thayer dealt in much greater detail with topics Bigelow had treated more briefly in his work on procedure. He agreed with Bigelow that the inquisition, introduced to England by the Normans and developed by the royal courts, superseded the older Anglo-Saxon law and was the source for the modern jury, in which the juror became differentiated from the witness. But as Bigelow critically observed, Thayer accepted Brunner's view that King Henry II, relying on earlier reforms in Normandy, had transformed the recognition into a right of Englishmen. In concluding that the law of evidence is the "child" of the jury and that the king was the great reformer of the law, Thayer recognized that his own detailed research supported views Maine previously asserted. Without citing Maine directly, Thayer also echoed his views about stages of historical development. Maitland subsequently relied heavily on Thayer's work and corresponded extensively with him, though he did not develop as close a personal relationship with Thayer as with Bigelow.

In *A Preliminary Treatise on the Law of Evidence*, Thayer practiced in the context of the law of evidence what he preached in his address "The Teaching

---

[1] James Bradley Thayer, A Preliminary Treatise on Evidence at the Common Law (Boston: Little, Brown, and Company, 1898), pp. 3, 50.

[2] In addition to numerous citations of these scholars throughout his book, Thayer specifically acknowledged his debts to Brunner and Bigelow. Id. at viii, 3, 50.

of English Law in Universities."[3] After reconstructing the connections between the laws of evidence and the emergence of the jury, he concluded that many lingering evidentiary rules had become dysfunctional and should be reformed. He thought judges should take the lead in undertaking this reform, but he also saw a role for the legislature in providing the authority and the broad principles under which the judges could operate. Even while stressing the role of history as a resource for changing the law, Thayer, like Adams and his students, declared that fundamental and attractive characteristics of the English race, such as commitments to popular justice, could be traced in a continuous historical link back to Germanic roots and forward to the United States.

Thayer opened his book by observing that he had initially planned to write a practical treatise on the law of evidence. "But in setting out to do this, many years ago," he reported, "I found at once the need of going much deeper into the history of the subject, and into an exact analysis of many familiar terms, than I had supposed would be necessary." He quickly realized that he could not satisfy his own scholarly standards "without a careful examination of the older law of trials, and without adding to this a critical study of a considerable number of related topics, crudely developed and half understood," which "overlie and perplex" the law of evidence. His book was "preliminary" because it dealt with these historical and other "auxiliary" topics rather than with the full law of evidence itself.[4] Emphasizing his fundamental belief in the relationship between historical reconstruction and legal reform, Thayer expressed his hope "that those who attentively consider the long and strange story of the development of the English jury and the immense influence it has had in shaping our law, will find here a basis for conclusions as to the scope and direction of certain much-needed reforms in the whole law of evidence and procedure."[5] In the language of his address, the law of evidence could be restated only after its history had been thoroughly studied. This historical study would reveal previously unobserved relationships and clear up various confusions, ambiguities, unintelligible phraseologies, and false theories.[6]

Thayer's treatise, though "preliminary," was a long book that culminated years of research and writing. As early as 1882–3, he spent a year in England to research the history of the jury, recruiting his two favorite students to teach his courses at Harvard Law School during his absence, Brooks Adams for evidence and Louis Brandeis for constitutional law.[7] Thayer published the results of his English research in a series of articles in the *Harvard Law Review* between 1889 and 1893. He combined these articles in the first version of his treatise, published in 1896 as part I, *Development of Trial by Jury*, and added substantial material for the final version of the *Preliminary Treatise* published in

---

[3] James Bradley Thayer, The Teaching of English Law in Universities, 9 Harv. L. Rev. 169 (1895).
[4] Thayer, supra note 1, at 1.
[5] Id. at 3.
[6] Thayer, supra note 3, at 178–9.
[7] Jay Hook, A Brief Life of James Bradley Thayer, 88 Nw. U.L. Rev. 1, 5 (1993).

1898.[8] The material in part I was overwhelmingly historical, linking the rise of the jury with the development of the law of evidence. The remainder, and ultimately the majority, of the book focused on untangling the confusion caused by "the habit of assuming, whenever evidential matter was rejected or received, that the result was attributable to some principle of the law of evidence." Thayer sought to demonstrate instead that many of the rules governing evidence were based on independent principles of substantive or procedural law rather than the law of evidence itself. The widespread failure to recognize the major role of substantive and procedural law, Thayer complained, caused the law of evidence to become "monstrously overloaded" and "to swallow up into itself much which belonged to other branches of law, or to the wide regions of logic and legal reasoning." As a result, "the law of evidence itself was intolerably perplexed" and analysis of substantive and procedural law was "clouded and thrown out of focus."[9] Though this volume was less historically oriented than the first part of the *Preliminary Treatise*, Thayer often resorted to history to explain how this confusion arose and to suggest doctrinal alternatives.

Underlining his own commitment to historical analysis of the law of evidence, Thayer criticized other scholars for their inattention to history even as he expressed his debts to legal historians such as Adams, Bigelow, and Brunner. He complained that Blackstone's explanation of trial by witnesses "shows little knowledge of its history," which led him into anachronistic misinterpretations of case law.[10] More broadly, he called the writings by J. F. Stephen, a leading English commentator on the law of evidence, "injured by the small consideration that he shows for the historical aspect of the matter."[11] "One who would state the law of evidence truly," Thayer emphasized, "must allow himself to grow intimately acquainted with the working of the jury system and its long history."[12] Such familiarity makes clear "the many practical considerations which the jury system brought vividly home to the judges as they shaped our rules of evidence in the daily administration of it."[13] Thayer dedicated himself to exploring these crucial historical considerations that Stephen ignored.

The Law of Evidence as "the Child of the Jury"

The English law of evidence, Thayer stressed, "is the child of the jury,"[14] an insight he attributed to a comment by Maine thirty years before.[15] From the beginning

---

[8] Id.; James Parker Hall, James Bradley Thayer, in Great American Lawyers (Philadelphia: The John C. Winston Company, 1909) (William Draper Lewis, ed.), vol. VIII, pp. 345, 355; John Chipman Gray, 15 Harv. L. Rev. 601, 601–2 (1902); Jeremiah Smith, 15 Harv. L. Rev. 602 (1902).

[9] Thayer, supra note 1, at 4.

[10] Id. at 24.

[11] Id. at 266 n. 1.

[12] Id. at 267 n. 1.

[13] Id. at 268 n. 1.

[14] Id. at 47.

[15] Id. at 508.

of his book, he emphasized that the jury "accounts for the common-law system of evidence."[16] Without the jury, he maintained, there would have been no law of evidence. He observed that where the jury never existed, or where it died out, as in continental Europe, no separate law of evidence arose.[17] But with a jury, where "ordinary, untrained citizens are acting as judges of fact,"[18] courts had to address numerous practical questions about whether these citizens were equipped to evaluate evidence. The answers to these questions, he declared, produced the English law of evidence, which provided for the exclusion of otherwise logically probative evidence that might confuse, mislead, or have other dangerous effects on the jury.[19] Because these answers were "worked out in the daily forge of experience in the trial of causes, not created, or greatly changed, until lately, by legislation, not the fruit of any man's systematic reflection or forecast," the law of evidence was "sure to exhibit at every step the marks of its origin."[20] Echoing Holmes's assertion in *The Common Law*, "The life of the law has not been logic: it has been experience," Thayer concluded that the "law of evidence is the creature of experience rather than logic."[21] That experience, for the law of evidence, was the history of the jury. Challenging Greenleaf, the "distinguished author" who closed his "famous treatise" on evidence by observing its "symmetry and beauty," Thayer maintained instead that "our law of evidence is a piece of illogical, but by no means irrational, patchwork." The law of evidence is not irrational because it can be explained historically, by understanding its connection to the development of a jury.[22]

Like Adams and his students, Thayer connected his discussion of the history of English law to democratic political traditions embedded in race. Immediately after pointing out the "constant, anxious," even "overanxious" efforts of the law of evidence to exclude evidence from the jury, Thayer addressed those who might wonder about the value of maintaining a tribunal "which has needed so much watching and so many safeguards." He responded by stressing "the deep political significance of the jury and its relation to what is most valued in the national history and traditions of the English race."[23] Thayer did not immediately elaborate this statement. Yet in contrast to Bigelow, who starkly differentiated Germanic Anglo-Saxon law from the Norman law, which had accumulated many Roman elements, Thayer soon stressed that the Normans and Anglo-Saxons were "cousins of the Germanic race." Within this Germanic tradition, he asserted, "the conception of popular courts and popular justice" was the "great fundamental thing ... out of which all else grew." Citing works by Maine and Henry Adams's essay "The Anglo Saxon Courts of Law," Thayer

---

[16] Id. at 2.
[17] Id. at 268–70.
[18] Id. at 509.
[19] Id. at 2, 266, 509.
[20] Id. at 3.
[21] Id. at 267.
[22] Id. at 508–9.
[23] Id. at 2.

reiterated that nothing among the Germanic races "was more ancient than the idea and practice of popular justice." As Henry Adams had suggested to Herbert Adams, Thayer connected the New England town-meeting to the ancient Germanic courts, called moots. These ancient courts, Thayer asserted, "were a sort of town-meeting of judges." The "whole company," not just the presiding officers, served as judges, "as if in a New England town-meeting, the lineal descendant of the old Germanic moots, the people conducted the judicature, as well as the finance and politics, of the town."[24] Less directly, Thayer also seemed to be connecting the jury to the "conception of popular courts and popular justice" at the core of the Germanic tradition that extended to England and, ultimately, to the United States.

When the Normans conquered England, Thayer observed, "much of what they brought was already there." This identity, he added, was not surprising since the Normans and Anglo-Saxons were Germanic cousins. Yet the inquisition, which Thayer called "the parent of the modern jury," did not already exist in Anglo-Saxon England. Instead, like the judicial duel, which it superseded, the inquisition was a "novelty" introduced to England by the Normans as an aspect of their royal power. Thayer defined the inquisition as "the practice of ascertaining facts by summoning together by public authority a number of people most likely and most competent, as being neighbors, to know and tell the truth, and calling for their answer under oath." On the Continent, the Frankish kings and the Norman dukes used the inquisition as a general method of public administration, including the work of the courts carried out under royal authority.[25] For more than a century after the Norman Conquest, the use of the inquisition grew simultaneously in Normandy and England. But in the early thirteenth century, when the Normans lost Normandy to the French, the inquisition started to die out slowly on the Continent while it "began its peculiar, astonishing development in England."[26]

Covering much the same ground as Bigelow but with different points of emphasis, Thayer in his early chapters first described the older forms of trial and then discussed their eventual replacement by the jury that emerged from the inquisition. He focused on four of the older forms of trial: by witnesses on behalf of a party; by oath, often with oath helpers, called compurgation or wager of law; by ordeal; and by battle.[27] These older forms "were companions of trial by jury when that mighty plant first struck its root into English soil, and some of them lived long beside it." Eventually, however, they "dwindled and died out" while trial by jury "grew and spread,"[28] though they often persisted for centuries as "a relic of barbarism."[29] Hostility to trial by battle, a

---

[24] Id. at 7–8.
[25] Id. at 7; see id. at 2–3.
[26] Id. at 50.
[27] Id. at 16–46.
[28] Id. at 16.
[29] Id. at 45; see id. at 77.

"dangerous, costly, and discredited mode of proof," in particular contributed to the introduction of juries.[30] To call these older forms "trials," Thayer noted, was anachronistic because in all of them, unlike in the modern trial, people "tried" their own issues instead of submitting them to the independent body the jury became.[31] The word "trial," moreover, was rarely applied to these older forms in their own era. "I use the word 'trial,'" Thayer explained, "because it is the word in common use during recent centuries."[32] What became the modern trial by jury began as an alternative to these older forms of proof, and Thayer apparently decided that it would be helpful to apply the word "trial" to all of them even as he recognized the anachronism.

Like Bigelow and Brunner before him, Thayer ascribed the growth of the jury to the power of the Crown. Thayer identified the origins of the inquisition in efforts by Frankish kings to collect revenue. In the ninth century, for example, Louis I ordered that inquiries related to the royal fisc should not be made through witnesses produced by interested parties, but through the sworn statements of persons selected from the neighborhood of parties potentially subject to taxation or other services to the Crown. These neighbors were likely to know facts related to the royal inquiry, such as who possessed land and by what title. Their role, Thayer emphasized, was not simply to ascertain facts, but to decide the result of a controversy through a trial. Thayer considered the inquisition a much better procedure than "the rude, superstitious, one-sided methods" that the popular courts used to collect royal revenues. Once this "enlightened principle had come in as regards revenue," it "was likely to extend and did extend to judicature, for that was only another part of royal administration."[33]

Only royal power, Thayer emphasized, "could have accomplished so great an innovation as this."[34] Only the Crown could have ended the traditional methods of the popular courts, through which parties produced their own witnesses, in effect trying their own cases, and forced the parties instead to submit their disputes to a body of people selected from the community by public authority. Only the Crown, moreover, could have forced members of the community to take an oath and serve as inquisitors.[35] Thayer underlined "the extraordinary nature of the actual achievement" and declared it "a wonderful thing."[36] He also observed that this innovation provided an excellent illustration of Maine's general assertion that in early times the king was the great reformer of the law.[37]

Borrowing many of his examples from Bigelow, Thayer maintained that in the century following the Norman Conquest the inquisition was used in many

---

[30] Id. at 41.
[31] Id. at 56.
[32] Id. at 16 n. 1.
[33] Id. at 48.
[34] Id. at 49.
[35] Id. at 49, 56.
[36] Id. at 56.
[37] Id. at 49.

aspects of "ordinary administration" as well as in judicature. He observed that the famous Domesday Book of 1085–6, which contained numerous details about local customs in England as well as facts related to landownership and taxation, was itself compiled through a form of inquisition. The commission responsible for the Domesday Book took sworn testimony from men in neighborhoods throughout the country.[38] The use of the inquisition was irregular and unorganized, Thayer added, until it took permanent shape during the reign of Henry II, "a great and sagacious king,"[39] from 1154 to 1189. Prior to Henry II, kings granted inquisitions as a matter of royal favor in a particular instance. Under Henry II, the inquisition became a matter of right, an entitlement to the king's writ ordering an inquisition in specific categories of cases. At this point, the term "recognition" became attached to the inquisition, the inquisition referring to the inquiry that the recognition answered through impartial members of the community. Noting the disagreement between Brunner and Bigelow about the origins of the recognition as a matter of right, Thayer supported Brunner's position that Henry II had begun to establish it as a right while he was still duke of Normandy.[40] Over time, successive kings created new forms of action, all of which required the jury as the only method of trial. "By its intrinsic fairness as contrasted with older modes, and by the favor of the crown and the judges," the jury "grew fast to be regarded as the one regular common law mode of trial, always to be had when no other was fixed."[41] Thayer observed the rapid growth of trial by jury after the introduction of printed records[42] and traced its slow extension to criminal cases.[43]

In examining the development of trial by jury, Thayer discussed how twelve jurors and unanimity became requirements[44] and devoted substantial attention to the history of methods for both informing and controlling the jury. Under the heading of informing the jury, he discussed the selection of jurors, the combined deliberations of jurors and witnesses, the presentation of written documents to the jury, statements by parties or their counsel, the judicial charge to the jury, and the beginnings of special pleading.[45] In the context of this discussion, he pointed out that methods of informing the jury had reached their current forms well before the modern conception of trial by jury had matured.[46] Under the heading of controlling the jury, he began with the attaint, which for a long time was the only means to remedy a false verdict. The attaint involved a new trial based on the theory that the jury in the original trial had willfully falsified the evidence and should therefore be punished.[47] Yet the attaint became

[38] Id. at 51.
[39] Id. at 53.
[40] Id. at 55.
[41] Id. at 60.
[42] Id. at 66.
[43] Id. at 68–84.
[44] Id. at 65–70.
[45] Id. at 90–136.
[46] Id. at 134.
[47] Id. at 137.

unworkable because people, recognizing that innocent jurors could reach false verdicts, did not want to punish the innocent jurors as the price of remedying the false verdicts.[48] Thayer traced the decline of the attaint over centuries as the function of the jury changed and new means of controlling it arose. These new means included setting aside a verdict as being contrary to the evidence, without any need of finding willful jury misconduct.[49] The most significant method of controlling the jury, Thayer emphasized as the culmination of his chapters on its history, was the development of "that body of excluding rules which chiefly constitute the English 'Law of Evidence.'"[50] The topic of controlling the jury thus enabled Thayer to make his major point that the law of evidence could only be understood as an outgrowth of the history of the jury.

Interwoven throughout his treatment of the history of the jury, Thayer identified the steps by which the original inquisition became over centuries the type of trial by jury that produced the distinctively English law of evidence. The complicated transformation of the jury from community witnesses who met in private to triers of fact who heard evidence in open court lay at the heart of this process. Originally, jurors were witnesses from the community summoned by the sheriff. Presumed as members of the community to have personal knowledge of the facts of the case, their selection by a public official made them seem more impartial, more independent, and, therefore, more trustworthy than the witnesses produced by parties to the dispute.[51] These jurors were both witnesses and triers of fact.[52] Although other witnesses produced by the parties could inform the jury, they rarely seemed necessary and were infrequently used at a time when the jurors themselves were presumed, as members of the community, to know the relevant facts and felt free to disregard their testimony.[53] Yet in some cases witnesses who were not jurors themselves conferred privately with the jurors to share their distinctive knowledge of the relevant facts. This use of "business" or "transaction" witnesses to inform the jurors, most common in cases when witnesses to a deed testified about its genuineness, extended to other areas, such as dower.[54]

Over time, the practice of jurors meeting in private with transaction witnesses ended and witnesses who were not jurors increasingly testified in public to the jury in open court supervised by judges.[55] Thayer conceded that he could not specifically trace this major change from private to public testimony by witnesses to the jury,[56] but he offered several possible explanations for it. The very practice of private meetings between transaction witnesses and jurors,

---

[48] Id. at 138–9.
[49] Id. at 172.
[50] Id. at 180.
[51] Id. at 130–2, 137.
[52] Id. at 130–2, 137, 168–9, 519.
[53] Id. at 132, 137.
[54] Id. at 97, 100–4, 500.
[55] Id. at 137–40.
[56] Id. at 123.

he pointed out, lent itself to corruption and abuse. In certain types of trials, involving challenges to the honesty of jurors, witnesses were examined in open court from an early period, and this practice eventually spread to the regular jury trial.[57] A statute in the middle of the sixteenth century enabled parties to require the appearances of witnesses in open court and protected the witnesses who testified.[58] And when judges began to reverse jury verdicts as inconsistent with the evidence, without any need of punishing the jury as in the attaint, it became apparent that judges needed access to the same evidence as jurors. Providing similar access encouraged testimony by witnesses in open court and discouraged juror reliance on private knowledge, whether from private meetings with witnesses or from their own experience in the community. The role of the jurors as witnesses declined and eventually ended as other witnesses increasingly testified before judges in open court and jurors were precluded from relying on private knowledge, including the very knowledge for which jurors as community witnesses initially were selected. The role of the jurors as impartial triers of fact based on the evidence of others gradually became their chief, and ultimately their only, function.[59]

As witnesses became differentiated from jurors and testified to them in open court, rules governing testimony proliferated,[60] generating the English law of evidence. To underline this point, Thayer contrasted the grand jury in criminal cases, which continued to operate in private despite efforts that almost succeeded at the end of the seventeenth century to force it as well to receive its evidence publicly in open court.[61] If the jury, like the grand jury, had retained its old methods of hearing witnesses "privately and without any judicial supervision," he speculated, "it is easy to see that our law of evidence never would have taken shape." The "judicial oversight and control of the process of introducing evidence to the jury" gave "birth" to the Anglo-American system of evidence, and "he who would understand it must keep this fact constantly in mind."[62]

In his subsequent discussion of hearsay, which he treated under the general heading of the "best evidence" rule, Thayer most specifically illustrated the connection between the history of the jury and the law of evidence. In the early days of the jury, when business or transaction witnesses deliberated in private with the jurors who were community witnesses, their testimony was designed to provide the direct knowledge they had of the transaction, most frequently as witnesses to the making of a deed. This direct knowledge was the reason they joined the jury. While the jurors themselves, as community witnesses, were encouraged to rely on their general knowledge, including hearsay, the business and transaction witnesses were supposed to limit themselves to what they had

[57] Id. at 12–23, 500.
[58] Id. at 102, 503. See id. at 126–30 (discussing previous dangers of testifying).
[59] Id. at 137–40, 172–4.
[60] Id. at 137.
[61] Id. at 180 and 180 n. 4.
[62] Id. at 181.

directly seen and heard.[63] This limitation on witnesses continued when witnesses testified in open court and jurors were no longer allowed to rely on their own personal knowledge. Thayer observed that "as the scope of the jury's function narrowed and they became merely judges on what was furnished them by witnesses, the original discrimination between the jury and the witness lost its old application, and had a new form. Now the contrast was between witnesses, and a jury who were judges, knowing nothing of the fact."[64] The emphasis in Anglo-American law on the prohibition against hearsay, Thayer emphasized, is "traceable in its origin and continuance to the fact that witnesses at common law testify mainly to juries, persons who were formerly themselves witnesses, and not merely to judges."[65]

At the end of his long discussion of the development of the jury, Thayer raised two questions whose answers made historiographical points. Why, he asked, did not the English learn from the Romans, who after a long struggle had produced "enlightened ideas of proof"? Instead, the English "repeated all over again the ancient experience of Rome in its days of barbarism." Thayer provided two general explanations that transcended the distinctive situations of Rome and England. He first cited "the astonishing persistence of national habits," which made it difficult for one nation ever to learn from another. Second, he declared that "human experience is incommunicable when men and nations are not prepared to learn from it." Although Thayer did not cite Maine, he invoked a theory of stages of historical development that resembled Maine's discussion in *Ancient Law*. He stressed that civilization is not simply a chronological progression through the centuries but reflects "a particular stage of human development." Maine had indicated that the return of barbarism after the fall of the Roman Empire had reduced Europe to an earlier stage of development than the classic Roman civilization had previously achieved.[66] Without addressing Maine's particular theories about the return of barbarism to Europe, Thayer did agree that medieval England, though later in time than Rome at its peak, had not reached Rome's more advanced stage of civilization. Apart from the inevitable difficulty of changing national habits at any time, medieval England was insufficiently advanced to learn from the Roman example.[67]

Even granting that medieval England was at the wrong stage of development to be able to learn from Roman experience, Thayer added, why did it take the English centuries to recognize the implications of principles they themselves had come to understand? These principles could have enabled them to revise old laws and traditions whose function and meaning no longer made sense and to which they had become "enslaved." Thayer did not fully specify

---

[63] Id. at 500, 519.

[64] Id. at 500.

[65] Id. at 501.

[66] Sir Henry Maine, Ancient Law (Washington, D.C.: Beard Books, 2000) (reprint of 1861 ed.), pp. 79–80.

[67] Thayer, supra note 1, at 181.

either the principles or the old laws and traditions to which he was alluding. Presumably, by principles he meant "the enlightened ideas of proof" introduced by the inquisition, and by the old laws and traditions he meant the older forms of proof that he often characterized as "relics of barbarism."[68] Thayer's explanation, similar to his reliance on "the astonishing persistence of national habits" in discussing England's failure to learn from Rome, assumed a general human incapacity to change easily. He maintained that history provided many illustrations of "this fumbling and wandering of the human mind," citing as one example the long period between the invention of the printing press by Gutenberg and its practical use. Remembering these other examples helps to understand "the strange lingering, just out of reach, of conceptions and modes of proof which seem to us the only possible ones."[69]

The Lessons of History: Revising the Modern Law of Evidence

Although Thayer's title emphasized that his treatise was "preliminary," he did suggest some general revisions of the law of evidence based on his analysis of its connection with the history of the jury. Given this connection, he acknowledged, it was natural to ask whether the jury, whose development created the law of evidence, should continue at all. Ending the jury as a mode of trial would also end the need for the law of evidence, which, as Thayer had demonstrated, had became enormously complex and confused. He observed that in England, as well as in Massachusetts and other American states, the jury system already had been substantially modified, particularly in limiting jury trials in civil cases. The experience in these jurisdictions, Thayer reported, had been satisfactory. He recommended additional reductions of jury trials, though he opposed their elimination in all civil and especially in criminal cases.[70]

Thayer did not elaborate why he wanted to retain trial by jury or why he believed it especially important in criminal cases. The most probable explanation lies in his assertion at the beginning of the book that trial by jury has "deep political significance" rooted in "the national history and traditions of the English race," particularly "the conception of popular courts and popular justice."[71] An anonymous reviewer made this point explicitly in a statement Thayer probably would have endorsed. The reviewer anticipated with approval that the jury trial would fall into increasing disuse "in its application to the thousand and one petty disputes which occupy the courts," such as "ordinary matters of contract or property." By contrast, where life and liberty, "those grand questions of human right," are at stake, "our deepest instincts incline us to resort of a popular tribunal of fact." The reviewer believed that eliminating the jury in petty disputes, which a judge could handle as well or better, would

---

[68] See, e.g., id. at 45, 77.
[69] Id. at 181–2.
[70] Id. at 534–5.
[71] Id. at 2, 7–8.

increase its dignity and influence where it was most needed as a safeguard of fundamental popular rights against abuse by despotic power.[72]

Under the assumption that the jury system would and, indeed, should in reduced form continue, Thayer tried to identify "regulative and excluding precepts" that should govern the system of evidence administered by judges.[73] He based his suggestions on two "leading principles": "(1) that nothing is to be received which is not logically probative of some matter requiring to be proved; and (2) that everything which is thus probative should come in, unless a clear ground of policy or law excludes it."[74] The practical danger of giving a jury information which it might misunderstand or misuse had been one of the clear grounds of policy excluding otherwise probative evidence.[75] Thayer endorsed many of these exclusions as "full of good sense," the result of numerous rulings over centuries "by sagacious lawyers, while settling practical questions, in presiding over courts where ordinary, untrained citizens are acting as judges of fact." But too often, Thayer immediately added, that good sense did not prevail.[76] He particularly stressed that "old conceptions of a jury's incapacity, and of the need of so much exclusion, were overstrained, and that they are largely inapplicable to modern juries."[77]

Thayer's discussion of hearsay best illustrates his use of history both to understand existing law and to enable its restatement. After pointing out how the prohibition against hearsay evidence arose when transaction witnesses deliberated privately with a jury of community witnesses, he stressed that "a steady and rigid adherence to the general doctrine of hearsay prohibition" continued in the vastly transformed context of witnesses testifying in open court to a jury whose role was limited to determining the facts.[78] Over the years, Thayer added, numerous exceptions to the prohibition against hearsay arose. The combination of widespread failure to understand these exceptions and uncertainty about the extent to which they could be further developed[79] had produced "an instructive spectacle of confusion" under "the curse of hearsay." Much of this confusion derived "from the desire, on the one hand, to hold to the just historical theory of our cases; and, on the other, to resort to first principles, without being aware of the size and complexity of the task which is thus unconsciously entered upon."[80] The "just historical theory" was to treat the prohibition against hearsay as the rule, subject to exceptions.[81] Yet Thayer, probably influenced by his belief that assumptions about jury incapacity were

---

72 The Nation (August 16, 1896), pp. 126, 127.
73 Thayer, supra note 1, at 535.
74 Id. at 530; see id. at 265–6.
75 Id. at 266; see id. at 516.
76 Id. at 509.
77 Id. at 535.
78 Id. at 519.
79 Id. at 521.
80 Id. at 523.
81 Id. at 265–6.

"overstrained" in the past and "largely inapplicable" in the present,[82] maintained as a better first principle that the hearsay rule should be the exception to a general rule that all relevant evidence is admissible. He assumed that this principle would allow the admission of substantially more hearsay evidence than under the prevailing historical theory.[83] Presumably, realistic rather than "overstrained" evaluations of jury incapacity would be among the grounds of policy that would justify the hearsay exception under Thayer's alternative approach. If adopting his suggestion "shall bring about a restatement of some material parts of the law of evidence," Thayer declared, "that, perhaps, will only turn out as it should."[84]

In encouraging restatement of the law of evidence, Thayer emphasized that judges, not legislators, should take the primary role. He acknowledged that judges needed some help from the legislature in the form of legislation granting them authority to change the rules of evidence subject to some broad fundamental principles endorsed by the legislature.[85] He also acknowledged that legislative law reform is often difficult to achieve and that lawyers are particularly conservative and resistant to change. But he was confident that "a few enlightened and resolute lawyers" in a legislature could obtain such legislation.[86] Even without legislative help, he added, judges had always had great discretion in shaping the rules of evidence and could accomplish most revisions on their own.[87] Informed by history, judges should simplify the law of evidence along the lines he recommended,[88] which would make it "a far worthier instrument of justice than it is."[89] In addition to his two "leading principles" focused on the admission of probative evidence,[90] these recommendations included retaining many existing general principles, such as oral public testimony by witnesses, the exclusion of material that would delay the trial or confuse the jury, provisions for expert witnesses, and judicial discretion to exercise a "restraining power," not to substitute its judgment for the jury's, but to set aside verdicts when necessary to prevent gross injustice or to insure conformity to the law.[91] He disagreed with his contemporaries who doubted the capacity of most judges to exercise this discretion effectively, pointing out that those judges who could not do so should and could be replaced.[92]

In addition to explaining the law of evidence as a product of the history of the jury and to suggesting some simplifying principles as the basis for its

---

[82] Id. at 535.
[83] Id. at 522.
[84] Id. at 266.
[85] Id. at 511, 531.
[86] Id. at 531–2.
[87] Id. at 533–4.
[88] Id. at 509, 511, 534.
[89] Id. at 511.
[90] Id. at 535.
[91] Id. at 536.
[92] Id. at 537–8.

restatement, Thayer, as he promised at the beginning of his book,[93] differentiated the law of evidence from other rules that had become confused with it.
Not all rules that exclude evidence, Thayer reiterated throughout, are part of
the law of evidence. Substantive law, procedural law, and general rules of reason, rather than the law of evidence itself, account for a huge proportion of
these exclusions. Yet these exclusions are often misrepresented as part of the
law of evidence, further confusing an already perplexed subject.[94] By failing
to differentiate actual rules of evidence from these other rules excluding evidence, judges and authors of legal texts had been "working a sort of intellectual fraud," leaving the law largely "ill-apprehended, ill-stated, ill-digested."[95]
Thayer himself emphasized that "the law of evidence relates merely to matter
of fact offered to a judicial tribunal as the basis of inference to another matter of fact."[96] The law of evidence, he reiterated, "does not include all that
relates to the general topic of proof or legal reasoning, or all that is popularly
meant by the word 'evidence,' – all evidential matter, – but only such as it is
necessary to offer to use in court when a tribunal has to ascertain a matter of
fact unknown or disputed."[97] In chapters about judicial notice, presumptions,
burden of proof, and the "parole evidence" rule, Thayer stressed that most
rules excluding evidence under these headings were not based on the law of
evidence, but on substantive or procedural law or on general rules of reason.[98]
These rules, currently "disguised under the name of the law of evidence," must
be eliminated from it as "foreign matter," so that "the process of simplifying
and restating the rules of evidence, in the proper sense of the word, can go
forward."[99] Thayer included historical discussions throughout these chapters,
though to a lesser extent than in his primary focus on history in connecting the
law of evidence with the development of the jury.

Most directly connected to his central theme, Thayer relied on cases from all
periods of English legal history, particularly in his chapter on judicial notice,
to demonstrate the difference between laws of evidence and other rules excluding evidence.[100] More generally, he often invoked history to demonstrate the
origins of substantive rules. The presumption that a person not heard from for
seven years should be deemed to be dead, he observed, arose out of judicial
instructions to the jury in individual cases and only later became an affirma-
tive rule of law.[101] He called this transformation "a process of judicial legislation, advancing from what is a mere recognition of a legitimate step in legal

---

[93] Id. at 4.
[94] Id. at 269, 511–12, 523.
[95] Id. at 511.
[96] Id. at 388–9.
[97] Id. at 391.
[98] See, e.g., id. at 298 (judicial notice), 314–15, 331, 335–7, 351–2 (presumptions), 354, 389 (burden of proof), 390, 392, 397, 448, 468 (parole evidence).
[99] Id. at 531.
[100] Id. at 277–98.
[101] Id. at 319–24.

reasoning to a declaration of the legal effect of certain facts."[102] In discussing the "parole evidence" rule, he ascribed its liberalization in the eighteenth century to the emerging system of commercial law and to the role of ecclesiastical courts and courts of equity in developing conceptions derived from Roman law.[103] Thayer also looked to history as an alternative source of law. When prevailing law seemed overly rigid and confused, he occasionally found, as in his discussion of "parole evidence," enough precedents "to support juster and truer doctrines."[104]

Thayer claimed that some rules could only be explained historically. The distinction in "parole evidence" between using a direct statement of intention to illuminate a writing and using it as an independent means of proof, he asserted, was not based on reason, as earlier commentators had asserted, but on the history of ancient doctrines of pleading and substantive law.[105] Like Holmes, he believed that even if rules had lost their original historical justifications, they should be retained if they served useful functions in the present. For example, the practice of taking judicial notice of facts without proof arose at a time when the sovereign administered justice. Initially, the king sat personally in court. Later, judicial officers, who were his deputies or representatives, replaced him. Under this system, it made sense to take judicial notice of anything the king knew or did in his official capacity. Over time, new legal and political theories replaced the conception of the administration of justice as a concrete aspect of the king's sovereignty. Though the original justification was gone, Thayer approved the continuing and expanded practice of judicial notice, which had the practical benefit of shortening trials.[106]

International Critical Responses

A Preliminary Treatise was widely and favorably reviewed on both sides of the Atlantic. As one American review observed, Thayer's prior articles in the *Harvard Law Review* had already made him well known among scholars in Europe as well as in the United States.[107] Most significantly, Maitland had praised these articles privately to Thayer and publicly in *The History of English Law*. In a letter attached to the copy of *The History of English Law* that Maitland sent to Thayer in 1895, Maitland described his reliance on Thayer's earlier articles. "Long as it is," Maitland wrote, "it would have been much longer but for your announced intention of republishing three excellent papers that appeared in the Harvard Law Review." "With my share of the gift," he added, "goes my homage and fealty."[108]

[102] Id. at 324.
[103] Id. at 436.
[104] Id. at 461.
[105] Id. at 441–2.
[106] Id. at 299–300.
[107] Nation, supra note 72, at 126.
[108] Letter from Frederic Maitland to James Bradley Thayer (March 20, 1895) (James Bradley Thayer Papers, Harvard Law School Library) [hereinafter Thayer Papers].

Revealing the shared transatlantic interest in English legal history, Maitland and Thayer had been corresponding regularly for years.[109] In 1887, Maitland sent a copy of his edition of *Bracton's Note Book* to Thayer. "You have conferred a very great benefit upon all students of our ancient law," Thayer replied, adding that he had just written a review of it for the *Nation*.[110] The published review reiterated this praise. Thayer, who himself took extensive notes on the history of the German law of evidence, including many notebooks on Brunner's books,[111] and taught a course on the subject in the mid-1880s,[112] emphasized that Maitland's edition of Bracton would both inform and be illuminated by "the learned researches of the Germans into the old Frankish and Germanic law."[113] Indicating the community of legal historians in Boston, Thayer told Maitland that Ames "had been eagerly expecting the book" and was "better able to appreciate and profit by it, I expect, than any of our people, – hardly excluding Holmes or Bigelow."[114] Maitland soon became a candidate for a vacant professorship of English law at Cambridge and asked Thayer for permission to identify him as the author of the review in the *Nation*,[115] obviously believing that Thayer's name would impress the English. When Maitland received the professorship, he thanked Thayer "for your kind exertions on my behalf."[116]

After the publication of *A Preliminary Treatise*, numerous scholars echoed Maitland's earlier praise. Bigelow called it "noble," adding, "I am glad that anything I have done should have in any degree contributed to such a work."[117] Foreign reviewers indicated that Thayer had become one of the world's leading legal historians. A French review compared it to the great works of legal history written by Brunner in Germany and Maitland and Pollock in England,[118] and an English review predicted that the book "may possibly exert as great an influence on English legal thinking as 'Holmes on the Common Law.'"[119] Writing for the English *Law Quarterly Review*, Frederick Pollock maintained that Thayer's book "goes to the root of the subject more thoroughly, we venture to say, than any other textbook in existence."[120] In response to Thayer's

[109] Thayer Papers, supra note 108, at Box 18, Folder 14.

[110] Letter from James Bradley Thayer to Frederic Maitland (December 30, 1887) (Frederic William Maitland Papers, Cambridge University Library, add 7006).

[111] Thayer Papers, supra note 106, Box 12, Folders 1–4.

[112] Inventory to Thayer's Papers, p. 5, id.

[113] The Nation (March 22, 1888), pp. 241, 243.

[114] Letter from Thayer to Maitland, supra note 110.

[115] Letter from Frederic Maitland to James Bradley Thayer (June 1888) (Thayer Papers, supra note 108, Box 18, Folder 14).

[116] Letter from Frederic Maitland to James Bradley Thayer (September 15, 1888) (Thayer Papers, supra note 108, Box 18, Folder 14).

[117] Letter from Melville M. Bigelow to James Bradley Thayer (November 21, 1898) (Thayer Papers, supra note 108, Box 17, Folder 4).

[118] Revue Historique, no. 137, p. 155 (Thayer Papers, supra note 108, Box 17, Folder 3).

[119] 3 Law Journal 589 (December 3, 1898) (Thayer Papers, supra note 108, Box 17, Folder 3).

[120] Frederick Pollock, 15 Law Quarterly Review 86 (1899) (Thayer Papers, supra note 108, Box 17, Folder 3).

gift of part I, Brunner wrote that he was already familiar with Thayer's articles in the *Harvard Law Review* and praised "the scientific work which you have so excellently accomplished in your book." Brunner informed Thayer that for more than twenty years he had thought of taking a long research trip to England. "I heartily rejoice," Brunner could now report, "that the yawning gulf in the history of the jury has been filled by you better than I could have done." He closed his letter by expressing his appreciation "for the friendly way in which you have referred to me in your work."[121]

Beyond summarizing and agreeing with Thayer's central arguments, many reviews stressed his originality and attributed it to his innovative combination of history with traditional legal analysis.[122] Reviews pointed to his "more scientific treatment of the law of evidence"[123] and observed that the book should interest scholars of institutional history as well as lawyers.[124] The *Nation* described it as "at once practical and historical,"[125] a comment echoed by others. For some, Thayer's scholarly devotion to historical truth was itself highly practical. "When the reader discovers that every institution, every doctrine, every rule, is traced step by step from its first manifestation until it has attained its final form," one review concluded, "he feels that he is in the hands of a searcher after historical truth, and not of one who is manipulating history in the interest of a preconceived notion."[126] The reviewer remarked that the book was "the product of university life" in the library and the classroom, thereby seeming to link the professionalization of legal scholarship in university law schools with Thayer's historical approach. Challenging the common view that professors are dreamers whereas practitioners are realistic, he maintained that "nothing is as practical as *truth*."[127]

Also linking the historical and practical features of the book, others contrasted mere antiquarianism with Thayer's practical interest in using history to understand current law. In a letter commenting on Thayer's initial articles in the *Harvard Law Review*, John F. Dillon, an American judge and prolific author on various legal topics, wrote that "I have seen this subject in its historical aspect nowhere treated so satisfactorily. Many points in the interesting history formerly obscure have been illuminated and made clear by you. Nor is the subject one of antiquarian interest only," Dillon added, "for, as you point out, the English law of evidence, so unique in its character, is essentially the child of the jury, without which it never would have grown up,

---

[121] Letter from Heinrich Brunner to James Bradley Thayer (July 4, 1896) (Thayer Papers, supra note 108, Box 18, Folder 1).

[122] See, e.g., The Nation, supra note 72, at 126; The Nation (June 15, 1899), p. 459; 13 Law Quarterly Review 208 (1897); 2 Am. Hist. Rev. 341 (1897).

[123] 8 Yale L.J. 216, 217 (1899).

[124] 11 Political Science Quarterly 732, 734 (1896).

[125] The Nation, supra note 72, at 126.

[126] American Law Register (May, 1899) (Thayer Papers, supra note 108, Box 17, Folder 4), pp. 327, 328.

[127] Id. at 329.

and without which it cannot be adequately understood."[128] In his published review of Thayer's book, Frederick Pollock similarly stressed that Thayer's interest in history was practical rather than antiquarian. To the casual reader, Pollock observed, the book might seem to be "nothing but ancient history." Pollock emphasized, however, that Thayer was "a modern lawyer who is also an accurate historical scholar" and that his interest in history did not derive from "antiquarian predilection," but from the recognition that the existing law of evidence could only be understood through "a far-reaching search into its origins."[129] John Wigmore, who studied with Thayer at Harvard before beginning his own monumental work on the law of evidence, wrote to him that the book confirmed for all what his students already knew, that Thayer was the leading expert in the field. "As an achievement merely in the writing of history," Wigmore maintained, "it would be unique and pioneering, but I do not know when a work of history ever bore so immediately and practically upon concrete improvement in current practice." Wigmore added that he felt confident in the sincerity of his praise because he disagreed with Thayer on various "matters of classification and analysis." Yet even when he disagreed with Thayer, Wigmore assured him, "your achievements and example have, in the height of the standard set, alone made it possible for me to have true ideals of the work to be done."[130]

The only significant criticisms of Thayer were stated in private correspondence. Bigelow, unsurprisingly in light of his own prior scholarship, chided Thayer for relying too heavily on Brunner. In a letter responding to Thayer's earlier article on the jury, Bigelow began by declaring it "excellent in every way." Yet he immediately identified his "only criticism," which he elaborated at length. Bigelow believed Thayer had let himself "swallow Brunner too readily" in identifying Henry, either as duke of Normandy or subsequently as King Henry II, as a great law reformer. "Brunner, with his pro-Norman anti-Anglican feeling," Bigelow asserted, "can see nothing English of any account." According to Bigelow, the fragments of litigation that remained from Henry's reign revealed that he developed the inquisition as a fiscal reformer, not as a law reformer, which he no more resembled "than the man in the moon." Henry threw the "sop" of the recognition to the people simply to "help fill his Treasury; and that was enough." Referring to the relevant pages of his own *History of Procedure*, Bigelow maintained that Stephen Langton more than sixty years later, not Henry, was the great law reformer. Bigelow's more general point was that the English, not the Normans, were the first reformers of the law, a process that could only take place "when at length the English feeling had sufficiently revived." Writing that he had "incurred Brunner's displeasure"

---

[128] Letter from John F. Dillon to James Bradley Thayer (April 27, 1892) (Thayer Papers, supra note 108, Box 18, Folder 2).

[129] Law Quarterly Review, supra note 122, at 208.

[130] Letter from John Wigmore to James Bradley Thayer (November 23, 1898) (Thayer Papers, supra note 108, Box 19, Folder 6).

in making these points, Bigelow proudly proclaimed, "my only regret is that others have not incurred it also." Brunner, he complained, was "pig-headed."[131] Apparently regretting the tone of this letter, Bigelow wrote to Thayer again three days later, restraining his language while reiterating his basic point. "Of course Brunner's scholarship is of the highest order and his services are beyond praise," Bigelow acknowledged after referring to his earlier "hasty" letter. "It would have been enough to say that he is strongly pro-Norman, and that we must look out for that if there be occasion, as there is in regard to Hen. 2 as a law reformer."[132]

Hammond had a similar reaction to the same article. He wrote to Thayer in response to an invitation to contribute an article to the *Harvard Law Review* "in connection with yours on The Jury and its development." Commenting that he had just finished Brunner's book before reading Thayer's article, Hammond reported that the book "had not convinced me that the Norman share of the jury was so important as both B[runner] and you assume." "In fact," Hammond added, "his complete statement of the Norman case rather convinced me that it was not made out, especially in the important point of the legislation of Henry II as Norman or English."[133] In his extensive unpublished manuscript on the history of the common law, Hammond similarly and frequently criticized Brunner for overemphasizing the Norman and underestimating the distinctively English contribution.[134]

A. V. Dicey, professor of law at Oxford, challenged Thayer on other grounds. In a long letter to Thayer that was the most thorough critique of his book, Dicey combined great praise with respectful criticism. Dicey included Thayer as part of a general indictment of the legal scholarship being produced in the United States and particularly at Harvard Law School. He began by calling the *Preliminary Treatise* a work "of which any writer might be extremely proud. It is certain to be the leading and decisive work on its subject."[135] Dicey was extremely pleased that conclusions he had reached "on very inadequate investigation are confirmed in substance by your complete examination."[136] Dicey also complimented Thayer for "an elaborate piece of legal speculation and history" in which he avoided the excessive study of cases that frequently limited the scholarship of the Harvard law faculty.[137] Dicey then turned to his criticisms.

---

[131] Letter from Melville M. Bigelow to James Bradley Thayer (February 5, 1892) (Thayer Papers, supra note 108, Box 18, Folder 1).

[132] Letter from Melville M. Bigelow to James Bradley Thayer (February 8, 1892) (Thayer Papers, supra note 108, Folder 1).

[133] Letter from William Gardiner Hammond to James Bradley Thayer (February 26, 1892) (Thayer Papers, supra note 108, Box 18, Folder 1).

[134] William Gardiner Hammond, Notes of Lectures on History of the Common Law (1894) (Harvard Law School Archives).

[135] Letter from A. V. Dicey to James Bradley Thayer (March 28, 1899) (Thayer Papers, supra note 108, Box 17, Folder 3), p. 2.

[136] Id. at 5.

[137] Id. at 2.

In addition to some substantive suggestions on particular issues of evidence,[138] Dicey claimed that Thayer had not entirely escaped the faults of his Harvard colleagues and had devoted too much attention to judicial dicta. "After all," Dicey wrote, "a judge is only a lawyer seated on the judgment seat." Dicey maintained that his criticism "originates in my intense desire that your noble work should be completed." He assured Thayer that he would much rather learn his final conclusions about the law of evidence "than run a great chance of not perhaps living long enough" while Thayer provided "the almost needless assurances" that his "deductions are confirmed by the dicta of lawyers whom we are pleased to call authorities, but who will never carry half the weight with your reader that you already carry yourself." Blackstone's *Commentaries*, Dicey suggested, might never have been completed "if Blackstone had tried to strengthen all his positions by citing the judges who had preceded him." Reminding Thayer that life is short, Dicey wished "you could be imprisoned without law books for a year and compelled to complete your speculations."[139]

Dicey conceded that "at Oxford the literary power of the professors and teachers is a good deal in excess of our knowledge." But, he added, "I have sometimes thought that in the U.S. the literary, or speculative side of law fell a little below what might be expected from the vast knowledge, which I have never seen equaled, of your best teachers."[140] The very defects of the English, he delicately maintained, made him aware "of the opposite failings even when slight, of others." Dicey, therefore, felt confident in asserting that "the fallacy of authorities and excesses in the way of industry are the weak points of my Harvard friends," including Thayer.[141] Thayer's failure to complete his intended work on evidence for which his treatise was "preliminary" lends some support to Dicey's criticism.

Though Thayer died in 1902 without fulfilling this great ambition, his colleagues justly assessed his major scholarly contribution. John Chipman Gray, his colleague at Harvard Law School, reported that the *Preliminary Treatise* satisfied Thayer's own high standards and "gave him a distinguished place among those eminent jurists whose contributions to legal history have illustrated the closing years of the last century."[142] According to Ames, the book was a "worthy companion" to Brunner's classic work on the jury and provided Thayer "an immediate reputation, not only in this country, but in England, as a legal historian and jurist of the first rank."[143] In their own subsequent scholarly writing, Ames and Bigelow endorsed Thayer's central conclusions. Ames praised Thayer for recognizing that "our artificial rules of evidence were the natural outgrowth of trial by jury, and could only be explained by tracing

[138] Id. at 6–9.
[139] Id. at 3–4.
[140] Id. at 2–3.
[141] Id. at 4–5.
[142] Gray, supra note 8, at 602.
[143] J. B. Ames, 15 Harv. L. Rev. 599, 599–600 (1902).

carefully the development of that institution in England."[144] Bigelow, more dramatically, agreed with Thayer that the "devious course" of the law of evidence was "everywhere affected by the jury."[145] He relied on Thayer while concluding that the English law excluding hearsay evidence "has made it necessary, more and more down to the present day, to heap exception upon exception, until confusion is enough to baffle all but the persistent few who can follow the attenuating thread of history back to its obscure and distant beginnings." As a result, Bigelow maintained, the administration of law had become an embarrassment.[146] In a particularly devastating comment that ended with a citation to Thayer, Bigelow ridiculed "a process devoted to truth, which begins by turning away half the stream of evidence, and then sets to grinding out grist of rules for turning dribblings of the waste back to old, forgotten uses."[147]

Perhaps the most significant posthumous tribute to Thayer came from Wigmore, whose magisterial multi-volume treatise on the law of evidence, published in 1904, was the kind of work Thayer himself had hoped ultimately to produce. Wigmore dedicated his treatise to Thayer, "Historian and Teacher." In discussing the history of the subject, Wigmore called Thayer its "one master," who "set the example and marked the lines for all subsequent research in this part of the subject." Wigmore added that his own aim in treating the history of evidence was simply to "fill out the missing places, accepting the results already reached by him."[148]

---

[144] Id. at 599.

[145] Melville M. Bigelow, The Old Jury, in Papers on the Legal History of Government (Boston: Little, Brown, and Company, 1920), pp. 152, 170 n. 2.

[146] Id. at 170.

[147] Id. at 184 and n. 1.

[148] John Henry Wigmore: A Treatise on the System of Evidence in Trials at Common Law (Boston: Little, Brown, and Company, 1904), vol. 1, p. xii.

IX

Ames on the History of the Common Law

James Barr Ames, Thayer's colleague at Harvard Law School, completes the group of late nineteenth-century American scholars who made important original contributions to the history of English law. Unlike Bigelow, Holmes, and Thayer, Ames did not produce a major book. Diverted by teaching, by preparing casebooks, and later by his duties as dean of Harvard Law School, Ames did not even write many articles. Yet the articles he did write on English legal history attracted widespread attention and respect, even though they were extremely technical and dense, making them difficult to read. When Maitland saw the list of articles to be published in a three-volume set entitled *Select Essays in Anglo-American Legal History*, a friend reported, he "scanned it carefully for several minutes and then remarked: 'Ames' essays are the best of the lot.'"[1]

From the beginning of his career in the early 1870s, Ames took the English Year Books to his summer home and worked his way through them. His notes on the Year Books formed the basis for the lecture course in legal history he occasionally taught at Harvard Law School and for the articles derived from some of those lectures.[2] Henry Adams taught at Harvard during Ames's early years at Harvard Law School and took a great interest in his parallel research in early English legal history.[3] Ames served on Bigelow's dissertation committee,[4] was in close contact with Holmes and Thayer as well as Bigelow, and corresponded with Brunner and Maitland about shared interests in legal history.

Like his contemporaries who wrote about the history of English law, Ames was most interested in the relationship between past and present law, what he

[1] H. D. Hazeltine, Gossip about Legal History: Unpublished Letters of Maitland and Ames, 2 Cambridge L.J. 1 (1924).

[2] Samuel Williston, James Barr Ames – Services to Legal Education, 23 Harv. L. Rev. 330 (1910).

[3] Letter from Henry Adams to Henry Cabot Lodge (January 2, 1873), in Letters of Henry Adams (1858–1891) (Boston: Houghton Mifflin Company, 1930) (W. C. Ford, ed.), pp. 235, 236–7.

[4] The original copies of all doctoral theses are on file at Harvard University.

sometimes called "genealogy."[5] Ames introduced his lectures on legal history by informing his students that he would treat "the origin and development of the ideas of crime, tort, property, and equity in our law."[6] He occasionally used metaphors of family descent. For example, he declared that "the action of account is father of the count for money had and received."[7] In a late essay, "Law and Morals,"[8] Ames made the broad historical claim that the common law had become increasingly moral over time. He saw the law professor, who uniquely has the time for systematic, comprehensive, and comparative investigation, as the chief vehicle for further improvement.[9]

Ames joined the consensus that the common law had Teutonic rather than Roman origins. He acknowledged that Bracton had introduced some doctrines of Roman law into the English common law while cautioning that this Roman influence was less than previously assumed. The main impact of Roman law, he added, was through the Ecclesiastical Courts and various doctrines of equity. He particularly stressed that there had been no counterpart in England to the substantial influence of Roman law in Germany and France. Just as Lodge had emphasized the purity of Germanic law in England, Ames maintained that "English law is more German than the law of Germany itself." Like Thayer but unlike Bigelow, Ames identified Anglo-Saxon and Norman law as the two related sources of Germanic law in England. He pointed out that Norman law originated among the Franks and often called it Franco-Norman. Anglo-Saxon and Franco-Norman law, he added, exhibited many common characteristics derived from the Germanic roots they shared. Yet Ames, like Bigelow and Thayer, considered Franco-Norman law "vastly more important" than Anglo-Saxon law. To the extent they conflicted after the Norman Conquest, he stressed, the Franco-Norman law overwhelmingly prevailed, despite some notable exceptions. He, therefore, concluded that the origins of English law are best sought in Frankish law, whose earliest surviving examples are found in the law of the Salic Franks published around 475.[10] He cited Sohm's book as the fullest treatment of the procedural law of the Salic Franks.[11]

In much of his writing, Ames emphasized the modern implications of old law. Like Thayer, Ames viewed the study of legal history as a guide to understanding and, where needed, to improving current law. In his work on evidence, Thayer typically treated history as the basis for ridding current law of dysfunctional survivals from past law, though he occasionally invoked past doctrine as preferable to current law. Ames, by contrast, mainly treated past

---

[5] James Barr Ames, Express Assumpsit, in Lectures on Legal History and Miscellaneous Legal Essays (Cambridge, Mass.: Harvard University Press, 1913), p. 145.

[6] James Barr Ames, The Salic and Anglo-Saxon Courts, in Ames, supra note 5, p. 34.

[7] James Barr Ames, Account, in Ames, supra note 5, pp. 116, 121.

[8] James Barr Ames, Law and Morals, in Ames, supra note 5, p. 435.

[9] James Barr Ames, The Vocation of the Law Professor, in Ames, supra note 5, pp. 354, 366–7.

[10] Ames, supra note 6, at 34.

[11] James Barr Ames, Substantive Law before the Time of Bracton, in Ames, supra note 5, p. 39 n. 1.

law as the source of constructive rules that made analytic sense in the present. In several instances, however, Ames preferred old law to new law that threatened or superseded it. For example, he saw the old law of disseisin of chattels as informing the present, both in demonstrating the need to insulate from liability people who had received goods in good faith, and in warning against the "unsatisfactory results" of recent deviations from this view.[12] He similarly asserted the continuing viability of the old law of consideration while opposing an "innovation of the nineteenth century" that enabled courts to ignore the agreement of the parties about the value of an act and to determine a different value. According to Ames, the innovation was unsuccessful because it undermined reasonable bargains and encumbered the law with unreasonable distinctions. "It is not too late," he urged, "to abandon this modern invention and to return to the simple doctrine of the fathers, who found a consideration in the mere fact of a bargain, in other words, in any act or forbearance given in exchange for a promise." The old law provided the formality needed to guard against "thoughtless gratuitous promises," met the practical needs of businessmen, and was not burdened by the unnecessary subtleties of later law.[13]

Sometimes Ames recognized that a modern legal innovation with which he disagreed had become so firmly established "that it would be quixotic to attack it in the courts." The law allowing an undisclosed principal to sue and be sued regarding contracts made by his agent, he sadly concluded, fell into that category.[14] Ames nevertheless tried to prove that this law violated "fundamental legal principles" derived from centuries of past decisions, produced unjust results, and should be viewed as an anomaly.[15] Though he conceded that a legal challenge to the law itself would not be successful, Ames hoped that his analysis would convince judges to avoid relying on this unfortunate law as "the basis of analogical reasoning."[16]

In more fluid areas of legal development, by contrast, Ames invoked legal history as part of his effort to shape the emerging law. Modern codes of procedure, he observed, had eliminated much of the legal procedure and terminology that had previously underlined the distinction between law and equity. "These changes are commonly thought to have been beneficial," Ames reported without indicating any dissent from this consensus. He worried, however, that the changes produced by the modern codes could lead to undervaluing or overlooking the "essential and permanent difference between legal and equitable relief" reflected in centuries of English law. He emphasized that the distinction between a legal judgment that provides a remedy to the plaintiff in land, goods, or money and an equitable judgment that orders the defendant to do or not to

---

[12] James Barr Ames, The Inalienability of Choses in Action, in Ames, supra note 5, pp. 210, 218.

[13] James Barr Ames, Two Theories of Consideration, in Ames, supra note 5, pp. 323, 353.

[14] James Barr Ames, Undisclosed Principal – His Rights and Liabilities, in Ames, supra note 5, pp. 453, 456.

[15] Id. at 453, 456, 463.

[16] Id. at 453.

do a specified thing "is as vital and far-reaching as ever."[17] And he pointed out that equity can force a murderer to surrender title to land that the common law, despite his crime, would allow him to acquire.[18]

Former students recalled Ames as a "legal evolutionist,"[19] who believed in "using history as showing a progressive development in tune more or less with changing conditions, and as leading up to or falling short of modern needs."[20] One student remembered "that he sometimes went back into history, sometimes unfairly, to sustain some results which he felt the cases should have decided, or a result which he was anxious to establish." Ames did not leave the impression that "he was bound by history," but he did seem sometimes "to bolster up a very desirable present day result by old cases which hardly stood for the exact problem for which he wished to use them as support."[21] Another observed that Ames "used his great historical learning chiefly to account for infelicities and unethical developments of the law, which having a merely historical basis ought to be corrected."[22] These students generally recognized that Ames did not employ the "functionalist" approach later promoted by Pound. Ames did not discuss the impact of social conditions on legal development[23] and occasionally reminded students "that it was dangerous to resort to public policy to support a judicial decision."[24]

Among his writings on the history of the common law, I focus here on two articles by Ames in the early volumes of the *Harvard Law Review*. Published in 1888 and 1889, these articles well illustrate Ames's approach to English legal history and engage the work of two of his leading contemporaries, Holmes and Maitland. "Express Assumpsit," one of several articles Ames wrote on the history of assumpsit, effectively and influentially challenged Holmes's interpretation of the origins of the concept of consideration in contract law. The article hurt Holmes's sensitive feelings and remained an irritant to him for decades. "The Disseisin of Chattels," building on Maitland's article "The Seisin of Chattels" in the 1885 volume of the *Law Quarterly Review*, generated an extended correspondence between Ames and Maitland about the history of property law. The correspondence and published exchanges between Ames and Maitland were filled with mutual respect even when they disagreed about specific legal interpretations. Though more difficult to follow than any of the other

---

[17] James Barr Ames, Can a Murderer Acquire Title by his Crime and Keep It? in Ames, supra note 5, pp. 310, 310–11.

[18] Id. at 321.

[19] Extracts from letters by onetime students under Deans Langdell and Ames, relative to the attitude of those teachers toward the law (James Barr Ames Papers, Harvard Law School Library, Box 1, Folder 34), XVI. These letters were solicited by Charles Warren, who wrote a history of Harvard Law School. Charles Warren, History of the Harvard Law School and of Early Legal Conditions in America (New York: Lewis Publishing Company, 1908).

[20] Id. at XLIX.

[21] Id. at XLII.

[22] Id. at VI.

[23] Id. at VIII.

[24] Id. at XIII.

scholarship I discuss in this book, these articles repay attention by illustrating the kinds of doctrinal issues and complex, technical analysis that engaged the most prominent legal historians on both sides of the Atlantic in the late nineteenth century.

Ames and Holmes on the History of Consideration

At the end of "Implied Assumpsit," the sequel to his article "Express Assumpsit," Ames summarized his treatment of assumpsit in a paragraph that captured his close analysis of the complicated evolution of legal doctrine and his confidence in the flexibility and autonomy of the common law.

In its origin an action of tort, it was soon transformed into an action of contract, becoming afterwards a remedy where there was neither tort nor contract. Based at first only upon an express promise, it was afterwards supported upon an implied promise, and even upon a fictitious promise. Introduced as a special manifestation of the action on the case, it soon acquired the dignity of a distinct form of action, which superseded debt, became concurrent with account, with case upon a bailment, a warranty, and bills of exchange, and competed with equity in the case of the essentially equitable quasi-contracts growing out of the principle of unjust enrichment. Surely it would be hard to find a better illustration of the flexibility and power of self-development of the Common Law.[25]

Without exploring all of these topics, I will examine how Ames's treatment of assumpsit challenged Holmes's conclusions about the history of consideration. As Pollock and Maitland noted,[26] the history of consideration was one of the most debated topics in contemporary scholarship on English legal history, and it has continued to generate substantial scholarly commentary.[27]

The introductory paragraph of Ames's article "Express Assumpsit" signaled that Holmes was his primary target. After observing that scholars of the English law of contract had been particularly fascinated by the "mystery of consideration," Ames summarized three recent views, beginning with Holmes. By noting that the other two authors published after his own article was in manuscript,[28] Ames indicated that he would be focusing on Holmes, and he did. Ames quoted Holmes, who maintained that "the requirement of consideration in all parol contracts is simply a modified generalization of *quid pro quo* to raise a debt by parol."[29] Ames, by contrast, disagreed with all theories that found a single source for consideration, including those of the two other scholars he mentioned but did not pursue in detail.[30]

---

[25] James Barr Ames, Implied Assumpsit, in Ames, supra note 5, pp. 149, 166.

[26] Frederick Pollock and Frederic Maitland, The History of English Law before the Time of Edward I (Cambridge University Press, 1899) (2d ed.), vol. II, p. 214 n. 2.

[27] See A. W. B. Simpson, A History of the Common Law of Contract: The Rise of the Action of Assumpsit (Oxford, England: Clarendon Press, 1975), p. 317 n. 1.

[28] Ames, supra note 5, at 129 n. 5.

[29] Id. at 129 (quoting Holmes article on "Early English Equity" and The Common Law). Ames noted that Langdell previously had expressed a similar view. Id. at 129 n. 2.

[30] Id. at 145 (Hare), 147–8 (Salmond).

According to Ames, the modern doctrine of consideration had two very distinct sources, detriment and precedent debt. Detriment arose as part of the history of special assumpsit. Precedent debt arose as part of the history of indebitatus assumpsit. Because these two forms of assumpsit had such independent histories, Ames treated them separately and consecutively. He spent most of the article on the history of special assumpsit. Yet even in his discussion of indebitatus assumpsit, which required the quid pro quo Holmes considered essential to consideration, Ames disagreed with Holmes's analysis.[31] The modern definition of consideration, Ames stressed, has a different meaning than either of these sources. He warned against anachronism, stressing that the modern definition "would not have covered the cases of the sixteenth century," when these sources of consideration emerged.[32]

Again alert to anachronism, Ames maintained that understanding the early role of assumpsit required sensitivity to the "radical difference between modern and primitive conceptions of legal liability." The primitive conception of a tort viewed it as an injury to a person or to property caused by a stranger. In contrast to modern tort law, if the person injured had allowed contact with another, there was no tort.[33] Assumpsit became a way to extend tort liability beyond strangers to those who had made an express promise to assume the risk of injury. Undertaking that express promise constituted the assumpsit.[34] Because assumpsit arose in tort actions, Ames added, consideration, a contractual concept, was not an issue.[35]

Ames proceeded to examine the use of assumpsit in four categories of tort cases, which antedated and eventually led to the emergence of special assumpsit. Frustratingly, he never clearly defined special assumpsit, but in context he seemed to mean a form of action in contract,[36] similar to a modern parol contract,[37] based on a parol promise.[38] The first category was the original use of assumpsit to extend tort liability beyond strangers. Ames gave examples of cases in which undertakings by defendants who were not strangers to the plaintiffs constituted assumpsits that justified liability. A ferryman who undertook to transport the plaintiff's horse across a river was liable because his overloading the boat caused the horse to drown. Surgeons who undertook to cure the plaintiff or the plaintiff's animals were liable for the injuries they caused by not exercising adequate skill. Similarly, carpenters who undertook to build but who did not do so skillfully were liable for their poor performance. All of these cases, Ames emphasized, involved active misconduct by the defendant.[39]

---

[31] Id. at 129–30.
[32] Id. at 129.
[33] Id. at 131.
[34] Id. at 130–2, 136–7; Ames, supra note 25, at 149.
[35] Ames, supra note 5, at 130, 133, 137.
[36] Id. at 133.
[37] Id. at 139.
[38] Id. at 144.
[39] Id. at 130.

A second category of assumpsit developed in cases accusing bailees of negligent custody of items given to them by plaintiffs. Unlike the first category,
the cases in which bailees were defendants involved nonfeasance rather than
misfeasance. Ames stressed, however, that the nonfeasance of bailees was more
than simply a breach of promise. The bailee was an actor. By the act of taking
possession of the plaintiff's goods, the bailee had undertaken to keep them
safely.[40] The third category was composed of "the actions of deceit against
the vendor of a chattel upon a false warranty."[41] To prevail, plaintiffs had to
prove that the vendor had undertaken an express warranty of quality.[42] The
fourth category, like the third, was framed as an action of deceit,[43] "the deceit
in breaking a promise on the faith of which the plaintiff had been induced to
part with his money or other property."[44] These four categories of assumpsit,
Ames repeatedly observed, both preceded special assumpsit and overlapped in
time with each other.[45]

While introducing his discussion of the fourth category of assumpsit, Ames
stressed that it was the most direct source of special assumpsit. "However
much the actions against a surgeon or carpenter for misfeasance, those against
a bailee for negligent custody, and, above all, those against a vendor for a
false warranty, may have contributed, indirectly, to the introduction of special
assumpsit, there is yet a fourth class of cases which seem to have been more
intimately connected with the development of the modern parol contract than
any of those yet considered."[46] This quotation seems to link special assumpsit
with parol contract, helping to define what Ames meant by special assumpsit.
Ames did not, however, elaborate the "indirect" ways in which the three categories contributed to its introduction. Instead, he traced the development of
this fourth category from cases that involved misfeasance through innovations
that brought it to the verge of a contract action in special assumpsit.

In an early case of deceit involving the loss of money based on a broken
promise, the defendant took money from the plaintiff to purchase property as
his counsel. Yet the defendant purchased the property for a third person after
informing him of the plaintiff's intent. Although the act of the defendant did
not injure the person or physical property of the plaintiff, the traditional basis
for tort liability, the court upheld the plaintiff's action for deceit. In this case,
Ames observed, it was not difficult to extend the principle of misfeasance to the
betrayal of the plaintiff's secrets by his counsel.[47] A more difficult case arose
when a plaintiff brought an action of deceit, claiming that he had bargained
with the defendant for the purchase of land and paid the agreed price, but that

[40] Id. at 132–3.
[41] Id. at 136.
[42] Id. at 137.
[43] Id. at 139, 140.
[44] Id. at 142.
[45] Id. at 132, 136, 141.
[46] Id. at 138–9.
[47] Id. at 140–1.

the defendant had nevertheless granted rights in the land to another and had thereby deceived him. Here the defendant was the vendor, not the agent of the plaintiff. Under existing law, the promise to perform the agreement was not binding in itself. Where was the misfeasance, traditionally an essential element of the tort of deceit, in this case? The defendant claimed there was none. As Ames remarked, judges had great difficulty extending the action of deceit to this situation, but eventually they did so, finding a misfeasance.[48] Over time, the very distinction between misfeasance and nonfeasance seemed "altogether too shadowy to be maintained" and was abandoned.[49]

In the definitive modern treatment of the "history of the common law of contract," echoing Ames in its subtitle, "the rise of the action of assumpsit," A. W. B. Simpson, like Ames almost a century before, remarked that this extension of deceit "was quite a new departure." This departure required "very strained reasoning," forcing judges into "considerable flights of ingenuity" to distinguish deceit from "the mere failure to perform the agreement."[50] Simpson's discussion helps explain Ames's unelaborated comment that "actions of deceit against the vendor of a chattel upon a false warranty" were the most important of the other three forms of assumpsit in the development of special assumpsit. The new departure involving deceit in the context of selling land, Simpson observed, "may have owed something to the earlier development of the seller's liability for deceit in the sale of goods; if the seller of goods was chargeable for deceit, there was no very good reason why the seller of land should not be chargeable."[51] And though Ames did not elaborate the way in which assumpsit against bailees contributed "indirectly" to the changes that led to special assumpsit, it seems probable that its recognition of nonfeasance made it easier to relax and then abandon the distinction between misfeasance and nonfeasance in the assumpsit of deceit.

Ames stressed that the fourth category of assumpsit, like the other three, involved a detriment to the plaintiff, the loss of money or other property induced by the deceit. Criticizing Holmes again for misinterpreting the history of consideration in *The Common Law*,[52] he reiterated that it was not material whether the benefit of the deceit was received by the defendant who made the deceitful promise or a third person.[53] In the early sixteenth century, Ames added, actions in deceit extended to the breach of a promise even if money was not exchanged at the time of the bargain. The detriment to the plaintiff that supported the action in deceit, moreover, extended to loss of time or labor as well as loss of money or property.[54] Parallel developments in equity, which granted

[48] Id. at 141.
[49] Id. at 142.
[50] Simpson, supra note 27, at 256–7.
[51] Id. at 256.
[52] Ames, supra note 5, at 143 n. 3 (also criticizing Langdell).
[53] Id. at 142.
[54] Id. at 142–3.

relief to plaintiffs who relied to their detriment on promises by defendants, reinforced the extension of the action of deceit in the common law.[55]

Even as a breach of a parol promise became remediable as a deceit, Ames reported, courts continued to differentiate assumpsit based in deceit from contract. Yet the distinction between assumpsit and contract did not last, and a new term, "special assumpsit," was conceived as a contractual action. Frustratingly, Ames compressed his discussion of this crucial change into two sentences. "By a natural transition," he wrote, "actions upon parol promises came to be regarded as actions *ex contractu*. Damages were soon assessed, not upon the theory of reimbursement for the loss of the thing given for the promise, but upon the principle of compensation for the failure to obtain the thing promised."[56] Though he had spent pages describing the development of the four categories of assumpsit in tort that led to special assumpsit, Ames did not elaborate at all the crucial "natural transition" of assumpsit from a tort to a contract action. Rather, he ended his treatment of the history of special assumpsit by observing that it retained traces of its origin as a tort action of deceit. The allegation of deceit, for example, was retained until the nineteenth century, "an unmistakable mark of the genealogy of the action." The requirement in contract law that consideration must go from the plaintiff to the defendant, he added, derived from the tort action of deceit, which could be maintained only if the plaintiff incurred a detriment based on the defendant's promise.[57] In his companion article "Implied Assumpsit," Ames remarked that this entire history illustrated the continuing vitality of medieval legal conceptions and revealed the "extraordinary conservatism" of the common law. Though many were familiar with rules of real property and pleading that reflect "the persistency of archaic reverence for form and of scholastic methods of interpretation," Ames maintained that this conservatism could be found in virtually any branch of the law at the beginning of the seventeenth century.[58]

After his discussion of the emergence of special assumpsit from the four categories of assumpsit that preceded it, Ames much more briefly addressed the history of indebitatus assumpsit. Unlike special assumpsit, which created a new substantive right to sue for a breach of a parol promise based on detriment, indebitatus assumpsit only allowed a new procedure for the enforcement of an existing right.[59] The existing right, in actions of debt, was based on "*quid pro quo*, or benefit" received by the defendant. The quid pro quo in indebitatus assumpsit, Ames stressed, was identical to its use in actions of debt.[60] The main procedural advantage of indebitatus assumpsit, Ames explained in his companion article, was the right to a trial by jury, which was unavailable in actions of debt. Indebitatus assumpsit also had the advantage of allowing the plaintiff to

---

[55] Id. at 143–4.
[56] Id. at 144–5.
[57] Id. at 145.
[58] Ames, supra note 25, at 149.
[59] Simpson, supra note 27, at 316, reached a similar conclusion.
[60] Ames, supra note 5, at 146.

assert the debt created by the benefit without the specificity required in actions of debt.[61]

In a short paragraph, Ames connected his treatment of special assumpsit and indebitatus assumpsit to the history of consideration, the topic with which he began his article. As assumpsit became a technical action in itself, as opposed to an aspect of a tort action, people felt the need for terminology to indicate what made promises enforceable. Promises were not "binding of themselves." What made them binding? Two answers, from two very different areas of the law, special assumpsit and indebitatus assumpsit, were available: "the detriment or the debt for which they were given." According to Ames, "a need was naturally felt for a single word to express the additional and essential requisite of all parol contracts." The best word for that purpose was "consideration," which "became the peculiar mark of the technical action of assumpsit, as distinguished from other actions on the case against surgeons or carpenters, bailees and warranting vendors, in which, as we have seen, it was still customary to allege an undertaking by the defendant."[62]

This explanation, Ames concluded, demonstrated that Holmes's theory of the origins of consideration was "not tenable." Holmes maintained that consideration in all parol contracts derived from the quid pro quo used in debt. He did not even consider the huge role played by detriment, which developed in an area of law far removed from debt. Ames found it "impossible to believe" that detriment evolved from debt. Even regarding the element of consideration connected with debt, the quid pro quo, Ames disagreed with Holmes. Holmes claimed that consideration in contract "modified" the quid pro quo used "to raise a debt by parol." But Ames did not believe there was any substantive modification of the concept of quid pro quo as it moved from debt to contract. According to Ames, "the consideration of indebitatus assumpsit was identical with the *quid pro quo*, and not a modification of it."[63]

Holmes wrote a defensive letter to Ames acknowledging his basic criticism while minimizing its importance and objecting to his tone. "I read your articles on assumpsit with much interest," Holmes told Ames, observing that "I had noted to develop the element of deceit – but frankly admit that my account leaves something to be desired." Holmes explained that "I have had no time" and doubted he would "ever have again to read the Yearbooks." Based on his past reading of the Year Books, however, Holmes declared, "I am pretty confident that the main core of my discussion is sound." He then protested Ames's treatment of him. "I think you exaggerate the importance of what I left out." Becoming more personal, Holmes complained "of a slight note of asperity when you refer to me. I had to cover a great deal of ground in my book – my ideas on each subject," he bragged, "so far as I know were new and have been accepted as such." "It would be remarkable," he added defensively, "if in some

[61] Ames, supra note 25, at 153.
[62] Ames, supra note 5, at 147.
[63] Id.

matters of detail I did not err." Holmes assured Ames that he was "as ready to accept a correction as another." But, he immediately added, "with a man whose opinion I value and whose learning I respect I cannot but feel hurt if his only public expressions sound as if written with a slightly irritated adverseness." Somewhat softening his own irritation, Holmes told Ames, "I make too much of it by writing it down – but I like to be frank to an old colleague." As apparent evidence of continued respect for Ames, Holmes closed his letter by reporting that he had recommended the articles to "one or two intelligent foreigners in search of light" and added a postscript asking Ames to let him know whether his research uncovered "anything curious in the history of fraud."[64]

Ames immediately sent a conciliatory response. Holmes's hurt feelings about the tone of his criticisms, he wrote, "came upon me as a painful surprise." Ames told Holmes that he was "wholly unconscious" of the spirit Holmes read into them. He conceded that he had expressed his dissent "somewhat baldly," a fault he attributed to the influence of German scholarship. "Much reading of German law books," he wrote, "probably accounts in large measure for my doubtless too blunt manner of putting things." Trying to assuage Holmes, Ames maintained that he had used the same unfortunate manner in criticizing others. Yet this defense was rather unconvincing, for most of Ames's criticisms were directed at Holmes, and he did not use as stark language as "not tenable" and "impossible to believe" about other scholars. Ames went on to stress his respect for Holmes. "No one, I am sure, values your work in the field of legal history more than I do." Ames added that "it has been in my mind to dedicate to you my book on the 'History of Tort and Contract,' with your permission." Tellingly invoking the German scholars they both read and respected while trying to minimize the significance of his criticisms, Ames said that the idea of the dedication to Holmes came from "the example of Bruns in dedicating to Jhering his book on 'Possession' notwithstanding the many differences of opinion between the two."[65] Ames never wrote the book, but lectures on these topics were published posthumously in his *Lectures on Legal History*.[66]

"Forget what I wrote," Holmes told Ames in a gracious reply, "yet I am glad that I did write for the sake of your kind answer. I dare say the very high value I set on your opinion made me over sensitive. Of course you understand I don't deprecate criticism."[67] "I did not say to you the other day," Holmes soon added, "how delighted I was at the prospect of your publishing the book you mention which I know no man in this country or England equally competent

---

[64] Letter from Oliver Wendell Holmes, Jr. to James Barr Ames (December 1888) (Ames Papers, supra note 19, Box 1, Folder 12).

[65] Letter from James Barr Ames to Oliver Wendell Holmes, Jr. (December 5, 1888), microformed on reel 27, 0720–1 (University Publications of American, Oliver Wendell Holmes Papers).

[66] Mark DeWolfe Howe, Justice Oliver Wendell Holmes: The Proving Years, 1870–1882 (Cambridge, Mass.: Harvard University Press, 1963), p. 231 n. 17.

[67] Letter from Oliver Wendell Holmes, Jr. to James Barr Ames (December 6, 1888) (Ames Papers, supra note 19, Box 1, Folder 12). Howe, supra note 66, at 230–1, discusses this exchange.

to write."[68] Two years later, Holmes informed Ames that he had been rereading his articles on disseisin of chattels. "In most respects," Holmes declared, "I had nothing but praise," though he concluded by mentioning unspecified "points which some day I hope we may discuss."[69] Perhaps remembering this incident, Holmes also sent Ames a draft essay and, in apparent recognition of Ames's expertise as a legal historian, asked him whether it was good enough to be published. Acknowledging the limitations of his own research, Holmes confided to Ames: "I can't help feeling that the early historical part might have much light thrown upon it by researches outside the regular printed sources – but my impression is that the piece was solid work when it was written."[70] Despite this evidence of reconciliation, in private correspondence decades later Holmes indicated lingering resentment toward Ames. He wrote to Wesley Hohfeld, a professor at Yale Law School, that "Ames always had a whack at me when he could" even though they "were very good friends."[71] "Ames always wanted to pitch into me," he similarly told his English friend Harold Laski, "but he wasn't an enemy – he was almost a friend."[72] A few years later, Holmes added to Laski that Ames had a "prejudice" against him "although we got on very well together."[73]

Other critical references to Holmes throughout Ames's work provide support for Holmes's sense of hostility from Ames. Ames devoted his lecture "Simple Contracts prior to Assumpsit" to demonstrating that Holmes's unconventional interpretation of this subject was unconvincing.[74] His article "The Origin of Uses" similarly focused on disproving Holmes's "novel and interesting" conclusions about this subject.[75] Even in lectures and articles that did not take on Holmes directly, Ames challenged his interpretations of legal history.[76] Only rarely did Ames cite Holmes favorably,[77] though he sometimes tempered his criticisms by calling Holmes "distinguished."[78] Of the many other

---

[68] Letter from Oliver Wendell Holmes, Jr. to James Barr Ames (January 7, 1889) (Ames Papers, supra note 19. Box 1, Folder 12).

[69] Letter from Oliver Wendell Holmes, Jr. to James Barr Ames (February 12, 1891) (Ames Papers, supra note 19, Box 1, Folder 12).

[70] Letter from Oliver Wendell Holmes, Jr. to James Barr Ames (February 7, 1891) (Ames Papers, supra note 19, Box 1, Folder 12).

[71] Howe, supra note 61, at 231.

[72] Letter from Oliver Wendell Holmes, Jr. to Harold J. Laski (May 1, 1919), in Holmes-Laski Letters: The Correspondence of Mr. Justice Holmes and Harold J. Laski (Cambridge, Mass.: Harvard University Press, 1953) (Mark DeWolfe Howe, ed.), vol. 1, pp. 199, 200.

[73] Letter from Oliver Wendell Holmes, Jr. to Harold J. Laski (March 22, 1924), in Holmes-Laski Letters, supra note 72, at 727.

[74] James Barr Ames, Simple Contracts prior to Assumpsit, in Ames, supra note 5, pp. 122–8.

[75] James Barr Ames, The Origin of Uses, in Ames, supra note 5, pp. 233–42.

[76] James Barr Ames, Detinue, in Ames, supra note 5, pp. 71, 79 n. 4.; James Barr Ames, Covenant, in Ames, supra note 5, pp. 97, 100; Ames, supra note 12, at 211 n. 4.

[77] James Barr Ames, Specialty Contracts and Equitable Defenses, in Ames, supra note 5, pp. 104, 113.

[78] Ames, supra note 74, at 124; Ames, supra note 12, at 211 n. 4.

contemporary legal scholars Ames discussed, none received as many negative comments.

Ames's article on assumpsit that criticized Holmes generated high praise from Maitland and Pollock. Maitland wrote that he had just been reading it "with very great interest," called it "most valuable," and declared that it "will go far to settling the question."[79] Pollock similarly congratulated Ames for getting "at last to the bottom of that puzzle, or at any rate much nearer to it than anyone before." Pollock added that Ames's article would help him with his forthcoming work on contract law.[80] Pollock later wrote to Ames that preparing his lectures on the history of contract at Oxford "caused me to go more carefully through your articles on Assumpsit and I was confirmed in agreement with you."[81] In *The History of English Law*, Pollock and Maitland, after noting that they disagreed with an "ingenious theory" of Holmes about the history of quid pro quo, added that Ames had put the history of consideration "on a new footing."[82]

Ames and Maitland on the History of Property Law

Just as Ames's article "Express Assumpsit" responded to Holmes's prior work on the history of consideration, his article "The Disseisin of Chattels" addressed an earlier article by Maitland, "The Seisin of Chattels." Yet in contrast to his criticism of Holmes, which yielded an alternative explanation of the history of consideration, Ames had only praise for Maitland and portrayed his own article as extending Maitland's basic conclusions. Its publication provoked a lengthy and respectful correspondence between Maitland and Ames about its contents and conclusions, which echoed in the section on movable goods in *The History of English Law*. In addition to engaging another important contemporary scholar and contributing to the transatlantic discussion of the history of English law, Ames's article revealed the breadth of his interests and knowledge. His work on assumpsit dealt with the history of tort and contract. "The Disseisin of Chattels" and several related articles dealt with the history of property.

Ames began "The Disseisin of Chattels" by summarizing Maitland's "admirable" article. Maitland's readers, Ames declared in his opening sentence, "were doubtless startled" by its title, "The Seisin of Chattels." As Maitland himself stressed, previous scholars had assumed that the term "seisin" referred to a feudal concept of interest in land that differed from possession and that had no application to movable goods, called chattels. Even to refer to "the

---

[79] Letter from Frederic Maitland to James Barr Ames (May 6, 1888) (Ames Papers, supra note 19, Box 1, Folder 30).

[80] Letter from Frederick Pollock to James Barr Ames (June 23, 1888) (Ames Papers, supra note 19, Box 1, Folder 32).

[81] Letter from Frederick Pollock to James Barr Ames (December 7, 1889) (Ames Papers, supra note 19, Box 1, Folder 32).

[82] Pollock and Maitland, supra note 26, vol. II, at 214 n. 2.

seisin of chattels" was, therefore, startling, apparently "a really bad blunder," to use Maitland's own words. "There is hardly a rule of our legal terminology," Maitland admitted in his opening sentence, "better settled than that which is broken by the title of this paper."[83] Yet by providing conclusive evidence that the terms "seisin" and "possession" were synonymous and were both applied to chattels as well as land, Maitland convinced Ames that his "title was aptly chosen." "In a word," Ames wrote, "seisin was not a purely feudal notion." Ames's title raised analogous issues about "disseisin," which was also considered a feudal concept that applied only to land. And Ames reached analogous conclusions to Maitland's, declaring that disseisin was not "a peculiarity of feudalism" and that it applied to chattels as well as land. [84]

Maitland's article, one of the first he published, indicated the large issues he perceived in his research, most importantly, the very value of original scholarship in English legal history. Maitland ascribed the existing misconception of seisin to the broadly accepted position of Lord Mansfield, who wrote that it was "a technical term to denote the completion of that investiture by which the tenant was admitted into the tenure, and without which no freehold could be constituted or pass." This description of seisin, Maitland observed, presented it as a "distinctly feudal notion," differentiated it as a technical term that was not equivalent to possession, and left the impression that the distinction between possession and seisin was "of very ancient date, an outline of immemorial common law." Based on feudal conceptions of land tenure, it could not apply to movables, since there was "no tenure of movables."[85]

Responding to Mansfield, Maitland first observed that Mansfield had supported his own conclusion by referring to "certain ancient Lombards and a modern Scotchman" rather than to any English sources. Understatedly calling this sourcing "a little strange," Maitland indicated that it should provoke skepticism about Mansfield's conclusion.[86] He also warned that it was too easy to attribute to the irrationality of feudalism legal terms that are difficult to understand in the present. "Seisin and disseisin seem so mysterious a matter," he observed, "that, in despair of rational explanation, we are glad to have so satisfactory a word as feudalism wherewith to hush the questioner."[87]

By his own example, Maitland wanted to illustrate that careful research in original sources could provide a rational explanation for what seems mysterious. Through these sources, he challenged Mansfield's conclusions. Begging his reader's patience for his extensive citations, he attempted to prove that seisin, "so far from having any very close connection with those ideas and institutions which we call feudal, had not even any exclusive reference to land." Rather, from time immemorial until the fifteenth century, English lawyers frequently,

---

[83] F. W. Maitland, The Seisin of Chattels, 1 Law Quarterly Review 324 (1885).
[84] James Barr Ames, The Disseisin of Chattels, in Ames, supra note 5, at 172.
[85] Maitland, supra note 83, at 324.
[86] Id.
[87] Id. at 325.

sometimes habitually, referred to the seisin of chattels, indicating that the gulf between real property and personal property was not as "wide and deep and ancient" as was commonly supposed.[88] A complicated history that "is particular to England"[89] and has nothing to do with Lombardy,[90] Maitland added, explains why people stopped referring to seisin of goods.

After praising and indicating his agreement with Maitland's treatment of seisin, Ames similarly used original historical sources to extend Maitland's conclusions to disseisin. Ames acknowledged that the term "disseisin" was typically used in connection with land. A disseisor of land, Ames wrote, is someone who has wrongfully ousted the owner of land and who gains by this tort an estate in fee simple.[91] The disseised owner retains a right of action and a right of entry. But "as long as the disseisin continues, the disseised owner is deprived of the two characteristic features of property, – he has neither the present enjoyment nor the power of alienation."[92] In contrast to Maitland, who found numerous allusions to seisin of chattels, Ames acknowledged that he had found only three references to disseisin of chattels,[93] though Bigelow soon wrote to Ames citing additional examples in *Placita*.[94] These three examples, however, were sufficient to convince him that disseisin applied to chattels as well as land, that a strong analogy existed "between the tortious taking of chattels and the wrongful ouster from land."[95] As to chattels as well as land, the wrongdoing of the disseisor deprived the disseisee of rights to his property. Indeed, Ames observed, the disseisor of chattels gained more rights than the disseisor of land because the disseisee of chattels, unlike the disseisee of land, had no right of action to recover his property. The disseisee of chattels, though the victim of a tort, suffered a total loss and had no legal interest in what subsequently became of his chattels.[96] Following Maitland's conclusion about seisin, Ames maintained that "the doctrine of disseisin belongs not to feudalism alone, but to the general law of property." He ended his article by indicating that in subsequent work he would attempt to show that the law of disseisin "is not a mere episode in English legal history, but that it is a living principle, founded in the nature of things, and of great practical value in the solution of many important questions."[97]

Maitland read Ames's article "Disseisin of Chattels" with great interest and responded to him at length. Maitland and Ames had already begun an extensive

[88] Id. at 324–5.
[89] Id. at 337.
[90] Id. at 338.
[91] Ames, supra note 84, at 172.
[92] Id. at 174.
[93] Id. at 172.
[94] Letter from Melville M. Bigelow to James Barr Ames (April 20, 1889) (Ames Papers, supra note 19, Box 1, Folder 5).
[95] Ames, supra note 84, at 174; see also id. at 190–1.
[96] Id. at 179–80.
[97] Id. at 191.

exchange of correspondence, apparently initiated by some critical notes Ames wrote on Maitland's edition of *Bracton's Note Book*. Thayer sent these notes to Maitland,[98] and Maitland wrote back to Ames expressing gratitude for his "criticisms, which are very just." Maitland added "a few notes in return," which elaborated his views and attempted to clear up possible misunderstandings of them by Ames.[99] Ames then responded to Maitland in a letter that apologized for his delay by explaining that he had wanted to consult his "History of Tort and Contract" lectures, which he had lent to Holmes. After thanking Maitland for clearing up his "misapprehension" that Maitland "countenanced" some "altogether erroneous" theories of Holmes about "the introduction of 'uses' into our law," Ames commented at length on Maitland's article on seisin.[100] As the correspondence continued about the details of early English law, Maitland expressed disappointment that he could not interest his students in the field. "I very much wish that I could train up a few Cambridge men to use the Record Office," he wrote Ames, "but they all believe that they are going to succeed at the Bar."[101] Becoming increasingly close through their correspondence, Ames and Maitland exchanged invitations to visit in person,[102] though neither apparently did so.

As soon as Ames informed Maitland that he had written an article on the disseisin of chattels, Maitland expressed his eagerness to read it.[103] Soon after it was published, Maitland wrote to Ames that it gave him "real pleasure." Maitland reported that he had been familiar with many of the sources Ames cited and that his mind had been "flickering round" the subject of disseisin, but that he had "not had the courage to write about it." Praising Ames for arraying the authorities "in so solid a phalanx," Maitland told him that he easily accepted many of his conclusions. But Maitland added that he had difficulty agreeing with some conclusions to which the Year Books seemed to lead, particularly the view that the owner of chattels lost all rights to recovering them. "I must confess," he wrote to Ames, "that the evidence known to me is in your favour." Nevertheless, he added, "I cannot bring myself to believe that all this is the natural outcome of the English substantive law, that it truly expresses the notion that our ancestors had of the ownership of goods."[104]

---

[98] Letter from James Bradley Thayer to Frederic Maitland (March 20, 1887) (Frederic William Maitland Papers, Cambridge University Library, add 7006).

[99] Letter from Frederic Maitland to James Barr Ames (January 30, 1888), in Hazeltine, supra note 1, at 4.

[100] Letter from James Barr Ames to Frederic Maitland (March 24, 1888) (Frederic William Maitland Papers, supra note 98).

[101] Letter from Frederic Maitland to James Barr Ames (May 6, 1888), in Hazeltine, supra note 1, at 5, 6.

[102] Letter from Frederic Maitland to James Barr Ames (May 3, 1889), in Hazeltine, supra note 1, at 9, 11; letter from James Barr Ames to Frederic Maitland (November 27, 1889), in Hazeltine, supra note 1, at 11, 14.

[103] Letter from Frederic Maitland to James Barr Ames (October 14, 1888), in Hazeltine, supra note 1, at 8.

[104] Letter from Maitland to Ames, supra note 102, at 9.

As Maitland starkly asked in another letter, "In what sense can a thief have property?"[105]

Maitland then suggested a possible reason why his intuition, in spite of the evidence of the Year Books, might be correct. Stressing how few cases dealt with disseisin of chattels, he suggested that most cases involving the recovery of stolen goods were heard in the local courts, rather than in the king's courts, the courts whose results the Year Books reported. "I can't help thinking," Maitland wrote to Ames, "that the law of the King's courts is only a part of the law, and that the lawyers in those courts, having to do only with the remedies there given, get into a way of speaking about 'property' which really is misleading." The difficulty in recovering stolen goods in the king's courts, Maitland added, depended more on the king's interest in obtaining them through forfeiture than on any legal rules. Citing the king's power, Maitland observed that "it was ill arguing with a King." He asked Ames to respond to his theory. Is the disseisin of chattels described in Ames's "excellent paper," Maitland wondered, "the natural outcome of very ancient ideas of 'property,'" as Ames had indicated at the end of his article, "or is it due to the fact that our King's courts begin by administering only a part of the law, which part, however, is in course of time regarded and indeed actually becomes, the whole, owing to the decadence of the local tribunals."[106] Perhaps influenced by Maitland's letter, in his two subsequent related articles Ames did not reiterate the distinction in "Disseisin of Chattels" between disseisin of land and disseisin of chattels. Indeed, in contrast to his conclusion in "Disseisin of Chattels" that the disseisor of chattels has "absolute property in the chattel taken,"[107] his next article, "The Nature of Ownership," asserted that in a disseisin "no one could be said to be the full owner."[108]

After publishing his companion articles, Ames replied to Maitland's letter about "Disseisin of Chattels." He claimed that he had not intended to leave the impression that the owner of chattels lost all rights to recover them,[109] though his article clearly did so, particularly in emphasizing that the disseisee of chattels was in a worse position than the disseisee of land and had no legal interest in what became of his goods after they were wrongfully taken from him.[110] Maitland graciously accepted Ames's clarification,[111] even writing that "I am very glad to find that I was stupid enough to misunderstand your view, and that I can make my submission." Maitland added that his work on the book that became *The History of English Law* would prevent him from further study of the subject for what he feared would be a long time.[112]

---

[105] Letter from Maitland to Ames, supra note 103.

[106] Letter from Maitland to Ames, supra note 102, at 10.

[107] Ames, supra note 84, at 179.

[108] James Barr Ames, The Nature of Ownership, in Ames, supra note 5, pp. 192, 193.

[109] Letter from Ames to Maitland, supra note 102.

[110] Ames, supra note 84, at 179.

[111] Letter from Frederic Maitland to James Barr Ames (March 23, 1890), in Hazeltine, supra note 1, at 15, 16.

[112] Id. at 17.

Yet Maitland did return to the subject of movable goods in the second volume of *The History of English Law*. Rather than the "submission" of his letter, his text reiterated his original reservations about Ames's conclusions and elaborated his alternative explanation. As in his correspondence with Ames, Maitland observed that much of the litigation over chattels took place in local courts, which kept no written records or whose records had been lost or remained unpublished.[113] Yet from a variety of sources, primarily Bracton and Glanvill, Maitland concluded that the substantive law of thirteenth-century England allowed stolen goods to be recovered "not only from the hands of the thief, but from the hands of the third, the fourth, the twentieth possessor, even though those hands are clean and there has been a purchase in open market."[114] In a discussion that Maitland noted "had in view" Ames's work on the disseisin of chattels,[115] Maitland traced how procedural changes in the king's courts, largely involving the development of the writ of trespass, produced what he called the "lamentable result" that limited the rights of persons disseised of chattels to recover them from third parties.[116] Maitland also wrote, as he had suggested in his earlier letter, that people ascribed property in stolen goods to a thief because "the king has acquired a habit of taking them and refusing to give them up."[117]

Though Maitland referred to Ames as a "learned author" whose articles on disseisin of chattels were "masterly," he criticized him for failing to provide a sufficient explanation of his own observation that the disseisee of land had an action against a "third hand" but the disseisee of chattels did not. In contrast to Ames, Maitland maintained that "this difference can not be regarded as being of vast antiquity or as having its origin among the ideas of substantive law." After all, he reiterated, in the thirteenth century the disseisee of chattels "had an action against the twentieth hand." Whether or not his argument about the development of trespass was accepted as the explanation for the loss of this action, its existence in the thirteenth century convinced Maitland that the relatively weak position of the disseisee of chattels did not derive from a "defective conception of ownership," but from "an unfortunate accident." Maitland thus directly contradicted Ames, who had stressed that disseisin "was not an accident of English legal history, but a rule of universal law" that should be applied in the present.[118] This "unfortunate accident," Maitland added, "has momentous effects because it happens just at the time when the writs are crystallizing for good and all. The old action disappears; a new one is put in its place, but can not fill that place."[119] The entire episode provided evidence for

---

[113] Pollock and Maitland, supra note 26, at 150.
[114] Id. at 165.
[115] Id. at 168 n. 2.
[116] Id. at 167–8.
[117] Id. at 166.
[118] Ames, supra note 12, at 218.
[119] Pollock and Maitland, supra note 26, at 168 n. 2.

Maitland's more general point that "it is only through procedural forms that we can penetrate to substantive rights."[120]

In his articles on the history of the common law that engaged Holmes and Maitland, Ames displayed his characteristically close attention to the technical evolution of legal doctrine. His interactions with Holmes, Thayer, Pollock, and Maitland illustrate the shared transatlantic commitment to original research in the history of English law. The historical investigations begun by Adams and his students extended through the end of the nineteenth century. As English scholars gracefully recognized, Americans undertook more of this research than the English themselves. This shared transatlantic project culminated in England with the prodigious scholarship of Frederic Maitland. In his own work, Maitland generously acknowledged his substantial reliance on the previous contributions of Bigelow, Holmes, Thayer, and Ames.

[120] Id. at 160.

X

The History of American Constitutional Law

Reflecting their primary interest in the origins of Anglo-American law, late nineteenth-century American legal scholars wrote much more about the early history of English law than about the legal history of the United States. Their treatment of American legal history mostly appeared in casebooks that illustrated the historical development of their subjects in the United States as well as in England. In contrast to Bigelow's *History of Procedure in England*, Holmes's *The Common Law*, and Thayer's *A Preliminary Treatise on Evidence at the Common Law*, no American scholar wrote a major book on American constitutional history. Indeed, only Thayer wrote articles about American constitutional history comparable in scope to the *Essays in Anglo-Saxon Law* by Adams and his students or the articles by Ames on the history of various common law subjects. Although Thayer relied on and cited Cooley's earlier work in constitutional law, scholarship in constitutional history did not produce anything like the transatlantic collaborative inquiry into shared questions about the history of the English common law.

Yet several late nineteenth-century American legal scholars wrote about the history of American constitutional law in revealing detail. I examine outstanding examples in this chapter to demonstrate how much their study of American constitutional history resembled their substantially more extensive work on early English legal history. They used evolutionary theories of historical origins and development to understand and, on occasion, to suggest revisions of existing constitutional law. They maintained that history often reveals the original intent or underlying purpose of a constitutional doctrine. They also observed that constitutional law, often in response to popular demands produced by changing times, becomes transformed over time, sometimes into doctrines that are logically inconsistent with, or even diametrically opposed to, the ones they replaced. In addition to detecting the same historical phenomena exhibited by the history of the English common law, they stressed the historical context of distinctive features of American constitutional law. Most significantly, they identified popular sovereignty as the constitutional embodiment of the American victory in the Revolutionary War and viewed it as a key to constitutional interpretation. Although they occasionally addressed the constitutional ramifications of the Civil War and Reconstruction, as the correspondence between Holmes and Pomeroy and their related articles illustrate, these major recent developments did not provoke extended scholarly discussion or seem to alter the approach to the historical analysis of law they adapted from their European predecessors. Indeed, they cited the expansion of the war power to destroy slavery during the Civil War, the abolition of slavery by the Thirteenth Amendment, and limits on the meaning of citizenship in the Fourteenth Amendment as examples of the general theme that evolving custom is the source of law.

In both his scholarship and his teaching, Thayer focused on constitutional law and evidence. His work in constitutional law, like his work on evidence, reflected the historical approach to legal understanding he advocated in his address "The Teaching of English Law in Universities." The preface to his casebook on constitutional law announced that it would use "what scientific men call the *genetic* method of study, which allows one to see the topic grow and develop under his eye."[1] Through this method, whose application to legal study he generously attributed to Langdell,[2] Thayer hoped "to promote a deeper, more systematic, and exacter study of this most interesting and important subject, too much neglected by the profession." He stressed that constitutional law, while a technical subject of law composed of principles and rules applied by courts to decide litigated cases, is also "allied not merely with history, but with statecraft, and with the political problems of our great and complex national life."[3] As a result of these complicated relationships, legal doctrines that once seemed adequate "melt away in the light of later experience," often gradually and "almost unperceived," as "other doctrines take their place." The "orderly tracing" of the history of case law, Thayer concluded, best reveals to the student "the nature of this process, the large scope of the questions presented, and the true limitations of the legal principles that govern them."[4]

Intriguingly, Thayer intended to write a book on constitutional law analogous to his *Preliminary Treatise on Evidence*. According to his son, Ezra Ripley Thayer, he had collected much of the material for this book, which remained unpublished at his death. Ezra Ripley Thayer, himself a professor and dean at Harvard Law School, felt that it "would be little short of desecration" for someone else "to shape" this material for posthumous publication, given his father's high standards and ceaseless revision of his work. Yet Thayer's essays on constitutional law, his son added, contained much of the material that he would have incorporated into the unpublished book.[5] In these essays, as well

---

[1] James Bradley Thayer, Cases on Constitutional Law (Cambridge, Mass.: Charles W. Sever and Company, 1895), vol. I, p. v.

[2] Id. at vi.

[3] Id. at v.

[4] Id. at vi.

[5] Ezra Ripley Thayer, Prefatory Note, James Bradley Thayer, Legal Essays (Boston: The Boston Book Company, 1908), p. v.

as in his biographical sketch of Chief Justice Marshall, Thayer applied his historical approach to constitutional law.

Although Thayer's essays are the most extensive historical treatments of American constitutional law, other late nineteenth-century American scholars examined its history. Responding to a request from Lord Acton, Bigelow contributed a lengthy essay to the volume on the United States in the multi-volume *Cambridge Modern History*, planned by Acton and published after his death.[6] Acton described the project as "the universal modern history which this university is preparing" and wrote that they were trying to get "the most competent men we can find, and are especially anxious that the American volume shall be the work of Americans."[7] Bigelow's essay focused on the history of the Constitutional Convention and the structure of the new Constitution. In addition, late nineteenth-century treatises on constitutional law, though mostly concerned with the description and analysis of constitutional doctrine, included some discussions of constitutional history.

In this chapter, I rely on three examples, chosen for their quality and detail, to convey late nineteenth-century American original scholarship on the history of constitutional law. Thayer's classic essay, "The Origin and Scope of the American Doctrine of Constitutional Law," first published in the *Harvard Law Review* and later included in his posthumous *Legal Essays*, frequently invoked history as a central part of its analysis. Cooley's chapter "Liberty of Speech and of the Press" in his enormously influential treatise *Constitutional Limitations* contained perhaps the most extensive historical treatment of any American constitutional treatise and harnessed it to constitutional interpretation. And Tiedeman's chapter "The Inviolability of Corporate Charters and of Charter Rights" in his book *The Unwritten Constitution of the United States* provided a detailed example of his general theory of evolutionary legal change in the context of the constitutional prohibition against the impairment of contracts.

Thayer on Judicial Power to Declare Legislation Unconstitutional

In "The Origin and Scope of the American Doctrine of Constitutional Law," as in his *Preliminary Treatise on Evidence*, Thayer used historical reconstruction to analyze current legal issues. "How," he began his article by asking, "did our American doctrine, which allows to the judiciary the power to declare legislative Acts unconstitutional, and to treat them as null, come about, and what is the true scope of it?"[8] The combination of a written constitution and

---

[6] Melville M. Bigelow, The Constitution (1776–1789), in The Cambridge Modern History: The United States (New York: The MacMillan Company, 1903) (A. W. Ward et al. eds.), vol. 7, pp. 235–304.

[7] Letter from Lord Acton to Melville Madison Bigelow (June 11, 1897) (Bigelow Collection, Howard Gotlieb Archival Research Center, Boston University, Bigelow Collection, Box 2, Acton Folder).

[8] James Bradley Thayer, The Origin and Scope of the American Doctrine of Constitutional Law, 7 Harv. L. Rev. 129 (1893), reprinted in Thayer, Legal Essays, supra note 5, p. 1.

of judges sworn to uphold it, he maintained, cannot, in itself, explain this judicial power. He pointed out that in other countries with written constitutions, including France, Germany, and Switzerland, judges had no such power.[9] The answer to his opening question, he declared, was historical, not structural. The judicial power to declare legislation unconstitutional grew out of the political experience of the American colonies. The charters from the English Crown that governed the colonies were essentially written constitutions. These charters contained restraints on colonial legislatures that were enforced by various means in England, including revocation of the charter, acts of Parliament, annulment of legislation by the Crown, and judicial proceedings. Just as the English courts disregarded as null acts by colonial legislatures that violated the charters, colonial courts assumed this power for themselves.[10]

The continuation of this practice of judicial review after the American Revolution, Thayer believed, was natural but not inevitable. Just as he emphasized historical contingency while connecting the development of the jury with the emerging law of evidence, he pointed out that the American Revolution fundamentally transformed theories of government in ways that challenged existing justifications for judicial review and jeopardized its future. Under the colonial structure of government, the superior authority of English institutions, including courts, to enforce the written charters was axiomatic and fully recognized. Enforcement of the written charters by the colonial courts seemed a natural extension of this superior authority.[11] The American Revolution, Thayer stressed, replaced the external sovereign in Great Britain with the American people, who "took his place" and became "their own sovereign." The new state constitutions and the federal constitution were not external orders from a new government, but "precepts from the people themselves" addressed to themselves and to the officials in the new structures the constitutions created. "The sovereign himself," as Thayer put it, "having written these expressions of his will, had retired into the clouds; in any regular course of events he had no organ to enforce his will, except those to whom his orders were addressed in these documents."[12]

But what if these orders were not followed? How, then, could the written constitutions be enforced? These questions, Thayer stressed, arose out of the new conditions produced by the American Revolution and could not be answered by pre-Revolutionary colonial theories based on the existence of an external sovereign.[13] Nor did the new written constitutions contain provisions that answered them. Members of the federal Constitutional Convention, Thayer noted, debated whether or not judges would have the power to declare

[9] Id. at 2.

[10] Id. at 3. Christopher G. Tiedeman, The Unwritten Constitution of the United States (Buffalo, N.Y.: William S. Hein & Company, Inc. reprint ed. 1974) (original ed. 1890), pp. 38–40, takes a similar position.

[11] Thayer, supra note 8, at 3.

[12] Id. at 4.

[13] Id.

laws unconstitutional and decided to leave this important issue unresolved. Like other contentious questions debated at the convention, he concluded, "it was left in order not to stir up enemies to the new instrument; left to be settled by the silent determinations of time, or by later discussion."[14] As a result, the Constitution did not clarify how its provisions should be enforced against violations by the agencies it created.

Ultimately, the prior colonial practice of judicial review continued under the new structure based on popular sovereignty. But Thayer stressed that the continuation of judicial review was hotly contested in the decades following the American Revolution and the ratification of the United States Constitution. Just as some members of the Constitutional Convention denied that the new Constitution authorized judicial review, some state legislatures and courts assumed that independence simply substituted the American legislature for the British Parliament and thereby invested the legislature with the same supremacy that Parliament enjoyed in England. Several state courts declared that they could not invalidate legislation, and at the end of the first decade of the nineteenth century the Ohio legislature impeached judges for declaring some of its legislation void. Opponents of judicial review argued that it was "anti-republican" and threatened liberty and property.[15] Yet most American jurisdictions followed the colonial practice of allowing courts to nullify legislation and, apparently by the second or third decade of the nineteenth century, the power of judges to declare legislation unconstitutional became accepted in all American jurisdictions.[16] Thayer speculated that the prevalence of theories of natural law, which viewed legislation contrary to natural law as unenforceable, assisted the acceptance of judicial review.[17]

Even when judicial review became widely accepted, Thayer emphasized, its scope was extremely limited. Courts did not even consider the constitutionality of legislation unless someone brought a lawsuit challenging a particular exercise of legislative power. Efforts to provide a judicial role in reviewing and, if necessary, revising laws before they could take effect, as occurs in some countries and as a few American states briefly adopted in the first decades after independence, were overwhelmingly rejected in the United States. Thus, even a law with revolutionary implications remains safe from judicial scrutiny unless an individual decides it is in his personal interest to have a judicial determination of its validity. Litigation, Thayer also pointed out, often occurs only decades after important and constitutionally controversial legislation has already had its intended effect. The constitutionality of legislation chartering a bank of the United States, for example, divided the cabinet of President Washington and continued to divide political parties for more than a generation. Yet the first bank charter of 1791 was not challenged in court until after

---

[14] Id. at 5 n. 3.
[15] Id. at 5–7.
[16] Id. at 4, 7–8.
[17] Id. at 6.

it was renewed in 1816. During this long period, other branches of government determined its constitutionality.[18] This "incidental and postponed" power of the judiciary convinced Thayer that the people did not intend judges to be the main safeguard against unconstitutional legislation.[19] In the debates over the Constitution, he noted, the role of the judiciary played a relatively small role in efforts to limit the power of the new government to oppress the people. The most important protections against government power addressed in the debates were widespread suffrage, short terms of elective office, a Congress containing both a Senate and a House of Representatives, and the executive veto, not judicial review of the constitutionality of legislation.[20] "As the opportunity of the judges to check and correct unconstitutional Acts is so limited," Thayer concluded, "it may help us to understand why the extent of their control, when they do have the opportunity, should also be narrow."[21]

Having examined the origins of judicial review of the constitutionality of legislation and its function in the system of government established by the Constitution, Thayer proceeded to examine the history of its judicial interpretation. He believed that many early decisions upheld judicial review too easily, without confronting the difficult and distinctive issues posed by constitutional analysis. He protested that too many decisions simply asserted that interpreting the constitutionality of legislation did not differ in any significant respect from other cases in which judges have to interpret potential conflicts between written documents. The reasoning of the judges read "as smoothly as if the constitution were a private letter of attorney, and the court's duty under it were precisely like any of its most ordinary operations."[22] Thayer included Chief Justice Marshall's famous opinion in *Marbury v. Madison* among these disappointing decisions. He regretted that Marshall's "short and dry treatment" of judicial review of the constitutionality of legislation, in contrast with the brilliance of his greatest opinions, treated the subject "as being one of no real difficulty." Marshall did not even address any of the many powerful arguments against judicial review.[23]

Fortunately, however, other judges did address the more complicated issues posed by judicial review and developed what Thayer called "a very significant rule of administration" that supplemented these disappointing decisions. He claimed that this "rule of administration" had become widely recognized by 1811, when Chief Justice Tilghman of the Pennsylvania Supreme Court effectively formulated it. The judicial power to declare legislation void, Tilghman declared while refusing to exercise it, should only be invoked if "the violation of the constitution is so manifest as to leave no room for reasonable doubt."[24]

---

[18] Id. at 9–11.
[19] Id. at 11.
[20] Id. at 11 n. 2.
[21] Id. at 11–12.
[22] Id. at 15.
[23] Id. at 15–16 n. 1.
[24] Id. at 17.

After quoting similar judicial statements both before and after Tilghman's decision,[25] Thayer stressed that these "early, constant, and emphatic"[26] reiterations demonstrated that they were "something more than a mere form of language, a mere expression of courtesy and deference," but a true "rule of administration."[27] Even more telling, Thayer added, courts adhered to this rule in the face of contrary arguments by some of the most eminent lawyers in some of the most important litigation of the early nineteenth century. For example, Daniel Webster unsuccessfully argued in the *Charles River Bridge* case that judges should take a more active role in reviewing the constitutionality of legislation.[28] "A rule thus powerfully attacked and thus explicitly maintained," Thayer concluded, "must be treated as having been deliberately meant, both as regards its substance and its form."[29]

Following his own advice that historical reconstruction should assist the restatement of law, Thayer frequently rephrased this "rule of administration" in his own words. Toward the end of his article, Thayer emphasized that he was "not stating a new doctrine, but attempting to restate more exactly and truly an admitted one."[30] Indeed, throughout his article he cited Cooley's *Constitutional Limitations* as well as prior judicial decisions to support his own views.[31] For example, after stating that the Constitution is subject to multiple plausible interpretations and that judges should therefore uphold the constitutionality of any legislation that is rational, Thayer invoked Cooley's assertion that judges should vote to sustain legislation they would have opposed had they been legislators.[32] Thayer clearly hoped his restatement would influence judges in his own day. "If what I have said be sound," he urged, "it is greatly to be desired that it should be more emphasized by our courts, in its full significance." He cited with approval the observation by others that legislatures in countries without a written constitution had afforded more protection to "private rights" than had legislatures in the United States.[33] Part of the explanation for this difference, Thayer believed, lay in excessive judicial review of the constitutionality of legislation in the United States. American legislatures felt little responsibility for determining the constitutionality of their own legislation because they relied on the courts to determine when legislation exceeded constitutional limits. Excessive reliance on judicial review, moreover, encouraged popular quiescence as well as legislative irresponsibility. "Under no system," Thayer maintained, "can the power of courts go far to save a people from ruin." He believed that the people themselves, not the courts, must be the primary guard against the

---

[25] Id. at 17–19.
[26] Id. at 22.
[27] Id. at 21.
[28] Id. at 23–5.
[29] Id. at 25.
[30] Id. at 38.
[31] Id. at 7 n. 4, 22 and 22 n. 1, 27 n. 4.
[32] Id. at 22 and n. 1.
[33] Id. at 38.

abuse of legislative power by their representatives.[34] Thayer's support of the "rule of administration" he highlighted and restated thus seemed historically grounded in the new theory of popular sovereignty that he identified as emerging from the aftermath of the American Revolution.

In an excerpt from his biographical sketch of Chief Justice Marshall, appended as a long footnote at the end of his article, Thayer elaborated his current worry about the "vast and growing increase of judicial interference with legislation" by declaring it unconstitutional. This situation, he emphasized, constituted "a very different state of things from what our fathers contemplated, a century and more ago, in framing the new system." Acknowledging the value of a properly limited judicial power to review the constitutionality of legislation, Thayer observed that its exercise, "even when unavoidable, is always attended with a serious evil." The evil is that "the correction of legislative mistakes comes from the outside, and the people thus lose the political experience, and the moral education and stimulus that come from fighting the question out in the ordinary way, and correcting their own errors."[35] Thayer was glad that the Supreme Court had upheld legislation that many people considered unconstitutional, such as the national banking law passed during the Civil War and the Granger legislation of the 1870s, which had regulated the rates charged by railroads, warehouses, and grain elevators.[36] Had the Court held this legislation unconstitutional, he acknowledged, the country "should have been saved some trouble and some harm." But he believed that "the good that came to the country and its people from the vigorous thinking that had to be done in the political debates that followed, from the infiltration through every part of the population of sound ideas and sentiments, from the rousing into activity of opposite elements, the enlargement of ideas, the strengthening of moral fibre, and the growth of political experience that came out of it all, – that all this far more than outweighed any evil which ever flowed from the refusal of the court to interfere with the work of the legislature."[37] Exercising the judicial power to declare legislation unconstitutional "should be a solemn, unusual, and painful act." The judiciary "cannot rightly attempt to protect the people, by undertaking a function not its own."[38]

In this article on constitutional law, as in his book on evidence, Thayer used historical analysis to suggest reforms of current law. But he reached different conclusions about the value of past law. Much of the current law of evidence, Thayer concluded, was inadequate because rules that made sense in the past had become dysfunctional survivals in the transformed conditions of the present. With respect to judicial review of the constitutionality of legislation, on

[34] Id. at 39.

[35] Id. at 40 n. 1.

[36] Id. at 40. For background on the Granger and legal tender cases, see Lawrence M. Friedman, A History of American Law (New York: Simon & Schuster, 1973), pp. 386, 391–2.

[37] Thayer, supra note 8, at 41 n. 1.

[38] Id. at 41.

the other hand, Thayer believed that the theory and practice of the early republic should be revived in the face of changes that deviated from the commitment to popular sovereignty at the core of American democracy. Thayer believed that history could teach lessons, but the lesson was not always the same.

Cooley on Freedom of Speech and Press

Cooley's chapter on "liberty of speech and of the press" in *Constitutional Limitations* in many respects resembled Thayer's essay "The Origin and Scope of the American Doctrine of Constitutional Law." He viewed constitutional law as evolving in response to changing historical circumstances. He used historical reconstruction as the basis for evaluating existing constitutional law. And he stressed the popular sovereignty that emerged with the new American structure of government following the Revolutionary War as the touchstone of constitutional analysis.

Cooley reasoned that the purpose of the American constitutional guarantees of free speech and a free press is best derived from the prior history of the repression of opinion in England and the American colonies.[39] Under the traditional common law, he observed, "liberty of the press was neither well protected nor well defined."[40] Throughout most of English history, the common law viewed publications by private persons as potential threats to public order. The government used censors to determine whether or not a book could be published, and publication of any book without the approval of the censors was criminal. Even after the English revolution of 1688, the government engaged in "cruel and relentless" prosecution of many books that would seem harmless to subsequent generations. The press was not allowed to publish news about current affairs that the government wanted concealed, and people who criticized public officials about their official performance were often punished for contempt and for disrupting good order. Parliament did not publish a record of its debates and punished unofficial publications about them.[41]

The treatment of the press in the American colonies was at least as restrictive as in England. For decades, the colonial laws themselves were not published, and in 1682 a printer in Virginia was arrested for publishing the laws passed in the most recent legislative session. Authorities frequently burned books on political and religious subjects as threats to good order. Even the Constitutional Convention of 1787 met behind closed doors, its members pledged to secrecy. The first open debate in the Senate did not take place until 1793.[42]

---

[39] Thomas M. Cooley, A Treatise on the Constitutional Limitations which Rest upon the Legislative Powers of the States of the American Union (Boston: Little, Brown, and Company, 1868), p. 422.

[40] Id. at 417.

[41] Id. at 417–18.

[42] Id. at 418–20.

Based on this history, Cooley asserted that protection for freedom of expression had arisen relatively recently. Many commentators in England and the United States, he acknowledged, understood liberty of the press simply as the abolition of government censorship, the ability to publish without the permission of the state. He referred to Blackstone's *Commentaries* as a standard statement of this view. "The liberty of the press," Blackstone wrote in the section cited by Cooley, "consists in no *previous* restraints upon publications, and not in freedom from censure for criminal matter when published."[43] Elaborating this statement, Blackstone added:

To subject the press to the restrictive power of a licenser, as was formerly done, both before and since the revolution [of 1688], is to subject all freedom of sentiment to the prejudices of one man, and to make him the arbitrary and infallible judge of all controverted points in learning, religion, and government. But to punish (as the law now does) any dangerous and offensive writings, which, when published, shall on a fair and impartial trial be adjudged of a pernicious tendency, is necessary for the preservation of peace and good order, of government and religion, the only solid foundations of civil liberty."[44]

Cooley recognized that leading American authorities on constitutional law, including Story and Kent, had interpreted the guarantees of free speech and a free press in the First Amendment and in analogous provisions of state constitutions as merely incorporating Blackstone's view of the English common law.[45]

Cooley, however, considered this definition of liberty of the press insufficient, particularly in light of American conceptions of popular sovereignty. He conceded that "liberty of speech and of the press does not imply complete exemption from responsibility for everything a citizen may say or publish." Yet "the mere exemption from previous restraints," he reasoned, "cannot be all that is secured by the constitutional provisions." If public authorities could punish people for "harmless publications," then "liberty of the press might be rendered a mockery and a delusion."[46]

In determining the line between protected and unprotected speech, Cooley stressed that the effective exercise of popular sovereignty depends on freedom of expression. The constitutional guarantees of free speech and a free press, he asserted, were intended "to protect parties in the free publication of matters of public concern, to secure their right to free discussion of public events and public measures, and to enable every citizen at any time to bring the government and any person in authority to the bar of public opinion by any just criticism upon their conduct in the exercise of the authority which the people have conferred upon them."[47] The evils that the constitutional guarantees guarded against "were not the censorship of the press merely, but any action of the

---

[43] Blackstone's Commentaries, vol. 4, p. 151.
[44] Id. at 152.
[45] Cooley, supra note 39, at 420.
[46] Id. at 421.
[47] Id. at 421–2.

government by means of which it might prevent such free and general discussion of public matters as seems absolutely essential to prepare the people for an intelligent exercise of their rights as citizens." Against this background of the centrality of freedom of expression to the operation of a system of government based on popular sovereignty, Cooley maintained that the constitutional liberty of speech and of the press "implies a right to freely utter and publish whatever the citizen may please, and to be protected against any responsibility for the publication, except so far as such publications, from their blasphemy, obscenity, or scandalous character, may be a public offence, or as by their falsehood and malice they may injuriously affect the private character of individuals."[48]

Cooley elaborated his understanding of the constitutional protections for free speech and a free press in the context of discussing common law rules affecting expression. Unfortunately, Cooley was unclear, and occasionally even inconsistent, in his treatment of the relationship between the common law and the constitutional guarantees. At times, he simply equated the constitutional guarantees with the common law in effect when they were adopted. At the beginning of his chapter, he asserted that the constitutional guarantees "do not create new rights, but their purpose is to protect the citizen in the enjoyment of those already possessed. We are at once, therefore, turned back from these provisions to the common law, in order that we may ascertain what the rights are which are thus protected, and what is the extent of the privileges they assure."[49] Immediately after setting forth his own broad definition of the constitutional guarantees as protecting all expression except blasphemy, obscenity, scandal, and malicious falsehoods that injure private character, he reiterated that for more specific standards "we must look to the common-law rules which were in force" when these guarantees were established.[50] Consistent with his criticism of Story and Kent for limiting the constitutional guarantees to Blackstone's definition of the English common law, Cooley maintained that the "English common-law rule, which made libels on the constitution or the government indictable, as it was administered by the courts, seems to us unsuited to the condition and circumstances of the people in America, and therefore to have never been adopted in the several States."[51] Yet Cooley also objected to the prior and existing common law in various American states regarding criticism of public officials and liability of the press. He maintained that this common law did not sufficiently protect expression about matters of public concern.

For example, in discussing the American common law of "libels upon the government," Cooley reluctantly acknowledged that "the common-law rules on this subject were administered in many cases with great harshness, and quite beyond any reasonable construction which those rules would bear." He particularly criticized the Sedition Act of 1798, under which opponents of the

[48] Id. at 422.
[49] Id. at 416–17.
[50] Id. at 422.
[51] Id. at 429.

policies of President John Adams were fined and jailed for "false, scandalous, and malicious" statements or publications against the government or government officials. Cooley provided a historical explanation for the Sedition Act. It was enacted "when the fabric of government was still new and untried, and when many men seemed to think that the breath of heated party discussions might tumble it about their heads."[52] Pointing out that many disputed the constitutionality of the Sedition Act at the time, Cooley added that it was certainly misguided. In practice, the Sedition Act increased the very criticism of government it was intended to prevent, and it played a key role in destroying the Federalist Party, which had been responsible for its enactment and enforcement. According to Cooley, "it is impossible to conceive, at the present time, of any such state of things as would be likely to bring about its re-enactment, or the passage of any similar repressive statute."[53]

Although Cooley never explicitly asserted that the Sedition Act and similar common law rules were unconstitutional, he applied the themes of his constitutional analysis in discussing them. Presenting his own views on the subject of "libels upon the government," Cooley repeatedly invoked popular sovereignty as the justification for narrowly limiting this offense. "When it is among the fundamental principles of the government that the people frame their own constitution," he asserted, "and that in doing so they reserve to themselves the power to amend it from time to time, as the public sentiment may change, it is difficult to conceive any sound basis on which prosecutions for libel on the system of government can be based, except when their evident intent and purpose is to excite rebellion and civil war."[54] "Repression of full and free discussion," he added, "is dangerous in any government resting upon the will of the people."[55] He stressed that this reasoning should apply with greatest force to "those classes who, not being admitted to a share in the government, attacked the constitution in the point which excluded them."[56] The protected expression of the excluded classes, he believed, should correspond to the intensity of the wrongs they felt. If their mode of expression seems extreme to others, "the consolation must be, that the evil likely to spring from the violent discussion will probably be less, and its correction by public sentiment more speedy, than if the terrors of the law were brought to bear to prevent the discussion."[57]

Despite their thematic similarities, Cooley did not directly attach this forceful defense of expression that criticizes the government to his interpretation of the First Amendment and analogous guarantees in state constitutions based on American conceptions of popular sovereignty. Instead, he skirted constitutional analysis by asserting, despite the Sedition Act and other evidence

[52] Id. at 427.
[53] Id. at 428.
[54] Id.
[55] Id. at 429.
[56] Id. at 428.
[57] Id. at 429.

to the contrary, that the early common law in the United States, unlike the English common law, allowed such criticism, "however sharp, unreasonable, and intemperate it might be."[58] This unconvincing assertion allowed Cooley to adhere to his position that the constitutional provisions reflected the American, though not the more restrictive English, common law of the time. In discussing the specific application of the constitutional provisions to the common law, he simply maintained that the common law of libel and slander could be modified, but only to the extent that the changes conformed to the justifications for liability at the time the constitutions were framed and ratified.[59] "The constitutional freedom of speech and of the press," he concluded, "must be as broad as existed when the constitution which guarantees it was adopted."[60]

Pursuing his general emphasis on the importance of protecting expression on matters of public concern, Cooley also urged expanded protection at common law for "criticism upon officers and candidates for office" and for "publication of privileged communications through the press." He criticized the common law of New York for refusing to recognize any exceptions to the presumption of malice from false statements about people.[61] The application of this rule to criticism of public officials and candidates for office, Cooley believed, did not provide sufficient protection for free speech about public affairs. A privilege for such criticism, he emphasized, did not require absolute immunity for false statements.[62] A better rule, suggested by one judge, would distinguish between public and private conduct and limit the privilege to the public conduct of public officials and candidates.[63] But Cooley observed that even this broader protection remained overly narrow, reasoning that private conduct may reveal character traits relevant to the assessment of qualifications for public office. Instead, he advocated a privilege for false statements about public officials and candidates for office limited only "by good faith and just intention."[64]

A similar privilege based on good faith, Cooley asserted, should free publishers of news about public figures from the general rule presuming malice from falsity.[65] As a practical matter, he observed that publishers rarely have personal knowledge of the information they publish and that efforts to verify its accuracy would typically delay publication beyond its use to readers.[66] Cooley regretted that "the plastic rules of the common law" had not accommodated themselves to emergence of the newspaper as an important institution in the discussion of public affairs. The common law, he observed, had changed in recognition of the fact that the railway had superseded the king's

---

[58] Id.
[59] Id. at 429–30.
[60] Id. at 429.
[61] Id. at 437.
[62] Id. at 438.
[63] Id. at 439.
[64] Id. at 440.
[65] Id. at 455.
[66] Id. at 454.

highway. Yet courts did not treat publishers of newspapers any differently from the village gossip of two centuries ago, "with no more privilege and no more protection."[67]

As in his discussion of "libels against the government," Cooley did not maintain that the constitutional guarantees of free expression required the changes in common law he advocated. Whether the New York courts "have duly considered the importance of publicity and discussion on all matters of general concern in a representative government," he wrote while criticizing their failure to create a privilege for criticisms of officials and candidates, "must be left to the consideration of the courts as these questions shall come before them in the future." Trying to influence the courts, he observed that "the general public sentiment and the prevailing customs allow a greater freedom of discussion" than the earlier decisions.[68] Apparently less hopeful about judicial protection of newspapers, Cooley concluded that publishers seeking a privilege for news reports should appeal to public opinion or to the legislature for modification of the common law.[69]

Tiedeman on the Constitutional Prohibition against the Impairment of Contracts

Although Tiedeman's discussion of changes in the judicial construction of the constitutional provision forbidding the impairment of contracts was less extensive than either Thayer's analysis of judicial review or Cooley's treatment of freedom of expression, it provides a particularly vivid example of the use of constitutional history to support evolutionary theories of constitutional interpretation. Historical investigation, Tiedeman maintained, clearly revealed the original intent of the prohibition against any law "impairing the obligation of a contract." Oppressed by the indebtedness incurred during the Revolutionary War, many Americans urged its repudiation. The framers of the Constitution inserted this provision simply to prevent state legislation allowing the repudiation of either public or private debts.[70]

Despite this clearly limited original intent, the Supreme Court dramatically expanded the impairment of contract clause in the famous *Dartmouth College* case, decided in 1819. That case arose when the New Hampshire legislature passed a law creating a new corporation to govern Dartmouth College. In his opinion for the Supreme Court, Chief Justice Marshall identified as a contract the state's original charter of incorporation to Dartmouth College. The law creating a new governing corporation, he reasoned, impaired that contract and, therefore, violated the Constitution. The New Hampshire legislature, he pointed out, could have passed the law creating the new corporation only if it had reserved the right of amendment in the initial charter of incorporation.[71]

---

[67] Id. at 452.
[68] Id. at 438.
[69] Id. at 457.
[70] Tiedeman, supra note 10, at 54.
[71] Id. at 55.

Applying the reasoning of Marshall's opinion in the *Dartmouth College* case, numerous decisions of federal and state courts held that subsequent legislatures must honor previous legislative contracts exempting individuals and corporations from taxation. However much the enforcement of such contracts would harm the public interest, the decisions reasoned, the Constitution prevents their impairment. Intimating future modification of the *Dartmouth College* holding, dissents in many of these cases maintained that a state legislature cannot deprive itself of political power through a contract and identified taxation as a political power.[72]

Under the leadership of Chief Justice Taney, the Supreme Court subsequently limited the impact of the *Dartmouth College* holding. In the *Charles River Bridge* case, decided in 1837, the Supreme Court rejected the argument that the legislative authorization of the construction of a second bridge, near a current bridge over the Charles River, impaired the charter of the different company that built the first bridge. The initial charter authorized the company to build the bridge and charge tolls for its use during a fixed period, after which the bridge would become public. The construction of the second bridge before the expiration of that fixed period, the company argued, unconstitutionally impaired its contract.[73] Chief Justice Taney reasoned that the original charter did not constitute a promise to create an exclusive monopoly and, therefore, that no unconstitutional impairment of contract occurred. Tiedeman, by contrast, viewed the loss of profits caused by the construction of a second bridge as an obvious impairment of contract. He attributed Taney's decision to the pressure of public support for the second bridge. "Public opinion was not yet ripe for an open repudiation of the Dartmouth College case," Tiedeman observed, "and hence the end was attained by the employment of a technicality."[74]

Further technical limitations on the reach of the *Dartmouth College* decision, Tiedeman added, arose as a result of the rapidly increasingly power of private corporations, facilitated by the industrial use of scientific advances. Public concern that corporations, particularly railroads, would usurp control of the government became too great for either the Congress or the courts to ignore. Congress passed legislation subjecting them to extensive regulation, which the courts upheld while rejecting arguments that the regulations unconstitutionally impaired the contractual obligations in the original corporate charters. As in the earlier dissents in the taxation cases, the courts reasoned that the legislature could not contract away its political power to regulate corporations in the public interest. The original charters, they maintained, were subject to the reasonable exercise of what the courts now called the "police power" of the state.[75]

Tiedeman observed that Chief Justice Marshall's opinion in *Dartmouth College* did not include "the slightest hint" that corporate rights were subject "to an indefinable and elastic power, called police power," whose exercise could

[72] Id. at 56.
[73] Id. at 57.
[74] Id. at 58.
[75] Id. at 58–9.

jeopardize corporate interests. But the actual facts of the case, he observed without elaboration, did not require any discussion of the police power, and "technicalities and refinements of verbal meanings" enabled early decisions upholding the police power of the state to avoid repudiating its holding.[76] Two subsequent Supreme Court cases relying on the police power, by contrast, could not be reconciled with *Dartmouth College*. In the first case, the Court upheld, as a valid exercise of the police power, a new provision in a state constitution that repealed the existing charter of a lottery company.[77] The second case arose when the growing population around a factory manufacturing fertilizer, complaining that it was a nuisance, convinced the state legislature to pass a law ordering its closing within two years, well before the end of fifty-year period of operation granted in the corporate charter. The Court again invoked the police power while sustaining this law.[78]

The facts of these cases, as well as others, Tiedeman maintained, could not be distinguished from those in *Dartmouth College*. In the later cases, the Court reasoned that the welfare of the community, threatened by corporate activity, justified the use of the police power by the state. But precisely the same reasoning, Tiedeman stressed, could have been used in *Dartmouth College* itself. The New Hampshire legislature could have plausibly claimed that the heavy representation of Tories on the old board of trustees so threatened the education of students that the public welfare justified the creation of a new governing corporation.[79] The "contradiction" between *Dartmouth College* and the later decisions, Tiedeman maintained, "arises out of a change in public opinion, and a consequent change in the constitutional rule." He closed his chapter by claiming that these later cases substantially modified, and arguably abrogated, the holding in *Dartmouth College* even while claiming to endorse it out of respect for its author, Chief Justice Marshall.[80] For Tiedeman, this series of cases clearly illustrated the extent to which constitutional interpretation evolves in response to popular pressure and social change.

Though the late nineteenth-century American legal scholars focused their original research on the early history of English law, they also investigated the history of constitutional law in the United States. Throughout their historical research, they sought to explain how current law evolved from the past, reflecting changes in society and in dominant popular views. They also suggested revisions of existing law based on insights derived from their historical explanations. Scholarship in constitutional law demonstrates law how far American legal scholars took the historical turn.

---

[76] Id. at 59–60.
[77] Id. at 60.
[78] Id. at 62.
[79] Id. at 65–6.
[80] Id. at 66.

XI

The Historical School of American Jurisprudence

Henry Adams and his students, Melville Madison Bigelow, Oliver Wendell Holmes, Jr., James Barr Ames, and James Bradley Thayer were the most important American legal historians during the last three decades of the nineteenth century. They largely created the field of professional legal history in the United States. Together with their counterparts in Germany and England, they formed a transatlantic community of legal historians, who accurately perceived themselves as engaged in a shared intellectual project. Their interests most overlapped in exploring the Teutonic origins of English law. As the examples of the previous chapter illustrate, the historical turn extended to significant work on the history of constitutional law in the United States. Yet the emphasis on the importance of history in understanding law was not limited to the relatively few who wrote legal history. American legal scholars generally viewed history as the key to legal analysis. Like Maine and probably influenced by him, they often identified their historical approach to law as a distinctive jurisprudential school, contrasting it with prior schools of natural law and analytic jurisprudence and associating it with inductive science. Among the most eminent of these scholars were James Coolidge Carter, Thomas McIntyre Cooley, William Gardiner Hammond, John Norton Pomeroy, Christopher G. Tiedeman, and Francis Wharton. This chapter focuses on their historical interpretation of law, a subject they typically discussed in more detail than did the legal historians themselves.

American legal scholars frequently expressed and elaborated in the context of legal analysis the key themes of the evolutionary historical thought that pervaded Western intellectual life in the nineteenth century. They generally viewed history as an evolutionary process of development that organically connected the past with the present. They often referred to the "seeds" or "germs" of legal doctrine "ripening" into the more developed "fruit" or "offshoots" of current law,[1]

---

[1] See, e.g., John Norton Pomeroy, An Introduction to Municipal Law: Designed for General Readers and for Students in Colleges and Higher Schools (San Francisco: A. L. Bancroft, 1883) (original ed., 1865), p. 19.

or to the "genealogy"[2] of law from its original "parents" to its "lineal descendents" among its living "children."[3] They often used evolution as a synonym for development rather than in its more specific Darwinian sense as a theory of natural selection extending over many generations. Indeed, evolutionary historical thought had become pervasive well before Darwin published his theories of biological evolution.[4] The late nineteenth-century American legal scholar Francis Wharton cited Burke and Savigny to support his assertion that "the doctrine of juridical evolution was taught long before that of physical evolution came prominently before the public eye."[5] Rather than stimulating evolutionary conceptions of time, Darwin's theories of biological evolution reinforced and helped diffuse them.[6]

Like most evolutionary historical thinkers, and in contrast to Darwin's identification of natural selection as the mechanism behind biological evolution, the late nineteenth-century American legal scholars did not generate theories that accounted for evolutionary change. A few referred to evolutionary historical change as reflecting a divine plan, but they did not elaborate, sometimes asserting that any attempt to uncover its details would be an act of extreme presumption, even irreverence. Understanding current law, they believed, depends on tracing its evolution from its earliest origins. They focused on the history of a nation, which they often identified with race, and viewed all aspects of national culture, including law, as related parts of its historical development. Occasionally, they explicitly differentiated meaningful history, which contributes to understanding the connections between past and present, from superficial history, which does not. Just as Cooley emphasized the importance of getting "beyond the surface facts of history," the accounts of battles and even of political revolutions, to the more important history of race,[7] Pomeroy took care to contrast his focus on "the life of the races" from mere "outside history" that recorded the history of dates and events, of battles, dynasties, and politics.[8] Exhibiting what current historians characterize and typically deprecate as "presentism," they made clear that they concentrated on meaningful history. As the work of the legal historians highlighted, they frequently dismissed history that does not help explain the present as irrelevant and merely

[2] See, e.g., James Barr Ames, Express Assumpsit, in Lectures on Legal History and Miscellaneous Legal Essays (Cambridge, Mass.: Harvard University Press, 1913), p. 145.

[3] See, e.g., James Bradley Thayer, A Preliminary Treatise on Evidence at the Common Law (Boston: Little, Brown, and Company, 1898), pp. 7, 11, 47.

[4] J. W. Burrow, Evolution and Society: A Study in Victorian Social Theory (Cambridge University Press, 1966), pp. 21, 135, 152–3; Maurice Mandelbaum, History, Man and Reason: A Study in Nineteenth-Century Thought (Baltimore: Johns Hopkins Press, 1971), pp. 77–8; John Higham, Theory, in John Higham with Leonard Krieger and Felix Gilbert, History (Englewood Cliffs, N.J.: Prentice-Hall, Inc., 1965), p. 94; see generally Peter Stein, Legal Evolution: The Story of an Idea (Cambridge University Press, 1980).

[5] Francis Wharton, Commentaries on Law 69 (Philadelphia: Kay & Brother, 1884), p. 69.

[6] Burrow, supra note 4, at 114.

[7] Thomas M. Cooley, Sources of Inspiration in Legal Pursuits, 9 Western Jurist 515 (1875).

[8] Pomeroy, supra note 1, at 9.

"antiquarian." Particularly interested in the history of their own legal system, the American legal scholars often endorsed the "Teutonic-germ theory" that was popular among English and American scholars in many fields.

While applying evolutionary thought to legal analysis, American legal scholars frequently emphasized that evolving custom is the source of law. In making this point, they sometimes explicitly rejected Blackstone's famous assertion that the common law consists of "immemorial custom."[9] They conceded that positive law does not always reflect the prevailing customs in a society, but they stressed that in these circumstances the positive law will not be obeyed and cannot be effectively enforced. While observing that judicial or legislative error in recognizing existing custom can produce "inoperative" positive law, they devoted particular attention to the evolutionary phenomenon of new customs superseding the earlier customs on which current law is often based. When evolving custom advances beyond existing law, they maintained, the law must change. They believed that judges are usually in the best position to conform law to changes in custom, and that judges typically do so subtly and even unconsciously in ways that escape detection. Yet they recognized unusual circumstances when discrepancies between law and custom require legislative action. Several of these scholars took pains to make clear that evolving custom is the ultimate basis for constitutional law as well as for common law and statutory law. They were confident that their scholarship, by demonstrating whether legal survivals should be retained or abandoned, would be an aid to judges and legislators. Based on their historical research, they hoped to reconceptualize the legal system to make it more functional for their own time and place.

The American legal scholars reflected the variations as well as the central themes of nineteenth-century evolutionary historical thought. They recognized discontinuity as well as connection between past and present. While some acknowledged periods of decline, they generally viewed evolution as progressive, often portrayed as a movement from barbarism to civilization. They lauded the growth of liberty, democracy, and morality as nations, particularly their own, became increasingly civilized. A few explicitly associated the racial consciousness of the Teutonic-germ theory with racial superiority, but most did not, assuming instead the distinctiveness of different races. Some detected immanent principles or governing laws that determined the evolutionary process, though they rarely elaborated these principles or laws. Others, however, viewed evolution as a sequence of contingent events. Frustratingly, like evolutionary thinkers in other fields, they often were unclear or expressed inconsistent positions about these and other issues.

Many American legal scholars self-consciously referred to themselves as legal scientists while stressing that they used the inductive method to extract meaning from evolving history. The scientific method of induction, they pointed out, derives and classifies principles from the observation of empirical data. They

[9] Blackstone's Commentaries, vol. 1, p. 65.

repeatedly stressed that the history of law, particularly of case law, provides the empirical evidence for inductive legal science, just as natural and physical facts provide the empirical evidence for inductive sciences such as biology, chemistry, physics, and astronomy. In developing their conception of law as an inductive historical science, they differentiated it both from the deductive science of mathematics and from prior speculative and unscientific theories of law, especially natural law and analytic jurisprudence. Although the theory of evolution itself can be derived inductively, as Darwin did in biological science, the legal scholars, like many nineteenth-century evolutionary scholars in other fields, did not claim that they had induced the full range of their evolutionary thought. Yet they did connect induction and evolution by frequently observing that the legal principles they induced from historical data had evolved over time. Many assumed, and some explicitly stated, that legal principles would continue to evolve in the future. In their amalgam of induction and evolution, the legal scholars resembled their counterparts in departments of history at American universities, who believed that they had transformed history from a "literary" and "speculative" field populated by amateurs into an inductive science based on the study of original sources. Like the historians, the legal scholars focused much more on the initial collection and classification of historical evidence than on attempts to derive broader conclusions from it.

Although they self-consciously identified with the historical analysis of law that had originated in Germany and England, American scholars also asserted their intellectual independence from their European predecessors and contemporaries. Some Americans complained that European scholars in what they called the "historical school" tended to accept current law precisely because it emerged from the past. Just because current law can be explained historically, Hammond observed, does not mean that it should be treated uncritically. He maintained that people should reflect self-consciously about whether "we *ought* to continue the custom or the precedent" derived from the past, a point many writers in the historical school had "overlooked."[10] Wharton agreed with Burke and Savigny that legislation can be effective only if it is consistent with the prevalent sense of right of the people, which is derived from their historical experience. Yet he immediately added that "the historical school has led, as it certainly did in Burke's case, to an undue reverence for those institutions which a nation has outgrown." In making this criticism, Wharton emphasized that he was not challenging the historical approach to law that he shared with Burke. "Undue reverence," he maintained, "is not a necessary incident of the theory on which that school rests." "On the contrary," he added, "the recognition of the continuousness of the existence of a nation, composed, as is necessarily the case, of elements constantly changing and developing, involves the corresponding and sympathetic change and development of the laws" emanating

---

[10] William G. Hammond, Supplementary Notes, by the Editor, in Francis Lieber, Legal and Political Hermeneutics (St. Louis, F. H. Thomas and Company, 1880) (3d. ed., William G. Hammond, ed.), p. 313.

from this national history. He used the transformation of views about slavery, defended by eminent moralists of the relatively recent past, but "universally reprobated" in his own time, to illustrate how the evolution of "national culture" had terminated an institution that the nation had "outgrown."[11]

At the same time that he recognized the continuous existence of nations, Wharton maintained that Savigny had exaggerated the similarity between a nation and "a continuous perpetual person." He particularly objected to the German conception of a Volksgeist, which "too arbitrarily" ascribed to nations "constant and distinct tendencies such as those which separate individuals from individuals."[12] While elaborating his own historical approach, Tiedeman identified with Jhering rather than with Jhering's predecessors, Savigny and Puchta. Citing Jhering as authority and including a quotation from him in the original German, Tiedeman maintained that changes in the prevalent sense of right involve "vigorous contest between opposing forces," rather than the "quiet, smooth, uneventful development," analogous to changes in language, postulated by "jurists of the Savigny-Puchta school."[13]

Evolutionary Legal Thought

Just as the nation was the organism whose origins and development attracted the attention of most nineteenth-century evolutionary historians, the American legal scholars typically associated legal history with national history. Also like their contemporaries in other fields, many of them equated national history with racial history. "No fact is more palpable in history," Pomeroy asserted, "than that the characteristics of race, by some means stamped indelibly into the individual and upon the common brotherhood, are preserved, modified, perhaps, but not obliterated, through centuries of change, through the rise and overthrow of governments and empires."[14] As did Savigny before him, Pomeroy often compared law to language as similar products of national and racial evolution. He observed that law, like language, steadily develops in "an unbroken chain" that "connects the forms and principles of today with those of the most remote periods."[15] "As languages indicate their descent through the most radical convulsions of the state and the people," he wrote, "so do the tribal institutions and customs perpetuate themselves from generation to generation."[16] Because a "jurisprudence must be the product of the ideas and life of the people over which it dominates," he stressed, "it must spring from the soil." It is impossible to incorporate even the best foreign laws, he added, unless they can be assimilated with the "habits and thoughts" derived from a

---

[11] Wharton, supra note 5, at 94.

[12] Id. at 93.

[13] Christopher G. Tiedeman, The Unwritten Constitution of the United States (Buffalo, N.Y.: William S. Hein & Company, Inc., reprint ed. 1974) (original ed. 1890), pp. 11–12.

[14] Pomeroy, supra note 1, at 250.

[15] Id. at xiii–xiv.

[16] Id. at 250.

nation's "primitive stock." As an example, he cited the failure of the attempt by some American states to "engraft" the French law of marriage.[17]

Wharton similarly maintained that each nationality had its own jurisprudence, adapted over time to its own needs and "congenial" to its own "soil."[18] American law, he concluded, reflects "the silent and spontaneous evolution of the nation, past as well as present, adapting itself to the conditions in which in each epoch it is placed."[19] He viewed law as "the instinctive and unconscious outgrowth of the nation," which he defined as "that people as wrought up in one continuous body with those who preceded it as part of a common race," rather than as "the majority of a particular people as it exists at a particular time."[20] In discussing the fundamental principles of the American Constitution, Tiedemann praised their "complete harmony" with "the political evolution of the nation,"[21] finding them "embedded in the national character" and "developed in accordance with the national growth."[22] Carter traced law to the accumulated wisdom of the race since its infancy.[23] "Law," Cooley tersely stated, "begins with the race."[24] He proceeded to associate race with the "people" and the "nation."[25] He emphasized that every people has its own laws. Even nations at equivalent levels of accomplishment, he observed, had very different laws and institutions, which were "fitted" to their distinctive histories.[26]

Expressing the Teutonic-germ theory while focusing on the evolution of Anglo-American law, Pomeroy observed that the Saxons "have bequeathed to us a strong and vigorous race life," including the personal freedom, self-reliance, and self-government that characterize modern England and the United States.[27] Pomeroy discussed both the Saxon and the feudal sources of subsequent English and American law. He identified the Saxon period as the origin of the English parliament and the American legislatures. He also traced various modern legal practices from the Saxons, including the jury trial, the bail system, and the remedy of pecuniary damages.[28] The continuing impact of feudal law, Pomeroy added, is revealed in lingering distinctions between real and personal property,[29] the modern law of inheritance,[30] and the principle of no taxation

---

[17] Id. at 209–10.

[18] Wharton, supra note 5, 69.

[19] Id. at iv.

[20] Id. at iii.

[21] Tiedeman, supra note 13, at 19.

[22] Id. at 16.

[23] James Coolidge Carter, Law: Its Origin, Growth and Function (New York: G. P. Putnam's Sons, 1907), p. 127.

[24] Cooley, supra note 7, at 516.

[25] Id. at 522.

[26] Id. at 516.

[27] Pomeroy, supra note 1, at 214–15.

[28] Id. at 240–41.

[29] Id. at 243–4.

[30] Id. at 289.

without consent.[31] Yet Pomeroy, despite his adherence to the Teutonic-germ theory, warned against exaggerating the similarities between England and the United States. He maintained that various factors, including the lack of "class distinction" in the United States, accounted for significant differences.[32] Cooley similarly identified the "genius for law and settled institutions" and the "willingness to submit to rule" as Saxon traits that "in time developed into the law-respecting and law-abiding Englishman and American."[33] Although he acknowledged various "harsh and repulsive" features of the common law and took care not to "eulogize" it, he praised it for reflecting the maxims of "a sturdy and independent race, accustomed in an unusual degree to freedom of thought and action, and to a share in the administration of public affairs."[34] The American system of municipal government, he added, "seems a part of the very nature of the race to which we belong," adopted from England "as if instinctively" by the first settlers.[35]

For some legal scholars, as for some historians generally, the proud race-consciousness of the Teutonic-germ theory had racist implications. By invoking the Teutonic-germ theory to justify restrictions on immigration, Pomeroy became the legal scholar who most explicitly conveyed racist views. Ironically, Pomeroy saw more racial mingling in Anglo-American history than did most of his contemporaries. He believed England and the United States, to a greater extent than modern European nations, were composed of multiple races. He identified Celtic, Saxon, Danish, and Norman "streams of blood" that combined to form the English nationality and its law. In addition, Roman jurisprudence "penetrated" these amalgamated streams.[36] In contrast to the influence of Roman law in French jurisprudence, Pomeroy emphasized that no element dominated the composite law of England and the United States. Yet he also insisted that Anglo-American law had become distinctive. "Whatever is drawn in from foreign sources, loses its individuality, and becomes blended with the general mass as though it were the product of native growth." The foreign sources "suffer a change and are made English," not as a "patchwork," but as a "mutually dependent" whole.[37] Most significantly, Pomeroy emphasized that while "related races" may "mingle" and "coalesce," "races entirely dissimilar cannot unite and attain to that homogeneity necessary for a single people and stable government."[38] As an illustration, he

---

[31] Id. at 293.

[32] John Norton Pomeroy, An Introduction to the Constitutional Law of the United States (Boston: Houghton, Osgood and Company, 1879) (4th ed.) (original ed., 1868), p. 139. See also id. at 108, 122.

[33] Thomas M. Cooley, Comparative Merits of Written and Prescriptive Constitutions, 2 Harv. L. Rev. 341, 343 (1889).

[34] Thomas M. Cooley, A Treatise on the Constitutional Limitations which Rest upon the Legislative Powers of the State of the American Union (Boston: Little, Brown, and Company, 1868), p. 22.

[35] Id. at 189–90.

[36] Pomeroy, supra note 1, at 13.

[37] Id. at 172.

[38] Id. at 422.

observed that American Indians, however much they have associated with whites and adopted some of their customs, "are as completely Indian in their ethnic peculiarities, as when the first Europeans landed on the American shores." Pomeroy, therefore, concluded that only "races nearly affiliated with our own Germanic stock" should be admitted to American citizenship. On this basis, he argued against citizenship for Africans, most Asians, and probably the Slavs of Eastern Europe.[39]

None of the other American legal scholars expressed similar views in his published work, but the later opposition to immigration by Henry Cabot Lodge echoed Pomeroy. In his essay on Anglo-Saxon land law written while a student of Henry Adams, Lodge did not go beyond his scholarly emphasis on the Teutonic origins of modern English common law. Yet after abandoning his brief academic career and becoming a senator, Lodge invoked the Teutonic racial origins of England and the United States to justify restrictions on immigration. In a 1909 speech, he defended a bill that established an "illiteracy test" for potential immigrants. Under the bill, those who failed the illiteracy test would be added to the existing categories for excluding immigrants: paupers, diseased persons, convicts, and contract laborers.[40]

Lodge approved the illiteracy test because it would overwhelmingly exclude "races with which the English-speaking people have never hitherto assimilated, and who are most alien to the great body of the people of the United States," but who had emigrated to the United States in "enormous proportions" in recent decades.[41] Like Pomeroy, he recognized that there is no "pure" race, that different races have mingled together. This mingling produced what Lodge called "artificial races," which have formed over centuries of shared history.[42] Also like Pomeroy, he maintained that this mingling can only occur among "kindred people," who share the "same blood,"[43] or at least people who share the same language and history. Lodge contrasted the philologist and ethnologist, who studied ethnic divisions at the beginning of human history, with the "scientific modern historian," who focused instead on the gradual development of "sharply marked race divisions" over the past thousand years.[44] As a student of Henry Adams, Lodge had trained as a scientific modern historian. He apparently believed that as a senator he was applying this training to his analysis of immigration.

The "English-speaking race" of England and the United States, Lodge concluded, was formed over centuries, overwhelmingly by people of the "same race stock," descended from the "great Germanic tribes." Though "derived from different channels," it had "attained a fixity and definiteness of national

[39] Id. at 422–3.
[40] Henry Cabot Lodge, The Restriction of Immigration (March 16, 1896), in Henry Cabot Lodge, Speeches and Addresses 1884–1909 (Boston: Houghton Mifflin Company, 1909), p. 243
[41] Id. at 247.
[42] Id. at 252.
[43] Id. at 253; see id. at 254.
[44] Id. at 252.

character unknown to any other people."[45] Lodge emphasized that racial qualities are moral much more than they are intellectual.[46] Even the most intelligent and well-educated Hindu, though a member of the same Indo-European family as the English, cannot be made into an Englishman. No amount of intelligence and learning can "efface" the differences produced by six thousand years of history, differences as marked as physiological ones. "The men of each race," Lodge observed, "possess an indestructible stock of ideas, traditions, sentiments, modes of thought, an unconscious inheritance from their ancestors, upon which argument has no effect."[47]

Lodge made clear, moreover, that he considered the "English-speaking race" superior to as well as different from the potential immigrants the illiteracy test would exclude. The lesson of history, he warned, is that the "lower race will prevail" if there is significant interbreeding with a "higher" one. He emphasized the limited "capacity of any race for assimilating and elevating an inferior race."[48] Because widespread immigration of the lower races to the United States dated only from around 1875,[49] he observed, this danger, though begun, remained small. It might not even have registered for Lodge in 1876, when he published his contribution to the *Essays in Anglo-Saxon Law*. But by 1909 Lodge believed that "the peril is at hand," which made passage of the illiteracy test crucial for the future of the United States. Lodge was confident that "the unerring instinct of the race will shut the danger out, as it closed the door upon the coming of the Chinese."[50]

It is conceivable that other legal scholars who subscribed to the Teutonic-germ theory agreed with Pomeroy and Lodge, even though they did not express these views in writing. But others apparently did not. As his correspondence with Lewis Morgan reveals, Henry Adams was open to the possible equality or even superiority of other races, including the American Indian and African. By comparing his own commitment to "democracy and radicalism" with Lodge's "federalist and conservative" views, Adams provided some additional, though indirect, evidence that they may have disagreed about issues relating to race. Yet Adams often expressed anti-Semitic views.[51] "I have now seen enough of Jews and Moors," he wrote to a friend while traveling in Spain, "to entertain more liberal views in regard to the Inquisition, and to feel that, though the ignorant may murmur, the Spaniards saw and pursued a noble aim."[52] Thayer, the son of a prominent abolitionist, became active in reform efforts on behalf of American

---

[45] Id. at 260.

[46] Id. at 264.

[47] Id. at 262.

[48] Id. at 264.

[49] Id. at 259.

[50] Id. at 265.

[51] Ernest Samuels, Henry Adams: The Major Phase (Cambridge, Mass.: Harvard University Press, 1964), pp. 129–30, 167–70, 182–4, 243, 356–9, 426–7.

[52] Ernest Samuels, Henry Adams: The Middle Years (Cambridge, Mass.: Harvard University Press, 1958), p. 115.

Indians, confident that they could become typical Americans committed to the values of the common law.[53] He argued that American Indians should be "absorbed" into American society "under the cover of our Constitution with the rest of us."[54]

Addressing major themes within general evolutionary thought, leading late nineteenth-century American legal scholars, like their colleagues who produced original work on the history of English law, reflected on whether legal evolution had been continuous or punctuated, progressive or undulatory, determined or contingent. Many identified evolutionary progress, especially in the Anglo-American legal tradition they believed the United States shared with England, and even more so in the United States, which several believed had advanced this tradition beyond the English law it inherited. Some associated legal progress with increased morality and order that reflected Christian conceptions of a perfected universe. Many assumed distinct stages of legal progress. Yet scholars who stressed progressive evolution warned against mistaking resemblance for continuity. They also identified irregularities and breaks in historical continuity and stressed the need to eliminate dysfunctional survivals inherited from earlier laws. While a few scholars maintained that underlying laws determined evolutionary change, more indicated or even explicitly proclaimed the contingency of history.

American legal scholars shared the widespread nineteenth-century view that historical evolution is progressive as well as continuous. Their images of organic growth, such as seeds maturing into fruit, themselves implied continuous progress. The Teutonic-germ theory, which many of them endorsed, expressed this view of progressive evolution in the context of their own national and racial development. Among all these scholars, Pomeroy most emphasized the progress of law over time. He claimed that the "prolific germ which can be traced back into the swamps and forests of Germany among the fierce and independent Saxons, has developed a growth, which, surviving the invasions of Danes and Normans, has given to England its free constitution, and is working out its perfect fruit in the individual liberty and local governments of the United States."[55] More specifically, he described "the general order of progress" from the Anglo-Saxon assemblies of freemen to the modern jury trial. Although he was unable to determine precisely when the jury trial began, he was confident that his account was able to portray "the transitions which prepared the way and finally ended in the perfected institution."[56]

American scholars occasionally observed that English law had progressed further in the United States than in England itself. Pomeroy praised English

[53] Jay Hook, A Brief Life of James Bradley Thayer, 88 Nw. U.L. Rev. 1, 7 (1993).

[54] James Bradley Thayer, Report of the Law Committee, Proceedings of the Sixth Annual Meeting of the Lake Mohonk Conference of Friends of the Indian (1888), reprinted in Americanizing the American Indians: Writings by the "Friends of the Indian," 1880–1900 (Cambridge, Mass.: Harvard University Press, 1973) (Francis Paul Prucha, ed.), pp. 172–3.

[55] Pomeroy, supra note 1, at 250.

[56] Id. at 70.

law for having grown from "an incomplete and meager system" into what is "now a structure, vast, symmetrical," and "equally harmonious in its minutest details."[57] But he claimed that in the United States the "seeds of liberty" planted by the Saxons "finally triumphed over the crown in the progress of development into a complete representative form of government."[58] Cooley also stressed that American law had advanced beyond its English origins. In the United States, English law "was raw material to be worked over," initially by relieving its hierarchical, class-based structure. Life, liberty, and property, principles long recognized in England, received broader and more comprehensive protection in the United States.[59] Under the rulings of American judges, the common law "lost many of its harsh and cruel features before they had been removed in England."[60]

The assumption that progress occurred in distinctive stages from barbarism to civilization, a frequent theme of evolutionary theories of history in the nineteenth century, attracted many of the American legal scholars as well. Without citing Maine but perhaps influenced by him, Pomeroy seemed to agree with his view that all progressive societies undergo similar stages of development. "A careful examination of the history of all nations which have progressed from comparative barbarism to a condition of high culture," he maintained, "will disclose a general resemblance in the forms by which this progress has been made evident in the law, through its development from rudeness and simplicity to refinement and comprehensiveness." Among these progressive nations, he included the ancient Roman state and many modern European countries as well as England and the United States.[61] He referred to stages of development, which he did not specify, while describing legal progress in general and Anglo-American law in particular.[62] In England and the United States, he believed, the "earlier stages" had been "passed through" and the last stage toward perfection had already begun.[63] Hammond[64] and Carter[65] similarly referred to stages of historical progress.

Some of these scholars associated progress with increasing morality. Pomeroy was confident that England and the United States, though not yet reaching perfection in morality and law, were well on their way to achieving it.[66] Contrasting the "morality of law," which is "commonly and habitually practiced by the people," with the "morality of ethics," the "rules of

[57] Id. at 176.

[58] Pomeroy, supra note 32, at 105.

[59] Cooley, supra note 33, at 348.

[60] Cooley, supra note 7, at 519.

[61] Pomeroy, supra note 1, at 17.

[62] Id. at 69, 103.

[63] Id. at 103.

[64] William Blackstone, Commentaries on the Laws of England, Edited for American Lawyers by William G. Hammond (San Francisco: Bancroft-Whitney Company, 1890) [hereinafter Hammond's Blackstone], vol. 1, p. 217.

[65] Carter, supra note 23, at 252.

[66] Pomeroy, supra note 1, at 103.

morality set forth by our moral teachers," Tiedeman called the morality of ethics "an idealistic conception, something to be striven for, and more and more approximated, but perhaps never to be fully realized before the days of the millennium."[67]

Scholars occasionally asserted that all societies would eventually progress to a morality that reflected the divine order of the universe, as understood by the Christian religion. Despite his concern about racial mingling in America beyond Germanic peoples, Pomeroy repeatedly maintained that law develops from simple, rude, and arbitrary forms to refined and comprehensive principles of pure ethics and abstract right.[68] "The original arbitrariness, the once complete nationalism," he wrote, "are gradually softened, and those innate principles of natural justice common to all times and peoples, which the Romans called *jus gentium*, have freer play." No actual system of laws, Pomeroy observed, had reached "strict harmony" with the principles of abstract right and natural justice that he associated "with the law of nature and with Christian morals."[69] The legal system of every nation still displayed distinctive characteristics based on its ethnic life, which fell short of "this natural order."[70] Yet he remained confident in progress toward "the maxims of a perfect morality," which he compared to "the spirit of the ethical portion of the Christian religion." This progress, he maintained, should be led by judges "evolving the new out from the old."[71] Like Pomeroy, Carter emphasized the extent to which law is "an emanation from Order"[72] and asserted that it reaches perfection as society advances and improves. He, too, believed that judges should "enlarge and refine" legal rules in response to "developing moral thought."[73]

Instead of focusing on the progress of law toward the perfection of a divine moral order, Hammond emphasized the progress in human understanding of the divine moral order that had always existed. He observed that people in the past, unwilling "to surrender entirely the belief that there is a Divine order in the moral as well as physical constitution of the world," too often mistakenly assumed that moral principles "were perfectly understood by them, and that the law of reason, of nature, or of God, as they understood it and could formulate it in words, was the standard of *jus* for all time." He stressed instead that human understanding of moral as well as of physical laws develops over time, based on increasing knowledge and education, even though the underlying moral and physical laws themselves do not change.[74]

---

[67] Tiedeman, supra note 13, at 15.
[68] Pomeroy, supra note 1, at 8, 17, 103.
[69] Id. at 8.
[70] Id. at 9.
[71] Id. at 179.
[72] Carter, supra note 23, at 345.
[73] Id. at 329.
[74] Hammond, supra note 10, at 327–30.

Even as they focused on continuity and progress as central themes in evolutionary legal history, late nineteenth-century American legal scholars frequently warned about mistaking resemblance between past and present law for continuous historical development, the danger often highlighted by the American historians of English law. "There can be no greater error in historical investigation," Pomeroy wrote, "than the conclusion that, because of a resemblance between institutions of two different nations, not contemporaneous, the later in time has borrowed from the former." Such resemblances, he stressed, are often "entirely casual." Both Roman and Saxon law, for example, required that the transfer of property take place in public before witnesses and public officials. According to Pomeroy, to infer from this similarity that the Saxons borrowed the practice from the Romans would be an unjustifiable "extravagance."[75] Writing about the history of English law in his edition of Blackstone's *Commentaries*, Hammond cautioned against inferring a "genetic relation" from resemblance. He observed that the "bocland" of the Saxon period shared many characteristics with the "fee tail" of the later common law. He emphasized, however, that "the resemblance must not be mistaken for identity." Though both dealt with hereditary land, the fee "is entirely a different institution." "Only errors and fallacies," he wrote, "result from confusing them or supposing any genetic relation between them."[76] In his unpublished work, Hammond warned more generally against "carrying back" modern ideas or terms "for the interpretation of ancient law." While urging scholars to focus on "the genealogy of legal rules and institutions," he maintained that they "cannot rely on surface resemblances or analogies as proving anything."[77] He specifically criticized scholars who used "modern notions" to investigate the early jury instead of "patiently ascertaining" how it was regarded in its own time.[78] Although he acknowledged that Anglo-Saxon institutions had their "counterparts" in the New England town meeting, he maintained that there is "no historical connection between them" and that even "the resemblance has been greatly exaggerated" by historians at Johns Hopkins and elsewhere.[79]

Sensitivity to the difference between resemblance and continuity did not distract American legal scholars from their primary goal of uncovering evolutionary connections between past and present law. They pointed out instances in which resemblance did not reflect continuity as a cautionary reminder to be careful and accurate in establishing the true historical origins and development of present law. They concentrated overwhelmingly on the law of the past they

---

[75] Pomeroy, supra note 1, at 247–8.

[76] Hammond's Blackstone, supra note 64, vol. 2, at 205–6.

[77] William Gardiner Hammond, Lecture I, The Historical Method, p. 47, William G. Hammond Papers, University of Iowa College of Law, Box I [hereinafter cited as Hammond Papers].

[78] William Gardiner Hammond, Chapter X, History of the Jury, p. 15, Hammond Papers, supra note 77, Box I.

[79] William Gardiner Hammond, Lecture III, The Anglo-Saxon Period, p. 40, Hammond Papers, supra note 77, Box II.

determined to be part of the evolutionary process that led to current law and presumably would help explain it. Correspondingly, they rarely discussed past law that did not form part of this evolutionary process.

While retaining the confident belief in continuous and progressive evolution that pervaded nineteenth-century Western intellectual thought, many of the American legal scholars also observed lack of progress, discontinuity, and decay in the history of law. Wharton maintained that legal evolution, like evolution in other sciences, is not a process of "fixed and unbroken advance," but is "undulatory." The law "swerves and curves to allow for obstacles by which its movement in a straight line might be blocked."[80] Even Pomeroy, who stressed the continuity of evolutionary progress more than any other American scholar, described the growth of the law as "irregular and unscientific" as well as slow.[81] He acknowledged that "the English law was for a long time bound up and hampered in its progress by a too nice regard for the technicalities of form."[82] And though he emphasized the extent to which law had neared perfection in England and especially the United States, he subscribed to a cyclical theory of evolutionary history in which progress is followed by decline and death as part of a natural, organic process.[83] He often used Rome to illustrate this entire cycle. Roman law began with the barbarous Latin tribes, culminated during the early empire, and declined until its death and "entombment" in the Justinian codes.[84] It thus provides an "example of the complete life and natural and necessary progress of a national jurisprudence, from its birth to its death."[85] Modern English and American law, he believed, remained full of vitality and capable of further growth toward perfection.[86] Yet he suggested that even in these unusually progressive countries, growth would be followed by decline, recapitulating the pattern of ancient Rome.[87]

Reflecting reservations about the progress of law, late nineteenth-century American legal scholars, like evolutionary thinkers in other fields, frequently identified dysfunctional survivals from the past, a focus of those who did original research on the history of English law, particularly Holmes and Thayer. They criticized a wide range of current legal rules as remnants of old laws that previously may have made sense but had become illogical and repressive as times changed. In a note to Blackstone's treatment of heirlooms, Hammond complained that the "senseless repetition" of "obsolete forms of law" produced "much of the uncertainty and error in the application of the law to actual cases which constitute the greatest and best-founded reproach against the law in the

---

[80] Wharton, supra note 5, at 71.
[81] Pomeroy, supra note 1, at 57.
[82] Id. at 102.
[83] Id. at 168–9.
[84] Id. at 170, 208–9, 296.
[85] Id. at 209.
[86] Id. at 170, 209.
[87] Id. at 211.

minds of laymen."[88] The "extremely artificial" distinction between real and personal property, Cooley observed, is not inherent in the nature of property but is a survival based on historical circumstances. The distinction arose at a time when virtually everything of value was in the freehold estate and the heirlooms inherited with it.[89] He pointed out as well that contemporary family law sadly retains rules derived from "the barbarous condition of society when the common law was forming." At that time, wives and children were considered the servants and dependents rather than the equals of fathers and husbands and were expected to rely on men for their protection. The husband and father was the legal representative of the entire family. Unfortunately, Cooley concluded, recent rapid social changes in family relationships had not been matched by modification of the common law of family rights, which remained substantially as it was in the primitive days of its origins.[90] Only Pomeroy expressed unqualified confidence in the ability of the legal system to eliminate precedents that no longer functioned effectively. He believed that judges, as part of "the national progress," realized that various old legal rules, while "once valuable," were now "useless and cumbrous rubbish," "unfitted" for the present. Judges constantly "laid aside" these rules, gradually replacing them with new ones, which "in turn, suffer the same fate" as progress continues.[91]

As did other evolutionary thinkers, legal scholars differed about the extent to which evolution was determined or contingent and sometimes gave contradictory signals about their own views. The English legal history written by Americans often revealed the contingency of history, most dramatically in discussing the impact of the Norman Conquest, and most explicitly in Bigelow's analysis of the feud between Becket and King Henry II. Many other American legal scholars observed the contingency of evolutionary change. Carter was the major exception. By describing society as having "passed through many successive stages of progress in accordance with natural laws," he indicated that he perceived evolution as determined by those natural laws, which he did not name or elaborate.[92] Carter saw no conflict between the eventual emergence of human control over social change and the existence of governing natural laws. The "success of man's administration of that control," he wrote, "lies in his correct perception of those fundamental laws which it must necessarily follow, and shaping the exercise of his limited power to aid and not to supersede those laws."[93]

The frequent invocation of organic metaphors to describe legal evolution, most typically the image of the germ or seed maturing into the fruit, may also imply a predetermined evolutionary plan. Yet even Pomeroy, who used this

---

[88] Hammond's Blackstone, supra note 64, vol. 2, at 653.
[89] Thomas M. Cooley, A Treatise on the Law of Torts (Chicago: Callahan, 1880), p. 426.
[90] Id. at 222.
[91] Pomeroy, supra note 1, at 183.
[92] Carter, supra note 23, at 252.
[93] Id. at 252–3.

image more than anyone, indicated the contingency of organic evolution. He maintained that the practice of freemen acting as judges was "the germ of the English jury."[94] This practice prevailed throughout the early Germanic tribes. Yet it only matured into the jury in England. "It may be asked why," Pomeroy recognized, "as the same germ of the institution existed among the primitive laws and customs of the affiliated peoples extending over the whole of Western Europe, did not the jury trial grow up by natural sequence of events in France and Italy and Spain, as well as in England?" The answer, he maintained, was that preexisting Roman law influenced continental Europe, eventually recasting the primitive Germanic laws "in a Roman mould."[95] The free tribunals of the ancient Germans gave way to the Roman imperial model of professional judges. England, by contrast, was much less affected by Roman law. "Thus in England," Pomeroy concluded, "we have the jury trial as the fruit of the ancient German assemblages of freemen in the courts; on the continent the same seed has produced a growth of a far different form, perpetuating the ideas and policy of the later Roman emperors."[96] In other words, contingent historical events, not a predetermined process of growth, accounted for development of the German germ into the English jury.

Wharton explicitly denied that evolution followed an inevitable path. Invoking Burke and Savigny, he maintained that "there is no inexorable law, physical or spiritual, binding either men or nations to specific destinies." According to him, laws change as a people's circumstances change, fit laws survive as unfit ones die out, and what may be fit for one nationality may be unfit for another. Disclaiming deterministic conceptions of evolution, he stressed that "with nations, as well as with individuals, spontaneity is the basis for growth."[97]

Evolving Custom as the Source of Law

In elaborating their evolutionary legal thought, many of these scholars identified evolving custom as the source of law. Carter devoted much of his major work, posthumously published as *Law: Its Origin, Growth and Function*, to this proposition, which appropriately led scholars in his own time[98] and in ours[99] to recognize him as its leading American proponent. Cooley, Hammond,

---

[94] Pomeroy, supra note 1, at 67.

[95] Id. at 68.

[96] Id. at 69.

[97] Wharton, supra note 5, at 69.

[98] John Chipman Gray, The Nature and Sources of the Law (New York: The Macmillan Company, 1927) (original ed. 1909), pp. 235–6, 283–91; Roscoe Pound, Book Review, 24 Harv. L. Rev. 317, 319–20 (1909).

[99] Morton J. Horwitz, The Transformation of American Law 1870–1960 (New York: Oxford University Press, 1992), pp. 119–20, 121–3; Lewis A. Grossman, James Coolidge Carter and Mugwump Jurisprudence, 20 Law and History Review 577, 579, 604, 605–19, 625–6 (2002); Kunal M. Parker, Context in History and Law: A Study of the Late Nineteenth-Century American Jurisprudence of Custom, 24 Law and History Review 473, 505–8 (2006).

Tiedeman, and Wharton developed various formulations of the relationship between custom and law that, while not identical to Carter's, often echoed and occasionally extended them, including to the interpretation of constitutional law. Although Carter analyzed custom in most detail, many scholars shared his view that law enforces some customs through the power of the state and evolves with them. Recognizing that customs often evolve faster than law can catch up, they addressed the process by which law conforms to new customs. Like Savigny, they frequently portrayed this process as gradual, smooth, and even unconscious. But they also acknowledged and occasionally praised conscious efforts to change the law, and Tiedeman, following Jhering, emphasized that these efforts often involved struggles between competing forces.

Carter stressed that custom is part of "the great process of Evolution."[100] He believed that an enlightened minority typically generates the evolution of custom. An improvement in the moral nature of "the more cultivated and intelligent" members of society, he maintained, spreads "in ever widening circles" until "higher forms of conduct ripen into new customs."[101] Like Carter, Wharton observed that custom begins with a sense of right and need initially be felt by only a few people. Gradually, others follow, creating a "general acceptance" that becomes a custom and eventually a law.[102] Tiedeman similarly attributed the "growth and evolution" of "the popular sense of right" to "the increasing enlightenment of the ethical teachers" in a society. He added that "even in the land of democratic rule and of universal suffrage, only a few persons really mould and fashion public opinion."[103]

Law, Carter believed, is "nothing but enforced custom."[104] "But while all Law is Custom," he added, "all Custom is not necessarily Law." He observed that the law does not take notice of all customs in a society but only regulates some of them.[105] Using criminal law as an example, he pointed out that though not every violation of custom is a crime, every crime is a violation of custom. Because the purpose of the criminal law is to protect society from violence, he agreed that violations of custom should be made criminal only when they threaten violence and are not merely "social offenses." Other violations of custom should be left outside the legal system, "subject to the jurisdiction of the moral forces of society."[106]

Carter invoked the history of conquest to support his position that custom is the source of law. He observed that even the Norman Conquest did not change the laws of England. Rather than producing new legal rights, he maintained, the courts established by the Normans continued to enforce existing customs,

---

[100] Carter, supra note 23, at 321.
[101] Id. at 129.
[102] Wharton, supra note 5, at 99.
[103] Tiedeman, supra note 13, at 9.
[104] Carter, supra note 23, at 313; see id. at 85.
[105] Id. at 120.
[106] Id. at 241–2.

often affording them better protection.[107] More generally, Carter asserted that no conquering nation had ever abrogated the private law of the peoples they had subdued. "This is significant proof," he concluded, "that the Private Law is self-existent and irrepealable in custom." He did acknowledge, however, that conquering nation could and did impose new laws in the public sphere when necessary to maintain their political sovereignty.[108]

Just as Carter described law as "enforced custom," Wharton maintained that all "operative" laws are "merely declaratory," "the products and not the molders of custom."[109] He emphasized that "custom makes the law, and not law custom."[110] Whereas Carter referred occasionally to Savigny throughout his book, Wharton invoked him explicitly to support this point. Wharton observed that "tracing the origins of law to local custom" was the "distinguishing feature of the historical school, of which Savigny is the most able and prominent representative."[111] Like Carter, Tiedeman observed that "not every moral rule commonly practiced by the mass of people, becomes a legal rule, obedience to which is enforced by a legal sanction."[112] He identified "moral suasion" and "physical force" as the two fundamentally different yet supplementary forces that control society. Moral suasion influences character and operates through church, home, and social life. Law invokes the threat of physical force by the government. "Those wrongful, immoral acts, which are properly called crimes or trespasses upon the interests of others," Tiedeman observed, "are generally regulated by law, but, except so far as they likewise have the character of trespasses, vices are left to the correction of the moral influence of public opinion."[113] He concluded that "the same social forces which create and develop the ethics of a nation create and develop its law; that the substantive law is essentially nothing more than the moral rules, commonly and habitually obeyed by the masses, whose enforcement by the courts is required for the public good."[114] Hammond similarly claimed that "law is not the independent creation of the judicial mind." The judge, he maintained, is only the "instrument" for applying "the popular sense of right" in a particular case.[115]

Twentieth-century scholars, particularly those interested in the sociology and anthropology of law, have debated whether the term "law" should be extended from binding rules enforced by the government to all binding rules enforced by various social groups within society.[116] The nineteenth-century American legal

[107] Id. at 58–60.
[108] Id. at 85–6.
[109] Wharton, supra note 5, at iii.
[110] Id. at 22 n. 1.
[111] Id. at 6.
[112] Tiedeman, supra note 13, at 13.
[113] Id. at 14.
[114] Id. at 15.
[115] William Gardiner Hammond, Dates and Topics, pp. 14–15, Hammond Papers, supra note 77, vol. 2.
[116] Sally Falk Moore, Law as Process: An Anthropological Approach (London: Routledge & K. Paul, 1978), p. 17.

scholars did not anticipate this debate. In contrasting custom from law, they indicated that the enforcement of rules through the legal power of the state is fundamentally different from the regulation of conduct through custom alone. Rather than engaging in the subsequent debate over whether "law" extends beyond the rules enforced by government, the nineteenth-century scholars were most interested in how law enforced by government responds to evolving custom.

Carter stressed that as transformations in society subject customs to "incessant change," the "law resting upon custom must change in accordance with it."[117] Custom, he believed, is not a vestige of the past that continues to influence the present, but a source of law that is perpetually renewed.[118] Hammond agreed. "If new customs arise under changing circumstances of a community, and are of such a nature that the public weal requires them to be enforced," he asserted, "this conviction operates at once upon them, and converts the mere custom into law."[119] Wharton maintained that "there is scarcely a maxim or a custom now recognized as part of the common law of England in our own times which is not, in its present exact shape, of an origin comparatively modern." Giving many examples, he concluded that virtually none of the common law that existed during the reign of Richard I had survived.[120] And in the United States, new customs effectively repealed prior English common law without needing any judicial or legislative action. The old law, based on old customs, simply "ceased to be in force."[121] Cooley declared that the common law is "the outgrowth of the habits of thought and action of the people, and was modified from time to time as those habits become modified, and as civilization advanced, and as new inventions changed the modes of business."[122] Even conceptions of natural rights, Tiedeman stressed, are not "fixed" or "invariable." They "vary and their characters change with the development of the ethical conceptions of the people, the development of the legal rights keeping pace with, and following behind, the development of natural or ethical rights." The natural rights proclaimed in the Declaration of Independence to be endowed by the Creator, he observed, were in fact "developed within the historical memory of man" and were unknown in earlier patriarchal societies.[123]

The evolution of new customs, some scholars emphasized, can conflict with existing law that had been generated by the superseded customs of the past. Carter observed that in such circumstances people "become dissatisfied with the standards which the existing law applies." The essential task of the legal system becomes "conforming the law to the actual custom of the

[117] Carter, supra note 23, at 258.
[118] Id. at 119.
[119] Hammond's Blackstone, supra note 64, vol. 1, at 213.
[120] Wharton, supra note 5, at 24.
[121] Id. at 22.
[122] Cooley, supra note 34, at 21.
[123] Tiedeman, supra note 13, at 73.

present."[124] Tiedeman made the same point in discussing the "evolution" of "the popular sense of right." "Although the legal rule reflects the popular sense of right, prevalent when it was formulated, it may not, and usually does not, conform altogether to the popular sense of right in its later stages of development, and very frequently there is so great a variance between them as to cause serious popular dissatisfaction."[125] Yet eventually, Tiedeman maintained, law will conform to the new sense of right through legal fictions or legislation, factors previously identified by Maine in *Ancient Law* for bringing law "into harmony with society."[126]

Several of these scholars emphasized that judicial decisions and legislation are ineffective when they do not conform to evolving custom. Carter differentiated correct precedents, which are "authenticated custom,"[127] from incorrect precedents, which are not rooted in custom and are not followed by the people. Custom is always the controlling power, whether the precedent is right or wrong. Judges, he added, tacitly recognize this point by reexamining decisions that do not turn out to govern conduct. They confess error by admitting either that something held in accordance with custom actually was not, or, conversely, that something classified as a departure from custom actually comported with it.[128] "A judicial precedent," he concluded, "is not law *per se*, but evidence of it only. The real law is custom."[129] Nor can legislation trump custom. When legislative power "is exerted to reinforce custom and prevent violations of it, it may be effectual, and rules or commands thus established are properly called laws; but if aimed against established custom they will be ineffectual."[130]

Tiedeman similarly asserted that some legislation does not reflect the prevalent sense of right and, therefore, "cannot be enforced." He called such legislation "deplorable" and "a misuse of power" because "it tends to lessen the popular reverence or respect for law, and habituates the people to the repeated violation, not only of those laws which do not reflect the prevalent sense of right, but also those which are so sanctioned."[131] Yet judges, to the extent possible within the letter of such legislation, typically construe it in ways that "conform" to this sense of right, thereby enforcing an entirely different result from the legislative intent. As an example, he cited the judicial construction of the English Statute of Uses, which produced most of the modern law of trusts.[132] Wharton gave eleven examples of laws that are "inoperative" in a "civilized society" because they do not respond to "national conscience and national

---

[124] Carter, supra note 23, at 129.
[125] Tiedeman, supra note 13, at 9.
[126] Id. at 12–13. Tiedman did not cite Maine. See Sir Henry Maine, Ancient law (Washington, D.C.: Baird Books, 2000) (reprint of 1861 ed.), p. 15.
[127] Carter, supra note 23, at 65–6.
[128] Id. at 82–3.
[129] Id. at 84.
[130] Id. at 130.
[131] Tiedeman, supra note 13, at 7 and n. 1.
[132] Id. at 8.

need."[133] They included laws imposing religious or political tests, "exacting social equality" or "prescribing equal division of property," regulating currency or fixing prices, establishing perpetuities, and prohibiting self-defense.[134]

While elaborating their own position that evolving custom is the source of law, the Americans occasionally emphasized their disagreement with important English and German scholars, whose treatment of the relationship between custom and law failed to recognize that custom evolves. Carter criticized Blackstone for asserting that the unwritten common law of the present is based entirely on "*ancient* custom, reaching so far back that its beginning is not known." Evolution demonstrated to Carter that "*present* custom" is the foundation of current law.[135] Wharton went further, claiming that Blackstone had erred not only in portraying the English common law as "running back indefinitely through times unknown," but in assuming that, as interpreted by him and his predecessors, it "had reached a perfection which it would be sacrilege to touch."[136] Hammond, by contrast, tried to reconcile his own evolutionary views with Blackstone. He differentiated the customs enforced by the common law, which "may change almost with every generation," from "the system of common law as a whole," which may "truly be styled of immemorial antiquity."[137]

Americans also stressed the evolution of custom in opposing theories that viewed custom and law as distinctive and successive stages of development. Carter criticized Maine for maintaining that Austin's view of law as the command of the sovereign, while incorrectly ignoring the underlying role of custom in primitive European and current oriental societies,[138] would eventually become "as true in fact as it is elegant in theory"[139] when progressive Aryan nations developed into centralized states. Reiterating "the supremacy of custom"[140] in the present as well as the past, Carter called Maine's conclusion "as erroneous as it is remarkable."[141] Hammond similarly criticized German scholars, particularly Beseler, who differentiated legal development into distinct stages of customary law, or *Volksrecht*, followed by "reflective" law, or *Juristenrecht*.[142]

Evolving Custom and Constitutional Law

Just as the original constitutional history written by Americans reflected the approach to legal history that dominated the much more extensive scholarship

---

[133] Wharton, supra note 5, at 56.
[134] Id. at 56–8.
[135] Carter, supra note 23, at 71; see also id. at 62, 75.
[136] Wharton, supra note 5, at 134.
[137] Hammond's Blackstone, supra note 64, vol. 1, at 207; see also Cooley, supra note 34, at 21.
[138] Carter, supra note 23, at 199.
[139] Id. at 200.
[140] Id. at 203.
[141] Id. at 199; see also id. at 187–90.
[142] Hammond, supra note 10, at 313.

on the early history of English law, several American scholars made clear that their general analysis of evolving custom as the source of law applied to constitutional law as well. They seemed to feel that the novelty of the written Constitution of the United States, in contrast to the unwritten constitution of Great Britain, posed challenges to this theory that required attention. Tiedeman wrote a short book, *The Unwritten Constitution of the United States*, on the role of evolving custom in constitutional interpretation, and others addressed this issue throughout their writings. Though they occasionally acknowledged that the literal language of a written constitution imposes some limits on its construction, they overwhelmingly emphasized the extent to which evolving custom remained the major determinant of constitutional meaning.

Wharton introduced his treatment of the Constitution by using language that was virtually identical to his earlier discussion of evolving custom as the basis for law. He maintained that constitutional laws, "like all other laws, are the product of the conscience and the necessities of the people from whom they emanate and by whom they are accepted."[143] They are effective only if they are "declaratory," if they "penetrate to the people," who construct as well as adopt them. The evolution of constitutional law, as of law generally, is mostly unconscious, instinctive, and unobserved. It must be understood historically, by examining the forces and environments that shaped it.[144] Cooley observed repeatedly that a good constitution evolves gradually out of the national experience of a people and reflects their prevailing views about government.[145] Tiedeman similarly pointed to national character and will, developed through national growth, as the real source of a constitution. Constitutions imposed by government edict or developed through philosophical speculation, he stressed, are likely to be out of harmony with historically evolved popular principles and, therefore, are unlikely to work.[146]

Both Wharton and Tiedeman cited the constitution John Locke drafted for the Carolina colonies as an example of a failed constitution, of the "impotence," in Wharton's words, "of paper law when brought into conflict with customary law." A constitution, Wharton insisted, cannot "be framed in the closets of English philosophers to be adapted to the wants and meet the convictions of the settlers of a new world."[147] Conversely, Tiedeman observed, the English and American constitutions work well, not because they have any "inherent and abstract excellences," but because, despite their imperfections, they are the "natural products of Anglo-American civilization" and "are in complete correspondence with the political sentiment of the respective nations."[148]

---

[143] Wharton, supra note 5, at 409–10.
[144] Id. at 410.
[145] Cooley, supra note 33, at 346, 349, 356.
[146] Tiedeman, supra note 13, at 16–19.
[147] Wharton, supra note 5, at 33; see Tiedeman, supra note 13, at 19.
[148] Tiedeman, supra note 19, at 20.

Many of the late nineteenth-century American scholars stressed that the written Constitution of the United States had not prevented transformations of constitutional interpretation in response to evolving custom. Pomeroy used the electoral college as an example. The Constitution, Pomeroy asserted, contemplated that electors would exercise their own judgment in voting for president. Typically chosen by state legislatures, they were supposed to be independent of the people. With the rapid growth of political parties and of demands for popular sovereignty, however, the system intended by the Constitution soon became obsolete. The people obtained control over electors by voting for them directly and by having electors pledge in advance to vote for the presidential candidate of a particular political party. "This complete change," Pomeroy observed, "is a remarkable instance of the way in which written laws and constitutions however carefully guarded may be made to yield to a change in popular feelings and wishes, so that while not a clause is repealed or modified, the effect of the whole is completely transformed." He attributed this change to an "unwritten law," which enforced the will of the people through the political process without any involvement of the courts.[149]

Cooley observed that a written constitution will have to be applied to many subjects "not present to the minds of the framers in drafting it."[150] In the United States, though the "bounds of power" expressed in the Constitution have not changed, "the gradual march of events" produced an enormous, almost infinite, increase in the power of the federal government. Cooley used the analogy of the conveyance of a lot of land to illustrate his views about constitutional interpretation. "When one conveys the lot upon which a palatial dwelling has been erected," Cooley wrote, "he may use the same descriptive terms of metes and bounds as when the lot had value for little more than a playground for school-boys; the dwelling is a mere incident to the lot, and it goes with it in conveyance without question, and also without specification."[151] As examples of "how vast is the edifice that may rightfully be erected within the bounds of single federal powers, which at first seemed of little importance,"[152] Cooley mentioned the application of the war power to destroy slavery and the extension of the power to regulate interstate commerce. John Quincy Adams, Cooley observed, was ridiculed when he initially maintained that in an emergency the war power could be used against slavery. Yet during the Civil War the people by "common consent" took precisely that position. The power to regulate interstate commerce, Cooley added, initially was so unimportant that it received little attention when the Constitution was adopted. Yet the "application of steam to locomotion and of electricity to correspondence has worked relatively as great a change in government as it has in the industrial world."

---

[149] Pomeroy, supra note 1, at 427–8.
[150] Cooley, supra note 33, at 354.
[151] Id. at 355.
[152] Id. at 356.

Federal power became necessary to regulate "public conveniences" that vitally affect citizens.[153]

Wharton similarly pointed out that the meaning of constitutional language "is unfolded under the action of changing conditions."[154] Citing Cooley, he stressed that the power of Congress had expanded "to specific objects which were not dreamed of by the framers."[155] In addition to Cooley's examples of changes in constitutional interpretation, Wharton mentioned the transformation of the function of the electoral college and the use of the "dormant" treaty power to annex territory.[156] While interpreting the constitutional amendments added after the Civil War, Wharton reiterated that constitutional meaning reflects social evolution. The abolition of slavery by the Thirteenth Amendment, he declared, represented "an organic change of public sentiment."[157] Though "nominally effected by an amendment to the Constitution, it was really effected by the spontaneous and instinctive action of the people as a whole when the civil war closed." The people "felt that after what had taken place, slavery could no longer exist." The textual amendment "recorded, and did not create, abolition."[158] Even southerners, though often reluctant to express this position and worried about the practical consequences of freeing the slaves, recognized abolition "as a necessity as fully as at the north."[159] Wharton also stressed popular understandings that limited the scope of the Fourteenth Amendment to the "negro race." He emphasized that its definition of citizenship "grew distinctively out of the late civil war" and must be understood in that context. There was no popular support, he asserted, for extending citizenship to Indian tribes or to Chinese immigrants. Indeed, the people would have rejected any amendment that explicitly would have done so.[160]

The framers themselves, Carter maintained, recognized that the Constitution must be interpreted differently in light of unanticipated subsequent developments. Only a "feeble minority" of the framers, he conceded, would have voted for constitutional provisions enabling the exercise of broad federal power that subsequently took place under the authority of the Constitution, including chartering banks, constructing railroads, fighting a war against seceding states, denying the mail service to state lotteries, and exerting authority over people in distant territories. Yet Carter maintained that had the framers lived into the present, they might have acquiesced in such extensions of federal power "as authorized by their own language."[161]

---

[153] Id. at 355.
[154] Wharton, supra note 5, at 449.
[155] Id. at 28.
[156] Id. at 28–9, 449.
[157] Id. at 659.
[158] Id. at 32–3.
[159] Id. at 659.
[160] Id. at 663–4.
[161] Carter, supra note 23, at 319.

Among the many late nineteenth-century scholars who stressed the role of evolving custom in constitutional law, only Tiedeman devoted an entire book to this subject. In *The Unwritten Constitution of the United States*, published in 1890, Tiedeman stressed that "the great body of American constitutional law cannot be found in the written instruments, which we call our constitutions." Rather, it is "unwritten" in the legal sense of that term, "to be found in the decisions of the courts and the acts of the National and State legislatures, constantly changing with the demands of the popular will."[162] While maintaining that the constitutional understandings of the people are more important than those of the framers, Tiedeman stressed that these popular understandings change over time. "The present popular will," not the will of those who either framed or voted for the Constitution, "must indicate which shade of meaning must be given to the written word." Tiedeman insisted that "the intentions of our ancestors cannot be permitted to control the present activity of the government."[163]

Tiedeman emphasized throughout his book that "all political constitutions undergo a constant and gradual evolution, keeping pace with the development of civilization, whether there be a written constitution or not." He added that "these changes generally take place without formal amendments to the written constitution."[164] Rather, they evolve through what he called the "unwritten constitution." Tiedeman concluded that the adoption of a written Constitution had "not materially altered the law of constitutional development" in the United States, which "follows and registers all material changes in public opinion as unerringly as the needle follows the magnetic meridian."[165] He devoted most of his book to demonstrating "striking examples of the mutations of constitutional law"[166] without formal amendments. These examples included the contradictory constructions of the constitutional provision prohibiting the impairment of contracts, discussed in the previous chapter, and the one identified by Pomeroy and Wharton, the transformed function of the electoral college.

The Constraints of a Written Constitution

While invoking changes in circumstances and popular understandings as justifying interpretations of the Constitution that deviate from its original meaning, many scholars conceded that a written constitution imposes some limits on subsequent interpretation. Despite the transformed understanding of the role of the electoral college, Pomeroy and Tiedeman observed, its continued existence mandated by the text of the Constitution hindered the implementation

---

[162] Tiedeman, supra note 13, at 45.

[163] Id. at 144.

[164] Id. at 155.

[165] Id. at 41.

[166] Id. at 45.

of the popular sovereignty the people desired. The unwritten law, in Pomeroy's opinion, did not fully solve the problem of the electoral college. "Under our present customs," he felt, "the choice of presidential electors has become a mere idle and useless form." Unless people wanted to return to its original meaning, "it would be better to abandon it altogether and permit the people to vote directly for the President."[167] Tiedeman agreed. The changed interpretation of the electoral college, he complained, had not sufficiently deprived the written constitutional text of its restraints on popular sovereignty. Under the changed construction, the people still vote for electors to the electoral college, not directly for the presidential candidate. As a result of differences in state populations, he observed, the electoral college has elected candidates who received a minority of the popular votes, thereby preventing "a full realization of the demand for a popular election" of the president.[168]

More generally, Pomeroy recognized the "essential difference" between the written Constitution of the United States and the unwritten constitution of England. "It may be," he conceded, "that an unwritten, traditional, elastic constitution, capable of continuous development, able, like the Common Law, to adapt itself to the changing needs of society and the state, is superior to the written." But he was certain that the American people preferred their written constitution to an unwritten one and that this preference had interpretative consequences. He maintained that a written constitution is subject to the same limiting principles of textual interpretation as a statute. Yet he also maintained that while a "careful, textual, lawyer-like mode is indispensable in construing the fundamental law of the United States, there is still room for the more free, wide, and statesmanlike methods," which should be employed by members of all branches of government as well as by the people themselves. These freer methods, he observed, allowed constitutional interpretation to incorporate both the "lessons taught by history," including the history of other nations, and "principles of justice and equity."[169]

Despite his concession that an unwritten constitution may be preferable to a written one, Pomeroy praised the combination of these interpretive techniques. He objected to the two opposing schools who favored either the strict textual method or the freer "statesmanlike" approach. "Each is in error," he wrote, "and disasters would surely follow were either to obtain a permanent supremacy." Under the exclusively textual method, "the Constitution loses its character as the fundamental, organic law of a government, and sinks to the level of an ordinary private statute, to be expounded with all the technical and literal precision which would be appropriate to a penal code." Under the exclusively statesmanlike approach, "the Constitution loses its character of law at all, and becomes simply a starting-point from which to construct a system unwritten and traditional." While the exclusively textual method "would

---

[167] Pomeroy, supra note 1, at 428.
[168] Tiedeman, supra note 13, at 50.
[169] Pomeroy, supra note 32, at 14–16.

cramp and dwarf the energies of a growing nation," the exclusively statesman-like approach "would remove all the barriers which have been set up lest those energies should finally become self-destructive." In the United States, Pomeroy happily concluded, the combination of the textual method and the statesman-like approach had prevailed, allowing "national development" to proceed "uninterrupted by arbitrary restraints, and unbroken by sudden shocks."[170]

Like Pomeroy, Wharton contrasted Great Britain, where no written constitution constrains government power, to the United States. Wharton was more specific than Pomeroy in identifying how the written Constitution of the United States limits interpretation. While conceding that the text of the Constitution allows substantial leeway in its construction, he emphasized that it contains some language that is "not only absolute but precise" and that must be followed.[171] Changed conditions, he observed, cannot abrogate explicit constitutional provisions prohibiting the establishment of religion, restrictions on freedom of petition and speech, deprivations of civil equality, or the taking of life, liberty, or property without due process of law. Other constitutional provisions, by contrast, "are in the nature of blank powers, to be filled in by the unconscious legislation of eras." As examples, he cited "the clauses conferring on the Federal government prerogatives essential to its empire," including the "dormant" powers over commerce and treaties.[172] As a general matter, he differentiated the "elasticity" of interpretation regarding "imperial powers" from the "rigor" necessary to construe constitutional language "securing state sovereignty and individual rights."[173]

In the chapter of *Constitutional Limitations* addressing the construction of state constitutions, Cooley took a much stricter approach to the interpretation of written constitutions. He stressed the "cardinal rule" that written instruments, including constitutions, "shall receive an unvarying interpretation," yielding a uniform practical construction. A major goal of a written constitution, he maintained, is to place the "fundamentals of government" beyond the control of "the varying moods of public opinion," which include the "temporary excitements and passions among the people" that prompt oppressive legislation in violation of fundamental constitutional rights. He directly contrasted the common law, where changes in public opinion should guide the courts, from construction of a written constitution, where judges and legislators "would be justly chargeable with reckless disregard of official oath and public duty," if they similarly deferred to public opinion. "The meaning of the constitution is fixed when it is adopted," Cooley concluded, "and it is not different at any subsequent time when a court has occasion to pass upon it." In interpreting a constitution, judges must "*declare the law as written*, leaving it to the people to make such changes as new circumstances require,"[174] presumably through the

---

[170] Id. at 16.
[171] Wharton, supra note 5, at 448.
[172] Id. at 449.
[173] Id. at 450 n. 1.
[174] Cooley, supra note 34, at 54-5.

formal amendment process. If a written constitutional provision seems unjust, Cooley added, judges should do everything possible to construe it in ways that prevent the injustice, often by interpreting it in light of the general purposes of the Constitution. But if such an interpretation cannot legitimately be made, the remedy "must rest with the people themselves, through an amendment of their work when better counsels prevail."[175]

Writing in the newly established *Harvard Law Review* approximately twenty years later, Cooley explicitly examined the "Comparative Merits of Written and Prescriptive Constitutions." A written constitution, he maintained, has the major advantage of imposing checks on legislative power by apportioning authority among different branches of government. In countries with an unwritten constitution, by contrast, the legislature is "necessarily supreme" and can abuse its power by changing the constitution at will, a strong temptation during periods of "temporary excitement."[176] He added that the steps required to amend a written constitution avoid the perils of "popular caprice and passion" by imposing delays, which allow "temporary passions to cool" and "excitements to pass away."[177] The major advantage of an unwritten constitution over a written one, Cooley maintained, lies in its capacity to respond to "the history and experiences of the people,"[178] to reflect "the principle of growth and expansion," the "most important principle of all."[179] The most excellent constitution, he stressed, "is obviously that which is the natural outgrowth of the national life, and which, having grown and expanded as the national thought has matured, is likely at any particular time to express the prevailing sentiment regarding government, and the accepted principles of civil and political liberty."[180] Failure to incorporate the historical progress of the people had been the "radical vice" of most written constitutions in Europe.[181]

Yet Cooley did not think this vice was inherent in the very structure of a written constitution. Indeed, he cited the United States Constitution as a written constitution that is as much of a growth as the unwritten constitution of England. Based on the general principles of government and liberty that over a long period had emerged in England,[182] the United States Constitution "was framed on the principle and with the purpose of preserving in America everything in the British constitution which was suited to the condition and circumstances of the new world; and there is not in all history a fundamental law which is a more genuine growth."[183] In contrast to countries with unwritten constitutions, where growth is often settled "at the point of a sword," as in

---

[175] Id. at 73.
[176] Cooley, supra note 33, at 347, 350.
[177] Id. at 350–1.
[178] Id. at 349.
[179] Id. at 347.
[180] Id. at 356.
[181] Id. at 347.
[182] Id.
[183] Id. at 349–50.

England at the time of the Magna Carta and the Revolution of 1688, a written constitution provides a mechanism, the amendment process, to accommodate growth peacefully.[184] While acknowledging that the last four amendments to the United States Constitution "were born of the Civil War," Cooley maintained that the Civil War was not fought to obtain them and that they would have been enacted anyway. "It was to escape an inevitable reform, not, as yet, imminent, but clearly foreshadowed, that the war was begun; and the four years of bloodshed only precipitated a purification of National and State constitutions, that would otherwise have come more slowly and peacefully, and as a necessary step in national progress."[185] Cooley concluded that the United States Constitution is essentially conservative, "the most conservative instrument of government known to the world," which in its very conservatism has enabled the United States to become "the chief representative of political progress." The "binding inflexibility" of the written constitution, "subject to safe amendment," works "in harmony" with "the progressive spirit of the people."[186]

More than other American scholars, Tiedeman minimized the impact of a written constitution. He declared that the "unwritten constitution of the United States, within the broad limitations of the written Constitution, is just as flexible, and yields just as readily to the mutations of public opinion as the unwritten constitution of Great Britain." The qualifying language indicated that even Tiedeman, who stressed the primacy of "the unwritten Constitution of the United States" in the title of his book, recognized that the written Constitution had some force. Yet Tiedeman took pains to stress how few restraints the written Constitution actually imposed. He anticipated that opponents of his theory would construe the qualifying language of this "savings clause" as undermining his fundamental point that the unwritten constitution dominates constitutional interpretation even in countries with a written constitution. Tiedeman responded by referring to the actual changes in judicial interpretation of written constitutional provisions, which "are made to mean one thing at one time, and at another time an altogether different thing" in reaction to "the stress of public opinion or private interests." These dramatic judicial transformations proved to Tiedeman the weakness of the written constitutional restraints. "The only obstacle in the way of an untrammeled popular will," he maintained, "is the bald letter of the Constitution." And even the baldest constitutional constraint, he added while referring to his subsequent chapter on the Civil War, "does not chain the popular will in times of great excitement and extreme necessity."[187] For Tiedeman, the only way to account for this otherwise "inexplicable contradiction" was to recognize that the "prevalent sense of right furnishes, in war as well as in peace, the norm for the formulation of rules of law."[188]

[184] Id. at 351.
[185] Id. at 352.
[186] Id. at 353.
[187] Tiedeman, supra note 13, at 43–4.
[188] Id. at 89.

Tiedeman's focus on the predominance of unwritten constitutional inter-pretation, even in a country with a written constitution, did not prevent him from asserting the superiority of the written United States Constitution to purely unwritten constitutions.[189] He applauded the checks and balances of the Constitution,[190] but he was most impressed with judicial review of the constitutionality of legislation. In contrast to Cooley and Thayer, who favored judicial deference to legislative determinations of the constitutionality of legis-lation, Tiedeman argued for much more extensive judicial review under a writ-ten constitution. He encouraged judicial invalidation of legislation and even judicial deviations from the constitutional text. Although he did not believe that the Constitution itself explicitly granted the judiciary the power to review the constitutionality of legislation, Tiedeman asserted that the structural role of the courts in the written constitutional system required them to make this determination.[191] According to Tiedeman, judicial review serves the fundamen-tal purpose of "protecting the minority against the absolutism of a democratic majority." Judges can reject popular legislation whenever they determine that it violates a constitutional provision. "This," Tiedeman declared, "is the real value of the written Constitution."[192]

Yet the judicial power to declare legislation unconstitutional, he immedi-ately added, is a barrier not to popular will, but to the people's "whims and ill-considered wishes" that result in "the evils of hasty and passionate legisla-tion." Consistent with his general theory that law must ultimately conform to the prevalent sense of right, Tiedeman was confident that the true popular will, rather than the passing popular whim, would ultimately prevail.[193] Various checks on judicial power, he pointed out, make declarations of unconstitu-tionality "only a dilatory proceeding."[194] For example, if the Supreme Court persists in resisting the popular will by declaring legislation unconstitutional, Congress can increase the number of Supreme Court justices and the presi-dent can appoint new ones "who will do the people's bidding."[195] The written Constitution of the United States, Tiedeman happily concluded, "succeeded in establishing, what exists nowhere else, a popular government without demo-cratic absolutism."[196]

Tiedeman praised the Supreme Court's narrowing interpretation of the Fourteenth Amendment in the *Slaughter-House* cases as a specific example of how judicial review can check passionate and ill-considered congressional action, even in the form of a constitutional amendment. The original American constitutional innovation of dual national and state citizenship, he observed,

---

[189] Id. at 155.
[190] Id. at 158–9.
[191] Id. at 160.
[192] Id. at 163.
[193] Id. at 164–5.
[194] Id. at 164.
[195] Id. at 161–2.
[196] Id. at 165.

did not clarify the relative strength of these two forms of citizenship.[197] This issue remained unexplored until agitation over slavery became significant.[198] Both the majority and dissenting opinions in the famous *Dred Scott* decision, he pointed out, agreed that citizenship of the United States derived from citizenship of a state. The dispute in *Dred Scott* was over the power of a free state to invest a slave from another state with the rights of national citizenship by first making the slave a citizen of the free state.[199] Worried that the analysis of dual citizenship in *Dred Scott* would undermine enforcement of the abolition of slavery, Congress passed the Fourteenth Amendment after the Civil War. The Fourteenth Amendment, Tiedeman asserted, did more than reverse *Dred Scott* and make state citizenship subordinate to national citizenship.[200] Its literal language, reflecting the intent of its framers in Congress, gave the Supreme Court, in Tiedeman's words, "the power at any time to inquire into the effect of State legislation on the fundamental privileges and immunities of the citizen, which, before the adoption of the amendment, were exclusively within the control and protection of the State governments."[201]

Tiedeman pointed out that Republicans in Congress, "flushed" with victory in the Civil War and "inflamed" by the repressive black laws enacted in the South, invoked the authority of the new Fourteenth Amendment to pass "far-reaching" legislation "which would be strong enough to protect the negro in his freedom."[202] The congressional Republicans wanted "to deprive the Southern people of all legal opportunity to keep the negro in political and social subjection, and, thus, to frustrate the realization of what they considered the legitimate results of the war." Unfortunately from Tiedeman's perspective, "this special end could not be attained without putting an end, everywhere, to local self-government in the American sense."[203]

The Supreme Court's decision in the *Slaughter-House* cases, Tiedeman maintained, "happily" averted this "disastrous result."[204] It limited the scope of the words "privileges and immunities of citizens of the United States" in the Fourteenth Amendment to an enumerated list, ascribing all other privileges and immunities to state citizenship.[205] Tiedeman had no doubt that this limited interpretation violated the literal meaning of the Fourteenth Amendment.[206] But the literal meaning, if enforced, would have reduced the states to insignificance and granted the federal government "supervisory control over the smallest concerns of life."[207] Unlike Cooley, Tiedeman did not believe the judiciary

---

[197] Id. at 107.
[198] Id. at 94.
[199] Id. at 97.
[200] Id. at 98.
[201] Id. at 99; see id. at 100.
[202] Id. at 101.
[203] Id. at 102.
[204] Id.
[205] Id. at 103–6.
[206] Id.
[207] Id. at 108.

should be limited by the Constitution's literal meaning. The Supreme Court's decision, Tiedeman asserted, was "noble."[208] Believing that the people had been "blinded with passion" in approving the Fourteenth Amendment, the decision narrowed the amendment's literal meaning to what the Court judged the people would have ratified in "their cooler moments."[209] The absence of any outcry against the decision or attempt to overrule it proved to Tiedeman that it reflected the people's "prevalent, but perhaps then unexpressed, sense of right." Whereas Wharton approved the *Slaughter-House* decision as a proper interpretation of the original meaning of the Fourteenth Amendment,[210] Tiedeman called it a "successful modification" of the literal language of the Fourteenth Amendment, which continued to serve "as a bulwark to the States in their struggle for autonomy and self-government."[211]

The Preference for Adjudication over Legislation

Because they believed that judges are better able than legislators to detect evolving customs and transform them into law, late nineteenth-century American legal scholars, like Savigny before them, generally preferred judicial decision-making over legislation as the locus for declaring the law. The underlying consensus that judges have the primary role in translating evolving custom into law was shared by scholars who disagreed with each other about whether judges "make" or "find" law, a major debate in late nineteenth-century American legal thought. Scholars who maintained that judges appropriately make law defended "judicial legislation" as the method of conforming law to evolving custom. Scholars who vigorously opposed "judicial legislation" and who insisted that judges only "find" law construed the judicial identification of evolved custom as "finding" the law.

Pomeroy and Carter were the scholars who expressed the preference for the judicial decision over the statute in greatest detail. Pomeroy stressed that both individual statutes and complete codes can only reflect the conditions of the age that produces them. They are unable to anticipate the needs and demands of a developing society.[212] Because their meaning depends mostly on the "mere language" of which they are composed, they are often difficult to understand and are arbitrarily applied.[213] The judicial decision, by contrast, "has an inherent power of expansion, unlimited except by the national life of the people, of whose civilization it is the product and exponent."[214] It is "superior" to the

---

[208] Id. at 106.
[209] Id. at 108; see id. at 102–3.
[210] Wharton, supra note 5, at 667 n. 1.
[211] Tiedeman, supra note 13, at 108–9.
[212] Pomeroy, supra note 1, at 201, 202, 206.
[213] Id. at 186.
[214] Id. at 202.

statute because judges, unlike statutes, can "bring forth new rules from the old premises, and apply them to the ever-changing circumstances of society."[215]

Carter, who was well known as an active opponent of the codification movement in the United States, similarly emphasized that judges, not legislators, are in the best position to conform law to evolving custom. Judges, he declared, are the experts in detecting and authenticating advances in custom and enforcing fair expectations based on those advances. They provide the "process by which the unwritten private law recognizes the advance in morals and manners and affixes upon advancing forms of custom the authenticating stamp of public approval."[216] As illustrations, he cited approvingly developments in the laws of sales, contract, and property. This continuing judicial process, he maintained, improves the law without legislative help. In specifically opposing Field's defense of codification, Carter relied heavily on Savigny.[217] He objected that codification declares rules that will be applicable in the future to situations that have never previously arisen. These rules could easily produce unanticipated results that are irrational and unfair.[218] Codification, he emphasized, is fundamentally inconsistent with his theory that evolving custom is the source of law.[219]

Ames and Thayer also expressed their preference for the judicial decision over legislation while stressing the value of legal history as a guide to reforming current law. The original historical investigations by professors, Ames maintained, would provide useful advice to judges, who are in a better position to develop the law than legislators. While conceding that legislation is occasionally necessary, Ames warned that it is a "dangerous weapon." He cited two pieces of legislation in New York as examples. The disastrous experience under a New York law dealing with trusts, he observed, eventually led to the restoration of the English common law. Ames also endorsed John Chipman Gray's severe criticism of the radical change made by the New York legislature in the common law rule against perpetuities. He recognized that "the spirit of codification is abroad," but he hoped at least that it could be "held in check" until, as in Germany, "where by far the best of modern codification is to be found," professors had been able to develop through extensive historical and comparative analysis "a body of legal literature resting upon sound generalizations."[220] While maintaining that his historical investigations had disclosed the need to restate the law of evidence, Thayer emphasized that "our law of evidence is ripe for the hand of the jurist," not for "the hand of the codifier."[221] In his general discussion of the importance of history in understanding law, he warned

[215] Id. at 198.
[216] Carter, supra note 23, at 327.
[217] Mathias Reimann, The Historical School Against Codification: Savigny, Carter, and the Defeat of the New York Civil Code, 37 Am. J. Comp. L. 95, 103–7 (1989).
[218] Carter, supra note 23, at 275.
[219] Id. at 263.
[220] James Barr Ames, The Vocation of the Law Professor, in Ames, supra note 2, pp. 354, 367–8.
[221] Thayer, supra note 3, at 511.

against premature codification and claimed that he knew of no successful codifications either in the United States or abroad.[222] Most codifiers, he asserted, made terrible, though honest, mistakes by attempting to legislate before they had sufficient knowledge, which historical research would provide.

Although they generally preferred the development of law by judges, which they frequently called "judicial legislation," late nineteenth-century legal scholars approved statutory legislation in narrowly specified conditions. They asserted that sometimes, particularly in periods of rapid social transformation, the statute is more effective than the judicial decision in enforcing changing customs. They also recognized the value of statutes in promoting legal certainty and uniformity. Yet even when they acknowledged a limited role for the statute, they stressed that it could not deviate from prevailing custom. Carter, the most visible opponent of codification, was also the person who devoted the most attention to the circumstances in which legislative action is appropriate. He maintained that "the consequences of misguided legislation should not blind us to its beneficent uses."[223] Though he often worried that legislation poses dangers to liberty, he praised its use within its "just province,"[224] including to enforce custom when courts are unable to do so.[225]

Carter repeatedly distinguished between private law, where legislative action should generally be avoided, and public law, where it is often justified and effective. After observing that over the course of history, as well as in contemporary England and the United States, legislative action typically related to the business of the state,[226] he called public law the "special province" of the legislature.[227] Much appropriate legislative action in the field of public law, Carter declared, deals with the political organization of the state into executive, legislative, and judicial branches of government; the division of territory into subdivisions such as counties and towns; the establishment of a system of taxation; and the maintenance of prisons, schools, courts, and other state institutions.[228] Carter also viewed the criminal law, designed "to preserve society from violence,"[229] as a proper field for the legislature. He asserted as well that "the necessities of civilized, industrial society in modern times have required an extension of the province of penal law by the positive enactment of numerous commands and prohibitions not to be found in the law of custom."[230] He agreed, for example, with the many statutes that specified "positive safeguards" in the operation of new and dangerous machinery, often used in increasingly

---

[222] James Bradley Thayer, The Teaching of English Law at Universities, 9 Harv. L. Rev. 169, 181 (1895).
[223] Carter, supra note 23, at 228.
[224] Id. at 135.
[225] Id. at 136.
[226] Id. at 115–7.
[227] Id. at 253.
[228] Id. at 238.
[229] Id. at 242.
[230] Id. at 244.

crowded urban areas. He approved penal legislation designed to prevent "evils which arise from the competitive struggles of modern life in industrial pursuits" and specifically endorsed statutes that restricted child labor and regulated tenement buildings to preserve health.[231]

More generally, Carter maintained that in the most advanced civilizations, customs, and therefore the laws produced by customs, "are subject to incessant change."[232] Judges, Carter believed, "are unable to break suddenly from the past"[233] and, therefore, cannot react fast enough to deal with these changes, whereas legislative action can resolve uncertainty about the state of custom by declaring any changes "an accomplished fact."[234] To illustrate, he cited favorably statutes providing rights to married women. These statutes, responding to advances in the treatment of women, overturned "harsh" laws that merged the legal existence of the wife in her husband and thereby gave him her property and income.[235] Carter also favored statutes designed to address class conflict, such as between employers and employees. Though he did not provide any specifics, he maintained that a wise legislature could remove the violence from class war by enacting laws that would allow the stronger party to prevail without needing the use of force.[236]

Other scholars who were generally skeptical of legislative action identified some limited exceptions. Like Carter, they believed that the need for rapid change or certainty justified a legislative response. While distinguishing the evolutionary function of judicial legislation from the more revolutionary function of statutory legislation, Wharton indicated that statutes are sometimes necessary. "Undoubtedly," he wrote, "from the legislature must come revolutionary changes in the law, such as make a catastrophic transition from one era to another."[237] Though generally favoring the gradual judicial development of the law, even at the expense of certainty,[238] Pomeroy conceded that legislative action is superior in those few situations when certainty is the highest value. He particularly stressed the need for certainty in criminal law, where the risk to life and liberty is so high, and, therefore, favored statutory definitions of crimes and punishments.[239] While maintaining that judges rather than legislators should take the lead in reforming the law of evidence, Thayer recognized that the judges could benefit from "slight" legislative cooperation, mostly through clear delegations of authority to judges limited only by "a few large and simple principles which are the skeleton of our present system."[240]

[231] Id. at 245.
[232] Id. at 257.
[233] Id. at 136.
[234] Id. at 258–9.
[235] Id. at 259.
[236] Id. at 261–2.
[237] Wharton, supra note 5, at 63.
[238] Pomeroy, supra note 1, at 198.
[239] Id. at 196.
[240] Thayer, supra note 3, at 511, 531.

Both Tiedeman and Cooley justified legislative action when a particularly large gap exists between the current common law and needed reform.
Sometimes, Tiedeman observed, even "fictional construction" of precedent
cannot stretch sufficiently to conform the common law to "the existing sense
of right, and the variance is so great as to cause great discomfort or arouse the
disapprobation of the people." Under such circumstances, changing the law
by statute is the only effective remedy.[241] Cooley made a similar point in his
treatise on torts. While generally preferring judicial development of the law, he
recognized occasional situations "in which improvement by judicial decisions
is impossible, and where legislation alone is adequate to the purpose."[242] He
urged legislative action, for example, if the common law is "distinctly adverse"
to the need for a new legal remedy.[243] In his treatise on constitutional limitations, Cooley also approved legislation both to pronounce authoritatively
common law principles that had been weakened by usurpation or abuse and
to accommodate the law to changes in society, such as the growth of wealth
and commerce. He placed the Magna Carta and the English Bill of Rights in
the first category, and the Statute of Wills and the Statute of Frauds in the
second.[244]

Consistent with their general position that law is effective only when rooted
in custom, while approving legislative action in limited circumstances these
scholars frequently reiterated that legislators, like judges, must conform the
law to prevailing national custom. Pomeroy declared that legislators as well
as judges must follow "the leadings of national life."[245] Wharton observed that
legislative action "emanated from the people as a customary law,"[246] that statutes "are the products of national conscience and necessities."[247] Carter similarly maintained that statutes convert "growing customs into positive rules."[248]
They "aid the unwritten law of custom and make it more effective" rather
than "furnish a substitute for it."[249] Legislation can "supplement and aid the
operation of custom," but it "can never supplant it."[250] While praising reforms
"accomplished by distinct and striking acts of legislation," particularly "the
establishment of the federal government of the United States" and "the emancipation of the American slaves," Cooley warned that legislation, however
excellent in the abstract, cannot operate effectively in advance of custom by
prompting people to "rise to its own level." He expressed as "a mere truism

[241] Tiedeman, supra note 13, at 12–13.
[242] Cooley, supra note 89, vol. 2, at 15.
[243] Id. at 16.
[244] Cooley, supra note 34, at 23.
[245] Pomeroy, supra note 1, at 176.
[246] Wharton, supra note 5, at 51.
[247] Id. at 750.
[248] Carter, supra note 23, at 245.
[249] Id. at 228–9; see 119–20.
[250] Id. at 120; see 313.

that the moral standards of the people must determine that of the laws instead of being determined by them."[251]

External Influences and the History of Legal Doctrine

Both the general conception of law as part of a broader evolution of national culture and the more specific view that custom is the source of law presume that external forces underlie legal development. Just as the American legal historians who wrote original scholarship on the history of English law discussed the impact of the Norman Conquest on the evolution of the common law, the many other American law professors who analyzed law historically alluded to external influences on the history of legal doctrine. Pomeroy, for example, stressed the decline of feudalism and the growth of cities to explain the emergence of personal property as a distinctive and important legal concept. During the feudal period, he pointed out, virtually all wealth was in land, whereas personal property was generally "simple and mean." Feudal law, therefore, ignored personal property as "too insignificant to merit attention." With the growth of powerful free cities, especially the maritime towns, personal property increased in value and sometimes even exceeded the worth of real property. As a result, the legal treatment of personal property became a crucial issue, while the law of real property receded in importance.[252]

In discussing the history of American law, scholars often stressed the distinctiveness of conditions in the United States. Hammond pointed to an unelaborated "entire change in the convictions and circumstances of the people" in explaining why the right of the poor to glean after the harvest and the right to hunt ravenous beasts, both protected under English common law, had disappeared completely in America.[253] Cooley similarly observed that the "rights in common" granted by English common law did not transfer to America. "The circumstances attending to the settlement of America," he declared, "were not favorable to the establishment of similar rights." Those who cultivated the land in America, he added more specifically, typically owned independent estates.[254] In another context, Hammond declared that under the influence of "changed customs of agriculture," California and other American states "evolved a law of irrigation," which recognized a property right in running water that had not been part of the common law of England or the original American states.[255] Cooley indicated that the invention and development of the railroad produced a departure from the old common law rule that the owner of property does not

---

[251] Thomas M. Cooley, Law as an Educating Force (Commencement Address, University of Michigan Law and Dental Schools, 1884) (Thomas M. Cooley Papers, Box 7, Bentley Historical Library, University of Michigan).

[252] Pomeroy, supra note 1, at 281–2.

[253] Hammond's Blackstone, supra note 64, vol. 3, at 295.

[254] Cooley, supra note 89, at 336.

[255] Hammond's Blackstone, supra note 64, vol. 1, at 213.

have to fence his land. Though some American jurisdictions initially applied this rule to railroads, many eventually required railroad companies to fence their land, either through legislation explicitly overruling the common law or simply through not following it.[256] More generally, Cooley contrasted the "aristocratic sentiment" that controlled English law with the democratic ideas underlying American law and government.[257] In America, Cooley stated, English law "was raw material to be worked over" under the influence of these broader democratic ideas. As a result, American law eliminated aspects of English law based on the special privileges or burdens of class and provided greater legal protection for life, liberty, and property.[258]

The political experience of the American colonists, scholars frequently stressed, accounted for key features of American constitutional law. Tiedeman stressed "the complete harmony" of the Constitution "with the political evolution of the nation."[259] Pomeroy's treatise on constitutional law contained a twenty-five-page chapter entitled "Historical Sketch of the Political Movements Which Terminated in the Adoption of the Constitution."[260] This chapter discussed events from the Declaration of Independence through the Revolutionary War, the Articles of Confederation, and the framing and ratification of the Constitution. Like Thayer in discussing judicial review and Cooley in discussing the First Amendment, Pomeroy stressed that a broadly accepted conception of popular sovereignty, forged through these events, formed the basis for the government created by the Constitution.[261] Only after sketching "the external history of the adoption of our Constitution" and examining "the nature of the various acts which preceded that event, to the end that the true national character of the political society and of its organic law might be discovered," did Pomeroy "interrogate the instrument itself."[262]

Just as Cooley cited experience under the Sedition Act of 1798 to analyze the emerging understanding of the recently ratified First Amendment and as Tiedeman cited popular concern about the growth of corporate power to explain apparent contradictions in Supreme Court decisions construing the constitutional prohibition against the impairment of contracts, scholars provided other examples of events after the ratification of the Constitution that influenced its subsequent interpretation. Pomeroy and Tiedeman pointed out that the functions of the electoral college set forth in the text of the Constitution had been dramatically transformed by the unanticipated development of political parties and by growing demands that presidential elections reflect the ideology of popular

---

256　Cooley, supra note 89, at 337–8.
257　Thomas M. Cooley, Suggestions Concerning the Study of the Law, in William Blackstone, Commentaries on the Laws of England (Chicago: Callaghan, 1872) (Thomas M. Cooley, ed.), vol. 1, pp. v, vi–vii.
258　Cooley, supra note 33, at 347–8.
259　Tiedeman, supra note 13, at 21.
260　Pomeroy, supra note 1, at 33–58.
261　Id. at 59.
262　Id. at 58.

sovereignty.[263] Carter and Wharton maintained that American territorial expansion generated novel constitutional interpretations to justify annexation.[264] As Wharton put it, "the logic of facts" had more to do with Supreme Court decisions justifying annexation of new territory than did "the logic of textual criticism."[265] Similarly, the escalation of the controversy over slavery prompted an expanded interpretation of the Constitution's war power.[266]

Although the late nineteenth-century American legal scholars clearly recognized and occasionally highlighted the importance of external influences to the evolution of law, they did not explore in any detail either these external influences themselves or their impact on the history of legal doctrine. Even Pomeroy, whose chapter-length "Historical Sketch of the Political Movements Which Terminated in the Adoption of the Constitution" devoted more attention to factual detail than did most of his colleagues, covered a lot of material quickly. In his crucial discussion of the weaknesses of the Confederation as background to the Constitution, Pomeroy tellingly did not provide his own independent account. Instead, he thought it sufficient to quote two long paragraphs from an article by a political scientist, which discussed the inability to enforce treaties, conflicting commercial regulations in different states, bankruptcy and other economic distress, rivalries among the states, and the panic produced by Shay's Rebellion in Massachusetts.[267] More strikingly, while asserting that American constitutional law "was the resultant of all the social and other forces, which went to make up the civilization of the people," Tiedeman simply asserted that elaboration "can be found in any respectable history of those times."[268]

In *The Common Law*, Holmes emphasized but did not elaborate the "special exigencies of commerce" while explaining the changing law of trespass. He wrote that the "absolute protection of property, however natural to a primitive community more occupied in production than in exchange, is hardly consistent with the requirements of modern business."[269] But that was the extent of his discussion of the external factors that influenced the law of trespass. Holmes did not analyze either the mode of production in primitive communities or the "special exigencies of commerce" that accounted for the "requirements of modern business." Nor did he try to explain the history of the economic transformation from production to exchange. He immediately returned to his doctrinal history of the law of trespass and the erosion of absolute protection for property.

These scholars seemed to believe that they should devote their technical skill as lawyers to analyzing the evolution of legal doctrine. They also seemed

---

[263] Pomeroy, supra note 1, at 427–8; Tiedeman, supra note 13, at 50–3.

[264] Carter, supra note 23, at 319; Wharton, supra note 5, at 449.

[265] Wharton, supra note 5, at 29.

[266] Carter, supra note 23, at 319; Tiedeman, supra note 13, at 89–90; Cooley, supra note 33, at 354–6.

[267] Pomeroy, supra note 32, at 51–52 (quoting J. H. McIlvaine).

[268] Id. at 41–2.

[269] Oliver Wendell Holmes, Jr., The Common Law (Cambridge, Mass.: Harvard University Press, 1963) (Mark DeWolfe Howe, ed.) (original ed. 1881), p. 80.

to consider this task both more difficult and more practically important than examining the interactions between external influences and distinctively legal categories. As Thayer stressed in his important address on the role of legal history in American legal education, they overwhelmingly studied the history of legal doctrine in order to understand, to restate, and, when historical research uncovered dysfunctional survivals from the past, to reform the law so that it could better serve society.[270]

Historical Legal Thought as a Distinctive Jurisprudential School

The late nineteenth-century American legal scholars frequently portrayed their historical conception of law as a distinctive jurisprudential school. Like the European scholars who initially turned to historical analysis as an alternative to the abstract speculation of the French Enlightenment, they extolled the benefits of history over theory. They often stressed that the prior schools of natural law and analytic jurisprudence, despite their many differences, shared a fatal weakness for theory.

Historical analysis, Wharton stressed, properly insisted that "no nation can be fitted out with a system of laws chosen for their speculative excellence."[271] Carter ascribed "love of a theory" to "human vanity." "The simple and beautiful forms in which consequences develop themselves when a sufficient cause is assumed, as in mathematics," Carter added, "furnish a pleasure which the mind desires to hold in its grasp, and it recoils from any scrutiny into facts from a secret fear that the possession will be endangered, and turns back to revel in the delights of theory." Carter himself preferred the more difficult "scrutiny into facts" revealed by evolving custom.[272] While stressing that knowledge of English history is essential for students of American law, Cooley similarly remarked that an "abstract consideration of rights may answer the purpose of the mere theorist, but it is not sufficient for the lawyer."[273] He criticized those who succumbed "to the winds of mere speculative abstraction" by assuming that the "enlightened wisdom" of their own age was more advanced than "the traditions and conclusions of the past."[274] Pomeroy also sought to prevent law "from being swept away by the force of caprice or mere theory."[275]

Like Maine in *Ancient Law*, numerous American scholars explicitly contrasted their historical understanding of law from the theoretical approaches of natural law and analytic jurisprudence. Carter made clear that his emphasis on evolving custom as the source of law entailed the rejection of two "commonly accepted theories of law." The first, the theory of natural law,

270 Thayer, supra note 222, at 179, 184.
271 Wharton, supra note 5, at 89.
272 Carter, supra note 23, at 217.
273 Cooley, supra note 257, at vii.
274 Cooley, supra note 7, at 517.
275 Pomeroy, supra note 1, at 26.

seeks "to establish law upon the basis of absolute Justice and Right" and "to enthrone over human conduct a rule of Order." The second views law as "a rule of Force," proceeding "from the arbitrary command of the Sovereign State." Carter associated Blackstone with the theory of natural law and Hobbes, Bentham, and Austin with the theory that "law is a command."[276] While referring explicitly to "what is known as the historical theory of law," Hammond also distinguished this approach both from Blackstone, who "was ever ready to sacrifice the historical basis of the law to the frigid common sense of the eighteenth century,"[277] and from "the school of analytic jurists in England."[278]

Those who view "the law as a body of rules proceeding from a supposed Law of Nature – an invisible fountain of right," Carter objected, "are simply indulging in hypothesis" that is not "open to our observation, and, consequently, not to our knowledge."[279] Guarding himself against charges of irreverence, he claimed that it is more irreverent to presume knowledge of God's laws than to dismiss "from our attention those theories which rest upon our feeble imaginations of the Divine Nature."[280] God's laws, he reasoned, must be as absolute as God himself, and "before we can know his laws we must be absolute – that is, equal with him." But humans are not equal to God and cannot know the absolute, so "science could scarcely find in the Sacred Scriptures rules of conduct which it was the duty of the State to enforce."[281] While granting the limits of human knowledge, Carter warned against concluding too soon that they have been reached. He cleverly maintained that the "rule of dramatic poetry, not to introduce a God upon the stage unless a crisis appears demanding the Divine intervention, should be the rule of philosophy also."[282]

Pomeroy took a somewhat different approach while advocating that law should be understood historically rather than as a system of natural law. He conceded that any civilized society would require a legal system "infused with the spirit of justice" that respects "the immutable distinctions between right and wrong."[283] He stressed, however, that no legal system "claims to be in exact agreement with the teachings of abstract right and natural justice." As examples of laws that are not "in strict harmony with the law of nature and with Christian morals" and that "would be unsupportable by any free and Christian people,"[284] he cited various legal restrictions on the free disposition of property.[285] Stressing the historical constraints on natural law, Pomeroy

[276] Carter, supra note 23, at 173–4; see id. at 11–13.
[277] Hammond's Blackstone, supra note 64, vol. 3, at 408.
[278] Id. at xviii.
[279] Carter, supra note 23, at 13.
[280] Id. at 175.
[281] Id. at 11–12.
[282] Id. at 175.
[283] Pomeroy, supra note 1, at 7.
[284] Id. at 8.
[285] Id. at 8–9.

observed that "the maxims of justice and pure right which enter into every system of municipal legislation, are and must be modified by the influence of the past, by the national history and institutions, by the manners, customs, and religions, in short, by the ethnic life of the people."[286] Cooley similarly maintained that customary law, though having "its secret springs in the nature of man," is nevertheless "molded and shaped by time, place, and circumstance of national development and growth."[287]

American scholars committed to historical understandings of law seemed to regard the more recent English school of analytic jurisprudence, especially the work of John Austin, as a greater threat than earlier theories of natural law. Carter observed that Austin's view of law as a command proceeding from sovereign power, despite substantial recent criticism of it, remained the dominant legal theory in England and America.[288] Wharton seemed to agree by singling out the English school of analytic jurisprudence, mentioning Hobbes and Austin by name, as able opponents of his own approach to law based on evolving custom.[289] Tiedeman, like Wharton, began his book by asserting his disagreement with the views of Bentham and Austin, which he called "false and misleading."[290] These scholars, however, did not devote much space specifically to refuting Austin and the English analytic school. They seemed to believe that such refutation was implicit in the elaboration of their own very different historical approaches. Carter came close to stating this point explicitly. After asserting Austin's views to be "radically and mischievously erroneous," Carter added that this point would "clearly appear if the views I shall hereafter endeavor to maintain be at all well founded."[291]

Yet a few American scholars, including Carter, elaborated somewhat their opposition to analytic jurisprudence. After stating Austin's theory of sovereignty, Hammond maintained that it is impossible to "give an intelligible account of any system of law, still less the history of any such system, without taking into view other factors entirely distinct from the will of the sovereign, real or fictitious." Except in legal treatises, he added, this impossibility has been well recognized since the days of Montesquieu and Burke.[292] Wharton stressed that "law is an emanation from the people to the sovereign, and not a command imposed by the sovereign on the people."[293] He described this view as the "distinguishing feature of the historical school, of which Savigny is the most able and prominent representative," while claiming that it also united "doctrinaire idealists," such as Jefferson; "shrewd political tacticians," such as Franklin; "philosophical economists," such as Edmund Burke and Adam

---

[286] Id. at 9.
[287] Cooley, supra note 7, at 517–18.
[288] Carter, supra note 23, at 8, 187.
[289] Wharton, supra note 5, at iv.
[290] Tiedeman, supra note 13, at 2; see generally id. at 1–3.
[291] Carter, supra note 23, at 8.
[292] Hammond's Blackstone, supra note 64, vol. 1, at 142.
[293] Wharton, supra note 5, at 5.

Smith; and "conservative traditionalists," such as Savigny and Puchta.[294] "To hold that law is created by a sovereign," Wharton maintained, "is as unreasonable and as inconsistent with our traditions as to hold that language is created by a sovereign."[295] While this passage implicitly invokes Savigny's famous analogy between language and law, Wharton explicitly cited Burke's position that all law is "declaratory" as the most "striking evidence of the want of universality of the rule of the analytical school that it is essential to a law that it should be imposed and enforced by a political superior."[296]

Carter was somewhat more sympathetic to Austin and other admittedly "powerful minds" in the analytical school. Emphasizing his view that evolutionary legal thought had superseded prior jurisprudential theories, he pointed out that in their era the "law of Evolution so dominating in its influence upon recent thought, had not been stated."[297] Had these great scholars been aware of the law of evolution, he clearly suggested, they would have accepted that law is based in custom and cannot be made or changed by statutory legislation.[298] Carter claimed that Bentham and Austin, like the proponents of natural law, were unscientific because they engaged in "a process of reasoning from assumed premises."[299] He tweaked Austin for his strenuous advocacy of codification even though Austin himself confessed "his inability to find anywhere in human experience a successful example of it."[300]

Legal History as Inductive Legal Science

In explaining their evolutionary legal thought, and sometimes more specifically in differentiating it from prior schools of natural law and analytic jurisprudence, many American scholars stressed that law is an inductive science, analogous to the physical and natural sciences. Historical evidence, particularly prior case law, provided the data for their inductions. They followed Maine by extending to law the English scientific tradition of induction from empirical evidence, most prominently identified with Francis Bacon, and emulated by American historians generally during the late nineteenth century.

As they extolled historical over theoretical analysis, many of these scholars emphasized that reliance on history allowed law to become an inductive science. Carter declared that the observation of cases over time "is the same kind of work which is performed in astronomy, geology, ornithology, and all other sciences." "The law," he stressed, "thus appears in its true character as an Inductive Science."[301] Sometimes quoting or citing Bacon as the source of his

---

[294] Id. at 6.
[295] Id. at 148.
[296] Id. at 42; see id. at 61.
[297] Carter, supra note 23, at 268.
[298] Id. at 268–9.
[299] Id. at 219.
[300] Id. at 303.
[301] Carter, supra note 23, at 84.

inductive conception of science, Carter emphasized that the method of scientific induction entails arrangement and classification as well as observation of empirical data.[302] He maintained that in all inductive sciences, including law, "the eventual classification," whether of a legal case, a plant, or an animal, must be determined "by the qualities which are really *found* in it," based on empirical observation, "not by qualities artificially imputed to it" by the investigator.[303] In criticizing natural law and analytic jurisprudence as unscientific, Carter complained that they did not sufficiently "hold in mind that the province of science was rigidly confined to the observation and orderly arrangement of facts."[304] Science, he insisted immediately after quoting Bacon, "is the orderly arrangement of things we can *know*, and not of things we cannot know."[305]

Hammond similarly asserted that the legal decision should be the means of determining legal principles "precisely as an observation or an experiment in natural science is the means by which a law of nature is learned."[306] Just "as the astronomer infers the true form of the planet's orbit from his observations of its position at many different times," the legal scientist infers the true meaning of the common law from his observations of case law over time. In contrast to earlier scholars who had based their understanding of law on reason, or nature, or God, as they understood those concepts, Hammond maintained that law "must be learned, like the laws of the physical world, inductively."[307] Cooley more simply maintained that law must be judged "by the act of observation rather than of introspection."[308]

Hammond's unpublished work most explicitly developed the contrast between the inductive historical method that had become prevalent in American legal scholarship and prior deductive approaches to legal analysis. In a lecture he frequently gave on "the historical method of studying law," he identified "the rival theories of a science of law deduced by reasoning from fundamental principles, and of a science of law inductively obtained by studying the facts of history." While differentiating these "two radically diverse views of law," Hammond emphasized that they reflected a more general division between the "deductive, or syllogistic and the inductive methods" that "pervades almost all the so-called moral sciences."[309] "The historical method," he concluded, "is simply induction employed in the moral sciences."[310] Since the beginning of the nineteenth century, Hammond observed, the relative popularity of the two competing views had dramatically changed. Whereas the deductive approach had prevailed in the past, since the turn of the nineteenth century the inductive

[302] Id. at 12–13, 84, 175.
[303] Id. at 192.
[304] Id. at 219.
[305] Id. at 175; see id. at 13.
[306] Hammond's Blackstone, supra note 64, vol. 1, at 220.
[307] Id. at 217.
[308] Cooley, supra note 7, at 518.
[309] Hammond, supra note 77, at 8.
[310] Id. at 27.

historical method increasingly became recognized throughout the moral sciences as "the only true one." Claiming that law is "proverbially a conservative science averse to all change or reform," Hammond acknowledged that the inductive historical method arrived later in law than in other moral sciences[311] before becoming "almost a fashion"[312] in law as well by the late nineteenth century. He observed in passing that the crucial contrast between the two methods concerned the derivation of legal principles. In the application of these principles to actual cases, he concluded without elaboration, "there is little difference between them."[313]

Hammond maintained that the deductive theory treated law as a mathematical science. Only "a few axioms" are used "to deduce all the general principles of law," which are then applied to decide particular cases.[314] The inductive historical theory, by contrast, "denies entirely the analogy between law and mathematics, but considers jurisprudence as a science more like the physical sciences, or like political economy, in which we learn the nature of things only by observation of their action." Examining "the entire past history of the race, and especially its legislative and judicial history, as a vast collection of facts," it analyzes and generalizes from these facts to discover legal principles. Rejecting a priori assumptions about the nature of society and law, it treats its conclusions "as only convenient provisional generalizations," subject to further historical study.[315] It recognizes that legal principles "have been reached by experience, which is but another name for induction, and that the way to make them more correct and to extend them still wider is to increase our experience by studying the history of the race."[316] Rather than "regarding each human law as an abortive attempt to reach or imitate an immutable standard, which would be the right law under all conditions and for all nations, this theory regards it as an experiment, by the repetition of which in different forms and under different conditions, man is enabled to approach nearer and nearer at every trial to the law which suits his circumstances at the time."[317] The inductive theory maintains that the general principles and doctrines of law "grow of themselves out of the soil in which they have their roots."[318]

In the final chapter of his unpublished book on the history of the common law, Hammond elaborated these contrasts while referring more specifically to particular legal concepts. The deductive theory of law that prevailed less than a century earlier "assumed that property, right, obligation, contract, and all such terms, stood for immutable conceptions, which had been present in men's minds from the earliest civilization – if not even from the savage state – and that

[311] Id. at 17.
[312] Id. at 25.
[313] Id. at 13.
[314] Id. at 10.
[315] Id. at 12.
[316] Id. at 14.
[317] Id. at 13.
[318] Id. at 45.

whatever other changes might be made in the law, these conceptions, at least, had the fixity of mathematical proof."[319] Yet current legal thinkers "no longer regard the law as a deductive science." They recognize that "law is inductive and like all inductive sciences it is constantly in process of construction."[320] They do not attribute differences between current and prior law to the subsequent correction of mistaken views.[321] Rather, they recognize that law can never be "a complete and finished body."[322] Hammond concluded that the "life of the law, as of the race to which it belongs, consists in a constant change of its constituent parts, the old dying out, the new taking its place, but the continuity of the whole being maintained throughout."[323]

Hammond was optimistic that the inductive historical method would overcome the widespread skepticism about all legal analysis. "The attempt to give logical reasons for rules of law which have a merely historical origin," he believed, "is responsible for much of the forced interpretation and false argumentation which has sometimes made all search for the reason of law distasteful to honest thinkers."[324]

Precisely because the inductive historical method "has been of late in so much vogue," Hammond took great pains to differentiate it from earlier uses of history in legal analysis. Identifying Coke, Selden, and Hale among the numerous prior English legal scholars who relied on the records of the past, Hammond maintained that "not one of them can be said to have had the faintest notion of what is now called the historical method."[325] Scholars had been able to detect the defects in the assumptions prevalent in centuries before their own. "But in all these repetitions of the same process of criticism, it had never occurred to any century that the truth which was formulated by itself was not the final and absolute truth to last for all time, and which its predecessors had been simply blind in overlooking." They employed the deductive method in arriving at their own legal theories, which they used to judge the past without any historical perspective on their own views. The "great merit" of the inductive historical method, Hammond stressed, "lies in its emancipation from fixed moral and jural truth, or rather from such assumed forms of such truth as had previously in every age been accepted as conclusive."[326] To underline his point, Hammond noted the difference between the German philosophical and historical schools of law. The philosophical school relied heavily on history "but used all history indifferently" as the basis for generating ideal laws and institutions. The historical school, by contrast, limited itself to "the details of their own

---

[319] William Gardiner Hammond, Theory of Law, p. 4, Hammond Papers, supra note 77, Box V.
[320] Id. at 3.
[321] Id. at 4.
[322] Id. at 11.
[323] Id. at 12.
[324] Hammond, supra note 77, at 38.
[325] Id. at 26.
[326] Id. at 27.

history." Its members focused on the history of Rome and Germany, the sources of modern German law, "because they thought it essential to trace institutions from the beginning as they actually existed and to learn all about them from the course of their own development."[327]

Occasionally, Hammond acknowledged that at some time in the indefinite future the inductive method would uncover moral laws of the universe that theories of logical deduction claimed to have discovered already through a priori reasoning.[328] The "historical school," he granted, assumes that moral as well as physical principles "probably" govern the universe but believes that "man is not yet in a position to understand them."[329] Hammond recognized that he might have been "unjust" to the inductive historical method "in saying that it does not recognize fixed moral truths." Rather, he clarified, it "simply denies that such truths have been attained."[330] After claiming that historical evidence refuted natural law theories of the eighteenth century, Hammond concluded that natural law "is the ideal to which all law is tending, not the source from which all law has sprung."[331]

Extremely interested in legal education, Hammond emphasized the importance of teaching the inductive historical method in law schools. He pointed out that when law was considered a deductive science, consisting of "a vast number of rules, all derived from a few leading principles," legal education focused on mastering those principles.[332] The recognition that "we have reached our present condition by a process of induction" that will continue "without limit" ended the expectation that students would learn "fixed, fundamental principles" from which they could reason for the rest of their career.[333] Having realized that "law is in its very nature a historical science, and therefore no man can know truly and philosophically what the law is, unless he knows also how the law has grown to be what it is now," the study of legal history must be "the one solid foundation upon which the whole structure of legal education can be built."[334] Hammond alluded to the "higher culture" that students would indirectly but almost certainly gain from the study of legal history,[335] yet he focused on its practical benefits. He reported that his students, and even more importantly his former students who had years of professional experience, confirmed his conviction "of the practical value of the historical method in the study of law."[336]

[327] Id. at 28.
[328] Id. at 12.
[329] Id. at 14.
[330] Id. at 27.
[331] William Gardiner Hammond, Divine and Natural Law, p. 2, Hammond Papers, supra note 77, vol. 2.
[332] Hammond, supra note 319, at 2–3.
[333] Id. at 4.
[334] Hammond, supra note 77, at 8.
[335] Id. at 41.
[336] Id. at 2–3.

Although Hammond had "watched anxiously" for the appearance of a good book designed to teach the historical method in law, he bemoaned the "complete lack" of one.[337] Existing legal treatises, he frequently complained, typically were mere "records of disconnected cases,"[338] assembled in "an illogical and disorderly manner, or whose statements of the law were so loose and inaccurate as to prove misleading."[339] He urged the production of new treatises that would examine

the history of the common law, tracing the growth and development of its institutions and principles from the forests of Germany through the events of fifteen hundred years, down to the form which they take in our own day and country, and thus laying the most firm and rational basis, for the settlement of its disputed questions, the clearing up of its dark places, the entire study and practice of the law of our own land.[340]

Like Henry Adams, Hammond regretted the fact that most of the material for such a history was contained in German scholarship. "It is a shame to our profession, on both sides of the Atlantic," he maintained, that it had not "even had enterprise to translate" the German contribution "to the early history of our own law."[341] Hammond repeatedly emphasized that the historical treatise he had in mind "need not be very bulky."[342] Indeed, "if presented in a systematic shape," in contrast to Holmes's "frequent and irregular" historical "digressions" in *The Common Law* "to explain a conception, or to interpret a rule,"[343] the relevant history could be "abridged and simplified."[344] A well-conceived historical treatise for students "economizes labor and time" by exposing "the great branches and trunks" of the law which had been hidden under "the labyrinth of minor details."[345]

By helping to portray legal scholarship as an inductive science, the turn to history played a vital role in gaining acceptance for legal studies in the emerging American research university. Charles W. Eliot, who became president of Harvard in 1869 and led its transformation into one of America's first major research universities, emphasized inductive reasoning as the essential skill universities should impart to students. Reviewing his years as president, Eliot proudly observed that "in all departments of the University," including the law school, "a careful observation of actual facts, an accurate recording of the facts determined, and a just and limited inference from the recorded facts have come to be the primary methods of study and research."[346] Throughout

[337] Id. at 3.

[338] Hammond, supra note 319, at 25.

[339] Hammond, supra note 115, at 16–16 ½.

[340] William G. Hammond, American Law Schools in the Past and in the Future, p. 13, Hammond Papers, supra note 77, vol. 3.

[341] Hammond, supra note 77, at 2.

[342] Id.

[343] Holmes, supra note 269, at 6.

[344] Hammond, supra note 77, at 41.

[345] Id. at 46–7.

[346] Anthony Chase, The Birth of the Modern Law School, 23 Am. J. Legal Hist. 329, 336 (1979).

the university, empirical studies replaced the lecture method of instruction. Shortly before he became president, Eliot provided a model for this transformation in his jointly authored book *Inorganic Chemistry*, the first chemistry textbook that took the form of a laboratory manual.[347]

Eliot viewed the case method of legal instruction as the counterpart to empirical studies in other fields.[348] In 1870, just a year after becoming president, Eliot appointed Langdell dean of the law school, later claiming that this appointment was one of his three major accomplishments during the forty years he served as president of Harvard.[349] In addition to supporting Langdell's efforts to raise the quality of Harvard Law School by requiring higher admissions standards[350] and by basing faculty selection on academic performance in law school rather than on the traditional reliance on professional achievement,[351] Eliot endorsed Langdell's innovative development of the case method of instruction from casebooks as an inductive pedagogy to replace lectures derived from treatises.[352] Whereas the treatise tradition cited cases, if at all, to illustrate legal doctrines and principles, Langdell prepared casebooks, presenting cases in chronological order and without headnotes or commentary, "to compel the mind to work out the principles from the cases,"[353] the method he used in classroom interaction with students.[354]

The understanding of legal science by Langdell and his colleagues at Harvard Law School underlines how extensively late nineteenth-century legal scholars viewed legal history, particularly the history of decided cases, as the empirical counterpart to the data from which scientists in other fields induced their conclusions. As the dean appointed to transform Harvard Law School into a respectable branch of a modern university, he encouraged "teaching law as a science," the title of an after-dinner speech he gave to the Harvard Alumni Association in 1887. After reporting that Harvard was following the continental practice of teaching law in universities, in contrast to the English tradition of legal training through apprenticeship, Langdell stressed that law must be studied scientifically in order to be accepted by universities. Announcing his two basic principles, Langdell stated "that law is a science, and that all available materials of that science are found in printed books."[355] He and his "associates," presumably his colleagues at Harvard Law School, had "constantly inculcated the idea that the library is the proper workshop of professors and students alike; that it is to us what the laboratories of the university are to the

[347] Id. at 334–5.
[348] Id. at 342.
[349] Bruce A. Kimball, The Inception of Modern Professional Education: C. C. Langdell, 1826–1906 (The University of North Carolina Press, 2009), p. 4.
[350] Id. at 7, 221.
[351] Id. at 166, 170.
[352] Id. at 141, 146; Chase, supra note 346, at 338.
[353] Kimball, supra note 349, at 89.
[354] Id. at 6–7, 88–9, 130–1, 141, 165.
[355] Christopher C. Langdell, Teaching Law as a Science, 21 Am. L. Rev. 123 (1887).

FIGURE 11.1. *Christopher Columbus Langdell.* Courtesy of Historical & Special Collections, Harvard Law School Library.

chemists and physicists, the museum of natural history to the zoologists, the botanical garden to the botanists."[356]

Langdell stressed that observation of cases must extend over time in order for the inductive method to work properly. In the preface to his 1871 casebook on contracts, which became the model for numerous other casebooks in many legal specialties, he wrote that legal science "consists of certain principles or doctrines," each of which "has arrived at the present state in slow degrees; in other words, it is a growth, extending in many cases through centuries. This

[356] Id. at 124.

growth is to be traced in the main through a series of cases."[357] He added that the induction of legal principles from the historical study of case law should enable the systematic classification and arrangement of current legal doctrine. He tried in his casebook "to select, classify, and arrange all the cases which had contributed in any important degree to the growth, development, or establishment" of the "essential doctrines" of current contract law. In explaining his selections, Langdell declared that "the cases which are useful and necessary for this purpose at the present day bear an exceedingly small proportion to all that have been reported." For purposes of "systematic study," the overwhelming majority of reported cases "are useless and worse than useless." Langdell maintained, moreover, that the number of "fundamental legal doctrines," like the number of "useful and necessary" cases, is relatively small, certainly "much less than is commonly supposed." The lack of prior scientific legal analysis, he added, accounts for the prevailing incorrect assumptions about the multiplicity of legal doctrines. "If these doctrines could be so classified and arranged that each should be found in its proper place, and nowhere else," he asserted, "they would cease to be formidable from their number." Langdell intended his casebook, tellingly entitled *Selection of Cases on the Law of Contracts*, to demonstrate these points, treating cases as "original sources."[358]

Langdell's casebooks were much more influential than the three treatises that he largely derived from his casebooks or the articles he occasionally published in the *Harvard Law Review*.[359] Ames observed that Langdell's best work, his short book summarizing equity pleading, demonstrated the practical benefits of legal history. Had English judges in the seventeenth and eighteenth centuries been familiar with the historical development of equity pleading that Langdell described in this book, Ames concluded, "suitors would have been saved from a mass of costly litigation, and the reports would not have been encumbered with what must be considered the least creditable judgments in the history of English equity."[360]

Thayer and Ames, Langdell's colleagues at Harvard Law School, endorsed his attempt to classify the legal principles he induced from the history of case law. Thayer reported in the preface to his own casebook on constitutional law that he and his colleagues at Harvard Law School all eventually accepted the approach with which Langdell's "name is so honorably connected, – that of studying cases, carefully chosen and arranged so as to present the development of principles."[361] At the end of his *Preliminary Treatise on Evidence*, Thayer

---

[357] Christopher Columbus Langdell, Selection of Cases on the Law of Contracts (Boston: Little Brown, 1871), p. vi.

[358] Id. at vii.

[359] For summaries of Langdell's writings, see Bruce A. Kimball, The Langdell Problem: Historicizing the Century of Historiography, 1906–2000s, 22 Law and History Review 277, 281–2 (2004); James Barr Ames, Christopher Columbus Langdell, in Ames, supra note 2, at 467, 474–6.

[360] Ames, supra note 359, at 476.

[361] James Bradley Thayer, Cases on Constitutional Law (Cambridge, Mass.: Charles W. Sever and Company 1895), vol. 1, p. vi.

urged that a restatement of the law of evidence should be the next step after the historical examination and criticism of cases that dominated his book. Just as Langdell emphasized that relatively few legal doctrines are fundamental for a systematic classification of the law, Thayer maintained that only a small number of "clear, simple, and sound" principles underlie what had become an "elaborate mass" of misleading and unnecessary complexity in the law of evidence.[362] Ames similarly believed that "the pursuit of legal doctrines to their source" would yield "some original generalizations, illuminating and simplifying the law."[363] Joseph Beale, another Harvard professor, declared that legal scientists, like scientists generally, "have abandoned the subjective and deductive philosophy of the middle ages" and instead "learn from scientific observation and historical discovery." The methods of "observation and induction," Beale added, had enabled legal scientists to provide the "intelligent statement of the principles of law."[364]

William Keener, who introduced the case method to Columbia Law School after teaching at Harvard from 1885 to 1890, similarly emphasized that studying cases over time made law an inductive science. In an article aptly entitled "The Inductive Method in Legal Education," he described a case as "both a laboratory and a library," an original source analogous to a scientific "specimen."[365] By examining the "growth and development"[366] of law through selected cases, Keener maintained, students could induce and classify its relatively few central principles.[367]

Just as Carter disparaged the theoretical comfort of mathematics while advocating that legal scholars must scrutinize the facts revealed by evolving custom, and as Lodge, Holmes, and Hammond rejected analogies between mathematics and law, some of these proponents of the case method specifically differentiated inductive legal science from deductive reason in general and mathematics in particular. "Law," Langdell stressed in his annual Dean's Report for 1876–77, "has not the demonstrative certainty of mathematics."[368] In describing the case method used by all his colleagues at Harvard Law School, John Chipman Gray, like Langdell himself, contrasted it with the pure logic of mathematics while asserting its connection with history. He asserted that the case method "accustoms the student to consider the law not merely as a series of propositions having, like a succession of problems in geometry, only a logical interdependence, but as a living thing, sloughing off the old, taking on the new."[369] By instructive

---

[362] Thayer, supra note 3, at 511.

[363] Ames, supra note 220, at 368.

[364] Joseph H. Beale, Jr., The Development of Jurisprudence during the Past Century, 18 Harv. L. Rev. 271, 283 (1905).

[365] William A. Keener, The Inductive Method in Legal Education, 17 ABA Rep. 473, 477 (1894).

[366] Id. at 489.

[367] Id. at 481.

[368] William P. LaPiana, Logic and Experience: The Origin of Modern American Legal Education (New York: Oxford University Press, 1994), p. 56.

[369] Letter from J. C. Gray to the editors of the Yale Law Journal, in Methods of Legal Education, 1 Yale L.J. 139, 159 (1892).

contrast, Savigny, the great German legal scholar, had famously equated law with geometry. Just as it is possible to "deduce" the whole triangle from "two sides and the included angle," the law has "points," which Savigny called "leading axioms," from which it is possible to "deduce" the entire legal system.[370] A former student recalled that Langdell and Ames were "practical lawyers, who had developed theories as to legal doctrines," which they "derived from the cases. They were not closet philosophers, who attempted to devolve a system of jurisprudence out of their inner consciousness; but they took the position that, considering the way in which our law is developed, emphasis must necessarily be laid on historical origins."[371]

The American legal scholars never suggested that their efforts to classify law were inconsistent with their conception of law as continuously evolving. They resembled Holmes, who sought a logical arrangement of law while criticizing Herbert Spencer and others for attempting to establish timeless theories "by a logical deduction from axioms," an effort that seemed to contradict their own evolutionary belief in "successive adaptations to the environment."[372] Gray explicitly stated the view that came through clearly though implicitly in the work of the others. He introduced his influential book, *The Nature and Sources of the Law*, by telling his readers that it would be devoted to "the analysis and relations of some fundamental legal ideas." He emphasized, however, that he was not "insensible to the value of historical studies, nor blind to the fact that legal conceptions are constantly changing." Like Hammond, he thought it valuable "to consider and analyze Law in the stage of development which it has reached, although we believe it neither possible nor desirable that the development should not go on in the future."[373] These scholars, in contrast to the position that Wharton ascribed to Blackstone and that later critics ascribed to them, did not believe that through their own analysis and classification law "had reached a perfection which it would be sacrilege to touch."[374]

Conclusion

The careers of leading American law professors during the last three decades of the nineteenth century demonstrate the pervasiveness of a historical school of American jurisprudence that extended well beyond the relatively few who

---

[370] Frederick Charles von Savigny, Of the Vocation of Our Age for Legislation and Jurisprudence (North Stratford, N.H.: Ayer Company Publishers, Inc., 2000) (reprint of 1831 English ed.), pp. 38–9.

[371] Extracts from letters by onetime students under Deans Langdell and Ames, relative to the attitude of those teachers toward the law (James Barr Ames Papers, Harvard Law School Library, Box 1, Folder 34), XXI.

[372] Oliver Wendell Holmes, Jr., The Gas-Stokers' Strike, 7 Am. L. Rev. 582 (1873), reprinted in The Collected Works of Justice Holmes (University of Chicago Press, 1995) (Sheldon M. Novick, ed.), vol. 1, at 323, 324.

[373] John Chipman Gray, The Nature and Sources of the Law (New York: The Macmillan Company, 1927) (original ed. 1909), p. 1.

[374] Wharton, supra note 5, at 134.

actually produced original scholarship in legal history. Like Savigny and Maine before them, many American legal scholars explicitly differentiated their historical approach from prior jurisprudential schools, particularly natural law and analytic jurisprudence. While focusing on the history of English common law, which they considered the main source of modern American law, they applied their historical analysis throughout the law, to American constitutional law as well as common law, to criminal law as well as civil law, and to legislation as well as adjudication. They emphasized that historical analysis is inductive, and, therefore, scientific, whereas prior jurisprudential schools, whatever the differences among them, were based on "mere" theory, which they variously deprecated as vain, abstract, speculative, subjective, a priori, deductive, and unscientific. They asserted that any attempt to create a general theory of law, including natural law and analytic jurisprudence, would inevitably fail because every country needed its own legal system, compatible with its distinctive historical experience. They believed that it is impossible to extricate legal analysis from historical context and pointed out that inattention to history had produced analytic errors by previous scholars. Challenging theorists of natural law, they stressed that even concepts of natural rights had been historically determined. Challenging analytic jurisprudence, they stressed that custom limits sovereign power. They invoked their understanding of law as a historically based inductive science to justify the inclusion of academic law schools, staffed by full-time scholars and teachers, within emerging American research universities. Extending their inductive approach to pedagogy as well as research, they developed the case method of instruction from casebooks organized historically as an alternative to traditional lectures based on treatises.

Influenced by the evolutionary social thought that dominated transatlantic intellectual life throughout the nineteenth century, the American legal scholars viewed history as a continuous organic process of development that connected the past with the present and the emerging future. They felt strongly that the present could not be understood without appreciating how it evolved from its earliest origins. Most interested in the nation as the key subject of historical investigation, they typically referred to it through biological metaphors, frequently associated it with a unified race, and sometimes asserted that unrelated races could not be assimilated into a national tradition. Though they emphasized the continuity of the evolutionary process and generally depicted evolution as progressive, particularly in Western Europe and the United States, they recognized that historical continuity, even in those countries, often was neither smooth nor progressive. Most believed that evolution was contingent rather than preordained, and even the few who assumed laws of evolutionary development did not speculate about what those laws might be, sometimes assuming that they were beyond human understanding. Sensitive to the differentness of the past, they were alert to the dangers of anachronism and often warned against mistaking resemblance between the past and present as evidence of continuous evolution. They also recognized that much of the past did not leave traces on subsequent developments. But they were generally uninterested in history that could not be connected to the present, often dismissing it as superficial and criticizing its study as antiquarianism.

In applying their evolutionary historical thought to legal analysis, the late nineteenth-century American legal scholars emphasized that law responds to evolving custom. They believed that social customs often evolve more rapidly than law, requiring law to catch up in order to be effective. They recognized that some old law remains functional over time, either because it serves the same purpose as in the past or because new and convincing justifications adapt it to changed circumstances. But they also stressed that old law, which was well suited to the customs under which it arose, sometimes cannot adapt to new customs and becomes dysfunctional.

Even as they recognized their major debts to the historical approach developed by their European predecessors, particularly Savigny and Maine, these American legal scholars also criticized the Europeans. They agreed with Savigny and Maine about the distinctiveness and superiority of a historical approach to legal analysis. Yet some complained that Savigny was too complacent in accepting evolved law as natural and inevitable. They maintained instead that the past need not govern or enslave future generations, that knowledge of the past can provide the wisdom to liberate the present. Some also objected that Maine had neither proved his many generalizations about legal evolution with sufficient evidence nor recognized the importance of Teutonic law as opposed to Roman law in the Anglo-American legal tradition. In contrast to Savigny, who was attracted to historical jurisprudence in reaction against the attempted imposition of French ideas and institutions on Germany during the Napoleonic wars, the Americans who took the historical turn in the last three decades of the nineteenth century seemed intellectually unaffected by the recent Civil War in their own country. Most strikingly, despite the Civil War, they continued to follow Savigny and Maine in viewing the presumably unified and racially homogeneous nation as the primary organ of historical evolution.

The conception of history shared by leading American legal scholars during the late nineteenth century directly informed their understanding of the professional function of the law professor. Primarily interested in making law as effective as possible for their own society, they emphasized that detailed knowledge of legal origins and evolution is a necessary prerequisite to understanding, evaluating, and reforming existing law. Because they believed that American law derived mostly from the English common law, they concentrated on investigating the extent to which English origins could be connected as part of a continuous process of development to current law. They generally recognized that the English common law continued to evolve in America and occasionally wrote about distinctively American legal history, both in private law and in the novel subject of American constitutional law. Given their evolutionary assumptions, it makes sense that at the beginning of professional American scholarship in legal history they were most interested in the earliest sources of their legal tradition. They were confident that their historical research would disclose which legal survivals remained effective, and should be retained, and which had become dysfunctional as society evolved, and should be eliminated. Many highlighted individual liberty and political democracy as the central, positive elements of a continuous tradition dating from the Teutonic forests of continental Europe, extended to England through various invasions of Teutonic tribes, and further developing in the United States, freed from the aristocratic constraints of British society and supported by popular sovereignty.

Consistent with their views that the prior evolution of law enables intelligent analysis of current law and that scientific induction entails classification as well as observation, many of the late nineteenth-century American legal scholars were eager to construct rational restatements of the law based on their historical investigations. Impressed by the influence of German legal scholars on judges and legislators in Germany, they hoped to have a similar impact in the United States. Because they assumed that evolution would continue indefinitely, they recognized that their restatements, however useful in the present, were necessarily temporary. As society evolved, some currently functional laws would become dysfunctional, just as laws that had been functional in the past had become dysfunctional in the present. New laws, new classifications, and new restatements would be needed in the future.

The historical school of American jurisprudence was not monolithic. Most leading American legal scholars during the late nineteenth century analyzed law historically, but only a few wrote original works in legal history based on detailed study of primary sources. Some of the legal historians who worked from primary sources, despite their emphasis on the continuities between past and present, became so fascinated with the law of the past that they explored its characteristics beyond what was necessary to explain current law. More than any other American scholar, Bigelow delved into the details of legal history for their own sake. Some were more intellectually honest than others in their use of history to analyze current law. Holmes, in particular, manipulated and even distorted legal history to support his analytical views. The American scholars differed about the extent to which legal history demonstrated that current law was functional. Some, such as Ames, more frequently invoked legal history to support current law, whereas others, such as Holmes and Thayer, more frequently invoked legal history to explain how legal survivals had become dysfunctional and urged their elimination. Most leading American legal scholars, following Savigny, viewed evolution as a relatively smooth and often unconscious process, but others, following Jhering, saw conflict and struggle as its fundamental characteristics. While identifying the nation, often identified with race, as the key organ of social evolution, they differed substantially about the extent to which various races could be assimilated into the American nation. Yet their self-consciously shared, and now largely forgotten, commitment to a distinctive historical school of jurisprudence, adapted from European scholars and distinguished from prior schools of natural law and analytic jurisprudence, dwarfs these differences.

PART III

MAITLAND, POUND, AND POUND'S SUCCESSORS

XII

Maitland

The Maturity of English Legal History

Frederic Maitland is widely acclaimed as the greatest legal historian ever to write in the English language. In a relatively short scholarly career from 1884 to his death at fifty-six in 1906, he focused on the history of medieval English law. Like Bigelow and for similar reasons, Maitland considered the medieval period the most important in English legal history. Between 1154 and 1272, he believed, English law was taking the form it would essentially retain until his own century. In contrast to Bigelow, who relied on previously printed records for his compilation of original sources in *Placita Anglo-Normannica*, Maitland published meticulously edited volumes of original sources that had been sequestered in archives, often in formats that were difficult to decipher. Based on these sources, he wrote interpretive histories, most impressively and influentially his massive two-volume work, *The History of English Law before the Time of Edward I*, published in 1895. Internationally recognized and praised in his own lifetime, he remains universally admired, including by those who have challenged some of his conclusions. Even scholars who generally deprecate the legal history written in the nineteenth century view Maitland as the exception, the one who met, and even established, modern professional standards for the field. S. F. C. Milsom, Maitland's most important late twentieth-century critic, claims that Maitland "had nothing to stand on. There was no legal history worthy of the name."[1] J. H. Baker reiterated that Maitland "inaugurated the scholarly study of English legal history."[2]

It does no damage to Maitland's well-deserved reputation to recognize, as he did himself with typical generosity, that he built upon others. Maitland's correspondence with Bigelow, Ames, and Thayer, discussed in the previous chapters on these American scholars, demonstrates his respect for them. In the introduction to *The History of English Law*, he listed eight scholars whose work he

---

[1] S. F. C. Milsom, F. W. Maitland, 66 Proceedings of the British Academy (Oxford University Press, 1982), pp. 265, 281.

[2] J. H. Baker, Why the History of English Law Has Not Been Finished, 59 Cambridge law Journal 62, 64 (2000).

admired and did not intend to duplicate by what he called "vain repetition."[3]
Four of these scholars were American: Holmes, Thayer, Ames, and Bigelow. Of
the others, two were German, Brunner and Liebermann; one was a Russian,
who immigrated to England, Vinogradoff; and only one, Stephen, was English.
The frequent citation of these eight scholars throughout the book's two volumes made clear that this prefatory praise was substantive and not merely
polite. While pointing out that substantial work on medieval English law "lies
scattered in monographs and journals," the introduction referred specifically
to only one journal, the *Harvard Law Review*, observing that it would have
been "ungrateful indeed" not to name it.[4] Signaling the *Harvard Law Review*
for special mention, like naming the four American legal historians, underlined
Maitland's high opinion of American scholarship.

In addition to relying on the previous work of the four Americans he cited,
Maitland shared many of their historiographical views. These similarities
challenge the long-standing and widespread image of him as a unique and
refreshingly modern exception to the otherwise discredited treatment of legal
history by nineteenth-century legal scholars. Like Holmes, another famous
nineteenth-century scholar frequently and misleadingly differentiated from his
contemporaries, Maitland reflected the fundamental evolutionary perspective
that dominated historical thinking in the nineteenth century. Typical of these
historians, he often conveyed his evolutionary thought through metaphors of
organic growth, portraying a continuous process of national development,
often tied to race, from early origins to maturity. Like many others, he recognized discontinuities as well as continuities in legal history, warned about
anachronistically mistaking resemblance between the present and the past for
evidence of continuity, observed both functional and dysfunctional survivals
of past law in the present, and stressed the contingency of history. Because so
many subsequent scholars viewed Maitland as distinctively interested in legal
history as a window into social and economic history, it is perhaps most striking that he himself emphasized his primary focus on the internal evolution of
legal doctrines, precisely the attribute they condemned in others. In his many
criticisms of Henry Maine, Maitland often echoed Henry Adams and his students, whose *Essays in Anglo-Saxon Law* he cited throughout *The History of
English Law*.

Maitland's achievements as an editor and author far surpassed in quantity
and scope the work on which he built. He made previously obscure archival
sources widely available, published the first comprehensive overview of English
legal history in its formative era, and opened up many potential new areas of
scholarly inquiry. Yet, as many subsequent scholars have recognized, Maitland
did not leave successors who built on his work. After his death, interest in

---

[3] Frederick Pollock and Frederic William Maitland, The History of English Law Before the Time
of Edward I (Cambridge University Press, 1899) (2d ed.) [hereinafter History of English Law],
vol. 1, at xxxvii.

[4] Id. at xxxv.

legal history waned in England as well as in the United States. Sadly, Maitland culminated rather than invigorated an era dominated by historical approaches to law.

Biographical Background

Born in 1850, Maitland had intellectually accomplished ancestors on both sides of his family. His father and his paternal grandfather were lawyers who had careers in other fields. His grandfather became a librarian and later wrote ecclesiastical history. His father, after writing pamphlets on tax law, became secretary of the Civil Service Commission. His maternal grandfather, the son and grandson of lawyers, was a distinguished chemist, a fellow of the Royal Society, and a professor at King's College, London. His mother died when he was a baby, and his father died when he was thirteen, six months before he started at Eton.[5] After Eton, he attended Trinity College, Cambridge, where, under the influence of the philosopher Henry Sidgwick, he shifted his intellectual attention from mathematics to moral philosophy. Like Maine before him, Maitland was an outstanding student and was elected to the Apostles, the exclusive intellectual club to which Maine previously had belonged. But unlike Maine, who moved directly from his undergraduate studies to an academic career, Maitland failed to win the fellowship for which he competed. The dissertation he submitted as part of the competition, "A Historical Sketch of Liberty and Equality as Ideals of English Political Philosophy from the Time of Hobbes to the Time of Coleridge," embarrassed the mature Maitland, but it addressed themes to which he subsequently returned, particularly in his late essays on corporations and trusts.[6]

After college at Cambridge, Maitland moved to London, where he entered Lincoln's Inn in 1872 and joined the bar in 1876. While practicing law, with an emphasis on conveyancing, Maitland read extensively. He was particularly influenced by Savigny's *History of Roman Law*, which he started to translate into English, and by Stubbs's *Constitutional History*. Though he never completed his translation of Savigny, he continued to read major German legal scholars, including Brunner and Grimm, whose books addressed issues in the history of property law that Maitland found interesting in relation to his practice in conveyancing. Maitland wrote several chapters of a projected book on property law but abandoned it when he heard that the government might try to reform the existing law. He did, however, address the law of property in his first published legal article, which appeared anonymously in the *Westminster Review* in 1879. The article proposed dramatic changes in the English law of property, including the abolition of the heir at law and the conversion of all

[5] H. A. L. Fisher, Frederick William Maitland: A Biographical Sketch (Cambridge University Press, 1910), pp. 2–5; C. H. S. Fifoot, Frederic William Maitland: A Life (Cambridge, Mass.: Harvard University Press, 1971), pp. 1–15.

[6] Fisher, supra note 5, at 6–12; Fifoot, supra note 5, at 35, 40, 42–3, 46–9.

FIGURE 12.1. *Frederic Maitland.* Published with permission of the Tarlton Law Library, Jamail Center for Legal Research, University of Texas School of Law.

property into personal property.[7] He also published articles on philosophical themes in *Mind*.[8]

While still in practice, Maitland undertook original research in the Record Office on the early plea rolls for the County of Gloucester. He had special interest in Gloucester, where he had often visited his grandfather and where he had inherited some property. In 1884, he published an edited volume, *Pleas of the Crown for the County of Gloucester before the Abbot of Reading, 1221*, which he hoped would interest students of English history as well as of English law. These pleas, he wrote in his preface, presented "a picture, or rather, since little imaginative art went to its making, a photograph of English life as it was early in the thirteenth century, and a photograph taken from a point of view at which chroniclers too seldom place themselves." He believed that "a large stock of examples, given with all their concrete details, may serve to provide a body of

---

[7] Fisher, supra note 5, at 18–20; Fifoot, supra 5, at 53–4.
[8] Fisher, supra note 5, at 20; Fifoot, supra note 5, at 57.

flesh and blood for the ancient rules which, whether in the pages of Bracton or in those of modern historians, are apt to seem abstract, unreal, impracticable."[9] While providing evidence of criminal activity, including murder, rape, and robbery, the pleas even more significantly revealed the political life of England. "We have here," he claimed, "a section of the body politic which shows just those most vital parts, of which, because they were deep-seated, the soul politic was hardly conscious, the system of government and police, the organization of county, hundred, and township." By using archival legal records as the route to historical conclusions that extended beyond the law, Maitland already exhibited key characteristics of his subsequent scholarly career.

Maitland applied unsuccessfully in 1883 for a readership in English law at Oxford. The following year, Maitland's former teacher, Sidgwick, agreed to fund from his own stipend a readership in English law at Cambridge. Maitland was elected to this readership just days before the publication of his *Pleas of the Crown* and began teaching in 1885.[10] In late 1886 and early 1887, he was part of a group of twelve members of the bar who established the Selden Society "to encourage the study and advance the knowledge of the History of English Law." Maitland was instrumental in convincing the society to focus on printing records rather than essays and became its first editor. He produced eight of the twenty-one volumes published by the society during his lifetime, and he supervised the rest. According to his brother-in-law, H. A. L. Fisher, among all of Maitland's achievements, the Selden Society "stood nearest to his heart." Twenty Americans were among the society's initial eighty-five subscribers, including Ames, Bigelow, Holmes, Langdell, and Thayer.[11] In 1888, Maitland became Downing Chair of the Laws of England at Cambridge,[12] the position he held until his early death in 1906.

Maitland's publications during his three years as a reader reflected his immersion in medieval English legal history. He wrote his first three articles on seisin, which he considered the key concept of English property law. He also published at his own expense *Bracton's Note Book*, a multi-volume collection of cases and annotations. Paul Vinogradoff had discovered the manuscript that became *Bracton's Note Book* in the British Museum and published a letter in the *Athenaeum* announcing his discovery. Vinogradoff suggested the manuscript's "close connection" to Bracton's treatise,[13] which he described as a statement of English law in the thirteenth century "so detailed and accurate that there is nothing to match it in the whole legal literature of the Middle Ages."[14] Vinogradoff, who had met Maitland in London, convinced him to edit

---

[9] Fisher, supra note 5, at 25–6; Fifoot, supra note 5, at 62.

[10] Fisher, supra note 5, at 29–30; Fifoot, supra note 5, at 63.

[11] Fisher, supra note 5, at 76–80; Fifoot, supra note 5, at 52.

[12] Fisher, supra note 5, at 35; Fifoot, supra note 5, at 91–2.

[13] Paul Vinogradoff, A Letter of Paul Vinogradoff Printed in the Athenaeum for 19 July, 1884, in Bracton's Note Book (London: C. J. Clay & Sons, 1887) (F. W. Maitland, ed.), vol. I, lpp. xvii, xix.

[14] Id. at xvii.

this manuscript. As Maitland's lengthy introduction and correspondence make clear, his editorial work was difficult and time-consuming. He had to travel to the British Museum or the Record Office. He copied the cases from the manuscript and tried to make sense of multiple abbreviations. He even tried to find whatever original plea rolls still existed in order to verify the extracts from them contained in the manuscript.[15]

Maitland deemed the results well worth the effort. Making the point that became a central theme in his scholarship, Maitland emphasized that the middle of the thirteenth century, when Bracton was working on his treatise, was "a critical moment in the history of English law, and therefore in the essential history of the English people." The law that would become the common law of England "was rapidly and definitely assuming the shape that it was to keep but little changed for long ages." No later than the death of Edward I in 1307, the "main outlines of the common law would ... be drawn for once and all." But during the first part of the long reign of Edward's father, Henry III, who ruled from 1216 to 1272, "the king's justices must have enjoyed such an opportunity of moulding a powerful, practical scheme of law as has rarely been given to men."[16] The common law "was not yet a struggling captive netted in the meshes of procedure."[17] One could detect "yet flexible law soon to lose its flexibility."[18]

The cases in the manuscript discovered by Vinogradoff, Maitland observed with delight, were extremely significant. Included for their importance and interest, they reflected the English law during this crucial period.[19] Maitland believed that Bracton himself selected and annotated them, although he was initially reluctant to say so in public. "I am endeavouring to keep an open mind," he wrote to Bigelow in 1885, "until the whole is legible in type and shall be quite ready to say that Bracton can not have been the annotator, for whoever may have made the collection and adorned it with notes the book is still valuable, a collection of leading cases made in the middle of the thirteenth century by a lawyer or judge, a collection containing many of the authorities cited by our great text writer."[20] Justifying the title, *Bracton's Note Book*, in the published version, Maitland made the case at length for Bracton's role[21] even as he stressed the manuscript's historical importance, whoever the compiler and annotator.[22] He concluded that "until evidence be produced on the other side, Bracton is entitled to a judgment, a possessory judgment" of responsibility for the manuscript.[23]

---

[15] F. W. Maitland, Introduction, Bracton's Note Book, supra note 13, at 1, 121–7; Fifoot, supra note 5, at 72–3.
[16] Maitland, supra note 15, at 1.
[17] Id. at 6.
[18] Id. at 7.
[19] Id. at 11–12.
[20] Fifoot, supra note 5, at 14.
[21] Maitland, supra note 15, at 71–117.
[22] Id. at 13.
[23] Id. at 71.

In the eighteen years between his election as Downing Chair and his death, Maitland, though hampered by chronic illness, produced an unprecedented and still unsurpassed body of work on the history of English law. He continued to prepare volumes of previously unpublished archival sources while writing interpretative histories that typically built upon those sources. Soon after publishing *Bracton's Note Book*, he edited the first three volumes published by the Selden Society: *Select Pleas of the Crown* (1888), *Select Pleas of the Manorial and Other Seigniorial Courts* (1889), and, with a coeditor, *The Court Baron* (1891). Among Maitland's other editions of archival sources, probably the most important were the initial three volumes of the Selden Society's *Year Book* series, covering the period 1307–11 and produced in the years immediately preceding his death. Maitland initially proposed this series to the Selden Society in 1896, and his work involved finding and translating the manuscripts, collating cases reported in the *Year Books* with entries on the plea rolls, and writing introductions to each volume.[24] As Vinogradoff observed in his eulogy for Maitland, "in order to read and publish *Year Books*, he had to build up a grammar of corrupt law French and to fathom the inadvertences and blunders of fourteenth-century legal students taking hurried notes in court."[25] Maitland even included a long discussion, "The Anglo-French Language in the Early Year Books," in one of his introductions. His attribution of the *Year Books* to the notes of students challenged previous theories that they were official records.[26]

Maitland's major work, *The History of English Law before the Time of Edward I*, was published in two volumes in 1895. In his introduction to *Bracton's Note Book*, Maitland commented that Bracton, whose book stopped abruptly in the middle of discussing the writ of right, "did not fulfill the whole of his splendid plan."[27] Maitland's two volumes did fulfill his own splendid plan "to set forth at some length the doctrines and rules of English law" during the crucial period between 1154 and 1272.[28] Although *The History of English Law* did not reach as wide an audience as Maine's *Ancient Law*, it achieved much greater and more lasting scholarly respect. From its publication to the present, scholars have regarded it as the best book on legal history ever published in the English language. Maitland's other books included *Domesday Book and Beyond* (1897), *Township and Borough* (1898), *Roman Canon Law in the Church of England* (1898), and *English Law and the Renaissance* (1901). He also wrote numerous important essays. Influenced by the German scholar Otto von Gierke, part of whose work Maitland translated into English as *Political Theories of the Middle Age*, Maitland emphasized in his late essays on corporations and trusts the key role of groups in promoting pluralism and

[24] Fifoot, supra note 5, at 250–2.
[25] Paul Vinogradoff, Frederic William Maitland, The Collected Papers of Paul Vinogradoff (Oxford: Clarendon Press, 1928), vol. I, pp. 253, 257.
[26] Fisher, supra note 5, at 166; Fifoot, supra note 5, at 258.
[27] Maitland, supra note 15, at 7.
[28] History of English Law, supra note 3, vol. I, at xxiii.

protecting individuals from the state, themes he first addressed in his unsuccessful dissertation for a postgraduate fellowship.

This support of pluralism was the closest Maitland came in his published work to revealing his political views. H. A. L. Fisher reported that Maitland, in contrast to the conservative Maine, was a Liberal Unionist, the name chosen by Liberals who refused to back Home Rule for Ireland. Fisher added that Maitland's "mind was far too independent to bear the strain of party allegiance and led him to differ upon some important questions from the principles upheld by the Unionist government." He "was in favour of what is called 'the secular solution' in education, and tried, but without success, to think well of the policy which brought about the South African War." Although he joined a committee in support of free trade, an issue that split Liberal Unionists, "he rarely spoke of politics," in part because his scholarly temperament made him reluctant to offer opinions on subjects he had not studied thoroughly. Fisher concluded that Maitland "was simply a scientific historian, with a singularly open and candid mind, and with a detachment almost unique from the prejudice of sect or party."[29] Unlike Savigny, Maine, or the many American legal scholars who became active in the Mugwump movement, politics was not a major factor in Maitland's life, which was fully immersed in scholarship, family, and friendship.

Maitland's Inaugural Lecture: "Why the History of English Law Is Not Written"

In his inaugural lecture as Downing professor, Maitland provided some answers to its title, "Why the History of English Law Is Not Written." But Maitland did not limit himself to explaining the unfortunate condition of his field. Appropriately for an inaugural lecture, he suggested a research agenda for the history of English law that should be written. While setting forth this agenda, he anticipated many of the key themes and conclusions of the actual history he would soon write himself.

Maitland contrasted the lack of scholarship on English legal history with the extensive literature on the history of other legal traditions. The history of Roman law, he observed, had been so thoroughly studied that "every shred of evidence seems to have been crushed and thrashed and forced to give up its meaning and perhaps somewhat more than its meaning," probably a sly deprecatory reference to the theoretical use of Roman law by German scholars and to Maine's speculations about general evolutionary development based on Roman law.[30] Even the history of German and French law, though not subjected to as intensive scrutiny as the history of Roman law, had received

---

[29] Fisher, supra note 5, at 174–5.

[30] Frederic William Maitland, Why the History of English Law Is Not Written, in The Collected Papers of Frederic William Maitland (Cambridge University Press, 1911) (H. A.L. Fisher, ed.) [hereinafter Collected Papers], vol. I, pp. 480, 482.

substantial scholarly attention.[31] The "unmanageable bulk" of primary materials, often unprinted or in a "hopeless mass of corruption," provided "some excuse, though hardly a sufficient excuse" for the neglect of the history of English law.[32] After all, scholars abroad had published impressive work on aspects of English legal history.[33] Referring to American scholarship on English legal history, Maitland declared himself "cosmopolitan enough to regret an arrangement of the universe which has placed our records in one hemisphere and those who would make the best use of them in another."[34]

The isolation of legal education in England and professional differences between lawyers and historians, Maitland concluded, helped account for "why the history of English law is not written." Law had only recently become a subject for study at English universities, and the study of law mostly attracted people interested in becoming practicing lawyers rather than legal scholars.[35] For practicing lawyers, Maitland stressed, past law is important as authority in the present, whereas for historians past law is important as evidence of the past. Lawyers and historians, therefore, have very different orientations to the familiar process by which legal principles and language acquire new meanings over time. For the lawyer, the process represents "an evolution of the true intent and meaning of the old law," but for the historian, "it is almost of necessity a process of perversion and misunderstanding." A lawyer, Maitland declared, "must be orthodox otherwise he is no lawyer." An orthodox historian, by contrast, is "a contradiction in terms."[36] Any attempt "to make history the handmaid of dogma," he added, "will soon cease to be history."[37]

Maitland believed that only a trained lawyer could deal with the technical material necessary to write good legal history.[38] He, therefore, placed his hope in a failed barrister, someone who "is weary of waiting for that solicitor who never comes."[39] That description fit Maitland's view of himself. As Vinogradoff reported in an essay published months after Maitland died, when the two men met in 1884, while Maitland was still a barrister in London, Maitland remarked "that he would much rather devote his life to the historical study of English law than watch in his chambers in Lincoln's Inn for the footsteps of the client who never comes," a comment he often repeated in subsequent years.[40] Fortunately, Sidgwick's endowment soon allowed Maitland to pursue the career he preferred.

[31] Id. at 482–3.
[32] Id. at 483–4.
[33] Id. at 484–5.
[34] Id. at 485.
[35] Id. at 487–8.
[36] Id. at 491.
[37] Id. at 492.
[38] Id. at 494.
[39] Id. at 496.
[40] Vinogradoff, supra note 25, at 254; see also, Milsom, supra note 1, at 273.

The publication of Glanvill's textbook in 1189, Maitland maintained, was the "date at which English law becomes articulate, begins to speak to us clearly and continuously." By the reign of Edward I a century later, a wealth of original sources provided the basis for a comprehensive account of English law.[41] A historian who studied the forms of action, which Maitland considered the core of English law, could write an interesting book about "the evolution of the great elementary conceptions, ownership, possession, contract, tort, and the like."[42] Technical legal documents, he added, could provide the best and sometimes the sole evidence for social, economic, political, and religious history. The conditions of English villagers in the late Middle Ages, he asserted as his example, could only be uncovered by mastering "an extremely formal system of pleading and procedure" containing "actions with repulsive names," topics beyond the competence of historians without legal training.[43] Maitland highlighted the "very early centralization of justice" in England after the Norman Conquest as crucial to the continuity and unity of English legal history. Reconstructing English law of the twelfth century, moreover, would provide a sound basis for understanding earlier periods.[44]

The History of English Law

In *The History of English Law before the Time of Edward I*, Maitland wrote the kind of legal history whose absence he bemoaned and whose contents he anticipated in his inaugural essay seven years earlier. Although the cover and title page listed Pollock and Maitland as joint authors, an introductory note by Pollock added that "although the book was planned in common and has been revised by both of us, by far the greater share of the execution belongs to Mr Maitland, both as to the actual writing and as to the detailed research which was constantly required."[45] In a letter to Holmes reporting "how little" he had contributed to the book, Pollock stated that he had written most of the introduction, the chapter on Anglo-Saxon law, and most of the chapter on the early history of contract,[46] less than a tenth of the entire manuscript. Writing to Vinogradoff in 1892, Maitland expressed his disappointment with Pollock's Anglo-Saxon chapter.[47] Perhaps this disappointment prompted Maitland to take as much responsibility for the book as possible. "The original scheme," Maitland wrote to a friend in 1894, "would have divided the work into approximately equal shares – but I soon discovered (as I suppose a 'collaborator' often

[41] Maitland, supra note 30, at 481.

[42] Id. at 484.

[43] Id. at 486.

[44] Id. at 482.

[45] History of English Law, supra note 3, vol. I, p. vi.

[46] Letter from Frederick Pollock to Oliver Wendell Holmes, Jr. (August 23, 1895), in Holmes-Pollock Letters (Cambridge, Mass.: Harvard University Press, 1941) (Mark DeWolfe Howe, ed.), vol. 1, pp. 60–1.

[47] Letter from Frederic Maitland to Paul Vinogradoff (May 29, 1892), in The Letters of Frederic William Maitland (Cambridge, Mass.: Harvard University Press, 1965) (C. H. S. Fifoot, ed.) [hereinafter Maitland Letters], pp. 102, 103.

will) that I wanted one thing while my yoke-fellow wanted another." Maitland, therefore, was pleased when other projects prevented Pollock from working on the book, allowing Maitland himself to write almost all of it.[48]

In explaining his focus, perhaps "written at wearisome length," on the relatively short period between 1154 and 1272, Maitland pointed out that "it is a luminous age throwing light on both past and future."[49] It also "deserves study for its own sake." He reiterated, in language that echoed his introduction to *Bracton's Note Book*, that it "was the critical moment in English legal history and therefore in the innermost history of our land and our race."[50] Emphasizing "the permanence of its work," he concluded that the law developed during these years ultimately governed the United States as well as England itself.[51]

Maitland divided *The History of English Law* into two books. Book I, entitled *Sketch of Early English Legal History*, covered in 225 pages "the growth of English law to the accession of Edward I, 'the English Justinian,'" in 1272.[52] It consisted of seven chapters: "The Dark Age in Legal History," "Anglo-Saxon Law," "Norman Law," "England under the Norman Kings," "Roman and Canon Law," "The Age of Glanvill," and "The Age of Bracton." Book II, entitled *The Doctrines of English Law in the Early Middle Ages*, covered the remaining 1,137 pages. It consisted of nine chapters: "Tenure," "The Sorts and Conditions of Men," "Jurisdiction and the Communities of the Land," "Ownership and Possession," "Contract," "Inheritance," "Family Law," "Crime and Tort," and "Procedure." Like the American legal historians who preceded him, Maitland stressed the importance of recognizing the differences between past and present law while also trying to indicate evolutionary connections between them.

At the beginning of book II, Maitland addressed the difficulties posed by writing about medieval law for modern readers. Arranging medieval law from the perspective of modern law would "run a great risk of ignoring distinctions which our ancestors saw, and a yet greater risk of insisting on distinctions which for them had no existence." For example, the distinction between public and private law, so central in modern times, made little sense in the Middle Ages, when feudalism essentially denied this distinction. Yet arranging medieval law from the perspective of the Middle Ages would run the corresponding risk of obscuring topics of greatest interest to a modern reader. For example, the emphasis in the Middle Ages on the "intricate mass of procedural rules" associated with the "forms of action" would distract attention from the modern concern about substantive law.[53] Asserting that the historian must simultaneously consider both medieval understandings and modern interests, Maitland confronted this dilemma by focusing on the "ideas and rules" in medieval law

---

[48] Letter from Frederic Maitland to Leslie Stephen (July 27, 1894), in id. at 138.
[49] History of English Law, supra note 3, vol. II, at 672–3.
[50] Id. at 673.
[51] Id. at 674.
[52] Id., vol. I, at 225.
[53] Id. at 229–30.

that seemed "elementary." He identified the law of land tenure as the most elementary part of medieval law and, therefore, began book II with a long chapter on this subject. Yet he divided his treatment of tenure into its public and private aspects, even as he stressed that this very division "is one that we make for our own convenience, not one that is imposed upon us by our authorities."[54]

From the beginning of *The History of English Law*, Maitland made clear some limitations on the ambitious scope of his project. Observing that most prior works about a particular legal system had included discussions of legal philosophy and jurisprudence, Maitland declared that he would avoid these topics. He considered them aspects of "the theoretical part of politics" rather than of "legal science," which he defined as "the actual result of facts of human nature and history."[55] Maitland also informed his readers that he would mostly ignore constitutional history and ecclesiastical law. He pointed out that for centuries English writers, most prominently and recently Stubbs, had addressed topics of constitutional history, including the history of parliament, of taxation, and, more generally, of government.[56] The medieval private law that he would be covering, by contrast, had not received much attention. Yet he indicated that he would comment on political events that influenced private law and remarked that attention to private law can disclose the importance of some political events that historians of public affairs had overlooked. Similarly, while not treating most aspects of ecclesiastical law, which related to the internal operation of the church, he would discuss topics of private law governed by ecclesiastical law and the courts of the church, such as marriage and inheritance.[57]

Underlining the approach he shared with most nineteenth-century legal historians but contrary to subsequent assumptions about him, Maitland emphasized that he would "be primarily concerned with the evolution of legal doctrine." He added that he would also "try to illustrate by real examples some of the political and economic causes and effects of those rules that are under our examination." But the evolution of those rules, rather than their "political and economic causes and effects," was his main focus. He described his book as neither "a practical hand-book of medieval law," which presumably would not have paid attention to the evolution of law, nor a description of "the whole of medieval life," which presumably would have paid more attention to the causes and effects of law. Consistent with his anti-theoretical bent, he added that "an abstract discourse about method is seldom very profitable."[58] Rather than elaborate the relationship between legal doctrine and external events, he turned immediately to the law of land tenure. Beginning with this subject,

---

[54] Id. at 231.

[55] Id. at xxiii.

[56] See letter from Frederic Maitland to James Barr Ames (March 23, 1890), in Maitland Letters, supra note 47, at 80, 81.

[57] History of English Law, supra note 3, vol. I, at xxxvii.

[58] Id. at 232.

the overwhelming majority of his two volumes dealt with the internal history of medieval legal doctrine in England. Though Maitland wrote well, his analysis could be difficult to follow, particularly for those lacking substantial familiarity with law in general and medieval law in particular. He addressed highly technical legal issues and, probably in order to cover the vast expanse of medieval private law, often compressed his discussion.[59] As Fisher persuasively commented in his memoir, "Maitland was undoubtedly over-allusive, not from ostentation but from absorption and from a tendency common to learned and modest men to credit the general reader with more knowledge than he is likely to possess."[60]

In discussing the scope of his project, Maitland indicated he would make careful though limited use of comparative legal history. He was extremely interested in why the English and continental legal systems, which were so similar in the thirteenth century, deviated so substantially from each other over the following centuries. He raised this issue in his introduction[61] and returned to it at the very end of the second volume.[62] "The first step toward an answer," he asserted, "must be a careful statement of each system by itself. We must know in isolation the things that are to be compared before we compare them." By referring to his own work as "preliminary labour," Maitland indicated that he would be focusing on a careful statement of the English system, "the first step toward an answer," rather than on more elaborate comparisons of English and continental law. Yet he added that prior work on French and German medieval law provided "many an invaluable hint for the solution of specifically English problems."[63] Like the American legal historians who preceded him, Maitland repeatedly highlighted the Teutonic origins of English law and supported his conclusions through extensive citations to European, mostly German, scholars of early Teutonic law on the Continent. This European scholarship allowed Maitland to point out differences as well as similarities between English and continental law. One important difference, he observed, was the greater role in England of temporal compared to ecclesiastical law.[64] Comparisons to medieval continental law also helped him demonstrate differences between medieval and modern English law. For example, in his discussion of movable goods, he invoked French and German medieval law to challenge the common assumption that in England the medieval law of chattels was very similar to its modern law.[65]

Maitland had strong opinions about the influence of other legal systems on the history of English law. In his most general statement, he wrote that "our laws have been formed in the main from a stock of Teutonic customs with

---

[59] Fisher, supra note 5, at 105–6.
[60] Id. at 106.
[61] History of English Law, supra note 3, vol. I, at xxxvi.
[62] Id., vol. II, at 673–4.
[63] Id., vol. I, at xxxvi.
[64] Id. at 131.
[65] Id., vol. II, at 150–6.

some additions of matter, and considerable additions or modifications of form received directly or indirectly from the Roman system."[66] He was adamant that Roman law did not have continuous influence in England and rejected the claim that the law of ancient Rome persisted after the Teutonic invasions ended the early Roman occupation of England. The laws and jurisprudence of imperial Rome, he maintained, like its language and religion, left no traces in Anglo-Saxon England.[67] As Bigelow had previously emphasized, he recognized that the law of Normandy introduced to England much later by the Norman Conquest contained elements of Roman law, derived from the last centuries of the Roman Empire. This later importation of Roman law, he pointed out, in no way supported the argument that English law contained "a continuous persistence of unadulterated Roman elements."[68] In addition to the Roman law that had been incorporated into Norman law, soon after the Norman Conquest a different Roman influence, the revival of the classical Roman law contained in the works of Justinian, reached England. For the century from roughly 1150 to 1250 this Roman law shaped and modified English law,[69] particularly through the canonical jurisprudence that affected temporal law either by attraction or repulsion,[70] but also in specific rules, such as the requirement of the delivery of the deed in the law of conveyance.[71] Yet in England, in contrast to the Continent, this Roman influence did not last. According to Maitland, "It taught us much; and then there was healthy resistance to foreign dogma."[72]

The development of original writs in England, Maitland observed, "would be the strongest bulwark against Romanism and sever our English law from all her sisters."[73] Ironically, these writs, while "the most distinctively English trait of our medieval law," in many respects resembled the forms of action of early Roman law. Maitland insisted that these resemblances should not be mistaken for imitation, as many had assumed. The English developed them on their own, in response to the actual conditions of medieval England.[74] The Roman law revived in the eleventh and twelfth centuries, he reiterated, was not the early Roman law that contained the forms of action, but the mature Roman law compiled by Justinian, which had eliminated them. The medieval scholars who revived the Roman law of Justinian would have rejected the earlier forms of action as obsolete impediments to the simpler and better system of justice found in Justinian. In the mature system of Justinian, a magistrate decides both the facts and the law without any need for either a jury or forms of action.[75] While

---

[66] Id., vol. I, at xxx.
[67] Id. at xxxi–xxxii.
[68] Id. at xxxiii.
[69] Id. at xxxiii–xxxiv.
[70] Id. at 116, 124, 131, 353; id., vol. II, at 335, 477.
[71] Id., vol. II, at 86.
[72] Id., vol. I, at 24 and generally at 111–35 (chapter entitled "Roman and Canon Law").
[73] Id., vol. II, at 558.
[74] Id. at 559.
[75] Id. at 559–60.

"the other nations of Western Europe were beginning to adopt as their own the ultimate results of Roman legal history," as reflected in Justinian, "England was unconsciously reproducing that history" by developing writs that resembled but did not borrow from the forms of action of early Roman law.[76] The causes of action under the English writs, moreover, became classified according to the relief demanded, as in old Germanic law, rather than according to the right relied on, as in old Roman law. "After a brief attempt to be Roman," Maitland concluded, "our law falls back into old Germanic habits."[77]

Although he agreed with the American legal historians about the Teutonic origins of English law, Maitland did not take a position on the different views expressed by the Americans about the relative importance of various Teutonic strains. He believed that before the Norman Conquest, English law was mainly "pure Germanic law."[78] He identified the Anglo-Norman law after the Norman Conquest as Germanic, deriving from Frankish law. Because Frankish law was "close to the root of Germanic tradition," it resembled other Germanic strains, such as the Anglo-Saxon, but it was also a "distinct variation." English princes, he pointed out, had been borrowing directly from Frankish law before the Norman Conquest. To decide the relative influence of these different Germanic strains on English law, he concluded, is often difficult and sometimes impossible. Disclaiming sufficient knowledge of the period before the Middle Ages, Maitland was satisfied simply to identify these strains and to emphasize that medieval English law, the area of his own expertise, derived primarily from Germanic sources.[79]

In discussing the impact of Norman law in England after the Norman Conquest, Maitland stressed that it was substantial but neither immediate nor inevitable. He called the Norman Conquest "a catastrophe which determines the whole future history of English law." Yet in 1066, the year of the Norman Conquest, this subsequent impact was not at all clear. Only a relatively small number of Normans entered England, the invading Normans had no legal code, and Norman law had no other "portable, transplantable shape." King William the Conqueror did not demonstrate any interest in imposing foreign law on England, and England already had its own law, much of it in writing.[80] During the reign of Stephen, the last Norman king, from 1135 to 1154, the course of English law remained uncertain.[81] Only during the reign of the first Angevin king, Henry II, from 1154 to 1189, did Norman law become English. "The reign of Henry II is of supreme importance in the history of our law," Maitland wrote, "and its importance is due to the action of the central power, to reforms ordained by the king."[82] Through his own involvement,[83] the king's court, which

[76] Id. at 558.
[77] Id. at 571.
[78] Id., vol. I, at xxvii.
[79] Id. at xxx–xxxi.
[80] Id. at 79.
[81] Id. at 110.
[82] Id. at 136.
[83] Id. at 159.

under the Norman kings was a court for great men, great causes, and matters
that concerned the king, became "an ordinary tribunal for the entire realm."[84]
The exceptional became normal.[85] "If we must choose one moment of time
as fatal" for the triumph of Norman law in England, Maitland asserted, "we
ought to choose 1166 rather than 1066, the year of the assize of novel disseisin
rather than the year of the battle of Hastings."[86] This assize, decreed by Henry
II, provided a remedy in the king's court for any man unjustly dispossessed of
his free tenement and a right to be heard by a jury.[87] Maitland emphasized that
the jury, long considered the "palladium of our liberties" in England, "is in its
origin not English but Frankish, not popular but royal."[88]

Maitland wrote about the development of medieval English law from these
Franco-Norman roots, pointing out that the custom of the king's court became
the distinctively English common law.[89] He maintained, for example, that no
later than the thirteenth century the English law of contract was already "taking a course of its own."[90] He stressed the rapid growth of English law during
the long reign of Henry III from 1216 to 1272, highlighting the substantial
increase in the number of writs that enabled people to bring cases to the king's
court,[91] which became the most important court in England.[92] Without directly
alluding to the debate among Thayer, Bigelow, and Hammond about the reception of Norman law, Maitland agreed with Bigelow and Hammond that its
influence was neither as early nor as extensive as Brunner had maintained. In
his own highly laudatory review of *The History of English Law*, Brunner maintained that Maitland, though he paid "constant attention" to Norman law and
its sources, should have "more strongly emphasized" its influence.[93] With typical modesty, Maitland responded that Brunner might be correct, noting that
the question of Norman influence "is very difficult." He was willing to "fully
admit that in any case our private law and law of procedure have many French
traits."[94] Yet with respect to some subjects, such as the inheritance of movable
property, Brunner saw Norman origins where Maitland, explicitly disagreeing
with him, did not.[95]

By the end of the reign of Henry III, Maitland stressed in language very
similar to his introduction of *Bracton's Note Book*, "most of the main outlines

---

[84] Id. at 153; see id. at 108.
[85] Id. at 144.
[86] Id. at 84.
[87] Id. at 146.
[88] Id. at 142.
[89] Id. at 184, 188.
[90] Id., vol. II, at 185.
[91] Id., vol. I, at 195.
[92] Id. at 202.
[93] Heinrich Brunner, Pollock and Maitland's History of English Law, 11 Political Science Quarterly 534, 535 (1896).
[94] History of English Law, supra note 3, vol. I, at 94, n. 2.
[95] Compare Brunner, supra note 93, at 543 with History of English Law, supra note 3, vol. II, at 349 and n. 1.

of our medieval law have been drawn for good and all." The subsequent centuries, he added, mostly filled in the details of this medieval scheme.[96] "So continuous has been our English legal life during the last six centuries," he asserted in explaining why he ended his chronological coverage in 1272, "that the law of the later middle ages has never been forgotten among us." England, he pointed out, did not suffer the disruption that the reception of Roman law inflicted on Germany. Whereas nineteenth-century historians of German law had to "disinter and reconstruct" medieval German law from the subsequent reception of Roman law, historians of English law had an unobstructed path from the medieval past to the present.[97] Reiterating the distinctiveness and continuity of English law, he closed his book by asserting that "it was for the good of the whole world that one race stood apart from its neighbors."[98]

Maitland recognized, however, that the continuous influence of medieval law in England also had deleterious effects. The law of inheritance, he believed, suffered most from medieval law, whose "evil consequences" continued in the division between real and personal property,[99] the division whose abolition he proposed in his first article while still a barrister in London. More generally, he conceded that "the modern excellences" achieved by medieval English law – uniformity, simplicity, and certainty – had been purchased at a heavy price – rigidity, hostility to innovation, and insularity.[100] While admiring the men who boldly created medieval English law, Maitland admitted that "a premature simplicity imposed from above is apt to find its sequel in fiction and evasion and intricate subtlety."[101]

Reliance on American Scholars

Consistent with his praise of Holmes, Thayer, Ames, and Bigelow in his introduction, Maitland relied on and engaged their previous scholarship on English legal history throughout the two volumes of *The History of English Law*. Most impressively, in the section of the book dealing with pleading and proof, he described three of Thayer's articles in the *Harvard Law Review* as "so full and excellent" that his treatment would be very brief, dealing only with "the more vital or the more neglected parts of the story."[102] This section cited Thayer extensively[103] both for specific details and for more general themes, such as the lack of an equivalent to the modern trial[104] and the "radically different" role of

---

[96] History of English Law, supra note 3, vol. I, at 174.
[97] Id. at xxxiv.
[98] Id., vol. II, at 674.
[99] Id. at 363.
[100] Id., vol. I, at 225.
[101] Id., vol. II, at 447.
[102] Id. at 604 n. 1.
[103] History of English Law, supra note 3, vol. II, at 598 n. 1, 601 n. 4, 606 n. 1, 629 n. 3, 632 n. 5, 634, n. 3, 637 n. 3, 638 n. 3, 650 n. 4, 652 n. 3, 654 n. 1, 654 n. 4, 665 n. 1.
[104] Id. at 592 n. 2.

witnesses[105] in the twelfth century. *The History of English Law* cited Bigelow
for evidence that Henry II had a significant role in the king's court,[106] to support the assertion that the use of the seal in contract law originated with the
Frankish kings rather than ancient folk law,[107] as authority regarding both the
substantive[108] and procedural[109] law of theft, and in discussing the allotment of
proof between litigants.[110] While analyzing seisin in the chapter on ownership
and possession, Maitland politely noted that he could not "wholly agree" with
Bigelow's conclusion that questions of possession could easily be transformed
into proprietary questions.[111]

   The History of English Law similarly cited Holmes and Ames on a variety
of issues. It invoked Holmes approvingly while observing that the relativity
of ownership in late medieval land law persisted in current English law,[112]
while pointing out that ancient law assigned liability to inanimate objects[113]
and while maintaining that much of the law of specific relief originated in the
thirteenth century and was not introduced by chancellors in the later Middle
Ages.[114] Maitland relied on Holmes in his discussions of the law of bailment[115]
and the role of an executor[116] but qualified one of his conclusions about bailment[117] and disagreed with some of his views about ownership,[118] assumpsit,[119] and the law of master and servant.[120] Maitland cited articles by Ames
about the history of assumpsit in his chapters on contract and on crime and
tort. Based on Ames's empirical research, Maitland accepted his conclusion
that before the seventeenth century plaintiffs could not use the action of covenant to recover a debt.[121] Maitland also commented in this chapter on the
disagreement between Ames and Holmes about the history of consideration,
siding with Ames. After noting that he disagreed with an "ingenious theory"
of Holmes about the history of quid pro quo and adding that the "history of
'consideration' lies outside the period with which we are dealing," Maitland
observed that Ames "has put the subject, from the fifteenth century down-
ward, on a new footing."[122] In his chapter on crime and tort, Maitland relied

---

[105] Id. at 601 n. 4.
[106] Id., vol. I, at 158 n. 2, 4, 159 n. 2.
[107] Id., vol. II, at 223 n. 4.
[108] Id. at 496 n. 3.
[109] Id. at 597 n. 4.
[110] Id. at 602 n. 2, 3; 603 n. 3.
[111] Id. at 59 n. 2.
[112] Id. at 78 n. 3.
[113] Id. at 474 n. 5.
[114] Id. at 596 n. 5.
[115] Id. at 156 n. 1, 172 n. 1, 5.
[116] Id. at 336 n. 1.
[117] Id. at 172 n. 1.
[118] Id. at 45–6.
[119] Id. at 214 n. 2.
[120] Id. at 531–2 and 532 n. 2.
[121] Id. at 219 n. 1.
[122] Id. at 214 n. 2.

on Ames to describe the slow and difficult extension of assumpsit to expand tort liability.[123] He also cited Ames's article on the history of trover to support the claim that the crime of larceny involved an action against a possessor and, therefore, could not be committed by a possessor.[124] The substantial correspondence between Ames and Maitland about Ames's article "Disseisin of Chattels," recounted in the previous chapter on Ames, informed Maitland's chapter on ownership and possession, which included a footnote respectfully criticizing Ames's conclusions.[125] In addition to the four American scholars he specifically praised in his introduction, Maitland occasionally referred to the *Essays in Anglo-Saxon Law* by Adams and his students[126] and to works by Langdell[127] and John Wigmore,[128] Thayer's student who became a preeminent scholar of evidence at Northwestern Law School.

Evolutionary Themes

Beyond praising and relying on the specific contributions to the history of English law by Ames, Bigelow, Holmes, and Thayer, Maitland exhibited the more general evolutionary legal thought that pervaded late nineteenth-century American legal scholarship. Throughout his book, Maitland discussed the origins and evolution of legal doctrine, often using organic metaphors. He identified the sworn inquest, transplanted from Normandy, as the "germ" of the English trial by jury.[129] He referred to the "infancy," "germ," and "embryonic history" of the law of agency,[130] and to the "germs" of trespasses as a class of torts.[131] He described the "beginnings of a doctrine of public or official capacities,"[132] of estates,[133] of primogeniture,[134] and of seisin as possession,[135] and he identified "the genesis of 'employer's liability.'"[136] Maitland addressed the "evolution" of military tenure,[137] of the idea of a corporation,[138] of ecclesiastical jurisdiction,[139] of possessory actions,[140] of various writs,[141] and of

---

[123] Id. at 527 n. 5.
[124] Id. at 498 n. 7.
[125] Id. at 168 n. 2. Maitland also cited Ames's articles id. at 166 n. 1, 166, n. 3, 167, n. 2, 172, n. 3, 175 n. 5.
[126] Id. at 156 n. 1, 159, n. 2, 251, n. 3, 252, n. 2, 253, n. 1, 364, n. 1, 426, n. 4.
[127] Id. at 205 n. 1, 221 n. 1.
[128] Id. at 186 n. 2, 470 n. 1, 474 n. 5, 476 n. 1, 528 n. 6, 531 n. 3.
[129] Id., vol. I, at 74, 93.
[130] Id., vol. II, at 228.
[131] Id. at 511.
[132] Id., vol. I, at 523.
[133] Id., vol. II, at 11.
[134] Id. at 312.
[135] Id. at 31.
[136] Id. at 528.
[137] Id., vol. I, at 253.
[138] Id. at 534.
[139] Id., vol. II, at 2.
[140] Id. at 46.
[141] Id. at 64, 69 n. 1, 77.

primogeniture.[142] In the context of his treatment of the law of movable goods, he illustrated "the evolution of legal remedies" lagging behind "the evolution of morality."[143] Maitland also used powerful evolutionary metaphors to underline the independence of English from Roman law. He described the English writs "not as the outcome of a classificatory process that has been applied to pre-existing materials," but as "living things" with their own histories. "A few are still-born, some are sterile, others live to see their children and children's children in high places. The struggle for life is keen among them and only the fittest survive."[144] In one of his broadest generalizations, he claimed that the law of property "being evolved" in medieval England had an "illustrious future" because it was "capable of becoming the land law of the England, the America, the Australia of the twentieth century."[145]

Like many nineteenth-century legal scholars, Maitland associated legal evolution with national and racial history while also indicating the limits of explanations based on nation or race. He referred to the continuous history of "our own Teutonic race."[146] Yet in analyzing why English law deviated from the law of France and Germany, countries "near of kin," he warned against "hasty talk about national character."[147] And in evaluating the law of England after the Norman Conquest, he maintained that determining what part was based on previous English law and what part was introduced by the Normans "should not be stated as though it were a simple ethnical question." He objected to metaphors of two ethnic traditions merging like rivulets into a river or elements into a chemical compound. "Other elements, which are not racial," he emphasized, "have gone into its making."[148]

The Relationship between Law and Society

In his treatment of the relationship between law and society, as in his interest in legal evolution, Maitland resembled other nineteenth-century legal scholars more than most recent commentators assume. Like the Americans, he recognized external influences on law while focusing on its internal evolution. He fulfilled his promise to concentrate on "the evolution of legal doctrine" without neglecting the "political and economic causes and effects" of legal rules.[149] He referred more to causes than to effects and typically treated both relatively briefly, without the detailed elaboration he lavished on the legal doctrines that were his primary concern. For example, Maitland identified the various factors that turned the Norman Conquest into a decisive influence on English law. He mentioned the individual characteristics of the Norman leaders who

[142] Id. at 325.
[143] Id. at 177.
[144] Id. at 561.
[145] Id. at 1.
[146] Id. at 448.
[147] Id., vol. I, at xxxvi.
[148] Id. at 79–80.
[149] Id. at 232.

subjugated the English, the rebellion of Norman barons against their king soon after the Conquest, and the fact that William the Conqueror left three sons, thereby making the grant of a charter of liberties in England much more likely than if he had left only one.[150] Most significantly, the aftermath of the Norman Conquest produced "an exceedingly strong kingship which proves its strength by outliving three disputed successions and crushing a rebellious baronage."[151] Yet Maitland did not elaborate these influences beyond identifying them. Readers who were not already familiar with the history of England in the centuries following the Norman Conquest could not have learned about it from his book. Nor did he even identify many of the "hundred forces which play upon our legal history" in this period. "We have not to speak here of all these causes," he wrote, because "they do not come within the history of law." His point in mentioning some of them was to correct the common but mistaken view that Norman and English law simply merged together. The diverging interests of the king and the nobles, he observed, became "as potent a cause of legal phenomena" as the prior legal traditions of different ethnic groups.[152] Even more broadly, Maitland pointed to factors beyond the Norman Conquest that influenced the development of medieval English law. "Everywhere in western Europe new principles of social and political order were emerging; new classes were being formed; the old laws, the only written laws, were becoming obsolete; the state was taking a new shape."[153] After mentioning these major external influences as part of his effort to demonstrate that the law in Norman England was not simply the merger of two legal traditions, Maitland, typically, did not elaborate them.

The emergence of a strong kingship in England, Maitland emphasized, largely explains the distinctiveness of English law. He maintained that the power of the English kings both produced the English common law and limited the influence of Roman law in England. Maitland particularly highlighted the importance of the reforms initiated under the centralized authority of Henry II[154] while making clear that he was "leaving the political and constitutional events of the reign for others."[155] Summarizing "the most durable and the most fruitful" legal results of his reign, Maitland declared that "the whole of English law is centralized and unified by the institution of a permanent court of professional judges, by the frequent mission of itinerant judges throughout the land, by the introduction of the 'inquest' or 'recognition' and the 'original writ' as normal parts of the machinery of justice."[156] These developments, Maitland maintained, especially the original writs, helped insulate England against the revival of Roman law, which was penetrating other countries of

[150] Id. at 79–80.
[151] Id. at 94.
[152] Id. at 80.
[153] Id. at 105.
[154] Id. at 136.
[155] Id. at 174.
[156] Id. at 138.

Western Europe during this period. Indicating his sensitivity to historical contingency, he speculated that if the Norman invasion had been repelled, a strong kingship might not have developed, and English law might have broken into numerous local customs. Under those counterfactual circumstances, the legal history of England might have resembled the actual legal history of Germany, with Roman law replacing a declining native tradition.[157]

The strong kingship that arose in the aftermath of the Norman Conquest, Maitland added, also produced a division between lay and ecclesiastical jurisdictions that had major consequences for the subsequent history of English law. Alluding to the quarrel between King Henry II and Archbishop Thomas Becket without describing it in any historical detail, Maitland characterized its outcome as an overwhelming and permanent, though not a total, victory for the lay courts over the religious courts.[158] Yet the few denials of jurisdiction to lay courts, he pointed out, impeded the development of several important areas of law. The English law of corporations and trusts, topics to which Maitland influentially returned in his late essays, was delayed because lay courts had no jurisdiction over the internal affairs of religious institutions. The concept of fictitious persons, so central to corporate law, arose primarily in these religious institutions, and the administration of money given to church officials for relief of the poor or other specified purposes raised issues that would subsequently be addressed by the law of trusts.[159] Religious courts, moreover, retained exclusive jurisdiction over sexual morality and had significant jurisdiction over defamation and usury.[160]

Maitland's discussion of criminal law further illustrates his general historiographical approach of identifying but not elaborating external influences on the evolution of legal doctrine. In just one introductory paragraph, he mentioned political, social, and economic causes that transformed criminal law in the twelfth century. They included the growth of vassalage that weakened the bond of kinship, the many foreigners in England for whom the king was their only kin, the various tariffs levied by different ethnic groups, and the impoverishment of peasants under laws that gave their lords claims to property that otherwise could have been used to pay for their misdeeds. After identifying some specifically legal influences on the transformation of criminal law, Maitland concluded this paragraph with the disclaimer that "it is not for us to describe all these converging forces." Consistent with his emphasis on the evolution of legal doctrine, he considered it "enough if we can detect the technical machinery by which they did their work."[161]

Though Maitland did not elaborate the external influences on legal evolution, he also repeatedly emphasized that they could not be ignored, and he occasionally criticized legal theories that assumed purely autonomous legal

---

[157] Id. at 79, 110.
[158] Id. at 124–5.
[159] Id. at 126.
[160] Id. at 130.
[161] Id., vol. II, at 462.

development. Maitland's discussion of seisin, the topic of his first three articles after becoming a reader at Cambridge, provided a particularly important example while also allowing him to stress the benefits of historical over purely theoretical analysis of legal doctrine that he emphasized in his introduction. He declared that no idea in the entire history of English law was more significant than seisin, which formed the basis of English land law.[162] In its origins, and for centuries after the Norman Conquest, seisin meant possession,[163] which was distinguished from, and sometimes opposed to, proprietary rights.[164] The relationship between possession and ownership had been a major issue in legal scholarship, particularly in Germany, ever since Savigny's influential treatise on the subject, and Maitland referred to this scholarship during his discussion of seisin. Pointing out that prior scholars had addressed the relationship between possession and ownership primarily by reference to the classical Roman law, he warned against basing conclusions on logic alone, without attention to considerations of space and time.[165]

"That the German jurists in their attempts to pin the Roman lawyers down to some one neat doctrine of possession and of the reasons for protecting it, may have been engaged on an impossible task," Maitland asserted, "it is not for us to suggest in this place." But Maitland seemed to be making precisely this suggestion by immediately adding that "so far as concerns our own English law we make no doubt that at different times and in different measures every conceivable reason for protecting possession has been felt as a weighty argument and has had its influence on rights and remedies." He pointed out that analogues to modern theories of Savigny, Jhering, and others had been invoked in the course of English legal history, sometimes together, at other times in conflict, until ultimately some prevailed over others. Maitland indicated that "there well may be a certain truth in all these theories,"[166] while insisting that historical factors, not logic or principles of justice, best explain their use and prevalence at different times. Maitland emphasized the importance of "motives and aims of which an abstract jurisprudence knows nothing," but that an understanding of politics in historical context can reveal. To illustrate, he observed that Henry II, when he protected possession by instituting the "possessory assizes," surely was thinking "of the additional strength that would accrue to him, and his successors, could he make his subjects feel that they owed the beatitude of possession to his ordinance and the action of his court."[167]

Yet most of Maitland's lengthy treatment of seisin, following the general approach he announced for the entire book, dealt with its evolution as a legal doctrine.[168] Tracing the growth of a set of possessory actions for the protection

---

[162] Id. at 29.
[163] Id. at 31.
[164] Id. at 33.
[165] Id. at 40–1.
[166] Id. at 44.
[167] Id. at 41.
[168] Id. at 46–80.

of seisin,[169] he emphasized, as had many of his predecessors, including Maine and Holmes, the connection between procedure and substance. Though they were complicated and difficult, "unless we understand the writs of entry we cannot understand seisin."[170] Not simply "matters of mere procedure," the rules about writs of entry "seem to be the outward manifestation of a great rule of substantive law"; the "graduated hierarchy of actions corresponds to a graduated hierarchy of seisins and of proprietary rights." Maitland understood this substantive rule to mean that seisin "generates a proprietary right – an ownership, we may even say – which is good against all who have no better, because they have no older, right."[171] In practice, the law operated to protect ownership until an older right could be proved. Because proof of an older right, rather than proof of ownership against all others, was sufficient to prevail in a proprietary action, Maitland emphasized "the relativity of ownership" in medieval land law.[172] This idea of relativity, he added, continued to govern modern English land law, even though the forms of action from which it emerged no longer existed.[173]

While Maitland accurately claimed that he was more interested in analyzing doctrine than in describing "the whole of medieval life,"[174] his meticulous and thoughtful analysis of legal documents often yielded important insights into the social and economic history of medieval England. In studying the crucial law of land tenure, he observed that many men who had the status of free men were, in practical effect, unfree because they were tenants of lords who could demand agricultural labor from them to an unpredictable extent. Maitland realized that it was very difficult to prove that a man was personally unfree.[175] Yet, he added, the "man who on going to bed knows that he must spend the morrow in working for his lord and does not know to what kind of work he may be put, though he may be legally a free man, free to fling up his tenement and go away, is in fact for the time being bound by his tenure to live the same life that is led by the great mass of unfree men."[176] Tenure, he concluded, was much more important than status.[177] Maitland also pointed out the social consequences of the king's leases of his manors to lords. The king had an interest in assuring that the tenants on these manors were well treated, for the tenants provided security for his rent.[178] Tenants on land retained by the king, moreover, continued to enjoy rights that preceded the Norman Conquest.[179]

---

[169] Id. at 46.
[170] Id. at 62.
[171] Id. at 75.
[172] Id. at 77.
[173] Id. at 78.
[174] Id., vol. I, at 232.
[175] Id. at 382–3.
[176] Id. at 398.
[177] Id. at 407.
[178] Id. at 398.
[179] Id. at 398–401.

Discussing the implications of the medieval law of inheritance for economic history, Maitland observed that the legal distinction between real property, which was inheritable, and chattels, which were not, did not in practice limit the heir to the inheritance of "bare acres, while the capital which has made them fertile goes to others." A detailed knowledge of medieval law revealed that a substantial amount of agricultural capital was considered realty that descends to the heir, including the right to require labor from tenants, who were treated as "annexed to the soil" and whose plows, oxen, and other chattels could be used by the heir. Various local customs, moreover, gave the heir rights to "heir-looms" that included the best chattels, such as animals and household goods. These legal rules, Maitland emphasized, enabled the intergenerational transfer of agricultural wealth during a period when "agriculture was almost the only process productive of wealth."[180]

Identifying and examining different legally constituted classes of persons, such as women and Jews, was another way in which Maitland's legal analysis revealed important aspects of medieval life. With respect to subjects of private law, unmarried women had the same rights as men, but public law did not recognize women as having either rights or obligations. Women, for example, did not serve on juries or participate in local government.[181] When a woman married, moreover, her previous ownership of land and chattels was transferred to her husband,[182] though Maitland emphasized the contingency of the legal treatment of the chattel of married women, pointing out that in the thirteenth century "our law had not decisively made up its mind against a community of chattels between husband and wife."[183]

Jews, Maitland reported, were legally free in relation to all other persons except the king, to whom they owed servitude. He observed that the kings of medieval England had economic incentives to give rights to Jews that were denied to Christians, particularly lending money at interest. As a result, many Jews became wealthy and were heavily taxed, thereby significantly financing the kingdom and subsidizing royal indigence. Because money owed to Jews to a substantial extent was also money owed ultimately to the kings, the kings often protected the Jews. The kings also allowed the Jews enormous autonomy regarding their internal affairs. Yet this system, though it provided Jews an important role in English life for roughly a century and a half after they arrived in England after the Norman Conquest, over time oppressed both Jews and Christian Englishmen, whose hatred of Jews on religious grounds became exacerbated by their economic role. Popular pressure prompted increasing restrictions on Jews from the middle of the thirteenth century. Eventually, Jews were prohibited from charging interest, cutting off their main source of income.[184]

---

[180] Id., vol. II, at 362–3.
[181] Id., vol. I, at 482–4.
[182] Id., vol. II, at 407, 427.
[183] Id. at 427.
[184] Id., vol. I, at 468–75.

The expulsion of the Jews from England in 1290, Maitland concluded, "looks like the only possible solution of a difficult problem."[185]

Codification

Consistent with his aversion to theory, Maitland did not address most of the jurisprudential implications of evolutionary legal thought that often preoccupied late nineteenth-century American legal scholars. In an essay published just months before he died, however, he recognized the value of codification, a subject the Americans considered at length, often in the context of evaluating the relative merits of codification and adjudication in conforming law to evolving custom. Maitland's essay "The Making of the German Civil Code" praised the substantial work over two decades that eventually produced the German Civil Code, passed by the Reichstag in 1896 and effective as of January 1, 1900. While making clear that he, like other Englishmen, did not admire "all things German,"[186] Maitland declared the new code "a great achievement, and ... a just cause for national pride."[187] Observing that the German code had become admired throughout the world and would undoubtedly influence other countries, Maitland hoped that it would serve as a model for England as well.

Disclaiming any theoretical interest in examining "the relative merits of codified and uncodified law," an issue many American scholars considered at length, Maitland stressed the value of the German code in bringing "their law up to date," able to face "modern times with modern ideas, modern machinery, modern methods."[188] Praise of the German code, he emphasized, was fully consistent with interest in legal history. He made the obvious point that he found legal history intrinsically interesting. He added that it was valuable as well as fascinating "to trace the origin of legal rules in the social and economic conditions of a by-gone age." Yet people with historical sensitivity, he maintained, should be particularly eager to eliminate dysfunctional survivals from inherited law. Law "unfitly surviving in a changed environment" was an "anachronism," offensive to taste as well as to reason. Pointing out that the Germans themselves were the pioneers and masters of legal history, he stressed that their interest in it had not prevented them from using codification to modernize their law. Indeed, Maitland felt that the German sensitivity to history "encouraged them to believe that every age should be the mistress of its own law."[189] Echoing Americans who viewed legislation rather than adjudication as appropriate when a large gap separates existing common law and needed reform, Maitland argued that a primary function of legislation is "to sweep into the dust-bin of

[185] Id. at 471.
[186] Frederic Maitland, The Making of the German Civil Code, in Collected Papers, supra note 30, vol. 3, pp. 474, 486.
[187] Id. at 484.
[188] Id. at 485.
[189] Id. at 486–7.

history the rubbish that inevitably accumulates in the course of legal history." Conceding that adjudication can go a long way in "accommodating old law to new wants," Maitland emphasized that judges "never can say that the old rule is rubbish and must go to the dust-bin."[190]

Maitland's Critique of Maine

Throughout *The History of English Law* as well as in his other scholarship and private correspondence, Maitland differentiated his methods and conclusions from Maine's. At some points, Maitland challenged Maine directly; at others, only by implication. Maitland's correspondence reveals extreme generosity in his assessments of others, but a letter from Pollock discussing Maine prompted one of Maitland's rare negative comments. "I always talk of him with reluctance," Maitland replied, "for on the few occasions on which I sought to verify his statements of fact I came to the conclusion that he trusted much to a memory that played him tricks and rarely looked back at a book that he had once read."[191]

In his inaugural lecture at Cambridge in 1888, Maitland referred to the recently deceased Maine as a "great man" who was the "prophet" and "herald" of "the science of comparative jurisprudence." But by quoting Maine's own comment about comparative jurisprudence "if it ever exists," Maitland made clear his own view that it had not yet arrived. "It is only through learning wide and deep, tough and technical," Maitland asserted while discussing Maine, "that we can safely approach those world-wide questions that he raised or criticize the answers that he found for them." Maitland acknowledged Maine's own broad learning[192] but seemed implicitly to challenge him by adding that "there is not much 'comparative jurisprudence' for those who do not know thoroughly well the things to be compared, not much 'comparative jurisprudence' for Englishmen who will not slave at their law reports."[193] Endorsing the idea of comparative jurisprudence, Maitland confidently maintained that examining the medieval law of continental Europe "would send us to our Year Books with a new vigour and a new intelligence."[194] Sixteen years later, removed from the context of an inaugural lecture following Maine's death, Maitland was less circumspect in his criticisms. "Who could forget," he wrote of Maine, "the penetrating glance, the easy grace, the pointed phrase? But, to blurt out an unfashionable truth, there were qualities in his work, or in his presentation of his work, which would have served to better purpose in a land of laborious pedantry than where men are readily persuaded that hard labour

---

[190] Id. at 487.
[191] Letter from Frederic Maitland to Frederick Pollock (January 21, 1901), in Maitland Letters, *supra* note 47, at 222.
[192] Maitland, *supra* note 30, at 486.
[193] Id. at 489.
[194] Id. at 490.

is disagreeable and that signs of hard labour are disgusting."[195] Unlike Maine, who, as Pollock remarked, ignored English legal materials because they "were not in a fit state,"[196] Maitland undertook to put them "in a fit state" and to "slave" at them.

At various points in *The History of English Law*, Maitland explicitly challenged Maine's conclusions. He criticized Maine and other "historical speculators" for drawing unjustified inferences from the exclusion of "the half-blood" in the common law of inheritance. Observing that this exclusion is neither ancient nor significant, Maitland rejected Maine's claim that it supported his theory of the primitive family based on descent through the male.[197] In correspondence with Pollock, Maitland called Maine's "story" about the half-blood "a mere dream" contradicted by historical evidence.[198] Maitland also attributed Maine's mistaken explanations of the law of theft to his theoretical position that ancient law punished criminals based on the resentment of the injured party rather than on the culpability of the criminal.[199]

Without referring specifically to Maine, Maitland denied his fundamental claim that legal systems in different countries exhibit parallel stages of growth. In discussing the medieval law of inheritance, Maitland cited documentary evidence of "an individualistic law of succession for movable goods" in medieval England as "quite sufficient to give us pause before we speak of 'family ownership' as a phenomenon that must necessarily appear in the history of every race."[200] "To suppose that the family law of every nation must needs traverse the same route," he concluded, "this is an unwarrantable hypothesis." "To construct some fated scheme of successive stages which shall comprise every arrangement that may yet be discovered among backward peoples," he declared more broadly, "this is a hopeless task. A not unnatural inference from the backwardness would be that somehow or another they have wandered away from the road along which the more successful races have made their journey." Maitland clearly considered this inference absurd, and he emphasized that "comparative jurisprudence" could not prove the "universal validity" of "dogma" refuted by specific historical evidence from a particular country.[201]

In a talk favorably comparing history to political science, Maitland similarly rejected the view that historians should strive for increasing levels of generality.[202] Again challenging Maine without mentioning him by name, Maitland expressed "a special dread of those theorists who are trying to fill

---

[195] Frederic Maitland, The Laws of the Anglo-Saxons, in Collected Papers, supra note 30, vol. 3, pp. 447, 460.

[196] Frederick Pollock, Introduction, Maine's Ancient Law (New York: Henry Holt and Company, 1889), p. xx.

[197] History of English Law, supra note 3, vol. II, at 302, 304.

[198] Letter from Maitland to Pollock, supra note 191.

[199] History of English Law, supra note 3, vol. II, at 496–7.

[200] Id. at 251.

[201] Id. at 255.

[202] Frederic Maitland, The Body Politic, in Collected Papers, supra note 30, vol. 3, pp. 285, 303.

up the dark ages of medieval history with laws collected from the barbarian tribes that have been observed in modern days."[203] He emphasized that different countries had different legal histories affected by numerous different local conditions, and that no legal system could fairly be described as typical or normal. Using the history of judicial procedure and the history of governmental organization as examples, he claimed that the very "idea of normalness" among different countries is "an inappropriate and a delusive idea; it implies a comparison that we cannot make." The legal history of one country, he declared, "is neither more nor less normal" than the legal history of another.[204]

Both in the contexts of the family and of communal affairs, Maitland detected evidence of individualism in medieval English law that contradicted Maine's assertion that all progressive societies move from communalism to individualism. "Still under the influence of modern theories about 'archaic' facts," Maitland warned, "we might exaggerate the amount of communalism or even of self-government which exists in the township."[205] He repeatedly stressed that the apparent communalism of medieval life is only "the thin cloak of a rough and rude individualism."[206] "The apparent communalism of old law covers an individualism which has deep and ancient roots."[207] What appears to be communal liability on closer inspection turns out to be the joint and several liability of individuals.[208] True communalism, Maitland maintained, first appeared centuries later in Elizabethan England.[209] Far removed from the subsequently developed law of corporations, in medieval England people would "listen in vain for any one to say that the lands of the city are not simply the lands of the citizens, or that a debt owed by the borough is not a debt owed by the burgesses. So long as such sayings are not said," Maitland concluded, "the personality of the group-person is latent and insecure."[210]

Similarly, Maitland emphasized the extent of individualism in medieval family law, thereby undermining Maine's invocation of the family as the embodiment of communalism. "It has become a common place among English writers," Maitland wrote, "that the family rather than the individual was the 'unit' of ancient law." Although Maitland again did not provide any citations, Maine was the English writer who was the source of this "common place." While conceding that the strength of the sacred bond of blood lent truth to this "common place," Maitland added that the terms "family" and "unit" are too vague to be useful to legal historians.[211] He rejected, again without citing Maine by name, many of his specific conclusions about the history of the

---

[203] Id. at 300.
[204] Id. at 302.
[205] The History of English Law, supra note 3, vol. I, at 620.
[206] Id. at 616.
[207] Id. at 688.
[208] Id. at 617, 627–8, 630.
[209] Id. at 617.
[210] Id. at 687.
[211] Id., vol. II, at 240.

family. While discussing and disagreeing with the "popular theory that land was owned by families or households before it was owned by individuals,"[212] Maitland was surely thinking of Maine as the originator of this "popular theory." In contrast to Maine, moreover, Maitland did not believe the ancient family was characterized by patriarchal descent though the male.[213] Maitland reinforced the individualism of medieval family law by emphasizing the lack of community property between a husband and wife. "Our own law at an early time," he wrote, "took a decisive step. It rejected the idea of community."[214] "Long ago," he reiterated at the end of his lengthy treatment of this subject, "we chose our individualistic path."[215]

In *Township and Borough*, published three years after *The History of English Law*, Maitland directly addressed and rejected Maine's statements in *Ancient Law* describing the family as a corporation and the father as a trustee. "This patriarchal trustee," Maitland wrote, "who represents a corporation, looks to me, I must confess, suspiciously modern." In the same passage, Maitland explained that his own analysis of history required many words and qualifications. "The outcome," Maitland conceded, "will not be so graceful, so lucid, as Maine's Ancient Law." But Maitland left no doubt throughout his work that he preferred his own meticulous historical scholarship to Maine's grace and lucidity, which, Maitland often reminded his readers, was the pyrrhic victory of style over substance.[216] Most directly challenging Maine's broadest conclusion, Maitland wrote: "If we look at the doings of our law courts, we may feel inclined to revise a famous judgement and to say that while the individual is the unit of ancient, the corporation is the unit of modern law."[217]

Maitland's Late Essays: The Legal Treatment of Groups and English Pluralism

Maitland reflected more generally on the function and legal treatment of groups in important late essays that connected his historical investigations, presented as the objective conclusions of rigorous research, to broader social concerns. Like the Americans Melville Bigelow and Roscoe Pound, Maitland wrote at the beginning of the twentieth century about the dangers of individualism and the attractions of collectivism in modern society. Maitland first worried about the vulnerability of individuals to the powerful modern state in his early thesis on the history of English political philosophy. The thesis criticized individualistic theories of natural rights as insufficient protection for minorities in a democracy. It considered as a possible alternative Coleridge's theory that representation should be based on interests rather than individuals. Yet it ultimately

---

[212] Id. at 245.
[213] Id. at 240.
[214] Id. at 402.
[215] Id. at 433.
[216] Frederic Maitland, Township and Borough (Cambridge University Press, 1898), pp. 21–2.
[217] Id. at 13.

rejected this alternative, reasoning that Coleridge's identification of only two interests, the landed and the commercial, was too narrow. In the thesis itself, Maitland did not propose a solution to the problems he identified. But his later reading of works by the German legal scholar Otto von Gierke prompted him to recognize groups independent of the state as vital to a healthy society.[218] Maitland translated a portion of Gierke's work into English, published in 1900 as *Political Theories of the Middle Age*, with an introduction that made clear the extent to which he endorsed Gierke's positions.[219] Informed by his reading of Gierke and by his own extensive knowledge of English legal history, Maitland wrote several essays in the few years between his translation of Gierke and his death in 1906 that developed his views on the importance of independent groups in the context of analyzing the English law of corporations and trusts. According to Maitland, the English law of trusts had happily evolved to provide meaningful protection for a wide range of groups, which largely accounted for the distinctive and admirable pluralism of English society.

Gierke argued that groups have a real personality of their own, developed organically over time independently of the state.[220] He specifically contrasted his view with the previous "concession theory," which treated corporations as created by the state and subject to the state's control.[221] Maitland's introduction specifically endorsed the position that the group is "no fiction, no symbol, no coercive name for individuals, but a living organism and a real person."[222] He identified both the state and the corporation as related species of a genus that he called "group-units," defined as permanently organized groups to which one can "attribute acts and intents, rights and wrongs."[223] Contrasting Maine's famous statement about the movement of progressive societies from status to contract, Maitland asserted in a lecture that the current "line of advance" was "to something that contract cannot explain, and for which our best, if an inadequate, name is the personality of the organised group."[224]

[218] J. W. Burrow, Whigs and Liberals: Continuity and Change in English Political Thought (Oxford University Press, 1988), pp. 135–7; J. W. Burrow, "The Village Community" and the Uses of History in Late Nineteenth-Century England, in Historical Perspectives: Studies in English Thought and Society, in Honour of J. H. Plumb (London: Europa, 1974) (Neil McKendrick, ed.) [hereinafter Village Community], pp. 255, 277; Ernest Barker, Maitland as a Sociologist, 29 The Sociological Review 121, 122, 126 (1937).

[219] David Runciman and Magnus Ryan, Editors' Introduction, F. W. Maitland, State, Trust and Corporation (Cambridge University Press, 2003) [hereinafter State, Trust, and Corporation], pp. ix, xi.

[220] Ernest Barker, Political Thought in England, 1848 to 1914 (London: Oxford University Press, 2d ed., 1928), p. 153; Barker, supra note 218, at 128; Burrow, Whigs and Liberals, supra note 128, at 135.

[221] David Runciman, Pluralism and the Personality of the Modern State (Cambridge University Press, 1997), pp. 93–4.

[222] Burrow, Village Community, supra note 218, at 277.

[223] Frederic Maitland, Extract from Maitland's Introduction to Political Theories of the Middle Age by Otto von Gierke, in State, Trust, and Corporation, supra note 219, p. 1.

[224] Frederic Maitland, Moral Personality and Legal Personality, in State, Trust, and Corporation, supra note 219, pp. 62, 69.

Unfortunately, Maitland observed in many of his essays, the history of the English law of corporations had impeded recognition of the real, organic nature of groups. He identified the concept of the "corporation sole," which he called "that curious freak of English law,"[225] as the main culprit. He pointed out that the corporation sole originated as a solution to the inability of English property law to deal with the property of the parish church. In negotiating the complicated relationship among the church, the parson, and the parson's patron, the corporation sole arose as a way for the parson to have meaningful, but limited, control of church property. The law recognized the parson as the owner of the church, not in his personal capacity, but as a corporation consisting only of himself, a corporation sole. Unlike an owner in his personal capacity, the parson did not have full control over church property. He could use it, but he could not alienate it. When the parson died, the church property went into abeyance until a new parson was appointed.[226] As a corporation sole, the parson became an artificial person.[227] Maitland called the corporation sole "a juristic abortion" because it was not given any personality of its own.[228] But the corporation sole did allow the parson some independent control over church property while indicating that he was not acting in his personal interest, but in the interest of his official capacity with responsibility to the church.[229]

Maitland observed that the corporation sole would not have become a problem had it been limited to the parson. Unfortunately, however, the concept was extended to the king of England and became "more abortive and infinitely more mischievous."[230] It "has persuaded us to think clumsy thoughts or to speak clumsy words about King and Commonwealth,"[231] to conclude that "the King of England ought to be brought into one class with the parson: both were to be artificial persons and both were to be corporations sole."[232] The king, he punned, became "parsonified."[233] The "foolish parson," Maitland sadly remarked, had thereby led English law astray.[234] As a result, "we have been, more or less explicitly, trying to persuade ourselves that our law does not recognize the personality or corporate character of the State or Nation or Commonwealth, and has no need to do anything of the sort if only it will admit that the King, or, yet worse, the Crown, is not unlike a parson."[235] This

---

[225] Frederic Maitland, The Crown as Corporation, in State Trust, and Corporation, supra note 219, p. 32.

[226] Frederic Maitland, The Corporation Sole, in State, Trust, and Corporation, supra note 219, pp. 9, 26–7; Runciman and Ryan, supra note 219, at xiv–xv.

[227] Maitland, supra note 225, at 36.

[228] Frederic Maitland, Trust and Corporation, in State, Trust, and Corporation, supra note 219, pp. 75, 98; Maitland, supra note 226, at 30; Runciman and Ryan, supra note 219, at xv.

[229] Runciman, supra note 221, at 98.

[230] Maitland, supra note 225, at 36.

[231] Maitland, supra note 226, at 30.

[232] Maitland, supra note 225, at 32.

[233] Id. at 33.

[234] Id. at 46.

[235] Id. at 33.

view, Maitland emphasized, had disastrous consequences. "We cannot get on without the State, or the Nation, or the Commonwealth, or the Public, or some similar entity, and yet that is what we are professing to do."[236]

In contrast to the corporation sole, a "mere ghost of a fiction," Maitland identified a "true corporation, a corporation aggregate," which is composed of many members.[237] Instead of viewing the king as a corporation sole, Maitland declared, he should be viewed as "the head of a complex and highly organized 'corporation aggregate of many' – of very many." Maitland saw "no great harm in calling this corporation a Crown," but he preferred the word "Commonwealth."[238] The fate of all corporations sole, Maitland believed, was to become corporations aggregate.[239]

Though Maitland preferred the "corporation aggregate" to the "corporation sole," he had reservations about the corporation itself as a legal concept. The main problem was the lingering vitality of the concession theory of the corporation, which subjected corporations to state control. Sometimes referring directly to "the concession theory from which we suffered,"[240] Maitland pointed out that this theory, derived from Roman law, made the personality of a corporation a legal fiction that was "the gift of the prince."[241] He elaborated by quoting a source from Gierke, "Only the prince may create by fiction what does not exist in reality."[242] This position, moreover, implies the illicitness of any group the prince has not authorized.[243]

Maitland pointed out that the "Roman doctrine of corporations was an apt lever for those forces which were transforming the medieval nation into the modern State." It undermined the system of federated groups that formed the structure of medieval society. "All that stands between the State and the individual," according to the concession theory of the corporation, "has but a derivative and precarious existence." Maitland provided historical illustrations. Charles II condemned all citizens of London for "presuming to act as a corporation." The best example, the history of France, revealed "the pulverizing, macadamizing tendency in all its glory, working from century to century, reducing to impotence, and then to nullity, all that intervenes between Man and State." In 1792, the revolutionary assembly declared: "A State that is truly free ought not to suffer within its bosom any corporation, not even such as, being dedicated to public instruction, have merited well of the country." Maitland understood this declaration "as one of the mottoes of modern absolutism: the absolute State faced the absolute individual."[244] He believed that the

[236] Id. at 38.
[237] Maitland, supra note 226, at 28.
[238] Maitland, supra note 225, at 41.
[239] Id. at 48.
[240] Maitland, supra note 228, at 123.
[241] Maitland, supra note 224, at 65.
[242] Id. at 65–6.
[243] Id. at 66.
[244] Id.

concession theory of the corporation, by treating the group as an artificial and fictitious creation of the state without any real personality of its own, provided an important intellectual justification for this modern absolutism.

The development of the trust, Maitland stressed, saved England from the evils of the concession theory of the corporation.[245] He called the trust "the greatest and most distinctive achievement performed by Englishmen in the field of jurisprudence."[246] It supplemented the "meagre law of corporations" by providing "a liberal substitute for a law about personified institutions."[247] The trust established unincorporated bodies "without troubling the State to concede or deny the mysterious boon of personality,"[248] freeing them to act without asking the state for permission.[249] It built "a wall of trustees,"[250] a "hard, exterior shell,"[251] that enabled the English "to construct bodies which were not technically corporations and which yet would be sufficiently protected from the assaults of individualistic theory,"[252] the view that the state is largely composed of individual units.[253]

Tracing the origins of the trust, Maitland pointed out that it arose as a way for the feudal landowner to avoid the restrictions the law of primogeniture placed on the inheritance of land. Primogeniture prevented the landowner from leaving his land by will, but he wanted to provide for all of his children, not just his oldest son. As a response to this predicament, the landowner conveyed land to some friends, who held it in trust for later use by his children. The emerging Court of Chancery approved this arrangement.[254] From these origins, Maitland stressed, the trust became "a most powerful instrument of social experimentation."[255] It allowed married women to own property,[256] enabled the formation of joint-stock companies with limited liability,[257] and was used by "barely tolerated sects" to shelter the preaching of their doctrines from charges of illegality. "All that we English people mean by 'religious liberty,'" Maitland observed, "has been intimately connected with the making of trusts."[258] Over the years, the trust protected groups as varied as the Inns of Court, the London

---

[245] Fisher, supra note 5, at 156.
[246] Frederic Maitland, The Unincorporate Body, in State, Trust, and Corporation, supra note 219, p. 52.
[247] Id. at 57.
[248] Id. at 59.
[249] Maitland, supra note 228, at 116. Maitland cited the Jockey Club as an example, id., observing that "in the eyes of a large number of my fellow-countrymen the most important and august tribunal in England is not the House of Lords but the Jockey Club." Id. at 110.
[250] Maitland, supra note 224, at 70.
[251] Maitland, supra note 228, at 105.
[252] Maitland, supra note 224, at 70.
[253] Barker, supra note 220, at 157–8; Burrow, Whigs and Liberals, supra note 218, at 143–4.
[254] Maitland, supra note 228, at 84–5; Barker, supra note 218, at 131.
[255] Maitland, supra note 246, at 56. See also id. at 59; Maitland, supra note 228, at 97.
[256] Maitland, supra note 246, at 56.
[257] Id.
[258] Maitland, supra note 228, at 102.

Stock Exchange, the London Library, the Jockey Club, and trade unions.[259] The elastic concept of the trust extended to government powers themselves, which came to be conceived as being held in trust. Ultimately, "the Trust presses forward until it is imposing itself upon all wielders of political power, upon all the organs of the body politic."[260]

Maitland acknowledged that English law did not have an adequate theory of the trust[261] and, more generally, that the English had not even attempted to answer many of the theoretical questions about the group that Gierke had posed and addressed. Yet in typically English fashion, he seemed to take pride in this lack of theory. Whereas in Germany "almost every conceivable question has been forestalled by scientific and controversial discussion,"[262] England muddled along with its "disorderly" jurisprudence. This very disorder, Maitland believed, gave English jurisprudence "something of the character of an experimental science," which he hoped "it will never lose."[263] The trust allowed "social experimentation"[264] that protected both groups and the individuals who formed them. This protection promoted the distinctive pluralism that made England great.

Maitland's Legacy

Unlike Maine, whose enormous influence was tempered from the beginning by serious reservations about his methods and conclusions, Maitland has been continuously recognized as a great scholar from his own lifetime to the present. As early as 1888, in a letter to Pollock a month after Maine's death, Holmes followed his guarded evaluation of Maine with high praise for Maitland. In contrast to his reservations about Maine, the brilliant popularizer who had been "impatient of investigation" and unlikely to "leave much mark on the actual structure of jurisprudence," Holmes described Maitland's work on legal history as "truly scientific," consisting of "accurate investigation of details in the interest of questions of philosophical importance," and, most rarely for Holmes, even conceded that Maitland had made a valid criticism of Holmes's own work.[265] When Maitland died, Vinogradoff called him "the greatest historian of the law of England, one who not only surpassed all predecessors in this domain but is not likely to be surpassed soon in the course of succeeding generations." Maitland, Vinogradoff declared, "has practically remodeled our knowledge of English law at the most important period of its existence."[266]

---

[259] Id. at 125.
[260] Id. at 126–7.
[261] Id. at 111.
[262] Id. at 112.
[263] Id. at 110.
[264] Id. at 97.
[265] Letter from Oliver Wendell Holmes, Jr. to Frederick Pollock (March 4, 1888), in Holmes Pollock Letters (Cambridge, Mass.: Harvard University Press, 1941) (Mark DeWolfe Howe, ed.), vol. 1, pp. 30, 31.
[266] Vinogradoff, supra note 25, at 263.

Subsequent eminent historians who did not specialize in legal history, including J. H. Hexter, R. G. Collingwood, and Marc Bloch, commented on Maitland's preeminence.[267] Even Maitland's major late twentieth-century critic, S. F. C. Milsom, echoed Vinogradoff in calling Maitland's work "still the last word on the history of English law in its most crucial period,"[268] "largely untouched, untouchable."[269] It has been regarded "almost as revelation" and "Maitland himself has been, and still is, not just revered but loved."[270] In his introduction to a reprinted edition of *The History of English Law*, Milsom described it "not as a dead masterpiece but as a still living authority," which remained the "starting-point" for current scholars.[271] Patrick Wormald, who recently wrote a major study of early English law,[272] called Maitland the "first and greatest of professional medievalists"[273] and marveled that "he was so seldom wrong."[274] According to G. R. Elton, Maitland set the standards for later historians in all fields.[275]

The uniform praise of Maitland, however, has not precluded challenges to aspects of his work. In ironic contrast to his general reputation as the first legal historian who extended his interests beyond the internal analysis of legal doctrine, many of these challenges attack his insufficient use of broader historical sources. Milsom, the major challenger, has asserted that Maitland incorrectly projected modern assumptions and legal concepts, such as ownership and possession, onto early medieval law and society;[276] focused too much on the king's courts at the expense of local jurisdictions, thereby distorting his understandings of medieval law;[277] relied too uncritically on Bracton, who was not representative of his own time;[278] and succumbed too easily to "the routine deception of legal records, of law itself,"[279] which, especially in the Middle Ages, "tell the investigator nearly everything except what he wants to know,"[280]

---

[267] Alan Macfarlane, The Making of the Modern World: Visions from the West and East (New York: Palgrave, 2002), p. 123.

[268] Milsom, supra note 1, at 259.

[269] Id. at 267.

[270] Id. at 266.

[271] S. F. C. Milsom, Introduction, Frederick Pollock and Frederic Maitland, The History of English Law before the Time of Edward I (Cambridge University Press, 1968) (2d edition, reissued), p. xxiii.

[272] Patrick Wormald, The Making of English Law: King Alfred to the Twelfth Century (Oxford: Blackwell Publishers Ltd., 1999).

[273] Patrick Wormald, Maitland and Anglo-Saxon Law: Beyond Domesday Book, in The History of English Law: Centenary Essays on "Pollock and Maitland" (Oxford University Press, 1996) (John Hudson, ed.), p. 1.

[274] Id. at 6.

[275] G. R. Elton, F. W. Maitland (Yale University Press, 1985), p. 102.

[276] Milsom, supra note 1, at 275; S. F. C. Milsom, 'Pollock and Maitland': A Lawyer's Retrospect, in Hudson, supra note 273, pp. 243, 257.

[277] Milsom, supra note 271, at xxvii–xxviii.

[278] Id. at lxxii–lxxiii.

[279] Milsom, supra note 1, at 279.

[280] Milsom, supra note 271, at xxv.

the external world of facts and ideas outside the law.[281] Other recent scholars have expressed similar criticisms, especially regarding Maitland's focus on the king's courts[282] and on legal records in general.[283] In analyzing the legal history of the family, for example, Maitland did not examine, as later scholars did, the influence of views about kinship by people other than judges.[284] By concentrating on the decisions of courts rather than on changes in the organization of the family, Maitland too easily attributed these changes to the influence of judges.[285] Subsequent historians, moreover, have examined disputes in a broader context, such as by recognizing their resolution by marriage alliances as well as by judicial decisions, by using vernacular as well as legal literature as sources, and by directing more attention to interpersonal relationships of power and honor than to legal rules enforced by courts.[286] Based on his expertise in the Anglo-Saxon period, Patrick Wormald claimed that Maitland "underrated the part played by the earliest Kings of England in shaping a distinctive English legal tradition."[287] And while subscribing to the general view that Maitland, in contrast to his contemporaries, examined the past in its own context, G. R. Elton observed that on occasion, particularly in his conviction that the medieval period laid the foundation for modern English law, Maitland fell into "the teleological error" of "the predominant climate surrounding him."[288]

Yet criticisms and corrections of Maitland are almost always tempered by reverent praise. According to Milsom, his most severe critic, "the very splendour of his achievement may have beguiled us into a too easy dependence." Milsom took care to describe his own revisionism as an essay in "pious heresy."[289] Milsom made clear, moreover, that many of Maitland's errors, particularly his occasional identification of "highly abstract notions of property too early," referred only to the beginning of the period discussed in *The History of English Law*. By the end of this period, what Maitland mistakenly wrote about the earlier period became true, prompting Milsom to acknowledge that "here the heretic is most disturbed by his own heresy." More generally, Milsom concluded that his revisions, however significant, "are not important when compared with the original picture" provided by Maitland himself, whose work had not been superseded.[290] Similarly, Richard Helmholz, after maintaining

---

[281] Id. at xxvii.

[282] John Hudson, Maitland and Anglo-Norman Law, in Hudson, supra note 273, pp. 21, 39–40; Henry Summerson, Maitland and the Criminal Law in the Age of *Bracton*, in Hudson, supra note 273, pp. 115, 143.

[283] Hudson, supra note 282, at 35–6; Wormald, supra note 273, at 18–19; Stephen D. White, Maitland on Family and Kinship, in Hudson, supra note 273, pp. 91, 109–10.

[284] White, supra note 283, at 94–5.

[285] Id. at 109–10.

[286] Hudson, supra note 273, at 35–6.

[287] Patrick Wormald, Frederick William Maitland and the Earliest English Law, 16 Law and History Review 1, 3 (1997).

[288] Elton, supra note 275, at 51.

[289] Milsom, supra note 271, at xxv.

[290] Id. at lxxiii.

that Roman and canon law had much less influence in medieval England than indicated by *The History of English Law*, requiring "considerable modification" of its conclusions,[291] emphasized that it "remains the best overall treatment" of these subjects.[292] Wormald believed that Maitland's flaws "were in fact effects of his virtues: lack of insularity, scorn for unfounded tradition, love of raw evidence."[293] Almost immediately after identifying Maitland's "teleological error," Elton added that he avoided it more than modern historians.[294]

Though highly respected, and even revered, Maitland, like Maine, did not leave a legacy of scholars who carried on his work in legal history. His one close collaborator, Mary Bateson, died only a few weeks before Maitland himself.[295] Maitland lectured to law students, who rarely were interested in scholarly careers, and professional historians rarely became interested in law.[296] In 1901, Maitland advocated changes within English universities that might stimulate more research in legal history. No doubt recalling Sidgwick's generosity in helping him begin his own academic career, he urged the establishment of fellowships and endowed professorships to enable lawyers to have a career "a little outside the beaten path that leads to briefs and fees." He lamented the examination system that kept the teaching of English law at "a pretty low level." Echoing the recommendations of the Select Committee in 1846, he advocated a division of responsibility in which the universities would teach legal theory and the Inns of Court would teach practical skills.[297] But Maitland's account at the beginning of his career of "why the history of law is not written" remained accurate after his death. Just as Maine's *Ancient Law* disappeared from the curriculum, English students in recent generations did not encounter Maitland.[298] Maitland's greatest work, *The History of English Law*, is currently out of print.

Like Maine, Maitland influenced scholars in other fields. His late work on the corporation and the trust inspired some English political thinkers who became known as pluralists to praise the independent group as needed protection against the increasingly powerful state. Though the biographical sketch of Maitland written by his brother-in-law, H. A. L. Fisher, described him as a "dissenter from all the Churches" who "rarely spoke of politics,"[299] both "socialist pluralists," such as Harold Laski and G. D. H. Cole, and advocates of clerical independence, such as John Figgis, relied on his work. While Maitland

---

[291] R. H. Helmholz, The Learned Laws in 'Pollock and Maitland,' in Hudson, supra note 273, pp. 145, 153.

[292] Id. at 168.

[293] Wormald, supra note 287, at 24.

[294] Elton, supra note 275, at 52.

[295] Fisher, supra note 5, at 171–2.

[296] Milsom, supra note 1, at 277.

[297] Frederic Maitland, Law at the Universities, in Collected Papers, supra note 30, vol. 3, pp. 419, 426–31.

[298] Macfarlane, supra note 267, at 7.

[299] Fisher, supra note 5, at 100, 175.

stayed close to the historical record and wrote in a scholarly voice, these scholars drew more speculative and overtly political conclusions from his discussion of groups.[300] Yet after World War I, political pluralism of all varieties lost influence and was even abandoned by former adherents.[301]

Very recently, however, scholars have directed renewed attention to Maitland. In 1996, on the centenary of the publication of *The History of English Law*, the British Academy published a group of essays assessing it. In 2003, Cambridge University Press published some of Maitland's important late essays as part of its series of texts in the history of political thought. Claiming that these essays are classics of political theory as well as of history, the frontispiece describes them as "a series of profound insights into the way the character of the state has been shaped by the non-political associations that exist alongside it."[302] Perhaps most impressively, in 2002 Alan Macfarlane, the eminent anthropologist, devoted half a book, ambitiously entitled *The Making of the Modern World*, to Maitland. Macfarlane reports that his own thirty-year study of the history of an English parish from 1350 to 1850 reinforced Maitland's earlier conclusions. "Maitland's vision," he writes, "fits the English case beautifully. I did not undertake the village study to test Maitland, but after the event, when we compare his hypothetical model against the superb documentation for one English parish for 500 years, it is impossible to find anything that he seems seriously to have misjudged."[303] Macfarlane describes Maitland as "the leading figure in the first archival revolution, when the central records became usable and used for the first time," and describes himself as the beneficiary of a second archival revolution after 1950, when much additional archival material became available. The new material demonstrated "how far Maitland's still somewhat intuitive conclusions were substantiated by microscopic work on how the system he postulated actually worked at the local level."[304] Macfarlane views Maitland not only as a great historian, but also, much more broadly, as a great political philosopher. Complaining that Maitland's work "has tended to be set within too small a frame,"[305] he compares Maitland to Montesquieu, Adam Smith, and Tocqueville as deep thinkers about "how to combine liberty, equality and fraternity." Better than any of the others, Macfarlane maintains, Maitland reconciled the tensions between groups and individuals, "using the history of English law as a way of trying to solve the problems of the origin and nature of the modern world."[306] Maitland recognized that the "essence

---

[300] Runciman, supra note 221, at 123; Stefan Collini, Public Moralists: Political Thought and Intellectual Life in Britain, 1850–1930 (Oxford University Press, 1991), pp. 303–4; Burrow, Village Community, supra note 218, at 276; Runciman and Ryan, supra note 219, at xxvi.

[301] Runciman and Ryan, supra note 219, at xxvi.

[302] State, Trust, and Corporation, supra note 219 (frontispiece).

[303] Macfarlane, supra note 267, at 129.

[304] Id. at 126.

[305] Id. at 133.

[306] Id. at 4.

of modernity lay in the separation of spheres, the tensions between religion, politics, kinship, and society."[307]

Maitland and his American colleagues hoped that their original research in English legal history would stimulate additional scholarship in their field. Just as Bigelow was optimistic that Maitland's work would prompt American law schools to establish chairs in legal history, Maitland hoped that the curriculum at Cambridge would include more courses on the history of English law. The recent emergence of American law schools as research institutions staffed by full-time scholars, Thayer believed, would enable the two generations of additional historical research needed as preliminary work to the effective restatement of current law. Thayer praised the "brave beginning already made"[308] in this historical work, but he made these comments toward the end, not the beginning, of a period of major scholarship on the history of English law. The substantial original work in English in this field, which began with Adams and his students, culminated in Maitland's scholarship. Contrary to the hopes of these American and English scholars, institutional and financial support for legal history did not materialize in either country. More significantly, the historical study of law, particularly the search for the evolution of legal doctrine that dominated the research of scholars from Maine through Maitland, lost its intellectual appeal in both countries. In law, as in many other fields, interest in social science, tied to social reconstruction, superseded historical analysis. This transformation is best revealed through the enormously important but insufficiently studied early scholarship of Roscoe Pound in the United States during the decade before World War I.

---

[307] Id. at 134–5.
[308] James Bradley Thayer, The Teaching of English Law at Universities, 9 Harv. L. Rev. 169, 183 (1895).

XIII

Pound

From Historical to Sociological Jurisprudence

Roscoe Pound was the key figure both in ending the dominance of historical explanation in American legal scholarship and in creating the influential, though often inaccurate, interpretation of late nineteenth-century legal thought that persisted throughout the twentieth century. Pound's crucial role in these major intellectual developments during the decade before World War I has been obscured by subsequent scholars, who have mostly focused on his nasty debate with Karl Llewellyn about legal realism in the 1930s. That debate, whose intellectual significance did not approach its emotional venom, occurred during the long twilight of Pound's career.[1]

After a short biographical section and an overview of his central goals, this chapter assesses Pound's critique of his American predecessors. It then explores Pound's underlying concern about the dangerous gap between the extreme individualism of the American legal system and the collectivism that the American people both needed and wanted in the early twentieth century. This gap provides the context for understanding Pound's criticism of historical jurisprudence, which he associated with individualism and deductive formalism, and his promotion of sociological jurisprudence, which he associated with collectivism, pragmatism, and social science. Sociological jurisprudence, Pound believed, would enable "legal justice" to provide "social justice."

---

[1] For discussions of the Pound-Llewellyn debate, see Morton J. Horwitz, The Transformation of American Law 1870–1960 (New York: Oxford University Press, 1992), pp. 172–80; N. E. H. Hull, Roscoe Pound and Karl Llewellyn: Searching for an American Jurisprudence (University of Chicago Press, 1997). For discussions of Pound's prewar scholarship, see Hull, at 36–75 (chapter on Pound's discovery of sociology); Michael Willrich, City of Courts: Socializing Justice in Progressive Era Chicago (Cambridge University Press, 2003), pp. 104–15 (relationship between Pound's conception of legal socialization and his concerns about urban judicial administration); Thomas A. Green, Freedom and Responsibility in the Age of Pound: An Essay on Criminal Justice, 93 Mich. L. Rev. 1915, 1949–2001 (1995) (evolution of Pound's criminal justice jurisprudence from 1905 to 1923).

Biographical Background

Pound's parents moved from upstate New York to Lincoln, Nebraska, where Pound was born in 1870. His father, a lawyer, was elected as a Republican to the state district court. While a judge, he served as a delegate to the Nebraska constitutional convention in 1875. Pound's mother taught briefly in an elementary school before deciding to instruct her children at home. She began teaching Pound German when he was six. Thanks also to a German maid employed by his parents and to his attendance at a Methodist Sunday school in a German community in Lincoln, Pound grew increasingly proficient throughout his childhood in the language that became crucial to his future scholarship.[2] After years of home schooling, Pound attended public school and then enrolled at the University of Nebraska when he was only fourteen. Starting in the university's demanding classical course of study, he switched to natural sciences as a junior. He worked closely with Charles E. Bessey, a nationally eminent botanist, an association that subsequently prompted some critics of his elaborate classifications of legal thought to attribute them to his early training as a botanist.[3]

The summer after his graduation from college in 1888, Pound read law with his father, who had recently resumed legal practice after his judicial career, and attended law classes given two evenings a week by a local lawyer. While continuing to work in his father's law office, Pound enrolled in graduate school in botany in the fall, becoming Bessey's research assistant.[4] At his father's urging, Pound spent a year as a student at Harvard Law School in 1889–90, returning to Lincoln the next summer, where he rejoined his father. After passing the Nebraska bar exam, he worked for a prominent local attorney, became a sole practitioner in 1895, and, by 1900, had established a partnership with two other lawyers in Lincoln that became a leading corporate firm in Nebraska.[5]

During his years in private practice, Pound was active in politics, the state bar, legal education, and, most remarkably, botanical research. As a publicist and speaker, he supported the 1896 presidential campaign of William McKinley. He strenuously opposed William Jennings Bryan and the Populists, objecting particularly to their class-based politics and attacks on the fairness of the judicial system. Pound remained active in local Republican politics after McKinley's election, serving two terms as chair of the Republican central committee in Lincoln. Through his work in the Nebraska State Bar Association, which soon took more of his time than Republican politics, he tried to raise the professional standards of the bar, especially through improved legal education.[6]

Beginning in 1895, Pound taught Roman law at the University of Nebraska. He received an appointment as an assistant professor in 1899. In 1900, Pound

---

[2] David Wigdor, *Roscoe Pound: Philosopher of Law* (Westport, Conn.: Greenwood Press, 1974), pp. 6–13.

[3] Id. at 17–19, 22, 24.

[4] Id. at 27–9.

[5] Id. at 27, 29, 31, 46, 70.

[6] Id. at 73–7.

FIGURE 13.1. *Roscoe Pound.* Courtesy of Historical & Special Collections, Harvard Law School Library.

became the youngest of nine commissioners appointed to the Nebraska Supreme Court Commission, a temporary body established by the legislature to help the three judges on the Nebraska Supreme Court clear its rapidly growing docket. The commissioners worked essentially as temporary judges. For the three years he served until the commission expired, Pound decided a wide range of cases. Consistent with the positions he subsequently took as a scholar, Pound exhibited flexibility in the application of legal rules and sensitivity to the social context of litigation.[7]

Throughout the 1890s, Pound remained active as a botanist. Inspired by a German scientist whose book he reviewed for the *American Naturalist*, Pound and a friend, working at night in the university herbarium, wrote a comprehensive volume, *The Phytogeography of Nebraska*. This book became a classic of American botany and helped create the field of ecology. It also served as the dissertation for his Ph.D., which he received in 1897.[8] Like Holmes, Pound was

[7] Id. at 77–83.
[8] Id. at 55, 66.

pushed into law by his father and as a young lawyer was attracted to another field while expressing reservations about the law. In 1895, Pound wrote to a close friend that he was a lawyer only "because my father wished it."[9]

Yet Pound, also like Holmes, became reconciled to his legal career and soon devoted much of his enormous ability and ambition to legal scholarship. Pound was appointed dean of the Nebraska College of Law in 1903. Like Bigelow at Boston University in the early 1870s, he worked hard as an administrator to improve the school's quality, raising admissions standards, extending the course of study from two to three years, and insisting on replacing the part-time faculty of practitioners with full-time scholars.[10] While serving as dean, Pound began producing the articles that made his scholarly reputation. Lured to Northwestern Law School by Wigmore in 1907, Pound moved to the University of Chicago in 1909 and to Harvard in 1910.[11] Ironically, in 1913 he was named Carter Professor of General Jurisprudence at Harvard,[12] the chair endowed by the man whose version of historical jurisprudence he had vigorously criticized in much of his previous work. Pound was appointed dean of the Harvard Law School in 1916, a position he held until his retirement in 1936.[13] Although Pound remained at Harvard until his death in 1964 and published continuously throughout his long life, he wrote his most important scholarship in the slightly more than ten years before becoming dean. Unlike Holmes's scholarship, which many readers understandably find extremely difficult to follow, Pound's work, though often repetitious, is relatively clear and accessible.

Pound's Project

Like Melville Bigelow's contemporaneous writings, Pound's legal analysis derived largely from his strong personal belief that the traditional individualism of American society had become dysfunctional. In articles that made him a leading American legal scholar, Pound maintained that the social problems of twentieth-century industrial society could only be solved by recognizing collective interests. He stressed that prior jurisprudential schools, including the school of historical jurisprudence that had prevailed in the United States since roughly 1870, both reflected and provided legal support for the excessive individualism that stood in the way of needed social reform. His articles frequently promoted what he called "sociological jurisprudence" as an emerging jurisprudential school. By focusing on collective interests, Pound believed, sociological jurisprudence offered the possibility that law could serve rather than hinder the public good in an increasingly interdependent society.

[9] Id. at 71.
[10] Id. at 103, 106, 108.
[11] Id. at 129–30, 146, 186.
[12] Id. at 207.
[13] Id. at 204, 254.

Throughout his critique of the "mechanical jurisprudence" he disparagingly attributed to prior jurisprudential schools, Pound linked individualism with deductive formalism. Mechanical jurisprudence, he claimed, artificially derived legal rules from fixed and unexamined conceptions by a process of logical deduction entirely divorced from reality. He identified the primacy of individual freedom as a major conception in the system of deductive formalism. Particularly discouraging for Pound, he concluded that in the United States the conception of individual freedom had migrated from the common law to constitutional law. The individualistic conception of "liberty of contract" became the foundation for the laissez-faire constitutionalism through which the courts invalidated progressive social legislation enacted in the collective public interest. Yet unlike many progressives who shared his dismay at these decisions, Pound did not attribute them to a self-interested alliance of conservative judges and entrepreneurs. He stressed that the intellectual pervasiveness of individualistic conceptions of law, rather than economic and political interests, best accounted for laissez-faire constitutionalism.

As Pound himself emphasized, his call for a collectively oriented and pragmatic sociological jurisprudence to supersede the individualism and deductive formalism of historical jurisprudence was part of a transatlantic intellectual trend. Both in Europe and in the United States, many maintained that collectivism should replace the individualism of the past in order to achieve necessary social and economic changes. Just as the general turn to history in many Western countries and scholarly disciplines affected American legal thought during the late nineteenth century, the movement from individualistic to collective perspectives across countries and disciplines affected it in the early twentieth century, especially through Pound's influential work. Pound generously made clear that his views about sociological jurisprudence derived substantially from three recent intellectual sources: anti-formalist German legal thought that challenged historical jurisprudence, particularly as formulated by Rudolph von Jhering; American pragmatism, especially the work of William James; and the new social sciences in the United States, most importantly the "social control" school of sociology led by E. A. Ross, who was a colleague at the University of Nebraska at the beginning of Pound's legal career.

Pound's opposition to historical jurisprudence as the dominant legal support of individualism prompted him to characterize it in some detail. His account of historical jurisprudence remains the fullest and most sophisticated analysis of the role of history in late nineteenth-century legal thought, although in many respects it is exaggerated, unfair, confusing, or simply incorrect. Subsequent American legal scholars have largely followed Pound's criticisms of his nineteenth-century predecessors while losing sight of his emphasis on the centrality of history in their thought.

In founding historical jurisprudence, Pound claimed, Savigny was as individualistic and as committed to formal deduction as the previous school of philosophical jurisprudence. Savigny simply substituted historical research for philosophical analysis as the method for identifying the legal principles from which to deduce a timeless legal structure. Just as philosophical jurisprudence derived individualistic legal principles from theories of natural rights, historical jurisprudence derived them from historical sources. It portrayed legal history as an unconscious and inevitable process that revealed the gradual unfolding of the idea of individual freedom. The historical search for fundamental legal principles, Pound emphasized, entailed an internal approach to legal history, focusing on the history of legal thought while ignoring the connections between law and society. This internal approach assumed that legal change is caused exclusively by legal phenomena and that current legal issues can be decided by logical deductions from past law.

These characteristics of historical jurisprudence, Pound maintained, impeded legal reform that could promote the collectivism America so desperately needed. Beyond reinforcing through historical analysis the preexisting individualism of the legal system, the focus on the internal development of law diverted attention from how law might benefit society. Treating history as an unconscious and inevitable process, moreover, left no room for human will. It produced a "juristic pessimism" incompatible with reform and oblivious to justice, thereby allowing the perpetuation of laws that did not serve current needs. The widespread hostility of historical jurisprudence to codification as a legislative infringement on personal liberty, Pound declared, exemplified both its individualism and its "juristic pessimism." Throughout his work, Pound made clear that he borrowed substantially from Jhering's earlier critique of historical jurisprudence in Germany in analyzing what he treated as an inferior, derivative version in the United States.

Despite his many criticisms of historical jurisprudence, Pound stressed that he valued the appropriate use of history in legal analysis. He warned that abandoning the historical method entirely would be even worse than the misuse of history by historical jurisprudence. In his own work, he wrote extensively about the history of legal thought. Occasionally, he even praised historical jurisprudence itself, particularly its emphasis on the use of primary sources as the basis for the comparative study of the origins and development of legal doctrines and institutions. More typically, he differentiated "legal history" as a general field from "historical jurisprudence" as a distinctive jurisprudential school. "Legal history," he wrote, while defining it as "the discovery and exposition of the actual course of development of a particular legal system or of a particular doctrine in a particular system, is not historical jurisprudence."[14] In a lengthy and generally laudatory review of Paul Vinogradoff's *Outlines of Historical Jurisprudence*, published in 1920, Pound emphasized the "real break" between Maine's historical jurisprudence and Vinogradoff's treatment of legal history, calling it "no less than the break which divides twentieth-century from nineteenth-century jurisprudence."[15] In dramatic contrast to Maine,

---

[14] Roscoe Pound, The Scope and Purpose of Sociological Jurisprudence, I, 24 Harv. L. Rev. 591, 616 (1911).

[15] Roscoe Pound, Book Review, 35 Harv. L. Rev. 774, 775 (1922).

Vinogradoff espoused a theory of history that was relativist, recognizing ideas as valid for a particular society rather than as universal. Unlike Maine, Vinogradoff did not attempt to uncover a single normal and continuous evolutionary process beginning with a universal primitive idea but instead appreciated the complexity of primitive cultures. Further differentiating himself from historical jurisprudence, Vinogradoff accepted the possibility of "creative juristic activity" and recognized collision of interests within society beyond mere conflicts of individual wills.[16]

Perhaps most significantly, Pound saw a crucial role for legal history in the new sociological jurisprudence that he hoped would supersede historical jurisprudence. By illustrating the impact of legal rules and principles in addressing concrete situations in the past, "sociological legal history"[17] could serve as a "functional critique"[18] that would assist both legislators and judges in evaluating how law could best meet present conditions. Correctly used, the historical method is the best way to determine which laws work in practice and which should be abandoned as dysfunctional survivals. Pound defended the incorporation of the social sciences within sociological jurisprudence by pointing out historical precedents for importing the insights of other disciplines into legal analysis. He asserted that the emphasis on "relation" in feudal and Germanic law proved that the English legal tradition was more collectivist than individualistic. He also provided historical examples of successful efforts to transform the law as models for sociological jurisprudence.

Unfortunately, Pound was not always consistent in his discussion of legal history. Using various terminology to convey the range of methodological approaches to the field, Pound typically equated "historical jurisprudence" with "the historical school"[19] while contrasting both with "legal history"[20] and "sociological legal history."[21] Yet at times he confusingly referred to "sociological legal history" as a branch of historical jurisprudence[22] or legal history.[23] Compounding this confusion, he occasionally praised scholars he identified with the historical school he otherwise disparaged. While placing Holmes, Bigelow, Thayer, Ames, and Maitland within the historical school, he maintained that they "have made us wiser with respect to law and history."[24] In a passage criticizing the historical school for its individualism and deductivism,

---

[16] Id. at 776.

[17] Roscoe Pound, The Scope and Purpose of Sociological Jurisprudence, III, 25 Harv. L. Rev. 489, 514 (1912).

[18] Pound, supra note 15, at 780.

[19] Pound, supra note 14, at 599–601; Roscoe Pound, The Scope and Purpose of Sociological Jurisprudence, II, 25 Harv. L. Rev. 140, 148 n. 31 (1912).

[20] Pound, supra note 14, at 616–17.

[21] Pound, supra note 19, at 154; Pound, supra note 17, at 514–15.

[22] Pound, supra note 14, at 618; Roscoe Pound, Theories of Law, 22 Yale L.J. 114, 137 n. 84 (1912) [hereinafter Pound-Theories]; Roscoe Pound, Legislation as a Social Function, 18 Am. J. Soc. 755, 764–5 (1913) [hereinafter Pound-Legislation]; Pound, supra note 15, at 777.

[23] Pound, supra note 19, at 147; Pound-Legislation, supra note 22, at 764–5.

[24] Pound, supra note 17, at 510–12.

Pound emphasized its association with Harvard Law School, where Thayer and Ames taught.[25] Yet Pound was consistent in his attack on Carter. He identified Carter as the most significant and representative figure in the American historical school, accusing him of a priori deductivism from historical sources, individualism, and hostility to legislative innovation.[26]

Assessing Pound's Critique of His American Predecessors

Previous chapters of this book demonstrate that Pound's account of historical jurisprudence, while accurate in part, presented a misleading picture of late nineteenth-century American legal scholars. As Pound maintained, historical interpretations of law did dominate American legal scholarship in the decades after 1870. American legal scholars did focus on the origin and development of legal doctrines and institutions, and they did try to organize and systematize legal materials based on their historical analysis. They did largely limit their investigations to the nature and content of law as revealed by doctrinal writings and legal decisions. Many of them did identify individual freedom, particularly the political freedom necessary to democratic government, as a central component of their own legal tradition. They did often oppose legislation in general and codification in particular.

Yet in many significant respects, Pound was misleading or inaccurate in characterizing his predecessors. Although he occasionally recognized in passing that some American scholars had done significant work in legal history, his generally brief and dismissive treatment of them as derivative inferiors to German scholars obscured their internationally admired original contributions to the history of English law. Contrary to Pound's major accusation that they used history to perpetuate the individualism and deductive formalism of traditional legal thought, they opposed deductive formalism while emphasizing their commitment to history as an inductive science and recognized that contemporary social conditions required limits on individualism. Pound erred in applying Jhering's critique of historical jurisprudence in Germany to the Americans. Though they were interested in classifying current law into a coherent structure, they believed that law would continue to evolve, preventing any legal structure from becoming timeless. Like Pound and Jhering, they criticized Savigny and other Europeans for using history to justify existing law and for treating law as an inevitable unconscious process beyond the power of human intervention to reform.

Though the late nineteenth-century American legal scholars often found traditions of political liberty at the core of Anglo-American legal history, they were not nearly as committed to individualism as Pound maintained. Many disagreed with Maine's assertion of a universal evolutionary progress from

[25] Roscoe Pound, Law in Books and Law in Action, 44 Am. L. Rev. 12, 27–8 (1910).
[26] Id. at 28–30.

collectivism to individualism and recognized important variations among different national traditions. Many accepted, and sometimes promoted, restrictions on individual rights, particularly when dramatic social and economic changes had produced gross inequalities. Recognizing collisions of interests in their own country between employers and employees and between landlords and tenants, many urged legal reforms designed to improve the condition of employees and tenants. Even Carter, consistently portrayed by Pound as the leading representative of the evils of historical jurisprudence, defended the income tax as a socially desirable measure to reduce economic inequality. Despite Pound's claim that their hostility to legislation reflected concern about reforms that would undermine individualism, they generally preferred adjudication to legislation because they believed that judges were better able than legislators to conform law to evolving custom. They also recognized exceptions, including during periods of rapid social change, when legislation could be more effective in responding to evolving custom than judicial decisions. As Carter's support for the income tax vividly demonstrated, they were even open to "class legislation," among other conscious and creative efforts to reform the law.

The work of these late nineteenth-century legal scholars, moreover, does not support Pound's influential claim that they denied external influences on law. From the Norman Conquest of England through the American Revolution and the industrialization of their own time, they highlighted the great extent to which law responded to external events. They stressed that American conditions had produced distinctive innovations in both private and constitutional law. They often focused on the internal study of legal doctrine not because they were oblivious to the relationship between law and society, as Pound maintained, but because they viewed their historical investigations as a necessary preliminary to legal reform in the public interest. By uncovering and then eliminating dysfunctional doctrinal survivals from the past, they believed they could restate law in ways that would enable it to function more effectively in the present.

Ironically, just as Pound described Savigny as retaining significant features of philosophical jurisprudence while developing historical jurisprudence in opposition to it, Pound himself displayed throughout his own work many of the evolutionary assumptions about legal history that characterized the late nineteenth-century American scholars he associated disparagingly with historical jurisprudence. Like them, he was interested in tracing the evolution of current law from past law. Like them, he frequently emphasized evolving customs as the source of law and believed that law must conform to the prevailing customs of a community. Like them, he asserted that in dynamic societies existing law, derived from previous social conditions, lags behind changing customs, often producing social friction. And like them, he maintained that law will inevitably respond by conforming to evolved community standards, either slowly, by unconscious judicial action, or more rapidly, by the conscious efforts of judges and, often most effectively, by legislators. Indeed, after reading one of Pound's articles in 1913, Charles Bessey, the Nebraska professor of botany with whom Pound had studied and collaborated, concluded that "in the matter of law, evolution is as great a factor as it is in Biology."[27] Pound himself, however, did not acknowledge or perhaps even recognize these affinities with his predecessors.

Despite the many similarities between Pound and his late nineteenth-century predecessors, he differed from them in several significant respects. Though the late nineteenth-century scholars recognized the interactions between law and society and often viewed their historical investigations as the foundation for contemporary law reform, their primary focus, as Pound accurately charged, was on the historical evolution of legal doctrine. Only by understanding this historical evolution, they believed, could scholars be in a position to identify the current law that needed reform. They often maintained that substantially more historical investigation, perhaps taking generations, was required before scholars could know enough to make responsible suggestions about legal reform in the social interest. While many of them were politically active, particularly in supporting the moderate reforms associated with the Mugwump movement, their concerns about municipal corruption and the growing materialism of American life did not directly inform their scholarship.

Pound, by contrast, considered early twentieth-century American society in a state of crisis and saw law as a pragmatic means to address contemporary social problems that required immediate attention. While legal history, particularly the legal history of the relationship between law and society, could contribute to this pragmatic use of law, he did not think that it was the only, or even the major, way to make law pragmatic. Pound was optimistic that the emerging social sciences could be used to identify social problems and solutions, which new laws could then help implement. The late nineteenth-century scholars were not nearly as committed to individualism or as opposed to collectivism as Pound indicated when he referred to them as the American school of historical jurisprudence. They did not, however, share his central concern about the evils of individualism and the benefits of collectivism.

The Gap between Legal Individualism and Popular Collectivism

Throughout his pathbreaking articles between 1904 and 1914, Pound emphasized the dangerous gap between the outmoded individualism of legal thought and the socially responsive collectivism of popular thought. In a 1906 address to the American Bar Association analyzing "The Causes of Popular Dissatisfaction with the Administration of Justice" in the United States, Pound highlighted "the individualistic spirit of our common law, which agrees ill with a collectivist age."[28] "No amount of admiration for our traditional system," he

---

[27] Letter from Charles E. Bessey to Roscoe Pound (January 13, 1913) (Roscoe Pound Papers, Box 217, Folder 5, Harvard Law School Library) [hereinafter Pound Papers].

[28] Roscoe Pound, The Causes of Popular Dissatisfaction with the Administration of Justice, 40 Am. L. Rev. 729, 736 (1906).

maintained in another early article, "should blind us to the obvious fact that it exhibits too great a respect for the individual, and for the entrenched position in which our legal and political history has put him, and too little respect for the needs of society, when they come in conflict with the individual, to be in touch with the present age."[29] He asserted elsewhere that the individualism of American law "exaggerates private right at the expense of public right"[30] and "is against the genius of the time and the interest of the modern industrial community."[31]

As a result of this discrepancy between the individualism of law and the collectivism of the people, Pound tried to convince his readers, "a struggle is in progress between society and the common law."[32] He famously contrasted the divergence between "the law in action," reflecting "popular thought and feeling," and "the law in the books" made by judges.[33] Criticizing American law schools for perpetuating "the sturdy resistance of common-law individualism to the collectivist tendencies of modern thought," he warned about "creating a permanent gulf between legal thought and popular thought."[34] Pound similarly contrasted the individualism of "legal justice" with the collectivism of "social justice."[35] While the exaggerated individualism of American law, which Pound frequently called "ultra-individualism"[36] or sometimes "over-individualism,"[37] derived from the protection of individual rights through the common law, he observed that it had also spread to American constitutional law.[38] Quoting Jane Addams on the "growing distrust of the integrity of the courts" among working people, Pound asserted that judicial decisions invoking liberty of contract to declare social legislation unconstitutional are "so out of the range of ordinary understanding" and "so academic and so artificial in their reasoning, that they cannot fail to engender such feelings."[39]

While identifying and bemoaning the gap between legal and popular thought, Pound, like the late nineteenth-century scholars who viewed evolving custom as the source of law, emphasized that law must ultimately conform "to the moral sense of the community." He acknowledged that in the past the individualism of the law matched the community's moral sense, which viewed justice "as the liberty of each limited only by the like liberties of all."[40] To illustrate the legal formulation of this moral sense of individualism, Pound repeatedly

[29] Do We Need a Philosophy of Law? 5 Colum. L. Rev. 339, 344 (1905).
[30] Roscoe Pound, Liberty of Contract, 18 Yale L.J. 454, 457 (1909).
[31] Roscoe Pound, Puritanism and the Common Law, 45 Am. L. Rev. 811, 829 (1910).
[32] Pound, supra note 29, at 345.
[33] Pound, supra note 25, at 21, 24.
[34] Roscoe Pound, The Need of a Sociological Jurisprudence, 19 Green Bag 607, 611 (1907).
[35] Pound, supra note 25, at 30–1; Roscoe Pound, supra note 31, at 828.
[36] Pound, supra note 31, at 815; Roscoe Pound, Justice According to Law, III, 14 Colum. L. Rev. 103, 111–19 (1914); Pound, supra note 34, at 613; Pound, supra note 25, at 21.
[37] Pound, supra note 25, at 21.
[38] Pound, supra note 29, at 345.
[39] Pound, supra note 30, at 487.
[40] Pound, supra note 34, at 612.

quoted Blackstone's statement that "the public good is in nothing more essentially interested, than in the protection of every individual's private rights."[41] The legal individualism of the common law, Pound added, served society well in the sixteenth and seventeenth centuries, when judicial recognition of individual rights protected the English people in their struggle against royal power.[42]

As Pound frequently stressed, however, "times have changed." Individuals, who in England once needed protection from their kings, had become secure in America against the state. Alluding to the judicial ascription of individual identity to corporations as well as to their owners, Pound complained that the individualism of the common law had evolved to protect "individuals, natural or artificial, that need no defense but sally from beneath its aegis to injure society."[43] When the judiciary in the United States "assumes to stand between the legislature and the public and thus again to protect the individual from the state," he asserted, "it really stands between the public and what the public needs and desires, and protects individuals who need no protection against society which does need it."[44] Under these changed circumstances, the people no longer support individualism. Instead, they "look to society for protection against individuals" and "resent doctrines that protect these individuals against society for fear society will oppress us." The continuing individualism of the law had become a barrier between "the people, or large classes of the people, and legislation they desire" to control the excesses of the individualism that now harmed rather than helped them. By enforcing legal individualism contrary to the new moral sense of the community, "the courts have been put in a false position of doing nothing and obstructing everything, which it is impossible for the layman to interpret aright."[45]

Unfortunately, the individualism of "legal theory and doctrine reached a degree of fixity before the conditions with which law must deal to-day had come into existence."[46] The "individualistic conception of justice," moreover, "reached its complete logical development after the doctrine itself had lost its vitality."[47] Pound found it "remarkable" that the common law, which historically had exhibited enormous "tenacity and vitality," had remained so "intensely individualist in an age that looks more and more to social control for the solution of its problems and is succeeding in the socialization of pretty much everything except the law."[48] Despite the recent inflexibility of the common law, Pound insisted that law is too closely related to everyday life to be treated as a "sacred tradition" immune from change.[49] Like many nineteenth-century legal

[41] Pound, supra note 29, at 347; Pound, supra note 30, at 461.
[42] Pound, supra note 29, at 349; Roscoe Pound, Common Law and Legislation, 21 Harv. L. Rev. 383, 403 (1908).
[43] Pound, supra note 29, at 349–50.
[44] Pound, supra note 42, at 403.
[45] Pound, supra note 28, at 738.
[46] Pound, supra note 34, at 608.
[47] Pound, supra note 30, at 460.
[48] Pound, supra note 31, at 811.
[49] Roscoe Pound, Mechanical Jurisprudence, 8 Colum. L. Rev. 605, 606 (1908).

scholars attracted to evolutionary thought, Pound conceded that in any rapidly changing society the law never fully reflects the moral sense of a community. In explaining "the inevitable difference in rate of progress between law and public opinion,"[50] he observed that law "does not respond quickly to new conditions. It does not change until ill effects are felt; often not until they are felt acutely. The moral or intellectual or economic change must come first." To the extent that existing law has not responded to the ill effects of such change, friction between popular and legal thought necessarily arises. The greater the change without a legal response, he added, the greater the probability of friction. In a period of rapid change, "this friction can not fail to be in excess."[51] And the United States during the late nineteenth century, the period just before Pound began his legal career, had experienced extraordinarily rapid change while the law remained individualistic.

Over history, Pound observed, law tended more than other areas of intellectual life to remain out of touch with general changes in thought. In the classical period, law was the last field in which Greek learning influenced Rome. In early modern Europe, philosophy freed itself from Aristotle and theology escaped the church fathers more than a century before law achieved independence from the Roman law of Justinian. And in Pound's own day, when virtually every field, led by the natural sciences, had "abandoned deduction from predetermined conceptions," jurisprudence retained this traditional methodology.[52]

Despite the traditional lag in legal thought, Pound was convinced that legal change would be produced by the excessive friction between the individualistic legal system and popular support for a collectivist response to the needs of a dramatically transformed American society. Sooner or later, Pound asserted, the collectivist ideology of the public will prevail over legal individualism and will be enforced by the courts. Lawyers trained in and committed to legal individualism "may retard but cannot prevent progress" toward collectivism. Pound urged lawyers to do more than cease their obstruction of this inevitable progress. Rather than simply let law unconsciously follow popular thought, lawyers should consciously try to assist the transformation to collectivism, even if that meant challenging the individualism of most of their colleagues. They should help "insure that the common law remain, what its exponents have always insisted it is – the custom of the people," which had changed from individualism to collectivism under the pressure of new conditions.[53]

Particularly annoying to Pound was the persistence in legal thinking "of nineteenth-century ideas of the futility of effort at a time when the efficacy of effort had become part of the sociological and political creed." Such fatalistic thinking, he believed, significantly impeded the prospect of law reform and was the source of much of the popular hostility to law.[54] Lawyers, he maintained,

---

[50] Pound, supra note 28, at 733; Pound, supra note 25, at 26; see also Roscoe Pound, Justice According to Law, 13 Colum. L. Rev. 696, 713 (1913).

[51] Pound, supra note 28, at 734.

[52] Pound, supra note 25, at 25.

[53] Pound, supra note 34, at 615.

[54] Pound, supra note 17, at 507.

should not become "legal monks" who sanctify legal texts until they become irrelevant. Rather, they should try to close the gap between law in action and law in the books "by making the law in the books such that the law in action can conform to it."[55] They should develop new law by studying the relationship between law and society.[56] To do so, Pound believed, they had to become educated in contemporary social sciences.[57]

Examples of Individualism in American Law
Pound provided many illustrations to support his general critique of the excessive individualism of American law. Perhaps his most famous example was the judicial development of liberty of contract as an individual constitutional right that invalidated progressive social legislation, especially labor legislation. In 1909 Pound devoted an entire article to this subject, which he opened by quoting from Justice Harlan's 1908 opinion for the Supreme Court in *Adair v. United States*. This opinion, Pound observed, culminated a generation of Supreme Court decisions on liberty of contract by holding unconstitutional a federal law that prohibited carriers in interstate commerce from discharging an employee because of his membership in a labor union. According to Harlan, "the right of an employee to quit the service of the employer, for whatever reason, is the same as the right of the employer, for whatever reason, to dispense with the services of such employee." Any legislation that "disturbs" this "equality of right," Harlan maintained, "is an arbitrary interference with the liberty of contract, which no government can legally justify in a free land."[58]

To anyone who knew anything about industrial conditions in the United States, Pound maintained, Harlan's language about the equal rights of employers and employees would ring hollow and false. "Why," Pound asked, "is the legal conception of the relation of employer and employee so at variance with the common knowledge of mankind?" How could learned Supreme Court justices be so clueless as to treat the employment relationship "as if the parties were individuals – as if they were farmers haggling over the sale of a horse?"[59] Pound rejected the frequent explanation that judges were simply projecting their own social and economic views into the law, the explanation used by many of the populists he opposed while supporting McKinley for president in 1896. Observing the widespread use of liberty of contract by judges throughout the United States, Pound claimed that it must have deeper roots,[60] "the currency in juristic thought of an individualist conception of justice."[61] In

---

[55] Pound, supra note 25, at 35.
[56] Pound, supra note 34, at 611.
[57] Pound, supra note 29, at 352–3.
[58] Pound, supra note 30, at 454.
[59] Id.
[60] Id. at 454–5.
[61] Id. at 457; see also Pound, supra note 25, at 33; Pound, supra note 31, at 823.

England, Pound observed, modern legislation had mitigated the excessive individualism of the common law. In the United States, by contrast, the individual rights guaranteed by common law had become established in state and federal constitutions, making constitutional law a barrier to the kind of modern legislation passed in England.[62]

Pound also detected pervasive individualism in criminal law and tort law. He emphasized that criminal law focuses on the criminal as an individual rather than on the impact of crime on society. The retributive theory of justice at the core of American criminal law, he maintained, seeks to punish the evil will of the individual criminal as a form of revenge. It views the criminal as a free moral agent who voluntarily chose wrong instead of right. This individualistic approach, Pound protested, neglects the social context of crime and "hampers the efficiency of penal legislation intended to protect society." Rather than worrying about the moral blameworthiness of an individual, criminal law should try to prevent actions that harm society.[63] Similarly in tort law, the doctrines of assumption of risk and contributory negligence focus on the choices of an individual free agent, not on relevant social statistics, such as the fact that most industrial accidents occur during the last hour of work, "when the mind is numbed and the operative has ceased to be the free agent which our law contemplates."[64] Though Pound, like Holmes, opposed moral theories of law rooted in individualism, Pound, who often cited Holmes as a precursor of his own views, did not himself observe this parallel.

More generally, Pound attributed broad characteristics of the American legal system to its pervasive and destructive individualism. The antipathy of the common law to legislation, he maintained, reflects the view that less law is better because law restricts individual freedom.[65] To illustrate this attitude, Pound quoted Carter, who wrote that it is important "to leave each man to work out in freedom his own happiness or misery, to stand or fall by the consequences of his own conduct."[66] According to Pound, Carter "died in the harness writing an elaborate argument against legislation, and made generous provision in his will for a professor in a leading American law school to teach – I had almost said to preach – the doctrine of no legislation."[67] Only three years after publishing this article, Pound himself became the beneficiary of the provision in Carter's will when he was named Carter Professor of General Jurisprudence at Harvard Law School, an appointment that did not change his views about Carter.[68] In the same article, Pound asserted that individualism also accounted for the hostility to equity in the American legal system. Equity, he pointed out, coerces the free will of individuals by acting preventively, instead of allowing

---

[62] Pound, supra note 28, at 738.
[63] Pound, supra note 31, at 823–4; Pound, supra note 25, at 33.
[64] Pound, supra note 31, at 822–3.
[65] Pound, supra note 30, at 457, 462; Pound, supra note 31, at 821.
[66] Pound, supra note 31, at 822.
[67] Id. at 821.
[68] Wigdor, supra note 2, at 207.

individual action and imposing a legal penalty afterward. Equity also gives judges enormous discretion, thus increasing their power over individuals.[69]

Historical Sources of Legal Individualism

Displaying his interest in the history of legal thought, Pound identified what he considered to be the more general sources of legal individualism. They included the Teutonic character, Puritan theology, Coke's emphasis on the individual rights of Englishmen during the struggle against the Crown in the late sixteenth and early seventeenth centuries, eighteenth-century jurisprudence, the reaction against eighteenth-century absolutism and the French Revolution, laissez-faire economics, and Maine's work in legal history during the nineteenth century. In addition, Pound cited distinctively American sources of legal individualism, such as the framing of American constitutions at the height of the influence of natural law and the growth of American law when individualism predominated in ethics and economics. Pound only listed or barely described some of these sources, but he treated others at greater length, especially Puritanism, to which he devoted an entire article and which he frequently mentioned throughout his work.

Pound praised Coke as "the great light of our legal system,"[70] whose "indefatigable zeal and uncompromising dogmatism" protected the individual rights of Englishmen "from subversion by royal authority."[71] Writing in the late sixteenth and early seventeenth centuries, Coke led the transformation of the feudal duties of lords to their tenants into the legal duties of kings to their subjects and helped establish the supremacy of law.[72] Grotius and his followers in the seventeenth century, Pound added, reinforced Coke's individualism. Basing their theory in reason rather than the authority of tradition, they emphasized that individuals have natural rights independent of the state, which the state should secure by law but may not abridge.[73] The victory of the judiciary against the Crown in England during the seventeenth century "seemed to establish that the law was something that stood between the individual and organized society and secured his natural rights."[74] Despite his admiration of Coke, Pound maintained that by reading all of English legal history in the context of the struggle against the Crown in his own era, Coke misread earlier cases and exaggerated the individualism of the English legal tradition. Coke's influence on eighteenth-century commentators and nineteenth-century judges, moreover, extended the exaggerated individualism he incorrectly ascribed to the entire history of the English common law.[75]

---

[69] Pound, supra note 31, at 825.

[70] Pound, supra note 30, at 459.

[71] Pound, supra note 29, at 350.

[72] Roscoe Pound, The End of Law as Developed in Juristic Thought, 27 Harv. L. Rev. 605, 617 (1914).

[73] Id. at 617–19.

[74] Id. at 622.

[75] Pound, supra note 30, at 459–60 and 459 n. 34.

Developing the emphasis by Grotius and his followers on natural rights accessible to reason, eighteenth-century jurisprudence became "ultra-individualist."[76] It asserted the existence of universal natural rights valid for all peoples at all times and places, and it regarded natural law as the rules that guarantee these rights through the state.[77] Under the influence of this approach, many in England began to identify rights at common law with natural rights. Eventually, "the common-law limitations upon royal authority became natural limitations upon all authority and the common-law rights of Englishmen became the natural rights of man."[78] Perceiving the common law as the system for protecting individual natural rights, people identified the threats to those rights as arising not just from other individuals, but, even more dangerously, from the larger society and the state.[79]

In the late eighteenth and early nineteenth centuries, Pound believed, economic and political theories reinforced the legal individualism that had been developing for more than two hundred years. The laissez-faire views of Adam Smith and other major economists promoted individualism in the economic sphere. The widespread reaction against absolute governments, particularly against the excesses of the French Revolution, similarly made political individualism popular.[80] Later in the nineteenth century, the legal histories written by Henry Maine, whose themes derived from Savigny's individualistic interpretation of Roman law,[81] more directly supported legal individualism by depicting the history of law as the progressive development of individual liberty.[82] "In the nineteenth century," Pound concluded, "the idea of justice as the maximum of individual self-assertion, which begins to appear at the end of the sixteenth century, reached its highest development."[83]

While acknowledging that individualism has been a feature of many legal systems, Pound highlighted Puritanism, a religion practiced only in England and America, as the most important source of the distinctive "ultra-individualism" of Anglo-American law. Puritanism is as important in understanding Anglo-American legal thought, Pound declared, as Stoicism is in understanding Roman law.[84] He contested theories that the emancipation of the middle class or Protestantism generally accounted for legal individualism. Cultures with a strong middle class, he observed, had not uniformly developed individualistic legal systems. Puritanism, he claimed, "has given a peculiar character to the middle class of England and America." Nor could Protestantism more generally

---

[76] Pound, supra note 36, at 119.

[77] Pound, supra note 72, at 623.

[78] Id. at 618.

[79] Id. at 625.

[80] Roscoe Pound, The End of Law as Developed in Juristic Thought, II, 30 Harv. L. Rev. 201, 206 (1917).

[81] Id. at 221.

[82] Id. at 210.

[83] Id. at 225.

[84] Pound, supra note 31, at 815; see also Pound, supra note 30, at 459.

account for legal individualism. Most strikingly, Luther himself, the original Protestant, believed that personal freedom could best be achieved through a strong state and society rather than through individual legal rights against the state. Only the combination of "a peculiar phase of the emancipation of the middle class and a peculiar phase of Protestantism" known as Puritanism can account for the individualistic "spirit of our common law."[85]

In two of his major early articles, Pound used identical language to describe Puritan individualism.

The fundamental proposition from which the Puritan proceeded was the doctrine that man was a free moral agent, with power to choose what he would do and a responsibility coincident with that power. He put individual conscience and individual judgment in the first place. No authority could coerce them; but every one must assume and abide the consequences of the choice he was free to make.[86]

In terms of religious organization, this view led to "consociation" rather than subordination. As a Puritan leader wrote, "We are not over one another, but with one another."[87] Pound observed that consociation in religious life was itself a very legalistic concept, a type of contractual agreement, and that the Puritans extended this contractual theory to the political relationship between individuals and the state. "If men were to be free to act according to their consciences and to contract with others for consociation in congregations, it was a necessary consequence that the State – as a political congregation – was a matter of contract also; and liberty of contract was a further necessary deduction." The Puritans who settled New England, Pound stressed, put theory into practice by establishing their political and their religious communities as covenants or compacts whose continuation as well as formation depended on the consent of each individual.[88] For the Puritan, "law was a device to secure liberty, its only justification was that it preserved individual liberty, and its sole basis was the free agreement of the individual to be bound by it."[89] The theory of consociation, moreover, "demanded that a fixed, absolute, universal rule, which the individual had contracted to abide, be resorted to; and thus the moral and the legal principle were to be applied in the same way, and that the legal way."[90]

Pound maintained that there have been only "two great growing periods of our common law system," the era of Coke in England and the period in the United States that ended with the Civil War. The first period consisted of developing a system of law out of prior legislation and judicial decisions. The second period required determining which aspects of English law applied to conditions in America. In both periods, Pound stressed, Puritan religious influence

---

[85] Pound, supra note 31, at 816.
[86] Id. at 819; Pound, supra note 25, at 32–3.
[87] Pound, supra note 31, at 819; Pound, supra note 25, at 33.
[88] Pound, supra note 31, at 819.
[89] Pound, supra note 25, at 33.
[90] Pound, supra note 31, at 820.

was strong. The "age of Coke was the age of the Puritans in England and the period that ends with our Civil War was the age of the Puritans in America." According to Pound, "it is not an accident that the great periods of common law history, the periods of growth, the periods when doctrines were worked out and took shape, were periods in which religious thought was a prime form of mental activity and were periods in which the Puritan was a potent force in religious thought." In America, Pound emphasized, Puritans were substantially more powerful than in England because they did not have to contend with a powerful establishment and could create their own institutions without interference. It is thus again "not an accident that common-law principles have attained their highest and most complete logical development in America, and that we are and long have been more thoroughly a common-law country than England herself."[91]

In addition to the special strength of Puritanism, Pound cited other conditions in the United States that made American law particularly individualistic. He stressed that the United States achieved independence when theories of natural law were at their zenith. Underlining the extent to which the common law had become identified with natural rights in the United States, Pound pointed out that in 1774 the Continental Congress asserted the legal rights of Englishmen, whereas just two years later the Declaration of Independence relied on the natural rights of man. Pound maintained that "each claimed the same things," using interchangeably the legal rights of Englishmen and the natural rights of man.[92] Even more significantly, he emphasized, the Constitution of the United States and the first state constitutions date from this period dominated by natural law.[93] Thus natural law not only became identified with the common law as part of an assumed universal legal order, as in England; natural law in America also became incorporated into federal and state constitutions, especially their bills of rights.[94] American courts struck down a wide variety of useful and popular laws by treating constitutional references to liberty, most prominently in the Fourteenth Amendment, as "declaring a natural liberty which was also a common-law liberty."[95]

After the American Revolution and the Constitution, Pound maintained, economic thought reinforced the individualism of American law. Just as natural law had its greatest influence during the formative period of American law, individualism in economics prevailed during its subsequent period of growth during the nineteenth century. Economists confirmed for lawyers the individualism that pervaded the classics of the common law. In the education of a nineteenth-century American judge, Pound observed, his course in political

[91] Id. at 817–19; Pound, supra note 25, at 31–2.
[92] Pound, supra note 72, at 625.
[93] Pound, supra note 30, at 460.
[94] Id. at 466–7.
[95] Pound, supra note 72, at 626.

economy reinforced the individualism he learned from reading Blackstone in a law office.[96] Pound concluded that this combination of legal and economic individualism promoted a purely negative conception of the function of law, which emphasized preventing or eliminating barriers to individual self-assertion instead of the positive goal of using law to encourage social progress.[97] Law exalted individual freedom over both the state and society.[98]

Historical Jurisprudence: Individualistic and Deductive

In much of his early scholarship, Pound combined his desire to reform the "ultra-individualism" of American law with his interest in the historical evolution of legal thought. He viewed previous stages of legal thought as supporting individualism, but also as laying the groundwork for the new, more collectivist school of "sociological jurisprudence" in which Pound placed his hopes for the future. Pound developed numerous classifications of legal thought, which were not entirely consistent with each other[99] and which have frustrated subsequent scholars, who occasionally claim that Pound's training as a botanist both reflected and reinforced his obsession with classification.[100] Though not accounting for the full variety of his classifications, Pound himself maintained that distinctions among methods and schools of jurisprudence depend to some extent on the purpose for making them.[101] Yet Pound's early scholarship does reveal a basic classification that followed many of his American predecessors in identifying three successive, though overlapping, schools: philosophical jurisprudence, analytical jurisprudence, and historical jurisprudence. Finding pervasive individualism and deductive formalism in all three, he devoted most of his attention to historical jurisprudence, the most recent and the one that continued to dominate jurisprudential thought in the early twentieth century, particularly in the United States.

Reflecting his historical orientation, Pound prefaced his analysis of historical jurisprudence with discussions of the earlier schools. The theories of natural rights that dominated philosophical jurisprudence in the eighteenth century, he maintained, were "thoroughly individualist," viewing the protection of individual interests as the end of the law.[102] Although Kant influentially shifted the focus of philosophical jurisprudence from natural rights, he extended its individualism by detecting an "ultimate metaphysical principle" in "freedom of will." For Kant, the end of law meant "the securing of freedom of will to

---

[96] Pound, supra note 30, at 460; Pound, supra note 36, at 120.

[97] Pound, supra note 80, at 203.

[98] Pound, supra note 31, at 816.

[99] See, e.g., Pound, supra note 34, at 608–9; Pound, supra note 14, at 591–2; Pound, supra note 80, at 203.

[100] Wigdor, supra note 2, at 24; Alan Hunt, The Sociological Movement in Law (Philadelphia: Temple University Press, 1978), p. 12 and 154 n. 10.

[101] Pound, supra note 15, at 780–1.

[102] Pound, supra note 72, at 624–5.

everyone so far as consistent with the freedom of all other wills," and justice consisted of "the securing of a maximum of individual self-assertion."[103] Kant believed that "we realize individual freedom through rules of law."[104]

The analytical jurisprudence developed by English utilitarians in the nineteenth century, Pound added, reinforced individualism even as it challenged philosophical jurisprudence. Pound observed that the principle of utility did not entail individualism. Indeed, it easily could have been interpreted to promote a "social utilitarianism" measuring each person's conduct by its contribution to the happiness of the majority. Yet when Bentham and other English utilitarians were writing, Pound sadly observed, "individualist ideas were too firmly fixed in men's minds to be questioned." Bentham himself assumed that the greater the individual self-assertion, the greater the general happiness. Like metaphysical jurists such as Kant, he advocated "the maximum of free individual action consistent with general free action."[105]

Just as analytical jurisprudence reinforced the individualism of the philosophical jurisprudence it otherwise challenged, Pound asserted that historical jurisprudence exacerbated the individualism of these prior schools despite its many criticisms of both. He claimed that Savigny, the founder of historical jurisprudence in Germany in the early nineteenth century, found historical sources for the individualism that philosophical jurisprudence had associated with natural rights. Maine, Pound believed, later adapted Savigny's historical justification for individualism to the English context. Treating Savigny and Maine in much more detail than any American, Pound left the impression that historical jurisprudence in the United States was inferior to as well as derivative of the work of these two leading European scholars. While recognizing that previous scholars had written about legal history, he indicated that only with the development of historical jurisprudence did historical analysis become the prevailing mode of legal thought. Nineteenth-century historical jurisprudence, moreover, was "radically different" from earlier approaches to legal history, such as the reconstruction of classical antiquity by Renaissance humanists, the attempt by English writers to demonstrate the immemorial antiquity of the common law in order to establish its continuing authority,[106] and the "pseudo-history" of eighteenth-century universal legal history based on rational conjecture.[107]

Pound described historical jurisprudence as the comparative study of the origin and development of legal doctrines and institutions.[108] Without providing details, he praised it for laying "the foundations of a sound comparative legal history" and for providing "a sounder and more critical" history of Roman, German, and English law by conducting research "with a high feeling for the

---

[103] Id. at 628.
[104] Pound, supra note 80, at 204.
[105] Id. at 206–7.
[106] Pound, supra note 15, at 774.
[107] Roscoe Pound, Interpretations of Legal History (Cambridge University Press, 1923), p. 68.
[108] Pound, supra note 14, at 599.

intrinsic value of the original sources."[109] All jurisprudential schools in the nineteenth century sought to organize and systematize the law; historical jurisprudence did so "by principles derived historically from the legal materials by study of their development" rather than "analytically from the legal materials themselves, or by principles derived metaphysically."[110] Unfortunately, Pound believed, the legal materials of interest to historical jurisprudence consisted of doctrinal writings and legal decisions, presumed to express the gradual development of the life of a people.[111] Keeping "religiously within the limits of the legal materials,"[112] this internal focus proceeded "as if the causes of change in the law were always to be found in the legal phenomena of the past." It assumed that "systematic deduction" from past law would provide complete answers to current legal issues, as if law "were a system without hiatus and without antinomies."[113] Historical jurisprudence, moreover, was more interested in the nature and content of law than in the ends law should serve.[114]

While agreeing with historical jurists that law frequently reflects principles derived from the historical experience of a people, Pound also stressed that law is equally likely to be a contingent product of whatever analogy happened to be available during the formative stages of a particular institution or doctrine. Once the analogy is accepted, subsequent legal thought often adheres to it with striking and even irrational persistence, though it may become ineffective in practice and inconsistent with the developing experience of the community.[115] "Indeed," Pound concluded, "it has been recognized repeatedly that law represents commonly not customary models of popular action, but customary modes of judicial decision or juristic thinking, rooted in either case in a purely juristic tradition."[116] Rather than building on their historical research to advocate that modern law rid itself of historical accidents divorced from the developing life of a community, historical jurists too often provided justifications for their continuance.[117]

Illustrating these points, Pound observed that the modern law of partnership derives from Roman law, whose theory of partnership originated in the closest analogy then available, the *consortium* of a family, which retained an undivided inheritance after the death of the paterfamilias. Although the better analogy of the juristic person subsequently developed, and although recent commercial codes treated mercantile partnerships as entities, modern partnership law preserved the original Roman analogy to the consortium. Rather than reflecting the actual experience and practice of merchants,

---

[109] Pound, supra note 107, at 780.
[110] Pound, supra note 15, at 775.
[111] Pound, supra note 14, at 599.
[112] Pound, supra note 15, at 780.
[113] Pound, supra note 17, at 515.
[114] Pound, supra note 80, at 209.
[115] Pound, supra note 14, at 603.
[116] Id. at 604.
[117] Id. at 608.

modern partnership law thus remained trapped in an ancient but outmoded tradition dating from republican Rome.[118] As an example of elevating "juristic tradition" over efficient custom, Pound cited Savigny's discussion of the provisions on stolen property in the French Civil Code. Savigny criticized these provisions for misunderstanding and misstating Roman law, even though they accurately reflected the customary law of France and more effectively met the needs of modern France than Roman law, which was based on the very different conditions in ancient Rome. This example, Pound sadly observed, typified the dismissive attitude of historical jurisprudence toward the practical problems law should address.[119]

Throughout his analysis of historical jurisprudence, Pound emphasized that it was an idealistic interpretation of history, akin to earlier theories of natural law. As their shared emphasis on individual liberty revealed, whereas philosophical jurists had deduced universal principles from their interpretation of natural law, historical jurists deduced them from their study of history.[120] Like the school of natural law, the historical jurists "worked *a priori* and gave us theories fully as absolute." Both "deduced from and tested existing doctrines by a fixed, arbitrary, unchangeable standard."[121] While tracing the gradual development of ideas over time, Pound added, historical jurisprudence treated history as an unconscious process that cannot be altered through conscious human intervention. It assumed that law is found, not made.[122] He quoted the observation of the French scholar Saleilles that historical jurisprudence "had clipped its wings and as it were disarmed itself in declaring that scientifically it could exert no effect upon the phenomenological development of law; it had only to await, to register, to verify."[123] This "juristic pessimism,"[124] Pound declared, accounted for a key feature of historical jurisprudence he repeatedly highlighted and criticized, its hostility to law reform, especially through legislation, aimed at transforming existing law.[125] Pound viewed historical jurisprudence as a lethal combination of individualism, formal deduction, and resistance to conscious change at a time when society needed and the public wanted pragmatic law reform based on collective values.

Savigny and Maine: Founders of Historical Jurisprudence
Pound identified Savigny's work in the early nineteenth century as the real beginning of historical jurisprudence, though he mentioned Cujos, a scholar in

---

[118] Id. at 603–4.
[119] Pound, supra note 15, at 770; Pound, supra note 107, at 15.
[120] Pound, supra note 14, at 600–1; Pound, supra note 22, at 133–4; Pound, supra note 79, at 209–10; Pound, supra note 15, at 774–5.
[121] Roscoe Pound, The Spirit of the Common Law (New Brunswick, N.J.: Transaction Books, 1999) (original ed. 1921), pp. 155–6.
[122] Pound, supra note 14, at 599.
[123] Pound, supra note 80, at 222 n. 65.
[124] Id. at 221.
[125] Pound, supra note 14, at 599–601.

Bourges at the beginning of the sixteenth century, as the pioneer of the field.[126] The development of historical jurisprudence by Savigny, Pound emphasized, must be understood in the more general context of the French Revolution and its aftermath. Savigny reacted against the extraordinary confidence in the power of reason during the period of the French Revolution, whose legal manifestations included theories of natural law and efforts to write logically perfect constitutions and codes. Just as Edmund Burke protested the French elevation of abstract reason over historical tradition in his *Reflections on the Revolution in France*, Savigny criticized the similar displacement of history by reason in French law.[127] Rather than deriving formulaic legal principles from the abstractions of natural law, as in the French Declaration of the Rights of Man, Burke and Savigny maintained that the law should emerge from the historical experience of a nation. And laws that emerged from the historical experience of France, they agreed, could not be effectively exported to other countries with different historical experiences, such as, of course, England and Germany.[128] Savigny particularly opposed codification, whose supposed logic he undermined by revealing how many codes were based on misunderstandings of earlier laws from different historical periods and thus could not be effective at a later time in another place.[129]

Yet Savigny, Pound also maintained, unconsciously remained under the influence of the theories of natural law that he had learned as a student but had expressly rejected while developing historical jurisprudence. Savigny simply substituted historical for philosophical foundations of law and assumed the gradual realization of legal ideas over time. He believed that historical research would discover these ideas, whose implications could then be pursued through logic.[130] Echoing Holmes, Pound maintained that the most fundamental idea Savigny discovered through historical research was the progressive realization of Kant's philosophical view of individual freedom as right. Just as Roman jurists gave legal content to Greek philosophy, Pound concluded, "Savigny put Kant's definition of right in terms of ordering the activities of free beings, co-existing in a condition of free contact with each other, by means of rules determining the boundaries within which each might securely exercise his freedom, and gave us a theory of law."[131] As a Romanist, Savigny discovered these legal implications of Kantian philosophy in the historical study of Roman law, whose principles he interpreted as universally as any scholar of natural law interpreted principles deduced from reason.[132] Without providing illustrations, Pound asserted that Savigny and his followers in Germany accepted "a metaphysical method of deducing a whole system

---

[126] Pound, supra note 14, at 598–9.
[127] Pound, supra note 107, at 13–14; Pound, supra note 15, at 780.
[128] Pound, supra note 107, at 19; Pound, supra note 15, at 780.
[129] Pound, supra note 107, at 14–16.
[130] Id. at 17–18.
[131] Id. at 28; see Pound, supra note 15, at 775.
[132] Pound, supra note 107, at 19; Pound, supra note 19, at 148.

from an assumed fundamental idea, which, when applied in jurisprudence, led to a method of rigorous deduction from principles discovered through historical investigation."[133]

Pound complimented Savigny's historical jurisprudence for demonstrating how much current law consisted of survivals from the past that no longer served any useful function and often undermined the goals of justice. Savigny's historical research usefully exposed as specious the reasons invented by philosophical jurists of the eighteenth century to justify these survivals. But by developing an idealistic interpretation of legal history focused on the realization of ideas over time, Savigny assumed an inevitable process that thwarted the critical promise of his own use of history against philosophical jurisprudence.[134] For him, it made no sense to try to change and improve the law because law, like language, is the product of unconscious evolution rather than human will.[135] Like the philosophical jurists who preceded him, Savigny ultimately justified current law at the expense of seeking justice.[136] And as a historian, he viewed the legal past through the distorting lens of ideas he assumed were being realized in the present.[137] The attempt by Savigny and his successors to "Romanize" law, Pound protested, misrepresented both the original Roman law and the history of modern law. By treating Kantian interpretations of law as originating in ancient Rome, they projected their own nineteenth-century views backward. The actual Roman law of the first and second centuries, Pound insisted, bore little resemblance to the idealistic nineteenth-century version of it. Roman law proceeded from the Stoic conception of duty, not from individual freedom and will.[138]

After identifying Savigny's work in the early nineteenth century as the real beginning of historical jurisprudence, Pound treated Henry Maine as the key figure in the next generation.[139] Just as Savigny employed historical jurisprudence against the dominant school of natural law in Germany, Maine employed it against the dominant analytical school in England.[140] In many respects, Pound observed, Maine's historical jurisprudence "was essentially the same" as Savigny's, particularly in viewing law as the realization of Kant's individualistic theory of right. Yet Savigny focused on "the ethical idea of human freedom as right,"[141] whereas Maine developed a more political interpretation, expressed most concretely in his famous general principle that law in progressive societies has "been a movement from status to contract."[142] According to Pound,

---

[133] Pound, supra note 19, at 148.
[134] Pound, supra note 107, at 42.
[135] Pound, supra note 19, at 156.
[136] Pound, supra note 107, at 42.
[137] Id. at 19–20.
[138] Id. at 27, 55–6.
[139] Id. at 55.
[140] Id. at 142, 145; Pound, supra note 14, at 592–3.
[141] Pound, supa note 15, at 775.
[142] Pound, supra note 80, at 209–10 and n. 31.

Maine understood the movement from status to contract "as a progress from limitations of freedom or liabilities existing or imposed independently of will toward a complete freedom of contract and liability only to willed undertakings or culpable conduct."[143] The constraints of status and social institutions are replaced by the voluntary actions of individual will. Maine conceived of political progress as the "unfolding of the idea of liberty; as a gradual limitation and direction of state action so as to make possible the maximum of individual self-assertion which is taken to be the maximum realization of the idea of liberty."[144]

Stressing Maine's debt to the interpretation of Roman law by Savigny, Pound pointed out that the widespread acceptance in England and the United States of Maine's theory of progress from status to contract had "Romanized" interpretation of the common law. Yet Maine's famous theoretical generalization, Pound emphasized, derived entirely from his flawed understanding of Roman law and neither was based on, nor could draw any support from, the actual history of Anglo-American law.[145] In contrast to the focus on individual freedom and will falsely imputed to Roman law by the nineteenth-century "Romanists" who wrote historical jurisprudence, Pound insisted that the fundamental idea of the common law, in both public and especially private law, is relation.[146] In particular, the importance of the relation between lord and tenant in the formative period of English law made the idea of relation central in English legal thought and was the analogy, conscious or unconscious, by which English law analyzed other legal relationships.[147] Pound called this emphasis on relation the "feudal" element in the Anglo-American legal tradition and suggested that it "should be called the Germanic element,"[148] thereby following the many American scholars who stressed the Germanic rather than the Roman origins of English law.

Historical Jurisprudence in America

In tracing the history of historical jurisprudence, Pound commented on its prevalence in the United States in the second half of the nineteenth century, especially after 1870.[149] "So far as American legal scholars trouble themselves with juristic theory at all," Pound wrote in 1910 while implying that they did not trouble themselves much, "their point of view is usually historical."[150] He asserted that the American historical jurists at the end of the nineteenth century very much resembled Savigny and his German

---

[143] Pound, supra note 107, at 60.
[144] Pound, supra note 80, at 210.
[145] Id. at 211, 218–19, 220–1; Pound, supra note 107, at 56.
[146] Pound, supra note 80, at 212–18; Pound, supra note 107, at 56–8.
[147] Pound, supra note 80, at 217–18; Pound, supra note 107, at 58.
[148] Pound, supra note 80, at 217.
[149] Pound-Theories, supra note 22, at 135, 139.
[150] Pound, supra note 25, at 27.

colleagues.[151] He also emphasized Maine's influence in the United States. The widespread American acceptance of Maine's theory of legal progress from status to contract, Pound believed, provided the primary explanation for American judicial decisions on subjects such as liberty of contract and labor relations, cases many progressive scholars attributed, incorrectly in Pound's opinion, to economic factors, including the class bias of judges.[152]

Throughout his writings, Pound associated many late nineteenth-century American scholars with historical jurisprudence, including Ames,[153] Bigelow,[154] Carter,[155] Hammond,[156] Holmes,[157] and Thayer.[158] Pound identified Carter as "the greatest American lawyer of recent times" and as the "authoritative" representative of historical jurisprudence in the United States.[159] Carter's conception of law, Pound observed, "comes from Savigny through Sir Henry Maine."[160] And although Holmes eventually abandoned historical jurisprudence, he did "notable work" during its "heyday" in applying "the best possibilities of its methods" to the history of Anglo-American law.[161]

Pound offered many explanations for the dominance of historical jurisprudence in the United States during the late nineteenth century. Tying his discussion of historical jurisprudence to his emphasis on the pervasive individualism of American law, he observed that Maine's theory of progress from status to contract perfectly reinforced this individualism.[162] The American tradition of judicial power to declare legislation unconstitutional, moreover, bred a distrust of legislation that made Savigny's opposition to codification attractive.[163] Pound observed that historical jurisprudence reached its greatest influence in the United States in the decades after 1870, when many American students began to study in Germany with the great German scholars in the field and subsequently returned to become law professors in the United States.[164] Writing in the decade before World War I, Pound stressed "the almost uncontested supremacy"[165] of historical jurisprudence in American law schools, which he attributed in large part to the preeminence of Harvard Law School in American

---

[151] Pound, supra note 19, at 148 and n. 31.

[152] Pound, supra note 80, at 210–11, 218–19; Pound, supra note 107, at 62–3.

[153] Pound, supra note 107, at 17, 42, 119–20; Pound, supra note 14, at 603 n. 43; Pound, supra note 17, at 512.

[154] Pound, supra note 107, at 17; Pound, supra note 17, at 512.

[155] Pound, supra note 107, at 34–5; Pound, supra note 14, at 593 n. 10; Pound, supra note 25, at 29.

[156] Pound, supra note 14, at 593 n. 10.

[157] Pound, supra note 17, at 512.

[158] Pound, supra note 107, at 17; Pound, supra note 17, at 512.

[159] Pound, supra note 25, at 28–9.

[160] Roscoe Pound, Book Review, 34 Political Science Quarterly 317 (1909).

[161] Pound, supra note 107, at 10; Roscoe Pound, Justice Holmes's Contributions to the Science of Law, 34 Harv. L. Rev. 449, 450 (1921).

[162] Pound, supra note 80, at 210–11.

[163] Pound, supra note 19, at 148; Pound, supra note 25, at 27; Pound, supra note 22, at 139.

[164] Pound, Theories, supra note 22, at 135.

[165] Pound, supra note 14, at 603; Pound, supra note 25, at 28.

legal education.[166] Presumably, Pound was referring to the popularity of historical jurisprudence among the Harvard faculty and to the substantial number
of Harvard graduates who taught at other law schools throughout the country.
More generally, Pound added, practicing lawyers, who typically assume the
legal ideas they learned as students reflect a natural legal order, spread historical jurisprudence from the law schools to the broader legal culture.[167]

In the United States, as previously in Germany, Pound maintained, historical jurisprudence provided a new foundation for natural law. In Germany,
Savigny and his successors deduced principles of natural law from the history
of Roman law. In the United States, the historical justification of natural law
became even more pronounced than in Germany, with American scholars relying mostly on the classical English common law of the seventeenth through
the first half of the nineteenth centuries, and sometimes on English law as far
back as the medieval Year Books, as the historical basis for natural law. Having
deduced natural law from the classical common law, historical jurists in the
United States evaluated all subsequent situations, doctrines, and statutes by its
principles, thereby precluding legal innovation.[168]

Focusing on Carter, Pound criticized American historical jurists for objecting to proposed statutory reforms of commercial law, the law of partnership,
and procedure simply because the proposals departed from historically developed existing law.[169] Such resistance to legal change, Pound observed, elevates
"juristic tradition" over the actual customs of the people,[170] which, at least in
theory, historical jurisprudence considers the proper foundation of law. Noting
that Ames, "the greatest of our historical jurists" on the subject of equity, had
criticized American judges for the "unwarranted assumption of equitable
powers," Pound asked: "Why must we insist that all power of growth in this
regard came to an end in the eighteenth century?"[171] In his classic article "Law
in Books and Law in Action," Pound warned that "if we admit the doctrines
of the historical jurist and take the juristic principles of the Roman law or of
Anglo-American common law as the basis from which to make logical deductions, the law in the books will more and more become an impossible attempt
to govern the living by the dead."[172]

Although Pound linked individualism with deductive formalism throughout his discussion of historical jurisprudence, he highlighted this connection
in his critique of the use of "freedom of contract" in American constitutional
law. Pound claimed that historical jurisprudence, like the previous schools
of philosophical and analytical jurisprudence, constituted "a jurisprudence

---

[166] Pound, supra note 25, at 27.
[167] Pound, supra note 14, at 602–3.
[168] Id. at 600–1; Pound, supra note 19, at 148; Pound, supra note 107, at 119–20; Pound, supra
note 25, at 29–30; Pound, supra note 31, at 811.
[169] Pound, supra note 14, at 601–2.
[170] Id. at 604.
[171] Id. at 603 n. 43.
[172] Pound, supra note 25, at 25.

of conceptions,"[173] the term Jhering used to attack historical jurisprudence in Germany. He then declared that the Supreme Court's application of the Fourteenth Amendment to protect "freedom of contract" provided a "striking instance" of the "jurisprudence of conceptions."[174] "The conception of freedom of contract is made the basis of a logical deduction" about the equality of the relationship between employers and employees. Yet the Court does not examine the consequences of this deduction, thus failing to observe that its logic, in the context of the actual employment relationship, defeats liberty in practice and obstructs social progress.[175]

Sociological Jurisprudence: Collectivist and Pragmatic

While criticizing the individualism and deductive formalism of historical jurisprudence, Pound promoted what he called "sociological jurisprudence" as a collectivist and pragmatic alternative. He described sociological jurisprudence as an emerging jurisprudential school that provided legal support for the "collectivism" or "socialism" most Americans needed and wanted in the early twentieth century. Like many progressive intellectuals of the time, Pound used the term "socialism" as the equivalent of collectivism and the opposite of individualism, rather than as a term denoting class consciousness or central state control.[176] Edward A. Ross, the eminent sociologist who became friendly with Pound when both taught at the University of Nebraska,[177] urged Pound to combine his many articles into a book,[178] which "is sorely needed to provide the intellectual backing for our movement."[179] After moving to the University of Wisconsin, Ross recommended to his new colleague, the economist Richard T. Ely, that he publish Pound's forthcoming book in a series Ely edited.[180] Ely read Pound's outline "with a great deal of care and interest" and wrote to Pound that the book "is going to prove an extremely valuable work and I venture to hope even an epoch-making one."[181] Over several years, Ross repeatedly implored Pound to finish the book.[182] Expressing similar frustration while thanking Pound for

[173] Pound, supra note 49, at 613.
[174] Id. at 615–16.
[175] Id. at 616.
[176] See Daniel T. Rodgers, Atlantic Crossings: Social Politics in a Progressive Age (Cambridge, Mass.: Harvard University Press, 1998), p. 100.
[177] Wigdor, supra note 2, at 111–13.
[178] Letter from E. A. Ross to Roscoe Pound (November 14, 1907), in Pound Papers, supra note 27, Box 227, Folder 28.
[179] Letter from E. A. Ross to Roscoe Pound (February 8, 1911), in Pound Papers, supra note 27, Box 227, Folder 28.
[180] Letter from E. A. Ross to Roscoe Pound (December 3, 1907), in Pound Papers, supra note 27, Box 227, Folder 28; letter from Richard T. Ely to Roscoe Pound (December 4, 1907), in Pound Papers, supra note 27, Box 220, Folder 9).
[181] Letter from Richard T. Ely to Roscoe Pound (August 17, 1908), in Pound Papers, supra note 27, Box 220, Folder 9.
[182] See, e.g., Letters from E. A. Ross to Roscoe Pound (July 15, 1909, February 8, 1911, March 13, 1914), in Pound Papers, supra note 27, Box 227, Folder 28.

sending him an article, another eminent sociologist, Albion W. Small of the University of Chicago, stressed that the article did not "make me forget that your *magnum opus* is due, and as I have been advertising it all over the country, I hope it will materialize before a great while."[183] Somewhat more subtly, Ely, six years after his initial correspondence with Pound, sent Pound his new book, observing that he had quoted Pound and that "I often thought of you and the importance of the work you are doing while writing it."[184] Pound spent years revising and expanding his own manuscript[185] while referring in several of his articles to "a forthcoming book, to be entitled 'Sociological Jurisprudence.'"[186] As late as 1916 and 1917, he indicated to his publisher that it was nearing completion[187] and, in explaining to Wigmore his decision to abandon another project, wrote, "I have my book to finish – which I have twice put off for other things."[188] Pound never published his eagerly anticipated book, but his many, often overlapping articles in the decade before World War I conveyed the central themes he associated with sociological jurisprudence.

The title of one of Pound's earliest articles asked in 1905, "Do We Need a Philosophy of Law?" Pound answered affirmatively, claiming that lawyers, in order "to keep abreast of our time," should be trained in a new philosophy that would "lead our law to hold a more even balance between individualism and socialism."[189] "The Need of a Sociological Jurisprudence," an article he wrote two years later, named this new philosophy. Its opening paragraph protested that the "individual standards" of American law were applied "in the teeth of the collective standard" that the law ought to express.[190] Emphasizing in another article that "social justice is asserting itself against legal justice," Pound maintained that "our legal system must temper its individualism,"[191] which is "against the genius of the time and the interest of the modern industrial community," and recognize the "collectivist principles" that the public desires.[192] Sociological jurisprudence, he believed, would align legal justice with social justice and remove the gap between the individualism of the legal system and

---

[183] Letter from Albion W. Small to Roscoe Pound (January 30, 1914), in Pound Papers, supra note 27, Box 228, Folder 19.

[184] Letter from Richard T. Ely to Roscoe Pound (November 28, 1914), in Pound Papers, supra note 27, Box 220, Folder 9.

[185] Letter from Roscoe Pound to E. A. Ross (February 13, 1911), in Pound Papers, supra note 27, Box 227, Folder 28.

[186] See, e.g., Pound-Theories, supra note 22, at 114 n. 1; Roscoe Pound, The End of Law as Developed in Legal Rules and Doctrines, 27 Harv. L. Rev. 195 note (1914); Pound, supra note 72, at 605 note.

[187] See Pound Papers, supra note 27, Box 226, Folder 7a (correspondence with MacMillan Company).

[188] Letter from Roscoe Pound to John Wigmore (June 14, 1916), in Pound Papers, supra note 27, Box 231, Folder 10.

[189] Pound, supra note 29, at 352.

[190] Pound, supra note 34, at 607.

[191] Pound, supra note 31, at 828.

[192] Id. at 829.

popular collectivism. Pound expressed confidence that sociological jurisprudence was in the process of arising from the "breakdown"[193] of the older philosophical, analytical, and historical schools. Hoping to stimulate this process, he devoted much of his prolific early scholarship to explaining and advocating sociological jurisprudence.

Pound defined sociological jurisprudence more by contrasting it favorably with the prior jurisprudential schools it was superseding, particularly the dominant school of historical jurisprudence, than by elaborating what he meant by collective interests or social justice. In addition to differentiating the collectivism of sociological jurisprudence from the individualism of the prior schools, Pound stressed that sociological jurisprudence rejected other major characteristics of historical jurisprudence that posed obstacles to legal reform in the public interest. Whereas historical jurisprudence focused on the internal contents of law, attempting to answer legal questions by formal deduction from historically derived principles, sociological jurisprudence focused on the relationship between law and society, especially on how law could be a pragmatic instrument in achieving social justice. Historical jurisprudence portrayed the evolution of legal doctrine as an unconscious and inevitable process, emphasizing the futility of human efforts to change the law, particularly through legislation. Sociological jurisprudence, by contrast, challenged this "juristic pessimism" by encouraging the conscious transformation of law and praising legislation as an agency of social progress.

Pound drew on three recent intellectual trends in his formulation of sociological jurisprudence. First, within legal thought itself, German jurists, led by Jhering, criticized German historical jurisprudence and created a social theory of law. The same criticisms, Pound believed, applied to American historical jurisprudence, itself an inferior imitation of its German predecessor. Second, American philosophical pragmatism provided an independent attack on formalism throughout intellectual life while urging attention to practical social realities, an approach Pound extended to legal thought. Third, the new social sciences in America, particularly sociology, enabled law to become pragmatic by assessing collective interests and indicating how law could contribute to them.

Jhering's Teleological Jurisprudence
Pound constantly differentiated Jhering's "social theory of law" from the "individualist" theories that preceded it. He emphasized the "capital importance" of Jhering's shift in focus from viewing law as rights the individual can invoke against society to viewing law as something created by society as a means of securing interests or protecting relations society itself recognizes.[194] Jhering's "teleological" approach to law, Pound maintained, introduced a

---

[193] Pound, supra note 14, at 594.
[194] Pound, supra note 19, at 143.

"radical change in jurisprudence" as "epoch-making" as Savigny's development of historical jurisprudence. Shifting the emphasis of legal scholarship from "the nature of law to its purpose," Jhering and his followers replaced the "jurisprudence of conceptions" at the core of Savigny's historical jurisprudence with what Pound variously called a "jurisprudence of actualities,"[195] a "jurisprudence of realities,"[196] or a "jurisprudence of results."[197] Whereas the jurisprudence of conceptions deduced a legal system based on fundamental conceptions derived from the historical development of Roman law, Jhering's teleological approach "began at the other end" by first asking, "How will a rule or decision operate in practice?"[198] By the end of the nineteenth century, Pound asserted, the individualistic conceptions German historical jurists had extracted from Roman legal history were losing "touch with practical life" and had become purely "academic."[199] Jhering reconnected law with practical life by examining the "human ends" law should promote and by treating law as a means to achieve those ends. Jhering, Pound observed, saw the legal implications of even the most trivial aspects of daily life. Rather than finding law from the evidence of legal history, Jhering believed in consciously shaping law in the social interest.[200]

Pound emphasized the relevance of Jhering's analysis to his own critique of American law. The Germans whom Jhering ridiculed for their attachment to the "jurisprudence of conceptions," Pound asserted, "have their counterpart in American judges who insist upon a legal theory of equality of rights and liberty of contract in the face of notorious social and economic conditions." Jhering's view "of law as a means toward social ends," his insistence that "abstract considerations do not suffice to justify legal rules," and his requirement that jurists "keep in touch with life" undermined the decisions of these American judges and pointed the way to different results, which would enable legal justice to implement social justice.[201] In Germany, Pound observed, Jhering's theories had become part of the reform movement that "lead to the downfall" of historical jurisprudence and its individualist theory.[202] Clearly viewing Jhering as a model, Pound obviously hoped that his adaptation of Jhering's theories into his own formulation of sociological jurisprudence would have a similar beneficial impact in the United States.

American Pragmatism
While emphasizing Jhering's "enduring value for sociological jurisprudence,"[203] Pound identified additional, more distinctively American sources. He frequently

---

[195] Id. at 140.
[196] Id. at 142.
[197] Pound, supra note 49, at 610.
[198] Id.; see also Pound, supra note 19, at 142.
[199] Pound, supra note 14, at 142.
[200] Id. at 141.
[201] Id. at 146–7.
[202] Id. at 145, 143.
[203] Id. at 146.

associated sociological jurisprudence with philosophical pragmatism and quoted William James, the great American philosopher of pragmatism, in support of his jurisprudential views.[204] In two of his most famous early articles, Pound used identical language while describing sociological jurisprudence as the application of pragmatism to law. "The sociological movement in jurisprudence is a movement for pragmatism as a philosophy of law; for the adjustment of principles and doctrines to the human conditions they are to govern rather than to assumed first principles; for putting the human factor in the central place and relegating logic to its true position as an instrument."[205] For Pound, sociological jurisprudence was pragmatic precisely in the ways that it differed from the "mechanical jurisprudence" of the past, which focused on the internal logic of artificial and technical rules deduced from a priori conceptions, often without regard, or even contrary, to factual evidence.[206] The vices James found in metaphysics, Pound found in jurisprudence. After quoting James's attack on metaphysics for invoking God, Matter, Reason, the Absolute, and Energy as "so many solving names" that prematurely ended inquiry, Pound complained that mechanical jurisprudence similarly used legal terms such as "estoppel," "malice," and "privity" as talismanic "solving words" that ended "juristic search."[207] And just as James maintained that philosophical theories should be "instruments, not answers to enigmas," Pound urged jurisprudence to view law as a pragmatic means toward social ends, such as the fair administration of justice.[208]

"Jurisprudence," Pound repeatedly stressed, "is the last in the march of the sciences away from the method of deduction from predetermined conceptions."[209] The deductive method, he observed, had prevailed in all areas of inquiry, even in the natural sciences. Drawing on his own scientific background, Pound pointed out that Linnaeus had deduced a theory of homologies between the organs of animals and vegetables without any empirical study. Eventually, actual investigation of the organisms themselves overthrew his basic theory. "The substitution of efficient for final causes as explanations of natural phenomena," Pound added, "has been paralleled by a revolution in political thought," in which "practical utility" has replaced "assumed principles of human nature" in the analysis of institutions. Yet no similar transformation had occurred in legal analysis. Pound, therefore, challenged jurisprudence "to attain a pragmatic, a sociological legal science" that would match the accomplishments already achieved in other fields.[210]

In an impassioned paragraph, Pound expressed confidence that his challenge would be answered.

A swing of the pendulum toward liberality at this time is but part of a general movement in all departments of mental activity away from the purely formal, away from hard and

---

[204] Pound, supra note 49, at 607, 608, 620–1.

[205] Id. at 609–10; Pound, supra note 30, at 464.

[206] Pound, supra note 49, at 607–10; Pound, supra note 30, at 462.

[207] Pound, supra note 49, at 621.

[208] Id. at 605, 608.

[209] Id. at 610; Pound, supra note 30, at 464.

[210] Pound, supra note 49, at 609.

fast notions, away from traditional categories which our fathers supposed were impressed upon the nature of things for all time. This movement is remaking the natural and physical sciences, is rewriting history, is recasting political theories, is making over economic theory, and, under the name of sociology, is changing our attitude toward all problems of social life.

"It is inevitable," he added, "that jurisprudence, and ultimately the law itself, be affected profoundly. For whatever its validity in other fields, pragmatism must be the philosophy of the lawyer." He was confident that pragmatism would supersede historical jurisprudence.[211] Although Pound did not try to equate pragmatism with Jhering's jurisprudence, he stressed that both rejected deductive formalism while seeking to address practical realities in the social interest.

The Promise of Social Science

The new social sciences that emerged in the late nineteenth century, Pound maintained, enabled law to become pragmatic by providing empirical data about the social facts that should inform legal rules and about the effects of law on society. In his discussion of the new social sciences, Pound repeatedly differentiated their commitment to "social justice" from the lingering individualism of American "legal justice," a distinction made by many social scientists themselves.[212] He cited leading American social scientists throughout his articles. Like Bigelow at Boston University during the same period, Pound encouraged the legal system in general and law professors in particular to incorporate their insights.

Pound emphasized that the basis for legal doctrines should be sought "not in Blackstone's wisdom of our ancestors, not in the apocryphal reasons of the beginnings of legal science, not in their history, useful as that is in enabling us to appraise doctrines at their true value, but in a scientific apprehension of the relations of law to society and of the needs and interests and opinions of society to-day." Pound made clear that by science he did not mean the "traditional legal pseudo-science" of the past, but the new social sciences of sociology, economics, and political science. Modern law professors should not abandon study of the legal principles that guide judges in reaching decisions, but they should also examine the social and economic conditions in which the law actually operates. If law professors remain "legal monks," studying "pure law" in an atmosphere from which "every worldly and human element is excluded," they will be unable to develop "practical principles" suitable for "a restless world of flesh and blood." Noting a comment by Brunner about the impact of Roman law in Germany on peasant possessions, Pound stressed that the "most logical and skillfully reasoned rules may defeat the end of law in their practical

---

[211] Roscoe Pound, A Practical Program of Procedural Reform, Proc. Il. State Bar Assoc. 372, 375 (1910).

[212] See Pound, supra note 25, at 30–1 and n. 18 (citing Commons, Ward, and Willoughby).

administration because not adapted to the environment in which they are to be enforced."[213]

Legal education, Pound therefore stressed, should include training in contemporary social science,[214] even if that requires professors to "take issue with courts and practitioners and books of authority as to the nature of justice and of rights and the basis of current legal conceptions and of received principles." Even when they teach "the law that the courts administer," professors should do so "in the spirit and from the standpoint of the political, economic, and sociological learning of to-day." In other words, they must "create in this country a true sociological jurisprudence."[215] If they do not, Pound warned, "their legitimate hegemony in legislation and politics" will devolve to social scientists and engineers.[216] Perhaps to reassure the same readers he was warning, Pound observed that by enabling lawyers to understand actual social conditions and popular thought, sociological jurisprudence based on the social sciences would help "insure that the common law remain, what its exponents have always insisted it is – the custom of the people."[217]

Pound followed his own advice. He quoted, cited, and relied on leading American social scientists throughout his work, including Edward A. Ross, Albion W. Small, John R. Commons, Richard T. Ely, Lester F. Ward, and Westal W. Willoughby.[218] He praised Ward for initiating the challenge to what he called "mechanical sociology," epitomized by Herbert Spencer and presumably analogous to the "mechanical jurisprudence" Pound attacked in law. He quoted approvingly Small's description of Spencer. According to Small, Spencer treated "social forces as though they were mills of the gods which men could at most learn to describe, but which they might not presume to organize and control."[219] Economic interpretations that portrayed law as the inevitable product of the interests of the dominant class, Pound maintained, were a version of mechanical sociology. Quoting at length from essays by Brooks Adams in *Centralization and the Law*, his collaboration with Melville Bigelow, Pound asserted that Adams exhibited the "most extreme form in America" of such economic interpretations.[220] In contrast to the mechanical sociology of Spencer and Adams, Pound declared, Ward emphasized that "social forces are essentially psychic."[221] Importantly for Pound, the psychological approach to social forces envisioned conscious effort to transform society. Ward contrasted "pure

---

[213] Pound, supra note 34, at 611–12.

[214] Pound, supra note 29, at 352–3.

[215] Pound, supra note 34, at 615.

[216] Id. at 612.

[217] Id. at 615.

[218] Id. at 612; Pound, supra note 17, at 491 n. 5, 493, 504, 506–10; Pound, supra note 42, at 406; Pound, supra note 49, at 609; Roscoe Pound, supra note 186, at 195 n. 1, 196 n. 1; Pound, supra note 25, at 30–1.

[219] Pound, supra note 17, at 493.

[220] Id. at 492.

[221] Id. at 506 n. 67.

sociology," which views social development as "unconscious, unintended, and undesired," a purely "spontaneous" process, with his own "applied sociology," which "assumes that effort is consciously and intentionally directed to the improvement of social conditions."[222] Before Ward, "social science had been content to study the laws by which social progress took place and had believed it possible to do no more than to observe nature realize itself."[223] Pound understood Ward to proclaim that "it is not enough to study and observe." Rather, study and observation disclose "efficient social forces," which should be applied "consciously to social ends."[224] Pound similarly praised the use of "social control," informed by the social sciences, to benefit society,[225] a concept most closely associated with his friend and former colleague Edward A. Ross.

Complaining that jurisprudence remained "in the rags of a past century, while kindred sciences have been reclothed,"[226] Pound asserted that jurisprudence is not "self-sufficient."[227] He bemoaned "the entire separation of jurisprudence from the other social sciences," insisting on "the unity of the social sciences and the impossibility of a self-centered, self-sufficing science of law."[228] Pound conceded that some American scholars had harnessed history to legal science but claimed that in the United States scholars had not otherwise even begun to unify law with the emerging social sciences.[229] As a result, legal science was intellectually impoverished and, more practically, was unable to meet, or even to recognize, social ends. These weaknesses accounted for "the gulf between legal thought and popular thought on matters of social reform."[230] Using Ross's book *Social Psychology* as a model, Pound yearned for a similar book, presumably his own, by a lawyer about Anglo-American law. Such a book, Pound believed, "would be worth many volumes of the conventional analytical and historical jurisprudence."[231]

While criticizing American jurists for their individualistic interpretation of legal justice, Pound quoted and endorsed leading American social scientists who challenged it. What jurists praised as individualism, sociologists, in the words of Lester F. Ward, viewed as "the enforcement by society of an artificial equality in social conditions which are naturally unequal."[232] Pound also quoted with approval the economist John R. Commons, who wrote, "Justice is not merely fair play between individuals, as our legal philosophy would have it – it is fair play between social classes." Judicial decisions based on liberty

---

[222] Id. at 507 n. 70.
[223] Id. at 506.
[224] Id. at 507.
[225] Pound, supra note 25, at 30.
[226] Id.
[227] Pound, supra note 25, at 36; Pound, supra note 17, at 510–11.
[228] Pound, supra note 17, at 511.
[229] Id.
[230] Id. at 510.
[231] Id. at 509.
[232] Pound, supra note 34, at 612 (quoting Ward).

of contract, Pound immediately added, demonstrate that courts endorsed the individualistic conception of justice that Commons rejected.[233]

Urging "the absorption into law of ideas developed in the social sciences," Pound advocated "the socialization of law." He maintained that law should gradually transfer its emphasis "from individual interests to social interests." Law should recognize that individual interests are not higher than social interests and, more significantly, that social interests should generally determine which individual interests the law protects. Without citing Jhering, who had quite similar views, Pound added that a movement from individual interests to social interests had been occurring in legal systems throughout the world.[234] Sociological jurisprudence, Pound emphasized, would overcome nineteenth-century notions about the futility of effort, the source of so much popular dissatisfaction with law, and replace them with a belief in the "efficacy of effort" that had already permeated sociological and political thought.[235]

In an apparent attempt to make his proposal to unify law with the new social sciences seem less dramatic and, therefore, more acceptable, Pound returned to the historical analysis with which he was so comfortable. He observed that law had previously been revolutionized "through the infusion into the legal system of something from without" when the "purely professional development of law" had become overly rigid. In the sixteenth and seventeenth centuries, the common law developed in the king's courts had become so paralyzed by systematic logic that it could not address the moral issues presented in litigation. "With equal impartiality," Pound commented, "its rules fell upon the just and the unjust." The development of equity in the Court of Chancery by chancellors who were clergymen rather than lawyers responded to this predicament by infusing ethical notions into the law. Similarly in the eighteenth century, the professional development of the law had become too inflexible for an era in which commerce was rapidly expanding. By the end of the eighteenth century, the law responded by absorbing practices based on the actual experiences of merchants.[236] "May we not be confident," Pound asked, "that in the same way the law of the twentieth century will absorb the new economics and the social science of today and be made over thereby?"[237] Reminding his readers that economists in the nineteenth century had been ahead of the law in promoting individualism, Pound maintained that there should be nothing troubling in the fact that contemporary economists and sociologists urged a social version of justice before the law had accepted it.[238] In his own era, Pound maintained, the "infusion of social ideas" from the social sciences into the law was as necessary to overcome the prevailing legal individualism as the

233 Pound, supra note 25, at 30–1.
234 Pound-Legislation, supra note 22, at 760–1.
235 Pound, supra note 17, at 507.
236 Pound, supra note 36, at 116.
237 Id. at 117.
238 Id. at 120.

infusions from religion and commerce were necessary to overcome the legal rigidities of the past.[239]

Challenging the contemporary "legal muckraker," who attributed the problems of the legal system to sinister influences and bad judges, Pound located them instead in the persistence of outmoded individualism. Rather than a conflict between good and bad men, Pound emphasized a conflict between old and new ideas, "a contest between the conceptions of our traditional law and modern juristic conceptions born of a new movement in all the social sciences." According to Pound, the application of the social sciences to fundamental problems, "not reversion to justice without law through changes in the judicial establishment or referenda on judicial decisions, is the road to socialization of the law."[240]

The Emergence of Sociological Jurisprudence

Although Pound believed that the United States lagged substantially behind Europe in the development of sociological jurisprudence,[241] he did see some glimmers of hope both in legal thought and in positive law. He treated Holmes as an important forerunner of sociological jurisprudence in the United States. "The sociological movement in jurisprudence, the movement for pragmatism as a philosophy of law, the movement for the adjustment of principles and doctrines to the human conditions they are to govern rather than to assumed first principles, the movement for putting the human factor in the central place and relegating logic to its true position as an instrument," Pound declared in his famous 1909 article attacking the judicial use of "liberty of contract" to declare social legislation unconstitutional, "has scarcely shown itself as yet in America." Holmes's dissent in *Lochner v. New York*, Pound immediately added, could be "the best exposition of it we have,"[242] though he also noted Holmes's essay "The Path of the Law" as another example.[243] Reviewing Holmes's *Collected Papers* in 1921, Pound reiterated his praise of Holmes for his pioneering contributions to modern legal thought without specifically describing it as sociological jurisprudence. Claiming that Holmes had "anticipated"[244] and "shaped" modern American jurisprudence, in contrast to the immediate past, Pound asserted that the essays Holmes wrote in the 1890s could have been written between 1910 and 1920.[245] Contrasting Holmes with Carter, Pound observed that Holmes had moved beyond the historical approach of his earlier writings.[246] Rejecting historical jurisprudence and its slavery to legal traditions, "deductions from liberty," the "pseudo-concept"

---

[239] Id. at 119.
[240] Id. at 120–1.
[241] See Pound, supra note 49, at 613; Pound, supra note 17, at 511.
[242] Pound, supra note 30, at 464.
[243] Id. at 464 n. 63.
[244] Pound, supra note 161, at 451.
[245] Id. at 449.
[246] Id. at 450.

of rights, the futility of legislation, and intellectual autonomy of jurisprudence, Holmes endorsed a functional approach to law focusing on its proper ends based on considerations of policy; recognized the importance of social interests; believed in the efficacy of effort, including through legislation; and understood that jurisprudence was not self-sufficient.[247] While emphasizing Holmes's rejection of late nineteenth-century American legal thought, Pound also observed that Holmes did not go to the opposite "extreme," represented by the "progressives" at the turn of the twentieth century.[248] Pound thereby associated Holmes with Pound's own contrast between the reforms he advocated through sociological jurisprudence and the "legal muckrakers" he attacked.

In addition to Holmes's intellectual contributions to sociological jurisprudence, Pound detected significant signs of progress in the American legal system from "the individualist justice of the nineteenth century, which has passed so significantly by the name of legal justice, to the social justice" he hoped sociological jurisprudence would promote.[249] In two of his articles, Pound identified seven such signs of the "infusion of social ideas"[250] into law: (1) limitations on the law of property as a vehicle for the antisocial exercise of rights, (2) limitations on freedom of contract through both legislation and judicial decisions, (3) limitations on the power of a husband to dispose of property without the consent of his wife, (4) limitations on the powers of creditors and injured parties to obtain compensation or repayment, (5) imposition of liability without fault, (6) increasing recognition of property such as running water as belonging to the state, and (7) increasing recognition of social interests in protecting dependent children.[251] Elaborating some of these points, Pound observed that many statutes had survived constitutional scrutiny even though they limited freedom of contract by creating legal rights and obligations that could not be bargained away.[252] Much recent legislation, Pound added, had reintroduced "*status* or something very much like it" by basing the legal treatment of people on their occupation or position in society.[253] Without referring specifically to Maine, Pound claimed that this legislation belies "the famous individualist generalization of the nineteenth century that the growth of the law is a progress from *status* to contract."[254] He also identified the doctrine of "the police power," associated with the authority of the sovereign people, as gaining a foothold in constitutional law and providing an "antidote" to the traditional

---

[247] Id. at 451–2.
[248] Id. at 451.
[249] Pound, supra note 36, at 118.
[250] Id. at 119.
[251] Pound, supra note 186, at 226, 228–34; Pound, supra note 36, at 118; see Pound, supra note 34, at 613–15.
[252] Pound, supra note 34, at 613.
[253] Id. at 615.
[254] Pound, supra note 50, at 118.

individualism of American constitutional law.[255] Despite these signs of progress, Pound concluded that sociological jurisprudence "is still formative" not just in the United States, but also in Europe.[256]

Sociological Legal History

Even as he extolled the contributions of the new social sciences to the collectivism of sociological jurisprudence and disparaged the individualism and deductive formalism of historical jurisprudence, Pound made clear that he viewed legal history, properly conceived, as a vital component of sociological jurisprudence. Legal history, he maintained, could support sociological jurisprudence by demonstrating the sources of legal collectivism, the efficacy of human effort in the past, and the relationship between law and society over time, yielding lessons about how best to achieve social justice in the present and future. "If modern jurisprudence were to lose the historical method," Pound declared, "it would prove even more sterile than the much-abused historical jurisprudence of the last century."[257] Sometimes referring to the proper historical method as "sociological legal history,"[258] and differentiating it from historical jurisprudence,[259] Pound maintained that legal history is the study "not merely of how doctrines have evolved and developed, considered solely as jural materials, but of what social effects the doctrines of the law have produced in the past and how they have produced them."[260] Legal history should demonstrate how law emerged from and accommodated itself to social, economic, and psychological conditions. This historical evidence, he added, should help people determine whether or not they should retain or abandon law inherited from the past.[261] "The function of legal history," he concluded, "comes to be one of illustrating how rules and principles have met concrete situations in the past and of enabling us to judge how we may deal with such situations in the present, rather than one of furnishing self-sufficient premises from which rules are to be obtained by rigid deduction."[262] Further differentiating sociological legal history from traditional historical jurisprudence, Pound maintained that legal history should recognize the role of human activity in legal reform.[263] Such a perspective, he emphasized, does not imply a "great-lawyer interpretation" of the past[264] but only rejects the view of historical jurisprudence that law somehow evolves by itself, according to historical forces in which individuals have no meaningful role.[265] Pound

---

[255] Pound, supra note 29, at 350–1.
[256] Pound, supra note 17, at 489.
[257] Pound, supra note 19, at 155.
[258] Pound, supra note 17, at 514.
[259] Pound, supra note 19, at 154–5 and n. 53.
[260] Pound, supra note 17, at 514.
[261] Id. at 515.
[262] Pound, supra note 19, at 147.
[263] Id. at 149; Pound, supra note 107, at 68.
[264] Pound, supra note 107, at 140.
[265] Id. at 118.

simply urged "the importance of looking at the events of legal history in terms of the men who took part in them and of the personalities and characters and prejudices of these men as a factor in the results."[266]

Pound cited examples of creative individual effort from Roman, French, English, and American law. His American examples included Marshall, whose early interpretation of the Constitution helped make it effective, and Kent and Story, who contributed significantly to the reception of English law in the United States.[267] But he used Coke as his primary example. Writing on behalf of the power of the English common law courts in their contest against the Stuart kings, Coke asserted that the Magna Carta and a long subsequent succession of statutes and judicial decisions had recognized the immemorial common law rights of Englishmen. Many recent scholars of English law, Pound observed, had convincingly demonstrated that in making this argument Coke had seriously misinterpreted English legal history. But for Pound, Coke's partisan perversion of history only demonstrated the extent of his creative power. Underlying the potential of individuals to change the law, Pound also speculated that if Bacon had preceded rather than followed Coke, or if the king had supported Bacon's subsequent proposals for codification, the legal history of the next three centuries would have been very different. The victorious Coke, through the force of his personal determination, detailed legal knowledge, and high professional standing, was able to create a common law in England that was administered by the courts and that protected the individual subject from the king and his agents. This English law, moreover, became the foundation of American law.[268] Coke, Pound concluded, "actually made law as perhaps it was never made to so great an extent by one man before or since."[269]

Attempting to emulate these illustrious predecessors, Pound himself tried consciously, through his own creative individual efforts, to reform the destructive ultra-individualism of American law. He associated his claim about the centrality of the idea of relation in Anglo-American legal history with his emphasis on social interests as the foundation of sociological jurisprudence. "If we cast aside the Romanist prejudices of the nineteenth-century historical school," which incorrectly identified Roman law with legal individualism, "we may perceive that in the idea of relation, in the characteristic common-law mode of treating legal problems which we derived from the analogy of the incidents of feudal tenure, we have an institution of capital importance for the law of the future, a means of making our received legal tradition a living force for justice in the society of today and of tomorrow."[270] Sometimes Pound maintained that all legal history, and not just the Anglo-American common law, recognized the primacy of social interests. Primitive law, he asserted, arose

[266] Id. at 140.
[267] Id. at 139.
[268] Id. at 8–9, 52, 128, 132, 139–40.
[269] Id. at 139.
[270] Pound, supra note 80, at 221.

to protect "the social interest in general security," and the gradual development of individual rights was only a means to further this underlying social interest. Pound urged scholars to "rewrite our legal histories accordingly," to "make historical jurisprudence more effective."[271]

Throughout his early writings, Pound generously recognized others who had begun to develop the "sociological" approach to legal history he favored. Focusing particularly on Jhering and Josef Kohler, described by Pound as the greatest living legal scholar,[272] Pound maintained that in Germany historical jurisprudence assumed "the name and something of the character of a sociological jurisprudence."[273] Pound portrayed Jhering as a great scholar of Roman law who successfully led a reform movement against historical jurisprudence that was as important as Savigny's original development of the field. In Jhering's "jurisprudence of realities," Pound observed, "the function of legal history comes to be one of illustrating how rules and principles have met concrete situations in the past and of enabling us to judge how we may deal with such situations in the present, rather than one of furnishing self-sufficient premises from which rules are to be obtained by rigid deduction."[274] This approach thus appreciates the role of conscious human action in fashioning law to meet human ends.[275] In abandoning the "jurisprudence of conceptions" of Romanist historical jurisprudence, Pound emphasized, Jhering also abandoned the individualism it attributed to Roman law.[276]

Pound maintained that Kohler followed Jhering in stressing the necessity of conscious human effort to adjust laws inherited from the past to the changed culture of the present.[277] Kohler focused on the "philosophical study of the evolutionary processes by which law is formed."[278] Pound admired Kohler for interpreting law in terms of the entire social history of a people, whereas previous legal historians had related law more narrowly to political history.[279] Kohler, moreover, understood that creativity in reforming current law is constrained by social and legal history and thus avoided the "confident rejection of the past and faith in rational abstract schemes" that plagued natural law in the eighteenth century.[280] Pound worried that Kohler retained, or could easily be interpreted to retain, aspects of idealistic legal history inconsistent with the instrumental approach Pound himself preferred.[281] But he praised Kohler for preserving and developing the best methodologies of legal history.[282]

[271] Pound-Legislation, supra note 22, at 764–5.
[272] Pound, supra note 19, at 155.
[273] Pound, supra note 14, at 614.
[274] Pound, supra note 19, at 147.
[275] Id. at 141.
[276] Id. at 140, 143.
[277] Id. at 156, 158; Pound, supra note 107, at 10–11, 49.
[278] Pound, supra note 14, at 617.
[279] Pound, supra note 19, at 158.
[280] Pound, supra note 107, at 150; see Pound, supra note 19, at 156.
[281] Pound, supra note 107, at 150–1.
[282] Pound, supra note 19, at 147, 155.

Pound also identified Gierke as an important German scholar whose use of history advanced sociological jurisprudence. Like Maitland, Pound praised Gierke for his focus on groups and associations. While employing historical methodology, Pound observed, Gierke broke with the individualism of the historical school. Gierke "struck the sociological note" by attributing real personality to groups and associations and by emphasizing their historical importance. "What man is," Gierke wrote in an introductory passage quoted by Pound, "he owes to the union of man with man." Gierke added that associations not only enhance the power of individuals, "but above all, through their permanence, surviving the personality of the individual, bind the past of the race to those to come." Associations allow "the possibility of the development of history." After quoting this passage, Pound concluded that Gierke's theory of associations "became as strong an attack on the individualist jurisprudence of the nineteenth century upon one side as Jhering's theory of interests was upon another."[283]

Although Pound emphasized the German scholars who tried to salvage a constructive approach to legal history from the deductivism, individualism, and passivity of historical jurisprudence, which itself originated and was most fully developed in Germany, he recognized similar efforts by American scholars. Pound particularly praised Holmes, who even in contributing to historical jurisprudence when it dominated legal scholarship at the beginning of his career[284] rejected its typical assumption that the principles of Roman law apply universally to all legal systems. In *The Common Law*, for example, Holmes maintained that the common law of bailment did not derive from Roman law.[285] More significantly, Holmes presciently criticized many of the basic premises of historical jurisprudence in essays written in the 1890s that, according to Pound, had unequaled influence on the next generation of American legal thought.[286] Pound directly contrasted Carter, the most representative exponent of historical jurisprudence, with Holmes.[287] Unlike Carter, but like Jhering and Kohler, Holmes believed in "the functional use of legal history," in consciously applying legal traditions "for the ends of today instead of remaining slaves to them."[288] He did not think a law should be enforced in the present simply because it existed in embryonic form in the past,[289] and he saw through the legal fictions that produced a false impression of historical continuity.[290] He focused on social interests rather than individual rights[291] and was not hostile to legislation.[292] Yet unlike the American progressives at the turn of the

---

[283] Pound, supra note 17, at 504.
[284] Pound, supra note 107, at 10; Pound, supra note 161, at 450.
[285] Pound, supra note 80, at 218 n. 56.
[286] Pound, supra note 161, at 449.
[287] Id. at 450.
[288] Id. at 451.
[289] Pound, supra note 107, at 10.
[290] Pound, supra note 161, at 450.
[291] Id. at 452.
[292] Id. at 451.

twentieth century who advocated reform without attention to legal precedent, Holmes understood that history provides the materials with which reformers must work.[293] Without similarly examining the scholarship of John Wigmore, Pound's contemporary and mentor, Pound noted approvingly that in turning increasingly to legal history in his recent work, Wigmore was attracted to its "practical or sociological side" rather than to the outmoded views of historical jurisprudence.[294]

Adjudication and Legislation in Sociological Jurisprudence

As part of his exposition of sociological jurisprudence, Pound addressed the relative merits of adjudication and legislation, a topic to which late nineteenth-century American legal scholars had devoted substantial attention. Pound's writings exhibit ambivalence, and even some inconsistency, about the implications of sociological jurisprudence for adjudication and legislation. At times, he indicated that sociological jurisprudence could assist adjudication as well as legislation and that both are valuable means of advancing law. At least as frequently, however, he maintained that sociological jurisprudence is more conducive to legislation than to adjudication and that legislation should be the preferred method of lawmaking in the twentieth century, with adjudication in a subordinate role.

Pound attributed the past failures of American law equally to legislation and adjudication. Legislation typically failed because it was based on the false assumption that the command of the state is sufficient to make law effective and had not been preceded by preparatory study of the conditions to which it would apply. As a result, it could not reflect social needs or standards and was often inoperative in practice. Pound insisted that these faults, and not the frequent claim that legislation was the wrong approach to subjects of private law, accounted for the history of bad legislation in the United States. He also maintained that the record of American adjudication, which had similarly ignored the needs of the people, was no better. In practice, Americans disregarded judicial decisions as well as statutes.[295] "Failures," Pound observed, "are not confined to legislative law-making." He concluded that "crudity and carelessness have too often characterized American law-making both legislative and judicial. They do not inhere necessarily in the one any more than in the other."[296]

Sociological jurisprudence, Pound emphasized, was trying to encourage both legislation and adjudication to pay more attention to "the social facts upon which law must proceed and to which it is to be applied."[297] He maintained that absolute theories asserting the supremacy of either legislation or adjudication

---

[293] Id. at 450–1.
[294] Pound-Theories, supra note 22, at 137 n. 84; see also Pound, supra note 17, at 515 n. 100.
[295] Pound, supra note 49, at 613–14.
[296] Pound, supra note 42, at 405–6.
[297] Pound, supra note 17, at 512–13.

must be abandoned and replaced by an analysis of which approach is better suited in various circumstances to advancing the proper ends of law.[298] He preferred statutory codification for delimiting and securing "interests of substance" and adjudication for matters involving moral assessments of human behavior, which require the exercise of substantial discretion. Based on this reasoning, he advocated legislation covering inheritance and succession, property, and commercial transactions but considered adjudication the proper method for resolving issues of tort law.[299]

Pound was confident that the common law could incorporate the insights of the social sciences, just as in the past it had incorporated the insights of religion and commercial practice. "Given new premises," he observed, "our common law has the means of developing them to meet the exigencies of justice and of molding the results into a scientific system."[300] Consistent with his differentiation of sociological jurisprudence from the general hostility of progressive activists to judges, Pound opposed progressive efforts "to tinker with our courts and with our judicial organization in the hope of bringing about particular results in particular kinds of cases, at a sacrifice of all that we have learned from legal and judicial history." Pound instead urged patience during a period in which the new anti-individualistic premises of sociological jurisprudence would be developed by scholars and gradually accepted by judges. "What we should insist upon," Pound declared, "is not recall of judges, but recall of much of the juristic and judicial thinking of the last century."[301] Pound recognized that the fundamental transformation from individualism to "socialization of the law" would be "tedious and painful" even with the support of "zealous and friendly courts." But he was confident that adjudication would eventually adjust to the methods of sociological jurisprudence.[302] Arguing against the rigid traditional division between administration and adjudication in the American legal system, Pound urged courts to incorporate within their work the collection of social facts that should inform their decisions. Rather than "a sort of slot machine into which the facts of a controversy are put above and from which the decision is taken out below," the metaphor Jhering invoked to ridicule the German legal formalists and what Pound called "mechanical jurisprudence,"[303] a court should become "a bureau of justice," analyzing social data to reach fair and effective results. He singled out for approval the Municipal Court of Chicago, which kept and studied statistics for lessons that could be transformed into legal rules.[304]

At other times, however, Pound portrayed legislation as the more appropriate vehicle for sociological jurisprudence and suggested that it should

[298] Pound-Theories, supra note 22, at 148.
[299] Id. at 149–50.
[300] Pound, supra note 36, at 118.
[301] Id. at 119.
[302] Id. at 120–1.
[303] Pound, supra note 19, at 146.
[304] Pound-Legislation, supra note 22, at 768.

supplant adjudication as the primary focus of the American legal system. He stressed that American law needed "a new starting point that only legislation can afford." Research bureaus and hearings under the auspices of legislatures, Pound declared, are "furnishing abundant material for legislation of the best type," thereby demonstrating "the sociological, the pragmatic theory behind legislation." Despite his claim that the Muncipal Court of Chicago had illustrated the way in which courts could become bureaus of justice, Pound elsewhere denied that courts had the resources to perform the investigative functions necessary to implement sociological jurisprudence. Adjudication, he therefore concluded, "cannot serve us." He envisioned a golden age of American legislation, analogous to the great classic era of legislation in Rome, in which legislators informed by the social sciences would rescue law from the "mechanical jurisprudence" that reinforced the destructive individualism of American law.[305]

Lacking the means to ascertain the actual social facts, Pound concluded, courts have become "less and less competent to formulate rules for new relations which require regulation." Because courts must resolve the cases before them, rather than determine the law that best serves society, they often produce decisions that, however just in a particular case, operate "unfairly and inequitably in a complex social organization." Pound agreed with the popular view that "objects to the settlement of questions of the highest social import in private litigations between John Doe and Richard Roe." Legislation, he reiterated, "must be the chief reliance of modern society."[306]

As part of his argument that legislation should replace adjudication as the dominant mode of American lawmaking, Pound tried to undermine the widespread belief, frequently articulated by late nineteenth-century American legal scholars, that the common law as determined by judges reflects evolving popular custom better than legislation ever could. In the United States of his own day, he asserted, judges were out of touch with the people. What defenders of the judiciary call custom "is a custom of judicial decision, not a custom of popular action." Legislation based on sociological jurisprudence, by contrast, actually uses the methods of the "sociological laboratory" to determine the "general will" of the public. It is, therefore, a better gauge of popular custom and a "more truly democratic form of lawmaking" than adjudication, which does not have similar access to the public.[307] Pound warned that "the public cannot be relied upon permanently to tolerate judicial obstruction or nullification of the social policies to which more and more it is compelled to be committed."[308]

Yet even when Pound preferred legislation to adjudication, he did not deny that adjudication should continue to play an important role in American law. He often maintained that legislation is the most effective way to implement

---

[305] Pound, supra note 49, at 621–2.
[306] Pound, supra note 42, at 403–4.
[307] Id. at 406.
[308] Id. at 407.

sociological jurisprudence and to overcome the traditional individualism of American law. He also recognized, however, that this new legislation would generate judicial interpretation. Adjudication in the United States, Pound asserted, could not escape its "mechanical jurisprudence" and outmoded individualism "until it is given a new starting point from without." He was confident that legislation, which could more easily incorporate sociological jurisprudence, would provide this new starting point.[309] Pound seemed to envisage a reciprocal relationship between legislation and adjudication in which legal scholars would play a crucial role. By analyzing the social conditions in which law must function, legal scholars would be able to evaluate the existing common law and, in the many places where necessary, propose legislative restatement. Such legislation, in turn, would produce a fresh round of adjudication on an improved foundation. "Herein," Pound exhorted, "is a noble task for the legal scholars of America."[310]

Conclusion

As recent scholars have observed, Pound was more an advocate than a practitioner of sociological jurisprudence. Urging examination of the interactions between law and society through empirical studies grounded in the social sciences, he did not undertake such studies himself.[311] Nor did he try to relate the successive changes in legal thought he so thoroughly explored to broader social change.[312] Like the legal scholars he frequently criticized, Pound also remained essentially a "legal monk" removed from the "restless world of flesh and blood."[313] Even in his advocacy of sociological jurisprudence, his treatment of sociology was partial, impressionistic, and functional, oriented more toward practical law reform than theoretical sophistication.[314] The sociological approach Pound knew best and relied on most, the "social control" school led E. A. Ross, his early colleague at the University of Nebraska, emphasized that society must limit individual self-interest for the public good and tied academic research to social reform.[315] This approach encouraged Pound to view law as a form of social control and gave him a sociological justification for concentrating on legal issues.[316] Pound identified Jhering's teleological jurisprudence, philosophical pragmatism, and the emerging social sciences as the foundations of sociological jurisprudence, but in his own work he relied more on Jhering's legal thought and the sensibility of pragmatism than on the theory or practice of social science.

---

[309] Pound, supra note 49, at 614.
[310] Id. at 622.
[311] Green, supra note 1, at 2012.
[312] Hunt, supra note 100, at 29–31.
[313] Pound, supra note 34, at 611–12.
[314] Hunt, supra note 100, at 19–21, 35–6; Green, supra note 1, at 1918, 1965.
[315] Dorothy Ross, The Origins of American Social Science (Cambridge University Press, 1991), pp. 230–1, 235–7, 249,
[316] Hunt, supra note 100, at 19–20.

Pound, moreover, did not pursue the pedagogical implications of his call for a sociological jurisprudence. He approved efforts by Ely to establish a school of jurisprudence at the University of Wisconsin that would emphasize the connections among economics, political science, and law.[317] According to a statement by Ely in 1916, the year Pound became dean at Harvard, Pound took the position "Smash the artificial separation of these subjects and keep it up."[318] Ely wrote that the school of jurisprudence did not materialize because the president who appointed Ely and was sympathetic to his proposal left before it could be implemented.[319] Though many predicted that Pound would be a reforming dean,[320] he did not attempt to implement anything similar at Harvard and subsequently refused an offer to become president of the University of Wisconsin.[321] By the time Johns Hopkins established an interdisciplinary Institute of Law in 1928, Pound actively opposed such programs. Indeed, no significant curricular innovations occurred during his two decades as dean of Harvard Law School.[322] Congratulating Pound on his appointment to the Harvard law faculty in 1910, Wigmore took the "liberty" to "express the hope that you will not allow the traditions and inertia and complacency of an age-honored institution to congeal or ossify your living zeal or any of your well-defined views. You know what the usual fate of the opposition is when it accepts office as the Party in Power."[323] Whether or not Pound was influenced by joining the faculty of Harvard Law School or soon becoming its dean, he did not follow through on his own hopes for sociological jurisprudence and by the late 1930s eventually manifested what Morton Horwitz convincingly calls an intellectual "about-face."[324]

Yet by attacking the individualism and deductivism of successive jurisprudential schools and by arguing for reliance on the social sciences to assist the legal analysis of social interests, Pound helped subsequent scholars develop both the empirical and the theoretical possibilities of the sociological jurisprudence that he strenuously advocated but barely pursued himself. Pound's effective promotion of sociological jurisprudence helped free his successors from the historical analysis of law that remained a key component of his own thought.[325] As legal scholars became increasingly interested in social science during the early decades of the twentieth century, the study of legal history

---

[317] Letter from Richard T. Ely to Roscoe Pound (July 9, 1915), in Pound Papers, supra note 27, Box 220, Folder 9.

[318] Letter from Richard T. Ely to Roscoe Pound (June 9, 1916), in Pound Papers, supra note 27, Box 220, Folder 9.

[319] Letter from Ely to Pound, supra note 317.

[320] Wigdor, supra note 2, at 204–5.

[321] Id. at 239–40.

[322] Id. at 252–3.

[323] Letter from John Wigmore to Roscoe Pound (March 29, 1910), in Pound Papers, supra note 27, Box 231, Folder 10.

[324] Horwitz, supra note 1, at 217–19.

[325] Id. at 33; Green, supra note 1, at 1959, 1962, 1996, 2013.

entered a long period of decline.[326] Just as the emerging social sciences moved away from historical exploration, especially from evolutionary theories of historical change,[327] so did legal scholarship. Legal history became a peripheral part of legal scholarship, a minor, often undistinguished, subfield. Pound was both the last major figure who shared the historical understanding of law that dominated American legal scholarship in the decades after 1870 and the person who did most to bring that era to a close. Despite the spectacular revival of legal history in the United States since 1970, history has not regained the central role in legal scholarship it had in the late nineteenth century. While Pound recognized the importance of history in late nineteenth-century American legal thought, subsequent legal scholars, including many legal historians themselves, have often minimized, or even denied, this historical influence. By contrast, Pound's mistaken ascription of deductive formalism to his predecessors, derived largely from Jhering's critique of historical jurisprudence in Germany, persisted throughout the twentieth century.

[326] Robert W. Gordon, J. Willard Hurst and the Common Law Tradition in American Legal Historiography, 10 Law & Soc'y Rev. 9, 12, 21 (1975).
[327] Ross, supra note 315, at 299, 303, 388–9.

XIV

Pound's Successors

Twentieth-Century Interpretations of Late
Nineteenth-Century Legal Thought

Scholars throughout the twentieth century perpetuated Pound's disparaging emphasis on the deductive formalism of late nineteenth-century American legal thought, usually without citing Pound himself. Like Pound, they typically observed that deductive formalism promoted conservatism while rejecting the stronger assertion by progressive historians of a nefarious alliance between legal thinkers and conservative business interests. Yet the twentieth-century scholars did not generally follow Pound in linking deductive formalism with individualism and historical jurisprudence. The tension between traditional individualism and socially desirable collectivism, which underlay Pound's analysis of legal thought, was not a major theme for his successors. Nor did they follow his identification of historical jurisprudence as the dominant juris-prudential school in the United States in the generation after 1870. Even the few twentieth-century American legal historians who explored the history of their field did not share Pound's view about the centrality of history in late nineteenth-century legal thought, though they occasionally elaborated criti-cisms similar to those Pound had levied against historical jurisprudence. They viewed the "Law and Society" school of legal history founded by J. Willard Hurst at the University of Wisconsin in the 1940s as the origin of professional legal history in the United States. They frequently indicated that prior work on the internal history of legal doctrine was worthy of contempt but not study, not even qualifying as real legal history, although they occasionally offered passing praise of Holmes, Ames, Thayer, and Bigelow.

Beginning with Duncan Kennedy's pioneering work in the 1970s on the struc-ture of "classical legal thought,"[1] some commentators have treated their late

---

[1] Duncan Kennedy, The Rise and Fall of Classical Legal Thought (Washington, D.C.: Beard Books, 2006). Though not published until 2006, the original manuscript of this book was prepared in 1975 and was widely circulated through the late 1970s and 1980s. Id. at vii–viii, xli.

For general discussions of classical legal thought, see William M. Wiecek, The Lost World of Classical Legal Thought (Oxford University Press, 1998); Neil Duxbury, Patterns of American Jurisprudence (Oxford: Clarendon Press, 1995), pp. 9–65 (chapter entitled "The Challenge of Formalism").

nineteenth-century predecessors more respectfully and in greater detail, even as they often reiterated many earlier criticisms of their work. Especially since 1990, when Stephen Siegel published his groundbreaking article "Historism in Late Nineteenth-Century Constitutional Thought,"[2] legal historians have redirected attention to the importance of history in late nineteenth-century legal thought while providing more extensive and nuanced explorations of its content.

My goal in this chapter is to place my own findings about late nineteenth-century American legal thought in the context of previous scholarship. I, therefore, will focus on the three major subjects discussed by twentieth-century scholars that are most directly implicated by my research and conclusions: deductive formalism, political conservatism, and the role of history. Some twentieth-century scholars, especially those who have published since 1970, have written extensive accounts of late nineteenth-century American legal thought that are neither limited to nor primarily interested in these three subjects. Whether convinced, agnostic, or skeptical, I find much of this scholarship provocative and intriguing. Yet I address additional aspects of it only when I feel they help explain a scholar's position about the three subjects on which I focus. For example, I refer to Duncan Kennedy's elaborate structuralist account of classical legal thought, but only to the extent that it helps clarify his conclusions about deductive formalism, politics, and history. By examining commentary by Pound's successors on late nineteenth-century American legal thought, this chapter demonstrates how much my own analysis, building on recent scholarship, asserts an alternative understanding. Far from being mechanical deductive formalists who provided intellectual support for conservative interests, the disparaging image presented by most twentieth-century commentators, the late nineteenth-century American legal scholars were historically sophisticated thinkers in the mainstream of transatlantic intellectual life, often dedicated to legal reform, and sometimes in the vanguard of original scholarship in legal history.

Deductive Formalism

Like Pound, many subsequent twentieth-century scholars have asserted the emphasis on deductive formalism in late nineteenth-century American legal thought without providing much detail about how it deduced specific rules from general principles. Indeed, they often defined their own jurisprudential views by differentiating them from deductive formalism. They generally agreed with Pound that law should address important issues of public policy, which the internal logic of deductive formalism ignored. In the 1970s, Duncan Kennedy tried to "decenter" formalism while focusing on other aspects of classical legal thought he considered more important.[3] Some recent scholars have stressed the

---

[2] Stephen A. Siegel, Historism in Late Nineteenth-Century Constitutional Thought, 1990 Wis. L. Rev. 1431.

[3] Kennedy, supra note 1, at xxxiv.

centrality of induction in late nineteenth-century legal thought, downplaying and occasionally even denying entirely its reliance on formal deduction.

Like Pound, the scholars grouped under the heading "legal realists," who attained prominence in the 1920s and 1930s, rejected the deductive formalism they attributed to late nineteenth-century American legal thought. They believed that deductive formalism maintained its pernicious intellectual influence in their own day and saw their work as part of an increasingly successful effort to supplant it. The legal realists were inspired by the dramatic contrasts made by Holmes between logic and experience and by Pound between law in the books and law in action, often using them as slogans for their movement.[4] More than Holmes and Pound themselves, many legal realists actually looked to experience and to law in action, rather than to logic or to law in the books, as the foundation of both scholarship and law reform. The legal realists focused on the elaboration of their alternative vision, but some of them addressed the deductive formalism they disparaged.

In a concise summary of the legal realist position, written in 1960 toward the end of his career, Karl Llewellyn used the term "Formal Style" to describe "the orthodox ideology" that had prevailed from the 1870s and "against which all modern thinking has played." Llewellyn's characterization of the Formal Style largely paralleled the prior views of Holmes and Pound. Judicial opinions proceeded "in deductive form with an air or expression of single-line inevitability." They used the term "principle" as "a generalization producing order" on as large a scale as possible. Llewellyn added, as Holmes and Pound had not, that principle functioned to prune away anomalous cases or rules that did not fit this ordered scheme. The Formal Style, moreover, admonished judges to avoid considerations of policy in reaching their decisions, stressing that policy is the exclusive role of the legislature.[5]

For Llewellyn, Langdell's "dazzling contract-construct" was the "American archetype" of the Formal Style. Through a set of formal principles, he asserted, Langdell created a system of contract law that excluded common sense, the ordinary meaning of words, and the actual practices of businessmen. For example, by requiring consideration for a contract and by defining consideration only as a bargained-for detriment that moves from the promisee, Langdell's construct eliminated all enforcement through reliance or by beneficiaries and ignored all matters that occurred before a promise was made. Llewellyn lamented that generations of law students had been introduced to legal studies through these "strange ideas" and that judges used them in reaching their decisions, often taking "pleasure as the pretty little puzzle-pieces lock together to leave for hundreds of good business practices no legal container but the garbage can."[6]

---

[4] See Morton J. Horwitz, The Transformation of American Law 1870–1960 (New York: Oxford University Press, 1992), pp. 187–8.

[5] Karl N. Llewellyn, The Common Law Tradition: Deciding Appeals (Boston: Little, Brown, 1960), pp. 38–9.

[6] Id.

Without citing Holmes or Pound, Llewellyn thus vividly illustrated the problems of invoking logic over experience, law in the books over law in action. Alluding to cases involving labor injunctions and constitutional law, Llewellyn observed that the Formal Style had not prevented sudden and far-reaching doctrinal innovations, though he added that it did "drive conscious creation all but underground."[7]

Writing about Pound with some bewilderment, Llewellyn praised him for sounding warnings against the evils of the Formal Style, particularly in his famous speech to the American Bar Association in 1906. Yet in 1914, Llewellyn observed, Pound wrote that the necessity of "propagandist agitation" against the Formal Style had ended because the "task of awakening has been achieved." In Llewellyn's view, by contrast, Pound's attack "had died out on the inert resistant air" as appellate judges continued to apply the Formal Style.[8] At least in the three decades after 1930, Llewellyn happily added, the Formal Style, though still influential, had "lost its grip."[9]

The most elaborate realist critique of prior legal thought was the aptly entitled "Transcendental Nonsense and the Functional Approach," published in 1935 by Felix Cohen. By using the term "transcendental nonsense" to describe what he associated with "mechanical jurisprudence" and otherwise called "traditional" or "classical" legal thought,[10] Cohen made clear his contempt for it. Reiterating points made by Holmes and Pound, Cohen criticized "transcendental nonsense" for treating legal concepts, such as corporations or property rights, as "supernatural entities which do not have a verifiable existence except to the eyes of faith."[11] Commenting that no person has ever seen a corporation, Cohen asked, "What right do we have to believe in corporations if we don't believe in angels?"[12] The rules of law that employ these legal concepts, he maintained, function as "theorems in an independent system" removed from both empirical social facts and moral ideals.[13] Classical jurists devoted themselves "to the taxonomy of legal concepts and to the systematic explication of principles of 'justice' and 'reason,' buttressed by 'correct' cases."[14] While teasing Pound for his classification of jurisprudential schools "with sub-species too numerous to mention,"[15] Cohen largely echoed Pound's exhortation for a more "functional approach," analogous to modern developments in science and philosophy.[16] He explicitly rejected the traditional view of a legal decision

---

[7] Id. at 39–40.

[8] Id. at 40 and n. 33.

[9] Id. at 41.

[10] Felix S. Cohen, Transcendental Nonsense and the Functional Approach, 35 Colum. L. Rev. 809, 821 (1935).

[11] Id. Cohen cited Holmes and Pound among his predecessors. Id.

[12] Id. at 811.

[13] Id. at 821.

[14] Id. at 833.

[15] Id. at 829.

[16] Id. at 821–2.

"as a logical deduction from fixed principles," which treats law "as a system of pure geometry."[17]

Just as Pound applied Jhering's critique of German formalism to late nineteenth-century American legal scholars, Cohen began his article by repeating the "dream" imagined by Jhering to attack the formalism of nineteenth-century German legal scholars. As reported by Cohen, Jhering dreamed that he had died and gone to heaven, where he encountered jurisprudential concepts in their absolute purity, divorced from all connection with human life. Logical instruments, including a "dialectic-hydraulic-interpretation press," could manipulate and transform these legal concepts into an infinite number of meanings. To qualify for entry into the "heaven of legal concepts," jurists had to drink water that induced forgetfulness of earthly matters. The most accomplished jurists, however, had no need of this drink, for there was nothing for them to forget.[18] Jhering's heaven of legal concepts was the "transcendental nonsense" divorced from reality that Cohen detected in classical American legal thought.

Happily, Cohen concluded, the dominance of classical legal thought had ended. He cited the Restatement of the Law by the American Law Institute as "the last long-drawn-out gasp of a dying tradition." He granted that some classical jurists had helpfully clarified the logic of legal doctrine, often pointing out inconsistencies. But he was confident that even this useful analysis would be superseded by more creative legal thinkers who would have interests beyond simply "restating" the "dogmas of legal theology." He looked forward to more investigation of the "hidden springs" and "social forces" that influence judges and to greater consideration of statistical methods and social values in legal analysis.[19] These methods, incorporating material previously considered "non-legal,"[20] would contribute to the "functional approach" he contrasted with "transcendental nonsense" in the title of his article.

The ascription of formalism to late nineteenth-century legal thought was reinforced by Morton White's widely read book *Social Thought in America: The Revolt against Formalism*, published in 1949. As his subtitle makes clear, White viewed "the revolt against formalism" as a fundamental characteristic of American social thought across many disciplines.[21] He equated this revolt with "liberal social philosophy" and covered its history from its beginnings in the late nineteenth century to its end in the 1930s.[22] Illustrating the lingering influence of Holmes's distinction in *The Common Law* between logic and experience, White identified Holmes, along with the philosopher John Dewey and the economist Thorstein Veblen, as "the leaders of a campaign to mop up the remnants of formal logic, classical economics and jurisprudence in America,

---

[17] Id. at 844–5.

[18] Id. at 809.

[19] Id. at 833 and n. 68.

[20] Id. at 834.

[21] Morton White, Social Thought in America: The Revolt against Formalism (New York, Oxford University Press, 1976) (paperback ed.), pp. 11–12.

[22] Id. at 4, 10.

and to emphasize that the life of science, economics, and law was not logic but experience in some streaming social sense."[23] White acknowledged difficulty in defining formalism, which had somewhat different meanings in different fields. Yet he found "a strong family resemblance" among anti-formalists, and he used this resemblance to define formalism by contrast. Creating a somewhat strained variant of Marx's famous conclusion to *The Communist Manifesto*, White declared that the anti-formalists "called upon social scientists in all domains, asked them to unite, and urged that they had nothing to lose but their deductive chains."[24] He identified Holmes as the oldest of the "anti-formalist revolutionaries" and called *The Common Law* the first "mature and clear statement" of its position.[25] In discussing *The Common Law*, White emphasized Holmes's "conviction that deductive logic did not suffice."[26]

Beginning with his pioneering manuscript, *The Rise & Fall of Classical Legal Thought*, written in the 1970s, Duncan Kennedy has generated substantial reconsideration of late nineteenth-century American legal thought, including its relationship to deductive formalism. In great contrast to Pound and the legal realists, Kennedy treated its contents at length and with respect. Kennedy agreed with Pound and the legal realists that deductive formalism was its preferred mode of reasoning. But he challenged their view that deductive formalism was its defining characteristic. Indeed, Kennedy indicated that virtually all legal thought contained elements of deductive formalism. He rejected "the conception of 'formalism' as an aberrational interlude" between the alleged "instrumentalism" that otherwise characterized American legal thought before the Civil War and after 1937.[27] By labeling late nineteenth-century American legal thought as "classical," he self-consciously differentiated himself from the many twentieth-century scholars who had equated it distinctively with deductive "formalism."

Especially for such an influential work, Kennedy's manuscript has had an extremely odd history. Completed in 1975 and widely circulated and read among legal scholars, it was not published until 1998, and then by an obscure publisher, AFAR. Its first chapter, however, was published as an article in 1980, with the imposing title "Toward an Historical Understanding of Legal Consciousness: The Case of Classical Legal Thought in America, 1850–1940."[28] In 2006, Beard Books republished the book with a fascinating preface by Kennedy, who reflected on "the ideas in the manuscript that seem to me still of interest, the context for the writing of it, and its fate."[29] Kennedy's position on the relationship between deductive formalism and classical legal thought,

---

[23] Id. at 11–12, citing Holmes at 13.

[24] Id. at 12.

[25] Id. at 15.

[26] Id. at 16.

[27] Kennedy, supra note 1, at 3.

[28] Duncan Kennedy, Toward an Historical Understanding of Legal Consciousness: The Case of Classical Legal Thought in America, 1850–1940, 3 Research in Law and Sociology 3 (1980).

[29] D. Kennedy, supra note 1, at ix.

though addressed in his original manuscript, comes through most clearly in his recent preface.

In his original manuscript, Kennedy introduced the concepts of "operativeness" and "the blocking level" in analyzing legal thought. Operativeness provides that "a number of more concrete subrules are somehow implicit in a legal principle or concept." The blocking level demarcates "the level beyond which concepts are inoperative." Above the blocking level, "appeals to morality or natural rights or utility" are appropriate.[30] Below the blocking level, "judges could draw the line in particular cases by deductively elaborating the general principles into specific subrules."[31] Simply put, deductive formalism is operative below the blocking level but not above it.

Classical legal thought, Kennedy maintained, substantially raised the blocking level from its preclassical position. It thereby dramatically increased the "potency of the method of deduction based on abstract operative concepts."[32] Within the huge area below the blocking level, moreover, classical legal thought largely assimilated law "to a single subsystem dominated by the concept of a power absolute within its judicially delineated sphere."[33] According to Kennedy, classical legal thought integrated into a single structure the four qualitatively distinct legal relationships that had arisen before the Civil War, which he described as "private citizen to private citizen, private citizen to state, legislature to judiciary, and federal government to state government." Before the Civil War, different analytic principles governed each of these legal relationships. The common law governed the relationship between private citizens, "sovereignty limited by written constitutions" governed the relationship between the private citizen and the state, "the equilibrium of forces between separate governmental powers" governed the relationship between the legislature and the judiciary, and "the union of sovereign states" governed the relationship between the federal and state governments.[34]

In classical legal thought, by contrast, each of these distinctive relationships became an example of a new unifying principle, "the delegation of legal powers absolute within their spheres." The absolute power of the judiciary was to police the boundaries between the other spheres.[35] Once its sphere had been delineated by the courts, each of the other participants in the four relationships from before the Civil War could act without legal constraints.[36] "The striking characteristic of Classical rights," Kennedy asserted, "is that they referred not to the maintenance of a body of pre-existing legal rules, but to areas of autonomy within which the individual was free of rules."[37]

[30] Id. at 247–8.
[31] Id. at 103.
[32] Id. at 249; see also id. at 25.
[33] Id. at 25.
[34] Id. at 2.
[35] Id. at 3.
[36] Id. at 25, 41.
[37] Id. at 87.

Kennedy used the term "the will theory" to describe how judges applied the new unifying principle of absolute power within separate spheres. After choosing whose will was absolute among those contending for judicial approval, the judge must enforce that actor's will by interpreting it and applying it in a particular case. The actor whose will the judge chooses to enforce can be a private individual, a state legislature, or the Congress.[38] As the neutral agent of the chosen actor, the judge does not independently evaluate the substantive merits of a legal dispute[39] or consult his personal moral views.[40] The judge, therefore, differs from the other actors in the legal system by being the only one who does not exercise will but instead carries out the will of others. This "impersonal, neutral character of the judicial function," Kennedy stressed, "was what differentiated it from the legislative, and what justified the enormous power of judges in an otherwise democratic political system." [41]

The systematic ordering and formal deduction that Kennedy, like his predecessors, found in late nineteenth-century legal analysis were, distinctively for Kennedy, the way in which judges performed their unique functions in Kennedy's own highly original structural interpretation of what he called "classical legal thought." Systematic ordering and formal deduction allowed a judge, objectively and with very limited interpretive discretion,[42] to police the boundaries among other legal actors and to enforce the will of the actor chosen by the judge. "Judges could define the limits of everyone else's powers/rights, without usurping sovereignty, because those limits were always implicit in the general principles they merely interpreted and applied."[43]

In the preface written for the 2006 edition of *The Rise & Fall of Classical Legal Thought*, Kennedy was more explicit than in his original manuscript about the relationship between deductive formalism and classical legal thought. Describing his innovative analysis of deduction as "phenomenological," Kennedy convincingly asserted that it jettisoned the approach to legal "formalism" that had pervaded interpretations of late nineteenth-century American legal thought since Pound. He reiterated his concept of the blocking level, below which deduction operates but above which concepts are merely "indicators" or simply "convenient labels for items without intrinsic logical connection." He asserted that the "blocking level can vary over time within a given discourse, so that one period's 'deduction' is another period's 'abuse of deduction' or 'formalism.'" This analysis, he emphasized, "turns 'formalism' into a relative term." In the traditional twentieth-century view, stated in its most extreme form by Felix Cohen, the concepts of legal formalism lacked any meaning. For Kennedy, by contrast, "all systems are deductive but they vary in the level of

---

[38] Id. at 242.
[39] Id. at 105–7.
[40] Id. at 254.
[41] Id. at 253.
[42] Id. at 107; see id. at 242.
[43] Id. at 255.

abstraction at which deduction is experienced as convincing."[44] Underlining his innovative approach, Kennedy maintained that the goal of his book was to "decenter" both Langdell, portrayed by many twentieth-century commentators as the leading example of late nineteenth-century American legal thought, and, more generally, ""the whole issue of formalism as a supposed jurisprudential theory."[45]

While Kennedy has continued to identify the role of deduction in classical legal thought,[46] he has recently maintained that the "classics were as various in their actual practices as we are in ours." Within the shared legal consciousness that was classical legal thought, individuals displayed the full spectrum of "competing jurisprudential theories" and "conflicting ideological orientations." In particular, he observed that classical legal thinkers only sometimes resolved questions by deduction. At other times, they "acknowledged gaps, conflicts, or ambiguities" that precluded deduction and looked instead to policy, equity, history, philosophy, or economics. According to Kennedy, "what defined classicism was the possibility that difficulty might yield to precedent and principle, rather than anything like formalism."[47] In another passage, he similarly divorced classical legal thought from deductive formalism. He observed that some people endorsed the "will theory," which for Kennedy was a foundation of classical legal thought, without also believing that it had to be applied deductively. "What made you a will theorist was that you saw will as the 'governing principle,' even if it was tricky and nondeductive to apply it, and you sometimes had to compromise it with other factors."[48]

Throughout his work on classical legal thought, Kennedy emphasized the irony that its impressive structure ultimately failed. The ambitious attempt of classical legal thinkers to create a comprehensive and coherent conceptual system that would address problems their predecessors "had preferred to duck"[49] ended up by undermining confidence that reason could ever explain law.[50] Kennedy's most extended account of this process, toward the end of *Rise & Fall*, highlights the role of deductive formalism and merits extended quotation. In classical legal thought, Kennedy emphasized, "the judge had no choice but to abandon appeals to right, morality, utility or practicality where they conflicted with the results of deduction."[51] Yet "the increasing potency of the method of deduction based on abstract operative concepts" proved "disruptive."[52]

[44] Id. at xxxiii.

[45] Id. at xxxiv.

[46] Duncan Kennedy, The Disenchantment of Logically Formal Legal Rationality, 55 Hastings L.J. 1032, 1033 (2004).

[47] Duncan Kennedy, From the Will Theory to the Principle of Private Autonomy: Lon Fuller's "Consideration and Form," 100 Colum. L. Rev. 94, 107 n. 33 (2000).

[48] Id. at 118–19 n. 76.

[49] Kennedy, supra note 1, at 264.

[50] Duncan Kennedy, Legal Formalism, 13 International Encyclopedia of the Social & Behavioral Sciences 8634, 8637 (Neil J. Smelser and Paul B. Baltes eds. 2001).

[51] Kennedy, supra note 1, at 250.

[52] Id. at 249.

The irony was that the very success of the enterprise of subsuming all legal relationships under a single small set of concepts eventually destroyed belief that it was the concepts themselves that determined the outcomes of their application. When the abstractions had performed their task of integrating legal thought, it became apparent that while pre-Classical particularity had been irrational, the new unity was merely linguistic – a verbal trick – rather than a substantive reconstruction. We came gradually to see that there were an infinity of possible results that might all plausibly find expression in the new conceptual language, and, what was worse, might all claim to be derivations of the abstract governing principles. The concepts, then, could be nothing more than a vocabulary for categorizing, describing and comparing, rather than the elements in a method for deriving outcomes. The famous principles, taken together, appeared either self-contradictory or so vague as to be worthless as guides to particular decisions.[53]

This passage connects Kennedy's impressive account of classical legal thought to his leadership of the critical legal studies movement. If even the heroic efforts of the classical legal theorists could not provide a rational method of legal analysis, the role of reason itself becomes suspect, and the line between law and politics is blurred.

Since Kennedy wrote *The Rise & Fall of Classical Legal Thought*, and probably provoked to a significant extent by it, many scholars have explored late nineteenth-century American legal thought in substantial detail while continuing to stress its reliance on deductive formalism.[54] Like Kennedy, but unlike Pound and the legal realists, these scholars treated the ideas of their nineteenth-century predecessors with respect. Some of them specifically condemned the unfair dismissal of the nineteenth-century thinkers by twentieth-century critics. The "very persistence and intensity of the polemical assault on classical orthodoxy," Thomas Grey astutely observed, indicated that "it was a powerful and appealing legal theory, not the feeble dogma portrayed in the critics' parodies."[55] Stephen Siegel similarly rejected both "the realists' caricature of classicism"[56] and twentieth-century scholars who treated late nineteenth-century constitutional thought not simply as mistaken, but as based on premises that could not have been taken seriously even by those who claimed to accept them.[57]

Morton Horwitz and Robert Gordon have reiterated the importance of deduction in late nineteenth-century legal thought while endorsing key themes of Kennedy's innovative analysis. Horwitz, who has acknowledged Kennedy's substantial influence on his own analysis of classical legal thought,[58] echoed Kennedy by referring to "the creation of increasingly abstract and general

---

[53] Id. at 250–1.
[54] Many others, including those in whose work Kennedy himself takes great pride, have applied his critical theoretical and structural approach without revisiting the classical legal scholars themselves. Id. at xlii (citing subsequent scholarship).
[55] Thomas C. Grey, Langdell's Orthodoxy, 45 U. Pitt. L. Rev. 1, 5 (1983).
[56] Stephen A. Siegel, John Chipman Gray and the Moral Basis of Classical Legal Thought, 86 Iowa L. Rev. 1513, 1517 (2001).
[57] Siegel, supra note 2, at 1543.
[58] Horwitz, supra note 4, at 273.

classifications,"[59] "the structure of legal reasoning,"[60] and "the categorical mind."[61] Like Kennedy, Horwitz stressed that late nineteenth-century legal thought self-confidently relied on "deduction from general principles and analogies among cases" as part of its aspiration to achieve "certainty and logical inexorability."[62] And like Kennedy, Horwitz concluded that classical legal thought ultimately exposed contradictions in legal reasoning it hoped to contain.[63] Its "compartmentalizing mechanisms" became "stretched to the breaking point," prompting legal thinkers to search for new ways of understanding law.[64]

Also echoing Kennedy, Robert Gordon claimed that late nineteenth-century American legal thought defined boundaries among zones of legal autonomy in which individuals could act freely but also specified the legal consequences of violating those boundaries if one acted in another's zone.[65] Legal science helped judges determine these consequences by demonstrating "how all of the subrules of the law could be derived from the core principles by deduction."[66] Eventually, however, "the aim of formal realizability through the deductive process of neutral adjudication appeared increasingly silly and unjust in the attempt to practice it." The goals of abstraction and generality that initially seemed so attractive in late nineteenth-century legal thought became its greatest weaknesses.[67] Although they reinforced Kennedy's "narrative of conceptual construction and disintegration," Horwitz and Gordon did not join his attempt to direct attention away from deductive formalism in analyzing late nineteenth-century American legal thought.[68]

In developing his distinctive analysis of late nineteenth-century American legal thought as "classical orthodoxy," Thomas Grey provided another angle of inquiry into the role of deduction. Whereas Kennedy wanted to "decenter" Langdell,[69] Grey focused on him, entitling his article "Langdell's Orthodoxy." At its heart, Grey observed, classical orthodoxy insisted that law is a science.[70] "The core notion of classical legal science," he maintained, "can be grasped through the analogy to geometry, as that subject was understood in the late nineteenth century,"[71] a structure of "induction of axioms, deduction of

[59] Id. at 11.
[60] Id. at 16.
[61] Id. at 17.
[62] Id. at 16.
[63] Id. at 15
[64] Id. at 19.
[65] Robert W. Gordon, Legal Thought and Legal Practice in the Age of American Enterprise 1870–1920, in Professions and Professional Ideologies in American (University of North Carolina Press, 1983) (G. Geison ed.), pp. 70, 88.
[66] Id. at 89.
[67] Id. at 94.
[68] See Kennedy, supra note 1, at xxxiv.
[69] Id. at xxxiv.
[70] Grey, supra note 55, at 5.
[71] Id. at 16.

theorems." In the legal context, a relatively small number of inductively derived general principles, typically but not always induced from previously decided cases, became the basis for deducing a much larger number of rules. These rules, in turn, determined the results of future cases.[72] Grey provided somewhat more detail than others who ascribed deductive formalism to the late nineteenth-century scholars. Langdell derived his rule that an acceptance by mail can only be effective upon receipt, Grey observed, from his general principle of consideration. Starting with the "top-level" principle that a contract can only be formed through a "consideration," either a promise or performance bargained by the parties, Langdell reasoned that a promise must be communicated to its promisee and that a communication by letter is only accomplished when the letter is received and read.[73] In the increasingly complex and disruptive American society following the Civil War, Grey surmised, "the dry geometry of classical legal orthodoxy had a certain paradoxical quasi-religious appeal to the educated elite." At a time when traditional religion no longer provided meaning and order for many, the principles and certainties of legal science took its place.[74] Like Pound, Grey claimed that the American Langdellians and the German Pandectists had similar commitments to deductive formalism, though he noted that the Langdellians achieved "a more nearly autonomous system" by not following the Pandectists' efforts to ground their jurisprudence in broader philosophical justifications.[75]

Particularly in a long article about Holmes, Grey differentiated the deductive formalism of classical orthodoxy from a broader theory of "conceptualism." He defined conceptualism as the view that law should be coherently ordered into abstract concepts. Formalists such as Langdell additionally believed that these concepts, once induced from prior cases, constitute axiomatic general truths, and that a deductive system of formal reasoning can apply them to decide new cases. According to Grey, conceptualism was virtually universal among Anglo-American legal scholars during the "classical period" between roughly 1870 and 1920, whereas legal formalism was not. Holmes and Pound, he pointed out, were conceptualists who criticized Langdellian formalism.[76] In contrast to Langdell, "Holmes did not believe that doctrinal conceptualization could produce a deductive system that would make legal reasoning formal and scientific."[77] Grey filled out the membership in these two intellectual camps by including Thayer, Wigmore, and Gray as conceptualists who rejected deductive formalism, and Beale, Ames, and Williston as Langdellian formalists, although Grey noted some differences among them regarding the

---

[72] Id. at 19.

[73] Id. at 12.

[74] Id. at 36.

[75] Thomas C. Grey, Judicial Review and Legal Pragmatism, 38 Wake Forest L. Rev. 473, 491, 496, 498 n. 10 (2003).

[76] Grey, supra note 55, at 49 n. 177; Thomas C. Grey, Holmes and Legal Pragmatism, 41 Stan. L. Rev. 787, 816, 819, 822–5 (1989).

[77] Grey, supra note 76, at 816.

extent of their insistence on objectivity and formality.[78] He asserted that the legal realists who later dismissed conceptualism as well as formalism wrongly conflated them, adding that scholars since the realists have similarly assumed that conceptualism entails formalism. This conflation, Grey sadly observed, has confused analysis of late nineteenth-century legal thought, obscuring the ways in which major figures like Langdell and Holmes agreed as well as differed.[79] Yet Grey introduced some unfortunate confusion of his own by using the word "classical" and even the phrase "classical legal science" to apply both to the general period of legal thought between 1870 and 1920 and to the particular type of legal thought that was the formal "classical orthodoxy" of Langdell and his followers.

Recent revisionist scholarship on Langdell[80] has emphasized the inductive aspects of his thought, minimizing or sometimes denying entirely the dominant conception of him as the exemplar of deductive formalism. Langdell's conception of legal science, revisionists have observed, typified late nineteenth-century views of science generally, replicating the focus on induction from empirical evidence and on the evolution of organic principles.[81] Whereas traditional scholarship on Langdell often stressed the mathematical or geometric structure of his legal thought, the revisionists detected a much closer analogy to experimental biology.[82]

Revisionist scholars agreed with the conventional view that Langdell and his colleagues tried to create from the principles they induced an autonomous legal structure composed of logical and orderly classifications.[83] They also agreed that Langdell and his colleagues selected only a very few cases for detailed treatment, considering the vast majority unsuitable for logical analysis and using those they did select to demonstrate the evolution of a legal principle.[84] Their revisionism consisted in emphasizing the inductive basis for this system. The conventional view, by contrast, emphasized the deductive aspects of Langdell's thought even when acknowledging inductive elements. Some revisionists denied that Langdell's thought contained any deductive aspects at all.[85] Without going quite this far, G. Edward White suggested a division of responsibility in the

---

[78] Grey, supra note 55, at 11–12 n. 36; Grey, supra note 75, at 501; Grey, supra note 76, at 825.

[79] Grey, supra note 76, at 823–4.

[80] See generally Bruce A. Kimball, The Langdell Problem: Historicizing the Century of Historiography, 22 L. & Hist. Rev. 277 (2004).

[81] Marcia Speziale, Langdell's Concept of Law as Science: The Beginning of Anti-Formalism in American Legal Theory, 5 Vermont L. Rev. 1, 2, 13, 29; G. Edward White, The Impact of Legal Science on Tort Law, 78 Colum. L. Rev. 213, 217–18, 229.

[82] Anthony J. Sebok, Legal Positivism in American Jurisprudence (Cambridge University Press, 1998), pp. 92–3, 96 (1998); Speziale, supra note 81, at 20–5; Mathias W. Reimann, Holmes's *Common Law* and German Legal Science, in The Legacy of Oliver Wendell Holmes, Jr. (Stanford, Calif.: Stanford University Press, 1992) (R. Gordon ed.), pp. 72, 108.

[83] A. Sebok, supra note 82, at 106; Speziale, supra note 81, at 34, 37; White, supra note 81, at 228.

[84] White, supra note 81, at 226, 228; see Reimann, supra note 82, at 108.

[85] A. Sebok, supra note 82, at 91, 101; Speziale, supra note 81, at 20, 35.

late nineteenth century between legal scholars, who focused on the inductive extraction of principles from past cases, and judges, who applied these principles to new cases without paying much attention to their sources.[86] The revisionist description of Langdell and his colleagues resembles the conceptualism that Grey differentiated from the deductive formalism he attributed to them.

Political Conservatism

Just as scholars since Pound have overwhelmingly reinforced his identification of deductive formalism with late nineteenth-century American legal thought, they have also largely followed his conclusions about the relationship between deductive formalism and political conservatism. Like Pound, they rejected widespread claims that late nineteenth-century legal thinkers formed a conscious alliance or conspiracy with conservative business interests, the view that Pound associated with "legal muckrakers" in his own time and that his successors often described as liberal or progressive historiography. Yet they agreed with Pound that the intellectual content of late nineteenth-century American legal thought, including its focus on deductive formalism, had conservative political effects.

The doctrines available to the "Formal Style" in the late nineteenth century, Llewellyn maintained, were "afflicted" with "preindustrial concepts" that lagged substantially behind rapidly changing conditions, prompting courts to invalidate statutes that could have reformed the law. Far from portraying an evil alliance between judges and conservative interests, Llewellyn indicated that the "Formal Style" prevented judges who wanted legal change from implementing it. He asserted that "the urge for felt right which no judge of conscience can ever wholly escape tended more and more into clash with prevailing doctrine and with the death's-head duties of the prevailing pattern of judicial ideal." Llewellyn acknowledged that widespread opposition to prevailing legal decisions had produced a "public revolt," which resulted in many new state court judges who replaced those "whose feeling for justice had merged in peace with obsolete and otherwise unhappy doctrine." Yet even these new judges, "whatever their political or social or economic outlook," had been socialized into the "Formal Style." Some of these judges "wanted to go right, and did not know how to." Others "though felt justice cried loud, could yet deafen their ears as they remembered duty to 'the law.'" They frequently proceeded with "almost random irregularity" and with "devastating" effects to ignore existing law "by way of bad logic, or by distortion of authority or fact, or by main strength."[87] By happy contrast, Llewellyn observed, judges in the middle of the twentieth century had largely abandoned the "Formal Style" and had become primarily interested "in getting the case decided *right* – within the authorities," though

---

[86] White, supra note 81, at 234–5.
[87] Llewellyn, supra note 5, at 40.

he acknowledged that they sometimes paid too little attention to the continuity of legal doctrine.[88]

Without alleging a conscious alliance between judges and political conservatism, Cohen presumed a consensus that American courts are "a generally conservative social force, and more like a brake than a motor in the social mechanism." He asserted as uncontroversial general knowledge that dominant economic forces influence judicial analysis, that judges reflect the attitudes of their class on social questions, and that many judges had previously served as counsel for "special interests," thereby shaping the law in ways desired by those who could pay most. Yet he asserted as equally uncontroversial general knowledge that judges are "craftsmen, with aesthetic ideals," who want their theories and decisions to satisfy the professional standards of practicing lawyers and law professors. Following his interest in the "hidden springs" and "social forces" behind legal decisions,[89] Cohen urged more "scientific" study of these various influences on judges beyond the mere "guesswork" of the past.[90] Unlike Llewellyn, Cohen did not maintain that deductive formalism had produced conservative results. But he did indicate that his own vision of legal science was necessarily political. Claiming that most "realists" generally denied the importance of values or maintained that facts must be gathered before they are evaluated, Cohen asserted instead that "a critical theory of social values" must be combined with "objective legal science."[91]

Kennedy began *The Rise & Fall of Classical Legal Thought* by denying what he described as "an article of faith" in "liberal historiography" from the late nineteenth century through the New Deal of the 1930s. Liberal historiography, he maintained, portrayed legal outcomes during this period as the result of an alliance between the conservative legal profession and "a class of despoiling entrepreneurs and politicians against the working class, the farmers, and the 'public interest.'"[92] In contrast to this crude reductionism, Kennedy insisted on recognizing the "relative autonomy of legal consciousness" as part of "larger structures of social thought and action." He did not deny that economic interest and political power affected legal results, as did the general ideology of laissez faire. But he emphasized what he believed liberal historiography ignored, that "legal consciousness, which has its own structure, mediates their influence on particular results."[93] Kennedy's long manuscript was his interpretation of the structure of the consciousness that was "classical legal thought." He did not, however, get to the relationship between classical legal thought and the "larger structures of social thought and action" in the late nineteenth century, the "external dialectic" that would supplement the "internal dialectic"

[88] Id. at 41.
[89] See supra text accompanying note 19.
[90] Cohen, supra note 10, at 845.
[91] Id. at 848–9.
[92] Kennedy, supra note 1, at 1.
[93] Id. at 2.

of classical legal thought itself. The "second part" of the book promised in his 1975 manuscript[94] was not written.

Throughout his book, Kennedy rejected political explanations of classical legal thought. He pointed out, for example, that the crucial "will theory" did not entail either laissez-faire economics or individualism, evils liberal historiography claimed to expose in classical legal thought. Because a judge applying the will theory could choose to enforce the will of the legislature or the will of a private citizen, it was a theory of statutory interpretation as well as a way to enforce private rights.[95] The emphasis by American classical theorists on objectivism in contract law, Kennedy asserted in a later article, had more to do with Anglo-American historical identity than any "mundane" political interest in the emerging definition of liberty of contract under the Fourteenth Amendment.[96]

Kennedy's treatment of the Supreme Court's decision in *Lochner*, often cited as the most prominent example of the conservative manipulation of legal reasoning to invalidate reform legislation, reveals how far he distanced himself from "liberal historiography." Rather than attribute conservative motives to the majority's holding that legislation limiting maximum working hours violated the due process clause of the Fourteenth Amendment, Kennedy used *Lochner* to illustrate some of his structural claims about classical legal thought. He portrayed the majority decision by Justice Peckham and the dissenting opinion by Justice Harlan as a disagreement within the shared rubric of classical legal thought rather than as a more fundamental divide. Both Peckham and Harlan, Kennedy observed, believed that judges had to engage in the objective and limited task of classifying the boundary between the powers of the state and the rights of individuals. They both believed, moreover, that the state's "police power" could not be recognized unless it were exercised in a "reasonable" way. They disagreed only about whether the legislation was reasonable and about whether the state had the burden of proving its reasonableness. Kennedy concluded that these disagreements were minor compared to the underlying "legal consciousness" that they shared.[97] Harlan's citation of *McCulloch v. Maryland* to support his view that the burden of proof rests with those who challenge the validity of a statute, Kennedy added, underlined his immersion in classical legal thought. *McCulloch* drew a boundary between state and federal power. Kennedy maintained that in 1819, when Chief Justice Marshall wrote *McCulloch*, it would have been "bizarre" to cite it in a case, like *Lochner*, involving the boundary between individual rights and state power. Yet Harlan "very Classically assumes that the concept of a power is essentially the same in the two systems," namely, relationships between the state and federal governments, and relationships between the private citizen and the state.[98]

---

[94] Id. at 253.
[95] Id. at 105–6.
[96] Kennedy, supra note 47, at 142 n. 155.
[97] Kennedy, supra note 1, at 9–15.
[98] Id. at 16.

In his discussion of *Lochner*, Kennedy conceded that the structural similarities between Peckham's majority opinion and Harlan's dissent might have been "a kind of compulsory curtsy to the audience before the 'real' battle, which is over whether the judiciary should favor capital or labor in the struggle for social justice."[99] Liberal historiography often viewed *Lochner* as precisely such a battle, but Kennedy's emphasis on the shared legal consciousness of Peckham and Harlan and his more general attention to the relative autonomy of legal consciousness indicated that he disagreed. He mentioned but tellingly did not endorse the "modern legal consciousness" of *Lochner* as "a horrible reminder of the bad consequences of Supreme Court justices letting their 'subjective' and 'political' passions draw them into a kind of judicial review that is both anti-democratic and institutionally suicidal."[100]

Kennedy, moreover, treated debates over codification as contained within the fundamental assumptions of classical legal thought, whereas liberal historiography portrayed them as a battle between conservatives who opposed codification and progressives who supported it. Under this "liberal" view, codification was a movement for reform legislation that would trump the undemocratic judicial enforcement of economic power under the pretense of legal logic.[101] Kennedy observed, by contrast, that both opponents and proponents of codification shared the classical consensus that the legislature and the judiciary had radically different roles and that each had absolute power within its respective sphere. Proponents of codification of private law sought to promote the classical goals of simplicity and clarity in the legal system out of the morass of judicial decisions. Opponents of codification nevertheless recognized occasions when it was necessary to undo the occasional mistakes of judges in applying the classical system or when rapid changes made legislative modifications of existing rules desirable.[102]

Gordon joined in dismissing the fading though "probably still dominant" view of "Progressive historians" that legal formalism "functioned simply as a smoke screen" or a "weapon" for "factional, class, or occupational interest."[103] Such an "instrumental" approach, he agreed, failed to take seriously the internal contents of law.[104] In his pioneering revisionist study of laissez-faire constitutionalism, Siegel emphasized that late nineteenth-century understandings

---

[99] Id. at 15.

[100] Id. at 9.

[101] See, e.g., Horwitz, supra note 4, at 117–19, 221; Clyde E. Jacobs, Law Writers and the Courts: The Influence of Thomas M. Cooley, Christopher G. Tiedeman and John F. Dillon Upon American Constitutional Law (University of California Press, 1954), p. 12; Mathias Reimann, The Historical School Against Codification: Savigny, Carter, and the Defeat of the New York Civil Code, 37 Am. J. Comp. L. 95, 114–19 (1989). But see Lewis A. Grossman, James Coolidge Carter and Mugwump Jurisprudence, 20 L. & Hist. Rev. 577, 588–90 (2002) (discussing contemporary views that the codification movement in New York after the Civil War favored the interests of railroads and other corporations).

[102] Kennedy, supra note 1, at 254–5.

[103] Gordon, supra note 65, at 71, 92.

[104] Id. at 71.

of history, rather than the social and economic views falsely attributed by the progressives, were its primary source.[105] And Grey claimed that the scholars he grouped within "classical orthodoxy" largely ignored public law, where the most politically charged legal issues typically arose. They believed that public law, unlike private law, was not amenable to the "scientific" analysis they advocated.[106] Indeed, Grey added, they agreed, though often reluctantly, that in a democracy the legislative majority has the power to pursue political and policy objectives that are "too vague for legal-scientific definition."[107]

Limiting classical legal science to private law gave Grey a unique vantage from which to join the consensus among legal scholars against progressive historiography, which associated classical legal thought with political conservatism and big business. The progressives and their later twentieth-century successors, Grey asserted, "successfully convinced themselves, and other American jurists generally, that a critique developed to undermine Langdellian private-law theory, first given influential statement by Holmes in a few quotable paragraphs of *The Common Law*, applied as well to laissez-faire constitutionalism."[108] Yet Grey pointed out that when lawyers in the 1880s started criticizing conservative judges for invalidating laws that protected labor and regulated business, they did not connect this criticism with the formalism and conceptualism that characterized classical legal thought about private law.[109] Holmes, Grey added, did not address issues of public law in his review of Langdell or in *The Common Law*. Grey conceded that Holmes, from his earliest legal writing in the 1870s, praised judicial deference to legislation dealing with "political economy." Grey stressed, however, that Holmes in no way linked his opposition to aggressive judicial review with his criticism of the deductive formalism of Langdell and the Germans in areas of private law.[110] The ascription and critique of the link between classical legal thought and the judicial activism of laissez-faire constitutionalism, Grey maintained, originated with Holmes's 1897 essay "The Path of the Law." As elaborated by Pound in the early twentieth century and reinforced by the legal realists, this mistaken view persisted throughout the twentieth century as part of an attempt, conscious or not, to undermine both Langdell and *Lochner*.[111]

Among the major twentieth-century successors to Pound, Horwitz exhibited most sympathy to progressive historiography. Horwitz wrote about late nineteenth-century legal thought in both of his volumes entitled *The Transformation of American Law*, one of the major accomplishments of American legal scholarship in the twentieth century. Even though published in 1977, Horwitz's discussion of "the rise of legal formalism" in his first

---

[105] Siegel, supra note 2, at 1436, 1445, 1542-3.
[106] Grey, supra note 55, at 33-4.
[107] Id. at 35.
[108] Grey, supra note 75, at 507.
[109] Id. at 494.
[110] Id. at 492-3.
[111] Id. at 494-6, 507.

volume reads very much like a version of the "liberal historiography" Kennedy ascribed to the period between the late nineteenth century and the New Deal of the 1930s. More than any of the earlier legal scholars who had studied late nineteenth-century American legal thought, Horwitz connected legal formalism with economic interests. In the seventy or eighty years following the American Revolution, Horwitz claimed, the American legal system changed from one based on protection, regulation, paternalism, and community morality to one that encouraged economic development. During this period, law "actively promoted a legal redistribution of wealth against the weakest groups in the society," such as farmers, workers, and consumers, and established doctrines that "maintained the new distribution of economic and political power."[112]

Horwitz correlated the rise of legal formalism with this new distribution of power. As the American legal and economic system was being transformed, law had to be flexible and instrumental. But once this transformation had occurred, its major beneficiaries were threatened by the same flexible and instrumental conception of law they once needed. Having achieved their objectives, they were better off if they could hide the extent to which they had been helped by many innovative laws driven by policies they favored. "There were, in short, major advantages in creating an intellectual system which gave common law rules the appearance of being self-contained, apolitical, and inexorable." Quoting Holmes and Llewellyn, Horwitz added that this system, "by making 'legal reasoning seem like mathematics,' conveyed 'an air ... of ... inevitability' about legal decisions."[113] Yet Holmes and Llewellyn, unlike Horwitz, did not connect this intellectual system to economic interests, and Llewellyn stressed that judges followed the "formal" style "whatever their political or economic or social outlook."[114]

Legal formalism, Horwitz pointed out, arose within the legal profession before it became aligned with broader economic interests. He asserted that the codification movement of the 1820s and 1830s, which attempted to transform substantive law by codifying it,[115] put both law and the legal profession on the defensive by asserting that they were essentially political. In response, "orthodox legal thought began to retreat from self-conscious policy-making goals, emphasizing more and more the apolitical, deductive, and 'scientific' character of legal reasoning." Yet this formal approach, while soon reflected in legal treatises, did not at first gain broader support because emerging commercial, mercantile, and entrepreneurial interests still needed legal change. By the 1840s, however, these interests were sufficiently established to encourage an alliance with legal formalism. Freezing legal doctrine in "a fixed and inexorable system of logically deducible rules" would minimize the likelihood of

---

[112] Morton J. Horwitz, The Transformation of American Law 1780–1860 (Cambridge, Mass.: Harvard University Press, 1977), pp. 253–4.

[113] Id.

[114] See supra text accompanying note 87 (quoting Llewellyn).

[115] Id. at 265.

additional redistributions of wealth that might threaten their own recent gains. This alliance, Horwitz added, protected the autonomy and augmented the prestige of lawyers.[116]

In his second volume, Horwitz acknowledged Kennedy's substantial intervening influence on his own analysis of the history of American law.[117] Yet Horwitz did not lose sight of the link between legal thought and economic conflicts that pervaded his first volume and that was largely absent from Kennedy's analysis of classical legal thought.[118] After stating in his preface that he would give greater power to "cultural factors" than in his first volume, Horwitz added that he would "continue to insist that the development of the law cannot be understood independently of social context."[119] Even as he emphasized the autonomous structure of classical legal thought, he situated it in the general "search for order" in the wake of the trauma of the Civil War and the "social conflict produced by immigration, urbanization, and industrialization."[120] Unlike Kennedy, Horwitz ascribed malevolent intent to classical legal thinkers. Their distinction between public and private law, he maintained, was an important part of "the effort to create a private realm immune to the dangers of redistribution." Rendering public law neutral by deriving its doctrines from private law was for Horwitz more than a by-product of the classical system. He declared that it was the "aspiration" of classical thinkers "to depoliticize public law" in this way.[121]

In his treatment of the debate over codification, Horwitz revealed in greatest detail his continued emphasis on the alliance between legal thought and the economic interests of the rich. Highlighting the importance of this debate, Horwitz declared it "the functional equivalent of late nineteenth-century jurisprudence," before jurisprudence itself emerged as a specialized field of study in the early twentieth century.[122] No other topic, he maintained, generated as much attention from legal scholars.[123] Whereas Kennedy viewed the codification debate as internal to classical legal thought,[124] Horwitz saw it as a conflict between democratic reform and conservative reaction led by classical legal thinkers. Horwitz depicted the codification movement as an attack on the regressive common law. Succeeding in the late nineteenth century where its predecessor in the Jacksonian era failed, it produced major reforms through

---

[116] Id. at 258–9.

[117] Horwitz, supra note 4, at 273.

[118] Kennedy himself has observed that in his second volume Horwitz "reformulated the progressive critique." This language is in the 8/27/2000 draft of Kennedy, Legal Formalism, supra note 50, at 12, but does not appear in the published version.

[119] M. Horwitz, supra note 4, at vii.

[120] Id. at 10, citing, id. at 273, Robert W. Wiebe, The Search for Order, 1877–1920 (New York: Hill and Wang, 1967).

[121] Id. at 27.

[122] Id. at 117.

[123] Id. at 118.

[124] See supra text accompanying notes 101–2.

departures from the common law in areas such as the rights of married women, adoption, and the regulation of corporations.[125]

Horwitz identified James Coolidge Carter, vilified earlier by Pound as the exemplar of deductive formalism, as the leading opponent of codification in New York. Horwitz called Carter a member of the "Establishment Bar," whose writings "articulated the jurisprudence of American legal orthodoxy at the end of the nineteenth century." Carter and his allies emphasized the "objective, apolitical, and scientific character of common law adjudication" as the traditional and more attractive alternative to codification. Underlying this intellectual defense of the common law, Horwitz maintained, "was a long-standing fear of legislative intrusion into the distribution of wealth and privilege."[126] Carter "shrewdly sought to reconcile opposition to legislation with the democratic spirit" by insisting that judicial interpretation of "customary law" was more in touch with popular sovereignty than was legislation.[127] For Carter and other "orthodox" legal theorists, custom "legitimated social coercion without having to acknowledge that it was coercive"[128] and became a weapon "to defeat the democratic impulse for legislative supremacy."[129]

Contrary to Horwitz's identification of Carter as the leader of those concerned that codification would redistribute wealth and power, Lewis Grossman has more recently observed that Carter and his allies in the anti-codification movement in New York had the opposite concern. They worried that much of the proposed codification would have supported corporate interests.[130] Drawing on recent historical scholarship about the Mugwump movement, Grossman portrayed Carter as a leading Mugwump reformer rather than as an apologist for conservatism. Grossman described the Mugwumps as genteel, well-educated descendants of old New England families, typically working in business and the professions, especially law. They viewed their moralistic program of reform as an attempt to rescue the political process from its capture by an evil alliance of corrupt politicians and the new corporate plutocrats who had emerged during, and whose behavior defined, the "Gilded Age" in the decades following the Civil War.[131] More broadly, Gordon and Grey have stressed how many late nineteenth-century American legal scholars were Mugwumps, whose politics were moderate.[132] Revisionist historians had already challenged the claim by progressive historiography that laissez-faire constitutionalism, particularly associated with Cooley, developed in alliance with conservative business interests. The revisionists instead highlighted its Jacksonian origins based on

---

[125] Horwitz, supra note 4, at 118.
[126] Id.
[127] Id. at 119–20.
[128] Id. at 122.
[129] Id. at 121.
[130] Grossman, supra note 101, at 588–90.
[131] Id. at 581–2.
[132] Gordon, supra note 65, at 76, 97 ("mildly reformist"); Grey, supra note 55, at 34–35 ("moderately conservative").

principles of individual liberty, equal political rights, and government neutrality. They pointed out that the laissez-faire constitutionalists frequently relied on these principles to oppose business interests.[133]

Just as most twentieth-century scholars, with the prominent and partial exception of Horwitz, joined Pound in dismissing the emphasis in progressive historiography on a conscious alliance between legal theory and political conservatism, they also followed Pound in stressing the conservative effects of late nineteenth-century American legal thought. Like Pound, Llewellyn and Cohen stressed that the deductive formalism of the late nineteenth-century scholars excluded considerations of policy from legal analysis, a position that discouraged judges from adapting the inherited common law to social change.[134] Cohen added that the "circularity of legal reasoning" embedded in classical legal thought reinforced "economic prejudice masquerading in the cloak of legal logic."[135]

Without attributing the malevolent intent Horwitz continued to stress, Kennedy emphasized the conservative effects of the extension of private law doctrines to public law, a phenomenon he associated with the increasing abstraction of legal thought in the late nineteenth century. In elaborating the structure of classical legal thought, Kennedy observed that it extended to public as well as private law.[136] For example, it "conceived the property right as 'the same thing' whether exercised against a neighbor or against the state, and sovereignty as the same thing whether its object was the citizen or another government."[137] The abstractions that composed the classical system, such as property right and sovereignty, transcended any distinction between private and public. They were entities "from which both private and public law rights followed as deductions or implications."[138] In practice, classical legal thought applied the prior common law of contract and property to constitutional interpretation,[139] the point made by Pound before World War I. The legal definition of the individual rights the Fourteenth Amendment guaranteed against the state derived from the rules the common law developed to govern relations among neighbors.[140]

---

[133] See generally Howard Gillman, The Constitution Beseiged: The Rise and demise of Lochner Era Police Powers Jurisprudence (Duke University Press 1993); Michael Les Benedict, Laissez-Faire and Liberty: A Re-Evaluation of the Meaning and Origins of Laissez-Faire Consitutionalism, 3 L. & Hist. Rev. 293 (1985); Alan Jones, Thomas M. Cooley and "Laissez-Faire Constitutionalism": A Reconsideration, 53 J. Am. Hist. 751 (1967); Charles W. McCurdy, Justice Field and the Jurisprudence of Government-Business Relations: Some Parameters of Laissez-Faire Constitutionalism, 1863–1897, 61 J. Am. Hist. 970 (1975).

[134] Llewellyn, supra note 5, at 38–9; Cohen, supra note 10, at 833–4.

[135] Cohen, supra note 10, at 817.

[136] Kennedy, supra note 1, at 242.

[137] Id. at 257.

[138] Id. at 259.

[139] Id. at 260–1.

[140] Id. at 91.

The underlying unity of private and public law under the abstractions of classical legal thought, Kennedy stressed, made adjudication of constitutional cases seem as neutral and apolitical as in cases involving private law. "The process of abstraction made the unquestionable legality of private law available as a structure for public law rights that would otherwise have seemed too dangerously undefined for judicial administration." Abstraction "gave the theorists of the relatively weak public law sector access to the strength of the private law sector."[141] More specifically, by using the common law definition of contract as the basis for interpreting the constitutional meaning of the liberty of contract protected against state action by the Fourteenth Amendment, judicial review of social legislation could be presented more as a technical interpretation of law than as an undemocratic and inappropriate judicial exercise of political ideology.[142]

Gordon agreed that late nineteenth-century legal thought "was sometimes ideologically serviceable to powerful entrepreneurs" because their coercion and domination seemed to disappear as the natural result of "neutral rules of the game."[143] He stressed the harmonious structure of liberal legal science, the key role of deduction in deriving legal subrules from core principles, and the extent to which constitutional interpretation incorporated the presumed neutral principles of the common law.[144] Gordon observed as well that while structures of thought do not "determine" practical outcomes, they do establish the categories of discourse in which "political conflict will be carried out."[145] He urged legal historians to focus on the actual human beings who manufacture, use, and destabilize legal concepts. Following his own advice, in his essay on legal thought and legal practice between 1870 and 1920 he used two activities of corporate lawyers to illustrate how liberal legal science operated in the concrete world of legal practice: drafting state incorporation law and corporate charters, and corporate reorganization.[146] An important part of corporate practice, he maintained, consisted in aggressively pursuing a client's interests within existing legal boundaries while discouraging clients from crossing them. In this way, the liberal practitioner sustained the classical system by keeping its "boundaries in repair from the damage done by his own battering."[147]

From a different perspective, Grey agreed that classical legal scholars, whatever their personal politics or intent, provided ideological support for business interests. Consistent with his limitation of classical orthodoxy to private law, Grey did not identify the migration of common law definitions into laissez-faire constitutional interpretation, the phenomenon that intrigued previous scholars from Pound to Kennedy, Horwitz, and Gordon. Yet Grey did agree that

[141] Id. at 260.
[142] Id. at 261.
[143] Gordon, supra note 65, at 92–3.
[144] Id. at 89, 98, 106.
[145] Id. at 118.
[146] Id. at 100.
[147] Id. at 99.

classical legal thought helped business interests by treating "economic power relations as neutral, scientifically derived private law rights."[148] This help was significant because classical legal scientists placed most of the operation of the market and the system of private property into the category of private law rather than of public law, thereby making key economic issues subject to the legal analysis of classical orthodoxy.[149] Grey doubted, however, that this ideological support had much actual impact on judicial decisions. He observed that from 1870 to 1940 most important politically charged legal issues involved judicial review of reform legislation clearly within the public sphere, to which classical orthodoxy did not apply.[150]

The Role of History

Although they extended Pound's attention to the deductive formalism of late nineteenth-century American legal thought and to its conservative political implications, twentieth-century scholars did not share Pound's focus on the role of history in the system of deductive formalism. Whereas Pound identified historical jurisprudence as the dominant jurisprudential school in the late nineteenth century, they displaced history from the core of their analysis. Yet some twentieth-century scholars occasionally repeated some of Pound's criticisms of internal legal history, particularly its neglect of the relationship between law and society and its tendency to justify existing law. A few twentieth-century legal historians have elaborated these criticisms. They have emphasized that internal legal history is "lawyer's legal history," serving the practical needs of the legal profession rather than the intellectual requirements of professional historians. By using the doctrinal categories of the present to organize their investigation of the past, they claim, internal legal history provided a misleading continuity between past and present, making false analogies to the past, and ignoring how law actually functioned in past societies. Recent legal historians who have examined the work of the nineteenth-century American legal scholars have generated new interpretations of their understandings of history, which often challenge the traditional disparagement of their thought and overlap to varying degrees with my own conclusions.

Some subsequent twentieth-century scholars agreed with Pound that the deductive formalism of late nineteenth-century American legal thought did not recognize historical change. Just as Pound emphasized that American historical jurists found "unchangeable" sources for deductive formalism in the past history of the English common law,[151] Cohen claimed that "there are no temporal processes" in classical legal thought. By portraying a legal decision as simply

---

[148] Grey, supra note 55, at 33.

[149] Id. at 35.

[150] Id. at 33–4.

[151] Roscoe Pound, The Spirit of the Common Law (New Brunswick, N.J.: Transaction Publishers, 1999) (original ed. 1921), p. 156.

"a logical deduction from fixed principles," like "a system of pure geometry," classical thinkers attempted "to give an instantaneous snapshot of an existing and completed system of rights and duties."[152] Morton Horwitz described "the rise of legal formalism" as a successful effort by mercantile and entrepreneurial interests "to 'freeze' legal doctrine and to conceive of law not as a malleable instrument of their own desires and interests but as a fixed and inexorable system of logically deductible rules."[153] Kennedy similarly depicted classical legal thought as impervious to historical change. He referred to the "apparently ineradicable categories of Classicism" that had dominated private law by the 1870s and were soon extended to public law as well.[154] Classical legal thought, he conceded, recognized a historical process in the past, whereby legal principles had achieved increasing internal consistency "through a natural, organic, incremental evolution." But even if this historical process had not yet fully evolved, classical thinkers confidently concluded that total internal consistency would soon be reached.[155] Thereafter, the classical system would become closed, "self-perpetuating through time."[156] Unlike Pound, who stressed the influence of German historical jurisprudence in the United States while equating it with deductive formalism, Kennedy asserted that the historical school of legal scholarship in the nineteenth century, though a major force in Germany, "was a minor tendency" in the United States, Britain, and France.[157]

In his review of Horwitz's second volume, Gordon stressed that the "Classics" had a "historicist" conception of the extent to which the common law was "natural." He criticized Horwitz for frequently and erroneously claiming that they equated "natural" with "pre-political." Instead, Gordon maintained, they believed that "the common law ground rules were 'natural' in the sense that society was a naturally developing organism which gradually evolved customs that were 'naturally' adapted to every stage of its development." These customs became incorporated in the common law.[158] In other work, Gordon observed that the late nineteenth-century legal scholars, whatever their differences, typically assumed that "all societies undergo comparable processes of development from the simple to the complex, the primitive to the civilized." They often concluded that the United States manifested the culmination of a continuous process that began long ago in the Teutonic forests.[159]

---

[152] Cohen, supra note 10, at 844–5.

[153] Horwitz, supra note 112, at 258–9.

[154] Kennedy, supra note 1, at 105.

[155] Id. at 246.

[156] Id. at 260.

[157] Duncan Kennedy, The Disenchantment of Logically Formal Legal Rationality, 55 Hastings L.J. 1032, 1033 (2004).

[158] Robert W. Gordon, Book Review, 6 Yale J. L. and Humanities 137, 153–4 (1994). Gordon credits Siegel, supra note 2, as the "most comprehensive account" of the role of history and custom in classical legal thought. Id. at 154 n. 51.

[159] Robert W. Gordon, J. Willard Hurst and the Common Law Tradition in American Legal Historiography, 10 Law & Soc'y Rev. 9, 14–15 (1975).

For the "formalist" or "classical" legal scholars, Gordon maintained, legal history complemented analysis. Mostly confining their work in legal history to the origins and development of legal rules, they tried to relate this history to presumed enduring principles. If history demonstrated the relationship between the rule and the principle, it confirmed the analytic derivation of the rule from the principle. If history did not demonstrate such a relationship, the classical scholars treated the rule as an anachronistic survival that should be abandoned, often tracing its survival to a textual misreading by a judge that altered what would have been the natural evolution of law. Excising these survivals would promote the coherence of the classical structure. Gordon, like Kennedy, attributed to classical legal scholars the view that the common law had been evolving toward generality and internal consistency. This view, Gordon added, explains why they were more likely to find in history confirmation for principles rather than survivals requiring excisions.[160] Yet Gordon did not further maintain, as Kennedy had, that they believed this evolutionary process was reaching its conclusion, allowing the classical system to become "self-perpetuating through time" and thus eliminating any future role for history in legal analysis.[161]

Grey addressed the role of history in late nineteenth-century American legal thought while differentiating the formalism of classical orthodoxy from historical jurisprudence. Although both understood law as evolving progressively over time,[162] historical jurisprudence, best represented in the United States by Carter, viewed law as the contingent product of a nation's evolving customs. Classical orthodoxy, by contrast, did not rely on custom. Without elaborating his discussion of historical jurisprudence, Grey emphasized that classical orthodoxy used history, primarily the history of case law, as the empirical raw material for the operation of legal science, the induction of general principles, and the deduction from them of rules that would decide future cases. It accounted for legal change by ascribing a crucial role to the legal scientist, whose historical investigations can detect a principle that was immanent but previously unrecognized in past cases. Such a principle simultaneously reflects the slow evolution of society, explains past decisions convincingly, and contributes to the future progress of the law by making explicit on a scientific basis what had not previously been articulated. Once formulated scientifically, a legal doctrine might produce better results. History allowed classical orthodoxy to avoid the unscientific philosophical speculation it criticized in previous theories based on natural law but also to continue to focus, like natural law but unlike historical jurisprudence, on reason and principle.[163]

While emphasizing induction as the key to Langdell's conception of law as a science, revisionists have reinforced Grey's description of the role of history

---

[160] Robert W. Gordon, Historicism in Legal Scholarship, 90 Yale L.J. 1017, 1040–1 (1981).

[161] Kennedy, supra note 1, at 260.

[162] Grey, supra note 55, at 28–30.

[163] Id. at 30–1.

in classical orthodoxy. Yet in contrast to Grey, who commented in passing
that Langdell's innovation of the case method of instruction was inconsistent
with his commitment to the logical deduction of legal results from abstract
principles,[164] several revisionist scholars have maintained that his attempt to
induce evolving principles was the underlying goal that linked his scholarly
theories with his pedagogical innovation.[165] Because Langdell believed as a theorist that legal principles should be induced from the historical development
of case law, as a teacher he produced and taught from casebooks organized
chronologically.[166] Just as these casebooks replaced the treatises filled with
deductive logic that had previously been the staple of legal education, classroom interaction with students designed to induce the principles contained
in the cases replaced the prior practice of lectures that conveyed the predi-
gested deductive reasoning of the treatises.[167] The scholarly articles produced
by Langdell and his colleagues at Harvard similarly invoked the development
of case law as the scientific basis for their skepticism about the abstract dogmas
they found in the treatises.[168]

Langdell and his followers, the revisionists observed by contrast to Kennedy,
believed that the legal principles they induced and the classifications they created were themselves subject to further evolution and would never become
immutable.[169] The Langdellians may have been confident that evolution would
continue to refine legal principles, making them progressively better as well as
different, but they did not believe that the legal system would become frozen.[170]
And unlike Pound and Cohen, who had identified Langdell with the German
Pandectists, Mathias Reimann has emphasized their very different use of historical sources. The Roman legal authorities on which the Pandectists claimed
to rely, Reimann maintained, had been reduced to illustrations of principles
that were really derived from the a priori speculation of German philosophy.
Langdell, by contrast, did induce his principles from selected case law, consistent with the traditions of the common law. Whereas the Pandectists' principles
were timeless and static, Langdell's were organically rooted in the real world
and subject to evolutionary change.[171]

The Attack on Doctrinal Legal History
Like Pound, many twentieth-century American legal historians criticized their
predecessors for limiting their research to the internal history of legal doctrine.

---

[164] Id. at 24.
[165] See generally White, supra note 81, at 225–32.
[166] Reimann, supra note 82, at 108–9.
[167] Sebok, supra note 82, at 95–6; Paul D. Carrington, Hail! Langdell, 20 L. & Soc. Inquiry 691,
711 (1995); Speziale, supra note 81, at 3, 15–20, 37; see generally, Kimball, supra note 80.
[168] White, supra note 81, at 225–6.
[169] Reimann, supra note 82, at 108; Speziale, supra note 81, at 3, 34, 36, 37; see Sebok, supra note
82, at 96.
[170] White, supra note 81, at 229.
[171] Reimann, supra note 82, at 108.

As Gordon lamented in what remains the leading article on the history of American legal historiography, they not only took "legal things as their exclusive subject-matter, but whenever possible adduced as factors explaining the development of legal things only *other* legal things."[172] Late twentieth-century legal historians identified the "Law and Society" school of legal history, founded by J. Willard Hurst at the University of Wisconsin in the 1940s, as finally overcoming this traditional, historiographically unsophisticated, internal approach. By examining the relationship between law and society, they claimed, Hurst made legal history professionally respectable to historians and ended its isolation from general historiography.[173]

Beginning with his 1942 article setting forth a research program for legal history, Hurst urged American legal historians to "examine law not in terms of doctrinal classification, but in terms of a given economic or cultural function or activity."[174] By asserting that "we have not time to spend in antiquarianism," he suggested that prior doctrinal history suffered from this fault.[175] In a later survey of American legal history, Hurst observed that since 1870, when serious scholarship first began in university law schools, legal research, including in legal history, had only "a thin record of accomplishment," confined to "providing concepts and ordering judicial precedents for the immediate operating needs of bench and bar."[176] Indicating his affinity with Pound, Hurst complained that legal history "has made little response" to his "call for a sociological jurisprudence," but sadly "continues content on the whole to let the formal headings of the law fix its subject matter."[177] Even within the realm of doctrinal history, Hurst added, legal historians gave exaggerated attention to courts, treating them as if they were the entire legal system.[178]

In deploring the traditional internal approach, many twentieth-century legal historians placed particular emphasis on its use of the doctrinal categories of the present to govern the exploration of the past. Even before Hurst began to publish, Daniel Boorstin, who later abandoned legal history for a distinguished and prolific career as a generalist American historian, criticized English and American scholars for writing legal history as a kind of "legal embryology," a search in the rudimentary forms of the past for the origins and growth of the more fully developed law of the present, often treated as the inevitable culmination of this process.[179] The classifications of legal textbooks and treatises, such as contracts, torts, and crimes, became the classifications for research in legal history.[180] As a typical example, Boorstin quoted the opening sentences

---

[172] Gordon, supra note 159, at 20.
[173] Id. at 54.
[174] J. Willard Hurst, Legal History: A Research Program, 1942 Wis. L. Rev. 323, 329.
[175] Id. at 323.
[176] Willard Hurst, The Law in United States History, Proc. Amer. Phil. Soc. 518, 520 (1960).
[177] Id. at 522.
[178] Id. at 521–2.
[179] D. J. Boorstin, Tradition and Method in Legal History, 54 Harv. L. Rev. 424, 429 (1941).
[180] Id. at 426.

of the collected *Lectures on Legal History* by Ames, which announced that they would address "the origin and development" of various legal ideas.[181] Boorstin also cited Holmes as an able legal historian who generally engaged in legal embryology, while noting that many of his best contributions to the field occurred when he freed himself from subservience to the needs of the practicing lawyer.[182] Even Maitland, whose escape from this subservience contributed to his brilliance as a legal historian, unfortunately succumbed at times to the "lawyer's spell."[183] By contrast, Boorstin noted that in continental Europe, unlike in England and the United States, legal history was more a branch of history than a subsidiary of the practical professional focus of legal studies. He attributed this difference to the traditional interest in Roman law on the Continent and to the fact that law was part of a general education in continental universities.[184]

Legal embryology, Boorstin complained, provided a false simplicity and symmetry to legal history, analogous to the early writing of political history according to the reigns of kings and queens.[185] It often distorted the past and produced false analogies to the present. Organizing the data of legal history under modern legal categories, he observed, makes it harder to understand the role of legal concepts in earlier societies.[186] Even if the legal historian is interested in analogies between past and present, Boorstin added, functional analogies are much more significant than the conceptual ones sought by embryonic legal history. Using the development of contract from assumpsit as an example, he pointed out that the medieval functional counterpart to current contract law may be found in a medieval conceptual category that more closely resembles current tort law. Uncovering the functions performed by legal doctrines at different times, Boorstin maintained, is much more significant than tracing how those doctrines, which "are capable of manifold and unpredictable uses,"[187] developed over time. For example, whereas legal historians had extensively traced the history of the doctrine of consideration, Boorstin urged inquiry into why this doctrine arose in the eighteenth century as opposed to some other time, suggesting that the answer would reveal the function it served.[188] Much embryonic legal history, he added, seemed confused about whether it was searching for the ancient origins of modern concepts or the ancient, perhaps different, concepts that served similar purposes to the modern ones.[189]

Pointing out that most legal history in the United States had been written by and for lawyers, Horwitz frequently called the emphasis on origins and

---

[181] Id. at 425.
[182] Id. at 428 and n. 8.
[183] Id. at 428 n. 8 and 430–1.
[184] Id. at 424 n. 2.
[185] Id. at 426.
[186] Id. at 431–2.
[187] Id. at 433.
[188] Id. at 432.
[189] Id. at 433.

continuity "lawyer's legal history." As the most dramatic illustration, he cited Holmes's search in early English law for the sources of the fault principle of liability. He referred to the work of Langdell and Ames as additional examples. Yet Horwitz focused his attention and criticism on Pound, even though Pound himself had initiated the twentieth-century critique of the internal study of legal history while urging a new "sociological legal history." Horwitz called Pound the "single most influential representative of orthodox lawyer's legal history."[190]

In contrast to the earlier treatment of the doctrinal legal history by Boorstin and Hurst, Horwitz stressed that it advanced "fundamentally conservative political preferences dressed up in the neutral garb of expert and objective legal history."[191] Not mentioning Pound's attack on the socially destructive individualism of historical jurisprudence, Horwitz used Pound as his primary example, quoting repeatedly from two of Pound's major articles published before World War I.[192] He asserted that Pound relegated economic influences on legal doctrine to "some comfortable distance in the past," after which law became "functionally autonomous." To illustrate, Horwitz cited Pound's portrayal of the movement toward fault liability in the nineteenth century as the triumph of "some unhistorical and disembodied intellectual criterion of 'common sense.'" Pound himself criticized historical jurisprudence for simply substituting historical for philosophical premises in a misguided and socially destructive attempt to analyze law through formal reason, but Horwitz maintained that Pound equated common sense with "thinking as a lawyer," the traditional "self-serving and uncritical assumption" by lawyers that their work is governed by "Reason itself." Horwitz, by contrast, claimed that fault liability obviously developed as part of a more general effort to establish a system of legal thought that would reduce the costs of economic growth. Similarly, Horwitz observed, Pound's historical classification of jurisprudential schools presented legal ideas succeeding each other in a march toward the discovery of progressively better ones, "giving absolutely no clue of why they served to express the political, or cultural forces of the time."[193] Pound confidently assumed that the faculty of human reason is unaffected by history and that its application to legal analysis, as to all areas of scientific inquiry, provides right and wrong answers.[194]

This misplaced confidence in science and reason, Horwitz argued, enabled the differentiation of law from politics that made lawyer's legal history "inevitably

---

[190] Morton J. Horwitz, The Conservative Tradition in the Writing of American Legal History, 17 Am. J. Legal Hist. 275, 276 (1973).

[191] Id.

[192] Id. at 279–80.

[193] Id. at 279–80.

[194] Id. at 278. Horwitz subsequently developed a more complex and favorable assessment of Pound, contrasting his impressive early work developing sociological jurisprudence before World War I with his "about-face" by 1938, when he denounced the "administrative absolutism" of the New Deal. Horwitz, supra note 4, at 217–20.

conservative."[195] Failing to recognize that the American legal tradition is "itself a contingent and changing product of specific historical struggles," lawyer's legal history left the impression of "a kind of meta-historical set of values within which social conflict has always taken place."[196] To write lawyer's legal history, Horwitz complained, "is to pervert the real function of history by reducing it to the pathetic role of justifying the world as it is." Its practitioners ransack the past to applaud the history of the common law as the manifestation of professional craft. They dismiss the codification movement, the historical antagonist of the common law tradition, as an inappropriate, even demagogic, political intrusion into the rational and scientific development of the law.[197] Horwitz observed that Pound, his favorite example, extolled the triumphs of the common law in American history, first over the admirers of France in the decades after the American Revolution and again over their successors, the advocates of codification in the 1830s and 1840s.[198]

Horwitz was struck by the parallels between lawyer's legal history and the history of science written by scientists as famously described by Thomas Kuhn in *The Structure of Scientific Revolutions*. Both the lawyers and the scientists present history as a continuous process that has produced inevitable and universal understandings within their disciplines. In Horwitz's words, they "use history to justify and glorify the present." Yet historians of law, Horwitz pointed out, have a harder time than historians of science in excluding politics from their inquiry. The historian of science can plausibly attribute scientific change to the progress of reason in search for truth. The legal historian, however, cannot ignore the history of political movements that organized to change the law. According to Horwitz, lawyer's legal history responds by treating these broad political movements similarly to the more narrowly legal codification movement, as demagogic attacks on the legitimate categories of professional expertise. Borrowing the phrase that Boorstin had applied to Blackstone, Horwitz called this conception of professional expertise a "mysterious science, involving forms of reasoning and access to knowledge unavailable to ordinary men." As a result, "an elitist and antidemocratic politics pervades most of the traditional writings on American legal history."[199]

Writing two years after Horwitz, Gordon made many similar points without Horwitz's stress on the conservative political implications of lawyer's legal history. Gordon agreed with Horwitz that this scholarship was ideological in separating law from politics and in treating law as esoteric knowledge inaccessible to the untrained citizen. Yet whereas Horwitz equated this ideological scholarship with political conservatism, Gordon emphasized its value in promoting the professional interests of lawyers.[200]

[195] Horwitz, supra note 190, at 280–1.
[196] Id. at 278.
[197] Id. at 281.
[198] Id. at 276.
[199] Id. at 283.
[200] Gordon, supra note 159, at 31 n. 65.

Gordon also borrowed from Kuhn to describe the historiography of American legal history. He agreed with Horwitz that legal history written by lawyers bears striking parallels to Kuhn's description of the history of science written by scientists.[201] More specifically, Gordon invoked Kuhn's distinction between internal and external histories. Until very recently, Gordon asserted, scholarship in American legal history had been overwhelmingly internal, written from within the discipline, rather than external, written in relation to the wider society.[202] Like Horwitz, Gordon claimed that it was harder for historians of law than for historians of science to write about their field solely from an internal perspective. He quoted approvingly the great Italian historiographer Arnaldo Momigliano. Conceding that the histories of literature, art, science, and religion can be limited to those particular fields, Momigliano asserted that the history of law cannot maintain such disciplinary autonomy. Law, he insisted, is too rooted in multiple human activities and relations to be treated in isolation. If historical investigation uncovers an autonomous legal tradition, Momigliano added, its existence is itself a "social phenomenon" requiring interpretation.[203] Yet legal historians before Hurst, Gordon asserted, did not pursue external legal history because abandoning the internal approach would have jeopardized their professional identities as lawyers, which they were eager to preserve.[204] He pointed out that Ames regarded the historically informed legal scientist as the "expert confidant" to the judge and, in rare instances when statutory reform might be necessary, to the legislature.[205]

Twentieth-century legal historians who generally criticized their predecessors occasionally acknowledged that they had produced some excellent work. While decrying embryological legal history, Boorstin observed that some of the most able legal historians had endorsed this approach, citing Holmes and Maitland.[206] In an essay endorsing "the humane study of law," which he differentiated from both "pragmatic" and "social science" approaches,[207] he associated it with embryological legal history. Emphasizing the "notable fact, often forgotten, that nearly every American contribution to legal history which ought to be considered a classic" was written in a "broad humanistic spirit," Boorstin gave just three illustrations: Holmes's *The Common Law*, Ames's *Lectures on Legal History*, both of which he had explicitly identified as embryological legal history, and Thayer's *A Preliminary Treatise on Evidence at the Common Law*, which also fits into that category. Boorstin conceded that each had been corrected in some respects by subsequent scholarship, but he maintained that they "were all works of large conception and of scholarly integrity in the best tradition of history as humanistic study." He described the late nineteenth century

---

[201] Id. at 17 n. 22.
[202] Id. at 11 and 11 n. 5.
[203] Id. at 9.
[204] Id. at 30–6.
[205] Id. at 32.
[206] Boorstin, supra note 179, at 428 and n. 8.
[207] Daniel J. Boorstin, The Humane Study of Law, 57 Yale L.J. 960, 964 (1948).

as "the efflorescence of American legal history," speculating that assumptions of Anglo-Saxon supremacy and the genteel tradition of general historical scholarship in New England might have contributed to it.[208]

Gordon also praised late nineteenth-century American legal historians whose evolutionary approach he rejected. Identifying the 1876 *Essays in Anglo-Saxon Law* by Adams and his students as the beginning of professional scholarship in legal history in the United States, he observed that their evolutionary study of legal history flourished during the 1880s and 1890s, particularly at Harvard Law School. He highlighted the contributions to scholarship on early English law by Holmes, Bigelow, Thayer, and Ames.[209] Gordon agreed with the eventual "discrediting of evolutionary theories of history."[210] But immediately after naming the Americans who wrote about early English law from an evolutionary perspective during the classical period, he added that he did not intend "to deprecate the achievement of these men, who were among the few people Maitland found it worthwhile to correspond with on professional subjects." Rather, Gordon regretted the persistence of the evolutionary approach among legal historians after 1900, when it was being repudiated by historians in history departments.[211] In addition, while maintaining that the "generalizing feature" of classical legal thought was more important than its "empirical or factual side," Gordon made an important exception for the legal historians of the period. "To give them credit," he noted, "the classical generation *did* do far more rigorous work on one part of the empirical project – namely, legal history – than any of their predecessors."[212]

Beyond recognizing the achievements of late nineteenth-century American legal historians, Gordon seemed to absolve at least some of them of the fault of studying history internally. He generally treated the classical period as part of a longer tradition of internal legal history that extended until Hurst's work of the 1940s, endorsed prior criticisms of internal legal history, and happily reported that "the situation is rapidly improving" because American legal historians in very recent years had finally, and belatedly, abandoned it.[213] Yet during the classical period, Gordon pointed out, evolutionary legal history "had held out the promise of connecting the history of law and of society."[214] Indeed, he added without naming names, the great legal historians of the classical period had begun to fulfill this promise in their studies of medieval English law by giving it a context.[215] Elsewhere, he did name several great English and European scholars – Maine, Brunner, Maitland, and Vinogradoff – who, "among others," had

---

[208] Id. at 963.
[209] Gordon, supra note 159, at 14–15.
[210] Id. at 20.
[211] Id. at 15–16.
[212] Robert W. Gordon, Book Review, 93 Mich. L. Rev. 1231, 1238–9 n. 16 (1995).
[213] Gordon, supra note 159, at 11–12.
[214] Id. at 19.
[215] Id. at 19–21.

studied the impact of legal forms on local social environments.[216] Gordon never specifically named American legal historians as possible "others," although in favorably identifying Holmes, Bigelow, Thayer, and Ames as contributors to the study of early English law whose work interested Maitland, he at least allowed the implication that they, too, connected law to social context.

Despite this early promise of a social history of law, Gordon observed that in America it was soon cut short as "legal history was reduced to internal history." He dated this unfortunate reduction to the classical period itself, quoting from a book published in 1890 by Carter as evidence. The organic theory of culture at the core of evolutionary legal history, Gordon maintained, "paradoxically encouraged scholars to disregard the social context of the day."[217] His quotation from Carter attempted to explain this paradox. Carter asserted that legal rules had "sprung out of" prior judicial inquiries "into habits, customs, business, and manners."[218] In this way, Gordon maintained, social practice had become incorporated into legal rules. Studying the history of legal rules, therefore, could be considered to include the study of the social influences on law. Internal legal history, in other words, recognized social history without having to investigate it as a separate, external subject.

Rediscovering the Importance of History

Although major scholars throughout the twentieth century commented on the role of history in late nineteenth-century American legal thought, only in the last two decades did some return to Pound's emphasis on its importance. Stephen Siegel's article "Historism in Late Nineteenth-Century Constitutional Thought" was the first and remains the most significant work in redirecting attention to the historical orientation of classical legal thought. In his highly original interpretation of laissez-faire constitutionalism, Siegel maintained that it had substantial intellectual roots in the "historism" that characterized mainstream nineteenth-century social thought. In subsequent articles about various "classical" legal thinkers, he incorporated his interpretation of the role of history into his treatment of classicism. He ultimately concluded that historical jurisprudence, which he equated with what he called "historistic classicism," was the dominant, though not the only, form of classical legal thought.[219]

Because Siegel dealt with laissez-faire constitutionalism in a separate article from later individual articles discussing specific legal scholars in relation to classical orthodoxy, the originality of his general interpretation of late nineteenth-century American legal thought must be pieced together by considering all these articles as a whole. Among the many varieties of classical legal

---

[216] Id. at 17–18.

[217] Id. at 19.

[218] Id. at 20.

[219] Stephen A. Siegel, Joel Bishop's Orthodoxy, 13 L. & Hist. Rev. 215, 254 n. 165 (1995); Stephen A. Siegel, The Revision Thickens, 20 L. & Hist. Rev. 631, 636–7 (2002).

thought Siegel identified, he stressed an underlying belief, with the important exception of Langdell, that law is embedded in morality. According to Siegel, this moral basis was as important to classical legal thought as its geometric form.[220] During the course of the nineteenth century, he maintained, the source of morality shifted from religious to secular grounds, particularly at Harvard Law School in the decades after 1870. Crucially in Siegel's interpretation, history became the prevailing basis for morality. By enabling law to retain a moral foundation, Siegel maintained, history eased the transition to secularism, which would have been much more controversial and delayed if morality had been excised along with religion.[221]

By differentiating "historism" from "historicism," Siegel underlined the crucial role of morality in historism. Historicism shared with historism the belief that secular causes produce historical change. But historicism did not believe in the underlying moral ordering principles that were central to historism. Instead of historism's search for these principles over time, historicism emphasized moral relativity and focused on extracting the "differentness" of the past. Whereas historism was a transitional theory of history, historicism is the modern one.[222]

Applying historism to law, American legal scholars concluded that positive law was "determined by principles of 'ethnic spirit' that were revealed through historical study of the nation and its dominant racial group."[223] In his study of laissez-faire constitutionalism, in which he first identified the centrality of historism in late nineteenth-century American legal thought, Siegel emphasized that historism, rather than the social and economic views falsely attributed by the progressives, was the primary source of this interpretation of the Constitution. Directed by their belief in historism to search for moral principles in the evolution of Anglo-American culture, they found laissez-faire constitutionalism to be one of the key principles.[224] Siegel examined at great length the theoretical commitment to historism in private as well as public law by three prominent laissez-faire constitutionalists, Pomeroy, Cooley, and Tiedeman. Probably because he focused on the subject of laissez-faire constitutionalism, he barely discussed other principles they derived from their historism. Yet he noted in passing Pomeroy's identification of "individual freedom" as the central principle of the Anglo-Saxons and "national power" as the central principle of the Romans, pointing out that these were "stock historist examples."[225] In his subsequent articles, he similarly referred to the general historism of other classical legal scholars rather than to the specific morally ordering legal principles they derived from it.

---

[220] Siegel, supra note 2, at 1598.
[221] See id. at 1515–17.
[222] Id. at 1451 n. 84, 1545; see also 1439–40.
[223] Id. at 1437.
[224] Id. at 1543; see also 1436, 1445, 1542.
[225] Id. at 1459 n. 138.

Because Siegel had a broad definition of classical legal thought, he included within it almost every major legal thinker of the late nineteenth century. Some classicists, such as Bishop, were religious but not historist.[226] Other classicists, including Pomeroy and Wharton, were religious and historist.[227] Still other classicists, such as Gray, were historist but not religious. In addition to Pomeroy, Cooley, Tiedeman, Bishop, Wharton, and Gray, the scholars he dealt with at length in his various articles, he identified as classicists all of Gray's major colleagues at Harvard Law School – Langdell, Ames, Thayer, Williston, and Beale[228] – as well as additional people he associated with historical jurisprudence, Carter, Dillon, and Hammond.[229] He had some second thoughts about Carter, noting that his "idiosyncratic" version of historical jurisprudence "arguably places him outside the fold of classical legal thought"[230] but otherwise retained his broad grouping. Among major thinkers of the nineteenth century, he only excluded Holmes, who did not study history as the source of normative values, but as the basis for legal reform, and was, therefore, a modernist, not a classicist.[231] Siegel most specifically connected historical research with classicism in an article on John Chipman Gray. Identifying anachronistic historical remnants in current law and urging that they not be followed, Siegel observed, was part of Gray's effort to establish the ordered legal system that was crucial to classical legal thought.[232]

Siegel importantly reiterated that Langdell, though a classicist in his commitment to uncovering the geometric structure of law, was the only classicist, even among his secular colleagues at Harvard, who rejected the connection of law with morality. With Langdell, "classicism decayed into mere formalism."[233] In this crucial respect, Siegel stressed, Langdell was not the archetypical classical legal scholar portrayed by critics throughout the twentieth century.[234] Perhaps, he added, the critics focused on Langdell precisely because what made him "unusual also made him an easy target." After all, "a legal system substantially divorced from social life, mores, and morals is easy to lampoon."[235] Though Langdell was outside the mainstream of classical legal science, Siegel added, his version was its last surviving form, which may have independently contributed to its later portrayal as typical.[236]

As part of an article on the importance of German law schools and law professors as a model for Americans, published in 1993, Mathias Reimann called

---

[226] Siegel, Joel Bishop's Orthodoxy, supra note 219, at 254 and n. 165.
[227] Siegel, supra note 2, at 1461; Stephen A. Siegel, Francis Wharton's Orthodoxy: God, Historical Jurisprudence, and Classical Legal Thought, 46 Am. J. Leg. Hist. 422, 438.
[228] Siegel, supra note 56, at 1590.
[229] Siegel, supra note 227, at 434 n. 110.
[230] Siegel, The Revision Thickens, supra note 219, at 637.
[231] Siegel, supra note 2, at 1546–7; Siegel, supra note 56, at 1572.
[232] Siegel, supra note 56, at 1531.
[233] Id. at 1598.
[234] Id. at 1514–18.
[235] Id. at 1517.
[236] Siegel, The Revision Thickens, supra note 219, at 637.

additional attention to the significance of history in late nineteenth-century American legal scholarship.[237] In the emerging field of legal history, Reimann asserted, Americans recognized German professors as the intellectual leaders, revering them for using legal history as the foundation for a scientific study of law even as they sometimes criticized them for lacking practical sense.[238] Although many German legal historians influenced Americans, Savigny was the most important. Many leading American scholars viewed Savigny as the prototype they sought to follow.[239] They adopted for themselves Savigny's approach to legal history as the source for detecting fundamental legal principles.[240] The American historical school, which spread from Harvard to other law schools in the last decades of the nineteenth century, looked to German legal historians for guidance as they "explored the history of the common law in order to find the true underlying principles of its historical evolution."[241] Just as Savigny and his German disciples had relied on the history of Roman law to develop a systematic law for Germany, American and English scholars in the late nineteenth century strove for a similar systemization by historical examination of the English common law.[242] Reimann pointed out that many American legal scholars had studied in Germany and that some German scholars visited, and occasionally immigrated to, the United States.[243] He stressed that James Barr Ames, whose appointment to the Harvard law faculty in 1873 began the rapid trend toward the employment of professionally trained legal scholars in American law schools, had studied in Germany and included many references to German legal historians in his own work.[244]

In an earlier article, Reimann provided a concrete example of the influence of the German historical school in the United States by claiming that Carter's successful opposition to codification in New York in the 1870s and 1880s adapted Savigny's historical theory of law as evolving custom. Echoing Savigny's own opposition to codification in Germany after the defeat of Napoleon in 1814 while reframing it in the American context, Carter maintained that codification would stifle the flexibility and growth of the common law.[245] Concerned that legislation would harm the economic interests of his wealthy clients,[246] Carter developed "the anti-legislative, anti-democratic, and conservative laissez-faire implications of the historical theory of law, which had mostly lain dormant and

[237] Mathias Reimann, A Career in Itself: The German Professoriate as a Model for American Legal Academia, in The Reception of Continental Ideas in the Common Law World 1820–1920 (M. Reimann ed., Berlin: Duncker & Humblot, 1993).

[238] Id. at 170–2, 196.

[239] Id. at 170.

[240] Id. at 180.

[241] Id. at 166, 179.

[242] Id. at 180.

[243] Id. at 173–6.

[244] Id. at 166, 173–4, 184.

[245] Reimann, supra note 101, at 106.

[246] Id. at 115–16.

hidden in the writings of Savigny himself."[247] Without denying that Carter had been convinced by Savigny's arguments, Reimann stressed that they allowed Carter and others to rationalize and hide their political and personal motives within a respected intellectual tradition.[248]

More than a decade later, Lewis Grossman reinforced the connection between Carter's historical jurisprudence and his opposition to codification even as he challenged the claim that Carter manipulated this connection on behalf of the conservative interests of his wealthy clients. Carter's version of historical jurisprudence, Grossman indicated, complemented his reformist Mugwump politics, a point Grossman emphasized by calling it "Mugwump jurisprudence." Identifying Carter as the most prominent American proponent of Savigny's historical jurisprudence, Grossman observed that the importance of history in late nineteenth-century legal thought, though highlighted by Pound, had subsequently been largely neglected by scholars who focused on the structure of "classical" legal thought and had only recently been rediscovered.[249] From Savigny's theory of law as evolving custom, Grossman asserted, Carter reasoned that the common law reflected popular standards of justice, which revealed the gradual unfolding of eternal and objective moral principles. Judges could recognize and incorporate into their decisions the evolution of custom toward higher ethical norms. Carter worried that legislation, as static written law, frequently conflicted with changing custom. Legislation divorced from custom, he believed, was unenforceable and, therefore, encouraged unfortunate disrespect for law.[250] Carter's Mugwump contempt for the corruption of Gilded Age politics reinforced his intellectual skepticism about legislation and helped him suggest that judicial development of the common law is more democratic than legislation.[251]

More generally, other scholars in the last two decades have identified a distinctive historical school in the United States during the late nineteenth century. In his 1990 book on the history of American jurisprudence from 1870 to 1970, published the same year as Siegel's classic article on "historism," James Herget included a chapter entitled "The Evolutionists, 1880–1923." Evolutionists, Herget maintained, accounted for law historically.[252] He observed that the term "evolutionary jurisprudence" had been used interchangeably with "historicism," "the historical school," "legal evolution," "the Darwinian theory of law,"[253] and "historical jurisprudence."[254] This approach, he concluded,

---

[247] Id. at 118.

[248] Id. at 118–19.

[249] Grossman, supra note 101, at 578 and 579 n. 4 (citing Stephen Siegel, William LaPiana, and Thomas Grey).

[250] Id. at 578–9, 608, 611, 616.

[251] Id. at 612.

[252] James E. Herget, American Jursiprudence, 1870–1970 (Houston, Texas: Rice University Press, 1990), p. 4.

[253] Id. at 22.

[254] Id. at 118.

had played a main supporting role, but not a dominant one, in the history of American legal philosophy.[255] In the late nineteenth century, he added, the boundary between historical jurisprudence and legal history was often unclear. He found that some works purporting to explain law historically did not go beyond expository legal history.[256]

The appeal to history as a new way of studying law that emerged among many American legal scholars after the Civil War,[257] William LaPiana stressed in an article published in 1992, was a scientifically based "historical jurisprudence," derived largely from Maine.[258] LaPiana portrayed these American advocates of historical jurisprudence as engaged in a "confrontation"[259] and "clash"[260] with the analytic jurisprudence associated with John Austin, the influential English legal philosopher. Challenging Austin's concept of law as the command of a sovereign, the product of will, they viewed "law as a system of broad general principles resting ultimately on custom."[261] All of these scholars agreed that "the expression of law in rules changes as times change"[262] and accepted "a theory of historical change based on stages of development." At the same time, they asserted the "existence of unchanging principles." LaPiana recognized tension between their beliefs in both "historical change" and underlying "unchanging principles," commenting that it "casts doubt on the evolutionary nature of this approach to law." He concluded that "the goal of these writers seems to be the prevention of change, not accommodation to a changing world."[263] Just as Siegel identified "historism" as a pervasive mode of thought that flourished during the nineteenth century,[264] LaPiana made the intriguing but unelaborated suggestion that late nineteenth-century American historical jurisprudence was closely related to the general intellectual history of the period.[265]

A far-ranging article by Christopher Tomlins analyzed late nineteenth-century American scholarship in legal history while evaluating the changing uses of history to justify the authority of the American legal system. Drawing on Dorothy Ross's comprehensive book *The Origins of American Social Science*, Tomlins contrasted the "historicist" conception of time that emerged after the Civil War with the antebellum "Providential" or "Christian" conception of time, which emphasized progress in human knowledge of God's fixed laws that order history

---

[255] Id. at 22.
[256] Id. at 118 and n. 4.
[257] William P. LaPiana, Jurisprudence of History and Truth, 23 Rutgers L.J. 519, 541, 554 (1992).
[258] Id. at 536.
[259] Id. at 523.
[260] Id. at 554.
[261] Id. at 521–2; see also 552.
[262] Id. at 555.
[263] Id. at 556.
[264] Siegel, supra note 2, at 1436.
[265] Lapiana, supra note 257, at 552, 558.

as well as nature.[266] Before closing with an analysis of the "external historiography" that began with Hurst and flourished in the "critical legal history" written by Horwitz and Gordon, much of the article treated the period between the reorganization of Harvard Law School under Langdell in the 1870s and the work of Roscoe Pound in the early twentieth century. Without dealing in detail with the work of particular scholars, Tomlins discussed the "historical jurisprudence" of professors at Harvard Law School, in which "history played the essential but auxiliary role of outlining the path to the present."[267] He also addressed the influence of Maine and especially of the German historical school on American scholars, treating Carter in a paragraph and mentioning Hammond, Pomeroy, Cooley, and Tiedeman.[268] He considered Holmes "the last gasp of historical jurisprudence – at least in its nineteenth-century form – in the United States."[269]

Most recently, Kunal Parker examined "the late nineteenth-century jurisprudence of custom" in an article that, he recognized, extends the scholarship of the past two decades and "forms part of an ongoing attempt to reorient our understanding of the intellectual world of late nineteenth-century American lawyers *toward* the broad significance of historical thinking and *away* from the over-represented story of the 'revolt against formalism.'"[270] Legal thinkers during the late nineteenth century, Parker observed, "were obsessed with time."[271] While agreeing with others that many late nineteenth-century legal scholars viewed law as derived from custom, Parker distinctively stressed that these scholars perceived a perpetual "unbridgeable" gap or lag between custom and law. They believed custom was always "slipping ahead of law," making law "always behind" custom, "always a little dead."[272] This conception of the relationship between law and custom, Parker pointed out, differed from earlier views. Though Maine heavily influenced the subsequent American "jurisprudence of custom," he treated custom as a stage toward the eventual development of law, which then left custom behind. Whereas the Americans saw custom perpetually ahead of law, for Maine custom preceded law, though he did treat "the social" as forever in advance of law.[273] And unlike those, most famously Blackstone,[274] who equated custom with the common law and

---

[266] Christopher Tomlins, History in the American Juridical Field: Narrative, Justification, and Explanation, 16 Yale J. L. & the Humanities 323, 332, 333, 336 (2004).

[267] Id. at 349.

[268] Id. at 358–9.

[269] Id. at 364.

[270] Kunal M. Parker, Context in History and Law: A Study of the Late Nineteenth-Century American Jurisprudence of Custom, 24 L. & Hist. Rev. 473, 475 and n. 4 (2006). As examples of this attempted reorientation, he cites works by James Herget, Lewis Grossman, William LaPiana, David Rabban, and Stephen Siegel.

[271] Id. at 482.

[272] Id. at 482, 496.

[273] Id. at 497–8.

[274] Id. at 506.

invoked the antiquity of custom to give the common law added authority, the late nineteenth-century Americans "chipped" custom "off from law" and transformed it "into a context for thinking about law,"[275] the ground from which it emerged.[276] Just as other scholars had identified Carter as the key figure in the American turn to historical understandings of law in the late nineteenth century, Parker called him the most brilliant representative of the "jurisprudence of custom."[277] Parker also interpreted as a "code for custom" the extensive references to an "unwritten" constitution upon which the written constitution depended, a major theme in scholarship on constitutional law after the Civil War.[278]

Assessing the Twentieth-Century Critique

Like Pound himself, most of his twentieth-century successors, although correct in part, presented a substantially misleading account of late nineteenth-century American legal thought. Their critique substantially overlapped with Pound's. In brief, though they appropriately highlighted the nineteenth-century focus on the content and organization of legal doctrine, they erred in maintaining that the nineteenth-century scholars were oblivious to the relationship between law and society, applied deductive formalism to their analysis of law, and were hostile to legal reform. Because I discussed these issues in the previous chapter on Pound, I focus here on additional claims by the twentieth-century scholars, mostly made by legal historians about the role of history in late nineteenth-century legal thought. As in my treatment of Pound, I refer to material in the chapters about the late nineteenth-century scholars in assessing these claims.

To use Thomas Grey's helpful terminology, the late nineteenth-century American legal scholars were conceptualists rather than formalists. Grey convincingly contrasted conceptualism, based on the induction and coherent classification of legal principles, from formalism, which additionally tries to deduce from these classified principles logically correct results that would objectively decide all future cases.[279] Holmes himself had suggested a similar distinction when he differentiated deduction from the "humbler error" of attempting to demonstrate the "logical cohesion" of the legal system.[280] Grey was also correct in identifying conceptualism as an almost universal characteristic of Anglo-American legal thought during the classical period and in criticizing the many twentieth-century scholars who conflated conceptualism and deductive formalism while rejecting both.[281] Yet as revisionist scholars have

---

[275] Id. at 482.

[276] Id. at 494.

[277] Id. at 505.

[278] Id. at 510.

[279] See supra text accompanying note 76.

[280] Oliver Wendell Holmes, The Common Law (Boston: Back Bay Books, 1963)(original ed. 1881), p. 32.

[281] See supra text accompanying note 76.

demonstrated convincingly, Grey erred in calling Langdell a deductive formalist. Like so many of his contemporaries, Langdell was a conceptualist who rejected deduction.[282] Duncan Kennedy's late work, departing from his earlier inclusion of formalism as a characteristic of classical legal thought, reinforced Grey's distinction between conceptualism and formalism. Kennedy recognized that classical legal scholars, while hopeful that their conceptual constructions would help resolve legal issues, often viewed the application of these constructions as a much more complex and indeterminate process than deductive formalism.[283] Mathias Reimann's discussion of the relationship between Langdell and the German Pandectists similarly reflected the difference between the deductive formalism of the Germans and Langdell's conceptualism.[284]

The twentieth-century scholars were essentially accurate in claiming that their late nineteenth-century predecessors studied the internal history of law largely to connect past law to present law as a service to the professional interests of practicing lawyers and judges. Indeed, the nineteenth-century scholars often stressed this point themselves. As chairman of the Section on Legal Education of the American Bar Association, Thayer maintained that the study of legal history was a "necessary preliminary for first-rate work,"[285] the basis for understanding current law. Exemplifying his own general advice, Thayer wrote *A Preliminary Treatise on Evidence at the Common Law*, which emphasized the impact of the history of the English jury on the modern law of evidence. Although Thayer had originally intended to write a treatise for "practical use," he realized in pursuing this project that he could not accomplish his goal without first delving deeply into history, which explained numerous confusions in the modern law of evidence.[286] Holmes made similar points in the opening paragraphs of *The Common Law*. Elaborating his famous assertion that experience, not logic, is the life of the law, Holmes maintained that in order to know what law is, "we must know what it has been." Investigating the connection between past law and present law, Holmes stressed, was his only reason for studying history. "I shall use the history of our law," he wrote, "so far as it is necessary to explain a conception or to interpret a rule, but no further."[287] True to his introductory comments, throughout *The Common Law* Holmes alternatively justified his use of legal history as essential to understanding current law and explained his lack of attention to legal history by asserting that it had no bearing on current law. Holmes reiterated these points in his later essays, applauding the "practical"[288] use of legal history for "the light it throws on

---

[282] See supra text accompanying notes 80–6.
[283] See supra text accompanying notes 46–8.
[284] See supra text accompanying note 171.
[285] James Bradley Thayer, The Teaching of English Law at Universities, 9 Harv. L. Rev. 169, 176 (1895).
[286] James Bradley Thayer, A Preliminary Treatise on Evidence at the Common Law (Boston: Little, Brown, and Company, 1898), p. 1.
[287] Holmes, supra note 280, at 5–6.
[288] Oliver Wendell Holmes, Law in Science and Science in Law, 12 Harv. L. Rev. 443, 444 (1899).

the present" while warning against the "pitfall of antiquarianism,"[289] whatever the pleasure of history as "an end in itself."[290] Similarly, Lodge contrasted legal history that helped explain the present with mere "antiquarianism,"[291] and Bigelow explained that he ignored writs "not in the direct order of development toward" modern forms of action.[292] Other late nineteenth-century American legal scholars often contrasted the meaningful history that helps explain the present with the superficial history that does not.[293] Most generally, the concept of evolutionary history that pervaded nineteenth-century transatlantic thought itself connotes continuity between past and present, especially as illustrated by the frequent organic metaphors of family descent and germs or seeds maturing into fruit. Ames, Boorstin's leading example of "legal embryology," tellingly referred to his work in legal history as "genealogy."[294] Many of these nineteenth-century scholars, moreover, viewed evolution as progressive as well as continuous, particularly the development of American liberty and democracy from "Teutonic germs."

Their interests in continuity and progress, however, did not prevent these scholars from also recognizing numerous instances of discontinuity, lack of progress, and contingency. Wharton shared prevailing evolutionary theories of legal development, but he criticized Savigny and his German followers who, in developing the concept of a Volksgeist, ignored the differences between a nation and "a continuous perpetual person."[295] Nor did the evolutionary views of Adams and his students prevent them from challenging Maine's specific theory of progress in stages from collectivism to individualism. Even as they assumed general progress, especially in Anglo-American civilization, many of the American legal scholars took care to observe that it was not continuous. They referred to legal progress as "undulatory,"[296] "irregular and unscientific,"[297] marked by "vicissitudes,"[298] confronted by "obstacles,"[299] and often receding before ultimately prevailing.[300] Many claimed that the Norman Conquest, by introducing feudalism to England, produced a major "break" in the progress

[289] Oliver Wendell Holmes. The Path of the Law, 10 Harv. L. Rev. 457, 474 (1897).
[290] Holmes, supra note 288, at 444.
[291] H. Cabot Lodge, The Anglo-Saxon Land-Law, in Essays in Anglo-Saxon Law (H. Adams ed., Boston: Little, Brown, and Company, 1876), p. 54, pp. 56–7.
[292] Melville Madison Bigelow, History of Procedure in England from the Norman Conquest: The Norman Period (1066–1204) (Boston: Little, Brown, and Company, 1880), p. 166.
[293] See, e.g., John Norton Pomeroy, An Introduction to Municipal Law (San Francisco: A. L. Bancroft and Company, 1883) (2d ed.), pp. 9–10; Thomas M. Cooley, Sources of Inspiration in Legal Pursuits, 9 West. Jurist 515, 516 (1875).
[294] James Barr Ames, Lectures in Legal History (Cambridge, Mass.: Harvard University Press, 1913), p. 145.
[295] Francis Wharton, Commentaries on Law (Philadelphia: Kay & Brother, 1884), p. 93.
[296] Id. at 71.
[297] Pomeroy, supra note 293, at 57.
[298] Thayer, supra note 286, at 27.
[299] Wharton, supra note 295, at 71.
[300] Melville Madison Bigelow, Placita Anglo-Normannica: Law Cases From William I to Richard I (Boston: Soule and Bugbee, 1881), p. xxvi.

from Teutonic origins to contemporary Anglo-American civilization.[301] Writing more specifically about technical legal issues, they identified declines in the development of forms of action[302] and of criminal law[303] before subsequent progress prevailed.

Scholars, moreover, often identified decline that was not remedied by subsequent progress. Bigelow maintained that the Provisions of Oxford promulgated in 1258, by depriving the king and his chancellor of their traditional power to grant new writs, had produced "the endless train of subtleties" in English law, which even to the present "so often resulted in the perversion of justice."[304] Hammond complained that Blackstone and his contemporaries, by trying to substitute their own classifications for the historically developed common law, had abrogated an existing system of logical rules and introduced gratuitous inconsistency into the law.[305] Referring to recent developments in the United States, Pomeroy objected to reforms of the law of pleading in New York,[306] Ames disagreed with innovations in contract law,[307] and Thayer worried that judges in the United States were departing from their traditional deference to legislative determinations about the constitutionality of legislation.[308]

The frequent references to the contingency of history by American legal scholars support the conclusion that they did not believe that history neatly falls into narratives of either progress or decline. If history could have turned out differently, narratives of progress or decline could have been reversed. In perhaps the most dramatic example of contingency, Bigelow asserted that at the time of the controversy between Becket and King Henry II, "England stood at the parting of the ways" between collectivism, morality, and equity or selfish individualism and legal rigidity. This controversy, Bigelow emphasized, could easily have been avoided, thus leading to a different result. Instead of succumbing to individualism and rigidity, which Bigelow viewed as the path of decline, England could have endorsed collectivism, morality, and equity, which Bigelow viewed as the path of progress.[309] Reinforcing his recognition of contingency in history, Bigelow recognized that it was impossible to know whether Becket's legal collectivism, even if adopted, would have lasted.[310] Wharton

---

[301] See, e.g., Bigelow, supra note 292, at 3; Lodge, supra note 291, at 119; Pomeroy, supra note 293, at 70.

[302] Bigelow, supra note 300, at xxvi.

[303] Thayer, supra note 286, at 27.

[304] Bigelow, supra note 300, at xxx.

[305] William G. Hammond, Blackstone's Commentaries (San Francisco: Bancroft-Whitney, 1890), vol. 3, p. 408.

[306] Pomeroy, supra note 293, at 125.

[307] Ames, supra note 294, at 353.

[308] James Bradley Thayer, The Origin and Scope of the American Doctrine of Constitutional Law, 7 Harv. L. Rev. 129 (1883).

[309] Melville M. Bigelow, Papers on the Legal History of Government (Boston: Little, Brown, and Company, 1920), pp. 217–20.

[310] Id. at 220.

stressed that there was no "inexorable law" of evolution.[311] Pomeroy observed more specifically that the practice of freemen acting as judges, the "germ of the English jury,"[312] was prevalent among many German tribes that did not develop the jury system. Its distinctive development into the jury in England, Pomeroy maintained, was based on the contingent historical factors, primarily the relative absence of Roman law.[313] In his own extensive discussion of the relationship between the history of the jury and the law of evidence, Thayer pointed out that if the jury had retained its procedure of hearing witnesses in private and without judicial oversight or control, as the grand jury barely managed to do despite almost successful attempts to force it to receive evidence in open court, the modern law of evidence "never would have taken shape."[314] Recognizing contingency in a very different context, Thayer concluded that the distinctive American concept of judicial review, though "a natural result of" its colonial experience, "was by no means a necessary one."[315]

While properly emphasizing that the late nineteenth-century scholars often studied history to help the legal profession understand current law, twentieth-century legal historians made additional claims about the consequences of this approach that the late nineteenth-century scholarship clearly refutes. Many of the late nineteenth-century scholars themselves highlighted the very dangers of false analogies between present and past legal categories that the twentieth-century critics wrongly accused them of ignoring. They often warned against inferring a "genetic relation" from resemblances between past and present law, a point Pomeroy and Hammond made in reference to property law and Laughlin and Bigelow made in reference to procedure.[316] Holmes stressed that modern differences between contract and tort did not exist in the past, and Ames emphasized in his analysis of assumpsit that primitive conceptions of legal liability were "radically different" from modern ones.[317]

Nor did the late nineteenth-century scholars overwhelmingly invoke history to justify current law, as many twentieth-century legal historians claimed. Among the late nineteenth-century scholars, only Ames more frequently cited past law to support rather than to question current law. Others occasionally praised the extension of past law into the present. In *The Common Law*, Holmes gave examples of legal rules that no longer served their original justifications but that made "good sense" in the present because they promoted desirable social policy.[318] Thayer made the same point about many rules of

---

[311] Wharton, supra note 295, at 69.
[312] Pomeroy, supra note 293, at 67.
[313] Id. at 67–9.
[314] Thayer, supra note 286, at 181.
[315] Thayer, supra note 308, at 131.
[316] Bigelow, supra note 292, at 156, 160, 165; Hammond, supra note 305, at 205–6; Laughlin, The Anglo-Saxon Legal Procedure, in Essays in Anglo-Saxon Law, supra note 291, at 261; Pomeroy, supra note 293, at 247–8.
[317] Ames, supra note 294, at 131; Holmes, supra note 280, at 217–26.
[318] Holmes, supra note 280, at 94, 292.

evidence, also observing the "good sense" of numerous judicial rulings over centuries by "sagacious lawyers" settling "practical questions."[319]

Much more often, however, the late nineteenth-century scholars highlighted current laws as dysfunctional survivals of past laws that should be revised or eliminated. Holmes made this point throughout *The Common Law* and reiterated it in his essays during the 1890s. He stressed the "skeptical" role of legal history in prompting "reconsideration of the worth"[320] of legal rules and, when necessary, in "clearing away the rubbish"[321] of old laws that no longer served society. The central theme of Thayer's major work emphasized that the law of hearsay and numerous other rules of evidence are historical by-products of the development of the English jury system, which stand as unfortunate barriers to the creation of a proper scientific law of evidence designed to achieve justice. In his general essay on the value of legal history, Thayer maintained that studying the history of any legal topic demonstrates "the necessity of restating the subject in hand."[322] Cooley regretted that the rapid recent social changes in family relationships had not been matched by modification of the common law of family rights, which remained substantially as it was in the primitive days of its origins, still treating wives and children as the servants and dependents of husbands and fathers.[323] Hammond maintained that much of current property law perpetuated obsolete and artificial rules from the Middle Ages while thwarting fair results in the present.[324] Even Ames stressed that numerous legal rules demonstrated "the persistency of archaic reverence for form and of scholastic methods of interpretation."[325] Contrary to the subsequent assertions of twentieth-century critics, these scholars saw themselves in the tradition of the Germans they emulated, as the leaders, not the servants, of practicing lawyers and judges, as scientists whose historical analysis would enable others to reform the law rather than to justify it. Several of them emphasized, moreover, that they were more skeptical than their European predecessors about the continuing value of traditional law. Just as Wharton criticized Burke and Savigny for "undue reverence" for laws the nation had "outgrown," Hammond observed that previous authors in the "historical school" had "overlooked" whether the precedents they traced to the past should be continued.[326]

Other claims by twentieth-century commentators about the role of history in late nineteenth-century legal thought varied widely in their range and accuracy. Duncan Kennedy incorrectly asserted that historical legal thought, while widespread in Germany, was only a minor factor for classical legal thinkers in

---

[319] Thayer, supra note 286, at 509.
[320] Holmes, supra note 289, at 469.
[321] Holmes, supra note 288, at 452.
[322] Thayer, supra note 285, at 179.
[323] Thomas M. Cooley, A Treatise on the Law of Torts (Chicago: Callaghan, 1889), p, 222.
[324] Hammond, supra note 305, vol. 2, at 653.
[325] Ames, supra note 294, at 149.
[326] William G. Hammond, Appendix to Francis Lieber, Legal and Political Hermeneutics (St. Louis: F. H. Thomas and Company, 1880) (3rd ed.), p. 313; Wharton, supra note 295, at 94.

the United States.[327] Felix Cohen and Morton Horwitz made a similar mistake by maintaining that classical legal thinkers did not recognize "temporal processes" but successfully attempted to "freeze" law "in a fixed and inexorable system of logically deducible rules."[328] Thomas Grey seemed to overdraw his distinction between historical jurisprudence, which emphasized evolving custom, and classical legal science, which used the history of case law to extract immanent principles.[329] Most legal scholars in the late nineteenth century did not clearly differentiate between history as evolving custom and history as evolving principles because they viewed evolving principles as a response to evolving custom. Yet Grey contributed a major insight by stressing the initial independence of opposition to the judicial activism of conservative judges from opposition to deductive formalism, themes that Pound eventually linked.[330]

Robert Gordon accurately highlighted the "historicist" position of nineteenth-century legal scholars that law reflects evolving custom.[331] He convincingly observed, moreover, that their rigorous work in legal history was a major contribution to their empirical project, an important point that was generally overlooked by other twentieth-century scholars. Yet I disagree with Gordon's assertion that this empirical project was much less important than their generalizing project.[332] The late nineteenth-century scholars who did original research in legal history were much more devoted to empirical investigation than to generalizations. Some explicitly maintained that generalizations were fruitless and even dangerous without a proper empirical basis that would require substantially more historical research in original sources.

Stephen Siegel did more than any other scholar to emphasize the centrality of history in late nineteenth-century American legal thought and set forth in substantial and convincing detail the extent to which evolutionary theories, typically tied to nation and race, permeated the work of major scholars in both public and private law. I agree with many of his pioneering descriptions of their historical thought. Yet I do not find their historical views as pervasively rooted in the moral ordering principles that he associates with "historism" and considers fundamental to their thought. Often, Siegel seems to assume that proof of an evolving principle rooted in nation or race itself is evidence of a moral ordering principle. Laissez-faire constitutionalism, for example, does not strike me as morally ordering. Unlike Siegel, moreover, I found that many of the nineteenth-century scholars, particularly those who did original historical research, were sensitive to the "differentness" of the past, a position he attributed to a later "historicism" that he differentiated from the moralistic "historism" of classical legal thought.[333]

---

[327] See supra text accompanying note 157.
[328] See supra text accompanying notes 152–3.
[329] See supra text accompanying notes 162–3.
[330] See supra text accompanying notes 108–11.
[331] See supra text accompanying note 158.
[332] See supra text accompanying note 212.
[333] See supra text accompanying note 222.

I generally agree with the recent revisionist scholars who followed Siegel in redirecting attention to the significant role of history in late nineteenth-century American legal thought, who explored various aspects of its evolutionary approaches to law, including the complicated influence of prior German scholarship, and who emphasized its "Mugwump jurisprudence." I also share Kunal Parker's view that the gap between evolving custom and law highlighted by many late nineteenth-century scholars was a major element of their thought. Yet I disagree with Parker's further claim that they viewed the gap as "unbridgeable," making law always behind custom, "always a little 'dead.'"[334] By repeatedly describing law as "conforming" to evolving custom, they seemed to view it as always catching up, sometimes unconsciously, sometimes consciously. As custom continued to evolve, at different rates at different times and in different societies, new gaps would be created, producing new laws that would close those gaps. Rather than a perpetual, unbridgeable gap between custom and law, these scholars perceived a perpetual process of conforming law to evolving custom.

The historical turn reinforces many generalizations scholars of classical legal thought typically derived from other sources. An underlying commitment to historical analysis helps explain its unified approach to public and private law, which most commentators have attributed to the abstract conceptual categories that applied to both. This shared commitment to historical analysis also justifies grouping together a large number of late nineteenth-century American legal scholars and perceiving them as part of a transatlantic legal community, groupings that scholars of classical legal thought have ascribed mostly to a common search for conceptual order. The parallel development of the scientific study of law and university based legal education, an observation Thomas Grey made about the United States and England while citing Max Weber's original insight into this connection in Germany, relates directly to the historical turn. When universities established law schools in all three countries, they viewed history as the basis for the legal science that made law worthy of inclusion in a modern university. The need to examine the historical sources of law justified the commitment of resources to hire full-time scholars. And though the passing references by some scholars of classical legal thought to its associations with broader themes in Western intellectual life typically allude to liberal social ideology, the widespread adoption of historical explanation in the nineteenth century is the clearest link between law and other disciplines.

---

[334] See supra text accompanying note 272.

Conclusion

Roscoe Pound's promotion of sociological over historical jurisprudence, elaborating themes in the contemporaneous writing of Bigelow and, to a lesser extent, Holmes, reflected in American legal scholarship a broad transformation of Western social thought. Just as there was a transatlantic turn to historical explanation in many fields during the nineteenth century, there was a transatlantic turn away from it around the beginning of the twentieth. Like Pound, many scholars on both sides of the Atlantic focused on the social problems they associated with the excessive individualism of industrial capitalism. Yearning to become expert advisers on social policy, many looked to the emerging social sciences for collective solutions to those problems. They often treated history, particularly the evolutionary study of origins and development that was popular during the nineteenth century, as irrelevant or even counterproductive to this project. As Holmes and Maitland illustrate, attraction to the social sciences over history, concern about excessive individualism, and commitment to social reform did not always coexist in the same person. By the 1890s, Holmes was attracted to the explanatory power and policy analysis of the new social sciences, but he did not exhibit concern about the perils of individualism or the need for social reform. While addressing the dangers of individualism and the attractions of collectivism, Maitland remained committed to history and questioned the methods of the social sciences. Indeed, Maitland emphasized the historical sources of collectivism. But Pound was typical of the many transatlantic scholars who turned from history to the social sciences as part of an effort to reform society by taming individualism.[1]

---

[1] Dorothy Ross, The Origins of American Social Science (Cambridge University Press, 1991), p. 279; Daniel T. Rodgers, Atlantic Crossings: Social Politics in a Progressive Age (Cambridge, Mass.: Harvard University Press, 1998), pp. 100, 106, 110; Jurgen Herbst, The German School in American Scholarship: A Study in the Transfer of Culture (Cornell University Press, 1965), pp. 196–9; John Higham, American History, in John Higham with Leonard Krieger and Felix Gilbert, History (Englewood Cliffs, N.J.: Prentice-Hall, Inc., 1965), pp. 145, 171.

As the emerging social sciences separated themselves from history, focusing on the factors that influence and could reform contemporary society, the growing number of people interested in combining scholarship with social activism often decided to become social scientists rather than historians.[2] The "social control" school of sociology, which Pound found so attractive as a model for sociological jurisprudence, viewed social science as the source of insights about how to regulate rapid social change. Some recent scholars have emphasized, and deprecated as "scientism," efforts by early twentieth-century social scientists to provide broad generalizations about society analogous to the successful generalizations about nature in the natural and physical sciences.[3] Yet others have claimed that the early social scientists were less interested in general theories than in the empirical study of pressing social issues, such as urban slums and economic inequality.[4]

Comments by major figures in the United States and England highlight the transatlantic shift from history to social science. In his presidential address to the American Political Science Association in 1910, Abbott Lawrence Lowell complained that too much scholarship examined the history rather than the current functions of politics. Whereas Langdell had maintained that the historical study of legal doctrine in a law library provided the scientific analogy to the laboratories of chemists and physicists, Lowell emphasized instead that the "main laboratory for the actual working of political institutions is not a library but the outside world of public life."[5] Lowell, who graduated from Harvard Law School in 1880 before becoming a political scientist,[6] might have even been thinking of Langdell's famous analogy in formulating his very different approach, which soon dominated political science. While reversing Langdell, Lowell's comment to political scientists echoed Pound's advice that law professors should not remain "legal monks" but should study the "restless world of flesh and blood." In England, where the emergence of the social sciences similarly directed attention from evolutionary history to the examination of contemporary society, James Bryce bemoaned in 1921 that "schemes of social reconstruction" had superseded the traditional study of institutions that had been grounded in the comparative historical approach popularized by Maine. In contrast to Lowell, who represented the future direction of the social sciences, Bryce's comment, J. W. Burrow and Stefan Collini observe, was "the epitaph for a whole intellectual episode."[7]

---

[2] Ross, supra note 1, at xxi, 388; Herbst, supra note 1, at 158–9; Peter Novick, That Noble Dream: The "Objectivity Question" and the American Historical Profession (Cambridge University Press, 1988), p. 69; John Higham, The Historical Profession, in History, supra note 1, pp. 1, 71–2; John Higham, Theory, in History, supra note 1, pp. 87, 108–9; Felix Gilbert, European and American Historiography, in History, supra note 1, at 315, 340.

[3] Ross, supra note 1, at 303, 364–5, 367, 468.

[4] Higham, Theory, supra note 2, at 110.

[5] Ross, supra note 1, at 293.

[6] Id. at 290.

[7] John Burrow and Stefan Collini, The Clue to the Maze: The Appeal of the Comparative Method, in Stefan Collini, Donald Winch, John Burrow, That Noble Science of Politics: A Study in Nineteenth-Century Intellectual History (Cambridge University Press, 1983), pp. 245–6.

While many scholars gravitated from history to the emerging social sciences, even those who remained historians abandoned the nineteenth-century study of the state and its institutions as organisms that evolved over long periods. The Teutonic-germ theory, an especially popular version of evolutionary historical thought, came under attack by historians in England in the 1880s and the United States in the 1890s. These historians claimed that neither English villages nor New England towns developed from Teutonic origins.[8] Further undermining the Teutonic-germ theory, American historians increasingly studied the distinctively American aspects of their past, diverting attention from European origins.[9] After the United States joined England in fighting Germany during World War I, the concept of a common Teutonic heritage became untenable.[10] Beyond the demise of the Teutonic-germ theory itself, influential new approaches to American history emphasized environmental over organic factors. Social and economic history largely supplanted institutional history. Among the most prominent examples, Frederick Jackson Turner, beginning in 1893, stressed the role of the frontier in explaining American history, and Charles Beard's economic interpretation of the Constitution, published in 1913, highlighted the economic self-interest of the framers as the key to understanding the Constitution.[11]

At the beginning of the twentieth century, historians as well as social scientists in the United States often identified with the progressive movement and sought to harness their professional expertise to social reform.[12] Historians, like law professors such as Bigelow and Pound, sought intellectual alliances with the social sciences.[13] The historians invoked the insights of the social sciences to study recent history as a guide to reconstructing society. Reflecting on these trends in his 1965 history of the American historical profession, John Higham concluded that the early twentieth century, like the eighteenth-century Enlightenment, was an unhistorical age. Both the progressive "new historians" of the early twentieth century and the eighteenth-century "philosophes," Higham claimed, deployed history to foreshorten and emancipate themselves from the past.[14] Higham's terminology of emancipation recalls Holmes's statement in the 1890s about the "negative and skeptical" role of history in "clearing away" the "rubbish" of past law.

These broad developments help explain the twentieth-century dismissal of the late nineteenth-century American legal scholars who were committed to historical legal science as a distinctive jurisprudential school. The conception

---

[8] Ross, supra note 1, at 270, 282; Novick, supra note 2, at 88; Higham, American History, supra note 1, at 161–2.

[9] Higham, American History, supra note 1, at 172–3.

[10] Herbst, supra note 1, at 123.

[11] Novick, supra note 2, at 87–8, 96; Ross, supra note 1, at 270; Higham, American History, supra note 1, at 172, 180.

[12] Herbst, supra note 1, at 158–9.

[13] Novick, supra note 2, at 90.

[14] Higham, Theory, supra note 2, at 112.

of law as an organic evolutionary process, which placed the American school of legal history in the mainstream of nineteenth-century transatlantic thought, became outmoded in the early twentieth century, in law as in other disciplines, including history itself. More specifically, the demise of the Teutonic-germ theory extended to the American legal historians who emphasized the Teutonic origins of English common law. For the progressive early twentieth-century scholars, the study of history, particularly its organic evolution over long periods, diverted attention from the urgent social problems they wanted their scholarship to address. Many of the nineteenth-century American legal scholars were also social reformers, and many used their historical research to identify and urge the elimination of dysfunctional survivals that prevented law from responding to contemporary social needs. Many regretted the growth of industrial capitalism and complained about the increasing materialism and inequality in American society. They favored legislation that regulated employers and landlords and supported the progressive income tax. Unlike the progressive scholars of the early twentieth century, however, they did not identify excessive individualism as a major source of social problems in the United States. Nor did they experience the same sense of social crisis, display the same urgency about reform, or harness their scholarship as directly to their activism as the progressive scholars. Thayer's involvement in alleviating the conditions of American Indians and in civil service reform, for example, was not reflected in his scholarship. With respect to scholarship, Thayer predicted that at least two generations of historical legal research would be necessary before the law could be systematically restated, and he resisted earlier codification of law as premature. The progressive legal scholars of the early twentieth century, by contrast, did not feel they had the luxury of time. For them, historical scholarship was not required to identify dysfunctional law, especially when the tools of the new social sciences could diagnose and suggest responses to pressing social problems. They believed that dysfunctional law should be eliminated, whether it was a survival of past law that was once functional, or simply a more recent ineffective way to address current social needs.

The early twentieth-century scholars could have dismissed the late nineteenth-century school of historical legal thought as irrelevant, and even as a hindrance to needed social reform, without also mischaracterizing its contents. Why did Pound and his successors create such a distorted impression of the late nineteenth-century American scholars, and why did so many of these distortions persist throughout the twentieth century? In my opinion, the twentieth-century portrayals of the late nineteenth-century American legal scholars as deductive formalists and poor historians are two of the major lingering mischaracterizations of their work. To a substantial extent, I believe, both mischaracterizations can be attributed to improper inferences from the late nineteenth-century focus on internal legal doctrine, inferences distorted by the ideological commitments of the twentieth-century scholars.

There are numerous plausible explanations for the twentieth-century ascription of deductive formalism to their late nineteenth-century predecessors, from the very general to the idiosyncratically particular. Most broadly, generational intellectual rebellion, analogous to psychological rebellion by children against parents, is a frequently observed phenomenon in many fields. It often includes misrepresentation by the younger generation of the thought of the older generation.[15] Such a generational intellectual rebellion, captured by Morton White's description of a broad "revolt against formalism" by American intellectuals between 1890 and 1930,[16] could plausibly account for treating prior thought as more formalistic than it actually was in order to highlight the claimed innovations of the younger generation. Most specifically, Holmes's frequently observed ambition, which included exaggerating his own originality while disparaging others, might have contributed to his caricature of Langdell as an excessively formalistic "legal theologian," a comment made in the late nineteenth century but treated as gospel for much of the twentieth. Most persuasively to me, the internal study of legal doctrine could easily have been confused with deductive formalism, especially by the early twentieth-century scholars who rejected the internal study of law as a diversion from the real social problems law needed to address. For example, the distinction highlighted by Thomas Grey between the pervasive conceptualism of the late nineteenth century, which attempted to order legal concepts into a coherent system, and deductive formalism, which maintains that legal concepts can be applied to reach logically correct results,[17] might have been difficult to identify for scholars who were generally skeptical about any internal study of law. Yet as this very distinction illustrates, and as the variety of legal history written by the late nineteenth-century American scholars reinforces, there are many ways to study law internally without concluding that it is a formal deductive system. Although deductive formalism entails the internal analysis of law, the internal analysis of law does not entail deductive formalism. Indeed, many of the nineteenth-century American scholars explicitly rejected deductive formalism as inconsistent with their emphasis on induction from the internal history of legal data and associated deduction with the faults of prior jurisprudential schools they intended to replace with their historical science of law.

Pound's heavy reliance on Jhering contributed to his mistaken attribution of deductive formalism to late nineteenth-century American legal thought. Jhering presented his social interpretation of law in opposition to the deductive formalism of historical jurisprudence in Germany, which he studied as a student and followed in his early scholarly work. Pound repeatedly emphasized that

---

[15] See, e.g., David Cole, Agon at Agora: Creative Misreadings in the First Amendment Tradition, 95 Yale L.J. 857, 862–66 (1986) (summarizing Harold Bloom's "antithetical criticism," rooted in Sigmund Freud's analysis of the Oedipal conflict, and suggesting implications for understanding judicial interpretation of the First Amendment).

[16] Morton White, Social Thought in America: The Revolt against Formalism (Oxford University Press, 1976 ed.) (original ed. 1947).

[17] Thomas C. Grey, Holmes and Legal Pragmatism, 41 Stan. L. Rev. 787, 821–5 (1989).

Jhering's social interpretation of law was a major model for his own sociological jurisprudence. While incorporating Jhering's prescriptions for legal scholarship, Pound also extended Jhering's criticisms of historical jurisprudence in Germany to prior legal thought in America. To use Pound's own terminology against Pound himself, this extension seems "mechanical." Although Pound recognized that historical analysis dominated American legal scholarship in the late nineteenth century, he did not analyze his American predecessors in nearly the detail that he devoted to European historical jurisprudence, particularly Savigny and Maine. Perhaps he did not even read the Americans carefully.

It also seems plausible that Pound might have transposed his concern about deductive formalism in judicial decisions that undermined progressive social legislation to his analysis of legal scholarship. Given his underlying goal of helping law serve social ends, Pound was probably more worried about the practical impact of legal decisions than about the scholarship of law professors. In his famous article on "mechanical jurisprudence," which he identified with deductive formalism, he complained that Supreme Court decisions used "freedom of contract" as "the basis of a logical deduction" to invalidate labor legislation, without realizing that its holdings in practice would undermine the liberty of employees and obstruct social progress.[18] Pound also referred to civil procedure and evidence as subjects in which judges used the deductive logic of mechanical jurisprudence to reach disastrous results that inhibited the fair administration of justice.[19] Thomas Grey has argued that legal decisions involving "freedom of contract" did not exhibit deductive formalism and has pointed out that many contemporary critics opposed judicial decisions overturning progressive legislation without linking them to deductive formalism.[20] Because I have not myself examined extensively the legal decisions of the late nineteenth and early twentieth centuries, I do not have an independent opinion about their use of deductive formalism. Whether or not late nineteenth-century American judges used deductive logic, Pound thought that they did while reaching decisions he considered contrary to the public interest. His views about the judicial decisions might have contributed to his assumption of a pervasive deductive formalism that extended to legal scholarship as well, even though the legal scholarship itself did not support that conclusion.

Generations of scholars perpetuated Pound's association of deductive formalism with late nineteenth-century American legal thought. In his own analysis of deductive formalism, Pound focused on European rather than American scholars, treating the Americans as derivative imitators. Scholars after Pound barely explored nineteenth-century thought at all, invoking deductive formalism mostly as an epithet against which to define their own thought as anti-formalist.

---

[18] Roscoe Pound, Mechanical Jurisprudence, 8 Colum. L. Rev. 605, 616 (1908).
[19] Id. at 617–20.
[20] Thomas C. Grey, Judicial Review and Legal Pragmatism, 38 Wake Forest L. Rev. 473, 494–7 (2003).

Agreeing with Pound's general program of sociological jurisprudence yet lacking his interest in the history of legal thought, they apparently saw no need to study the nineteenth-century scholars whose presumed approach to law they so thoroughly rejected. From their perspective, Pound had already demolished the deductive formalism of the nineteenth century, enabling them to rely on his conclusions while refining the use of social science and policy analysis that he endorsed. Not until Duncan Kennedy in the 1970s did twentieth-century scholars actually engage the nineteenth-century scholars themselves and treat their thought as worthy of intellectual respect. Kennedy's structural analysis "decentered" legal formalism from his treatment of "classical legal thought,"[21] and Thomas Grey narrowed its scope to scholarship about private law[22] while distinguishing it from a broader conceptualism. Yet Kennedy and Grey, like most of their late twentieth-century contemporaries, continued to identify deductive formalism as a basic feature of late nineteenth-century American legal thought. Only in recent years have some scholars begun to question whether deductive formalism was even a characteristic of American legal thought in the generation before Pound.

The criticism by twentieth-century American legal historians of the poor quality of work in their field before J. Willard Hurst began his career in the 1940s, like the criticism of deductive formalism, can be attributed to improper inferences from the nineteenth-century focus on internal legal thought. It is similarly misplaced and similarly can be traced more to the ideology of the critics than to the nineteenth-century scholarship itself. Focused on broadening the scope of American legal history, Hurst and many of his followers drew an invidious distinction between the limited "internal" history that had prevailed in the United States since 1870 and the "external" legal history they hoped would supplant it. Just as Pound's exposition of sociological jurisprudence helps explain his inaccurate portrayal of his predecessors, understanding the ambitious prescriptions for an external legal history by twentieth-century legal historians helps explain their dismissive mischaracterizations of internal legal history.

In developing the "Law and Society" school of legal history, Hurst in many ways followed through on the "sociological legal history" that Pound urged as a component of sociological jurisprudence. At the beginning of his career, Hurst encouraged a broad scope for the study of "legal" history, using quotation marks apparently to indicate that his conception of what counted as legal was much more extensive than the views of his predecessors. He maintained that legal historians should investigate the use of official power "in the name of the politically organized community" and the subsequent reaction by the rest of the community.[23] More specifically, he encouraged attention to three aspects

---

[21] Duncan Kennedy, The Rise and Fall of Classical Legal Thought (Washington, D.C.: Beard Books, 2006), p. xxxiv.

[22] Thomas C. Grey, Langdell's Orthodoxy, 45 U. Pitt. L. Rev. 1, 33–4 (1983).

[23] Willard Hurst, Legal History: A Research Program, 1942 Wis. L. Rev. 323, 325.

of "social control," the same term Pound borrowed from the progressive sociologist Edward A. Ross. All three aspects, Hurst maintained, shared a "common concern with the interrelations of the law and other social institutions." First, legal historians should explore why "legal" rather than "non-legal" means are used to address particular social problems. Second, they should study "the causal interaction of legal and non-legal institutions." Like Pound before him, Hurst emphasized that this causal interaction goes both ways. Economic, political, and cultural activities influence legal behavior, as recent "realist" legal thought had stressed. But legal historians should also examine "the effect of legal upon non-legal conduct," which, he implied, had been neglected. Third, related to the study of the impact of law on society, legal historians should focus on how "superficially diverse" legal activities affect common areas of nonlegal conduct, whether economic, political, or cultural. He was confident that such a focus would disclose possible inefficiencies, irrationalities, and collateral impacts of legal regulations. This information in turn would allow both informed appraisals of the effectiveness of law in the past and better planning for the use of law in the future.[24]

By referring to the value of legal history for future planning, Hurst indicated that he had practical as well as intellectual goals for the field. He opened his essay by tying his research program in legal history to "the call for directed intelligence in community affairs."[25] He justified its inclusion in the curriculum by proclaiming its usefulness, but not in the narrow sense of addressing immediate needs, such as providing historical justification for a judicial opinion or statute. Rather, Hurst optimistically believed that legal history at its best examines "how life in community may become both a source and a guaranty of the full realization of the individual human spirit."[26] In achieving this lofty goal, Hurst maintained that historians must abandon prior "individualistic scholarship" and learn to work cooperatively in teams with social scientists.[27]

In his overview "The Law in United States History" much later in his career, Hurst provided several illustrations of the ways in which legal categories had dominated legal history. Despite the enormous literature on the history of doctrinal interpretation of the commerce clause, legal historians had neglected its impact on sectional or national marketing organization. More generally, they had ignored the influence of business history on constitutional principles. Formal histories of property law had not examined how the simple fee title actually affected land use. Essays on the history of contract law had not considered its relationship to the market and the provision of credit. The scattered writings about the history of corporate law and tax law had failed to investigate how they affected the accumulation and use of investment capital. Scholarship on the history of the Bill of Rights, while relatively extensive, had not explored

[24] Id. at 328–9.
[25] Id. at 323.
[26] Id. at 324.
[27] Id. at 326.

how legal doctrine concerning civil rights contributed to the shifting balance of power among individual citizens, private groups, and various agencies of the state. He regretted that legal history had not responded to Pound's "call for a sociological jurisprudence." [28] Offering prescriptions as well criticisms, Hurst gave examples of the kind of legal history he advocated. He encouraged studies of the movements for women's legal rights, including suffrage and property rights for married women, as part of the broader history of women in the United States. A meaningful social history of the business corporation, he maintained, required understanding how legal definitions empowered corporate owners and managers.[29] Histories of agrarian political revolt, he added, should include discussions of the laws that governed the disposal of land in the public domain.[30]

Hurst followed his own prescriptions while becoming the most influential legal historian of his generation. His most important book,[31] *Law and Economic Growth: The Legal History of the Lumber Industry in Wisconsin, 1836–1915,* focused on "the interaction of legal and economic institutions" to "yield a product relevant to broader social theory."[32] It emphasized that the legal history of the Wisconsin lumber industry depended more on legislation and executive action than on case law.[33] It highlighted the extensive social drift and inertia that posed barriers to deliberative planning.[34] And it contrasted "a bastard strain in the pragmatism that contented itself with churning out a flow of specific responses to specific pressures" with the "sound pragmatism," based on more reflection about the consequences of actions, that allows people "to enlarge their reach of purpose and control."[35] He observed that in disposing of land in the public domain during the nineteenth century, most people sought immediate economic returns rather than long-term interests.[36] Yet Hurst did not follow his early advice of cooperating in teams with social scientists. In his major book, and throughout his work generally, he maintained the tradition of "individualistic scholarship" in legal history. Though clearly sympathetic to the social sciences, moreover, he did not incorporate much of their methodology into his own scholarship.[37]

---

[28] Willard Hurst, The Law in United States History, in Proceedings of the American Philosophical Society (Philadelphia: The American Philosophical Society, 1960), vol. 104, pp. 518, 522.

[29] Id. at 519.

[30] Id. at 520.

[31] Robert W. Gordon, J. Willard Hurst and the Common Law Tradition in American Legal Historiography, 10 Law and Soc'y Rev. 9, 50 (1975).

[32] James Willard Hurst, Law and Economic Growth: The Legal History of the Lumber Industry in Wisconsin, 1836–1915 (Cambridge, Mass.: Harvard University Press, 1964), p. viii.

[33] Id. at xi.

[34] See, e.g., id. at 15, 23, 444, 572.

[35] Id. at 206.

[36] Id. at 23, 206.

[37] Stanley N. Katz, The Problem of a Colonial Legal History, in Colonial British America: Essays in the New History of the Modern Early Era (Johns Hopkins University Press, 1984) (Jack P. Greene and J. R. Pole, eds.), pp. 457, 464.

Writing in the early 1940s, just a year before Hurst's initial article, Daniel Boorstin similarly urged American legal historians to "be more concerned with the relationship at any time between legal institutions and the rest of society, and less concerned with the embryology of the professional vocabulary."[38] While making clear his view that there were many, virtually unlimited, possibilities for creative legal history within this general rubric of relating law and society, he provided a few specific examples. Legal historians, he suggested, could usefully study the ways in which law had facilitated economic processes. In contrast to the legal categories of embryonic legal history, works in this vein would be organized around economic categories, such as labor, technology, land, capital, and markets. The historian would discuss how a large variety of legal concepts were deployed within these economic categories. In examining technological change, for example, the historian would write about patent law, administrative law, labor law, and even the law of civil liberties. Organization of legal history around economic categories, Boorstin observed, would indicate the extent to which legal doctrines were socially valuable and illustrate the constant adaptation of traditional legal doctrines to new practical uses.[39] Not limiting himself to economic categories, Boorstin also suggested that it would be interesting to organize legal history around ethical ones, such as the role of agreement. Scholars in various academic fields, he speculated, would benefit from a legal history of community deference to private agreements, a topic that would draw upon numerous legal categories, including contract, criminal law, property law, tort law, and administrative law. He was confident that such studies would usefully reveal important variations in legal control of individual activity.[40] Legal history, he added, could contribute to political and intellectual as well as to social and economic history.[41] Once liberated from the embryonic model, Boorstin believed, legal historians would be able to open their imaginations "to the infinite possibilities of history."[42]

Several years later, Boorstin wrote an essay, "The Humane Study of Law," which, without referring specifically to Hurst, expressed reservations about the "pragmatic" study of legal history, and particularly about the attempt to integrate legal scholarship, including legal history, with the social sciences. He reiterated from his earlier article that legal history should "point outward in many directions from the development of legal institutions to intellectual, political, economic, and social history."[43] In his second essay, however, he placed more emphasis on the relationship of law to the overlooked spiritual, as opposed to the more frequently studied material, aspects of the past.[44] While encouraging

[38] D. J. Boorstin, Tradition and Method in Legal History, 54 Harv. L. Rev. 424, 434 (1941).
[39] Id. at 434–5.
[40] Id. at 435.
[41] Id. at 436.
[42] Id. at 429.
[43] Daniel J. Boorstin, The Humane Study of Law, 57 Yale L.J. 960, 973 (1948).
[44] Id. at 975 and generally at 967–75.

research on the role of law in the history of the automobile,[45] a very material subject, he was more interested in relating legal history to religion, science, metaphysics, and aesthetics.[46]

In his book on Blackstone, published the same year as his first essay, Boorstin wrote the kind of "humane" legal history he subsequently advocated. The full subtitle of his book, phrased in the style of Blackstone's own time, captures Boorstin's approach: "An Essay on Blackstone's COMMENTARIES Showing How Blackstone, Employing Eighteenth-century Ideas of Science, Religion, History, Aesthetics, and Philosophy, made of the Law at once a Conservative and a Mysterious Science." Boorstin stressed that his book highlighted the relationship "between legal thought and thought about things other than law."[47] His central point was that Blackstone used the ideas and assumptions of his contemporaries to make existing legal institutions seem coherent and rational and thus to prevent challenges to the social arrangements he wanted to preserve.[48] Accommodating the tension between the joint commitments to religion and science in eighteenth-century English thought,[49] Blackstone provided rational principles of law based on the data of experience[50] while asserting the mystery of law "to protect ultimate values from the devouring gaze of Reason."[51] Emphasizing Blackstone's instrumental political use of contemporary ideas, Boorstin observed that the same ideas could be, and in fact were, used to attack the very values Blackstone invoked them to support.[52] True to his programmatic essays on legal history, Boorstin also devoted an entire chapter to Blackstone's use of aesthetics.[53] By attempting to prove that the English legal system was both beautiful and sublime, qualities contemporary thought ascribed to nature, Blackstone reinforced his goal of portraying current law as natural[54] and, therefore, not needing human improvement.[55]

Hurst and Boorstin certainly had a much broader conception of legal history than the late nineteenth-century American legal scholars. Accurately describing the work of prior American legal historians as "legal embryology" focused on the history of legal doctrine, they convincingly contrasted this "internal" legal history with their own interest in studying the history of the relationships between law and the broader "external" society. In significant respects, their complaints about the internal legal history written by their American predecessors anticipated complaints in recent decades that Maitland focused too heavily

---

[45] Id. at 969.

[46] Id. at 967, 970.

[47] Daniel J. Boorstin, The Mysterious Science of the Law: An Essay on Blackstone's Commentaries (University of Chicago Press, 1996) (original ed. 1941), p. xviii.

[48] Id. at 5–6.

[49] Id. at 16–17.

[50] Id. at 23.

[51] Id. at 25.

[52] Id. at 188.

[53] Id. at 85–105.

[54] Id. at 90–1.

[55] Id. at 105.

on internal legal materials, especially on judicial decisions, and that he used modern legal concepts to govern his study of the past while slighting external factors such as changes in the organization of the family and interpersonal relationships of power and honor. Yet unlike Hurst, who emphasized the "thin record of accomplishment" of prior American legal historians, the critics of Maitland uniformly praised the uniquely high quality of his work, often seeming uncomfortable even expressing their reservations about so great a scholar. Boorstin, somewhat ambivalently, associated Maitland as well as Holmes and Ames with the embryological legal history he criticized[56] while praising their "classic" works as examples of the strengths of the "humane study of law,"[57] which he compared favorably to the emerging popularity of the social sciences as the method of addressing the relationship between law and society.

Just as Pound and his successors erred in concluding that the internal study of law by late nineteenth-century American legal scholars encompassed deductive formalism, one of many possible internal approaches, Hurst and Boorstin erred in concluding that it encompassed various additional historiographical assumptions compatible with an internal orientation but not required by it. Even in drawing the fundamental, and essentially accurate, contrast between their ambitious plans for external legal history and the internal legal history that preceded it, they left the misimpression that prior scholars were oblivious to the relationship between law and society. Not nearly that naive, the prior scholars recognized, often alluded to, and sometimes stressed external influences on law. They did not examine these external factors in detail, even when recognizing their importance, because they had a different intellectual project, which called on their distinctive expertise as legal scholars to clarify the origins and evolution of the law, often as a route to clarifying, organizing, and, if necessary, reforming contemporary law. Yet the sophisticated treatment of external factors by Hurst and Boorstin makes it easy to understand how they transformed the relative prior lack of attention to these factors into an exaggerated claim that the late nineteenth-century scholars ignored or denied external influences on legal history. Erroneous claims about the internal legal history actually practiced by the late nineteenth-century scholars are less easy to rationalize. Contrary to the unsupported claims of the external legal historians, while pursuing internal "legal embryology" the late nineteenth-century scholars did not simply allow the doctrinal headings of modern law to govern their investigations of the past and did not view the present as the inevitable culmination of the past. Although they were interested in the evolutionary connections between past and present law, they recognized the contingency of history, tried to understand past law in its historical context, and often warned against making false analogies from present law to past law.

Beyond succumbing to the temptation of highlighting the value of their own innovations by exaggerating the weaknesses of their predecessors, the external

---

[56] Boorstin, supra note 38, at 430.
[57] Boorstin, supra note 43, at 963.

legal historians might have unfairly ascribed their dismay about the internal legal history written by their contemporaries to the late nineteenth-century scholars. Hurst's own historiographical essays described the internal approach, though dating from the 1870s, as still dominant. He wrote those essays to combat existing methodology in legal history, not merely as an exercise in historiography. More specifically, while criticizing internal legal history in the 1970s, both Horwitz and Gordon identified recently published works as examples of its faults. Horwitz associated the internal approach with "The Conservative Tradition in the Writing of American Legal History" in a review essay of two recent biographies of Justice Joseph Story. While dismissing one of those biographies as merely "bland and conventional,"[58] he identified the other as the "culmination of this tradition of historiography."[59] Gordon affiliated Holmes, Bigelow, Thayer, and Ames with the "institutional-evolutionary" internal school whose historiographical assumptions he criticized, but he emphasized his concern that "these assumptions have continued to linger around the law schools to the present day, like radio-active matter with an abnormally long half-life," long after professional historians appropriately repudiated them.[60] Tellingly, as his example of the "extraordinary persistence" of the internal approach, he described a recent article on the history of promise by a specialist in contract law who was not a legal historian.[61] In an essay on the history of legal history, Lawrence Friedman, Hurst's most eminent successor, cited two books published in the 1950s to illustrate the focus on "purely internal legal materials," without much attention to "socioeconomic context," before Hurst "brought the field to life."[62] Analogous to Pound's possible transposition of his concern about the deductive formalism of judicial decisions to contemporaneous legal scholarship that did not display it, the twentieth-century external legal historians might have transposed their criticisms of recent internal legal history to the late nineteenth-century scholars who had more sophisticated views.

Beginning in the 1970s, a younger generation of scholars, often associated with the emerging "Critical Legal Studies" movement, criticized the "Law and Society" school of legal history. Often expressing a broader division between younger radicals and older liberals, they claimed that Hurst and his followers had presented an overly optimistic, even complacent, account of the history of American law and society. In addition to underestimating conflict and inequality, they charged, the Law and Society school had been methodologically unsophisticated in failing to recognize the relative autonomy of law from society.[63]

---

[58] Morton J. Horwitz, The Conservative Tradition in the Writing of American Legal History, 17 Am. J. Legal Hist. 275, 293 (1973).

[59] Id. at 283.

[60] Gordon, supra note 31, at 15–16.

[61] Id. at 24.

[62] Lawrence M. Friedman, American Legal History: Past and Present, 34 J. of Legal Educ. 563 (1984).

[63] See especially Michael Grossberg, Social History Update: 'Fighting Faiths' and the Challenges of Legal History, 25 J. Soc. Hist. 191 (1991). See also Friedman, supra note 63, at 567, 570–2

Lawrence Friedman reported his "intense shock" at this attack. Writing auto-biographically in 1984, Friedman recalled how excited he was to discover Hurst and to join him in "a necessary job of destruction – entering the lists against the old, nonsocial, nonquantitative doctrinal history," which struck him "as so old-fashioned, so arid, so ... establishment." Friedman and others in the Law and Society school, now finding themselves portrayed as "the Establishment," felt "in the front line, ready to be ripped apart by a new generation."[64]

The call for exploring the relative autonomy of law entailed a return to the internal study of legal doctrine that the Law and Society school had rejected and ignored. Friedman wrote that he would call this approach "neodoctrinal-ist" if he were "inclined to rake it over the coals" but immediately added, "That would probably be unfair."[65] Later in his essay, Friedman, without these qualifications, referred to "the dangers of the neodoctrinalists" in denying the instrumental functions of law.[66] While Friedman seemed to use the term "neodoctrinalism" pejoratively, others referred to the return of doctrinal legal history in purely descriptive terms,[67] and Duncan Kennedy, perhaps its earliest and most prominent proponent, happily described his work as "taking doc-trine seriously."[68]

Whatever their reactions to studying the relative autonomy of law, com-mentators agreed that it treated legal doctrine as ideology,[69] a very different kind of doctrinal history than the evolutional legal history practiced by the late nineteenth-century American legal scholars. Friedman accurately observed that the "neodoctrinalists" were not interested in doctrine "because of any reason Langdell would recognize" and did "not find much of interest in *any* dusty records."[70] Rather, they studied the relative autonomy of law as a mask that conceals its actual operation[71] or as a structure that mediates contradictions.[72] Adapting structuralism and critical theory to legal analysis,[73] Duncan Kennedy

---

(1984); Robert W. Gordon, Critical Legal Histories, 36 Stan. L. Rev. 57, 110–13 (1984); Robert W. Gordon, Hurst Recaptured, 18 L. & Hist. Rev. 167, 167–70 (2000); Michael Grossberg, Legal History and Social Science: Friedman's 'History of American Law,' the Second Time Around, 13 L. & Soc. Inquiry 359, 366–8, 381–2 (1988); Ron Harris, The Encounters of Economic History and Legal History, 21 L. & Hist. Rev. 297, 328–9, 333 (2003); William J. Novak, Law, Capitalism, and the Liberal State: The Historical Sociology of James Willard Hurst, 18 L. & Hist. Rev. 97, 140 (2000); Barbara Y. Welke, Willard Hurst and the Archipelago of American Legal History, 18 L. & Hist. Rev. 198, 200–1 (2000).

[64] Friedman, supra note 62, at 566–7.

[65] Id. at 567.

[66] Id. at 572.

[67] Gordon, Critical Legal Histories, supra note 63, at 116–17; Grossberg, Social History Update, supra note 63, at 195; Novak, supra note 63, at 140.

[68] Kennedy, supra note 21, at xxxii.

[69] Friedman, supra note 62, at 567; Grossberg, Social History Update, supra note 63, at 195; Gordon, Critical Legal Histories, supra note 63, at 101, 112, 120.

[70] Friedman, supra note 62, at 567.

[71] Id., Grossberg, Social History Update, supra note 63, at 194.

[72] Gordon, Critical Legal Histories, supra note 63, at 116.

[73] Kennedy, supra note 21, at ix, xiv, xxv.

took the latter approach. In his "modernist" conception, he wrote, "consciousness functioned to 'mediate the contradictions of experience,' rather than, as in the neo-Marxist formulation, to mask the internal contradictions of the capitalist mode of production."[74] Kennedy called *The Rise & Fall of Classical Legal Thought* "a history of American legal thought," which he considered "distinct from a history of the doctrines of American law."[75] This distinction indicates his different use of doctrine than the late nineteenth-century scholars whose work he took seriously in creating his own interpretation of "classical legal thought." Kennedy's legal history is as distant from the legal history written by the late nineteenth-century scholars as structuralism and critical theory are from evolutionary social thought.

There has not been any counterpart in the United States to the resurgence of histories of doctrine written by leading English legal historians, such as S. F. C. Milsom and J. H. Baker. David Ibbetson has identified Milsom's *Historical Foundations of the Common Law*, published in 1969, as the modern emergence of the kind of doctrinal legal history that can be traced back to late nineteenth-century scholars such as Holmes.[76] In his introduction, Milsom wrote that he hoped to depict "the growth of the common law." A lucky historian, Milsom observed, "can see why a rule came into existence, what change left it working injustice, how it came to be evaded, how the evasion produced a new rule, and sometimes how that new rule in its turn came to be overtaken by change."[77] Baker described his subsequent book, *An Introduction to English Legal History*, as a history "of the principal English legal institutions and doctrines." Knowing "the historical development of the law," he claimed, is "indispensable" to providing "a dynamic sense of legal evolution." "History alone," he added, "reveals the reasons – though it does not provide any justifications – for the present shape of the law and legal concepts."[78] These statements by Milsom and Baker closely resemble descriptions by the late nineteenth-century American legal scholars of their own work.

By contrast, Lawrence Friedman's *A History of American Law*, published in 1973 and, as Friedman correctly observed, the first general history of American law,[79] reflected his commitment to the Law and Society school. He underlined in his preface that he had written "a *social* history of American law." "This book treats American law," Friedman proclaimed, "not as a kingdom unto itself, not as a set of rules and concepts, not as the province of lawyers alone, but as a mirror of society." Taking "nothing as autonomous," it understood "everything

---

[74] Id. at xvii.

[75] Id. at ix.

[76] David Ibbetson, Historical Research in Law, in Oxford Handbook of Legal Studies (Oxford University Press, 2003) (Peter Kane and Mark Tushnet, eds.), pp. 863, 872–3.

[77] S. F. C. Milsom, Historical Foundations of the Common Law (Toronto: Butterworths, 1981) (2nd ed.), p. 7.

[78] J. H. Baker, An Introduction to English Legal History (London: Butterworths, 2002) (4th ed.), p. vii.

[79] Lawrence M. Friedman, A History of American Law (New York: Simon and Schuster, 1973), p. 9.

as relative and molded by economy and society."[80] In his later historiographical essay, Friedman graciously conceded that some of Hurst's disciples, adding "I may be guilty here," took "his thought to a logical (or illogical) extreme." As a result, "they may have, in some ways, killed off the idea of law altogether, or at least the idea that law makes much of a difference."[81] While subsequent American scholars rejected the Law and Society disparagement of doctrine, they did not, except for the relatively few interested in the history of English law, emulate the English scholars who have resurrected in modern form the nineteenth-century interest in the history of doctrine. Indeed, to the limited extent that the Americans have even been aware of the recent English legal historians at all, they have often treated their work with bafflement or condescension. A greater proportion of English legal historians have joined the Law and Society and Critical Legal History schools that have dominated in recent decades in the United States. Yet the dramatic recent revival of scholarship in legal history in both countries seems to have proceeded largely on independent tracks, a striking difference from the close community of American and English scholars during the late nineteenth century.

Even more striking, despite this impressive revival, legal scholars in both countries typically do not approach their research historically. Historical analysis today is only one of many methodologies, and legal historians are only a small fraction of the legal professoriate. Even among legal scholars attracted to interdisciplinary work, I suspect that many more are interested in law and economics than in legal history. Yet in the nineteenth century, historical understandings of law pervaded legal scholarship, whether or not a particular scholar undertook original historical research. After the eclipse of historical explanation in the early twentieth century, it never regained its prominence within legal scholarship generally.

This book, I hope, contributes both to the subject matter and to the methodology of legal history. It recovers the centrality of history in the legal thought of the founding generation of professional legal scholars in the United States during the last three decades of the nineteenth century. For these scholars, studying the origins and evolution of the law constituted a distinctive jurisprudential school, whose reliance on history made it inductive and, therefore, scientific, in contrast to the abstract and, therefore, unscientific theorizing of natural law and analytic jurisprudence. The book places the emergence of this historical school of American jurisprudence in the broader context of the general turn to history throughout transatlantic intellectual life during the nineteenth century. As a by-product of its recovery of this distinctive historical school, it challenges the condescending twentieth-century disparagement of late nineteenth-century legal thought. Contrary to the claims of twentieth-century American legal scholars, their nineteenth-century

---

[80] Id. at 10.
[81] Friedman, supra note 62, at 570.

predecessors were historically sophisticated thinkers who did not view law as a timeless structure based on deductive formalism.

In addition to recovering the historical school of American jurisprudence, this book highlights the major American contributions to original scholarship in English legal history at the end of the nineteenth century. Stimulated by Henry Maine's bold generalizations about legal evolution, disciplined by German methods of archival research, and informed by German studies of the history of Germanic law, American legal scholars studied the early history of English law. They stressed both its Germanic origins and its connections to current law in England and the United States. Frederic Maitland, the English scholar whose work is still regarded as the best legal history ever written in the English language, admired and built on the prior scholarship of these Americans while developing close personal relationships with several of them. Some American legal scholars also studied the history of American constitutional law through the lens of their evolutionary thought

By examining the scholarship of Roscoe Pound during the decade before World War I, this book also portrays the eclipse of the historical school by sociological jurisprudence. Just as the historical school of American jurisprudence was part of a transatlantic turn to historical explanation, sociological jurisprudence was part of a later transatlantic turn away from it, often as part of a pragmatic effort to address pressing social problems through the methods of the emerging social sciences. My discussion of Pound and his successors conveys and corrects their largely misleading account of the late nineteenth-century scholars whose work forms the core of this book.

In treating these subjects, my primary goal has been to understand prior legal scholars on their own terms. Immersed in the evolutionary social thought that dominated nineteenth-century Western intellectual life, the first professional legal scholars in the United States had confidence in the power of the past to explain, and potentially to reform, the present. Subsequent generations have lost this confidence, perhaps historians most of all. My attempt to recover the intellectual world and professional achievements of the late nineteenth-century American legal scholars, freed from the frequent misrepresentations and condescension of their successors, is a very different kind of history, reflecting very different assumptions and goals, from their own. I hope it provides insights into the intellectual history of legal thought and adds to the healthy diversity of methodological approaches among modern legal historians.

Index